OXFORD HISTORY OF
EARLY MODERN EUROPE

General Editor: R. J. W. Evans

CONTESTED ISLAND

CONTESTED ISLAND

IRELAND 1460–1630

S. J. CONNOLLY

OXFORD
UNIVERSITY PRESS

OXFORD
UNIVERSITY PRESS

Great Clarendon Street, Oxford OX2 6DP

Oxford University Press is a department of the University of Oxford.
It furthers the University's objective of excellence in research, scholarship,
and education by publishing worldwide in

Oxford New York

Auckland Cape Town Dar es Salaam Hong Kong Karachi
Kuala Lumpur Madrid Melbourne Mexico City Nairobi
New Delhi Shanghai Taipei Toronto

With offices in

Argentina Austria Brazil Chile Czech Republic France Greece
Guatemala Hungary Italy Japan Poland Portugal Singapore
South Korea Switzerland Thailand Turkey Ukraine Vietnam

Published in the United States
by Oxford University Press Inc., New York

First published 2007

British Library Cataloguing in Publication Data
Data available

Library of Congress Cataloging in Publication Data
Data available

Typeset by Laserwords Private Limited, Chennai, India
Printed in Great Britain
on acid-free paper by
Biddles Ltd., King's Lynn, Norfolk

ISBN 978–0–19–820816–7

1 3 5 7 9 10 8 6 4 2

For Richard

Author's Note

ANY historian who agrees to write a survey covering more than three centuries accepts the risks involved in stepping outside his or her area of expertise. The risk is compounded, in the present case, because the necessity of breaking a long manuscript into two manageable sections has required me to begin with a volume well removed, in terms of chronology, from the period that has been the focus of my own detailed research. In all parts of the work I draw on a reading of at least the major primary sources available in print. But I am the first to recognize that this can be no substitute for the patient examination of the full range of surviving sources that has allowed specialist scholars, over the past two decades or so, to transform our understanding of Tudor and early Stuart Ireland, and it is on their work that the pages that follow primarily depend. The experts, of course, have not always agreed. It has not seemed a good idea, in a book of this kind, to load the text with the details of specific debates. But my footnotes should make clear to anyone interested where I am summarizing generally accepted views, where I am choosing between conflicting assessments, and where I am venturing a judgement of my own.

Throughout the text I have followed the standard convention of using the Julian calendar current in early modern England, rather than the Gregorian calendar adopted, from 1582, across much of continental Europe, but in taking the year as commencing on 1 January rather than on 25 March. I have modernized the spelling of quotations from contemporary sources. I have also, more hesitantly, decided to anglicize Irish-language names. To do so risks giving new life to the tired and inaccurate gibe that history is written from the standpoint of the winners. But the difficulties created by even the modernized spelling of the Gaelic originals are a real barrier to all but the initiated. Hence Aodh becomes Hugh and Ruaidhri Rory. However, I have retained the Christian name Tadhg. The standard anglicization 'Timothy' seems somehow inappropriate for a Gaelic warlord, while 'Teague' is both inaccurate (based on the assumption that the name rhymed with 'league') and tainted by its contemporary use as a term of sectarian abuse.

In a few others cases, likewise, it has proved either pointless to remove a fairly familiar Irish name, or impossible to find a convenient English equivalent. For those who want to know what they are reading, the following brief guide to pronunciation, covering the majority of the words involved, may be of some assistance. The effect of an 'h' (in the original orthography a superior dot) is to render a consonant silent, so that *Tadhg* is pronounced like the first syllable in 'tiger' and *Aodh* to rhyme with 'hay'. Alternatively the 'h' can change the sound, so that *Garbh* (rough—in this society a term of praise when applied to a lord) is pronounced 'gorv' and *dubh* (black) as 'dove'. The first syllable in *bacach* (lame) is prounounced to rhyme with 'lock', the second with 'loch' as in lake. The effect of an accent is to lengthen the vowel, so that *Mór* (large, when used of a person senior) is pronounced 'more', *Óg* (young, when used of a person junior) to rhyme with 'rogue', while *tánaiste*, a lord's deputy and designated successor, is pronounced, roughly, 'tawn-ish-te'. *Gaeil* and *Gaill* are the plural forms of *Gael* (Irish person) and *Gall* (foreigner), the first being pronounced 'gale' and the second to rhyme with 'doll'. All these are the pronunciations current in the school and public service Irish of the present day. Their relationship to the spoken language of the early modern period is partly conjectural.

This book was begun during a semester of sabbatical leave granted by Queen's University, Belfast. It was completed, after a mind-numbing intervening period as head of department, during a further period of research leave, extended for a second semester by a grant from the Arts and Humanities Research Council. I am grateful to both bodies for their support. At Queen's I have benefited from the advice and encouragement of Professor David Hayton, whose own work as a historian of early modern Ireland remains a standard for others to aspire to. I have also received helpful comments and assistance from Dr Bernadette Cunningham, Dr David Edwards, and Professor Raymond Gillespie. The series editor, Professor Robert Evans, offered valuable advice and criticism. Dr Eric Haywood of University College, Dublin, directed me to the words of the future Pius II. Mavis Bracegirdle nobly read and commented on the entire manuscript, and repeatedly recalled me sternly to my self-appointed task of making early modern Ireland both interesting and comprehensible to those for whom it is not an obsession. In so far as I have succeeded, it is with her help.

S. J. C.

Belfast
October 2006

Contents

Maps

Tables

Abbreviations

Annals of Ulster	*Anála Uladh, Annals of Ulster*, ed. E. M. Hennessy and B. MacCarthy, 4 vols. (Dublin, 1887–1901)
Carew MSS	*The Carew Manuscripts Preserved in the Archiepiscopal Library at Lambeth 1515–1624*, ed. J. S. Brewer and William Bullen, 6 vols. (London, 1867–73). Five of these six volumes are identified on the title page by date; the exception, published in 1871, is referred to here as vol. v.
CSP	*Calendar of State Papers*
CSPI	*Calendar of the State Papers Relating to Ireland 1509–1670*, 24 vols. (London, 1860–1912)
IESH	*Irish Economic and Social History*
IHS	*Irish Historical Studies*
JRSAI	*Journal of the Royal Society of Antiquaries of Ireland*
LP Henry VIII	*Letters and Papers Foreign and Domestic, Henry VIII*, 21 vols. (London, 1862–1932)
NHI	*A New History of Ireland*, ii. *Medieval Ireland 1169–1534*, ed. Art Cosgrove (Oxford, 1987); iii. *Early Modern Ireland 1534–1691*, ed. T. W. Moody, F. X. Martin, and F. J. Byrne (Oxford, 1976); ix. *Maps, Genealogies, Lists: A Companion to Irish History, Part II* (Oxford, 1984)
PRIA	*Proceedings of the Royal Irish Academy*
SP Henry VIII	*State Papers, Henry VIII*, 11 vols. (London, 1832–52)

We ought now to deal with Hybernia, which is separated from Britain by a short stretch of sea, and is partly free, benefiting from the friendship and the alliance of the Scots, and partly subject to English rule. But since nothing worth remembering has taken place there—we understand—during the period we write about, we hurry on to matters Spanish.

(Aeneas Sylvius Piccolomini (later Pope Pius II), *De Europa*, *c*.1458)

Introduction

THIS is the first part of a book about the different peoples who became the modern Irish. It opens in 1504, when one of the regional magnates who ruled a politically fragmented island on the western periphery of the continent led a culturally and linguistically diverse force from one coast almost to the other, in order to assert both his personal power and that of the English king he represented as deputy. Its successor will end in the 1790s, in an Ireland now firmly established as a coherent political unit, whose capital was one of the dozen or so largest cities in contemporary Europe. Differences of language and culture still existed, but had long lost their political significance. Instead the great division within Irish society was between Protestant and Catholic, dominant minority and subject majority, a fault line that had first appeared in the early sixteenth century but had subsequently been reinforced by a massive transfer of wealth and power. By the end of the eighteenth century, however, this long-established polarity was in its turn being challenged by a new ideology that combined a secular patriotism with the novel watchwords of liberty, equality, and brotherhood.

What is offered in this book and its successor is thus a narrative of multiple transformations. The period covered takes in the rise of the modern state, the Renaissance, the Scientific Revolution and the Enlightenment, the Reformation and Counter-Reformation, the great shift in economic activity from the Mediterranean to the Atlantic, the beginnings of popular democratic politics and of large-scale factory-based industry. A popular image of Ireland is of a society dominated, to a self-destructive degree, by ideas and emotions transmitted unchanged across the centuries. What is emphasized in the pages that follow is the opposite: the capacity of successive generations to adapt their customs and behaviour, their political allegiances and aspirations, and their sense of who they were, in response to the pressures and possibilities they confronted in a changing world. The reinventions and redefinitions that occurred across the centuries did indeed frequently involve an appeal to earlier times: the writing and rewriting of history is itself a significant part of the narrative offered here. But this too was evidence, not of a society dominated by memory and tradition, but rather of an unfailing ability to reshape the past to meet the needs of the present.

A history of changing notions of identity is also, inescapably, a history of changing alliances and oppositions. To redefine who one was was also to accept a new relationship to other ethnic, social, or religious groups. The dramatic events of the 1790s, when a Protestant-led revolutionary movement took up arms in the cause of a democratic and independent Irish republic, were to have an enduring resonance for later generations, who saw in them an alternative to the dreary sectarian divisions that subsequently came to dominate Irish public life. But that short-lived episode was only one part of a longer story. The book opens in a society defined by the distinction between an indigenous Gaelic Irish population and the heirs of a partial English conquest some three centuries old. Two centuries later, in 1688–91, we find the descendants of both these groups, now united by a shared Catholicism, mobilized in defence of the ruling British dynasty, while the heirs of a more recent Scottish and English colonization support a rival claimant to the thrones of England, Scotland, and Ireland. By the last chapters of the book it is the political aspirations of a Protestant population descended from these more recent settlers that has become the main threat to the established political order, while a frustrated and apprehensive British government has begun to explore the political potential of Catholic loyalism.

History, Voltaire wrote, is a pack of tricks that historians play on the dead. In more recent times the dead have, vicariously, had their revenge. For some time now historians have been forced to come to terms with a range of disconcerting new ideas. What was once accepted as evidence is now seen instead as a set of texts, open to a multiplicity of readings. The working up of such texts into a piece of historical writing, equally, is now presented as an essentially fictive process: the organization of selected traces of the past into a coherent narrative or analysis involves the creation of meanings and relationships that are not inherent to the materials themselves. The act of writing, likewise, is not neutral, but is shaped by the conventions of a particular rhetoric and particular narrative modes. It is a vulgar error, rivalling any philosophical naivety of which empirically-minded historians have been accused, to jump from this recognition of the constructed nature of historical accounts to the assumption that all such accounts can therefore claim equal status. That a glass may be described as half full or half empty does not mean that the amount of water it contains is a purely subjective matter. That a text can be read in more than one way does not mean that one can invest it with any meaning one chooses. But the challenge to the historian's traditional self-image is nevertheless a formidable one. Most have found it easy enough to admit that no one particular account of the past will be free of error, bias, and preconception. What they are now required to swallow is more radical: not just that no one version of the past can be wholly true, but that the very idea of a true account, against which, in principle at least, these different imperfect versions can be measured and assessed, is itself a sad illusion.

These are sobering thoughts for anyone involved in the business of writing history. For someone who had just finished a book like the present volume, the implications are particularly alarming. Is it possible, against the background just outlined, for a book that presents a single, structured account of three and a half centuries of history, even the history of a small island, to represent anything more than the last bellowings of a dinosaur in its swamp? Many may conclude that it is not. Yet if the underlying philosophical difficulties cannot be wished away, some at least of the likely traps can be avoided. The work that follows concentrates where possible on incident and experience rather than generalization. There are deliberate changes of focus, with successive sections written from the perspective of different social groups. It avoids the passive voice, that great transformer of event into process. It eschews one at least of the seductive narrative modes, the scrutiny of the past for the origins of the present. Instead it takes time to explore, not just those ideas and alignments that had a relevance for the future, but those that made sense only within a particular time and place: there are few decisive turning points in the pages that follow, but quite a few dead ends. And at times it explicitly draws attention to the ways in which more than one narrative can be constructed around the same events. None of this gets away from the central challenge: that any description of the past of necessity creates something that is not present in the past itself. But if this book remains an exercise in a traditional genre, the general narrative survey, it is at least a self-conscious one.

1

Prologue: The Hill of the Axes 1504

On 19 August 1504 two armies, each numbering several thousand, faced each other at Knockdoe, the Hill of Axes, eight miles north-east of the town of Galway. On one side were the forces of Gerald Fitzgerald, eighth earl of Kildare and governor of Ireland. Kildare had brought his army west in a punitive expedition against a local magnate, Ulick Burke of Clanricard, who had invaded the territory of another lord, O'Kelly, and then occupied the town of Galway. To oppose him Burke had brought out his own armed followers, supported by those of a number of neighbouring lords, of whom the most important were the O'Briens, a powerful dynasty dominating the territory west of the lower Shannon, and their clients the MacNamaras, who ruled what is now the eastern half of County Clare.

According to the fullest near-contemporary account of the battle, Kildare positioned his main force, 'billmen' armed with hooked blades mounted on long poles, behind a low stone wall, with archers on either side. His cavalry were positioned to the left, clear of the wall. Elsewhere in the line were the lightly armed footsoldiers known as 'kern', and the mailed professional warriors known as galloglass. Burke, meanwhile, drew up his kern and galloglass in a single body, with his cavalry to the left, facing the wall. The fighting may have begun with an attack of some kind by Kildare's horse. But the main encounter was a charge by Burke's troops against the enemy centre. Kildare's archers inflicted heavy casualties ('such a shower of arrows that their weapon and their hands were put fast together'); the attackers too would have thrown light spears ('darts'). Thereafter, however, the battle resolved itself into hand to hand fighting, with sword, axe, and bill, reportedly lasting several hours. Burke's cavalry scored a minor success, skirting the battlefield to plunder Kildare's baggage train, left unprotected when the earl's 17-year-old son abandoned his post there to join in the fighting. Later what is presumed to have been one of these same horsemen rode back to the main field, where the fighting had now ended, and called out to know who had taken Kildare and other notables in his army prisoner. However, he had misread the signs: it was Burke's forces that had eventually retreated, leaving Kildare's men in command of the field. In reply to the horseman's question 'one Skquyvors, a soldier out of Dublin, struck him with a gun with both his hands, and so beat out his brains'.[1]

[1] This follows the reconstruction of the battle, partly conjectural, in G. A. Hayes-McCoy, *Irish Battles: A Military History of Ireland* (Belfast, 1990), 48–67. Quotations are from the fullest

The battle of Knockdoe was celebrated by contemporaries and near contemporaries for two main reasons. The first was the scale of the encounter. A subsequent account, given from the point of view of the victors and putting the total dead on Burke's side at 9,000, was clearly exaggerated: the combined forces engaged have been estimated at only 10,000.[2] Even that, however, made Knockdoe the largest encounter of its kind in late medieval Ireland, and the continuance of hand to hand fighting over several hours suggests that the battle was indeed a bloody one. A contemporary Irish annalist recorded that of nine battalions of galloglass in Burke's army 'there escaped not alive of them but one thin battalion alone. And it was impossible to put an estimate on the horsemen, or on the footmen there, so that the field became uneven from those heaps of slaughter. . . . And there fell many multitudes of the forces of the earl on the other side.'[3] Even this account, constructed as it is within the limits of annalistic convention, probably softens the reality. Near-contemporary descriptions of other battles fought with similar weapons suggest a grim scene of severed or half-severed limbs and heads, with the mutilated living hideously mixed in with the grotesquely battered dead.[4]

Knockdoe was important, secondly, as illustrating the ambiguities of political relationships within this western island. Ireland in 1504 was a dependency of the crown of England: when Henry Tudor became King Henry VII, following his victory at the battle of Bosworth in 1485, he thereby became lord of Ireland. Like other absentee rulers of scattered dynastic possessions, he delegated executive power to a local representative, the earl of Kildare, who governed with the title of lord deputy.[5] Two centuries earlier, this lordship of Ireland had had real meaning. Anglo-Irish lords yielding at least nominal allegiance to the crown had controlled almost all of Leinster and the greater part of Connacht, all but the most westerly parts of Munster, and the eastern part of Ulster. By 1504, on the other hand, three quarters of this territory had been lost, reclaimed by resurgent Irish lordships like the O'Briens, or held by families like the Burkes

contemporary description, in the sixteenth-century compilation 'The Book of Howth', printed in *Carew MSS*, v. 181 ff. An alternative transcription of the text gives the soldier's name as 'Kynyvers': Donough Bryan, *Gerald Fitzgerald: The Great Earl of Kildare (1456–1513)* (Dublin and Cork, 1933), 248.

[2] Hayes-McCoy, *Irish Battles*, 61–2.

[3] *Annals of Ulster*, iii. 471. A battalion would have consisted of 80 galloglass, each supported by two spearcarriers: Hayes-McCoy, *Irish Battles*, 52.

[4] For example, after the English defeat of the Scots at Pinkie in 1547: 'Dead corpses lying dispersed abroad. Some with their legs cut off; some but ham strung and left lying half dead; others, with the arms cut off; divers, their necks half asunder; many, their heads cloven; of sundry, the brains smashed out; some others again, their heads quite off; with a thousand other kinds of killing.' Quoted in Marcus Merriman, 'The High Road from Scotland: Stewarts and Tudors', in Alexander Grant and K. J. Stringer (eds.), *Uniting the Kingdom? The Making of British History* (London, 1995), 114.

[5] Technically Kildare was in fact deputy to Henry VII's son, the 13-year-old Prince Henry, who held the formal title of lord lieutenant of Ireland.

who had lapsed from even the most nominal English allegiance. Contemporaries routinely spoke of 'the four obedient shires', the east coast counties of Louth, Meath, Dublin, and Kildare, the only remaining area in which the king's laws were upheld and his commands attended to. Even these, it was claimed, were in constant peril from the hostile territories beyond their borders. The decision of the Irish parliament, in 1495, to enclose this east coast enclave, designated 'the English Pale', within a ring of defensive earthworks, gave physical expression to the new limits of English law and government.

Against this background Kildare's expedition to Knockdoe was at first sight a triumphant reassertion of royal authority. The king's deputy brought his forces a hundred miles west of Dublin, into the heart of Gaelic Ireland, to inflict a crushing defeat on a lord who had dared to invade one of the king's towns. Yet this was only part of the story. If Kildare's expedition to the west was a defence of the king's rights, it was also the product of a web of local political relationships centred on Kildare himself. Burke of Clanricard's other principal victim, O'Kelly, may or may not have been a client with a claim on Kildare's protection, either directly or through an intermediate overlord. What is certain is that both the Clanricard Burkes and the O'Briens had earlier been on the opposite side from Kildare in a struggle for control of another Irish lordship, the Butler territories in Kilkenny and Tipperary.[6] In addition Burke's army included troops sent by the midlands lord Ely O'Carroll, whose territories bordered those of the earldom of Kildare, making him almost invariably the earl's enemy at times of conflict.[7] Kildare's army, likewise, was only partly a royal expeditionary force. As lord deputy he was entitled to call on the inhabitants of the Pale to perform military service, and these levies made up a part of his army. But some of the gentry who led these forces also had personal connections with the deputy: the Flemings of Slane and Darcy of Platen, struck down by the leader of Burke's galloglass as the fight began, were both relatives by marriage, while others were clients or political allies. They were accompanied, moreover, by a group of Gaelic lords, drawn mainly from Ulster and the midlands, whose allegiance was quite clearly to Kildare rather than to any English king. The O'Neills, represented by their chief's designated successor or *tánaiste*, were related to Kildare through the marriages of his sister and daughter. The O'Connors of Offaly were likewise related through the marriage of the earl's son to a daughter of Cahir O'Connor. (Later, in a further ramification of the network of alliances, this daughter was to marry into the family of Clanricard Burke's recent victims, the O'Kellys.) Hugh Roe (*Ruadh*, 'the Red') O'Donnell, who attended in person, was foster-father to another of Kildare's sons. The Magennises and O'Hanlons of south Ulster were

[6] Below, Ch. 2, '*Virtù* and *Fortuna*'.

[7] Tim Venning, 'The O'Carrolls of Offaly: Their Relations with the Dublin Authorities in the Sixteenth Century', in William Nolan and Timothy P. O'Neill (eds.), *Offaly: History and Society* (Dublin, 1998), 182–3.

political allies of over a decade's standing.[8] Also present in Kildare's army were the Burkes of Mayo, a separate branch of the dynasty and long-standing rivals with their Clanricard kinsmen for political dominance in the west.

All this must raise the question of precisely whose authority was being upheld at Knockdoe. Was it the distant king, in whose name Kildare marched westward? Or was it Kildare himself, whose network of dependencies and marriage alliances brought together the army with which he acted to protect a client and curb an enemy? Nor is this an abstract question. Kildare had not always been a loyal servant of Henry Tudor. His original allegiance had been to the rival house of York. In the years after 1485 he had violently obstructed attempts to remove him, to the point where the king was in effect forced to turn a blind eye to treason. By 1504 the two men had reached an accommodation. Indeed Kildare was confident enough of the value of the service he had rendered at Knockdoe to send the chancellor of Ireland to London with news of his victory, and the king, in turn, signified his approval by making him a knight of the garter. Yet the difficulties involved in governing an outlying territory through an overmighty subject had not gone away. They were to reappear in the next generation, with consequences that were to be wholly disastrous for the house of Kildare, and scarcely less so for its royal master.

As might be predicted from the tangle of alliances, antagonisms, and dependencies that had brought them together, the two armies that clashed at Knockdoe were a highly varied assembly, in their ethnic origin, their language, and their physical appearance. The Clanricard Burkes had originally been English colonists, who had conquered a large part of Connacht in the thirteenth century. Since then, however, they had become almost wholly gaelicized: speaking Irish, administering Irish law, patronizing Irish poets, musicians, and genealogists. By the time of Knockdoe there would have been little to distinguish Ulick Burke or his close relatives from their counterparts among the O'Briens or the other Irish lords with whom they allied. The troops they led onto the battlefield would also have been identical: Gaelic Irishmen, distinguishable not just by their speech but by their dress, the distinctive long Irish shirt, gathered at the waist and worn over tight trews or bare legs, and by their shaggy hair and untrimmed beards. The same would have been true of the soldiers supplied by O'Neill, O'Donnell, and the other Gaelic allies of the lord deputy. By contrast the troops levied by Kildare from the 'obedient shires', men like 'Skquyvors, a soldier out of Dublin', would for the most part have been English by surname, language, dress, and culture. But there would also have been others, particularly from the outer Pale, whose Gaelic speech and dress belied their English surnames, as well as Irishmen who had to a greater or lesser degree conformed to English manners and appearance. On both sides, finally, there were detachments of galloglass, descendants of the mercenary soldiers imported from the fourteenth

[8] Below, pp. 68–70.

century onwards from the western highlands and islands of Scotland. Although long settled in Ireland, and holders of land in their own right, they were still distinguished by the name *gallóglaigh* ('foreign warriors'), and by their continued status as a military caste.

Distinctions of culture and ethnic origin were also reflected in weaponry and methods of fighting.[9] The Gaelic Irish troops on both sides would have been kern, footsoldiers armed with swords or long knives and with throwing darts, or else mounted spearmen, riding without saddles or stirrups so that they stabbed or threw overarm rather than couching their lance in the English fashion. For protection these infantry and horsemen relied only on the extravagant folds of their linen shirts, reputedly containing as much as 23–32 metres of cloth, and leather jackets reaching to mid-chest with hanging flaps over the arms. A contemporary account of the battle of Stoke, in June 1487, had noted that the Irish kern brought to England to support the Yorkist pretender Lambert Simnel had fought 'as well as any naked men would do'.[10] The galloglass, by contrast, were distinguished by their mail shirts and iron helmets and by their weapons, the two-handed sword and the long-handled battle axe.

The Pale levies who made up the core of Kildare's army should in theory have borne the standard equipment of a contemporary English force, protected by helmets and breastplates and armed with longbows or bills. However, there were numerous complaints that the military culture of the Pale, like its English language and mode of dress, was being subverted by Gaelic influences. Men were neglecting to equip themselves with proper armour, and were abandoning the longbow for the more easily used but less effective short bows and throwing darts of the Irish.[11] Such criticisms were often wide of the mark: standard English military equipment was not always best suited to the raids and ambushes in wooded and boggy terrain characteristic of Irish warfare. But they were nevertheless taken seriously. A bill prepared for the Irish parliament in 1515 complained that 'in default of long bows divers of the king's subjects apply themselves to Irish archery, as using Irish bows and Irish spears, which induces them to Irish disposition'. In future merchants were to be required, on pain of incurring fines, to import longbows to the value of 13*s*. 4*d*., and 6*s*. 8*d*. worth of arrows, with every £20 worth of goods, 'to be sold to the king's subjects here'.[12] An earlier act, in 1494, forbade men in battle to shout out the names of their lords, as in 'Cromabo' (after Croom, the first site of the Fitzgerald lordship) or 'Butlerabo'. Instead a combatant was 'to call only on St George, or the name

[9] For general accounts of warfare in this period see Thomas Bartlett and Keith Jeffery (eds.), *A Military History of Ireland* (Cambridge, 1996), chs. 5–7; S. G. Ellis, *Reform and Revival: English Government in Ireland 1470–1534* (Woodbridge, 1986), ch. 2.

[10] Mairead Dunlevy, *Dress in Ireland: A History* (Cork, 1999), 53–4; S. G. Ellis, *Ireland in the Age of the Tudors 1447–1603* (Harlow, 1998), 85.

[11] *SP Henry VIII*, ii. 12, 18–23.

[12] *The Red Book of the Earls of Kildare*, ed. G. MacNiocaill (Dublin, 1964), 171.

of his sovereign lord, the king of England'.[13] Such pronouncements reflect the concerns of a society organized for war, in which not only was the bearing of arms a widespread obligation, but the manner in which they were borne was itself a crucial indicator of identity and allegiance.

The battle of Knockdoe was an exceptional event. The variety of the forces brought together by the two sides, the scale and ferocity of the fighting, and the earl's success in asserting royal authority, so decisively and so far from the centre of government, all placed the encounter well outside the normal pattern of Irish affairs. The military outcome, too, despite the excitement it generated at the time, was by no means decisive. Clanricard power in the west was temporarily checked. But five years later the O'Briens were able to inflict a serious defeat on another Kildare army, in alliance once again with O'Donnell and also with the renegade English earl of Desmond, as it returned from an expedition against the MacCarthys of the south-west. Despite all this, the events of 19 August 1504 serve to highlight several important aspects of the character of late medieval Ireland: a militarized frontier society, in which power depended immediately on physical force, in which government authority and personal lordship were inextricably entangled, and in which cultural frontiers were clearly defined yet constantly crossed. To these points can be added the perspective of hindsight. Within thirty years of this, its greatest triumph, the power of the house of Kildare would be in ruins. Its downfall, moreover, was to be only the beginning in a series of radical changes, military, political, cultural, and economic, that was to transform out of all recognition the world in which that power had been exercised and in which the two armies at Knockdoe had fought one another to a bloody finish.

[13] Irish Statutes 10 Henry VII, c. 20. 'Abú' is an Irish language interjection, rendered by the Edwardian pioneer of Gaelic lexicography as 'to victory'. See P. S. Dinneen, *Foclóir Gaedhilge agus Béarla* (rev. edn., Dublin, 1927), 3.

2

'The Land of Banba is but Swordland': Late Medieval Ireland

THE IRISH

At the end of the middle ages the dominant language and social organization across some two-thirds of Ireland, containing perhaps half of the island's population, was that of an ancient and distinctive Gaelic culture. One reason for this distinctiveness was that Ireland, lying far out to the west, behind the larger island of Great Britain, was never formally part of the Roman empire. Nor, in consequence, had it suffered the huge discontinuities experienced elsewhere as that empire contracted and collapsed. There had, however, been contacts with the Roman world, most notably the introduction during the fifth century of Christianity. With Christianization came the Latin alphabet, whose adaptation to writing in the vernacular as well as in learned Latin gave a new permanence and sophistication to cultural forms that had already existed for centuries. The result was the survival into the era of the Renaissance of a society that was literate, highly organized, yet in some respects strikingly outside the mainstream of European cultural development.[1]

The distinctiveness of this society was clearly evident in its political and social structure. Gaelic Ireland in the late middle ages and into the sixteenth century has been characterized as a lineage society.[2] The term is intended to highlight the dominance within each of its separate lordships of a social and political elite, defined by their claimed descent from a common ancestor. Contemporary English writers, groping for suitable terminology to describe a culture very different from their own, generally used the term 'sept' (apparently

[1] The most complete survey of medieval and early modern Gaelic Ireland is K. W. Nicholls, *Gaelic and Gaelicized Ireland in the Middle Ages* (2nd edn., Dublin, 2003). See also Nicholls's chapter 'Gaelic Society and Economy' in *NHI*, ii. 397–438. The other major work is Katharine Simms, *From Kings to Warlords* (Woodbridge, 1987). Mary O'Dowd, 'Gaelic Economy and Society', in Ciaran Brady and Raymond Gillespie (eds.), *Natives and Newcomers: Essays on the Making of Irish Colonial Society 1534–1641* (Dublin, 1986), 120–47 is a useful shorter survey. Patrick J. Duffy, David Edwards, and Elizabeth Fitzpatrick (eds.), *Gaelic Ireland: Land, Lordship and Settlement c.1250–c.1650* (Dublin, 2001) is a valuable collection of essays accompanied by a long bibliographical review.

[2] Nicholls, *Gaelic and Gaelicized Ireland*, 8.

an adaptation of Irish *sliocht*, meaning a section or group of people) to refer to these extended family groups. Another possible term, again with the added advantage of being of Irish origin, would be 'clan' (from Irish *clann*, offspring). To be of any use, however, this must first be stripped of its lingering romantic connotation of a whole society vertically integrated by real, or even imagined, ties of kinship. In the Scottish Highlands of the sixteenth and seventeenth centuries the peasant population as a whole considered themselves to be members of particular clans. This identification, sometimes based on an actual blood relationship but often wholly fictitious in genealogical terms, implied acceptance of a chief's authority, a claim on his protection, and a degree of solidarity against outsiders.[3] In Ireland, on the other hand, the line between members of the ruling lineage and the large majority who made up the remainder of the population remained firmly drawn. One Gaelic notable of the early seventeenth century referred derisively to 'mere churls and labouring men, [none] of whom knows his own great-grandfather'.[4] Surviving records provide no statistical basis for estimating the relative size of the two groups, which may well have varied with economic conditions and the structure of individual lordships. But for some indication we may look to the midlands lordship of Ely O'Carroll, where taxation records compiled in 1659 suggest that only around one in ten of the inhabitants bore the once prized surname O'Carroll.[5]

These lineages, clans, or septs provided the basis for a fragmented political system of separate and internally self-governing lordships. Each lordship was ruled by a chief. Abandonment of the earlier term king (*rí*) left no one agreed term for this figure. The most common was *tighearna* or lord, but there was also *ceann phobail* (head of a lordship), as well as borrowings from the Latin (*princeps, dominus*). English observers spoke of 'captains' of 'nations'. In practice rulers were known simply by the surname of the lineage (the O'Neill, the O'Brien). Land within the lordship was allocated among the members of the ruling lineage, according to a variety of customs specific to particular regions. In some cases the chief and his immediate family controlled the greater part of the land; in others, possibly reflecting a different internal political balance, more or less generous provision was also made for other branches of the lineage. In addition there was frequently some requirement, again varying from lordship to lordship, for the periodic redistribution of land among members of the sept. In some cases this was done at fixed intervals, in others on the succession of a new chief, in others again on the death of any existing participant. But in all cases the principle

[3] R. A. Dodgshon, '"Pretence of Blude" and "Place of thair Dwelling": The Nature of Highland Clans 1500–1745', in R. A. Houston and I. D. Whyte (eds.), *Scottish Society 1500–1800* (Cambridge, 1989), 169–98.

[4] Quoted in Nicholls, *Gaelic and Gaelicized Ireland*, 10.

[5] Rolf Loeber, 'The Changing Borders of the Ely O'Carroll Lordship', in William Nolan and Timothy P. O'Neill (eds.), *Offaly: History and Society* (Dublin, 1998), 295.

was the same. Possession was temporary, or at best for life: ownership remained corporate, vested in the lineage as a whole.

The same emphasis on group over individual rights was evident in the arrangements for political succession. There was no fixed rule for identifying a single heir. Instead chiefs were in theory chosen by the members of the lineage from among the *derbfine*, the group comprising all those descended within four generations from an existing or earlier chief. The system was not in practice quite as open as this legal definition implied. Claimants were most commonly the sons or brothers of the deceased or superseded chief. In some cases, indeed, either the strength of existing rulers and their chosen heirs, or the accidents of demography, permitted a smooth succession across the generations. On six successive occasions between 1359 and 1508, for example, the lordship of MacCarthy Mór passed from father to son. The same thing happened in the case of seven generations of rulers over the Maguires of Fermanagh.[6] The institution of *tánaiste*, allowing a reigning lord to designate a deputy with right of succession, gave qualified support to this type of dynastic stability. But in other cases, where more than one credible claimant existed, or where the designated successor proved deficient, the outcome depended ultimately on the strength of the rivals involved.

The system had a rationale, based on the central role of the chief as military leader: minorities, the great weakness of a hereditary mechanism, could not occur, and no clan need fear being led by a weakling or incompetent. But the price paid was sometimes a bloody and destructive succession struggle. When Neil Garbh, chief of the O'Donnells, died in captivity on the Isle of Man in 1439, he was succeeded by his brother Naghten, followed by Naghten's sons Rory and Turlough. However, they were opposed by Neil Garbh's sons, who killed Naghten in 1452 and Rory in 1454. In 1461 they defeated Turlough and cut off a hand and a foot—mutilations that, since a chief was required to be physically whole, effectively eliminated him as a rival. Neil Garbh's son Hugh 'the red' now took power. In 1480, however, he was forced to accept another of Naghten's sons as his deputy and designated successor. It was only with the death of this rival at the hands of Hugh's son Conn in 1497 that the cycle of violence initiated by the death of Neil Garbh almost sixty years earlier came to a close.[7] Among the O'Carrolls of Ely some decades later, conflict was likewise between uncle, nephew, and cousin. Fearganainm, the eldest though illegitimate son of Mulrony, having succeeded his father in 1532, was opposed by his uncles Donough and Owny and by Donough's sons William Moyle, Tadhg, and Calvach. William Moyle was eliminated in 1538, trapped in a church that was set ablaze to drive him out. In 1541, however, Tadhg surprised Ferganainm in his castle and killed him. Ferganainm's son Tadhg Caoch succeeded as chief,

[6] O'Dowd, 'Gaelic Economy and Society', 123; Nicholls, *Gaelic and Gaelicized Ireland*, 27.
[7] *NHI*, ii. 573–4; Nicholls, *Gaelic and Gaelicized Ireland*, 137.

but was killed by Calvach in 1553. The following year Calvach was in turn killed by Tadhg Caoch's brother, William Odher.[8]

The territories that comprised this patchwork of individual lordships varied hugely in size. At one extreme were tiny units such as that ruled by the MacCarrons of Westmeath, estimated in the late sixteenth century to amount to some 1,200 acres.[9] At the other were the major regional lordships, such as the O'Neills in central Ulster or the MacCarthys in the south west. All of the smaller territories would have been subject to the dominance of a larger neighbour. The major Irish lordships, equally, derived their power not only from their own more extensive territories, but from the control which they exercised over lesser septs. Most commonly this took the form of regular tribute, in money, in food, or in lodgings and entertainment for the lord and his retinue. In addition overlords frequently exacted military services, requiring tributary septs to provide fighting men in time of need, or billeting their own soldiers on subordinate territories. For additional security they might take hostages or place their own garrisons in strongholds located in the subject territory. The overlords of smaller territories also played a part, along with leading members of the lineage, in the choice of a new chief. These relationships of dominance and surbordination might be expressed in formal rituals of submission. But they depended almost wholly on the continuous exercise of effective power. A small territory located close to a powerful neighbour had little choice but to accept a more or less permanent dependence. The chief of a larger or more distant lordship, on the other hand, might submit or assert his independence as immediate circumstances permitted. A lesser lordship might also find itself caught between rival overlords, as when the O'Donnells and the Mayo Burkes competed in the late fifteenth and early sixteenth centuries for dominance in north Connacht. An observer from English Ireland, writing around 1515, perceptively summed up the basis of such relationships. The 'captain' of each region 'has imperial jurisdiction within his room, and obeys to no other person, English or Irish, except only to such persons as may subdue him by the sword'.[10]

What all this meant in practice was a society dominated by constant, small-scale warfare. Just as the succession of one lord to another depended on an effective assertion of authority, so it was in the relationship between territories: right existed where one could successfully exact obedience or tribute; property was what one could defend. The primacy thus given to effective violence as the source of political legitimacy implied that every lord maintained his own military force, as substantial as his resources permitted. The normal practice was to maintain a retinue of armed followers in the lord's own household, while billeting the remainder on the inhabitants of the lordship and also, in the case

[8] Tim Venning, 'The O'Carrolls of Offaly: Their Relations with the Dublin Authorities in the Sixteenth Century', in Nolan and O'Neill, *Offaly*, 185–91.

[9] Nicholls, *Gaelic and Gaelicized Ireland*, 22.

[10] *SP Henry VIII*, ii. 1.

of an overlord, on any subordinate territory that could be coerced into yielding this form of tribute. The majority of the soldiers maintained in this way were the lightly armed kern, of limited value in battle but ideally suited to the hit and run raids across rough and wooded terrain that made up much Gaelic warfare. They were reinforced by smaller numbers of horsemen and also by troops of galloglass, present in Ulster and Connacht from the thirteenth century and in Munster and Leinster from the fifteenth. Some galloglass clans imported from Scotland became landholders in their own right, in exchange for the military service given to an overlord: the MacSweenys under O'Donnell in the north-west, the MacDonnells under O'Neill in mid-Ulster, and the MacQuillans, initially under the earl of Ulster, in north Antrim. Otherwise galloglass, like other soldiers, were billeted on the territories of the lord himself or on those of subordinate chiefs. A report in around 1490 estimated that the Gaelic chiefs, along with some Connacht lords of English extraction now seen as wholly gaelicized, between them controlled some 3,000 horsemen, 3,000 galloglass, and around 15,000 kern.[11]

The main functions of the chief were twofold: to provide military leadership, and to uphold the position of the lordship by hospitality and by his patronage of poets, genealogists, and other men of learning. Given these limited functions, the internal political structures of the Gaelic lordships were, by contemporary European standards, rudimentary. The principal administrative tasks, the collection of taxes and the marshalling and billeting of troops, were delegated to prominent followers or were vested, as a hereditary prerogative, in a particular family. In either case those concerned were rewarded for their service by a fixed share of the exactions in money or kind for which they were responsible. There was also provision for public assemblies at which disputes were submitted to arbitration and important issues discussed. Such assemblies, often held on hilltops and summoned either at fixed times or as occasion required, were councils of leading landowners and members of the lineage, although a wider cross section of the population might attend to watch the proceedings. Neither the chief nor the assembly of clan notables, however, had any power to make general laws. Instead legal administration was in the hands of a hereditary caste of professional lawyers, the brehons, whose ostensible task was to give judgment in conformity with a canon of authoritative legal tracts committed to writing in the seventh and eighth centuries.

If Gaelic lords did not make law, neither did they, in normal circumstances, enforce it. Instead the system was one of restorative justice. Those guilty of theft or other offences made restitution and compensated those they were held to have injured. Even homicide was resolved by the payment of an *eraic* (blood money), proportionate to the status of the victim, to the kin of the dead man. The lord

[11] L. Price, 'Armed Forces of the Irish Chiefs in the Early Sixteenth Century', *JRSAI*, ser. 7, 2 (1932), 201–7. For the date of this document, and the overall totals given above, see S. G. Ellis, *Ireland in the Age of the Tudors 1447–1603* (Harlow, 1998), 248.

of a territory might also demand a fine, but that was in cases where the offender had violated his protection. There were also instances of capital punishment. In 1500, for example, Maguire of Fermanagh hanged a notorious thief, while in 1534 a successor hanged a woman guilty of having murdered her husband, and also burned her two accomplices alive.[12] But these actions, against individuals whose crimes were particularly scandalous, or who had become a threat to the community as a whole, were extensions of the lord's general function as defender of the territory. A similar concept of crime as a wrong done by one person to another, and requiring rectification in those terms, had at one time been common across much of Europe. By the sixteenth century, however, it had in most cases given way to the alternative notion of an abstract rule of law, whose breach required punishment in the name of the ruler.[13] The survival in Gaelic Ireland of the older concept of compensatory justice was a striking example of the society's isolation from the European mainstream. To contemporary English observers, on the other hand, the licence given to thieves and murderers to escape the hangman's rope by a money payment was evidence simply of corrupt and lawless government.

The brehons were only one of several hereditary learned classes who, in the absence of centralized political structures, had a particularly important role in defining and maintaining the social order. Many families in these classes, reflecting the close interaction of secular and religious culture, were hereditary tenants of church lands. Others held lands within particular lordships, free of the usual exactions. The most important and prestigious of the learned classes were the poets. Their role was to provide propaganda for the ruling houses of Gaelic Ireland, in the form of eulogies, exhortations to military or political action, poems of celebration for victories, and elegies for the dead. However, they were never mere household employees. The professional poet had undergone a long training in order to master the specialized diction and intricate metre and rhyme scheme within which bardic poetry had to be written. The leading masters of the craft rarely composed for any except the most powerful patrons. Some accounts suggest that poets as a class were semi-sacred figures, their persons and property protected by powerful taboos, and their hostile satires against those who had offended them believed to operate as curse as well as ridicule. A more sober review of the evidence, however, suggests that even the most prominent bard thought twice about satirizing a really powerful individual.[14] A second important learned class were the genealogists, whose pedigrees, both real and fabricated, were important both in determining the membership of the ruling

[12] *Annals of Ulster*, iii. 451, 597.

[13] Bruce Lenman and Geoffrey Parker, 'The State, the Community and the Criminal Law in Early Modern Europe', in V. A. C. Gatrell, Bruce Lenman, and Geoffrey Parker, *Crime and the Law: The Social History of Crime in Western Europe since 1500* (London, 1980), 11–48.

[14] Compare Nicholls, *Gaelic and Gaelicized Ireland*, 82; Katharine Simms, 'Bardic Poetry as a Historical Source', in Tom Dunne (ed.), *The Writer as Witness* (Cork, 1987), 68–9.

lineage and in providing it with the prestige and legitimacy derived from a suitably distinguished ancestry. Other learned families devoted themselves to history (possibly in combination with poetry or genealogy), to medicine, or to music.

The burden of supporting this entire pyramid of ruling lineages, the specialized families that supported their prestige, and the military establishments on which their power depended, rested squarely on the anonymous mass that made up the remainder of the Gaelic population, the families so casually dismissed as those who did not know their own great-grandfathers. Gaelic lords drew from the territories under their control a wide variety of exactions. Fixed payments in kind or more rarely in cash were demanded from every unit of land. So too were specified labour services from men and horses. There was also the food and lodging demanded for kern and galloglass, as well as the horses, hounds, and huntsmen in the lord's retinue. In addition extraordinary levies could be imposed to finance recurrent outbreaks of warfare, to provide a dowry for the marriage of a chief's daughter, or to meet the demands of an overlord. Those living on the extensive lands held by the chief himself would have made these payments directly to his agents. Where land was held by a retainer or by another member of the ruling lineage the peasantry contributed both to the support of their immediate lord and to the fulfilment of his obligations to the chief, including the requirement that substantial freeholders should provide a fixed number of nights' entertainment and lodging for their lord and his retinue.

There were no laws to regulate the scale of these multiple exactions. The only restriction on a lord's demands, possibly of real importance in a thinly populated society, was that tenants, neither tied to the soil nor incorporated into the clan system, could move freely from one lord to another. An early seventeenth-century English account maintained that the exactions of the lords 'have caused divers rebellions and insurrections among themselves'.[15] The truth of this is impossible to check. The Gaelic sources testify eloquently to the contempt in which the upper classes and professionals held their social inferiors. But on the doings of the common people themselves, much more on their private resentments and aspirations, they remain largely silent.

In outward appearance, Gaelic Ireland at the beginning of the sixteenth century was an empty and impoverished wasteland. The population of the island as a whole in 1500 was probably around 750,000, compared to a peak of 1 million two centuries earlier, before the ravages of the Black Death.[16] Although no figures are available, it is likely that population density was greater in the more intensely cultivated regions of English settlement, while in the Gaelic lordships sparser numbers lived dispersed across a wooded, undrained, and only patchily

[15] Thomas Gainsford (1618), quoted in D. B. Quinn, *The Elizabethans and the Irish* (Ithaca, NY, 1966), 167.

[16] See Appendix below.

cultivated landscape. There were no towns, nor even villages. The fortified dwellings of chiefs and other leading figures, along with certain ecclesiastical sites, could in some cases become the centre of a cluster of houses, belonging to associates, tenants, and labourers. The largest such community recorded appears to have been the 200 houses noted in 1517 as surrounding the residence of the local bishop at Rosscarbery, County Cork. However, the twenty houses round a castle burned in County Galway half a century later has been put forward as more representative.[17] The landscape was not wholly unmarked by human hands. Across most of the countryside territorial divisions, the ancestors of modern townlands, had been established centuries earlier and remained important for both taxation and the allocation of land, their boundaries marked out by ditches. Yet this evidence of long-established and highly organized settlement contrasted sharply with the huge amounts of land remaining in or close to its natural state. In the midlands lordship of Ely O'Carroll, it has been estimated that only one-fifth of the total area was considered, even in the early seventeenth century, as profitable land.[18] Much of the remainder would have been woodland, in some cases forest, in others dense scrub: discussions of the defence of the English territories to the east regularly emphasized the need to cut passes through neighbouring woods, in order to facilitate the interception or pursuit of raiders. Other areas consisted of largely unexploited bog and undrained marshland. Elsewhere the long, laborious process of clearing ground strewn with geological rubble, reflected today in the distinctive landscape of small fields enclosed by dry stone walls encountered in much of the west and a small part of south Ulster, had not yet begun, so that much land was of little use for either tillage or pasture.

A visitor to Gaelic Ireland from continental western Europe would have found one familiar feature. The monasteries and churches of the religious orders that had spread throughout Gaelic regions in the fifteenth century were extensive structures, finished and decorated in a distinctively Irish version of late Gothic. As such they testified both to a capacity to mobilize economic resources, and to a level of architectural sophistication, not otherwise evident. Apart from these, the most substantial buildings to be found in Gaelic areas were the tower houses of the lords and other substantial figures: plain rectangular structures, four or five storeys in height, their walls broken only by narrow windows and by a wide variety of loopholes and similar defensive openings. In other cases, particularly perhaps in Ulster where the tower house was less common, lords lived instead inside a fort composed of a ditch and earthenbank, possibly surmounted by a hedge. A late sixteenth-century drawing of the O'Neill fort at Tullyhogue shows a substantial two-storey thatched house, presumably O'Neill's own residence, at the centre of such an enclosure. More commonly, however, houses in Gaelic Ireland were simple one-roomed dwellings: where they were larger, it was to accommodate animals as well as people. Building materials varied. In some areas

[17] *NHI*, ii. 399, 404.

[18] Loeber, 'Changing Borders of Ely O'Carroll', 293.

stone was used for all or part of the walls. Elsewhere walls were constructed of sods, clay, wattle or other timber, or some combination of available materials. Roofs were of thatch or sods, with no chimney, so that smoke escaped through door, windows or thatch. The English observer Fynes Moryson, writing at the start of the seventeenth century, commented on men of substance ('the very lords among them') living in 'a cabin made of the boughs of trees and covered with earth'.[19]

The thinly spread population and material poverty of Gaelic Ireland reflected its dependence on a rudimentary agrarian economy. There was some manufacturing, in the form of textiles. The city of Waterford, for example, acted as a centre for the export of woollen cloth produced in the Gaelic lordships beyond its walls. Galway, likewise, traded in linens produced in its even more wholly gaelicized hinterland. In places there were even small watermills for the finishing of cloth, as well as others for grinding corn. All such production, however, was on a small scale, and it may well be that the millers, spinners, and weavers concerned, as well as the carpenters, masons, and other craftsmen mentioned from time to time in contemporary records, were part-time workers otherwise engaged in agriculture. Agriculture itself was primarily pastoral. Frequent incidental references to crops being ravaged in war, and to the hardship caused by harvest failures, make clear that there was rather more tillage than contemporary accounts suggested. But the main investment of Gaelic Ireland was nevertheless in livestock. This included sheep, especially in the south, along with pigs and horses. But above all it meant cattle. Herds of cows constituted the greater part of the personal wealth of the Irish upper classes and provided the main ingredients in the diet of all social groups. This meant that meat was more plentiful than would have been the case with most contemporary peasant populations, although the need to conserve stocks also led to the less conventional resource of blood drawn from the living beast and eaten mixed with grain. In addition, and more important in day to day terms, milk was consumed in its many forms: drunk as a liquid, eaten in the semi-solid form (curds or 'bonnyclabber') produced by the souring process, or made into cheese and butter, the latter regularly eaten as a food in its own right.

Neither of these forms of agriculture, tillage and pasture, involved an intensive exploitation of resources. The principal grain crop was oats, grown as food for both people and horses, with lesser quantities of wheat and barley, as well as flax for linen production. Crop rotation appears to have been unknown; instead land was tilled for two or three years then left fallow for a decade or more while it recovered its fertility. Small patches of ground were cultivated with spades. Larger areas were ploughed, using horses rather than oxen, and with the plough attached to the animals' tails, a practice reflecting not so much the barbarism

[19] Caoimhín Ó Danachair, 'Representations of Houses on Some Irish Maps of *c*.1600', in Geraint Jenkins (ed.), *Studies in Folk Life* (London 1969), 91–103; *NHI*, ii. 403–4.

denounced by English observers as the frequency with which the plough was likely to hit rocks or other obstacles and so suffer damage unless the plough team stopped at once. Tilled fields were not enclosed by permanent ditches or hedges; instead temporary barricades were put up to protect growing crops. Cattle rearing, meanwhile, was on a semi-nomadic basis. Transhumance, the movement of herds from lowland winter pasture to higher ground in summer, was common, as in other parts of early modern Europe. But even in lowland areas large herds were driven back and forth across the unfenced and largely empty countryside to take advantage of the scattered grazing available. Gaelic Ireland had no tradition of hay making, instead setting certain grasslands aside to serve as winter pasture.

If the political, social, and economic structures of Gaelic society can be reconstructed at least in outline, the quality of life of its inhabitants is a subject principally for speculation. A thin and apparently static population implies that something consistently cut back the potential for natural increase. The most likely constraints were famine and disease. In the late fifteenth century, annalists record famine in 1465, following the destruction of crops by frost and snow, widespread loss of cattle in 1473, and crops damaged by summer rain in 1487 and again in 1491. In 1496 bad weather brought loss of livestock and hindered their fattening, as well as damaging corn. The following year the Annals of Ulster recorded famine throughout all Ireland, 'for there was scarcely a recess in all Ireland wherein died not many persons of that hunger'. During the same period there were outbreaks of plague or other disease in 1462, 1466–8, 1470, 1477–8, 1484, 1488–9, and 1491–2. The 1488–9 outbreak was said to be so severe that the dead remained unburied throughout the country.[20] Constant low-level warfare, in which the spoiling of corn and driving off of cattle were preferred to set-piece battles, may also have played a part.

On the other side of the demographic equation, high mortality was balanced by high fertility. Irish females, one early seventeenth-century observer maintained, were 'women at thirteen and old wives at thirty'.[21] The evidence of later periods suggests that such extravagant claims, especially relating to what were perceived as inferior cultures, need to be treated with caution. The careers of women like Grace O'Mally (*c.*1530–*c.*1603), or Eleanor Butler, countess of Desmond (*c.*1545–*c.*1638), each twice married and the mothers respectively of four and six children who survived into adulthood, make clear that to be a woman in Gaelic (or, in the case of Eleanor, gaelicized) Ireland was not necessarily to be condemned to premature old age or an early death. But these were members of the ruling elite. Moreover both are visible precisely because they survived marriage

[20] *Annals of Ulster*, 423. The annalistic evidence on death and disease is usefully collated by Sir William Wilde in the introduction to his analysis of the mortality statistics for the census of 1851 (Parliamentary Papers 1856, vol. 29, 93 ff).

[21] Luke Gernon, 'A Discourse of Ireland', printed in C. Litton Falkiner, *Illustrations of Irish History and Topography, Mainly of the Seventeenth Century* (London, 1904), 357.

to achieve the autonomy and personal power that could come with widowhood, and the more extensive connections that could come with remarriage. They were probably exceptional in their own class, and much more so among Gaelic women as a whole. Although precise statistics do not exist, the fragmented pattern of landholding revealed when Gaelic land occupancy began to be recorded in terms of English property law has been taken as indicating that family size was in fact fairly large. One estimate is that half the population of Gaelic territories at any one time would have been under 2 years of age, and that few adults could expect to live beyond 40. [22]

The inner life that accompanied this harsh demographic regime is equally elusive. At the upper levels of Gaelic society, as in English Ireland and among other contemporary elites, wives and children were instruments of dynastic politics. Marriage, and the sending of sons to be fostered in the households of other lords, were a means of creating or reinforcing political bonds. Gaelic law differed from the practice in most parts of Europe in permitting women to hold property independently of their husbands. A Gaelic wife, on the other hand, had no right of inheritance from her husband; her sole entitlement, on his death, was to the recovery of the dowry she had brought with her. Gaelic law also differed from other west European systems, and from the canon law of the church, in permitting couples to dissolve unions that had become unsatisfactory or had ceased to serve a purpose, in recognizing the right of men to maintain concubines, and in according legal status to illegitimate as well as legitimate children.[23]

In the case of fosterage observers commented on the close ties of loyalty and emotion, continuing into adulthood, that developed between children and their foster parents. When Murrough O'Brien was executed as a traitor at Limerick in 1577, it was his foster-mother whose extravagant grief the poet Edmund Spenser claimed to have observed, as she took the severed head, 'and sucked up all the blood that run thereout, saying, that the earth was not worthy to drink it, and therewith also steeped her face and breast, and tore her hair, crying out and shrieking most terribly'.[24] Where marriage is concerned, the fragmentary evidence suggests that the texture of the relationships formed by a system dominated by dynastic considerations varied hugely from case to case. There are instances of wives abruptly discarded in response to a change in political alignments, but also of others who were regarded as an important influence on their husbands' doings. Richard Stanihurst, writing in

[22] Gearoid MacNiocaill, *Irish Population before Petty: Problems and Possibilities* (Dublin, 1981), 3; Christopher Maginn, *'Civilizing' Gaelic Leinster: The Extension of Tudor Rule in the O'Byrne and O'Toole Lordships* (Dublin, 2005), 22, citing the estimate of A. P. Smyth, *Celtic Leinster: Towards an Historical Geography of Early Irish Civilization* AD *500–1600* (Dublin, 1982), 5, who in turn draws on the age structure of modern Third World populations.

[23] Mary O'Dowd, *A History of Women in Ireland 1500–1800* (Harlow, 2005), 9–15.

[24] Edmund Spenser, *A View of the State of Ireland* (Oxford, 1997), 66.

1584, reported that at social gatherings 'The prime place at the table is bestowed upon the woman of the household. She wears an ankle length tunic with a long-sleeved saffron robe. In the presence of the guests, she and her husband share a strange silence, she alone of them being his intimate companion of the bed chamber.' Whether such silence really reflected intimacy or, as is perhaps more likely, the emotional distance of a union that was both expedient and contingent, is another matter. Nor is it clear where the Dubliner Stanihurst had got his information. Another observer, Fynes Moryson, whose participation during 1600–3 in the last and greatest English war against Gaelic Ireland had perhaps given him more first-hand information, emphasized instead the freedom with which women participated in social gatherings: 'the wives of Irish lords . . . often drink till they be drunken, or at least till they void urine in full assemblies of men.'[25]

Fynes Moryson's outrage at the toilet habits of Gaelic Irish ladies reflected the pervasive sense of contemporary Englishmen that they were dealing with an inferior civilization. Yet issues of refinement are always relative. Elsewhere, after all, he noted that the Irish themselves referred to the English as 'shite breeches', because of what they regarded as the loathsome habit of farting without lowering their trousers.[26] On occasion, moreover, more open-minded visitors had to confess themselves surprised by the level of civility they encountered in a supposedly barbarous land. Henry VIII's lord deputy, Sir Anthony St Leger, reporting in 1541 on his meeting with the west Ulster magnate Manus O'Donnell, advised his master that the only appropriate present he could be sent was a set of the formal robes worn to attend parliament:

> for I think him furnished of other apparel better than any Irishman; for at such time as he met with me, he was in a coat of crimson velvet, with aglets of gold 20 or 30 pair; over that a great double cloak of right crimson satin, guarded with black velvet, a bonnet, with a feather set full of aglets of gold, that me thought it strange to see him so honourable in apparel, and all the rest of his nation that I have seen as yet so vile.[27]

Manus's display of refinement was, as St Leger's comments made clear, exceptional, part of the equippage of a lord whose unusual degree of cultural and artistic interests have led him to be singled out as sixteenth-century Ireland's version of the Renaissance prince.[28] But other evidence also highlights the need

25 Richard Stanihurst, *De rebus in Hibernia Gestis* (1584), printed in Com Lennon, *Richard Stanihurst, the Dubliner 1547–1618* (Dublin, 1981), 150; Fynes Moryson, *An Itinerary*, 4 vols. (Glasgow, 1907), iv. 198.

26 *The Irish Sections of Fynes Moryson's Unpublished Itinerary*, ed. Graham Kew (Dublin, 1998), 111.

27 *SP Henry VIII*, iii. 320. An aglet was the pointed end of a lace, but in this context refers perhaps to ornaments attached to the dangling ends.

28 Brendan Bradshaw, 'Manus "the Magnificent": O'Donnell as Renaissance Prince', in Art Cosgrove and Donal McCartney (eds.), *Studies in Irish History* (Dublin, 1979), 15–36. Bradshaw's

to look beyond the undoubted limitations of a decentralized, war-torn political system, and a pastoral, exchange-based economy, and to recognize that Gaelic Ireland, for all the antiquity of its institutions and cultural traditions, was neither a static society nor a wholly inward looking one.

One obvious example is warfare. Here Irish lords had from an early stage borrowed freely from English allies and enemies. Their adoption of defensive architecture is reflected in the thousands of tower houses constructed during the fifteenth century, as well as in the erection of a few more substantial fortresses, like Bunratty Castle in County Clare, built by the MacNamaras around 1460. The same capacity for ambitious fortification is evident in the bridge across the River Shannon, the latest in a series of such structures, that by the 1530s allowed the O'Briens to control the passage into and out of their territory. The seven-arched structure was protected by castles at each end, of which that on the east

> builded all of hewn marble . . . was of such force that the ordnance did in manner no hurt to it, for the wall was at the least 12 or 13 foot thick, and both the castles were well warded with gunners, galloglass and horsemen, having made such fortifications of timber and hogsheads of earth, as the like have not been seen in this land.[29]

Defensive armour, meanwhile, had become a common prestige item in the households of the elite, although kern continued to fight in their shirts. When Hugh 'the Red' O'Donnell captured Castle Moly in County Tyrone from the O'Neills in 1498 he carried off no fewer than seventeen suits of armour.[30] A further innovation, this time originating in Gaelic Ireland itself, was the introduction of galloglass. In addition, although on a smaller scale, some coastal lords ventured into naval warfare. A report around 1490 noted that both the O'Driscolls of Baltimore in the far south-west and the O'Malleys on the southern side of Clew Bay maintained forces of kern 'who use long galleys'. In 1514 O'Donnell launched a fleet of boats on Lough Erne as part of his campaign to subdue Fermanagh. Two years later a French nobleman who had enjoyed his hospitality while on pilgrimage to the celebrated shrine of St Patrick at Lough Derg sent him a vessel full of firearms, including 'a large castle-breaking gun' which he used to take the fortress of Sligo.[31]

These modifications in methods of warfare involved not just a change of habits, but a substantial mobilization of new resources. In the case of fortification and the importation of galloglass it was possible to adapt traditional institutions to

deliberately provocative argument is enthusiastically elaborated in Darren MacEiteagáin, 'The Renaissance and the Late Medieval Lordship of Tír Chonaill 1461–1555', in William Nolan, Liam Ronayne, and Mairead Dunlevy (eds.), *Donegal: History and Society* (Dublin, 1995), 203–28. See also Mícheál MacCraith, 'Gaelic Ireland and the Renaissance', in Glanmor Williams and R. O. Jones (eds.), *The Celts and the Renaissance* (Cardiff, 1960), 57–89.

[29] *SP Henry VIII*, ii. 351; iii. 60.

[30] *Annals of Ulster*, iii. 431–3.

[31] Price, 'Armed Forces of the Irish Chiefs', 203, 204; *The Annals of Loch Cé*, ed. W. M. Hennessy (London, 1871), ii. 223, 225.

new purposes. A reinterpretation of the traditional requirement that subordinates and their tenants should contribute to the entertainment of the lord and his retinue made it possible to quarter both kern and galloglass on the inhabitants of a lord's own territories and any others he could dominate, the practice known as coyne and livery. The labour services required from tenants could likewise be extended to include work on the building and repair of tower houses and castles. Even here, however, some means would also have had to be found to hire and pay specialist craftsmen, while defensive armour must normally have involved an expensive commercial transaction.

A willingness to innovate in military matters is perhaps not surprising: survival, both political and physical, was at stake. But a capacity for change is also evident in other areas. Much of the work produced within the Gaelic learned tradition, as might be expected in a rarefied court culture, was highly stylized in character. Histories and genealogies shored up contemporary political aspirations by the formulaic manufacture of pedigrees and precedents; annalistic obituaries concealed real men, and occasionally women, behind layers of stereotypical praise. Yet intellectual life was not in fact wholly static. Indeed one branch of the Irish learned classes appears to have abandoned indigenous tradition entirely in order to join the European mainstream. Medieval Irish medical tracts consist entirely of translations of Latin texts produced in continental universities, leaving no trace of whatever native theory and practice had earlier existed.[32] Devotional literature combined lives of Irish saints and other material of local origin with Irish translations or versions of standard religious texts from continental Europe.[33] Even in the conservative field of hagiography the Irish language life of St Colmcille produced in 1523 for Manus O'Donnell has been seen as representing the influence of humanist scholarship in its concern to assemble a complete body of documentary evidence and to present previously inaccessible material in vernacular Irish.[34]

Even the brehons, or judges, theoretically charged with regulating society according to the unchanging principles of a centuries-old canon of legal texts, were in practice more flexible and creative, borrowing from both Roman civil law and contemporary English practice. Gaelic law, for example, made it almost impossible legally to alienate land. By the late middle ages, however, in a device probably inspired by the English mortgage, it was possible to make it the security for what was in practice an unredeemable loan.[35] In the late sixteenth century, similarly, at a time when chiefs were under pressure to bring law enforcement in their territories into closer conformity with English common law, certain jurists

[32] *NHI*, ii. 705.

[33] Samantha Meigs, *The Reformations in Ireland: Tradition and Confessionalism 1400–1690* (Dublin, 1997), 17–21.

[34] Bradshaw, 'Manus "the Magnificent"', 25–6.

[35] Gearóid MacNiocaill, 'The Interaction of Laws', in James Lydon (ed.), *The English in Medieval Ireland* (Dublin, 1984), 115–17.

can be found drawing selectively on previously obscure texts to find precedents for the use of capital punishment against thieves and murderers.[36]

Further, if more tentative, indications that this was not a wholly static society may be found in Gaelic Ireland's area of greatest weakness, its economic base. The external trade of the region consisted largely of the exchange of primary produce for goods unobtainable within it. The main exports were hides and fish along with a certain amount of wool and linen cloth, the main imports salt and wine. The organization of this trade was mainly in outside hands. In the southern half of the country the major coastal towns, themselves centres of English culture, acted as entrepôts, taking in produce from the Gaelic hinterland and importing goods to be sold there. However, there was also some direct trade by English, French, and Spanish merchants with the more remote Gaelic areas of the south-west. In the north and north-west, external trade depended almost entirely on such visits by foreign merchants. Yet there are also indications that Gaelic society was capable both of generating and of accommodating a degree of commercialization. The clearest example is the port of Sligo, which flourished in the fifteenth century as a centre for the export of herring and salmon, and provided a base for a native merchant dynasty, the Creans. Commercial centres of some kind also appear to have developed at Cavan, under the control of the O'Reillys, and at Longford and Granard. By the 1540s the O'Byrnes of Wicklow, who had long depended for subsistence on raiding the English territories near their mountain base, had become dependent instead on trade with the Pale through the town of Wicklow, one reason why they proved amenable at that point to offers of a new political relationship with the English crown.[37]

If Gaelic society was not static, neither was it wholly inward looking. Ireland's position as a westerly island permitted the survival of a distinctive culture. But at a time when travel by water was almost everywhere quicker and safer than extensive journeys overland, its geographical isolation should not be overstated. External trade, even if its organization was largely in foreign hands, nevertheless meant regular contact with a range of foreign visitors. An annalist noted in 1522 that news of the outbreak of a major European war, with England and the Empire engaged against France, had been brought by 'the distributors of news and the frequentors of harbours'.[38] Language too was not necessarily a barrier to contact with a wider world. If knowledge of English spread only gradually in the Gaelic heartland, Latin was, as elsewhere, generally understood by the educated

[36] Nerys Patterson, 'Gaelic Law and the Tudor Conquest of Ireland: The Social Background of the Sixteenth-Century Recension of the Pseudo-Historical Prologue to the *Senchas Már*', *IHS* 27 (1991), 193–215.

[37] *NHI*, ii. 419–21; Mary O'Dowd, *Power, Politics and Land: Early Modern Sligo 1568–1688* (Belfast, 1991), 149–64; Christopher Maginn, *'Civilizing' Gaelic Leinster: The Extension of Tudor Rule in the O'Byrne and O'Toole Lordships* (Dublin, 2005), 18–19.

[38] *Annals of Loch Cé*, ii. 235–7.

classes. In the 1560s a Fermanagh man conducting a secret correspondence with the English lord deputy in Dublin asked him to write in English rather than Latin, since there was less risk of other persons in his neighbourhood being able to read the letter.[39]

In addition to trading contacts, the more important lords at least were able to maintain diplomatic relations with foreign courts and aristocracies. In 1511 Hugh Dubh O'Donnell, lord of what is now Donegal, returning from a pilgrimage to Rome, spent four months at the court of Henry VIII, where he was knighted by the king. Both he and his son Manus also maintained regular contact with the kings of Scotland. St Leger, reporting on his meeting with Manus in 1541, noted that his entourage included a young man who had been brought up in the French court.[40] A few years later, in 1547–8, when members of the O'Connor Faly lineage were forced to flee following an unsuccessful revolt, the lord's son Cormac went to Scotland, where he remained for fifteen years, serving in the army of Mary of Guise, while two younger brothers went to the court of France.[41]

Perhaps the most intriguing question concerning the potential for change in Gaelic Ireland relates to its political development. Once again it is clear that tradition cannot be equated with stasis. The revival of Gaelic military and political power that took place during the thirteenth century, as native dynasties new and old expanded to fill the vacuum left by the faltering and contraction of the English colony, was no simple restoration. Instead, it has been argued, what took place was a selective revival of earlier political forms, behind a facade of conscious antiquarianism, in which pre-invasion notions of kingship were modified to reflect a more pragmatic concern with effective power.[42]Thereafter there were to be further changes in politics, culture, and economic life, in response variously to contact with English Ireland, to influences from continental Europe, and to pressures internal to Gaelic Ireland itself. By the fifteenth century the traditional royal offices, often held on a hereditary basis by particular families within the lordship, had in many cases been replaced by paid servants. There are references to secretaries, marshals, and constables. The use of seals likewise indicates a new reliance on written instruments, with a consequent concern for their preservation and authentication. It has also been suggested that by the fifteenth century, partly due to the influence of the clergy, the traditional emphasis on the chief as military leader had begun to be qualified by a new emphasis on the role of the lord in maintaining order within the territory under his control. This in turn made necessary the development of further administrative and military resources.[43]

39 Patricia Palmer, *Language and Conquest in Early Modern Ireland: English Renaissance Literature and Elizabethan Imperial Expansion* (Cambridge, 2001), 187.

40 Bradshaw, 'Manus "the Magnificent" ', 21–2.

41 Fiona Fitzsimons, 'The Lordship of O'Connor Faly 1520–70', in Nolan and O'Neill, *Offaly*, 221–2.

42 Simms, *From Kings to Warlords*, 16–17.

43 On these developments see ibid., ch. 6.

What is more difficult to determine is how far there was also the possibility of progress towards a greater degree of political centralization. Behind the endless tale of raids and battles that makes up the Irish annals of the period, it is possible to detect the rise of particular lordships to the status of regional powers. From the mid-fifteenth century, for example, the O'Briens extended their influence first over their eastern neighbours the MacNamaras, then across the Shannon into Limerick and Tipperary. Around the same time the O'Donnells began a highly successful southwards expansion into Fermanagh and north Connacht. In the past such expansion had come up against the limits imposed by weak political institutions and by an open system of succession. The Ulster lordship of the O'Neills, the largest political unit in Gaelic Ireland, split in the fourteenth century when the descendants of Hugh the Yellow (*Clann Aodh Buidhe*) established a separate eastern lordship (later anglicized as Clandeboye), and there were also recurrent difficulties in keeping together the territories north and south of the Sperrin Mountains. The question is whether the gradual development of more elaborate political structures, and the trend towards larger, more expensively equipped armies, might eventually have overcome these constraints. Could able and well placed rulers like Conn Bacach ONeill or Manus O'Donnell have taken on the role of state builders, expanding their lordships to absorb smaller territories and create an Ireland divided into five or six principalities, as was happening around the same time in Italy?[44] The question is impossible to answer. But it stands as a useful reminder that the actual outcome, the assimilation of Gaelic Ireland into an expanding English state, should not be taken without question as its only possible political future.

THE ENGLISH OF IRELAND

The English lordship of Ireland was a legacy of one distinctive phase in the history of medieval Europe. Its establishment at the end of the twelfth century was part of a great outward movement from the western European heartland to the periphery of the continent and beyond. The same tide that carried English warrior adventurers to Ireland had earlier carried their Norman ancestors to England itself and from there to Wales and Scotland. It had sustained the Christian reconquest of southern Spain, and permitted the establishment of crusader states in Palestine and Syria, as well as Norman colonies in Sicily, Cyprus, and Greece.[45] This varied array of conquests depended partly on

[44] Bradshaw, 'Manus "the Magnificent"', 36.

[45] For the European background, see Robert Bartlett, *The Making of Europe: Conquest, Colonization and Cultural Change 950–1350* (London, 1993). Ireland's place in this wider context is emphasized in C. A. Empey, 'Conquest and Settlement: Patterns of Anglo-Norman Settlement in North Munster and South Leinster', *IESH* 13 (1986).

military superiority: the use of heavy cavalry, the crossbow, and the castle, all supported by a social system effectively designed for the maintenance of the mounted knight and his auxiliaries. But it was also driven by a sharp rise in population. The pressure of numbers that pushed German and Flemish settlers into new territories east of the Elbe likewise brought to the newly conquered lands of southern and eastern Ireland not just a military elite but a large immigrant population. Settlement was inevitably uneven. In the north the earls of Ulster, whose domain at its peak extended round the north coast as far as Inishowen, were for the most part content with the role of overlords, exacting tribute and military service from a Gaelic population still living under local chiefs. In Connacht, English colonizers established a network of small urban settlements, but otherwise ruled over a predominantly Gaelic population. Across a large part of the south and east, on the other hand, conquest was followed by the settlement of a substantial English, Welsh, and Flemish population on a landscape dotted with new urban centres and reorganized along manorial lines.

From the early fourteenth century the demographic tide that had driven this immigration had turned. A population pressing against the ceiling of resources was drastically cut back by the classic Malthusian mechanisms of subsistence crisis and disease, most notably the Black Death of 1348–9. In Ireland there had already been indications, in military reverses and signs of political fragmentation, that the English colony might have reached its limits of expansion. Now, with settler numbers reduced by plague to as little as half their former level, and with no prospect of further recruitment from an equally diminished population in England itself, its borders began to contract. The most spectacular losses were in the earldom of Ulster, which by the end of the fourteenth century had been reduced to an enclave round Carrickfergus and a coastal strip of what is today County Down.[46] Elsewhere land was lost to different branches of the MacCarthys of the south west, to the O'Briens of Thomond, and to the MacMurroughs in south Leinster. In other cases, such as that of the Burkes of Connacht, territorial lords established by the conquest remained, but their ties to the Dublin government had largely disappeared and they ruled, according to Irish law and custom, over a countryside in which the villages and tilled fields that had marked earlier English settlement were no more than a memory. The legacy of the medieval colony was thus twofold: on the one hand, a long-established population highly conscious of its English identity; on the other, a preoccupation with decline from a more impressive past, and a sense of vulnerability in the face of continued pressure from Gaelic neighbours.

[46] The loss to local Gaelic lords of the greater part of the earldom followed the assassination in 1333 of the fourth earl, William de Burgh. Theoretical ownership, however, passed, through the houses of Mortimer and York, into the hands of the crown, creating a royal claim to Ulster that was to remain relevant for much of the sixteenth century.

At the end of the fifteenth century the centre of English Ireland consisted of a compact eastern region stretching from County Louth in the north through Meath and Dublin into County Kildare. From there a precariously narrow land corridor, squeezed between the Gaelic Irish of the Wicklow Mountains and those of the midlands, ran south through County Carlow into County Wexford. To the west lay a zone of less intensive but still significant English settlement in Counties Kilkenny and Tipperary.[47] In these regions the surviving evidence suggests the survival, in significant numbers though probably not numerically dominant, of a recognizably English population. Scattered statistics from Counties Meath, Dublin, Kildare, and Kilkenny indicate that half to three quarters of tenants and small farmers on certain estates had English surnames; the rent role of one abbey located on the River Liffey, as late as 1520, contains no Gaelic names whatever. Such evidence, however, dependent as it is on effective estate management, is likely to have survived from the most favoured areas. There is also the likelihood that the poorest sections of rural society, those least likely to appear in estate records, were more frequently of Gaelic origin than the better off. In Maynooth, at the very centre of the earl of Kildare's territory, the proportion of tenants identifiable as English was both lower and in decline, falling from just under half in 1451 to just over a third by 1518. [48]

The shifting balance between English and Irish settlement was inevitably reflected in language. In two areas, the baronies of Forth and Bargy in County Wexford and the district of Fingal just north of Dublin, comments by late eighteenth-century observers on the archaic features of the local dialect indicate a direct inheritance from the medieval colony. But the very frequency with which these two relatively small districts were cited must raise the question whether their history of unbroken linguistic continuity was exceptional. In the Tipperary lordship of Ormond, a series of ordinances drawn up in the 1440s at an assembly of rural freeholders makes clear that at that stage at least English, though of a variety that would already have been considered old-fashioned in England itself, was still in common use. It is less clear how far this remained the case over the next century. The Dubliner Richard Stanihurst, writing in 1577, insisted that the inhabitants of Meath, Kildare, and Louth 'speak to this day English'. But this was at a time when it had become politically urgent to reaffirm the English character of the Pale community, and Stanihurst's comment may well have applied to

[47] The most substantial study of the English lordship in the late fifteenth and early sixteenth centuries is S. G. Ellis, *Reform and Revival: English Government in Ireland 1470–1534* (Woodbridge, 1986), whose conclusions are restated in more summary form in idem, *Ireland in the Age of the Tudors*. Ellis builds on the important earlier work of D. B. Quinn (most conveniently approached through the latter's chapters in *NHI*, ii), but offers a more positive assessment, followed here with some qualification, of the workings of government within the lordship.

[48] Ellis, *Ireland in the Age of the Tudors*, 33; Mary Ann Lyons, *Church and Society in County Kildare 1470–1547* (Dublin, 2000), 18, 21, 25–6; Ellis, *Reform and Revival*, 6–7, offers some of the same figures as in his later work, with a rather different emphasis. For the unnamed abbey on the Liffey see Maginn, *'Civilizing' Gaelic Leinster*, 184 n. 10.

what he considered the better sort of people. Elsewhere in the same text, in fact, he lamented the cultural degeneracy whereby Irish was 'universally gaggled in the English Pale'.[49] Other evidence confirms that members of the Pale gentry and aristocracy—even the incoming English wife of a magnate like the earl of Kildare—found it necessary to acquire enough Irish to converse with servants, labourers, and others.[50]

In comparison to Gaelic Ireland the areas of English settlement represented a region of relatively advanced agricultural practice, based on a systematic combination of tillage and livestock. This was true not only of the four counties of the Pale, but also of at least the more fertile lands of Kilkenny and Tipperary, as well as parts of Carlow, Cork, Waterford, and Limerick. In some of these areas land was still laid out in large fields subdivided into strips, which were distributed among individual tenants or worked as demesne land on behalf of the lord. However, there had also been a steady process of enclosure, gradually replacing these communal fields with individual holdings. With a thin overall population, cultivation was not by later standards very intensive. Many areas still maintained a division between a constantly worked infield, taking in the best land, and a more episodically cultivated outfield on poorer ground. Even in the infield, moreover, extensive areas, a third or a half of the total depending on whether farming was by a two- or three-course rotation, remained fallow at any one time. Some calculations suggest that crop yields, even in the Pale, were undistinguished by comparison with contemporary England.[51] But this was nevertheless a settled landscape, shaped by enclosure, drainage, and land clearance, traversed by roads and bridges, and dotted with villages and market towns. In County Meath, the papal nuncio reported approvingly in 1574, 'there is scarce a mile in the country in which there is not either a large town or a castle or some lord's or gentleman's seat'.[52] By the late sixteenth century, in fact, the common complaint was that the English areas of the east coast, once as heavily wooded as other regions, were now too completely denuded of trees of any kind.[53] There was little rural manufacturing of the sort which supplemented agricultural incomes in the most developed parts of western Europe. But the presence of numerous water-powered corn mills was nevertheless testimony to a commercialized, tillage-based agriculture.

[49] Stanihurst, 'The Description of Ireland', in *Holinshed's Chronicles of England, Scotland and Ireland*, vi. *Ireland* (London, 1808), 5–6. For the background to Stanihurst's account see below, Ch. 5.

[50] For Forth and Bargy and Fingal see *NHI*, iii. 547–9. For the Ormond ordinances C. A. Empey, 'The Butler Lordship', *Journal of the Butler Society*, 1/3 (1970–1), 184–5.

[51] Nicholas Canny, *The Formation of the Old English Elite in Ireland* (Dublin, 1975), 3–5, using calculations by Gearóid MacNiocaill. For a more favourable assessment of agriculture in English Ireland see Ellis, *Ireland in the Age of the Tudors*, 35–6.

[52] *CSP Rome*, ii. *Elizabeth 1572–1578*, 152.

[53] *Holinshed's Chronicles*, v. 9; Thomas Gainsford (1618) quoted in Quinn, *Elizabethans and the Irish*, 163.

The other main legacy of English settlement in Ireland was the existence of cities and towns.[54] By international standards the urban network was poorly developed. There was as yet no clear-cut hierarchy in terms of size or volume of trade, and there was little economic interchange: instead each centre traded with its own hinterland and with external markets and suppliers. Town dwellers had been particularly hard hit by the Black Death, and their numbers had never fully recovered. The population of Dublin around 1500 has been estimated at between 5,000 and 10,000, compared to a late thirteenth-century peak of 20,000 or more. There and elsewhere late medieval accounts suggest a perceptible physical decay, with walls, wharves, and other amenities in poor repair and empty spaces inside the once densely crowded areas enclosed by the city walls. Even in this reduced state, however, the Irish towns remained important, in both economic and cultural terms. Dublin's suggested population of 5,000–10,000 would have put it somewhere between the largest provincial English town, Norwich, which had over 9,000 inhabitants in the early sixteenth century, and the eighth largest, Canterbury, which had just over 5,000. Stanihurst, an enthusiastic civic patriot, described it in 1577 as 'the beauty and eye of Ireland . . . commonly called the Irish or young London'.[55] Galway, with an estimated 4,000 inhabitants, would have been just within the twelve or so largest provincial towns in England. Limerick, with a population of around 3,000, would have compared with Gloucester, ranked twenty-fourth in the English urban hierarchy. Cork and Waterford, with around 2,400 persons each, would have been comparable to Lichfield, England's thirty-second town.[56]

In addition to these major centres there was a variety of lesser towns, with populations of 2,000 or so. Of these Carrickfergus and Drogheda, the latter described by Stanihurst as 'accounted the best town in Ireland, and truly not far behind some of their cities', were once again ports. On the other hand Kilkenny was a unique example of a well developed inland centre, 'the properest dry town in Ireland', its prosperity depending on the woollen industry of the surrounding countryside, the patronage of the powerful Butler dynasty, and its location on the navigable waterway of the Barrow and the Nore.[57] Of these towns, Dublin, Drogheda, and Kilkenny were centres serving a hinterland still marked by extensive English settlement. By contrast Galway, Limerick, Cork,

[54] The leading historian of Irish towns in this period is Colm Lennon. See his *The Lords of Dublin in the Age of Reformation* (Dublin, 1989), ch. 1; *Archbishop Richard Creagh of Armagh, 1523–1586: An Irish Prisoner of Conscience of the Tudor Era* (Dublin, 2000), ch. 1. See also Anthony Sheehan, 'Irish Towns in a Period of Change 1558–1625', in Brady and Gillespie, *Natives and Newcomers*.

[55] *Holinshed's Chronicles*, vi. 21.

[56] For the population of Dublin see Lennon, *Lords of Dublin*, 29–34. Other estimates of urban population, for about 1600, are those in *NHI*, iii. 390, and are based on counting the houses shown on contemporary maps. Data for English comparisons are taken from Alan Dyer, *Decline and Growth in English Towns 1400–1640* (London, 1991), 66, 72–4, as amended in Peter Clark (ed.), *The Cambridge Urban History of Britain*, ii. *1540–1840* (Cambridge, 2000), table 11.1.

[57] *Holinshed's Chronicles*, 30, 33.

Waterford, and Carrickfergus, along with the smaller but still important Youghal, were islands of English settlement in what was by this time a predominantly Gaelic hinterland, depending on the sea for communication with the rest of English Ireland.

An English visitor to an Irish town would probably have noted one immediate difference. In Dublin, surrounded by the relatively orderly Pale, the population had spread well beyond the medieval walls into suburbs. But elsewhere town walls remained an important defensive structure, still, in the sixteenth century, regularly added to and kept in repair. In other respects, however, such a visitor would have found much that was familiar. Streets were narrow and crooked, but the houses of the wealthier citizens were substantial two- and three-storey buildings. In Cork, Galway, and Limerick these were generally of stone; in Dublin and Waterford, up to at least the late sixteenth century, they were more commonly of wood, clay, and plaster. Well endowed churches and monasteries testified simultaneously to the prosperity, civic pride, and piety of the urban elite. Economic life was sophisticated and cosmopolitan, with merchants trading directly with England, France, Spain, Portugal, and Flanders, exporting fish, hides, wool, and textiles and importing such necessities and luxuries as salt, wine, iron, spices, and fine cloth. As in England, civic life was dominated by an elite of wealthy merchants—although Irish towns, to a much greater extent than their more economically dynamic English counterparts, tended to be ruled by stable cliques, with high levels of intermarriage within a small group of leading families and the same surnames recurring across the decades among holders of the highest civic offices. The speech of this urban patriciate struck English sophisticates as provincial. Sir John Harington, listening to two civic orations in Limerick in 1599, did not know 'which was more to be discommended, words, composition, and oratory, all of them having their particular excellencies in barbarism, harshness, and rustical both pronouncing and action'.[58] But their language, like their dress and manners, were unmistakably English. Those who had proceeded to a university education had done so at Oxford, Cambridge, or the Inns of Court in London.

If the physical appearance and social organization of the Irish towns would have been largely familiar to an English visitor, so too would their civic ritual. Events such as the annual riding of the franchises, where civic officers and members of the various trade guilds processed, in strict order of precedence, round the boundaries of the municipality, were simultaneously an expression of community, a reassertion of hierarchy, and a proclamation of collective privilege. Biblical dramas and morality plays are recorded in Kilkenny and Dublin, and may also have been performed in other towns. A further high point of the Dublin civic calendar, and a more explicit expression of English identity,

[58] Sir John Harington, *Nugae Antiquae, Being a Miscellaneous Collection of Original Papers in Prose and Verse*, 3 vols. (London, 1779), ii. 42–3.

was the annual procession organized by the guild of St Geoge, established in 1426 as the guild of the Dublin assembly, in which the saint vanquished an elaborately constructed dragon.[59] At the level of a less formal popular culture, the transmission of folk tradition across the Irish Sea is evident in the designation of a hill on Oxmantown Green as Little John's shot, commemorating a feat supposedly performed there by the legendary associate of Robin Hood.[60]

The role of the cities and towns as the primary centres of English culture was also reflected in the barriers they erected against the Gaelic world beyond their walls. In Dublin regulations introduced in 1454 required all 'men of Irish blood and women', including householders who had not been resident for at least twelve years, to leave the city within three weeks, and forbade the acceptance of Irish servants or apprentices for the future. In Galway, similarly, statutes introduced in the late fifteenth and early sixteenth centuries imposed a wide range of restrictions: no Irishman could practise in the courts of law or rent property in the town without a special licence, and it was illegal to sell them guns or boats. Irishmen entering the town had to surrender any weapons, and they were excluded altogether during public festivals. Members of certain Gaelic septs could be arrested on sight, and held to account for any injuries done to the citizens by them or their extended family. Other measures sought to preserve cultural identity. In Galway in 1527 the mayor and corporation forbade the inhabitants, on pain of a fine, to play handball or 'the hurling of the little ball with hockey sticks'; instead they were to play 'only the great football'. In Limerick the city council decreed in 1512 that no inhabitant was to be admitted to the franchise unless he maintained a decently equipped house and kitchen, 'could speak English well and be clothed in English apparel, viz. gown, doublet and hose'.[61]

Despite such restrictions the role of the towns as centres of English culture was difficult to sustain. Urban economic life depended on trade with what was, with the partial exception of Dublin, a predominantly Gaelic hinterland. Added to this was the well-known demographic deficit of medieval and early modern towns, whereby birth rates consistently lagged behind high urban mortality, so that numbers could be maintained or expanded only with regular immigration from the countryside. Even in Dublin, a list from 1514 of the members of the guild of carpenters and masons included the recognizably Irish names of Denis Obrune, Bren O'Hely, and Dermot McClanchy, as well as John Otoylls, whose surname

[59] Alan J. Fletcher, *Drama, Performance and Polity in Pre-Cromwellian Ireland* (Cork, 2000), chs. 3, 4.

[60] *Holinshed's Chronicles*, vi. 28.

[61] MacNiocaill, 'Socio-Economic Problems of the Late Medieval Irish Town', in David Harkness and Mary O'Dowd (eds.), *The Town in Ireland* (Belfast, 1981), 17; M. D. O'Sullivan, *Old Galway: The History of a Norman Colony in Ireland* (Cambridge, 1942), 386–7, 441; Lennon, *Archbishop Richard Creagh*, 19–20.

scarcely concealed his descent from the Gaelic sept of O'Toole, notorious for the periodic raids they launched from the mountains just south of the city.[62] To have been accepted as guild members all four must have been able and willing to adopt English language and dress. Indeed they may well have obtained patents entitling them to the legal status of Englishmen. But there were almost certainly others, unskilled workers and casual labourers, their numbers possibly fluctuating as ordinances against their presence were periodically invoked, who remained recognizably Irish in speech and appearance. In some cases, as in Limerick and Kilkenny, such immigration was reflected in the development of a separate Irishtown. Interaction with Irish-speaking servants and labourers, along with the need to trade with the Gaelic areas beyond the city walls, would in turn have meant that English-speaking townsmen found it convenient or necessary to become bilingual. Even Richard Stanihurst, anxious for political reasons to insist on the Englishness of the Irish towns, conceded that their inhabitants 'speak English, and Irish also because of their daily commerce with their Irish neighbours'.[63]

The gradual weakening of ethnic distinctions was also evident in the ability of some Gaelic families to enter the towns, not just as a replacement labour force, but as merchants, property owners, and even participants in urban government. The extent of such penetration varied considerably. In Dublin, at the heart of the most intensively colonized area, the urban oligarchy remained wholly and self-consciously English. Galway, besieged by what its citizens saw as the barbarous people to the west and by the power-hungry Burkes of Clanricard to the east, also maintained much of its separateness. Irishmen began to be admitted to the franchise from the late fifteenth century but these grants, unlike those to others, were rarely hereditary, and natives continued to be excluded from municipal office. In the Munster towns, by contrast, attitudes, by the fifteenth century at least, appear to have been significantly more relaxed. In Cork the Ronan or O'Ronayne family emerged as important members of the urban patriciate, with significant property both there and in the neighbouring towns of Kinsale and Youghal.[64] In Limerick the first member of the long-established Creagh family held urban office as early as 1351. This did not mean that awareness of ethnic differences had wholly disappeared. Edmund Sexton, whose family rose to prominence in Limerick in the early sixteenth century, was reportedly distrusted on account of his Gaelic birth. But then Sexton, a client of Thomas Cromwell

[62] Henry F. Berry, 'The Dublin Gild of Carpenters, Millers, Masons, and Heliers in the Sixteenth Century', *JRSAI* 35 (1905), 327.

[63] Stanihurst, *De Rebus in Hibernia Gestis* (1584), printed in Lennon, *Richard Stanihurst*, 145; cf. Vincent Carey, 'Bilingualism and Identity Formation in Sixteenth-Century Ireland', in Hiram Morgan (ed.), *Political Ideology in Ireland 1541–1641* (Dublin, 1999), 48.

[64] A. F. O'Brien, 'Politics, Economy and Society: The Development of Cork and the Irish South-Coast Region *c.*1170 to *c.*1583', in Patrick O'Flanagan and C. G. Buttimer (eds.), *Cork: History and Society* (Dublin, 1993), 133–4.

and early supporter of the Reformation, was also a new man in other respects likely to arouse hostility.[65]

The conscious efforts of urban elites to protect their towns from cultural contamination contrasts sharply with the behaviour of the English aristocracy and gentry in the outlying areas of English settlement. Here the threatened dilution or loss of cultural identity had been a cause of concern since at least the late thirteenth century. A statute enacted at the parliament held in Kilkenny in 1366, the best-known of a succession of measures of cultural defence, had required 'every Englishman' to use the English language, be called by an English name, and 'use English style in appearance, riding and dress, according to his position in society'.[66] Despite such prohibitions, the leading English families had to a large extent traded English for Gaelic custom. Their households spoke Irish as their normal language. They abandoned doublets and hose for mantles, short jackets, and flowing shirts. They rode their horses without saddles. They patronized poets, harpists, and other native performers. They intermarried with leading Gaelic families, and sent their children to be fostered in the households of Gaelic lords. Nor was the prohibition on taking Irish names observed. The eighth and ninth earls of Kildare were, respectively, 'Gearóid Mór and 'Gearóid Óg'. Thomas Fitzgerald, the eleventh earl of Desmond, who died in 1534, was 'Tomás Maol' (the Bald), while John, Lord Barrymore, who had died in 1486, was 'Seán Bacach' (the Lame).

Alongside this adoption of Gaelic dress and language, English lords had also turned to native practice in the management of the territories under their control. In addition to, or sometimes in place of, the rents in cash and kind and the labour services due to them from their tenants under English law, they extorted all or some of the customary entitlements of Gaelic society. These included 'cuddies' (from the Gaelic *cuid oíche*, a night's portion) and 'coshery' (from the Gaelic *cóisir*), varying forms of the obligation binding on substantial dependants to provide one or more night's entertainment for the lord and his retinue. There was also 'coyne and livery', a hybrid term derived from Gaelic *coinnmeadh* ('guesting') and the English term for the provision of fodder for horses. This normally referred to the billeting of troops and horsemen on the inhabitants of a territory, but could also be extended to the compulsory provision of lodgings and meals for a lord's servants or craftsmen or even, as in the lordship of Kildare, his hunting dogs. In the maintenance of law and order, likewise, English lords had long come to make use of brehon as well as English common law, to the extent in many cases of offering patronage and employment to one of the hereditary legal families as judges and advisers.

How is this adoption of Gaelic law and custom to be understood? Interpretations have varied over time, and remain hotly contested. To nationalist writers of the nineteenth and twentieth centuries the 'gaelicization' of the settler

[65] Lennon, *Archbishop Richard Creagh*, 19–20, 23, 28. [66] *NHI*, ii. 386–90.

population was a valuable means of smoothing over what would otherwise have been awkward discontinuities in the making of 'the Irish race', and confirming the primacy of a single 'national' culture. The descendants of the English conquerors, it was confidently proclaimed, had become 'more Irish than the Irish themselves'. Today it is recognized that the supposedly contemporary phrase dates only from the late eighteenth century, the Latin form (*Hiberniores ipsis Hibernis*) sometimes used to give it an authentic medieval ring from later still.[67] In place of the vision of colonists assuming an 'Irish' identity, meanwhile, recent accounts have offered instead a more sober vision of pragmatic adaptation to circumstances. For English lords ruling over a largely Gaelic population, and required to come to terms of some sort with the native rulers of adjoining territories, the employment of Gaelic minstrels, poets, and genealogists, and the adoption of local traditions of hospitality, feasting, and recreation, were obvious means of acquiring and preserving status. The use of local custom and practice in the management of estates and the resolving of disputes, involving recognized practitioners in the native legal tradition, was likewise no more than common sense. Coyne and livery was a serviceable means of maintaining armed retainers in an environment where money was scarce and violence common. Even the much criticized practice of permitting those guilty of capital offences to compound for their crime was likewise a practical accommodation to the needs of a thinly populated frontier society, compensating those who had suffered while avoiding the loss of a possibly valuable tenant and the destitution or alienation of his family.[68]

An emphasis on the practical reasons why English lords might have taken up elements of Gaelic practice provides a useful corrective to nationalist myth-making. At the same time it is important to emphasize that these multiple cultural adaptations were not simply a matter of a ruling elite dabbling in the 'little tradition' of their social inferiors, as ruling classes did all over Europe, by acquiring enough of a local dialect to converse with tenants, servants, and dependants, and bestowing a measure of patronage on popular festivals, performances, and rituals.[69] On the contrary the bards, historians, and jurists whose services were engaged by magnates like the earls of Ormond and Kildare were practitioners of a sophisticated if highly stylized court culture. What they produced for their new English patrons was not light entertainment, but odes celebrating their lordly and martial virtues, and genealogies providing them with

[67] Art Cosgrove, 'Hiberniores Ipsis Hibernis', in Cosgrove and McCartney, *Studies in Irish History*, 1–4.

[68] S. G. Ellis, *Tudor Frontiers and Noble Power: The Making of the British State* (Oxford, 1995), 57–68. For an alternative account, closer to the traditional emphasis on 'gaelicization', see Carey, 'Bilingualism and Identity Formation', and, for a direct critique of Ellis, Kenneth Nicholls, 'Worlds Apart? The Ellis Two-Nation Theory of Late Medieval Ireland', *History Ireland*, 7/2 (1999), 22–6.

[69] Bartlett, *Making of Europe*, 197–220; Peter Burke, *Popular Culture in Early Modern Europe* (London, 1978).

a pedigree stretching back to the heroes of the Gaelic, European, or biblical past. In this respect it seems necessary to think in terms, not just of pragmatic adaptation to a different environment, but of the emergence of a hybrid elite culture, as an aristocracy and gentry whose circumstances cut them off from their own centres of chivalric values and Latin learning turned instead to an alternative literate, Christian, and courtly culture that could be employed to legitimize their position within Irish society.[70]

If the supposed 'gaelicization' of the settler elite requires careful definition, it also demands close attention to variations in geography and social status. At one end of the scale magnates like the earls of Ormond and Kildare seem genuinely to have bestrode two cultural worlds, involving themselves deeply in Gaelic culture while in no way sacrificing their position as members of the English elite.The fourth earl of Ormond, ruling huge estates in Tipperary and Kilkenny, was a noted patron of Gaelic scribes and antiquaries. On his own lands he administered justice according to a mixture of English and Irish law, securing the services of the legal family of MacFhlannchadha by a grant of lands in County Kilkenny. Yet he was also the most important nobleman in the lordship during the first half of the fifteenth century, serving repeatedly as chief governor between 1420 and his death in 1452. In the same way the ninth earl of Kildare, a sophisticated product of the English royal court, where he had lived between the ages of 8 and 16, nevertheless supported Gaelic harpists and poets, preserved Irish manuscripts in his library at Maynooth, and continued his father's policy of cultivating close personal ties, reinforced by marriage alliances, with Gaelic chiefs. His first wife, Elizabeth Zouche, kinswoman of Henry VII, found it necessary on arrival in her new home at Maynooth to learn Irish, and a manual on the language, published over half a century later, paid tribute to the speed with which she did so.[71] Even the earls of Desmond, geographically more remote and estranged from the crown for more than half a century from the 1460s, retained a familiarity with English as well as Gaelic manners. The grandson of the deceased twelfth earl, brought before the lord deputy by his father-in-law Cormac Óg MacCarthy in 1535, 'speaks very good English, and keeps his hair and cap after the English fashion . . . and would be, as far as I can perceive, after the English fashion'. His rival for succession to the earldom, the twelfth earl's brother, also spoke 'very good English' and gave some indication of his own sense of identity when he denounced 'that Irish whoreson Cormac Óg'.[72]

At a different social level the lesser landowners of the eastern counties could likewise demonstrate a familiarity with Gaelic culture that did not compromise

[70] This follows the argument of Katharine Simms, 'Bards and Barons: The Anglo-Irish Aristocracy and the Native Culture', in Robert Bartlett and Angus MacKay (eds.), *Medieval Frontier Societies* (Oxford, 1989), 177–97.

[71] Mary Ann Lyons, *Gearóid Óg Fitzgerald, Ninth Earl of Kildare* (Dublin, 1998), 17; Carey, 'Bilingualism and Identity Formation', 51–2.

[72] Steven Ap Parry to Cromwell, 6 Oct. 1535 (*SP Henry VIII*, ii. 283, 285).

their Englishness. Sir William Darcy was reported around 1500 to be one of the few men remaining in County Westmeath who used a saddle and wore a gown and doublet. In a set of articles on the 'decay of Ireland' presented to the king and council in 1515, he identified among the causes of the problem 'the lords and gentlemen falling to Irish order and Irish habits'. Yet Darcy himself was able, in 1520, to join with Patrick Birmingham, chief justice of the King's Bench, in interrogating a prisoner who spoke only Irish.[73] Eight years later, another County Meath gentleman, Richard Nugent, baron Delvin, then acting lord deputy, was taken prisoner by O'Connor of Offaly. When the earl of Ormond's son obtained permission to visit him, O'Connor ordered the two to talk in Irish, so that he could monitor their conversation. It was clearly taken for granted that they would be able to do so; but the implication is also that they would otherwise have spoken in English.[74]

Biculturalism of this kind must be clearly distinguished from those cases in which Gaeldom involved a clear dilution of at least cultural Englishness. This was true of one great English family, the Burkes of Connacht, who by the late fifteenth century were regarded as having become almost wholly Irish in manners and allegiance, the one exception being that they continued to dispose of their property by primogeniture. Their defection can in part be attributed to the geographical remoteness of the Burke lands. However, it should also be noted that their connection with the English court and its local representatives was curtailed by political considerations. The Burkes had established themselves, by force of arms, on lands now theoretically belonging to the crown.[75] In other cases it was the minor branches of major families that proved vulnerable to assimilation into an alternative culture. The fourth earl of Ormond, despite his own unquestioned status as an English magnate, was alleged to have lamented that his brother's sons, who had now become heirs to the earldom, had not been prepared for this station by being brought up 'after the English fashion'.[76] More vulnerable still were the lesser gentry of outlying regions. By the late fifteenth century families such as the Haralds and Archbalds in the mountains south of Dublin city, the Berminghams in north west County Kildare, the Dillons, Delameres, and Daltons on the western borders of Meath, or the Barrys and Roches of County

[73] *Calendar of Ormond Deeds*, ed. Edmund Curtis (Dublin 1932–43), iv. 357; *Carew MSS 1515–1574*, 7; *SP Henry VIII*, ii. 44. See S. G. Ellis, 'An English Gentleman and his Community: Sir William Darcy of Platten', in V. P. Carey and Ute Lotz-Heumann (eds.), *Taking Sides: Colonial and Confessional Mentalités in Early Modern Ireland* (Dublin, 2003), 19–41.

[74] *SP Henry VIII*, ii. 130.

[75] Following the assassination of William de Burgh, the 4th earl of Ulster, in 1333, the title and ownership of his lands in Ulster and Connacht passed, through his female descendants, to other families and ultimately to the crown (see above, n. 46). However, de facto control of the Connacht lands passed into the hands of two other branches of the Burke family, the Lower MacWilliam or Clanricard Burkes to the south and the Upper MacWilliam or Mayo Burkes to the north.

[76] George Butler, 'Red Piers of Ormond', *Journal of the Butler Society*, 1 (1968), 40.

Cork, had not only shed almost all outward indications of their English origins; in most cases they had also, unlike the Burkes, abandoned primogeniture in favour of something closer to the Gaelic system of succession. The Berminghams had gone so far as to adopt a new, Gaelic surname, MacPheorais. In cases like this the line that had once separated settler and native had for all practical purposes ceased to exist.[77]

If the extent to which the adoption of Gaelic manners varied, so too did the implications for political behaviour. Figures like Ormond and Kildare were not only willing to play their part as the crown's servants in the management of the Irish lordship; they were also prepared to risk both their lives and their fortunes by taking part in the English factional struggles that culminated in the civil wars of 1455–87 between the houses of York and Lancaster. In 1462, for example, the earl of Desmond, who supported the Yorkists, defeated the Butlers, who had taken up arms in a last-ditch effort to regain the English throne for the Lancastrians, capturing, among others, Edmund MacRichard Butler, a nephew of the fourth earl of Ormond. Part of the ransom paid for his release was an intricately decorated Gaelic manuscript, the Book of Pottlerath, one of many that Butler had commissioned from the group of scribes that he maintained in his household.[78] In the same way the Nugents of west Meath in the early sixteenth century were simultaneously celebrated for their patronage of Irish poetry and for their achievements in pushing back the western frontier of the Pale at the expense of neighbouring Gaelic chieftains.[79] By contrast families such as the Daltons, the Haralds, or the Berminghams had by the late fifteenth century come to be regarded as having thrown off their allegiance. They had become 'English rebels and traitors' (as opposed to 'wild Irish'). Even here, however, it remains difficult to say how far what was seen as rebellious behaviour should be attributed to assimilation into a non-English culture, and how far to the indifference to the laws and requirements of central government that also existed in other peripheral areas, such as the Anglo-Scottish border.[80]

The adoption of Gaelic law and custom by sections of the settler community, then, was probably of less importance, in its own right or in its impact on political allegiances, than contemporaries feared or later generations persuaded themselves. Yet the issues of identity to which such allegiance potentially gave rise were only part of a wider set of tensions and contradictions arising from Ireland's status as a long-standing colony of settlement. The inhabitants of that colony described themselves as 'English' or, if finer distinctions were needed, as

[77] Christopher Maginn, 'English Marcher Lineages in South Dublin in the Late Middle Ages', *IHS* 34/134 (2004), 113–36; Lyons, *Church and Society in County Kildare*, 34.

[78] James Lydon, 'The Middle Nation', in James Lydon (ed.), *The English in Medieval Ireland* (Dublin, 1984), 16–17.

[79] Carey, 'Bilingualism and Identity Formation', 52–4.

[80] This comparison is developed in detail by Ellis, *Tudor Frontiers and Noble Power*.

'the English of Ireland', 'the English born in Ireland', or 'the English by blood'. They were also highly conscious of being the descendants of conquerors. The classic account of the exploits of the original settlers written in the late twelfth century by Gerald of Wales circulated widely in full and abridged versions, and was frequently cited as an authoritative text.[81] Yet this awareness of a shared history specific to Ireland in itself marked the English of the island out as a distinctive group. A degree of identification with their homeland was also evident in their willingness to adopt and extend the cults of local saints, such as Patrick and Bridget. The existence in Ireland of a separate parliament, a code of laws based on but not identical to those of England, and a separate court system further encouraged a sense of Irish as well as English identity.[82]

The emergence of a sense of distinctive identity among the people of the Irish lordship was further reinforced by the painful discovery that their claim to Englishness was not always accepted in England itself. In 1440 the Irish-born, regardless of nationality, were included in the poll tax levied on aliens. At other times doubts were raised about the allegiance of Irish-born students at the universities of Oxford and Cambridge. In Ireland itself, equally, reports from the mid-fourteenth century onwards testified to a mutual antipathy between the established settler population and more recent, English-born arrivals. Something of the tone of the exchanges that took place is suggested in the attempt of the statute of Kilkenny to lay down that 'no difference of allegiance henceforth be made between the English born in Ireland and the English born in England, by calling them *English hobbe* or *Irish dog*'.[83]

The clearest political expression of the sense of a separate identity that was thus developing among, or being forced on, the descendants of the medieval colony was in a declaration issued in 1460 by a parliament assembled at Drogheda. According to this

> the land of Ireland is and at all times has been corporate of itself, by the ancient laws and customs used in the same, freed of the burden of any special law of the realm of England, save only such laws as by the lords spiritual and temporal and the commons of the said land had been in great council or parliament there held, admitted, accepted, affirmed and proclaimed, according to sundry ancient statutes thereof made.[84]

This assertion of legislative autonomy had a specific background. The duke of York, who convened the Drogheda parliament in his capacity as lieutenant of Ireland, had been declared a traitor in England following a confrontation with the rival Lancastrian faction there, and several measures enacted at Drogheda

[81] Hiram Morgan, 'Giraldus Cambrensis and the Tudor Conquest of Ireland', in Morgan (ed.), *Political Ideology in Ireland 1541–1641* (Dublin, 1999), 22–44.
[82] Robin Frame, '"Les Engleys Nées en Irlande": The English Political Identity in Medieval Ireland', *Transactions of the Royal Historical Society*, ser. 6, 3 (1993), 83–103.
[83] Statute of Kilkenny (1366), printed in Edmund Curtis and R. B. McDowell (eds.), *Irish Historical Documents 1172–1922* (London, 1943), 53–4.
[84] Jocelyn Otway-Ruthven, *A History of Medieval Ireland* (London, 1968), 387.

were clearly designed to block any attempt to pursue him across the Irish Sea. The assertion of legislative autonomy, however, was phrased in terms more general than those used in other enactments, and has been seen as representing instead a concession extracted from York as the price of the support he received in Ireland. As such it can be taken as representing genuine constitutional aspirations.[85] In thus exploiting their political opportunity, York's Irish supporters were not in any sense compromising their English identity. Late medieval Europe was a society in which political rights and obligations were sectional and particular, and where states were typically an agglomeration of separate territories, each with its particular liberties and exemptions. The action of the parliament of Drogheda was in many respects on a par with the annual ritual whereby the mayor of Limerick threw a spear into the River Shannon, to symbolise the city's admiralty rights over the river and port, or the periodic resistance of urban corporations to attempted interference in their affairs by royal judges and officials. But it nevertheless made clear that English Ireland, if in no sense a nation, was nevertheless a political entity in its own right.

From another point of view, however, the real key to an assessment of the Declaration of 1460 is to recognize that the term 'political identity' is a modern abstraction, of only limited relevance to the late medieval world. Instead this was an age in which loyalties were most commonly defined in terms of personal, family, or dynastic loyalty, rather than nation. The standing force of 120 archers and 40 horse created in 1474 to strengthen the lordship's defences advertised its English identity by calling itself the Brotherhood of Arms of St George.[86] Yet twenty years later parliament found it necessary to legislate against those who in battle called out the names of Butler and Kildare, rather than of their king or patron saint. In this context the description offered of himself by the eighth earl of Kildare, writing in 1507 to what he believed to be distant kinsmen in Italy, is of particular relevance:

> Know then that my predecessors and ancestors passed from France into England, where they lived for a short time, and in the year 1140 [*sic*] came into this island of Ireland, in which by the power of their sword they obtained many possessions and performed great feats of arms, and have up to the present day increased and multiplied into divers branches and families. The consequence is that I, by the grace of God, and by hereditary right, possess the earldom, and am earl of Kildare, with many castles and possessions. And through the liberality of our most serene master, the king of England, I am viceregent

[85] This is the interpretation of Art Cosgrove, 'Parliament and the Anglo-Irish Commuity: The Declaration of 1460', in Art Cosgrove and J. I. McGuire (eds.), *Parliament and Community* (Belfast, 1983). For other assessments see J. F. Lydon, 'Ireland and the English Crown, 1171–1541'. *IHS*, 29 (1995), 281–94; S. G. Ellis, 'Nationalist Historiography and the English and Gaelic Worlds in the Late Middle Ages', *IHS*, 25 (1986), 1–18; idem, 'Historiographical Debate: Representations of the Past in Ireland—Whose Past and Whose Present?', *IHS*, 27 (1991), 289–308; Art Cosgrove, 'The Writing of Irish Medieval History', *IHS*, 27 (1990), 97–111.

[86] Ellis, 'Historiographical Debate', 300–1; cf. Ellis, *Ireland in the Age of the Tudors*, 72–4.

over all Ireland henceforth, at the pleasure of his majesty, a post held by my father and many of his predecessors.[87]

Kildare clearly had no difficulty acknowledging his allegiance to 'our most serene lord the king of England'. But the emphasis of his account was on his membership of an international military aristocracy whose conquests had at different times been in France, in England, in Ireland, and in Italy. And this was clearly of greater importance to him than any nationally based definition, whether 'English' or 'Anglo-Irish'.

THE PALE AND BEYOND

In the course of the fifteenth century the reduced area under the control of the English government in Dublin acquired a clear legal definition, and ultimately a new physical boundary. From about the 1420s the four counties of Dublin, Kildare, Meath, and Louth were recognized as a distinct administrative unit. Within this region later legislation distinguished between a land of peace or maghery (from the Irish *machaire*, a plain) and a march or border region that was to be fortified and defended. In 1495 an act of the Irish parliament required every inhabitant of the marches to erect a double ditch six feet high on the part of his land 'next unto Irishmen'. In addition the inhabitants of the whole four counties were to contribute to the building of similar ditches in the wasteland that lay between the marches and the territory of neighbouring Irish lords. It seems to have been only at this point that the enclosed area was for the first time referred to as 'the English Pale', possibly in imitation of Calais, where the term had recently been applied to a similar English enclave, and where Sir Edward Poynings, the lord deputy responsible for the act, had previously been governor.[88]

The construction of these elaborate defences reflected the vulnerability of the English territory to attack from the Irish lordships that lay beyond the march. Villages like Tallagh and Saggart, ten miles or less to the south of Dublin and today well within the greater Dublin area, were frequently raided by the O'Tooles and O'Byrnes of the adjoining mountains. At the other end of the Pale, County Louth suffered similarly from regular attacks by O'Hanlons, Magennises, O'Neills, and others, while there were also periodic raids into County Meath. To reduce the threat the four counties of the Pale made payments to regional Gaelic overlords. (In the case of Dublin the payment, to the MacMurroughs

[87] Kildare's letter is reprinted, from a seventeenth-century Italian compilation, in A. Fitzgibbon, 'Appendix to the Unpublished Geraldine Documents—the Gherardini of Tuscany', *JRSAI*, ser. 4, 4 (1876–8), 248–9.

[88] The fullest discussion of the creation of the Pale, and its significance, is in Ellis, *Reform and Revival*, 50–1; Ellis, *Tudor Frontiers and Noble Power*, 23–4. The act of 1495 is printed in Alice Conway, *Henry VII's Relations with Scotland and Ireland, 1485–1498* (Cambridge, 1932), 215–16.

of Wicklow, was paid directly by the royal exchequer.) Given the decentralized character of Gaelic Ireland these 'black rents' could be interpreted as subsidies to a military ally, as protection money paid to buy off a potential attacker or, perhaps most realistically, as involving something of both. Similar payments were made by towns outside the Pale. Wexford, for example, also made payments to the MacMurroughs, Limerick to the O'Briens, and Cork to MacCarthy of Muskerry.

The emergence of a fortified Pale and the payment of black rents to ward off Gaelic raids vividly illustrate how the English colony had contracted since its peak two centuries earlier. At the same time it is important to recognize that the decline was not continuous. The middle decades of the fifteenth century were a period of particular crisis. In England Henry VI was a weak ruler who from 1453 became mentally incapable, leading to several decades of sometimes violent internal conflict. In Ireland itself a succession of dynastic and political accidents affecting the earldoms of Ormond and Waterford, and for a time the earldom of Kildare, deprived the lordship of the magnate leadership required to organize and support its defence.[89] From the 1470s, on the other hand, the return of strong royal government in England and a revived magnate presence in the lordship itself made it possible not just to stop but to reverse the encroachments of the Gaelic Irish. The most impressive gains were made by the seventh and eighth earls of Kildare, who rebuilt their ravaged lordship in south Kildare and Carlow, and at the same time reasserted their control over the predatory inhabitants of the mountains south of Dublin. By 1488 the coastal town of Dalkey, earlier described as lying in the marches, was considered part of the maghery. Meanwhile the Butlers expanded their territories in Tipperary and Kilkenny, and the Nugents reasserted control on the frontiers of County Meath. Against this background the fortifications ordered by Poynings are better seen as consolidating an expanding frontier rather than as a further stage in a process of retreat. Expeditions by the earl of Kildare into Ulster in 1498, in defence of Galway in 1504, or into the south-west in 1510 likewise reveal as a misleading oversimplification the notion that English power on the island was confined to an ever-shrinking enclave on the east coast.

The emergence of the Pale as a distinct region had a political and administrative as well as a military significance. Dublin, Louth, Meath, and, with some qualification, Kildare were the four 'obedient shires' in which the normal processes of central and local government operated along lines broadly similar to contemporary English practice. Taxes, authorized by parliamentary grants of subsidy and levied according to a system rationalized in 1477–8, were collected regularly and transmitted to the royal exchequer. Customs revenue was likewise received from the ports of Drogheda and Dublin, with administrative reforms producing a marked improvement in yields from the 1460s onwards. Local

[89] For the fortunes of Ormond and Kildare see the concluding section of this chapter. After the death of John Talbot, first earl of Waterford, in 1453, his estates passed into the hands of absentees.

government in each county was supervised by a sheriff, assisted by a staff of clerks and lesser officials. Sheriffs were responsible for organizing defence and law enforcement within the county, for the execution of judicial writs, and for the maintenance of local records. They also collected local taxes, crown rents, and other royal entitlements, for which they accounted twice yearly at the exchequer. In addition they tried lesser offenders in their twice-yearly courts, known as tourns. More serious crimes were tried in the royal courts of King's Bench (which up to the 1490s was an itinerant court, sitting at different centres round the Pale) or Common Pleas. In both shire and royal courts cases were determined entirely according to the provisions of English law.[90]

Assessment of conditions outside the Pale is complicated by the distinction between those areas which enjoyed a degree of formally recognized administrative autonomy, and those which were in theory subject to the direct authority of the crown and its representatives. The towns of Dublin, Drogheda, Wexford, Waterford, New Ross, Youghal, Cork, Limerick, and Galway all held charters which allowed them to levy taxes and dispose of the resulting revenue, regulate trade and other activities, and deal with most forms of crime, all without reference to royal officials. Grants of liberties or palatinate jurisdiction, conferring broadly the same type of autonomy, had also been made to leading magnates. County Kerry was a liberty of the earls of Desmond, Tipperary of the Ormonds, and Wexford of the absentee earl of Shrewsbury. (The remains of the earldom of Ulster were also a liberty but in royal hands, so that its seneschal nominally reported to the Dublin administration much as county sheriffs did.) Limerick, Tipperary, Cork, and Galway, on the other hand, were in theory royal shires on the same basis as Meath and Louth. In practice the distinction between those outlying shires that were and were not liberties was of limited importance. The earl of Desmond's control over County Limerick was not significantly different from his control over County Kerry. The Ormonds, for their part, treated Kilkenny and Tipperary as a single administrative unit, assuming rights of liberty jurisdiction throughout. In the same way the eventual redesignation as a liberty of County Kildare, formerly one of the four obedient shires, was a belated recognition of the de facto dominance there of the increasingly powerful Fitzgerald earls—so much so that the change can be dated only approximately, to around 1514.

Observers within the Pale wrote in lurid terms of conditions beyond its boundaries. A report on the state of Ireland around 1515 listed Waterford, Cork, Kilkenny, Carlow, Limerick, and Kerry, as well as the whole of Connacht and Ulster, as 'counties that obey not the king's laws and have neither justice, neither sheriffs, under the king'.[91] Some twenty years later Patrick Finglas, law officer and

[90] For a detailed account see Ellis, *Reform and Revival.*

[91] 'State of Ireland and Plan for its Reformation *SP Henry VIII*, ii. 8. This long, unsigned document is generally dated to *c.*1515.

future judge, maintained in similar terms that 'all the land is now of Irish rule, except the little English pale'.[92] Modern accounts, on the other hand, emphasize the extent to which central government did in fact manage to exercise at least a residual supervision over the outlying parts of the lordship.[93] The chartered towns and other ports remitted some customs and other revenue, although the amounts were insignificant compared to those received from Dublin and Drogheda. Cases from the different city courts were referred to the royal judges for review or on appeal.[94] The sheriffs of outlying shires, the seneschals of the liberties, and the bailiffs of the cities appeared from time to time at the exchequer to account for receipts and payments and pay the dues required, known as 'proffers'. The alternation of years in which large numbers of proffers were received with others in which no local officials from outside the Pale came forward has been interpreted as indicating that irregular attendance was an officially sanctioned norm rather than as evidence of lack of control.[95] A further important mechanism for supervision was the periodic issue of general commissions empowering travelling judges to hold sessions in the outlying counties. By the early sixteenth century Cork, Kilkenny, Tipperary, Waterford, Wexford, and Carlow were being visited annually in this way. The precise competence of such itinerant commissioners varied. Even in areas of palatinate jurisdiction like Tipperary or Wexford, however, they were empowered to enquire into encroachments on royal rights, to hear cases involving the four pleas of the crown (arson, rape, treasure trove, and forestalling, the creation of artificial shortages to drive up prices), and to review other proceedings, while elsewhere they had a more general jurisdiction over both felonies and civil actions.

If the polemics of Pale reformers cannot be taken wholly at face value the evidence of the administrative archives must also be treated with a certain caution. There is the danger that formulaic and often fragmentary records may reflect bureaucratic routine rather than real events, or impose the appearance of system on a much less orderly reality. Nevertheless the image of a straightforward contrast between a Pale in which the king's laws were obeyed and normal administrative and judicial processes operated and a lawless wilderness beyond is seriously misleading. Instead the picture is of a series of gradations, from the reasonably well ordered inner Pale through a series of regions in which central government could hope to wield a greater or lesser degree of influence, to an outer frontier along which its authority was largely nominal. It is also important to recognize the extent to which the formalities of royal control masked a pragmatic

[92] Patrick Finglas, 'A Breviate of the Getting of Ireland and the Decay of the Same', printed in Walter Harris (ed.), *Hibernica, or Some Ancient Pieces Relating to Ireland* (Dublin, 1770 edn.), i. 84. Brendan Bradshaw, *The Dissolution of the Religious Orders in Ireland under Henry VIII* (Cambridge, 1974), 44, suggests a date of 1534 for this document.

[93] D. B. Quinn, 'Anglo-Irish Local Government 1485–1534, *IHS* 1 (1939), 354–81; Ellis, *Reform and Revival*, esp. ch. 7.

[94] Ellis, *Reform and Revival*, 74, 182–3.

[95] Ibid. 89.

accommodation with the facts of local power. Even in the relatively well ordered inner parts of the lordship sheriffs were either prominent figures in their own right, or clients of local magnates. In the far west successive Burke lords, in strict legal terms usurpers of the lands of the earldom of Ulster, were accepted as sheriffs of Connacht, even if their contact with Dublin remained nominal. In the same way the Savages, a gaelicized English family controlling the southern part of the Ards peninsula, generally held the title of seneschals of the earldom of Ulster. But when, in 1468–70, a new lord lieutenant bestowed this instead on the other main English family in the region, the Whites, the Savages went to war. In doing so they allied with the O'Neills of Clandeboye, while the Whites had the support of the O'Neills of Tyrone, so that a struggle for the endorsement of the Dublin government became entwined with the dynastic rivalries of Gaelic Ulster. Within a few years the government had capitulated to the realities of local power, and the Savages were once again seneschals.[96]

Similar ambiguities were evident in another area crucial to the government of the lordship, the upkeep and deployment of military force. All of the major lords beyond the Pale maghery maintained bodies of armed men. In itself this was not remarkable. The organization of defence was one of the traditional duties of magnates everywhere, and in border regions, whether in France, Cumberland, or Tipperary, this could be expected to be a substantial and permanent responsibility. But the military arrangements of the Irish lords were distinctive in three ways. First the forces they maintained consisted of professional soldiers, kern and galloglass, rather than simple musters of the able-bodied males among their tenants. Secondly the means by which these fighting men were maintained once again drew on the Gaelic custom of coyne and livery. Thirdly there was the way in which these private armies were used. English legal theory was uncompromising on this subject: there could be only one state of peace or war throughout the king's realms. In practice conditions in Ireland, where the fragmented territories of the outer lordship abutted onto the territories of an even more decentralized Gaeldom, made any such simplicity impossible to achieve. Instead frontier magnates dealt pragmatically with their Irish neighbours, making war or peace and concluding local alliances as circumstances dictated.[97] To unsympathetic observers, however, this placed them almost in the same category as the wild Irish themselves. An account of around 1515 wrote of 'more than 30 great captains of the English noble folk . . . every one of [whom] makes war and peace for himself without any licence of the king, or of any other temporal person, save to him that is strongest, and of such that may subdue them by the sword'.[98]

[96] Simms, 'The King's Friend: O'Neill, the Crown and the Earldom of Ulster', in Lydon, *England and Ireland in the Later Middle Ages*, 231–2.
[97] R. F. Frame, 'War and Peace in the Medieval Lordship of Ireland', in Lydon, *English in Medieval Ireland*, 130–40.
[98] *SP Henry VIII*, ii. 6.

KING'S FRIENDS AND IRISH ENEMIES

What, finally, of the relationship between the English lordship and those whom the Pale was constructed to exclude: the 'wild Irish' of the areas still under Gaelic rule? An act of 1331 had provided that the same law should apply to all free men, Irish and English, living within the lordship. Within a few decades, however, this ruling had fallen into disuse, possibly subverted by hostile judges. Instead what were referred to as 'mere' Irishmen were regarded as aliens, excluded from the operation of English law.[99] They could be debarred from proceeding with a civil action in the courts. Their wills were not recognized, and Irish widows of Englishmen did not have the normal entitlement to dowries. Clergymen of Gaelic birth were not eligible to hold benefices or to be admitted as members of religious communities in English areas. The killing of an Irishman was not a felony at law, although compensation might be due to his lord. This last provision has a particularly ominous ring. However, it existed as a logical consequence of the general principle that Irishmen, like foreigners in England itself, stood outside the protection of the law, rather than as a warrant for genocide. It must also be seen in the context of a society in which the real security of most men, English or Gaelic, depended more on the protection of a social superior than on abstract legal sanctions.

The real importance of the other legal disabilities that went with the status of a 'mere Irishman' is also open to question. In the late fifteenth and sixteenth centuries individuals bearing Gaelic names appear regularly in legal and administrative records, not as Irish enemies, but as tenants in good standing, as loyal petitioners of government, and as litigants and jurors in the royal courts.[100] Such individuals could have secured themselves against penalty and inconvenience by purchasing a charter of denization, declaring them and their descendants to be 'of free estate and condition', required to answer and be answered in the courts, and entitled to acquire and dispose of property. But the actual number of such grants was small: between 1461 and 1506 a total of 35 are recorded, 14 to laymen and the rest to clerics. Instead it would seem that the whole body of legal precept relating to English and Irish status was by this time largely a dead letter, except perhaps for those seeking a career in holy orders.[101]

[99] 'Mere' in this context meant 'purely' or 'fully' and had none of the derogatory connotations modern usage might suggest. It was also possible to be a 'mere' Englishman: see e.g. Stanihurst, in *Holinshed's Chronicles*, vi. 3.

[100] Ellis, *Reform and Revival*, 130, 193; Ellis, *Tudor Frontiers and Noble Power*, 33.

[101] Bryan Murphy, 'The Status of the Native Irish after 1331', *Irish Jurist*, 2 (1967), 116–38; Ellis, *Reform and Revival*, 129–31; idem, 'Racial Discrimination in Late Medieval Ireland', in Gudmundur Halfdanarson (ed.), *Racial Discrimination and Ethnicity in European History* (Pisa, 2003), 21–32.

The real 'wild Irish', of course, were not those who sought to creep into the lower levels of Pale society, but rather those who remained outside it, in the Gaelic lordships. Here the attitudes of the English of Ireland varied sharply. In the towns and inner Pale there is evidence of a deep rooted hostility, reflected in the tone of numerous civic ordinances directed against Gaelic interlopers and in a marked aversion to intermarriage. The aristocracy and gentry of outlying areas, by contrast, seem typically to have been involved in an intricate network of alliances, in conflict with some of their Gaelic neighbours and allied to others. Such alliances could be reinforced by fostering, where a child was sent to be brought up in the household of another family, and by what was known as gossiprid, a bond of association marked by the bestowal and acceptance of gifts, by an oath or by the taking of the sacrament.[102] To these were added the bonds of intermarriage—producing, for example, the complex web of alliances, embracing Gaelic Ireland as well as the Pale, that partly underpinned the army that the eighth earl of Kildare brought to Knockdoe. The earls of Kildare and Ormond contracted such alliances through daughters and younger sons, while they themselves and their heirs married wives of English birth or blood. The more peripheral earls of Desmond, and the lesser English lords, on the other hand, took Gaelic partners of their own. The eighth earl of Desmond, who died in 1487, had married Margaret, daughter of Tadhg O'Brien, lord of Thomond; William Barry, Lord Barrymore, who died in 1500, had married Sheila, daughter of Cormac MacCarthy of Muskerry.

Marriage alliances of this kind were no doubt an important contributor to the dissemination of Gaelic manners among the English elite that caused such concern to contemporary observers. But we must also consider their impact on Gaelic society. When Alice, daughter of the ninth earl of Kildare, married Brian O'Connor Faly, for example, their alliance did not solely build a bridge between the Gaelic midlands and the outer Pale. For Alice's mother had been Elizabeth Zouche, a kinswoman of Henry VII, whom the earl had brought back as his bride when he returned in 1503 from his upbringing at the royal court. A chain of direct personal influence thus stretched from the palace of Westminster to the O'Connor tower houses and castles of the central plain. The women who thus crossed ethnic and cultural frontiers, moreover, were not passive counters in the game of aristocratic aggrandizement and political management. Alice O'Connor acted as a trusted emissary for both her own and her husband's family. In 1528 she travelled from her father, detained in England, to her husband Brian O'Connor Faly, with instructions for him to attack the Pale. Later, following the defeat of the Kildare rebellion, she was sent to negotiate the surrender on terms of Brian and his relatives. A fuller knowledge of her story, and that of others like her, would do much to reveal the real

[102] Fiona Fitzsimons, 'Fosterage and Gossiprid in Late Medieval Ireland: Some New Evidence', in Duffy et al., *Gaelic Ireland*, 138–49.

workings of late medieval and early modern Irish society. But even as it stands her experience is a reminder of the complexities concealed behind apparently rigid legal formulae.

What, finally, can be said of the attitude of the Gaelic Irish to England, and to the English lordship that had violently established itself as their neighbour? The fullest evidence available is the literature of the period, the annals and genealogies of the professional learned classes, and more particularly the bardic poetry. This extensive body of verse, despite the rigid conventions of language and expression within which practitioners worked, has been convincingly presented as an authentic expression of attitudes and beliefs.[103] The poets, although a highly esteemed professional caste, wrote strictly to order. There is thus little risk, for once, of falling into the trap of mistaking the musings of a literary subculture for the voice of the age. Instead what we have are elaborate works of propaganda and self-justification, carefully tailored to the perceptions and prejudices of individual lords and their followers. The only note of caution must relate to what proportion of the population was thus represented. Propaganda implies an audience, and bardic poetry can thus legitimately be read as a reflection of the outlook, not just of Gaelic rulers but of their leading followers. Of the attitudes and aspirations of the Gaelic peasantry, on the other hand, we know, as in other areas, next to nothing.

Two characteristics are generally accepted as marking out late medieval Gaelic literature.[104] The first was an acute awareness of ethnic distinctions. Poets and annalists consistently distinguished between the native Irish and the descendants of the settlers who had come from England, Wales, and elsewhere in the twelfth century and after, generally referring to the former as the *Gaeil* and to the latter as the *Gaill* (foreigners). Thus when the earl of Kildare invaded Ulster in 1498, to join his nephew Turlough O'Neill in warfare against a rival branch of the family, the mixed force they commanded was described as '*slua Gall agus na Gaeil* [a host of foreigners and Gaels]'. An account of the ill-fated contingents that accompanied Lambert Simnel to England in 1487 likewise recorded the death both of the greater part of the Irish (in this case, interestingly, referred to as *Eireannaigh*, generally seen as a more inclusive term for the people of Ireland) and of many noble foreign youth (*Gallmacamhaibh*). When the north-western lord Aed O'Donnell visited the Pale in 1499, he was described as going into the *Galltacht* or land of the *Gaill.* At the same time these foreigners or *Gaill* were in their turn distinguished from the English of England, who were referred to

[103] Simms, 'Bardic Poetry'; Simms, 'Bards and Barons'.

[104] The extent to which Gaelic poetry of the late sixteenth century and after can be read as an expression of changing political attitudes has been the subject of much controvery. See below pp. 236–7. Assessments of the late medieval literature are, by contrast, in broad agreement. See, in addition to the work of Simms already cited: Joep Leerssen, *Mere Irish and Fíor-Ghael* (Cork, 1996), 151–77; Michelle O'Riordan, *The Gaelic Mind and the Collapse of the Gaelic World* (Cork, 1990), chs. 1, 2.

as *Sasanaigh*, derived from 'Saxon'. Sir Edward Poynings, sent from England in 1494 to impose order on the lordship, was *ridire Saxanaigh*, a Saxon knight.[105]

The terminology of ethnic identity was further complicated by proximity to a Scotland divided along very similar lines. In an age when travel by sea was considerably easier than travel by land there was a strong case for seeing Gaelic Ireland, or at least its northern half, as forming part of a single cultural region, and even a single, decentralized polity, with the Scottish islands and Highlands. Cultural links were maintained and reinforced by the regular passage back and forth of poets, musicians, and other artists and men of learning, as well as by the constant traffic in galloglass taking service under Irish lords. The overlap between Scottish and Irish Gaeldom was also given concrete expression in the existence of the lordship of Clan Donald, lords of the western islands and Highlands, who used their combination of land and maritime power to take advantage of the collapse of the earldom of Ulster by seizing a substantial territory along the north-east coast of Ireland. Irish writers describing or commenting on Scottish affairs distinguished between Scots and Gaelic speakers with the same terminology of *Gaill* and *Gaeil* that they applied to the division between English and Irish in Ireland itself, and in some cases wrote in terms of a single Gaeldom threatened by surrounding *Gaill*.[106]

The second main characteristic of late medieval Gaelic literature, however, is that this consciousness of divisions based on ancestry, culture and language coexisted with a pragmatic acceptance of the reality of an ethnically divided Ireland. When occasion suited, poets were happy to appeal to the concept of a united Gaelic kingdom, urging their patrons, especially if these were from formerly dominant dynasties like the O'Briens or the O'Neills, to recreate the glories of the ancient high kingship of Tara. But this was never more than a literary conceit. The same or other poets were equally willing to compose poems in honour of wholly or partly gaelicized patrons of English origin. Already in the fifteenth century these flexible propagandists had developed what was to be a favourite theme of later advocates of a more inclusive Irishness, from the Counter Reformation cleric Geoffrey Keating in the early seventeenth century to the Romantic nationalists of Young Ireland in the mid-nineteenth: the idea that Ireland had been the scene of a succession of invasions, of which the English incursion of the twelfth century had been only the latest. 'Of all the invasions of Ireland', a mid-fifteenth-century poem declared, 'that of the Geraldines, the last, was the best.'[107] Earlier still, in the late fourteenth century, the poet Geoffrey Fionn O'Daly had mocked the contradictory political posturings of his own profession. Addressing the third earl of Desmond, himself a noted practitioner

[105] These examples are taken from *Annals of Ulster*, iii. 437, 319, 439, 383.

[106] S. G. Ellis, 'The Collapse of the Gaelic World 1450–1650', *IHS* 31 (1999), 449–56; Ellis, *Ireland in the Age of the Tudors*, 243–54.

[107] Brendan Bradshaw, *The Irish Constitutional Revolution of the Sixteenth Century* (Cambridge, 1979), 22.

of Gaelic verse known to the Irish as '*Gearóid Iarla* [Gerald the earl]', Geoffrey urged him to pay no attention to poems that promised the Gael a kingdom they would never actually achieve. 'In poems to the *Gaill* we promise the driving of the *Gaeil* from Éire; in those to the *Gaeil* we promise the driving of the *Gaill* east overseas.'[108] As a telling example of this political flexibility, Katharine Simms offers the case of Tadhg Óg O'Higgin, who in 1442 exhorted Neachtain O'Donnell to avoid war with the O'Neills and concentrate instead on the *Gaill* whose occupation of so much of Ireland should be much more a cause of concern to him. But this was advice which Neachtain, in no position to resist the demands of the stronger O'Neills, would have been only too glad to take. In another poem, meanwhile, the same Tadhg Óg advised the chief of the O'Neills not to attack the English until he had subdued the other Gaelic lords of Ulster, which would of course have included the O'Donnells.[109]

The clear-headed political pragmatism concealed behind the rhetoric of bardic poetry should not surprise. The lords for whom they wrote allied with or made war on the representatives of the English community and the English crown as circumstances dictated, restrained by no national scruple. Instead their choices were determined by considerations of local politics. Successive O'Neills, for example, struggling to hold together their sprawling Ulster lordship and to fend off the challenges of the O'Donnells to the west and of recalcitrant lesser lordships to the east and south, repeatedly found it advantageous to seek the status of king's friend, allied with the local representatives of the English crown in order to organise the province of Ulster for their common advantage. In the same way the MacCarthys of the south-west, menaced by the (in English terms) renegade earl of Desmond, were consistently anxious to counter this threat by being on good terms with the Dublin administration.

The pragmatism of Gaelic poetry thus accorded closely with the actual political practice of a culturally unified but politically fragmented political system, in which consciousness of Gaelic identity coexisted with an intensely local politics. It was also consistent with both the theory and practice of Gaelic lordship, where legal and historical notions of right counted for far less than the ability to enforce one's claims to obedience and tribute. Another O'Higgin poet, writing in the late sixteenth century and addressing one of the Burkes of Connacht, made the point explicit:

> The land of Banba [Ireland] is but swordland
>
> . . . .
>
> To be under the rule of he who is strongest
> Is the law of this territory
>
> . . . .
>
> The father does not bequeath to the son
> *Fodla* [Ireland's] island of noble scions

108 *NHI*, ii. 696. 109 Simms, 'Bardic Poetry', 62.

Until it is obtained by force
It cannot be occupied.[110]

In this context it is easy to see how magnates of the *Gaill* such as Kildare, Ormond, and Desmond could be accepted as legitimate participants within a system of competing lordships, extending protection and exacting tribute on almost exactly the same basis as their Gaelic counterparts. This incorporation was all the easier because the lords concerned were willing to play their part, taking on the role of protectors, dispensers of hospitality, and patrons of poets and others. But it was also possible to accommodate, in general terms, the more distant figure of the English king. In 1503, for example, an annalist recorded the death of Henry VII's queen, Elizabeth of York, in a lightly adapted version of conventional terms: 'the wife of the king of the Saxons . . . the daughter of King Edward . . . a woman that was of the greatest charity and humanity from Italy to Ireland'.[111] This, however, was the token acknowledgement of a remote, theoretically conceived figure. In the century that followed, as the English crown came to exert a direct and increasingly assertive influence within all parts of Ireland, all sections of Gaelic society were to be forced to reassess their attitudes to national identity and political allegiance.

THE TALKING CRUCIFIX AND THE TURTLE DOVE

The ethnic division between Irish and English was also institutionalized in one further important institution, the church.[112] Even in the late fifteenth and early sixteenth centuries religious communities were still occasionally fined for having admitted fellow regulars of Gaelic origin, and it was more often priests than laymen who found it necessary to seek grants of English law. Ethnic divisions were also evident in episcopal appointments, with ten of the thirty-two Irish sees invariably held by Englishmen and another thirteen by Gaelic Irish bishops. In the archdiocese of Armagh, taking in both the whole of County Louth and a large tract of central Ulster extending to the west shores of Lough Neagh, ecclesiastical sources distinguished explicitly between the church *inter anglicos* and the church *inter hibernicos.* The archbishop, invariably English, resided in Drogheda, while a dean and chapter, all Gaelic Irish, controlled the formal centre of the archdiocese, in Armagh. Despite this observance of de facto divisions ethnic tensions appeared from time to time. In 1421, for example, the bishop of Waterford, John Geese,

[110] Quoted in Leerssen, *Mere Irish and Fíor-Ghael,* 175–6. I have slightly modified Leerssen's translation to retain the emphasis in the original.

[111] Annals of Ulster, iii. 465.

[112] For general accounts of the late medieval church see Canice Mooney, *The Church in Gaelic Ireland: Thirteenth to Fifteenth Centuries* (Dublin, 1969); John Watt, *The Church in Medieval Ireland* (Dublin, 1972); Henry Jefferies, *Priests and Prelates of Armagh in the Age of Reformation 1518–1556* (Dublin, 1997).

complained that Richard O'Hedian, archbishop of Cashel, 'made very much of the Irish, and that he loved none of the English nation', whom he refused to appoint to benefices.[113]

As in other areas of Irish life, however, ethnic divisions were in practice less clear cut than the letter of the law, or occasional flare ups of hostility between individuals, might suggest. Studies of Armagh diocese and province have demonstrated the remarkable ability of its archbishops to exercise real jurisdiction not only throughout the diocese, but within the whole province of Ulster. Most of the business recorded in the registers of the archbishops concerned the English areas of their see. But successive archbishops also made regular visits to Armagh and the rest of the territory *inter hibernicos*. In addition they occasionally visited other dioceses in the province, summoned the Gaelic bishops of north and west Ulster to provincial synods in Drogheda, and heard appeals from all parts of the province in their metropolitan court. They also maintained diplomatic relations with the O'Neill overlords of the region, at times clashing over encroachments on ecclesiastical liberties or property, but at others achieving mutual accommodation. In 1455 Archbishop John Mey officiated at the inauguration of Hugh O'Neill, lending his authority to a disputed succession in exchange for undertakings to uphold and protect the rights of the church.[114]

Armagh was in some respects a special case: its archbishops, Englishmen appointed by an English king, were nevertheless accepted in Gaelic Ireland as the heirs of St Patrick. Yet it was not only there that racial divisions were in practice often blurred. In the diocese of Dublin rigid enforcement of the exclusion of Irishmen allowed a self-consciously English elite to monopolize senior positions in the two cathedrals and the major religious houses. In rural parts of the diocese, on the other hand, Irish clergy frequently held lesser benefices, as they also did in Armagh *inter Anglicos*. In the neigbouring diocese of Kildare both the parish clergy and the cathedral chapter were ethnically mixed.[115] There was also some flexibility in episcopal appointments. If twenty-three of the thirty-two Irish dioceses were more or less permanently held by members of one nation or the other, that left nine in which the nationality of the bishop could change from one occasion to the next. It is also important to recognize that bishops, whether Irish or English, operated within a common institutional framework. They had received a similar training in law, canon law, or theology, either in a university in continental Europe or in Oxford or Cambridge. Moreover the establishment

[113] *NHI*, iii. 587.

[114] John Watt, 'Ecclesia Inter Anglicos et Inter Hibernicos: Confrontations and Coexistence in the Medieval Diocese and Province of Armagh', in Lydon, *The English in Medieval Ireland*, 46–64; Watt, 'The Church and the Two Nations in Late Medieval Armagh', in W. J. Sheils and Diane Wood (eds.), *The Churches, Ireland and the Irish* (Oxford, 1989), 37–54.

[115] James Murray, 'The Diocese of Dublin in the Sixteenth Century: Clerical Opposition and the Failure of the Reformation', in James Kelly and Daire Keogh (eds.), *History of the Catholic Diocese of Dublin* (Dublin, 2000), 92–111; Mary Ann Lyons, *Church and Society in County Kildare 1470–1547* (Dublin, 2000), 70–1.

from 1492 of an English Cardinal Protector at the papal court meant that the king was able to have a major say in the appointment of bishops in Gaelic Ireland, as he had long had in those areas under his direct or indirect control.

The institutionalization of the ethnic division, and the limited reach of the English crown, ensured that the church in Gaelic Ireland retained a number of distinctive features. These reflected the character of the society in which it operated, with its strong emphasis on inherited rights and functions. Most ecclesiastical lands were in the hands of two groups of office holders, coarbs and erenaghs. Both were survivors of the period before the creation of a regular territorial structure of dioceses and parishes in the twelfth century, when the Irish church had been organized primarily round monasteries. Coarbs, the more prestigious of the two, claimed descent from the founders of early monasteries, while erenachs were successors to the administrators of monastic lands. The role of both was to act as tenants and stewards of church lands, paying the bishop an annual rent, providing lodgings and entertainment for him and his retinue as he travelled through the diocese, maintaining parish churches, and in some cases providing hospitality for pilgrims and travellers. Coarbs might also serve as custodians of local relics. Both positions were hereditary, held by whoever was chosen in the ordinary way as head of the lineage group concerned. Although some of those so chosen took full priests' orders, others were in minor orders or none at all. However, coarb and erenagh families also provided many of the clergy. The same emphasis on hereditary right was evident in the appearance of successive members of the same family as incumbents of particular parishes or bishops in particular dioceses. One consequence of the priority thus given to dynastic succession was a widespread disregard both for the church's laws on consanguinity and for the obligation of clerical celibacy. In 1484, for example, a priest of the MacEgan family in the diocese of Clonfert, the son of an unmarried woman related to his father within the prohibited decrees, successfully applied for a dispensation from his dual defect to allow him to succeed his father as dean of the diocese. In 1498 the Annals of Ulster recorded the death of Cathal Óg MacManus Maguire, dean of Lough Erne and father of over a dozen children, saluting him as a gem of purity and a turtle dove of chastity. One of his sons, also a cleric, was later to marry the daughter of a bishop of Kilmore.[116]

A similar adaptation to the characteristic preoccupations of Gaelic society was evident in aspects of religious belief and custom. Saints, for example, were conceived of in terms derived from the role of secular lords as patrons and protectors. They were to be flattered by means of elaborate genealogies; their help could be claimed on the basis of kinship or clientage; alternatively, they could be coerced into rendering assistance by the moral blackmail of fasting; they provided effective sanctuary because any violation would be a slight on

[116] Watt, *Church in Medieval Ireland*, 189; Mooney, *The Church in Gaelic Ireland*, 59–60.

their honour which they would be bound to avenge.[117]At the same time it would be wrong to see Gaelic Christianity, at least among the educated elite, as wholly outside the European mainstream. In the great late medieval manuscript compilations, texts dealing with local saints and indigenous traditions appear side by side with material of continental origin on such standard themes as the passion of Christ and the life of the Virgin.[118] One rare glimpse into the interior religious life of a late medieval Irish ruler is provided by a petition submitted to Rome in 1439 by Thomas Óg Maguire, lord of Fermanagh, who recalled how he had found himself in grave danger of death while on a pilgrimage to the great shrine of St James at Santiago de Compostela in north-west Spain. At the time he had promised that if he survived he would retire from the world and live on alms. However, he now asked to be released from his vow, on the grounds that he had promised without securing the consent of his wife and children. The nature of Maguire's journey, to an internationally famous pilgrimage site, testifies to the orthodox character of his piety, just as his subsequent concern to obtain papal sanction for his abandoned vow indicates a well-developed sense of religious obligation. What gives the whole episode added significance is that in 1471, nine years before his death, Maguire is recorded as having in fact given up his lordship 'for the love of God'.[119]

The religious lives of the common people of Gaelic Ireland are more difficult to characterize with any confidence. Occasional glimpses from contemporary sources must be combined with the fuller evidence available from the early seventeenth century onwards, when clergy loyal to Rome began the task of reshaping popular religion along the lines prescribed by the Catholic Counter-Reformation. The broad picture that emerges is one familiar throughout pre-Reformation Europe, in which the rituals and symbols of Christianity had been combined with a variety of other traditions to create a body of belief and practice concerned primarily with achieving a sense of security in a world of unpredictable and often mysterious hazards. Thus saints became figures of power in their own right, whose intercession could be obtained by a variety of formulae. Shrines, wells, and other sites became sacred spots, where the proper observances could ensure health and good fortune. The person of the clergy, the consecrated host, and a variety of relics were likewise credited with supernatural powers. The official rituals of the church were of greatest relevance at turning points in the cycle of life: baptism, marriage, and the last sacraments administered to the dying were all of supreme importance. But here too the sacred mingled with the secular. Funerals in particular were accompanied by extravagant banquets, precursors of the later wake, at which feasting, drinking, and a degree of sexual licence served as an assertion of continuity in the face of mortality, as an ostentatious

[117] Meigs, *The Reformations in Ireland*, 28–37. [118] Ibid. 28–40.

[119] M. J. Haren, 'The Religious Outlook of a Gaelic Lord: A New Light on Thomas Óg Maguire', *IHS*, 25 (1986), 195–7.

display of family status, and as a means of creating or reinforcing social bonds. Marriage, too, subordinated religious to secular considerations. As in other societies, popular opinion placed more emphasis on betrothal, the formalizing of the contract before relatives and neighbours, than on its solemnization in church. If the family alignments that had underpinned the union changed, or if it did not quickly fulfil its function of producing children, the contract could be nullified. It was for this reason, rather than any hedonistic climate of sexual liberation, that illegitimacy carried little stigma in Gaelic society.

None of this, it should be emphasized, necessarily created a conflict between popular and official religion, of the kind that was to develop as the Protestant and Catholic Reformations took their parallel courses. The parish clergy, overwhelmingly locally recruited and trained by a system of apprenticeship to existing pastors, were likely to share many of the assumptions and preferences of the people to whom they ministered. The bishops and senior clergy, by contrast, represented a university-trained elite. But they too, having achieved their own synthesis of secular and religious preoccupations, were for the most part happy to prescribe or approve customs that allowed their flocks to do the same. They endorsed pilgrimages to holy wells and the shrines of local saints. In 1539, for example, the dean of Armagh, seconded by the archbishop, allowed a man who had strangled his son to do penance by visiting eighteen places of pilgrimage across a period of two years.[120] Bells and other relics were made available as needed to cure people or animals, or to test the truth of disputed statements; on occasion they could even be carried into battle. At other times the church deployed its magic for its own purposes, cursing and ringing bells against those who had encroached on its prerogatives, or simply quarrelled with its servants.

Church organization and religion in English Ireland in some respects differed significantly from the Gaelic pattern. Ecclesiastical affairs were subject both to the ultimate control of the crown and to English law, including the mid-fourteenth-century statutes of praemunire and provisors which imposed severe penalties on anyone cooperating in the assertion of papal jurisdiction against the rights of the monarch or of other patrons. Bishops and other senior dignitaries were nominated by the crown. Those at the centre of the lordship, the archbishops of Armagh and Dublin, and the bishop of Meath, were invariably English-born; bishops in the outer lordships were more commonly English of Irish birth, often in practice nominated at the behest of local magnates. The machinery of ecclesiastical discipline, through visitation and diocesan synods, was more highly organized. Open disregard for clerical celibacy was less common than in Gaelic areas, though instances nevertheless exist of clergy receiving dispensations for having lived with women or fathered children. Religious culture also differed, particularly in the central role of guilds and other fraternities, whose members partook together of the sacraments of the church, endowed and supported chapels

[120] Meigs, *Reformations in Ireland*, 39.

and shrines dedicated to their patron saint, commissioned masses and prayers for the souls of deceased brothers, and celebrated feast days and other festivals with mystery plays and pageants. These differences were in part a product of cultural inheritance—mystery plays and guilds modelled on English forms—but also of environment. A characteristic feature of late medieval Christianity everywhere in Europe was its corporate character: salvation was to be achieved through accumulated, collective merit, whether of the faithful as a whole or of a specific association, rather than through the efforts of a single individual. In the dispersed and lineage-dominated society of Gaelic Ireland this meant that occasions related to kinship, funerals, baptisms, and marriages assumed a central importance. In English Ireland, on the other hand, and more specifically in the towns, a more geographically concentrated and somewhat more individualized population created specific associations to achieve the same sense of collective security.

As in other respects, however, the division between religious cultures was by no means absolute. If the chief towns and the wholly Gaelic regions can be seen as two contrasting patterns, then the outlying rural areas of the Pale, with English social and ecclesiastical structures but a largely Gaelic population, must have represented some form of hybrid zone. Even between purely English and purely Gaelic Ireland, moreover, there were points of contact as well as difference. Whatever tensions existed between English and Irish clergy, they were part of the same ecclesiastical system, sharing both a common set of rituals and symbols and allegiance to a common spiritual hierarchy with the pope at its head. This was evident in the alternation of Gaelic and English bishops in some dioceses, in the employment of Gaelic clergy in parts of the lordship, and in the ability of the archbishops of Armagh to exercise authority on both sides of the ethnic frontier. Religious literature in both English and Irish drew on the same classic texts of medieval continental devotion. Where religious practice was concerned, the cult of saints, expressed particularly in pilgrimages to holy wells and other sites, was a prominent feature of both cultures. The enthusiasm that the English community developed for local saints such as Bridget and Patrick provided further common ground. The existence of a shared religious system, at both ideological and practical levels, was acknowledged by the corporation of Dublin, seconded by the Irish parliament, when they issued a safe conduct to pilgrims from any part of Ireland coming to Christ Church cathedral to see the *baculus Ihesu*, or staff of Jesus, that was preserved there with other relics, including a miraculous speaking crucifix.[121]

The Irish church of the late medieval period did not consist solely of the bishops and parish clergy. There were also the religious orders, divided between monks, theoretically devoted to a life of prayer and contemplation, and the mendicant orders, devoted to educational and pastoral work in return for alms. The monastic

[121] Kenneth Milne (ed.), *Christ Church Cathedral, Dublin: A History* (Dublin, 2000), 158.

orders were by the late middle ages largely moribund. Contemporary allegations of their scandalous worldliness and vice are now seen as exaggerated. But the evidence from English areas suggests a relatively small monastic establishment largely preoccupied with the administration of the substantial endowments of land and other property inherited from an earlier age. In Gaelic areas many houses had apparently abandoned any pretence of upholding the monastic life. Instead lay families and married nominal monks controlled their property on a hereditary basis. Among the mendicants, on the other hand, the fifteenth century saw a dramatic expansion. A total of ninety new houses were established between 1400 and 1508. These included forty-three houses of the Franciscan Third Order regular, a new and specifically Irish movement, originally designed for laity living in the world but later adapted to a communal life. Meanwhile the character of the main existing mendicant orders, Franciscans, Dominicans, and Augustinians, was being transformed by the extension from continental Euorope of an Observant movement committed to a return to the standards of discipline and commitment set by the original founders. The Observant movement was strongest in Gaelic Ireland, where most of the new houses were located. In the 1520s and 1530s, however, many of the mendicant houses in English areas also adopted the Observant rule, providing further evidence of the shared as well as separate elements in the two religious cultures.

What was the overall state of the late medieval Irish church? Older accounts have in general emphasized the instances of delinquency, and the departures from strict orthodoxy in areas like clerical celibacy, recorded in surviving administrative records. The most recent research, by contrast, suggests a more positive picture. There was indeed an endemic misallocation of resources. Much of the enormous wealth accumulated over centuries of Christian hegemony was held by cathedral chapters and other corporate bodies or by individual dignitaries, or alternatively had passed into the hands of lay patrons, while responsibility for pastoral work remained with a poorly paid lower clergy. Yet the evidence of visitation records suggests that these were for the most part reasonably closely supervised, that they had received a sound if not very sophisticated training in their priestly functions, and that most discharged their duties conscientiously enough. The proliferation of privately endowed masses ('chantries'), chapels of ease, and monastic houses may have promoted an untidy multiplication of places of worship. But it also ensured that pastoral services were readily available throughout both English and Gaelic Ireland. The growth of the Observant movement testified to a continued potential for spiritual revival. The continued vitality of guilds and confraternities, and the evidence of continued generous endowment of altars, shrines, chapels, and chantries, equally, serves as evidence of the continued strength of lay piety.

Another undoubted weakness of the church was the widespread secularization of ecclesiastical office. Bishops in English Ireland were royal nominees, often expected to act as administrators and political representatives. Other appointments were in the hands of lay patrons acting within a framework of clientage and the cultivation of dynastic power. In Gaelic Ireland ecclesiastical office of all kinds, from bishoprics and abbacies down to the simplest parish living, was so closely involved in the structures of a lineage society as to be in many cases hereditary. From a different point of view, however, the close integration of religious and secular concerns that was shortly to draw the censure of reformers can also be seen as a source of strength. There is no indication, in either cultural and political zone, of the anti-clericalism that already before the Reformation was so marked a feature of sections of English and German society. Instead the English patriciate of the towns found in the church an institution properly respectful of hierarchy, and able in its rituals to reflect and legitimize the urban social order. In Gaelic Ireland, likewise, the clergy enjoyed the status conferred on a hereditary caste with a clear-cut social function. And everywhere the poor found in the rituals of the church an easily understood system of values and beliefs which offered at least the hope of some protection from the multiple insecurities of their existence.

Having said this, it would be wrong to analyse the strength of late medieval religion solely in terms of its social functions, important though these were. There was also the rich symbolic world of Christianity itself. Three features in particular can be picked out. There was the complex economy of salvation, in which sins could be set against the merits acquired by one's own acts of piety and charity, by drawing on the storehouse of grace built up by the saints through indulgences, and by the prayers of others. There was the interchange between generations of the living and the dead reflected in the popularity of chantries and guilds, with all these implied for continuity and meaning. And there was the central mystery of the eucharist, when Jesus Christ, God made man, was once again manifested in the form of bread and wine. These elements made up the core of late medieval Christianity as it was understood by great numbers of men and women. And events were to show that any attempt to deny their truth, or to take away their external expression in ritual and institutions, was to meet with the fiercest resistance.

VIRTÙ AND FORTUNA: THE RISE OF THE KILDARES

In May 1507 Gerald Fitzgerald, eighth earl of Kildare, the victor of Knockdoe, wrote a letter of greeting to the Gherardini of Florence, whom he believed, presumably on the basis of the surname, to be his own distant relatives. This was six years before one of Florence's most famous citizens, living in rural exile, produced his treatise on the acquisition and management of political power. Machiavelli was content to find his model of successful statecraft in the person of Cesare Borgia, supplemented by precedents and examples derived from the history of classical Rome. Yet if he had by any chance wished to look further afield to illustrate his vision of the statesman endowed with audacity and willpower who bent the unpredictable currents of fortune to his advantage, he might have done worse than to turn to the career of the Gherardini's self-proclaimed relative.[122] Kildare, during a career of more than three decades, continued the work begun by his father, the seventh earl, to create an effective power base for himself on the foundations of a depleted patrimony; he captured and held control of central government in the lordship, and constructed a formidable network of alliances and dependencies extending through both English and Gaelic Ireland. He achieved all this, moreover, despite finding himself on the losing side in the brutal dynastic struggles that devastated the lands of the English crown between the 1450s and the 1480s.[123]

A few decades earlier, none of this could have been predicted. By the mid-fifteenth century two of the great magnate families that had dominated the affairs of medieval Ireland had withdrawn from direct involvement. The lands of the Mortimers, earls of Ulster and lords of Connacht and Meath, passed in 1425 to Richard, duke of York, and then, through Richard's son Edward IV, to the English crown. The Talbots, earls of Shrewsbury and Waterford and with lands in Wexford and Meath, were from the 1450s absentees. This left three Irish earldoms: the Butler earls of Ormond in Kilkenny and Tipperary, the earls of Kildare in Kildare and Carlow, and the other major branch of the Fitzgerald family, the earls of Desmond, in the more remote south-western counties of Limerick and Kerry. Of these the Ormonds were clearly the most important. James Butler, the fourth earl, was eight times chief governor between 1420 and 1452, while engaged in a lengthy contest for supremacy with the Talbots. For the Kildares, on the other hand, the mid-fifteenth century was a period of crisis. The death in 1432 of the fifth earl left the title in abeyance and the bulk of the family estates in the hands of the late earl's son-in-law, the powerful fourth earl of Ormond. In the absence of a resident magnate to organize the defence of the lands, the neighbouring Irish, O'Connors, O'Dempseys, and others, overran territory and castles in most of County Carlow and along the western side of County Kildare. When Ormond died in 1452, Thomas FitzMaurice, grand-nephew of the fifth earl of Kildare, challenged the claim of his successor to the Fitzgerald estates. In the short term the violent conflict that followed contributed further to the ravaging of the Kildare lands. By 1454, however, the English court had recognized Fitzmaurice as seventh earl. This allowed him to begin the task of reversing the losses of the last two decades, pushing back Gaelic interlopers,

[122] Machiavelli, *The Prince*, ch. 25. For Kildare's letter to the Gherardini see above, pp. 40–1.

[123] There are full accounts of the political events of Kildare's career by D. B. Quinn in *NHI* ii, chs. 21, 23; A. J.Otway-Ruthven, *A History of Medieval Ireland* (London, 1968), ch. 12; Ellis, *Ireland in the Age of the Tudors*, chs. 3–5. Ellis, *Tudor Frontiers and Noble Power* offers a more analytical account of the basis of Kildare's power, placed in the context of the government of the other English dominions. Donough Bryan, *Gerald Fitzgerald, the Great Earl of Kildare, 1456–1513* (Dublin, 1933) is a celebratory biography projecting onto the late fifteenth century the assumptions of early twentieth-century nationalism.

erecting castles and fortifications at strategic points, and settling tenants on the recovered lands.[124]

The recovery in Kildare fortunes had a wider political background. The fifth earl of Ormond, resident in England and also holding the English title of earl of Wiltshire, was closely associated with the Lancastrian faction at the English court. Fitzmaurice, on the other hand, was the leading Irish supporter of the Lancastrian's main rival, Richard, duke of York. His recognition as earl came during York's period as lord lieutenant, and he subsequently served as the duke's deputy. A renewed outbreak of civil war in England during 1459–61 completed the downfall of the Ormonds. The fifth earl, captured with other Lancastrian leaders following the decisive Yorkist victory at Towtown in 1461, was beheaded on the battlefield and his lands and title declared forfeit. York himself had died in battle the previous year, but Kildare could look to his son, now securely enthroned as Edward IV, to recognize the claims of a loyal supporter.

The rewards did not come immediately. Instead Kildare had first to serve as a secondary figure in an episode full of significance for the future. In 1463 Edward appointed as his deputy the seventh earl of Desmond. The Desmonds, the most remote and gaelicized of the Irish earldoms, had not provided a chief governor since the late fourteenth century. The seventh earl, however, had demonstrated his loyalty the previous year, when he had crushed a revolt by the Yorkist Butlers at the battle of Piltown in County Kilkenny. There may also have been hopes that his south-western power base would make him better placed than others to shore up the borders of the lordship against Gaelic incursions. The Pale elite, on the other hand, resented the intrusion into their affairs of a gaelicized border magnate. In 1467 their continued complaints led the king to replace Desmond with one of his leading English supporters, John Tiptoft, earl of Worcester. A few months later, in February 1468, Worcester suddenly had Desmond arrested and beheaded. A bill of attainder rushed through the parliament then sitting cited the earl's alliances with the king's Irish enemies. Later comment suggested that his real offence had perhaps been his billeting of troops, by coyne and livery, on the Pale. Yet these were precisely the assets—an independent military capacity and a network of alliances in both English and Gaelic Ireland—that had seemed to make him so well suited for the office of chief governor. Desmond's downfall, in other words, was a deadly lesson in a fundamental contradiction that was to persist into the sixteenth century. The only way in which the English crown could govern Ireland, without what it considered an unacceptable expenditure of men and money, was by relying on a local magnate powerful enough to keep the lordship secure and in good order. But magnate power on that scale posed potential dangers to the crown itself. For almost seventy years three successive earls of Kildare were triumphantly to manage that tension. In the end it was to destroy them.

[124] The reconstruction of the Kildare estates is examined in detail in Ellis, *Tudor Frontiers and Noble Power*, ch. 4.

Against this background the tangled events of the next few years become easier to follow. The earl of Kildare, as Desmond's deputy, had also been proclaimed a traitor, and briefly joined the dead earl's brother in a campaign of violent revenge. Within a year, however, the attainder had been reversed and Kildare restored to favour. Desmond's relatives and heirs had begun an estrangement from the crown that was to last over seventy years, and the Butlers remained in disgrace. The Leinster Fitzgeralds were thus the only major lords to whom the crown could turn for the management of its Irish concerns. Yet distrust remained. Kildare served as deputy from 1470 until 1475, when he was replaced by William Sherwood, bishop of Meath. When the seventh earl died, on 25 March 1478, he had just embarked on a jurisdictional conflict with Sherwood, exploiting the death of George, duke of Clarence, whose deputy Sherwood nominally was, to insist that the bishop's patent was now invalid and that he himself should take power as justiciar. The earl's son, the 21- or 22-year-old Gerald, quickly took up the cause, securing his own election as justiciar, and mobilizing his supporters to obstruct Lord Grey of Ruthin, whom the king had dispatched to take over as deputy. His confrontational tactics proved successful. At the beginning of 1479 the king summoned Kildare and others to London, negotiated a compromise settlement between the earl and his Irish opponents, and sent him back to Ireland confirmed in the office of deputy lieutenant.

The eighth earl's long dominance of Irish affairs, along with the dramatic later history of his family, was to make him a figure of larger-than-life legend. This, together with the obscurity of many key episodes in his dramatic career, makes the real man an elusive figure. Richard Stanihurst, a close associate of the house of Kildare but writing a century after the eighth earl's succession to the title, described him as 'open and plain, hardly able to rule himself when he were moved to anger . . . soon hot and soon cold . . . a warrior incomparable, towards the nobles that he fancied not somewhat headlong and unruly'.[125] A sixteenth-century compilation of anecdotes, much concerned with the earl's doings, went further: 'a man of no great wit . . . but half an innocent man, without great knowledge or learning, but rudely brought up according to the usage of his country'.[126] The comment of a modern historian, that the earl's signature on official documents took the form of 'cramped initials, unaccustomed to the pen', would at first sight seem to bear out these assessments.[127] Yet it is also important to remember that Kildare, throughout his career, was to prove capable of getting his way through parliamentary and administrative procedures and the use of legal instruments as well as on the battlefield. Overall what emerges is the tentative image of a man of unpolished charisma, who combined a capacity for violent and headstrong action with a sound sense of political realities and procedures.

[125] *Holinshed's Chronicles*, vi. 278–9.
[126] 'The Book of Howth', printed in *Carew MSS*, v. 179–80.
[127] Alice Conway, *Henry VII's Relations with Scotland and Ireland*, 1, 44, 93.

The upheavals of the next few years were to test to the limit the eighth earl's talent for survival. When Edward IV died in 1483, Kildare was elected justiciar in the name of his son, Edward V. Soon after, however, he accommodated himself without apparent difficulty to the seizure of the throne, and the probable murder of this nephew, by Edward IV's brother Richard. By summer 1485 it was clear that an invasion by Henry Tudor, heir to the Lancastrian claim to the throne, was imminent. Kildare took steps to protect his own position. An act of the Irish parliament, on the basis of a supposed statute of Henry II, reaffirmed the right of an inner group of councillors, who could be counted on to be mainly Kildare's supporters, to fill any vacancy in the chief governorship.[128] This meant that when Richard was killed at the battle of Bosworth in August 1485, and Kildare's patent as deputy lapsed, he was immediately elected justiciar. He seems to have delayed for some months offering formal recognition to the victorious king, although whether this was from genuine hesitation, or deliberate brinkmanship, is impossible to say. But by March 1486 he had come to terms with the new regime, and was confirmed in office as deputy to the king's uncle, the duke of Bedford.

This first accommodation with the new Tudor dynasty was short-lived. Early in 1487, the 10-year-old Lambert Simnel, whom exiled Yorkists claimed to be the son of the duke of Clarence and thus rightful heir to the English throne, arrived in Ireland. Irish supporters of the Yorkist cause, including Kildare's brother, quickly rallied to his cause. Kildare himself initially held back, but the arrival in May of 2,000 German mercenaries led him finally to commit himself. On 24 May he had young Simnel formally crowned in Christ Church cathedral in Dublin as king of England, France, and Ireland. Immediately afterwards he accepted a new commission as lieutenant to 'Edward VI', and organized a parliament in his name. On 4 June the Yorkist army, reinforced by kern raised among the Gaelic Irish, sailed for England, where they were decisively defeated at the battle of Stoke on 16 June. Kildare, still in control of the Irish administration, was initially defiant, but by October he seems to have offered some sort of submission. By June 1488 the two sides had moved close enough to an accommodation for the king to send Sir Richard Edgecombe to Ireland with letters of pardon for the earl and other leading lords.

Even at this stage, however, Kildare proved conspicuously unwilling to play the part of the penitent rebel. He initially kept Edgecombe waiting in Dublin for several days, before appearing with a retinue of 200 horsemen. Later he entertained Sir Richard with 'right good cheer' at his castle at Maynooth; a reference to Sir Richard 'always looking that the said earl would have done as was agreed overnight' suggests that at this stage Kildare may have sought to balance calculated off-handedness with non-committal bonhomie. Edgecombe, however,

[128] This was the so-called Statute of Henry Fitzempress. See Richardson and Sayles, *Irish Parliament in the Middle Ages*, 324–31.

pressed for unequivocal tokens of submission. In particular he demanded that Kildare and his associates enter into substantial financial bonds guaranteeing their future good behaviour. Bonds of this kind, exposing offenders to the immediate partial or complete confiscation of assets, were the principal means by which Henry VII had dealt with the parallel problem of over-powerful and unruly magnates in England. Kildare and his allies, however, refused point blank to agree to anything of the kind: he and his council gave 'plain answer' that, in a telling phrase, 'rather than they would do it, they would become Irish every [one] of them'. Edgecombe, for his part, 'gave short answers, with right fell and angry words'. But when news came that Henry VII's ally James III of Scotland had died in a battle against his own rebellious barons, he thought it better to close quickly with the best settlement he could achieve, in the form of a solemn oath of allegiance taken on the sacrament. His continuing distrust was evident not only in his refusal to deliver the earl's certificate of pardon until Kildare had supplied a written confirmation of the terms of his submission, but also in his attempt to guarantee the sacred nature of the bond by insisting that his own chaplain should consecrate the hosts on which the oaths were sworn.[129]

In the aftermath of this unsatisfactory settlement king and deputy remained predictably wary of one another. In 1489 Henry summoned Kildare and other temporal lords to England, where a later account claims that they were humiliated by having Simnel, now a servant in the royal household, wait on them at table. In 1491, on the other hand, Kildare fended off a demand to come to court again, producing letters indicating that the defence of the lordship required his presence. Later the same year a second Yorkist pretender, Perkin Warbeck, this time claiming to be the younger son of Edward IV, appeared briefly in Cork, where he received some support, including possibly encouragement from the earl of Desmond. Kildare made no open commitment to the pretender, but neither did he make any obvious moves against him. Henry VII's response was to send Sir James Ormond, illegitimate brother of the seventh earl, and Thomas Garth, an English soldier, to Ireland with 200 men. Initially they were commissioned to take control of the counties of Kilkenny and Tipperary, which were withdrawn from the deputy's jurisdiction. The Butlers of Ormond, whose territories these were, had been restored to their titles and estates following the Tudor victory in 1485. The earl of Ormond, however, was an absentee, and his Irish territories were managed on his behalf by Piers Butler of Polestown, head of a cadet branch of the family but also Kildare's son-in-law and ally. By displacing Piers, James Ormond, supported by the forces of his maternal relatives, the O'Briens, and of their allies, the Burkes of Clanricard, created a powerful counter to Kildare's authority while at the same time cutting his territories off from those of his

129 These details are taken from 'The Voyage of Sir Richard Edgecomb, into Ireland, in the Year 1488', printed from a manuscript then in Trinity College, Dublin, in Harris, *Hibernica*, 59–77.

potential ally the earl of Desmond. Next, on 11 June 1492, Kildare himself was dismissed as deputy. His successors were the archbishop of Dublin, Walter Fitzsimons, and James Ormond, governing jointly, the first as deputy, the second as 'governor of Ireland'.

Kildare's response to his supersession echoed the calculated displays of defiance with which he had asserted himself in 1478–9 and rescued his position in 1487–8, but in a form which was more reckless and considerably more bloody. A Gaelic annalist recorded that the earl 'resigned the protectorate of the foreigners of Meath, because he got not from them to aid him against the son of the earl of Ormond. And great evils came to the foreigners from that: to wit, the Gael plundered them and burned them generally from every point around them.'[130] There were also violent clashes, in Dublin and elsewhere, between Kildare's men and those of his opponents. Meanwhile Ormond and Garth had mounted a raid on another of Kildare's allies, O'Connor Faly, during which O'Connor's son had been killed. In revenge Kildare took Garth prisoner and hanged his son. The civic leaders of Dublin also appear, whether through the influence of Archbishop Fitzsimons or for other reasons, to have taken sides against Kildare. On 19 July 1493 Kildare, 'by craft and policy', induced leading citizens to assemble at Oxmantown Green, where his men attacked them, killing a former mayor and a number of others. Immediately afterwards, according to the later account of the Book of Howth, Kildare 'went through the English Pale, and where any of the earl of Ormond's race and friends was he robbed, spoiled, burned and killed them'.[131]

Henry VII's immediate response was to send 300 additional soldiers to Ireland in March 1493. In September he appointed two royal commissioners, supported by further reinforcements. A new lord deputy, Viscount Gormanstown, organized a meeting of the great council at Trim, where Kildare and others were required to provide bonds of security to keep the peace. Immediately afterwards Kildare, James Ormond, and others were summoned to court. The evidence for what followed is largely indirect. The most detailed recent examination suggests that Henry initially envisaged a pacification based on renewed pledges of allegiance and the settlement, in his presence, of past differences.[132] This was to include a pardon for the earl of Desmond, and in May Kildare signed an indenture agreeing to take custody of Desmond's son as a pledge of his good behaviour. In the event, however, Desmond remained in opposition, and there were reports of renewed intrigues on behalf of Warbeck. At this point, it is suggested, Henry was persuaded to adopt what had long been the remedy advocated by some of his Anglo-Irish subjects: a decisive intervention to strengthen the machinery of central government, reduce the Gaelic Irish to obedience, and so establish English

[130] *Annals of Ulster*, iii. 359. [131] 'Book of Howth', 176.

[132] S. G Ellis, 'Henry VII and Ireland 1491–1496', in James Lydon (ed.), *England and Ireland in the Later Middle Ages* (Dublin, 1981), 237–54.

law and good order throughout the island. The agent of this transformation was to be Sir Edward Poynings, an English soldier formerly in command of the English outpost at Calais, who now became deputy. Poynings landed at Howth on 13 October with 427 soldiers, soon supplemented by a further 226 recruited locally. He was accompanied by English-born appointees to key positions in the administration: Henry Deane, bishop of Bangor, who became chancellor, and three English lawyers to serve as treasurer and as chief justices.

Backed by these military and administrative resources, the new deputy moved quickly to assert his authority. By the end of the year he was said to have received the submission of both Gaelic and Anglo-Irish lords. In November he led his army north into County Armagh, devastating the lands of O'Hanlon and extorting his submission and that of his ally, Magennis. Between December 1494 and February 1495 Poynings presided over a parliament at Drogheda. Its enactments continued the programme of reform. A statute requiring that parliament should in future meet only after receiving the assent of the king and council, and his approval of all proposed legislation, was clearly intended to prevent future lords deputy using Ireland's legislative apparatus as an independent source of apparently legitimate authority, in the way that Richard of York had done in 1459–60 and Kildare, on behalf of 'Edward VI', in 1487–8. The broader concern to strengthen English control of the lordship was reflected in acts reserving control of the king's castles to Englishmen, and laying down that all officials should hold office during pleasure. Other acts sought to reduce magnate power, outlawing private war and regulating the maintenance of bands of armed retainers.

Kildare had accompanied Poynings from England, and subsequently to south Ulster. During this expedition, however, Poynings learned that Kildare had been in contact with O'Hanlon and Magennis, and accused the earl of treason. Over the next few months Kildare remained at least partly in hiding, possibly offering a degree of armed defiance. On 27 February 1495 he was arrested and immediately sent to England, where he was imprisoned. His brother, James Fitzgerald, responded by seizing Carlow Castle, expelling the royal garrison. In July, in an apparently unrelated development, Perkin Warbeck reappeared in command of a Yorkist fleet which blockaded the town of Waterford. He was supported by the earl of Desmond, who besieged the town from landward, by the city of Cork, and, nominally at least, by some of the Ulster Gaelic lords. Poynings captured Carlow Castle in July, and by the autumn had scattered the Yorkist expedition and driven Desmond back into his own territories. But these victories had been accomplished only with further soldiers and subventions of money from England. The original aim of Poynings's mission, a single, decisive intervention to establish a secure, orderly, and expanded lordship that from then on would finance its own defence and administration, was all too clearly not going to be realized in the immediate future.

It was against this background that Henry made moves towards a restoration of the more traditional pattern of government through leading magnates. In March

1496 the crown accepted Desmond's submission. In July James Fitzgerald submitted and was pardoned. Meanwhile Kildare was also being rehabilitated. As early as October 1495 the English parliament, presumably at the instigation of the crown, had reversed the act for his attainder passed, after his arrest, by the Drogheda parliament. By 1 April 1496 he had been permitted to marry Elizabeth St John, Henry's ward and cousin, receiving as a dowry lands in both England and Ireland. On 3–4 June O'Hanlon and Magennis made sworn declarations that Kildare had not had any treasonable communication with them, but on the contrary had urged them to submit to Poynings. On 6 August Kildare was appointed deputy for an initial period of ten years, having sworn to end his feud with James Ormond and others, to defend the kingdom against rebellion, and to observe the restrictions on the Irish parliament introduced under Poynings. He was also to leave his son in England, as a guarantee of his good behaviour.

Kildare returned to Ireland on 18 September 1496. He was reinstalled as lord deputy in a solemn ceremony at Drogheda, then went on to Dundalk where he received the submission of various Gaelic lords. Over the next year the two main outstanding issues left by recent upheavals were resolved. The first concerned Sir James Ormond, for whom Kildare's rehabilitation meant the end of his role as the crown's strongarm man in Ireland. Kildare and Piers Butler now presented Ormond, how truthfully it is hard to say, as engaged in armed defiance, allied to the violently anti-English O'Brien and also to Perkin Warbeck. On 17 July 1497 Ormond was killed in single combat by Piers Butler. Butler's account of the affair, in a letter to the earl of Ormond, was circumspect. He had come across Sir James 'suddenly in the open field not far from Kilkenny', and the two had 'fought together so long till God had wrought his will upon him'. Stanihurst, eighty years later, was more explicit:

> Piers having intelligence that his enemy, the base Butler, would have travelled from Donmore to Kilkenny, notwithstanding he were accompanied with six horsemen, yet Piers having none but his lackey, did forestall him in the way, and with a courageous charge gored the bastard through with his spear.[133]

There remained the challenge of Ormond's alleged ally Perkin Warbeck. Nine days after Ormond's death the pretender once again appeared at Cork, but met with little support. After a brief attempt on Waterford he retreated to England, where he was captured on 5 October. The king subsequently declared himself satisfied that not only Kildare but also Desmond would have moved against him had he stayed in Ireland any longer.

In subsequent mythology Kildare's triumphant return from captivity and disgrace marked the final demonstration of his position as 'all but king of Ireland': the moment when Henry VII allegedly proclaimed that if all Ireland could not

[133] Sir Piers Butler to Ormond, 7 Sept. 1497, in *Calendar of Ormond Deeds*, ed. Curtis iv. 332; *Holinshed's Chronicles*, vi. 278.

rule this man, then this man must rule all Ireland.[134] This was clearly a wild misrepresentation. In 1493–4, confronted with an English monarch determined to assert control, Kildare had submitted, going to England, composing his differences with the crown, and returning committed to giving his support to a new strategy of direct rule under Poynings. He had not sought the subsequent confrontation with the lord deputy; instead the indications are that it was Poynings, understandably influenced by his knowledge of the earl's past actions, who put the worst possible construction on his contacts with Magennis and O'Hanlon.[135] In restoring him, equally, the king was aware that Poynings's reforms had created new safeguards against the misuse of local power. At the same time Kildare had undeniably been allowed to get away with a great deal. To have been on the losing side in a complex and protracted succession struggle was perhaps pardonable. But having submitted to the victor, he had then betrayed the trust placed in him, at least once and quite possibly twice. He had also unleashed considerable violence, both directly and undirectly, against the king's representatives and subjects. Forty years later an official memorandum recalled as a tale current in Ireland the words supposedly spoken by a Fitzgerald retainer, Sir Gerald Shaneson, as he urged one of the earl's sons to stand firm in a subsequent confrontation with the crown:

> 'What, thou fool', said he, 'thou shalt be the more esteemed in Ireland to take part against the king; for what haddest thou been, if thy father had not done so? What was he set by, until he crowned a king here; took Garth, the king's captain prisoner; hanged his son; resisted Poynings and all deputies; killed them of Dublin, upon Oxmantown Green; would suffer no man to rule here for the king, except himself?'[136]

Apocryphal or not, the exhortation is a glimpse of how the eighth earl's exploits were remembered two decades after his death.

From the settlement of 1496 until his death in 1513 Kildare played a dual role in the government and politics of Ireland. At one level he acted as the crown's local representative. He showed no disposition to challenge the royal authority that had been forcefully reasserted during 1494–6. Parliament met and transacted business in accordance with the restrictions introduced by Poynings. Kildare himself maintained contact by infrequent but respectful letters. In 1503 he visited the court, staying for three months and returning, as visible proof of the trust he now enjoyed, with the son he had left there seven years before. In day to day terms, on the other hand, Kildare's rule amounted to the exercise of a personal lordship. He raised and spent the entire official revenue without the

134 'Book of Howth', 180; *Holinshed's Chronicles*, vi. 277.

135 This is the interpretation advanced by G. O. Sayles, 'The Vindication of the Earl of Kildare from Treason, 1496', *IHS* 7 (1950), 39–47. It does, however, depend rather heavily on the assumption that the later sworn statements of Magennis and O'Hanlon can be taken at face value.

136 Anonymous report to Thomas Cromwell and the king, 1533, in *SP Henry VIII*, ii (1834), 175.

requirement to present accounts of any kind. He ruled through a network of personal relationships of patronage and dependence. Most of all he repeatedly embarked, entirely on his own initiative, on military expeditions designed to crush challenges to his authority or to curb potential rivals.

The position of dominance that Kildare had thus established for himself was based first and foremost on his own estates. The eighth earl continued his father's work of reversing the losses that had been suffered in the period of neglect following the death of the fifth earl. In part this involved recovering further lands to the west and south of his patrimony by driving out Gaelic interlopers, constructing castles and other defences, and settling his own tenants on previously waste land. However Kildare accompanied this military expansion with the systematic acquisition of legal title to the lands coming into his possession, whether by purchase or by legal instruments conveying to him ownership of lands recovered from the Gaelic Irish. Other lands were acquired by purchase from fellow English proprietors, and by means of two advantageous marriages. The core of the property lay in Counties Kildare and Carlow, but there were also lands in Meath, Tipperary, Kilkenny, Limerick, and Cork, as well as along the east coast of what is now County Down. Altogether the income of the earldom in the early sixteenth century, between rents, tributes received from both English and Irish dependants, and the profits of office, has been estimated at well over £2,000 a year. This made Kildare by far the richest magnate in Ireland, and one of the ten richest nobles anywhere in the dominions of the English crown.[137]

Beyond the income and personal following derived from his estates, Kildare's power, like that of other late medieval magnates, depended on the creation and maintenance of a dense web of alliances and dependencies. In many cases these were established or reinforced by marriage. The eighth earl's first marriage was to the daughter of a local ally, the Fitzeustaces. His second, however, was to Henry VII's ward Elizabeth St John, while the ninth earl married first another royal relative, Elizabeth Zouche, whom he carried back with him from England in 1503, and then, in 1520, the daughter of a prominent courtier, the marquess of Dorset. Other marriages linked the Kildares to leading families in the lordship, such as the Flemings of Slane and the Plunketts of Dunsany. Most important of all in this context, the marriage of the eighth earl's daughter Margaret to Piers Butler brought a temporary cessation in the rivalry between the two great earldoms of Ormond and Kildare.[138] Other connections were given concrete form in the exchange of tributes and gifts. A 'rental' commenced by the ninth earl in 1518 contains details of payments received from some forty-five clergy, gentry and others, in exchange for his protection or his 'just favours' in their 'rightful causes'. The earl, for his part, made regular gifts of horses and harness

[137] Ellis, *Tudor Frontiers and Noble Power*, ch. 4.
[138] For Kildare's marriage alliances see Bryan, *Great Earl of Kildare*, 92–3.

to a wide variety of recipients. These had multiple purposes. Some were clearly fees to clients or retainers. Where the recipients were local gentry, there is a suggestion that they were expected in return to provide hospitality to the earl and his retinue. Where horses were sent to leading courtiers like the duke of Norfolk, or to the king himself, on the other hand, the aim would have been a less specific expression of goodwill. But in all cases these gifts, meticulously recorded and repeated annually, testified to the need to build up and maintain a complex network of vertical and horizontal relationships.[139]

This systematic use of marriage alliances, gifts, tributes, and fees was not by any means confined to the English of Ireland. Both the eighth and ninth earls also sought marriage alliances with leading Gaelic families, both in the midland region adjoining their own estates and in Ulster. A separate section of the 'rental' commenced in 1518 listed 'the earl of Kildare's duties upon Irishmen', setting out details of the payments in money, livestock, butter, honey, and hawks regularly made to him by Gaelic chiefs in return for his protection and favour. Kildare's dealings with these chiefs may not have differed much in principle from the protection he offered to lesser lords in the English areas. But they were expressed in the specific vocabularly of Gaelic Ireland. One entry, for example, records the forfeiture of sixty cattle by Ferrall MacOwen MacGeoghegan, according to a judgement attributed to two other MacGeoghegans, for having broken the ninth earl's *sláinte* or protection by an attack on the sept of Nele MacGeoghegan. In 1505, likewise, three different branches of the MacCoghlan family were required to give Kildare 100 cattle each as payment of the *eraic* due for the death of a Robert Nugent.[140] An even more striking example of Kildare's adaptation to Gaelic custom was his decision, in 1499, to send his son Henry to be fostered by the O'Donnells, Gaelic lords of the north-west.

The importance to both sides of the connections thus established was repeatedly demonstrated. After his sister Eleanor had married Conn Mór O'Neill, for example, Kildare not only obtained an act of parliament granting both husband and wife the legal status of English subjects; in the same year, 1480, he also joined with Conn Mór in attacking the castle of a recalcitrant member of a rival branch of the family, Shane Boy O'Neill. Later, in 1498, he came north with another army to help Conn Mór's sons, his nephews, capture Dungannon Castle from a dynastic rival. Cahir O'Conor, whose daughter Maeve married Kildare's son Oliver, was in 1485 awarded a levy on every ploughland in County Meath, to be raised by collectors of the crown's revenue. This was the same Cahir whose son's death in 1492 was avenged by the hanging of the son of Thomas Garth. The importance of marriage alliances and other connections, with both Anglo-Irish and Gaelic notables, was again evident in the mixed force that Kildare was

[139] Gearoid MacNiocaill (ed.), *Crown Surveys of Lands 1540–41* (Dublin, 1992), 256–63, 319–50. For an analysis see Ellis, *Tudor Frontiers and Noble Power*, 125–6, 137–8.

[140] MacNiocaill, *Crown Surveys*, 272, 352. For *eraic* or blood money see above, p. 14.

able to bring with him to confront Ulick Burke, himself apparently party to a marriage alliance that had failed to achieve its purpose, at Knockdoe. Six years later the earl led another mixed force into the south-west to ravage the territories of MacCarthy Mór and then destroy the bridge which the O'Briens had built to facilitate their expansion across the Shannon. This time his allies, as well as the earl of Desmond, included his son-in-law Donal MacCarthy Reagh 'the Swarthy' and Hugh O'Donnell, son of Hugh Roe, who had fostered the earl's son and joined him at Knockdoe. As the earl's army retreated from the O'Briens and their MacNamara allies O'Donnell joined with forces from Meath and Dublin in a highly praised rearguard action.[141]

Lordship, as each of these different examples makes clear, was a matter not just of wealth, retinue and clientage, but of effective armed force. Kildare could call on the tenants on his estates to provide military service. He also seems systematically to have used the labour services they owed him to construct and maintain strongholds and defensive boundaries on the west and south-west perimeters of his territory, facing the Gaelic areas. As lord deputy he could also call out the inhabitants of the Pale to provide service as required. These levies supplemented a standing force of professional soldiers. From around 1500 Kildare maintained a retinue of 120 kern and 120 galloglass, quartered on his tenants or on Gaelic clients whose tributes included the maintenance for specific periods of set numbers of troops. Somewhere in beween the two came a distinct group of tenants who held their land rent free in exchange for military service as horsemen. At its highest level, finally, lordship also involved personal leadership. Just as Sir Piers Butler defeated his rival James of Ormond in single combat, so the eighth and ninth earls of Kildare both regularly commanded their forces in the field. The eighth earl died on 3 September 1513, a few days after being shot while on his way to besiege Leap Castle, stronghold of his long-standing enemies the O'Carrolls of Ely. And the death of the ninth, in the Tower of London on 2 September 1534, was likewise attributed to the continuing effects of a gunshot wound he had sustained while attacking another O'Carroll stronghold, Birr Castle, in late 1532.

Lordship at its highest level was thus inextricably linked to the male world of weapons and warfare. Yet the dominance of personal lordship had another, less expected consequence. By emphasizing individual agency it conferred power on a small number of men, but also on some women. Richard Stanihurst, writing half a century after her death, recalled the formidable Margaret Fitzgerald, daughter of the eighth earl of Kildare. As wife of the militarily competent but clearly fairly rough and ready Sir Piers Butler, she had not only been 'the only means at those days whereby her husband his country was reclaimed from sluttishness and slovenry, to clean bedding and civility'. In addition, her husband, 'a simple gentleman', had been able to discharge the office of lord deputy only 'through the

[141] *Annals of Ulster*, 493–5.

singular wisdom of his countess, a lady of such a port that all estates of the realm crouched unto her; so politic, that nothing was thought substantially debated without her advice; manlike and tall of stature, very liberal and bountiful, a sure friend, a bitter enemy'. A document drawn up on behalf of her own brother, after he and Piers had fallen out, referred more brutally to the 'said earl, or my lady, his wife, by whom he is only ruled'.[142]

Such qualities, displayed too openly, were clearly seen as not wholly acceptable: Margaret Fitzgerald's virtues, for Stanihurst, were qualified by 'such a self-liking. . . such a majesty above the tenor of a subject', making her 'a rare woman, and able for wisdom to rule a realm, had not her stomach overruled her knowledge'. Yet Margaret was no isolated instance. Another daughter of the eighth earl, Eleanor, who had married the now deceased MacCarthy Reagh, emerged after the defeat of the Kildare rebellion as a central political figure in her own right, taking charge of the 9-year-old heir to the Kildare title and constructing a formidable alliance to support him, as part of the process concluding her own political marriage to the Ulster lord Manus O'Donnell. Later in the century there were to be further examples: Eleanor, the long-lived and resourceful wife of the fifteenth earl of Desmond; the Scottish noblewomen Agnes Campbell and her daughter Finola MacDonnell, whose marriages to Turlough Luineach O'Neill and Hugh O'Donnell made them major forces in Ulster Gaelic politics; and Grace O'Malley, whose family's naval power gave her an independent role even after her two marriages to an O'Flaherty and a Burke.

It is important to be clear on the different bases on which such power could rest. Occasionally, as with Margaret Fitzgerald and Piers Butler, it could arise from the accidents of personality or background. In the fragmented political system of Gaelic Ireland, it could be the military or other resources that a woman brought with her from her own family, like the Scottish mercenaries who accompanied Agnes Campbell and Finola MacDonnell, or Grace O'Malley's fighting ships. In English Ireland, on the other hand, a woman was likely to achieve real power only through demographic accident, as a widow with young or compliant sons. Joan Fitzgerald, daughter of an earl of Desmond, enjoyed such a position after the death in 1546 of her husband, the ninth earl of Ormond. But this was only until the crown, concerned at the safe custody of such a vital inheritance, forced her into a marriage with Sir Francis Bryan: 'While I was a widow and not married [to] an Englishman, I defended and kept my own, or at the least, no man went about to defeat me of my right. Well is the woman unmarried; I am bade to hold my peace, and that my husband shall have answer made unto him.'[143]

[142] Quoted in Elizabeth McKenna, 'Was there a Political Role for Women in Medieval Ireland?', in C. E. Meek and M. K. Simms (eds.), *'The Fragility of her Sex'? Medieval Irish Women in their European Context* (Dublin, 1996), 169. For Stanihurst's comments see *Holinshed's Chronicles*, vi. 280.

[143] John Kirwan, 'Lady Joan Fitzgerald, Countess of Ormond, Ossory and Desmond', *Journal of the Butler Society*, 4 (2000), 297.

Women's independent rule was thus both unusual and precarious. That it existed at all, in the face of such institutional and cultural obstacles, was nevertheless a further illustration of the extent to which late medieval Ireland was a society of personalized authority, in which even gender was less important than the facts of effective power.

3

From Lordship to Kingdom

The history of late medieval Ireland is haunted by three potent clichés. There is the image of the Pale, the fortified rump of a shrinking east coast colony. There is the figure of the earl of Kildare, permitted by a supposedly impotent English monarchy to rule all Ireland, because all Ireland could not rule him. And there is the assumption that Kildare and the other descendants of the medieval conquest had by this time lost any meaningful English identity, becoming instead 'more Irish than the Irish themselves'. All three of these familiar ideas, it now turns out, are seriously misleading. At the end of the fifteenth century the area under English control was expanding rather than contracting, while the crown and its leading Irish subjects had come through a period of crises to negotiate a mutually acceptable balance of interests, to which the accommodation of the latter to aspects of local law and custom offered no direct threat. To acknowledge these points, however, is to raise a new set of questions. The traditional image of a lordship in decline made it relatively easy to understand what happened next, when attempts by the crown to strengthen its fragile control provoked a disastrous political crisis. A more positive assessment of existing arrangements, by contrast, requires us to find new ways of explaining why these were so suddenly overthrown.

One partial answer is that the notion of an equilibrium between royal control and local power must be placed in context. English monarchs, aware of other calls on their resources, in France and on the Scottish border, may have accepted that Ireland should be largely left to manage itself. But this did not mean that they were satisfied with the limited power they enjoyed there. Richard III was willing, in the short term, to retain Kildare as his deputy. But during his short reign he also sent an emissary to establish direct contact with other magnates, and showed interest in reviving the crown's rights in the former territories of the earldom of Ulster, raising the question of how long he would have been willing to work through one all-powerful Irish servant. Henry VII, towards the end of his life, returned to the idea of a revived lordship under direct royal control, even proposing for a time to take personal charge of a major expedition to conquer the whole island. With the succession in 1509 of the young and ambitious Henry VIII the gap between the power English monarchs exercised and what they considered their due became wider still. In addition the new king aspired, as his father had never done, to cut a figure in European warfare and diplomacy. Ireland's potential role as a base from which to strike at England itself, already demonstrated in the Simnel and Warbeck episodes, now took on a new significance.

Changing policy towards the Irish lordship must also be put in the context of developments in the other possessions of the English crown. In 1485 Kildare was only one of many local magnates, each supported by their own military forces, with whom Henry VII had to reach an accommodation. Over the next two decades his political autonomy and control of an independent military force made him increasingly an anomaly, as the new king systematically stripped the English aristocracy of their armed retainers and forced them to accept the authority of royal judges and officials. The different political arrangements that prevailed in the Irish lordship continued to have parallels on England's Scottish and Welsh borders. But here the reign of the second Tudor king brought major change. The special legal jurisdiction of the Welsh marches disappeared in 1534. The remaining local franchises, giving particular districts legal and administrative autonomy, followed two years later, while in the same year Wales as a whole was incorporated into England. The creation of a new council of the north in 1537 imposed a new level of central control on another border region. The attack on Kildare hegemony in Ireland, commencing in 1520 and escalating in the mid-1530s, can thus to some extent be seen as part of a wider pattern, whereby central government extended its power over a hitherto autonomous periphery.

Having said this, however, it is important to emphasize that the transformation of the Irish lordship in the 1530s and after cannot be understood in simple whiggish terms, as the triumph of the 'modern' state over unruly feudal barons and unassimilated inhabitants of the periphery. In fact, it has been plausibly argued, the superficially modernizing thrust of Tudor policy concealed a great hollow at its centre. In both Ireland and the Scottish borders defence and the maintenance of a rudimentary level of law and order had traditionally been entrusted to local magnates, relying on their personal military and political authority. By the 1530s crown and ministers had come to find the level of independent military and political power implied by such arrangements increasingly unacceptable. But they remained unwilling to fund an alternative provision for defence and administration. Instead, by dismantling one system of management without providing a replacement, they consigned both regions, but more particularly Ireland, to decades of violence and disorder.[1]

The long-term aspiration to see Ireland brought properly under control, the development of a new concept of centralized authority, and the commitment to a more adventurous and dangerous foreign policy all had their origins in England. In addition, although their precise influence is harder to assess, there were pressures for change within the lordship itself. The main evidence for such

[1] This is the case argued in S. G. Ellis's important comparative study *Tudor Frontiers and Noble Power: The Making of the British State* (Oxford, 1995).

pressures lies in a series of tracts, the earliest dating from 1515, which set out what can be read as a common agenda for reform. The authors take as their starting point the decline of the colony from its medieval peak: it is in their work that the misleading concept of a shrunken and beleaguered Pale receives its most quotable expressions. They go on to identify the causes of this decline: the degeneracy and excessive power of magnates like Kildare, who ignored the king's laws, oppressed the population to maintain their private armies, and formed alliances with the Gaelic Irish.[2]

In reading these documents it is important to remember the faction-ridden political environment in which they were produced. One of the most colourful accounts of the failings of Kildare's stewardship, for example, was composed by Sir William Darcy, whom the earl had removed from the undertreasurership in order to replace him with his own father-in-law.[3] In addition, it has been pointed out, petitioners were forced to concentrate their attacks on the internal government of the lordship because of the impossibility of referring explicitly to what they must have recognized as the real problem: the unwillingness of the crown to take proper responsibility for its Irish possessions.[4] But it has nevertheless been plausibly argued that the memorials on the decayed state of the lordship that now began to reach the English court reflected the outlook of a specific section of Irish society, the lesser gentry, lawyers, and merchants of the Pale. These were groups naturally disposed to resent and distrust the power of the great territorial lords. Their closer contact with England, through education, travel, and participation in the Dublin administration, would have made them aware of the progress towards a more disciplined, law-abiding society made there over the previous half-century. There is also the suggestion, credible though difficult to test, that some of the same individuals would have been influenced by new ideas of Christian humanism then current in England, in which a just and orderly commonwealth, administered for the benefit of the whole community, was presented as both a religious and a political ideal.[5]

[2] The three best-known of these documents are: (*a*) articles by Sir William Darcy presented to the king's council at Greenwich, 24 June 1515 (*Carew MSS, 1515–1574*, 6–8); (*b*) Report on the state of Ireland and plan for its reformation (*SP Henry VIII*, ii. 1–30). This is normally dated to *c.*1515, and has been attributed to William Rokeby, archbishop of Dublin (Ciaran Brady, *The Chief Governors: The Rise and Fall of Reform Government in Tudor Ireland 1536-1588* (Cambridge, 1994), 249 n. 6, citing D. G. White); (*c*) Sir Patrick Finglas's 'Breviate', which evolved through several versions before reaching its final form in the early 1530s. The text most often cited is in Walter Harris, *Hibernica, or, Some Antient Pieces Relating to Ireland* (Dublin 1770 edn.). Note, however, that the final three paragraphs printed by Harris (pp. 102–3) are in fact from Darcy's articles.

[3] S. G. Ellis, 'An Engish Gentleman and his Community: Sir William Darcy of Platten', in Vincent Carey and Ute Lotz-Heumann (eds.), *Taking Sides? Colonial and Confessional Mentalités in Early Modern Ireland* (Dublin, 2003), 19–41.

[4] S. G. Ellis, *Ireland in the Age of the Tudors 1447–1603: English Expansion and the End of Gaelic Rule* (2nd edn; London, 1998), 116.

[5] Brendan Bradshaw, *The Irish Constitutional Revolution of the Sixteenth Century* (Cambridge, 1979), ch. 2.

These developments in English and Irish politics and society provide the background to the fall of the house of Kildare. They must not, however, be interpreted as indicating that its destruction was pre-planned, much less inevitable. The changing character and self-image of monarchy in England implied some alteration in the way in which Ireland was governed, and hence in the position of the Fitzgeralds. But to understand the form that alteration took it is necessary to turn from generalities to specifics, from the underlying pressures for change of some kind to the accidents and miscalculations that determined the actual outcome.[6]

THE FALL OF THE HOUSE OF KILDARE

The accession in April 1509 of the 18-year-old Henry VIII brought no immediate difference to the management of the Irish lordship that came with his new throne. The young king made clear from the start his enthusiasm for a more flamboyant style of monarchy. But his ambitions were firmly focused on overseas military adventure. At home he bought early popularity by the imprisonment and judicial murder of Richard Empson and Edmund Dudley, the two architects of his father's much hated regime of financial exactions. In Ireland, however, no similar gesture seemed to be required. Kildare, elected justiciar when his appointment as lord deputy lapsed with the old king's death, was instructed to present himself at court but was able to plead successfully that the state of the country required his presence. He was reappointed deputy in November 1510. When he died on 3 September 1513 his son, the 26-year-old ninth earl, succeeded him as deputy within less than three months, with the same extensive powers, including authority to raise and spend the Irish revenues without accounting for either receipts or disposal.

Gerald Fitzgerald, ninth earl of Kildare, widely known as Gearóid Óg or young Gerald to distinguish him from his father Gearóid Mór, was a very different figure from his predecessor. Where the eighth earl had apparently impressed contemporaries as a rude if highly capable provincial, the son, brought up at the English court between the ages of 9 and 16, was a polished Renaissance lord. His mansion at Maynooth and his other residences were lavishly furnished and ornamented. His library contained texts of contemporary scholarship and literature, in Latin and French, as well as works in English and Gaelic. A portrait from 1530 is sometimes attributed to Holbein. Yet this greater refinement should not be taken as implying that the ninth earl was necessarily less suited

[6] For general accounts of the events leading up to the Kildare rebellion see Lawrence MacCorristine, *The Revolt of Silken Thomas: A Challenge to Henry VIII* (Dublin, 1987); Mary Ann Lyons, *Gearóid Óg Fitzgerald* (Dublin, 1998); Ellis, *Tudor Frontiers and Noble Power*, 173–205; and D. B. Quinn's chapters in *NHI*, ii, chs. 23–4.

than his father to the brutal business of magnate rule. Squeamishness, as both the theory and the practice of contemporary Italy testified, was not one of the attributes of the Renaissance prince. In 1525, when the bishop of Leighlin was murdered on the orders of an ecclesiastical rival, Kildare gave ample proof of the other side of his character: he had the men responsible flayed alive and then disembowelled. On a larger scale he continued his father's work of pushing back the frontier with Gaelic Ireland, encroaching significantly on the midland Gaelic territories of O'Connor Faly and O'Carroll. He also led expeditions further afield: into Breifne, in 1514, where he killed O'Reilly and many of his leading supporters, and four years later into central Ulster, where he demolished the O'Neill fortress at Dungannon. Military power was underpinned by shrewd economic management. According to the earl of Ossory, a political opponent, the ninth earl was 'the greatest improver of his lands in this land'.[7]

The crisis of the Kildare dynasty began in 1519 when Kildare was again summoned to court and subsequently removed from office. The background to the decision can only be inferred. When Kildare had visited England four years earlier, the council had considered Sir William Darcy's highly critical account of the state of the lordship. But Kildare had returned to Ireland with a new patent as lord deputy, as well as grants of further lands and, apparently, permission to introduce an act in the forthcoming parliament conferring the status of a liberty on his lands in Kildare. In 1518-19, however, the king had entered on one of his periodic bouts of closer personal interest in matters of state, briefly taking up a range of ambitious projects at home and abroad. In addition to toying with the idea of becoming Holy Roman Emperor, and promoting his servant Cardinal Thomas Wolsey's pretensions to the papacy, he dealt personally with some Irish matters, including a dispute between Waterford and New Ross and reports of disorders in the liberty of Wexford. This direct contact may have made him more aware both of the general weakness of royal power in the lordship and of the specific complaints directed at Kildare's management. That Kildare was permitted to appoint his own deputy before leaving for London in autumn 1519 indicates that he was not at this stage in disgrace, although once there he may have damaged his standing by quarrelling openly with Wolsey at a meeting of the king's council.

The king's newly awakened interest in Irish affairs, however, went beyond the censure of an individual. Instead what he committed himself to was a radical, if short-lived, vision of a lordship managed on wholly new principles. An English viceroy, proceeding by a combination of force and diplomacy, was to secure a general submission to royal authority. The finances of the lordship were to be reorganized, with a new valuation of lands for taxation purposes and the cancellation of the fiscal exemptions granted to the major towns. Long-lost royal

[7] Quoted in Mary Ann Lyons, *Church and Society in County Kildare 1470–1547* (Dublin, 2000), 40.

lands were to be regained, and augmented by an act of resumption confiscating the lands of absentee proprietors. The Gaelic Irish, too, were to be induced, not just to make token submissions—the 'appearance only of obeisance'—but genuinely to observe the laws and seek justice from the royal courts. The agent of these multiple transformations was to be Henry Howard, earl of Surrey, a well connected courtier who had shared in his father's great victory over the Scots at Flodden in 1513 and had already served as lord high admiral. Appointed as lord lieutenant rather than to the lesser title of lord deputy, Surrey arrived in Dublin on 23 May 1520. He was accompanied, as planned, by a force of several hundred soldiers, including 220 members of the royal guard.

In issuing his ambitious orders for the complete reformation of not only English but also Gaelic Ireland, Henry VIII was inspired by a characteristic combination of idealism and an absolute belief in his own authority. Surrey was to point out to the Gaelic lords the benefits they would enjoy by conforming to English ways.

> you . . . should declare unto them the great decay, ruin and desolation of that commodious and fertile land, for lack of politic governance and good justice . . . For realms without justice be but tyrannies and robberies, more consonant to beastly appetites, than to the laudible life of reasonable creatures. And whereas wilfulness doth reign by strength, without law or justice, there is no distinction of property in dominions, nor yet any man may say, this is mine; but by strength the weaker is subdued and oppressed, which is contrary to all laws, both of God and man.

To secure acceptance of the new order, the lord lieutenant was authorized to bestow knighthoods on compliant Irish lords, and even to offer some flexibility in legal codes, approving Irish laws, if they were 'good and reasonable', and mitigating 'the rigour of our laws, if they shall think them too hard'. At the same time there was to be no ambiguity about the height from which these concessions were offered. Although Henry had no wish to take from any what rightfully belonged to them, the Irish chiefs were to be told, he was nevertheless 'their sovereign lord and prince' and 'of our absolute power . . . above the laws'. If any did not respond to 'virtuous admonitions, reasonable offers and charitable exhortations', moreover, 'we then shall have good ground, and can no less do, but, with our main power, put our self in readiness to subdue and exterminate them for ever'.

There were also other ambiguities. In instructing Surrey to proceed by 'sober ways, politic drifts and amiable persuasions', the king emphasized the need to inculcate true obedience to the laws, rather than an enforced appearance of submission. But he also hinted that conciliation was to be at least partly tactical, to be pursued only 'til such time as the strength of the Irish enemies be enfeebled and diminished, as well by getting their captains from them, as by putting divisions amongst them'. If he had no desire to take from his subjects what was rightfully theirs, he insisted that they in turn should restore 'such dominions as they unlawfully detain from us', a demand that held out the prospect of massive confiscations based on long dormant titles dating from the high point of the medieval colony. One early memorandum went further still, suggesting that the king regarded the whole existing pattern of land ownership in the Gaelic lordships as dispensable, since at present they 'live without order, not wealthy, nor being assured of any succession to their heirs'. Instead what he intended was a fair division of the land, at reasonable rents. Already at this early stage the two opposing principles that were to characterize Tudor policy towards Gaelic Ireland, conquest and reform, sat in ambiguous juxtaposition.[8]

Arriving in Ireland, Surrey was forced to deal with a wave of attacks by Irish lords, some taking advantage of the removal of Kildare's restraining hand, others, it seems clear, incited to make trouble by Kildare himself. In response he devastated the midland territory of the O'Mores, then, in mid-August, led a force into the territory of the Ulster lords O'Neill and MacMahon, 'where I did such annoyance as I might'. At the same time there were also apparent early successes for the policy of conciliation. Visiting Clonmel and Waterford in early October, Surrey found the earl of Desmond apparently submissive. He also received two south-western lords, MacCarthy Reagh and Cormac Óg MacCarthy of Muskerry, both clients of Butler. Meanwhile the Ulster chief Manus O'Donnell had come to Dublin to declare himself Henry VIII's 'true subject'. Surrey's private assessment of these submissions, however, remains difficult to establish. On 23 July 1520, after just two months in Ireland, he wrote to the king that the natives 'will not be brought to no good order, unless it be by compulsion, which will not be done without a great puissance of men, and great costs of money, and long continuance of time'. In September he told Wolsey that the Irish were quiet but could not be counted on to remain so, 'for there is small trust in their promises'.[9] He seems to have been genuinely impressed by the two MacCarthy lords, describing them as 'more conformable to good order than some Englishmen', and even claimed to know 'divers other Irishmen in like mind'. On the other hand Manus O'Donnell, whom Surrey had initially found 'a right wise man', eventually disappointed, launching an attack on O'Neill and McGuinness in late summer 1521 for the express purpose of preventing them from coming to terms with Surrey.[10]

By this time, in any case, the drive to remodel the lordship had already begun to falter. The king's enthusiasm had continued into the autumn of 1520, praising Surrey's achievements to date, but advising him to prepare for a long stay in Ireland while he carried through his mission of reform. As practical evidence of his continued commitment he advanced a further £4,000, to add to the £3,300 that Surrey had brought with him. But when Surrey, the following summer, applied for additional troops to meet new attacks on the Pale by O'Neill and

[8] *SP Henry VIII,* ii. 34, 52; *LP Henry VIII,* iii. pt. 1, p. 222.
[9] *SP Henry VIII,* ii. 37, 43. [10] Ibid. 57, 82–3, 64.

others, as well as a threatened invasion from Scotland, the reply was more equivocal. The king referred bravely to the need to conserve resources against the day 'when his grace should hereafter mind to send thither a great army, for the total and final subduing of that land'. But for the moment Surrey was to maintain himself, out of existing resources, within the four shires of the Pale.[11] Surrey's reply, at the end of June, reiterated that Ireland could be brought 'to good order and due subjection' only by conquest. His estimate of what would be required—either an army of 2,500 men to subdue the country county by county, or 6,000 to advance on several fronts at once, in a process extending over years, with further investment in fortresses, towns, and colonies of English settlers even when the military conquest was complete—may well have been intended to be prohibitive.[12] In any case the king, by the end of October, had agreed to his request to be recalled to England. The great Irish adventure was over.

This left the question of who was to take over the government of a dangerously destabilized lordship. The king rejected as too expensive the appointment of another English deputy. At the same time he refused to consider appointing Kildare. The earl had been imprisoned for a time in the spring and summer of 1521, but by the autumn he was free and re-establishing his influence at court. However, the king had given both Gaelic and English magnates firm assurances that he would not be permitted to return to take vengeance on those who had cooperated with his replacement. Instead Sir Piers Butler, who had worked closely with Surrey, took office, first as Surrey's deputy, then, in March 1522, as lord deputy in his own right. One complication here was the unresolved succession dispute that had arisen following the death in 1515 of the absentee seventh earl of Ormond. Sir Piers claimed the lands and title, but this was contested by the deceased earl's daughters, one of whom was the mother of a prominent courtier, Sir Thomas Boleyn. The king, agreeing to the appointment, had referred to 'Sir Piers Butler, pretending himself to be the earl of Ormond'. The new deputy's patent, however, gave him his title as 'Petrus Butteler . . . Comes Ormond'.[13]

Surrey had recommended Sir Piers to the king as 'not only a wise man, and hath a true English heart, but also he is the man of most experience of the feats of war of this country'.[14] His resources, in land and followers, were formidable, but his base in Tipperary and Kilkenny left him less well placed than Kildare to defend his own territories and at the same time protect the Pale. At the very beginning of his deputyship he recommended that Kildare be allowed to come back to Ireland to pacify his quarrelling kinsmen 'and reform his own lands'.[15] But when Kildare did return, in January 1523, the two earls were soon in conflict. Each contested the other's right to levy coyne and livery

[11] *SP Henry VIII*, 68. [12] Ibid. 73.
[13] Ibid. 89, 39 n. 1. [14] Ibid. 58.
[15] *LP Henry VIII*, iv. pt. 1, p. 32 (no. 81).

for the defence of the lordship, while Kildare also complained of attacks on his property and dependants. In November a council appointed by the king imposed a compromise formula recognizing the role of both earls in the defence of the lordship. But the vendetta resumed a few weeks later when Kildare's brother James Fitzgerald killed Robert Talbot, sheriff of County Dublin, as he rode south to spend Christmas with Ormond. In summer 1524 three commissioners, all senior English officials, arrived in Dublin in a new attempt to impose order. The two earls entered into bonds to uphold a settlement of their differences, while some forty other lords and gentry likewise bound themselves to keep the peace and uphold the law. But all this was only a prelude to Kildare's restoration. The patents for his appointment as deputy, with Ormond as lord treasurer, had been signed as early as May. The earl was required to hand over his brother James, to be paraded through London manacled and haltered with a hangman's noose before being pardoned for Talbot's death. But following this token submission he was triumphantly installed as deputy on 4 August.

Kildare's feud with Ormond introduced a new element of instability into the affairs of the lordship. Sir Piers Butler had been on good terms with the eighth earl, his father-in-law and one-time ally against James Ormond. His quarrel with the ninth earl appears to have begun after he had claimed the Ormond title. Kildare had enjoyed a share in the revenues of the earldom as long as it was held by an absentee, and Piers now refused his demand to be compensated for this loss. The real problem, however, was that the Leinster Fitzgeralds had now to cope, for the first time since the 1460s, with a resident magnate whose power was on a par with their own. Despite the settlement imposed by the English commissioners, both sides continued to prosecute the feud by the traditional method of raiding one another's territories. On one occasion, according to Kildare, Ormond's retainers attacked the village of Lyvetiston, County Kildare, 'where they cruelly murdered and burned seventeen men and women, divers of them being with child, and one of them, that fled out of the fire to the church, was slain at the high altar'.[16] Meanwhile the Butler territories were also under attack from the earl of Desmond in the south. Earlier, in 1523, Desmond had responded to Ormond's appointment as deputy by concluding a treaty with two French emissaries, committing himself to support a French-backed Yorkist candidate for the English throne. This reminder of Ireland's potential role as England's weak flank lost its immediate force with the defeat of the French at Pavia two years later. But Ormond was nevertheless able to complain that Kildare was not only abusing his power as deputy to destroy Butler supporters, but was treasonably unwilling to take action against his kinsman Desmond.

Faced with these continuing disorders, the king summoned both Ormond and Kildare to court. At the end of 1526 Kildare duly went to England, where he apparently underwent a hostile interrogation by Wolsey regarding his dealings

[16] *SP Henry VIII*, ii. 122.

with Desmond, before being released into the custody of the former earl of Surrey, now duke of Norfolk. Before leaving he had appointed his brother, Sir Thomas Fitzgerald, as his deputy. Sir Thomas was replaced, sometime before September 1527, by Richard Nugent, Lord Delvin. But this attempt to turn from overmighty subjects to the lesser Pale magnates, if that is what it was, was not a success. Lacking the territorial base of Ormond or Butler, and denied funding from England, Delvin proved unable to defend the Pale, as Kildare's agents encouraged O'Connor Faly and O'Neill to begin raiding once again. In May 1528 O'Connor Faly, aided by Sir Thomas Fitzgerald, took Delvin himself prisoner and held him for five months while he demanded black rents that had not been paid. However the king rejected suggestions that he should send Kildare, who was still legally deputy, back to Ireland, insisting that he would not tolerate attempts to show 'that his grace could not be served there, but only by him'.[17] Earlier that year Sir Piers Butler had prudently agreed to abandon the Ormond title to Sir Thomas Boleyn, whose daughter Anne was now Henry VIII's mistress, accepting in exchange the title of earl of Ossory, along with a favourable lease on a large part of the Ormond lands in Ireland. Now, in August 1528, he was once again appointed deputy. However, Kildare had already sent word to his two main Gaelic allies, O'Connor and Conn Bacach O'Neill, to resume attacks on the Pale, and Ossory, preoccupied by attempts to protect his own lands from Desmond, once again proved unable to provide effective defence.

In making use in this way of his Gaelic clients Kildare was continuing a strategy used by his father in 1492–3, and by himself during Surrey's lieutenancy. On his restoration to the deputyship in August 1524 he had blatantly acknowedged his debt to these kinsmen and allies by having Conn Bacach O'Neill carry the sword of state before him as he processed from Christ Church cathedral, where the council had met, to his mansion in Thomas Court. But it is important to recognize that Ormond, of the two earls the one more consistently willing to accommodate himself to the wishes of the English court, also had his Gaelic clients. When it was his turn to be inaugurated as deputy in 1528 he appeared with 'a great host of Irishmen'. These included both his long-standing ally O'More and also rival claimants to both the O'Carroll and O'Connor Faly lordships, whom he was backing in opposition to Kildare's friends. In this way the factional alliances of Gaelic and of English Ireland were inextricably linked. The main reason why O'Donnell had responded so willingly to Surrey's overtures, for example, was that his great regional rival, O'Neill, was closely linked to Kildare. Likewise the long-standing alliance of the MacCarthies with the Butlers of Ormond, and through them, at intervals, with the English crown, reflected their common enmity towards the other great regional power in the south west, the earls of Desmond.

[17] Quoted in Colm Lennon, *Sixteenth-Century Ireland: The Incomplete Conquest* (Dublin, 1994), 100.

Kildare's dealings with O'Connor and O'Neill earned him another spell in the Tower, but the crisis in the lordship continued. In June 1529 Wolsey devised a new expedient: a 'secret council' of three ministers who would govern the lordship with the master of the ordnance, Sir William Skeffington, advising them on military matters. Two of the three commissioners, however, were disposed to favour Kildare. Sir Thomas Boleyn, now earl of Wiltshire as well as Ormond, continued, despite the surrender of the Ormond title, to see Ossory as a rival, while the duke of Norfolk had by this time come round to the view that Ireland could not be governed without Kildare's cooperation.[18] The result was a compromise. Skeffington was appointed deputy and returned to Ireland in August 1530, accompanied by 200 soldiers and also by Kildare, who had undertaken to assist him in pacifying the country. For a time the new arrangement seemed to work. Expeditions to Ulster in early 1531 procured the submission of O'Neill and O'Donnell. But by May 1532 reports of renewed disorder led to Kildare, Ossory, and others being once again summoned to England. This time the royal council concluded that the fault lay with Skeffington, who had allegedly sought to counter Kildare's influence by creating new trouble between him and Ossory. How far this verdict reflected the continued influence of Wiltshire and Norfolk remains unclear. Certainly Kildare too was up to his old tricks. Around November 1531 the knight of the shire for County Kilkenny, at the heart of the Butler territory, had been kidnapped on his way to a meeting of parliament. The two burgesses for the city of Kilkenny were similarly abducted on their way home. However, Skeffington also faced accusations of financial irregularity, and the king made clear that he was dissatisfied at the return received for the cost of the deputy's army. In July 1532 Kildare was once more appointed deputy.

Kildare's second restoration, overlooking both his stubborn refusal to share power with other royal servants and his blatant collusion with the lordship's enemies, was the latest in a series of weak and inconsistent decisions. The dithering of the king and his ministers can in part be attributed to the competing demands on their attention. High spending on foreign adventures had depleted resources and produced a taxpayers' revolt in 1525. From 1527 there was the increasingly urgent search for a way of ending the king's marriage to Catherine of Aragon. In addition Irish policy, through the intervention of Wiltshire, Norfolk, and others, had now become entangled in the factional rivalries of the court. Above all, however, the problem lay in the king's contradictory attitude towards his Irish lordship. Reluctant to allow Kildare the degree of power he demanded, he was also unwilling to meet the cost of establishing and maintaining an alternative way of governing the lordship. A report during 1533 spelt out the consequences: the inhabitants of the lordship gave their allegiance to Kildare 'for

[18] The third member of the commission, John Alen, archbishop of Dublin, was also an opponent of Kildare.

dread and their own securities . . . accounting that room as inheritance to the earls of Kildare, and that the abode of any other, in that authority, should be but a short time, and that always finally they triumph and attain their purpose'.[19] At a personal level the results of the continued failure to develop a consistent strategy are evident in the case of Archbishop Alen of Dublin. An Englishman who became Wolsey's vice legate for Ireland, Alen was a zealous royal administrator who had challenged local vested interests, including those of Kildare, in his campaign to regain lost church lands. Thus he should have been a key figure in any comprehensive programme of reform, and had in fact been a member of the 'secret council' of 1529. Yet the king was prepared to see him sacrificed to the campaign of intimidation directed against the church in the aftermath of Wolsey's fall. As one of several leading churchmen prosecuted for violating the medieval legislation against papal provisions, Alen was removed from the lord chancellorship and subjected to a crippling fine. On Kildare's restoration he was replaced as chancellor by George Cromer, archbishop of Armagh, reportedly so under the thumb of the local nobility 'that he shows himself more like their chaplain, or parish priest, than the king's chancellor'.[20]

Any hope that Kildare's return would end the disorders that had now affected the lordship for more than a decade were quickly proved unfounded. The feud with Ossory continued. Some time in 1532 Kildare's retainers killed Ossory's son, Thomas Butler. Ossory, now supported by the displaced Skeffington, continued to lobby against Kildare in London. There are also indications of growing dissatisfaction with his rule among the English community in Ireland. Their restiveness may have been related to an apparent weakening of what had always been Kildare's greatest asset, his effectiveness in keeping Gaelic enemies at bay. In December 1532 the earl, assisting his son-in-law to assert his claim to the lordship of O'Connor Faly against a Butler-backed rival, was wounded in the side while directing the siege of Birr Castle, and 'was never whole again'. There followed a series of defeats and reverses, including a raid on Dublin itself by the O'Byrnes, who broke into the castle and rescued prisoners. Meanwhile events in England were also moving against Kildare. By the end of 1532 Thomas Cromwell had established himself as the king's main adviser, increasingly eclipsing Wiltshire and Norfolk. Cromwell's rise was due above all to his ability to resolve the problem of the royal divorce. But this would require far-reaching ecclesiastical change, in Ireland as well as England, which in turn made it more important than ever to put the government of the lordship in reliable hands. The possibility that the repudiation of queen and pope would provoke either internal revolt or foreign intervention also made king and minister more sensitive to the threat posed by disaffected magnates. The final confrontation with Kildare coincided

[19] *SP Henry VIII*, ii. 168.

[20] James Murray, 'Archbishop Alen, Tudor Reform and the Kildare Rebellion', *PRIA*, C, 89 (1989), 1–16. For Cromer, *SP Henry VIII*, ii. 168.

with the destruction of two other overmighty subjects: the execution in 1531 of the Welsh lord Sir Rees Ap Griffith, and the trial for treason of the nothern English peer Lord Dacre.

Cromwell's close interest in Irish affairs was evident from the start. He began a correspondence with Ossory and others within the lordship, sent two chaplains there to collect first-hand information, and had Irish merchants in Flanders questioned about dealings between Kildare and the Habsburg dominions. He also intervened in appointments. One of those he supported was an Englishman, John Alen (a cousin of the archbishop), who became Master of the Rolls. Others were Palesmen not aligned to Kildare: Christopher Delahide, a Butler supporter, who became a judge of the King's Bench; Patrick Finglas, whom Cromwell supported for the same court; and Thomas Cusack, for whom he also sought office. Beyond this, the exact nature of Cromwell's thinking on Ireland during 1532–3 remains unclear. It has been argued that he was from an early stage intent on a radical reform of its government. The alternative view is that Cromwell, while clearly distrustful of Kildare, had progressed no further than anyone else towards solving the problem of how he might be replaced without transferring to the crown what had already proved to be the prohibitive costs of direct rule. Instead his interventions in the affairs of the lordship were piecemeal and opportunistic.[21]

This latter view seems to be largely borne out by the manner in which what was to be the last, fatal trial of strength between the house of Kildare and the Tudor dynasty unfolded. In August 1533 the king reprimanded Kildare for obstructing the appointment of Cusack, Finglas, and others. Kildare's response was characteristically aggressive: he began transferring artillery from Dublin Castle to his own fortress at Maynooth. In September the king summoned Kildare, Ossory, and others to court. Kildare delayed, pleading the continued effects of his wound. By the time he finally reached England around the beginning of March 1534, Cromwell and the king had decided to replace him. However, they made no provision for a military force to allow the new deputy to enforce his authority. Meanwhile Kildare had secured his position by appointing his son Thomas, Lord Offaly, just returned from England, as his deputy. This move does not seem to have been anticipated by the king or his ministers, and indeed they seem later to have recognized that to allow Lord Thomas to return to Ireland, and so lose the opportunity of having both Kildare and his heir in their power, had been a serious tactical error.[22]

Kildare's motives in what followed can only be inferred. Obeying the king's summons was a rational gamble. By avoiding blatant defiance he kept open the

[21] Brendan Bradshaw, 'Cromwellian Reform and the Origins of the Kildare Rebellion 1533–4', *Transactions of the Royal Historical Society*, 27 (1977), 69–93; S. G. Ellis, 'Thomas Cromwell and Ireland 1532–1540', *Historical Journal*, 23 (1980), 497–519.

[22] Ellis, *Tudor Frontiers and Noble Power*, 197–8.

possibility of an accommodation with the crown. There was the clear risk of imprisonment or worse, but Kildare was by this time widely believed to be close to death, and his heir remained both safe and in a position of power. Cromwell's plans for the lordship, all the evidence suggests, did not include the destruction of the Kildares. Ossory had already signed an indenture binding him to maintain no armed forces and contract no alliances except on the orders of the king's deputy. The assumption is that Kildare was to be pressed to accept a similar agreement, and to cooperate with a new deputy. However, there is little doubt that Kildare perceived Cromwell as an enemy. At court he was aligned against Wiltshire and Norfolk. He was in correspondence with Ossory, and some of his appointments had favoured Butler supporters. His reform plans also discriminated, proposing the abolition of what he called the pretended liberty of Kildare but leaving Tipperary untouched. The choice of a deputy to replace Kildare was likewise highly provocative. Cromwell's choice was limited, in that no leading courtier wanted the job. But his selection of Skeffington, Kildare's avowed enemy, must have destroyed any lingering chance that the earl would cooperate. Cromwell's failure to give proposed changes an even-handed appearance has been cited as further evidence of the limits of his strategic vision towards Ireland at this time. At the same time it must be recognized that Kildare had responded to earlier attempts to remove or reduce his power, in 1521–3 and again in 1526–8, with armed resistance. There is no reason to believe that this time he would have reacted differently to even the most diplomatically packaged programme of reform.

By May 1534 preparations were under way to send Skeffington to Ireland as deputy with a retinue of 150 horsemen. Kildare was forbidden to leave the court and two of Cromwell's new appointees, Thomas Cusack and Thomas Finglas, were sent to Dublin to summon Offaly to London. In response the earl sent word warning his son not to obey. On 11 June 1534 Offaly rode to St Mary's Abbey, where he had summoned a meeting of the Irish council, at the head of a procession of 140 horsemen attired in leather jackets lined with silk.[23] There he delivered a speech denouncing the king, surrendered the sword of state to the chancellor, Archbishop Cromer of Armagh, and withdrew to join a force of some 1,000 soldiers assembled on Oxmantown Green. A generation later the chronicler Stanihurst, anxious to promote the political rehabilitation of the Leinster Fitzgeralds, popularized the story that Offaly was manipulated by enemies of the house of Kildare, who provoked him to ill-considered action by circulating a false rumour that his father had been executed. In reality, it now seems clear, Offaly was following a strategy agreed, in outline if not in detail, before his father's departure for England. His action fell into a familiar pattern:

[23] The jackets of the riders led an attendant Gaelic poet to celebrate '*Tomás na Sioda*' ('Silken Thomas'). The nickname, misunderstood as referring to Offaly's own habitual style of dress, formed the basis of the later image of a vain, frivolous young man, which in turn fitted neatly with Richard Stanihurst's misleading account of the origins of the revolt. (See n. 24.)

a display of determined defiance, backed up by actual and threatened violence, calculated to convince the king to abandon this latest attempt to undermine the family's local supremacy.[24]

This time, however, the calculation proved wrong. Times had changed: a blatant resort to violence of the kind that had worked so well under Edward IV or Henry VII were unacceptable to the new monarchy of Henry VIII and Thomas Cromwell. Moreover the domestic and international tensions created by the king's divorce and his break with the papacy made it easier to interpret any challenge to royal authority as treason or rebellion. How well the eighth or ninth earl might have adjusted their tactics to these new circumstances is open to question: the imperial ambassador reported in September that Garret Óg expressed complete approval of his son's actions, 'only wishing that he was older and more experienced in warfare'.[25] But what seems clear is that Offaly did not calibrate his challenge with the same sureness of touch that his predecessors had shown on earlier occasions. The decision to send Kildare to the Tower on 29 June is often cited as raising the stakes. But it is hard to see what else the Fitzgeralds could have expected, and the king went on to offer terms for their surrender. It was Offaly who pushed matters further. A letter sent from Dublin when his resignation of the sword of state was still fresh news reported that his followers had already 'committed infinite murders, burnings and robbings in the English Pale, about the city of Dublin, especially the king's lands and possessions'.[26] As on previous occasions, the demonstration of Kildare power also involved Gaelic allies: the midland chiefs O'Connor Faly, who was reported to have bound himself to Offaly by an oath, and O'More; the O'Byrnes, MacMurroughs, and O'Tooles, who menaced Dublin from their strongholds in the mountains to the south; and also Conn Bacach O'Neill, who declared his support after Offaly had marched north for a parley and surrendered to him the fortress of Greencastle in County Down. Meanwhile, on 27 July, Archbishop Alen, who had attempted to flee by ship, was driven ashore north of Dublin. Offaly and his men came to the house where he had taken refuge, 'brained him and hacked him in gobbets', and also slaughtered his servants and chaplains.

In addition to permitting this rapid escalation of violence, Offaly also linked his action to the recent breach with Rome, and to the international crisis that had resulted. The Habsburg emperor Charles V had for some time taken an interest in the affairs of Ireland. In 1529 he had sent his personal chaplain and confessor, Gonzalo Fernandez, to Dingle in County Kerry, where the earl of Desmond signed a treaty declaring himself the emperor's vassal. Now, in

[24] The image of Ossory as a hot-headed youth tricked into rebellion by the family's enemies originated with Richard Stanihurst, who was influenced both by his own connection with the Kildare family, where he had served as tutor to the 11th earl's children, and by his wider concern to emphasize the loyalty and civility of the English of Ireland. Its fictional character was first highlighted in Bradshaw, 'Cromwellian Reform and the Origins of the Kildare Rebellion'.

[25] *CSP Spanish 1534–5*, 256.

[26] *SP Henry VIII*, ii. 198.

June 1534, Fernandez returned on a second mission. Meanwhile the emperor instructed another agent, Eric Godscalke, bound for Scotland, to travel via Ireland, bringing with him two shiploads of munitions.[27] Offaly himself made no direct contact at this stage with the emperor or his agents. But as early as 7 July Eustace Chapuys, the emperor's ambassador in London, reported that he or his associates had been heard to say 'that were the Irish to rise in arms they would immediately get the assistance of 12,000 Spaniards'. Later, on 29 August, Chapuys passed on the news that Kildare's men were forcing the inhabitants of the towns to swear loyalty to pope and emperor.[28] One of Cromwell's correspondents, sending early news of the revolt, likewise reported that he and his followers 'do make their avaunt and boast, that they be of the pope's sect and band', and that they denounced the king as accursed.[29]

One further dimension of Offaly's revolt deserves mention. This was his proclamation ordering all those of English birth to leave Ireland immediately, on pain of death. Here Offaly may in part have expressed his own family's hatred of outsiders like Skeffington and Archbishop Alen, who had played such a prominent part in attempts to undermine their position. It is also unlikely that the announcement of a crusade against English interlopers caused much concern to his Gaelic allies. But its acceptance, at the very least, by his supporters in the Pale is nevertheless significant: the antagonism that can from time to time be glimpsed between the English of Ireland and the English by birth was clearly no trivial matter. The order, moreover, was enforced with characteristic Kildare ruthlessness. Reports circulating in London in mid-August indicated that Offaly 'spareth not to put to death man, woman or child which be born in England'. In addition his men summarily executed the crews of English fishing boats captured at sea, although Chapuys interpreted this as an effective means of crippling the important fisheries of south-west England, rather than mere ethnic malice. It was even reported that Offaly sent away his own wife, Elizabeth Zouche, declaring that 'he will have nothing to do with English blood'.[30]

By the autumn of 1534 the military situation in Ireland was desperate. Offaly—or Kildare as he became from 2 September, when his father died in the Tower of London—controlled the whole east coast region, from Drogheda to Wexford. Ossory continued to hold the Butler lands for the crown, but he was under attack from Desmond in the south as well as Offaly to the north. Otherwise the only remaining centres of resistance were the cities of Dublin

[27] For confusion over the different imperial missions to Ireland, see Micheál Ó Siochrú, 'Foreign Involvement in the Revolt of Silken Thomas', *PRIA*, C, 96 (1996), 53 n. 21.

[28] *SP, Henry VIII*, ii. 198; *Calendar of State Papers, Spanish 1534–5*, 248.

[29] *SP Henry VIII*, ii. 198

[30] S. G. Ellis, 'The Tudors and the Origins of the Modern Irish States: A Standing Army', in Thomas Bartlett and Keith Jeffery (eds.), *A Military History of Ireland* (Cambridge 1996), 128; *LP Henry VIII*, vii. 415 (no. 1064); *CSP, Spanish 1534–5*, 248; McCorristine, *The Revolt of Silken Thomas*, 68.

and Waterford. Meanwhile the crown was having difficulty raising, equipping, and transporting an adequate expeditionary force. However, Kildare's failure to capture Dublin Castle, where the garrison held out against overwhelming numbers, left him dangerously short of munitions. He also failed to prevent the landing of the royal army of 1,600 men, commanded by Skeffington, which arrived to the north of Dublin on 15 October. A smaller force of 800 had already arrived in Waterford. Kildare retreated to Maynooth and Skeffington, with winter approaching, was unable to move against him for several months. However, the majority of Kildare's supporters among the Pale aristocracy and gentry, faced with the arrival of a royal army, fairly quickly abandoned the revolt. Meanwhile the earl of Desmond had died in December, leaving his brother and grandson locked in a feud over the succession.

Once campaigning resumed in the spring Skeffington, despite continued shortages of horses, weapons, and supplies, and his own increasing infirmity, was thus able to make rapid progress. In March 1535 he captured Maynooth Castle after a ten-day siege. By this time Kildare had begun to search in earnest for foreign support. His chaplain, Charles Reynolds, was at the Scottish court in February 1535, before going on to Madrid and then, around May, to Rome. However, the emperor was now preoccupied with an expedition against north Africa; James V of Scotland, though sympathetic, was unwilling to risk war with England; the pope offered his blessing, and absolution for the unfortunate misunderstanding with Archbishop Alen, but nothing more. On 24 August Kildare surrendered to Lord Leonard Grey, his father's brother-in-law, who was now marshal of the army, having been promised that his life would be spared.

The response of the wider population of the English lordship to the Kildare revolt is difficult to assess. The only area to remain loyal to the crown, apart from the Butler territories, was the city of Waterford, whose record of consistent opposition to the Kildares went back to the days of Simnel and Warbeck. Some of those who took arms in support of the revolt would likewise have been motivated by ties of kinship or factional alignment, or even by religious principle. But there was also a strong element of self-preservation. Offaly, it was reported in late July, had announced that none of those who swore allegiance to him would suffer any hurt, 'whereof divers husbandmen aneareth ['join'] unto him, for fear of loss of their goods'.[31] Many of their betters presumably made the same decision. In Dublin the citizens initially mobilized to repel an attack by Kildare's Irish supporters the O'Tooles. Following a serious defeat at the hands of these raiders, however, they concluded a truce that allowed Offaly to besiege Dublin Castle without interference, returning to the conflict only when they were assured of rapid reinforcements from England. Even in December 1534, when the whole Pale was in royal hands, its gentry were reported to declare explicitly that they were not willing to take an active part against Kildare, 'in doubt he should have

[31] *SP Henry VIII*, ii. 200.

his pardon hereafter, as his grandfather, his father, and divers his ancestors have had, and then would prosecute them for the same'.[32] Indeed it was the legendary vindictiveness of the Fitzgeralds that was in the end their undoing. Kildare had been promised his life, and for almost a year the king and Cromwell remained uncertain as to what to do with him. The final decision to execute him, along with his five uncles, on 3 February 1537, was in response to demands from Ireland, where the Palesmen made clear that they were unwilling to cooperate fully with any alternative settlement while there remained even a possibility that the Fitzgeralds might yet again come to rule over them.

It is tempting to present the Kildare revolt, not just as a turning point in the government of the Irish lordship, but as of emblematic significance. Three themes that were to be central to the history of the next two centuries or more make their apparent appearance during 1534–5. There is the linking of religious loyalties to localist resistance to the extension of English power. There is the attempt by England's foreign enemies to exploit troubles in Ireland, and the anti-Reformation sympathies of its inhabitants. There is even the apparent beginning of an alliance between Gaelic Irish and English Irish, on the basis of a shared hostility to the intrusions into Ireland of the English-born. Yet it would be unwise to make too much of any of these superficially striking precursors. Although there was to be little positive enthusiasm in Ireland for the Anglican schism, its English population were to do their best, for several decades, to accommodate themselves to royal religious policy. Stanihurst may have unduly played down the involvement of the Pale in Kildare's revolt. But his recusant loyalism was nevertheless more typical of the political behaviour of the English of Ireland over the next three or four generations than Lord Thomas's anti-crown and anti-English rhetoric. The alliance of 'Old English' and Gaelic Irish was more distant still. All in all the conflicting evidence of the Kildare rebellion, combined with the events of the next few decades, suggests that loyalties and identity were highly fluid. Instincts had not yet hardened into clearly defined ideologies. Political responses were largely governed by the personal bonds and antagonisms of faction and lordship, as well as by pragmatic considerations of circumstance and self-interest. It was against this background that Henry VIII, his successors, and their ministers had now to find an alternative to the system of aristocratic delegation which they had finally and unwillingly abandoned.

GOOD AND GODLY REFORMATION

By the time the lengthy confrontation between the crown and the house of Kildare reached its climax, Ireland had also begun to be touched by the great crisis of European Christianity that had begun in Germany almost two decades

[32] *SP Henry VIII*, ii. 222.

earlier. A list of books in the library of the earl of Kildare included copies of Henry VIII's defence of the seven sacraments against the heresies of Martin Luther, as well as a book 'against the new opinions that hold against pilgrimages' by the king's lord chancellor, Sir Thomas More.[33] The presence of these officially sanctioned defences of orthodoxy were only what might have been expected of a loyal nobleman and former courtier. Over the next few years, however, religous and political loyalties were to be dramatically realigned. In 1530 Kildare was one of the peers who signed a petition to Clement VII asking him to permit the king's divorce from Catherine of Aragon. By 1532 the king's quest for a divorce had progressed beyond attempts to extort the pope's consent through a campaign of anti-clerical legislation to a determination to resolve the matter independently. The key legislation for a formal breach with Rome passed through the English parliament in 1533–4. Instructions drawn up around May 1534 in preparation for Skeffington's appointment as lord deputy required him to eradicate all tokens of the pope's authority in accordance with statutes already passed in England, 'and the like to be enacted there [i.e. Ireland] the next parliament'. Piers Butler's indenture with the crown, on 31 May, bound him to assist in this as well as in other reforming ordinances. Some similar commitment would presumably have been required from Kildare, if the crown had succeeded in its original plan of pressurizing him into cooperating in a new system of government. Instead Offaly's revolt postponed further action for the best part of two years.[34]

Offaly's decision to present his revolt as a Catholic rising against a heretical monarch can be seen as primarily a pragmatic political gesture, part of a long-standing pattern of conditional loyalty to a distant monarch: where his grandfather and his associates had told Sir Richard Edgecombe that they would turn Irish rather than place their fortunes in the king's hand, Offaly transferred, or threatened to transfer, his allegiance to pope and emperor. At the same time evidence of widespread support for the revolt among the clergy of the Pale indicates that the appeal to religious conservatism was successful. One of the most prominent clerical agitators, John Travers, the English-born chancellor of St Patrick's cathedral, was subsequently executed for treason. There were also strong suspicions that the archbishop of Armagh and chancellor of Ireland, George Cromer, had supported the revolt, although in his case the government seems to have thought it wiser not to enquire too closely.[35]

[33] Gearóid MacNiocaill (ed.), *Crown Surveys of Lands 1540–1* (Dublin, 1992), 314.

[34] There is no detailed, specialist study of the early Irish Reformation. R. D. Edwards, *Church and State in Tudor Ireland: A History of the Penal Laws against Irish Catholics 1534–1603* (Dublin, 1935) remains the only book-length study. For a modern critique see James Murray, 'Historical Revisit: R. Dudley Edwards, *Church and State in Tudor Ireland* (1935)', *IHS* 30 (1996), 233–41. There is a variety of article material on specialized aspects, usefully synthesized within a British Isles context in Felicity Heal, *Reformation in Britain and Ireland* (Oxford, 2002).

[35] For the religious aspects of the revolt see S. G. Ellis, 'The Kildare Rebellion and the Early Henrician Reformation', *Historical Journal*, 19 (1976), 807–30; H. A. Jefferies, 'The Early Tudor Reformations in the Irish Pale', *Journal of Ecclesiastical History*, 52 (2001), 44–7.

Unease at the king's breach with Rome can in part be seen as the response of a provincial society to unwelcome change being sponsored by the metropolitan centre. But it is also possible that circumstances had accustomed Irishmen of all kinds to develop a particularly strong sense of papal authority. In Gaelic Ireland the absence of a single, recognized centre of political authority had meant that clergy at all levels were accustomed to addressing their quest for patronage and advancement directly to Rome, the 'Rome running' so frequently commented on by contemporary observers.[36] There was also a remarkably tenacious historical tradition relating to the papal bull *Laudabiliter*, issued in 1155, which had authorized Henry II to conquer Ireland for the purpose of reforming religion there. Already in 1317 a group of Irish lords had addressed the pope protesting that the kings of England, by not discharging this duty of reform, had ceased to be their legitimate rulers. With Henry VIII's breach with Rome, the charge that the English crown forfeited its title to Ireland became more potent. Desmond, in 1529, had justified his transfer of allegiance to Charles V partly on these grounds. In April 1534 the imperial ambassador Chapuys had told his master that if the pope were to send an emissary to Ireland, or even publicize his condemnation of the king, 'some commotion might be created, since all the Irish consider themselves the subjects of the holy see'. And in December, after his rebellion had begun, Offaly was duly reported to have sent documents to Spain and Rome 'which should prove that the king holds this land of the see of Rome'.[37]

The next test of Irish responses to the early Henrician reformation came when a new Irish parliament met on 1 May 1536.[38] The Lords and Commons accepted without apparent difficulty a series of bills recognizing Henry VIII as supreme head of the Irish church, prohibiting appeals to Rome in ecclesiastical cases, and replacing annates, a papal tax amounting to the first year's revenue from bishoprics and other benefices, by a new levy, first fruits, paid to the king. Parliament did reject one bill, to authorize the granting within the realm of dispensations, licences, and faculties formerly dispensed by Rome. However, the issue here was not the repudiation of the pope, but the transfer of his jurisdiction to the archbishop of Canterbury; a revised bill, allowing for the issue of faculties by an Irish-based commission, passed without difficulty the following year. The

[36] John Watt, *The Church in Medieval Ireland* (Dublin, 1972), 188–93.

[37] *CSP Spanish 1534–5*, 131; *SP Henry VIII*, ii. 219. For Desmond, see D. M. Downey, 'Irish–European Integration: The Legacy of Charles V', in Judith Devlin and H. B. Clarke (eds.), *European Encounters* (Dublin, 2003), 108. See also James Murray, 'The Diocese of Dublin in the Sixteenth Century: Clerical Opposition and the Failure of the Reformation', in James Kelly and Daire Keogh, *History of the Catholic Diocese of Dublin* (Dublin, 2000), 99–102, which argues that even among those not disposed to political revolt the papal grant had become part of the origin legend of the English in Ireland, accounting for the strength of resistance to the religious policies of the crown.

[38] R. D. Edwards, 'The Irish Reformation Parliament of Henry VIII, 1536–7', in T. W. Moody (ed.), *Historical Studies*, vi (London, 1968), 59–84, is a minutely detailed account of proceedings. It must be supplemented by Brendan Bradshaw, 'The Opposition to the Ecclesiastical Legislation in the Irish Reformation Parliament', *IHS* 16 (1969), 285–303.

third house of parliament, in which six or seven proctors chosen from among the clergy of the dioceses of Dublin, Kildare, Meath, and Armagh kept alive the principle that the church represented a separate estate of the realm, refused its assent to the ecclesiastical bills. The government, however, took their passage through both Lords and Commons as sufficient to make them law.[39]

When parliament met again in September 1536, unease at the implications of the new religious policy became more evident. The Commons rejected three bills laid before it: the return to the crown of certain customs revenues formerly granted to the ports, a tax of one-twentieth on all land, and the dissolution of eight monasteries. Only the last of these was a religious issue. But it assumed central significance when the leading opposition spokeman, Patrick Barnewall, the king's serjeant at law, argued that the king's new role as head of the church, did not in fact give him 'so large a power as the bishop of Rome'. Specifically he argued that the king was entitled to provide for the spiritual reform of religious houses, but not to interfere with their temporal possessions. At a third session, in January and February 1537, the Commons reiterated their refusal to pass the three disputed bills. The bishops also joined the debate, arguing that legislation touching the church could not be valid without the consent of the proctors. However, a fourth session, in October to December, was more successful. Parliament now passed acts providing for the suppression of thirteen monasteries, imposing on the clergy a tax of one-twentieth of income, abrogating papal jurisdiction within Ireland, and imposing on all office holders an oath acknowledging the king's supremacy over the church. All this was facilitated by another act which resolved the issue of the clerical proctors by denying their right to be members of parliament.

The sequence of events is thus relatively clear. What is more difficult to decide is what conclusions can be drawn regarding the attitudes of different groups within Irish society to the Henrician reformation. The recalcitrance of the proctors, taken in conjunction with the involvement of so many clergy in Offaly's revolt, confirms that there was strong hostility among the clergy to the principle of the royal supremacy. The bishops too showed an inclination to obstruct the implementation of the new order; indeed the Dublin administration believed that the proctors acted from the start with their encouragement. That they surrendered more readily than their subordinates presumably reflects their more exposed position, and ingrained habits of obedience, as crown appointees. The ambiguities lie more with the laity. Even at the time it was suggested that the opposition of Barnewall and others to the suppression bill was motivated primarily by concern for their own economic interests, as tenants on monastic land, or paid administrators of monastic property. There were also other practical reasons why the Commons should have become less cooperative in the second

[39] For the evidence that the measures passed despite the proctors' opposition see Ellis, *Ireland in the Age of the Tudors*, 206 n. 47.

session of parliament than they had been in the first. The crown had failed to bring forward an act granting a general pardon to those involved in Offaly's revolt, which members had apparently been led to expect would be the reward for compliance in the first session. The proposed land tax and the transfer of customs revenue from the ports were also unpopular. As against this it has been pointed out that the monasteries initially selected for suppression were in border regions, where few Palesmen had the vested interests their opponents alleged. If Barnewall and others subsequently figured as purchasers of secularized monastic lands, moreover, they did so after it became clear that dissolution was unavoidable. Moreover he and others went on to return at least part of the land they acquired to the religious communities from whom it had been sequestered, or to other clergy. All this suggests that obstruction cannot necessarily be attributed solely to self-interest. Rather it reflected a real dislike of the royal supremacy, extending to laymen as well as clergy, possibly muted in a first session held in the aftermath of rebellion and suppression, but becoming more vocal as time went on.[40]

Whatever the precise motives of the opposition, the crown's response was a revealing mixture of menace and conciliation. By the time of the fourth and final session of the Reformation parliament, the king had sent four commissioners to resolve the stalemate. They brought with them a letter from the king himself demanding compliance, reinforced by the promise that 'if anyone will not we shall so look upon them with our princely eye as his ingratitude therein shall be little to his comfort'.[41] This not quite grammatical warning helps to account for the surrender of the bishops, and possibly of others. But it has also to be recognized that the threat of reprisals came only after substantial concessions. Barnewall was not only not penalized for his opposition; in early 1537 he and another member were permitted to travel to court to represent the Commons's reasons for rejecting the three measures. It is possible that they received assurances regarding the way in which the suppression bill would be implemented. Certainly on other matters the crown gave way. The customs bill was abandoned, the one-twentieth tax was applied only to clerical incomes, and a bill of general pardon for offences connected with the Offaly revolt was duly brought forward in autumn 1537. The lord deputy, Leonard Grey, also held a private meeting with a senior clergyman from Armagh, raising the possibility that he gave private assurances that the new ecclesiastical order would not be too rigorously enforced.[42]

Fully to appreciate the significance of this contest, and its eventual resolution, it is also necessary to be precise about the character of the changes that were

[40] Bradshaw, 'The Opposition to the Ecclesiastical Legislation in the Irish Reformation Parliament', emphasizes the lack of principled resistance to the new religious policy. See also Brendan Bradshaw, *The Dissolution of the Religious Orders in Ireland under Henry VIII* (Cambridge, 1974), 49–64. His dismissive attitude is challenged in Jefferies, 'The Early Tudor Reformations in the Irish Pale'.

[41] Edwards, *Church and State in Tudor Ireland*, 10.

[42] Jefferies, 'Early Tudor Reformations in the Irish Pale', 49–50.

at issue. The suppression of the monasteries accompanied the English and Irish Reformations, but did not necessarily involve a commitment to reformed doctrine. Modern studies suggest that the monasteries of early sixteenth-century Ireland were not the haunts of scandalous vice that has sometimes been assumed.[43] Indeed the mendicant foundations, first in Gaelic Ireland and subsequently in English areas, had been revitalized during the preceding century by the growth of the Observant movement. Yet the excessive wealth of many houses, the comfortably worldly lifestyle that prevailed within some among them, and the small size of many communities, made monasteries the target of much criticism. Well before the king's breach with Rome there had been suggestions that houses in border areas should be closed and their lands used to plant fresh colonists and military garrisons. That the Pale gentry accepted the suppression, and even participated enthusiastically in the division of the spoils, is thus not necessarily evidence of a slackening of religious allegiances. Renunciation of the pope's authority was another matter. But here too the issue was not presented in doctrinal terms. Instead the act proclaimed that the king had already been recognized as supreme head of the Church of England, and so should be likewise in Ireland, 'forasmuch as this land of Ireland is depending and belonging justly and rightfully to the imperial crown of England'.[44] The royal supremacy thus became inseparable from the framework of political relationships on which the very existence of the lordship depended. In this context what is remarkable is that its proclamation encountered even the resistance it did.

The formal acceptance of the royal supremacy thus achieved, with some difficulty, applied only to those bishops, exactly which ones is not known, who attended the parliament of 1536–7. The response of church leaders in the island as a whole to the religious changes largely reflected the political geography of early Tudor Ireland. In two of the four dioceses of the Pale circumstances permitted the appointment of bishops willing to conform to the new order: the English Augustinian George Browne, who had been appointed to succeed the murdered Alen in Dublin in 1536, and William Meagh, a local clergyman appointed to succeed the deceased Walter Wellesley in Kildare in 1540. In Meath Edward Staples, another Englishman, appointed in 1530, was a strong supporter of the supremacy, and later of Protestant reform. Archbishop Cromer, despite his earlier adherence to the Kildare revolt, seems also to have come to terms with the supremacy, for in 1539 he was deprived by Rome for heresy. The other bishops who conformed, apart from three absentee Englishmen holding the sees of Down and Connor, Elphin and Mayo, comprised two, Archbishop Butler of Cashel and Bishop Baron of Ossory, from the Butler sphere of influence, and three others, in Galway, Waterford, and Limerick, whose acquiescence reflected the continued role of the port towns as outposts of English identity. The remaining twenty

[43] Bradshaw, *Dissolution of the Religious Orders*, 8–38.
[44] Irish Statutes, 28 Henry VIII, c. 5.

bishops remained loyal to Rome. Over the next ten years, up to his death in 1547, the king was to appoint a dozen or so bishops, who by definition accepted the royal supremacy. However, the majority of these were also nominees of powerful local interests, and only one or two were to be committed advocates of religious reform. Meanwhile the pope made his own appointments both to vacant sees and to those held by defectors to the schismatic monarch. Yet polarization was not complete. Of forty-one bishops nominated by the pope between 1534 and 1553 some nine subsequently went through the ceremony of surrendering their bulls of appointment and begging pardon. All nine were then reappointed by royal grant, apparently with no attempt to make them take the oath recognizing the king's supremacy over the church. The papacy, for its part, made no attempt to replace those of its appointees who thus compromised with a schismatic king. As late as 1551 the bishop of Waterford and Lismore wrote seeking leave to resign his see and asking the king to prefer another clergyman to the vacancy 'by your honourable letter of recommendation to the pope': a striking demonstration of just how little the implications of the royal supremacy had penetrated even in an eastern county.[45]

The chief ecclesiastical agent of King Henry's new ecclesiastical order was Archbishop Browne. He had emerged from relative obscurity as prior of the London Augustinians by preaching in support of the royal supremacy and had headed the visitation which imposed an oath recognizing the new settlement on the mendicant orders in England. In Ireland he was initially inactive, although how far this reflected uncertainty as to his powers and responsibilities, and how far lack of real enthusiasm for reform, remains unclear. When a letter of rebuke from the king finally spurred him into a visitation of his diocese, in late 1537, the results were not encouraging. Most of the ordinary parish clergy were still using the traditional formulae invoking the pope's name at masses and on other public occasions. Meanwhile the members of the two cathedral chapters and the senior members of religious orders, the educated elite who might be expected to act as public spokesmen and leaders of opinion, were openly hostile. They were willing, when pressed, to take the oaths required, but flatly refused to preach in support of the royal supremacy. Instead, Browne complained, they worked to undermine his efforts 'in corners and such company as they liketh'.[46]

Confronted with the task of enforcing the new religious settlement in the face of indifference and outright hostility, the government was willing, where circumstances permitted, to demand at least outward conformity. In June 1538 the lord deputy, Lord Leonard Grey, made a formal progress through parts

[45] Edwards, *Church and State*, 101–8, 143.

[46] Brendan Bradshaw, 'George Browne, First Reformation Archbishop of Dublin 1536–1554', *Journal of Ecclesiastical History*, 21 (1970), 301–26; James Murray, 'Ecclesiastical Justice and the Enforcement of the Reformation: The Case of Archbishop Browne and the Clergy of Dublin', in Alan Ford, J. I. McGuire, and Kenneth Milne (eds.), *As by Law Established: The Church of Ireland since the Reformation* (Dublin, 1995), 3–51.

of Munster and Connacht, where he administered the oath of supremacy to the mayors and corporations of Limerick and Galway, and required them to do the same to the 'commonality'. In these cases, in fact, he went beyond the provisions of the recent legislation, which imposed the oath only on those taking up office.[47] At the end of the year a letter from the king complaining of the continued influence of the papacy in Ireland inspired a second major expedition. Archbishop Browne, accompanied by the Lord Chancellor, John Alen, the chief justice, Sir Gerald Aylmer, and other senior office holders, visited Carlow, Kilkenny, Ross, Wexford, Waterford, and Clonmel. Their progress appropriately symbolized the new union of church and state: at each centre Browne preached in favour of the royal supremacy, while next day the assembled dignitaries presided over a special court session and the execution of convicted prisoners. At Clonmel the commissioners reported that they had summoned all the bishops of Munster to attend, and that two archbishops and eight bishops had publicly taken the oaths of succession and supremacy.[48]

Formal gestures of this kind, reported in detail to London, allowed the king's Irish servants to assure him that they were vigorously upholding his authority. But they concealed a distinctly more pragmatic approach to day to day enforcement. In dispatches to London Browne complained of the refusal of the lord deputy to support him against dissident clergy. In particular he had released James Humphrey, a canon of St Patrick's cathedral, whom the archbishop had imprisoned for refusing to read new prayers proclaiming the royal supremacy. He had also, according to Browne, subverted the trial of the suffragan bishop of Meath, accused of openly upholding the pope's authority, by ostentatiously attending mass at the shrine in the diocese dedicated to the Virgin Mary. Grey's refusal to cooperate may have reflected his poor relations with Browne, while his performance at Trim raises the possibility that his private sympathies were with the religious conservatives. But it is also likely that he and others were concerned to balance obedience to the king's concern for his newly defined spiritual authority against a desire not to create martyrs or offend important local interests by too aggressive a policy against dissidents.[49]

Two other important changes took place in the early years of the royal supremacy. The first was the suppression of the remaining monasteries in the areas under direct royal control. Earlier measures had been aimed at specific targets. Thirteen houses, most of them small and run down, had been suppressed by the Irish parliament in 1537, while in 1538 the Augustinian house at All Hallows in Dublin, with a total of five inmates, had been dissolved at the request of the city corporation, which petitioned to be granted its assets as compensation

47 Edwards, *Church and State*, 85–6.

48 The two archbishops were presumably Edmund Butler, a half-hearted supporter of the religious reforms, and Christopher Bodkin, who had accepted a royal nomination to Tuam in 1536.

49 Murray, 'Ecclesiastical Justice'; Jefferies, 'Early Tudor Reformations', 53–5.

for losses suffered during Offaly's revolt. Now, in April 1539, the king issued a commission for the surrender of all monastic property. The commissioners began their work in the Pale in the second half of 1539, moving on to Wexford, Waterford, and the Ormond territories in March and April 1540. In all they suppressed forty-two monastic communities and fifty-one mendicant houses. Their proceedings enountered little resistance. One monastic superior, George Dowdall, prior of Ardee in County Louth, withdrew to the protection of the nearby O'Neill lordship. The nuns of Gracedieu in County Dublin continued their communal life on former monastic property made available to them by the grantee, Patrick Barnewall. A handful of mendicant communities likewise remained in existence, supported by sympathetic laymen. More commonly the promise of pensions to monks (though not mendicants) who surrendered without resistance was enough to ensure compliance. Most members of religious orders, in fact, had come to accept their suppression as inevitable, and the preceding two or three years had seen the widespread alienation of land in exchange for immediate cash sums. The acts legalizing the suppression sought to counter this asset stripping by invalidating all leases made during the two years preceding dissolution. But in practice most of the laymen to whom monastic property had been conveyed held on to their gains. As in the parliament of 1536–7, the need to secure the acquiescence of the laity in the suppression programme made necessary a pragmatic respect for vested interests.[50]

At the same time that the way was being prepared for the dissolution of the monasteries, the first serious attack began on popular religious practice. During December 1538 Archbishop Browne and his colleagues received orders, confirmed by a formal commission on 3 February 1539, to destroy all images that were the subject of popular veneration and pilgrimages. During the spring of 1539 the commissioners duly visited some fifty sites. Among the relics and shrines suppressed were the Baculus Ihesu, and the shrine of the Virgin at Trim. Once again there is no indication of resistance to the proceedings. This was partly because there was no campaign of aggressive iconoclasm: shrines and relics were quietly dismantled or removed, not publicly desecrated. However, the sums realized from the confiscated assets of suppressed shrines and relics were very low compared to yields in England. This suggests that in many cases venerated objects and their associated paraphernalia had already been removed, whether by conservative clergy or pious laymen. Certainly it is clear that many of the traditional devotions at holy wells and similar sites continued long after the suppression campaign had been completed.

In all of this it is important to remember that the Henrician reformation was primarily an act of schism rather than heresy. What was involved was a rejection of papal jurisdiction rather than of established doctrine or liturgy. Even the campaign against relics and pilgrimages was an attack, not on religious images as

[50] Bradshaw, *Dissolution of the Religious Orders.*

such, but on what was considered their superstitious or idolatrous use, a stand that would have been shared by many pre-Reformation churchmen. Archbishop Browne's 'Form of the Beads' introduced new prayers in English to be said before mass. Later he published official English translations of the creed, the ten commandments, and certain prayers, which the clergy were to teach their flocks by rote. In other respects, however, the mass remained unchanged. The English prayers, moreover, included the distinctly unprotestant 'Hail Mary'. Archbishop Browne's personal theological leanings remain unclear, but in general his main concern seems to have been to remain in step with the doctrinal pronouncements of the English church authorities.[51] If he did have ambitions to accompany jurisdictional with theological reform, these were in any case brought up short by the Act of Six Articles, passed by the English parliament in May 1539 to reaffirm the conservative position on transubstantiation, clerical celibacy, and other issues. For Browne this reversion to orthodoxy brought a personal crisis, because since his arrival in Ireland he had married a local woman, Elizabeth Miagh. To rescue his position he now had her remarried to his servant, Robert Bathe, providing for the upkeep of their three sons by a series of trusts created out of episcopal property. His allies in the complicated series of transactions required to achieve this settlement included several of the senior clergy with whom he had up to then been locked in conflict, and it has been suggested that the price of their cooperation was that he abandoned any further attempt to go beyond the facade of outward conformity and promote real religious change.[52]

THE STYLE AND TITLE OF KING

For confirmation that the destruction of the house of Kildare was in no way part of crown policy it is necessary to look no further than the confused and inconsistent actions of the king and his ministers following the defeat of Earl Thomas's revolt.[53] At the time of the earl's surrender in August 1535 he had already been declared a traitor by an act of the English parliament. Meanwhile a bill attainting his father was in draft, and was to pass through the Irish parliament in May 1536. By backdating the attainder of the deceased ninth earl to July 1528, when he had incited his son-in-law O'Connor Faly to revolt, the Irish act provided for the forfeiture not just of Earl Thomas (now styled plain Thomas Fitzgerald) but also of his father's other heirs. For the moment, however, Thomas

[51] See Bradshaw, 'George Browne', 312–13, which rejects Edwards's contention that Browne's 'Form of the Beads' moved ahead of the English bishops in rejecting works as one of the requirements for salvation (see Edwards, *Church and State*, 50).

[52] Murray, 'Ecclesiastical Justice', 49–50.

[53] The fullest account of the years 1535–44 is Bradshaw, *Irish Constitutional Revolution*. Brady, *Chief Governors*, provides an important corrective to Bradshaw's rather idealized depiction of government policy. Lennon, *Sixteenth-Century Ireland*, offers a sensible middle ground.

himself remained in the Tower, and it is clear that neither Cromwell nor the king was willing to rule out the possibility that he might eventually be restored to favour; in September 1535 he was even entertained briefly at court. In July 1536 a third act of attainder passed through the English parliament. But even then it was not until February 1537 that Fitzgerald was finally executed.

The indecision of king and chief minister reflected an acute political problem. The Kildares had guaranteed the security of the Irish lordship—on their own terms—not only by deploying their own formidable resources, but by means of a network of alliances and dependencies encompassing the Gaelic Irish both on the borders of the Pale and further afield. If the dynasty was to be eliminated, some new means would have to be found to uphold the lordship against its predatory neighbours. But prevarication also proved to be dangerous, as fears of the vengeance that might follow an eventual Kildare restoration made the inhabitants of the lordship reluctant to cooperate wholeheartedly with any alternative programme of government. Once the direction indicated by reasons of state became clear, the king and Cromwell acted with their customary ruthlessness. Along with Thomas died all five of his father's brothers, including two, Sir James Fitzgerald and Richard Fitzgerald, who had surrendered to Skeffington at an early stage, and had subsequently been pardoned in recognition of their service in suppressing the rebellion.

One solution to the government's dilemma would have been to return to the interventionist strategy which had been attempted under Surrey in the early 1520s, and whose subsequent abandonment had initiated the trail of calamities leading to the current crisis. During 1535–6 members of the Irish council brought forward ambitious schemes to take advantage of the defeat of the crown's enemies by extending royal control. Some of these concentrated on the reduction of the most immediate threat, the Gaelic lordships in the mountains of south Leinster, either by expropriation or assimilation. Others envisaged the reduction of the island as a whole. Cromwell himself, in autumn 1535, enquired in a memorandum 'whether it shall be expedient to begin a conquest or a reformation'.[54] Any such programme, however, would require heavy expenditure, at least in the short term. During 1536–7 the Irish parliament decisively rejected a series of measures intended to increase the crown's revenue. The Palesmen, in other words, were not prepared to pay for the interventionist strategy for which their representatives argued so eloquently. The king, for his part, ordered in mid-1537 that the army should be reduced to what the revenues of the lordship could support. As the practical constraints were reasserted, talk of a new conquest died away.

Changes to the management of the lordship, then, were to be piecemeal rather than radical. Between September 1537 and April 1538 four royal commissioners enquired into all aspects of Irish government. Their visit has been presented

[54] Quoted Ellis, *Ireland in the Age of the Tudors*, 145.

as the high point of a drive by Thomas Cromwell, then at the peak of his power in England, to reform the Irish administration as part of a wider process of establishing unitary, bureaucratic government throughout Henry VIII's realms.[55] Yet more recent accounts have retreated from the idea that Cromwell single-handedly revolutionized the machinery of English government. Moreover it now appears that in reality Cromwell, preoccupied with English religious and political affairs, paid only sporadic attention to Ireland, and that when he did so his main concern was to reduce costs and to use Irish patronage to develop a network of clients and dependants.[56] The commission of 1537–8 did not bring a revolution in Irish government. Instead the existing administrative machinery struggled inadequately to cope with the hugely increased responsibilities created by the sequestration of monastic property and the confiscation of the Kildare estates.[57] As for the vision of a revived colony, extending royal power over all or part of Gaelic Ireland, the commissioners looked instead to a strengthening of existing physical and cultural frontiers. They placed garrisons from the reduced standing army at strategic positions along the Pale, and made grants of land in border areas both to English military captains and to reliable local lords. They also called for new legislation forbidding residents of the English territories to use Gaelic language or dress, to intermarry with the Gaelic Irish, or to exchange children with them in fosterage.

All in all it seems clear that the confrontation with the Kildares left the crown with the worst of both worlds. It had crushed an overmighty subject but was unable, or at least unwilling, to construct an alternative means of providing for the maintenance of order in the region he and his ancestors had controlled. (A similar power vacuum was created in the Scottish borders when the king, at almost exactly the same time and for similar reasons, broke the power of the Dacre family.[58]) The man first called on to attempt the task of managing the lordship without the Kildares was Lord Leonard Grey. Grey, brother of the ninth earl of Kildare's second wife, Elizabeth Grey, came to Ireland as marshal of the army during Offaly's revolt; it was he who accepted his step-nephew's surrender, on what proved to be the false promise that his life would be spared. When Skeffington died in December 1535 Grey succeeded him as lord deputy. The army of 2,500 men deployed against Offaly had been reduced after his surrender to a garrison of 700 regulars. In 1537 this was again cut, to 340. Yet Grey used this diminished regular force, supplemented by levies from the Pale and men supplied by local lords, to embark on a series of ambitious military expeditions. In 1536 he invaded the south-west, capturing the castle at Carrigogunnell on the Shannon from the Desmonds and their allies the O'Briens. He also broke down the bridge built to facilitate incursions across the Shannon by the O'Briens, here

[55] Bradshaw, *Irish Constitutional Revolution*, 104–33.

[56] Brady, *Chief Governors*, 14–16.

[57] Ellis, 'Thomas Cromwell and Ireland', 507–11.

[58] This is the comparison developed in detail in Ellis, *Tudor Frontiers and Noble Power*.

emulating the actions of the eighth earl of Kildare a quarter of a century earlier. In 1537 he campaigned vigorously against the O'Connor Falys and the O'Carrolls to the west and the MacMurroughs to the south, destroying O'Connor's castle at Dangan and recovering Athlone. In 1538 he renewed the attack on O'Connor, and forced the submission of the MacMahons of south Ulster. Throughout he proved himself an ambitious and highly competent military leader. By cutting passages through the forests he was able to deploy wheeled artillery in previously impenetrable regions, allowing him to boast that he had entered regions where 'there never was deputy with carts'.[59] His campaign of political and military assertion reached a climax in the summer of 1538, when he made a thirty-day progress through Munster and Connacht, receiving the submissions of a variety of local lords.

All this took place in the power vacuum left by the destruction of the Kildares. The only surviving claimant to the title, following the execution of Offaly and his five uncles, was Gerald Fitzgerald, 14-year-old son of the ninth earl by his second marriage, who had been removed to the protection of his aunt, Lady Eleanor, daughter of the eighth earl and widow of MacCarthy Reagh. In 1538 Manus O'Donnell, who had recently succeeded his father as lord of the O'Donnell territories, married Lady Eleanor. Their diplomatic union provided the basis for a formidable political combination. By the following year O'Donnell had contracted an alliance with Con O'Neill and O'Connor Sligo. Lesser lords from the northern half of the island, like the O'Neills of Clandeboye and the Maguires, O'Cahans, and O'Rourkes, also declared their support.

Manus O'Donnell's motives in creating what came to be known as the Geraldine League may well have been primarily self-interested. He had taken power following a damaging internal struggle. Leadership of the new alliance put him on a more equal footing with Conn O'Neill, to whom he was politically indebted for his recent victory, and allowed him to reassert his family's weakened control over Sligo.[60] What allowed him to rally his fellow Gaelic lords in this new venture, however, was the widespread alarm created by the recent aggressive actions of Lord Grey. Reports forwarded to London by the Dublin administration presented the League as having two main objectives: the restoration of the Kildares and the repudiation of the crown's religious policy. There were also accounts of more exotic plans to inaugurate O'Neill as high king at Tara, with Kildare as his vassal. Such rhetoric need not necessarily be taken at face value. But the geographical extent of the coalition, reaching eventually into all four provinces, and the willingness of traditional rivals like O'Neill and O'Donnell to make common cause, suggests that there was real unease at the threat of an attempt to extend control over previously autonomous lordships. The declared hostility

[59] *NHI*, iii. 44.

[60] Brendan Bradshaw, '"Manus the Magnificent": O'Donnell as Renaissance Prince', in Art Cosgrove and Donal McCartney (eds.), *Studies in Irish History* (Dublin, 1979), 30–1.

to the Henrician Reformation, likewise, can be seen as in part a pragmatic device, winning valuable local backing from the clergy and possibly increasing the chances of gaining foreign support, and in part as an expression of genuine dislike of the royal supremacy.[61]

Grey's response to this challenge was characteristically vigorous. In May 1539 he marched north to demand that O'Neill and O'Donnell surrender young Gerald Fitzgerald, punishing their refusal with raids into south Ulster. In August the Ulster chiefs retaliated by attacking the Pale, sacking the towns of Ardee and Navan. Grey pursued them with a combined force of Pale levies and regular soldiers, defeated them in a dawn attack at Bellahoe south of Carrickmacross, and recaptured the cattle and other booty they had seized. Having spent November and December campaigning in Munster Grey once again entered south Ulster in January 1540, ravaging the countryside round Dungannon. In March Gerald Fizgerald left Ireland to take refuge in France. However, the League remained in existence, and there were reports in spring 1540 that its leaders were now talking of offering their allegiance to the king of Scotland.

That the reaction apparently provoked by Grey's incursions should have been under the ostensible banner of the Kildares was all the more anomalous because Grey himself, by this time, was under attack for his links to the fallen dynasty's former associates. Within the Dublin administration he had rehabilitated a number of officials compromised by their association with Offaly's revolt. In doing so he quickly alienated other office holders, notably John Alen, Cromwell's appointee as master of the rolls, and Gerald Aylmer, chief justice of the Common Pleas. Grey's provincial triumphs, likewise, had been achieved partly with the help of former members of the extensive network of alliances created by the Fitzgerald earls. When he made a second expedition against O'Brien's bridge in July 1538, for example, his main ally was none other than the Brian O'Connor Faly who twelve years earlier had kidnapped a lord deputy on behalf of his father-in-law Kildare, but who now, Grey assured the king, 'stuck as fast unto your Grace, and of your part against every one of them, even as he had been one of your English subjects'.[62] Around the same time Grey assisted another Kildare son-in-law, Fearganainm O'Carroll, who had joined in Thomas Fitzgerald's rebellion, in retaking two castles from his uncle Donough and his cousin William Moyle, both of whom had stayed loyal. Such alliances with men only recently in arms against the crown were not necessarily evidence of any sinister intention on Grey's part. Given his own meagre military resources, he could hope to uphold the king's authority across any substantial area of territory only with the help of local allies, and Kildare's former adherents, themselves in need of a new protector, were an obvious choice. Grey's own family links with the Fitzgeralds, though tarnished by the subsequent betrayal of his promise of mercy to Offaly, may

[61] The fullest discussion of the League is by Bradshaw, *Irish Constitutional Revolution*, 174–83.
[62] *SP Henry VIII*, iii. 62.

also have played a part. But association with figures like Brian and Fearganainm clearly left the deputy open to attack.[63]

The picture was further complicated by the existence of a rival network of influence, controlled by the Butlers of Ormond. The eclipse of their local rivals had greatly boosted the prestige and influence of the second great Anglo-Irish political dynasty. Almost immediately afterwards their position had strengthened still further, when the disgrace of Anne Boleyn undermined their leading rivals at court; in 1538 Piers Butler was able to reclaim the Ormond title he had been forced to surrender to Anne's father ten years earlier. Grey can hardly have wished to see one over-powerful local dynasty replaced by another. Indeed some of what was interpreted as a reconstruction of the Kildare interest may in fact have been primarily a strategy of containing the Butlers. In Leix, for example, he backed the sons of Connell O'More against their uncle, a client of Ormond, who sought to uphold his claim to succeed, as *tánaiste*, to the chieftainship. The assistance he received from Brian O'Connor was in exchange for supporting him against his brother, Cahir Roe, another Butler client, while Fearganainm's rivals Donough and William Moyle were also Ormond allies. In response the Butlers joined Alen and Aylmer in attacking the deputy's administraton. James Butler, son of Sir Piers, complained in June 1538 that Grey was 'the earl of Kildare newly born again', with O'Connor as his right hand.[64]

Explosive though they were, these charges had initially little effect. The arrival in September 1537of the four royal commissioners had seemed to provide Grey's enemies with their opportunity. The head of the commission, Sir Anthony St Leger, appeared to share the views of the deputy's critics and when he returned to England in April 1538 Alen, Aylmer, and James Butler went with him to press home their charges. In the event, however, Cromwell and the king chose to take Grey's energetic efforts to extend royal authority at face value, and gave him their continued support. In December 1539 Ormond, in a revealing gesture, renounced his opposition. Other opponents, like Alen and Aylmer, continued their campaign of character assassination, alleging that Grey's military operations against the Geraldine League masked an actual collusion with his nephew's protectors. But when Grey returned to England in April 1540 it was to plan the next stage of his campaign. What brought about his sudden downfall was an event wholly unrelated to Ireland: the palace coup which brought about Thomas Cromwell's arrest on 10 June. Given the close personal links between Grey and Cromwell, who had begun his career in the household of the deputy's father, the previously discounted charges of treachery were too useful to be ignored by those determined to ensure the secretary's destruction. Arrested on 12 June, Grey pleaded guilty to a series of acts of treason, including his dealings with Ferganainm O'Carroll and Brian O'Connor.

[63] This account follows the reassessment of Grey in Brady, *Chief Governors*, 13–25.
[64] *SP Henry VIII*, iii. 32.

The murderous intrigues of the Tudor court thus gave Ireland a new deputy. Sir Anthony St Leger, head of a Kentish gentry family, was an associate of Cromwell's main rival, the duke of Norfolk, who as earl of Surrey had made his own attempt to settle the affairs of Ireland twenty years earlier. Having supported Grey's critics during his period as head of the commission investigating Irish affairs in 1537–8, he had played a central role in the deputy's eventual downfall; indeed he was to continue the campaign against him until Grey's eventual execution some twelve months later. St Leger arrived in Ireland on 12 August 1540, and within a week had taken the field against the MacMurroughs in south Leinster. On 12 September he dispatched to the king a studiously matter-of-fact account of what seems in reality to have been a major innovation in policy. After his forces had ravaged the territory for ten days, the MacMurroughs had offered their submission. However, what they offered was no mere promise of peaceful obedience. They also undertook to abandon the chiefly title MacMurrough, 'and never more after that day to elect nor choose among them none to bear the same name, nor yet to be their governor, but only of your majesty and such as you shall appoint to the same'. In addition they were 'to take their lands of your majesty, to hold the same by knight service, and not only to serve you from henceforth according to their duties, but also to persecute all others of their nation that will disobey the same'.[65] At this stage the deputy and council were recommending that a second troublesome mountain sept, the O'Tooles, should be extirpated, as beyond reformation. Following a further short campaign, however, Turlough O'Toole offered to submit on the same terms as the MacMurroughs. In November, aided by £20 from St Leger's own pocket and accompanied by an interpreter, O'Toole travelled to court, where he did homage to Henry VIII, and agreed to hold lands from him by knight service, at a rent of 5 marks a year.

St Leger's dispatches artfully presented the terms of these submissions as originating with the Gaelic chiefs concerned. In fact the speed with which the deputy set to work, first in south Leinster and then elsewhere, suggests strongly that he had come to Ireland with a pre-prepared programme of action. Having pacified south Leinster, he went straight to the midlands, where he came to terms with the O'Mores of Leix as well as the Dempseys, MacNorrices, and other lesser lords, thus isolating the still defiant Brian O'Connor. In January 1541 he travelled to the Butler castle at Cahir, in County Tipperary, where he met James FitzJohn Fitzgerald, one of the claimants to the earldom of Desmond. James FitzJohn's position had strengthened considerably the previous March, when his brother Maurice had killed his rival James Fitzmaurice. In an

[65] *SP Henry VIII*, iii. 235–6. The MacMurroughs traced their descent to Dermot MacMurrough, the twelfth-century king of Leinster who had recovered his throne with the aid of what became the bridgehead for the first English colony in Ireland. Kavanagh and Kinsella were branches of this sept, but developed over time into surnames in their own right.

elaborate public ceremony he was recognized as the fourteenth earl and signed an indenture, similar to that accepted by Ossory seven years earlier, agreeing to promote royal government in his lordship. A week later Desmond and St Leger travelled together to Limerick, where the deputy began negotiations with the two most important western lords, McWilliam Burke and O'Brien. Next he turned his attention to Ulster and north Connacht. The most important of the Ulster lords, Con Bacach O'Neill, rejected two overtures, in March and May 1541. However, Manus O'Donnell met the deputy at Cavan in August and agreed terms, as did a number of lesser Ulster lords, and when O'Neill remained defiant St Leger joined with them in attacking his territories. In January 1542 O'Neill too submitted. The existing legal status of these different lords varied greatly. Desmond was a renegade feudal tenant of the crown. The Burkes were of English descent, but had no legal title to the lands they occupied. The O'Briens, O'Neills, and others were in theory the king's Irish enemies. What was now proposed, however, was that they should enjoy a common status as subjects of Henry VIII, holding their lands from him according to the same legal tenure.

None of this was entirely new. The commission of 1537–8, which had first brought St Leger to Ireland, had suggested offering English status and property titles to the Gaelic chiefs closest to the Pale, and Grey had negotiated arrangements along broadly these lines both with the O'Mores and with the MacGillpatricks. Earlier there had been Surrey's more loosely defined mission to induce Gaelic chiefs to accept the king's authority. However, the programme that emerged during the first three years or so of St Leger's deputyship went further than any predecessor. What was envisaged was not just a series of accommodations with border chiefs, but a reconstruction of Gaelic society along English lines. Irish chiefs were not merely to submit to the crown's authority. They were to surrender their lands to the king, and receive them back as grants under English law: the process subsequent historians referred to as 'surrender and regrant'. Having done so they were to take on the rights and duties of a gentry and aristocracy, attending parliament and participating in local government. In addition the redefinition of political and property relationships was not to be confined to the top layer of Gaelic society. St Leger's plans provided for an eventual process of arbitration and enquiry which would determine the relationship between overlords and lesser chiefs, and between chiefs and other members of the ruling family. What would emerge would thus be a complete social hierarchy of aristocracy, large and small gentry and independent freeholders, providing order and stability. Added to this was a programme of cultural and economic anglicization. Lords committed themselves and the inhabitants of their lands to adopting English dress and, as far as their knowledge allowed, language, to having their children educated in English ways and language, to cultivating such land as was fit for tillage, and to building houses for the accommodation of the new, fixed agricultural labour force thus created.

The initiative for this new strategy seems to have come primarily from the lord deputy and his circle, rather than from the court. St Leger's negotiations with the MacMurroughs and others in late 1540 pre-empted instructions to impose punitive terms on the Leinster chiefs. Thereafter Henry VIII appears to have been willing enough to have Gaelic chiefs submit to him as their sovereign lord; this, after all, was what he himself had tried to achieve, through Surrey, two decades earlier. However, he was repeatedly to stall the process by complaining that the terms of submission were too lenient and that some of the lands being surrendered and restored were in fact royal and other English possessions overrun during the late medieval Gaelic resurgence. Within Ireland St Leger's most important ally was Thomas Cusack, a lawyer from a Pale gentry family who had first come into government service as part of Cromwell's attempt to find an alternative to Kildare hegemony. Other supporters were Bishop Staples of Meath and George Dowdall, whom St Leger had appointed archbishop of Armagh in 1543.

The origins of this new policy have been much discussed.[66] Through Cusack and others, whom he had first encountered during his visit as a royal commissioner in 1537–8, St Leger was in touch with a body of ideas about the possible reform of Irish society that had been taking shape for three decades or more. One influential study suggests that these ideas, and St Leger's development of them, were shaped by a specific intellectual climate, Renaissance civic humanism, characterized by an optimistic assessment of human rationality and the potential for social and moral reform. An alternative analysis emphasizes instead the pragmatic advantages of the new strategy. Grey had sought to govern Ireland by building up a network of alliances and dependencies to replace that of the Kildares, but had found himself drawn into factional conflict and vulnerable to allegations of treachery. By building his policy round a new relationship between Gaelic lords and the king, St Leger was able to present himself as representing royal authority rather than faction, while at the same time protecting himself from the charges of personal aggrandizement that had finally destroyed his predecessor. It is also important to note the political background. Grey had dispersed the immediate threat of the Geraldine League at Bellahoe. But the appearance of a confederation of Gaelic chiefs united in support of the Geraldines and seeking links with England's continental enemies was another powerful reason to seek a long-term strategy for the pacification of the island.

The next stage in the programme was the appearance at court, to make their submission in person, of a succession of Irish lords. The first, after Turlough O'Toole, was the newly reconciled James FitzJohn, earl of Desmond,

[66] The account that follows draws mainly on Bradshaw, *Irish Constitutional Revolution*, and Brady, *Chief Governors*, ch. 1. Bradshaw argues for the roots of St Leger's policies in the philosophy of civic humanism, and brings out the implications of his strategy for government and administration as well as land holding. Brady pays more attention to the pragmatic political considerations behind St Leger's choice of strategy, and also emphasizes the extent to which it rested on a widespread distribution of the spoils of office.

in June 1542. The first major Gaelic lord was Con O'Neill, who arrived in mid-September accompanied by two leaders of the Magennises. The king, still prickly on the subject of his historic claims, refused O'Neill's request to be invested as earl of Ulster. Instead, on 1 October, Con Bacach Ó Néill, the O'Neill, became first earl of Tyrone, while his two Magennis clients were knighted. A further contingent arrived in June 1543, headed by Murrough O'Brien, whom Henry created earl of Thomond, and Ulick McWilliam Burke, who became first earl of Clanricard. They brought with them three minor Thomond lords, McNamara, O'Grady, and O'Shaughnessy, as well as McGillpatrick, an Ormond client who had supported the crown against the Geraldine League and had already been rewarded for his loyalty by being created baron of Upper Ossory. All four of these received knighthoods at the hands of the king.

Meanwhile St Leger had proceeded with another aspect of his programme, the incorporation of the Gaelic lords into the apparatus of central and local government. A session of the Irish parliament opened in June 1541. Only one chief, MacGillpatrick, ennobled two days earlier as baron of Upper Ossory, was as yet entitled to sit in the House of Lords. However, others—O'Reilly of Cavan, the MacMurroughs, O'Mores, McWilliam Burke, O'Brien—were present or sent representatives. They were joined by a further group of lords who, like Desmond, were English families long estranged from royal government: a Barry, a Roche, a Fitzmaurice, a Birmingham. The heterogeneous nature of the political community being conjured into existence was evident in the opening arrangements. The peers, St Leger reported, attended solemn mass, 'the most part of them in their robes, and rode in procession solemnly, in such sort as the like thereof hath not been seen here of many years'. But when they met next day for their first session the addresses of Thomas Cusack, speaker of the Commons, and of the lord chancellor, had to be 'briefly and prudently declared, in the Irish tongue to the said Lords, by the mouth of the earl of Ormond, greatly to their contentation'.[67]

Some of those who appeared, at this or later sessions, were living testimony to the numerous problems that had still to be resolved if a dynastic system based on the survival of the fittest was to be reconciled with English norms. Brian O'Connor arrived part of the way through the session, bringing with him Tadhg Caoch O'Carroll, son of Ferganainm, who had just been killed, along with Calvach O'Carroll, a brother of the assassin. Later petitioners included the killer of another of Henry VIII's new subjects, Turlough O'Toole, as well as contending groups from within the O'Neill lordship. From another point of view, however, what is significant is the willingness of such rivals to seek a settlement through the court of parliament, rather than on the battlefield. The decision to return to a peripatetic parliament, with sessions at Dublin,

[67] *SP Henry VIII*, iii. 304.

Limerick, and Trim, has been seen as a conscious attempt to strengthen this role as an arbiter of local disputes, while at the same time involving local lords in its judicial and administrative functions. A proposal to place such proceedings on a more permanent basis through the creation of regional councils that would oversee local government was never implemented, owing to the potential cost. However, royal sheriffs were appointed in Gaelic areas of the south and west (though not as yet in Ulster). Meanwhile the new earls of Thomond and Tyrone were added to the privy council, as was the former renegade Desmond.

St Leger's success in bringing so much of Gaelic Ireland into at least the beginnings of a new relationship with the crown was due to a combination of calculated military force, as against the MacMurroughs, the O'Tooles, and O'Neill, and patient, skilful diplomacy. This in turn required a pragmatic recognition of the limits of what could be achieved in the short term. Henry VIII's new subjects were required to offer tokens of submission to his authority, and in some cases to pay homage in person. However, the deputy and council firmly resisted the king's attempts to insist that they should be required to pay more than token sums in taxation. Indeed border lords required to renounce the black rents they had customarily levied on the Englishry were compensated by the grant of royal pensions. The introduction into Gaelic areas of the rudimentary structures of local government was likewise made acceptable by selecting the new sheriffs from the dominant local lineages. There were also concessions to Gaelic law and custom. A series of ordinances published for territories in the south and west set out a legal code assimilating aspects of Gaelic law. Although Irish chiefs had now become proprietors under English law, equally, the crown did not initially insist on the inflexible application of primogeniture. Instead the agreements with several individual lords recognized political reality by providing for the succession of an alternative whose claims were too strong to be ignored.

A similar pragmatic gradualism was evident in St Leger's religious policy. The agreements with the new lords bound them to join in resisting papal jurisdiction. In practice the deputy was once again content to accept a token submission to the royal supremacy. As part of the same strategy he recommended the appointment to vacant bishoprics of nominees of local lords, and accepted the submission on easy terms of men appointed by Rome. Even Richard de Burgo, representative of the dominant Burke lineage, who had seized the diocese of Clonfert from the crown appointee, Richard Nangle, subsequently received a royal grant admitting him to the see.[68] In extending the campaign to suppress religious houses beyond the Pale, Ormond, and Wexford, St Leger showed a similar circumspection. In Cork three mendicant houses were dissolved in 1541, and their property leased to local merchants. In Limerick, on the other hand, all three of the religious

[68] Edwards, *Church and State*, 95–7, 103–7.

houses in the city survived their legal dissolution through the intervention of local interests, in one case the combined influence of O'Brien and Desmond, in others members of the urban patriciate. In the earldoms of Desmond and Thomond themselves, the suppression campaign was largely nominal. In Desmond a survey in 1541 led to the formal dissolution of eight out of a total of fifty foundations. Once again some at least of the actual religious communities were in practice preserved by the new proprietors, including Desmond himself, to whom their lands were subsequently leased. In Thomond ownership of all mendicant and monastic possessions was transferred by royal patent to the O'Briens, who appear to have made no attempt to close down any of the communities concerned. In Lecale and Ards, remnants of the east Ulster colony, the crown accepted the submission of the papally appointed bishop of Down, Eoin Magennis, while leaving the religious life of the region undisturbed.

The generous distribution of the spoils that reconciled the local lords of Munster to the nominal implementation of the suppression policy was part of a wider pattern. On paper the confiscation of the Kildare estates and the sequestration of monastic property had increased the potential Irish revenue of the crown from around £5,000 to £14,000 a year. In practice receipts averaged only around £11,000. Royal officials leased confiscated and monastic land at the low valuation prevailing in the immediate aftermath of Offaly's rebellion, made allowance for annuities and pensions to former monks, friars, and nuns that would in fact continue to be paid by the crown, and undercollected even the low rents thus fixed: by 1547 arrears had risen to over £18,000. The man mainly responsible for this huge exercise in private profit at state expense was Sir William Brabazon, an English client of Cromwell's sent to Ireland as undertreasurer in 1534. Leading beneficiaries included Brabazon himself, St Leger and his brother Robert, and a number of the deputy's followers and allies, such as his private secretary John Parker, Brabazon's deputy Thomas Asgard, and Thomas Cusack. But a substantial share of the overall profits was distributed among a wide circle of office holders, Pale gentry, and local magnates. In this way, it has been suggested, St Leger found a solution to the problem that had destroyed Lord Leonard Grey. By tolerating and even encouraging this diversion into private hands of a large part of the crown's recent gains, he created an extensive and varied pro-government interest of the kind previously provided, at a price, by the Kildares. It would be unwise simply to redefine peculation entirely in terms of high political strategy. Brabazon's accounting practices, it should be remembered, first came under critical scrutiny as early as 1536, a full four years before St Leger's arrival. But at the very least both St Leger's own position and the strategy of reform on which he was engaged clearly benefited from what has been described as 'a conspiracy of remunerative silence'.[69]

[69] Brady, *Chief Governors*, 40.

This did not mean that St Leger did not make enemies. His willingness to come to terms with former Kildare supporters like Desmond left him open to exactly the same allegations he himself had used to destroy his predecessor. As early as August 1541 the master of the rolls, Robert Cowley, alleged that he was creating 'a new Geraldine breed'. Cowley was a Butler client, but on this occasion he received no support from the Ormonds or others, and he was disgraced and stripped of office. Before long, however, St Leger had fallen foul of the other inescapable political reality that had helped to bring down Grey: that any attempt to create an independent political interest meant containing, and at times directly opposing, the Butler faction. In 1546 St Leger faced charges from a much more dangerous coalition of opponents: John Alen, now lord chancellor, Ormond, and Robert Cowley's son Walter all came forward with charges that the deputy had failed to promote the king's true friends and had embezzled his revenues. Yet on this occasion too St Leger emerged triumphant. Too many powerful figures in Ireland were profiting from his administration, and far too few were anxious to see a detailed exploration of recent dealings in crown property. St Leger had also astutely divided his enemies, promising Walter Cowley an early restoration to favour if he would testify that Alen had maliciously promoted a feud between himself and Ormond. The isolated Alen, stripped of his offices, duly went to the Tower. Ormond, who had retreated from involvement as the case proceeded, went through the motions of a public reconciliation with St Leger. A few weeks later the earl was dead, opportunely but apparently not through foul play, having been taken fatally ill, along with seventeen members of his household, following a banquet at his London home.[70]

*

The parliament of 1541 transacted one other important piece of business. On the first day of the session St Leger proposed in the upper house a bill declaring Henry VIII and his successors to be kings of Ireland, 'with all manner honours, pre-eminences, prerogatives, dignities and all other things whatsoever they be, to the estate and majesty of a king imperial appertaining or belonging'. As with the opening addresses, the bill was not only read to the Lords but 'declared to them in Irish'. It passed through both houses at great speed, and without opposition, receiving the royal assent, through St Leger, the day after its introduction. Its passage was marked by extravagant public celebrations in the capital: 'great bonfires, wine set in the streets, great feastings in their houses, with a goodly sort of guns', as well as an amnesty for prisoners.[71]

[70] David Edwards, 'Malice Aforethought? The Death of the Ninth Earl of Ormond 1546', *Journal of the Butler Society*, 3 (1986–7), 30–41. Edwards rejects suggestions, not in any case contemporary, that St Leger had had the earl poisoned, mainly on the grounds that the deputy had already decisively won the political battle.

[71] *SP Henry VIII*, iii. 305.

The origins of the act for kingly title, like those of other aspects of government policy during these years, have to be inferred rather than reconstructed from explicit statements of intent. The initiative once again came from St Leger and the council. Indeed the king subsequently rebuked his servants in Ireland for investing him with a dignity which the revenues attached to it would not allow him to maintain appropriately. The preamble to the act explained that failure to give the king and his ancestors their proper title had prevented the inhabitants from showing them the full obedience that was their due. An obvious reason for the enactment, which could not be quite so openly acknowledged, was to counter claims that Henry VIII and his predecessors had owed their title to a grant from the pope, now nullified by his schismatic status. At the same time a formal proclamation of the king's position as ruler by right of the whole island was a logical accompaniment to the process whereby the Gaelic lords were induced to acknowledge him as their sovereign and to accept grants of their lands and, in some cases, titles of nobility. The emphasis on the king's commanding role, in this as in other respects, also helped to protect St Leger from charges of abusing his position.

The redesignation of Ireland as a kingdom, held as a dependent but separate crown by the rulers of England, was to provide the constitutional framework within which Ireland was governed for just over two and a half centuries. Its immediate importance is more difficult to assess. It has been argued that the adoption of the new style committed Henry VIII and his successors to new responsibilities towards their Irish inheritance, making it the core of a mid-sixteenth-century 'constitutional revolution'.[72] Yet this notion of a dramatic new departure is difficult to sustain. A body of legislation inherited from the medieval past distinguished between rebellious English subjects, like Desmond, and Irish enemies, like O'Neill. But already in 1522 Henry VIII had been quite clear, in his letters to the earl of Surrey, that he saw himself as 'sovereign lord and prince' over the Irish as well as the English inhabitants. When Grey, in 1536, took some of the leading O'Briens prisoner following a siege, he brought them to Limerick to be executed 'as traitors attainted of high treason'.[73] The acts of the following year, reiterating the prohibition on the wearing of Irish dress and intermarriage with the Irish, are at first sight a return to the principles of the statute of Kilkenny. But their emphasis was in fact subtly different. The complaint of the act against intermarriage was that by this means alliances had been formed, behind the screen of letters of denization, with enemies of the crown. The solution was not to forbid such unions, but to require the Irish parties to give better proof of their allegiance to the crown by oaths and bonds. The purpose of the act against Irish dress, likewise, was not to prevent the cultural contamination of the English community by the customs of Irish aliens, but to remove the distinction between the two ethnic groups. 'Diversity . . . in tongue, language, order and habit', the

[72] Bradshaw, *Irish Constitutional Revolution.* [73] *SP Henry VIII*, ii. 362.

act complained, made people believe that they 'were of sundry sorts, or rather sundry countries, where indeed they be wholly together in one body, whereof his highness is the only head under God'.[74] Seen in this context the statute of 1541 appears less as a revolutionary innovation than as one stage in the gradual development of thinking on the relationship between Gaelic Ireland and the English state.

Nor was this particular stage the final one. After 1543 the whole programme of submissions and the granting of new titles was suspended, leaving the negotiations with most individual lords only partially completed, because the king and his advisers were preoccupied with the war against France. In the longer term, likewise, visions of an Ireland transformed by radical and sustained intervention were to go on being undercut by an unwillingness to spend more money there than could be avoided. Meanwhile the law continued to recognize a distinction between English subjects and Irish aliens. Prosecutions against clerics and others of Gaelic ancestry who had intruded into English areas continued for some years after 1541, and applications to purchase grants of denization continued even longer. As late as 1575 the queen agreed to a petition from the citizens of Limerick for confirmation of their civic privileges, including a stipulation 'that none of the Irishry be preferred to any ecclesiastical living in the cathedral church of Limerick'. By 1611 the defeat of Hugh O'Neill and other Ulster lords had completed the extension of real military and political power over the whole island. At this point the attorney general, the historically minded Sir John Davies, wrote of the need for legislation confirming the inclusion of the native Irish under the king's law and protection. He made no reference to the statute of seven decades earlier.[75]

What of the Gaelic Irish who were the main objects of the new policy? The willingness of so many lords, including not only traditional friends of the English such as O'Donnell and MacCarthy but long-standing predators on the lordship such as O'Neill and O'Brien, to negotiate simultaneous agreements with the crown is undoubtedly striking. In 1544 the new relationship received concrete expression, when Gaelic and Anglo-Irish lords raised a force of 1,000 kern to support the war effort. Of these 600 men sailed to France, where they fought at the siege of Boulogne. The remainder fought on the Scottish border. The following year Ormond and the earl of Lennox led a further 400 galloglass and 1,500 kern and archers, along with 100 men from the crown retinue, to serve in Scotland. In both theatres the kern caused consternation among enemies and allies by their refusal to take prisoners alive. Some of the comment in government correspondence makes clear that their employment was seen partly as a means of ridding the country of violent and dangerous elements. But the episode was

[74] Irish Statutes, 28 Henry VIII, cc. 15, 28.

[75] For prosecutions and certificates of denization, see Ellis, *Ireland under the Tudors*, 175–6. For Limerick, Elizabeth I to Sir Henry Sidney, in *Carew MSS 1575–88*, 25–6. For the situation after 1603 see Ch. 7 below.

nevertheless a demonstration of the apparent potential for a new relationship between Gaelic Ireland and its newly acclaimed king.[76]

What is more difficult to determine is how exactly the Gaelic lords concerned viewed their participation in the whole process of surrender and regrant. Formal indentures by which particular lords had accepted the king of England as their overlord, bound themselves to keep the peace, and agreed to provide tribute or military assistance, had been a standard practice since the fourteenth century. It is possible that some saw the latest round of agreements in much the same light, ignoring the legal and political frills surrounding the procedure. On the other hand St Leger's comments on the political sophistication with which the lords approached the negotiations suggests that many were aware of the fuller implications—that they saw the advantages of regularizing their connection with the powerful political entity with which they had to share the island, and perhaps even of adopting some of the legal institutions and manners of a more orderly and economically developed neighbour. At the same time it is important to remember that only three or four years earlier a large number of the most important Gaelic lords had been engaged in a confederacy to resist the remorseless advance of English power. To this end they had played with the idea of recreating a native monarchy or of seeking a foreign protector in Scotland or elsewhere. They had also identified their political cause with resistance to the Henrician reformation. St Leger's policy of peaceful political and cultural assimilation can be seen as pointing the way towards one possible future. But it seems clear that for the moment political and religious allegiances were fluid and primarily pragmatic.

THE HANDLING OF WILD MEN

St Leger's triumph of autumn 1546 was short-lived. Henry VIII, though periodically grumpy and obstructive, had on the whole allowed his deputy to proceed with his strategy of reform, tempered by a level of pragmatic accommodation that at times shaded into outright bribery. On 28 January 1547, however, the old king died. The council ruling in the name of the 9-year-old Edward VI initially retained St Leger as chief governor. In May 1548, however, it replaced him with Sir Edward Bellingham, an experienced soldier who had come to Ireland the previous June as captain general of the army. The appointment followed an attack on St Leger's administration by his former ally, the undertreasurer William Brabazon, who accused him of being 'more favourable to Irishmen than to the king's subjects'. But it has also been seen as reflecting a shift in power within the English administration, in which the duke

[76] D. G. White, 'Henry VIII's Irish Kerne in France and Scotland 1544–5', *IHS* 3 (1957–8), 213–25.

of Somerset triumphed over the conservative element who would have been St Leger's natural allies. There followed a succession of rapid changes. Bellingham left Ireland in December 1549, three months after Somerset's fall from power. Government remained in the hands of two lords justices, one of them Brabazon, until September 1550, when St Leger returned to office. St Leger was replaced in May 1551 by Sir James Croft, another military man, who had earlier been appointed to inspect the coastal defences of the south. Croft left Ireland in December 1552. Once again the administration was left in the hands of two local lords justices until, in November 1553, St Leger returned for a final term as deputy.[77]

This rapid turnover in personnel coincided with a sharp increase in military activity. St Leger's quarrel with Brabazon appears to have begun when the undertreasurer, acting as lord justice during the deputy's absence in 1546, provoked the O'Connors by a punitive raid. Suggestions that this was a deliberate attempt to sabotage St Leger's conciliatory strategy seem to be unfounded. Instead, it has been argued, problems arose because the death of Ormond, leaving a minor as tenth earl, had created a power vacuum in the midlands. O'Connor Faly and O'More, both former Fitzgerald clients, seized the opportunity to ravage the western borders of Kildare, while there were also disturbances among the O'Byrnes, O'Tooles, and MacMurroughs.[78] Bellingham, remembered twenty years later as 'a good man-a-war', who 'wore ever his harness and so did all those whom he liked of', responded vigorously to the challenge.[79] By the end of 1548 he had captured and executed Cahir Roe O'Connor and sent his brother Brian, along with Rory O'More, as prisoners to London. In addition, adopting a strategy already favoured by Somerset's government along the Scottish border, Brabazon and Bellingham sought to consolidate the control thus established by placing fortified garrisons at strategic points. Brabazon established Fort Governor at Dangan in the O'Connor territory of Offaly in 1546, and the following year reconstructed the castle at Athlone. In 1548 Bellingham created Fort Protector in Leix, the territory of the O'Mores, on the site of what was to become the town of Maryborough, as well as a smaller forward post at Nenagh. The following year he established a garrison at Leighlinbridge, on the frontier with the MacMurroughs. To the north he established two military strongmen, Nicholas Bagenal at Newry and Andrew Brereton in Lecale, with grants of land requiring them to establish and maintain garrisons.

[77] The fullest narrative account of the period 1547–53 is D. G. White, 'The Reign of Edward VI in Ireland: Some Political, Social and Economic Aspects', *Irish Historical Studies*, 14 (1965), 197–211. However, this must be supplemented by the important reassessment in Brady, *Chief Governors*, ch. 2. See also Lennon, *Sixteenth-Century Ireland*, 164–76.

[78] This accounts follows Brady, *Chief Governors*, 56–7. For St Leger's quarrel with Brabazon see Ellis, *Ireland*, 158.

[79] 'Book of Howth', *Carew MSS*, v. 195.

This shift towards a more aggressive Irish policy can be attributed in part to the generally authoritarian character of the new Edwardian regime, where two successive rulers of military background, the dukes of Somerset and Northumberland, pursued unpopular military and religious policies with dubious legitimacy in the name of a teenage king. In August 1551, informed of the submission of certain Gaelic chiefs, the English privy council bluntly set out its programme of rule: 'we win them not by their wills, but by our power . . . then shall they obey because they cannot choose'.[80] But the new policy also reflected the particular danger which Ireland presented to a regime beset by enemies both at home and abroad. From 1547 England was at war with both Scotland and France, and even after 1550, when the Treaty of Boulogne ended formal hostilities, reports persisted of an imminent Franco-Scottish invasion. There were also contacts between these hostile powers and the Gaelic Irish. Two of the sons of the imprisoned Brian O'Connor took refuge in France, and a third at the Scottish court, while in 1550 there were reports that French envoys had visited the Ulster chiefs. This combination of internal and external threat made St Leger's cautious policy seem dangerously lax. His position was further weakened by the self-interested lobbying of Brereton, whom St Leger had removed from Lecale after he had offended Conn O'Neill, observing as he did so that 'such handling of wild men had done much harm in Ireland'. It was against this background that Northumberland first sent Croft to Ireland and then appointed him to replace St Leger.

Accompanied by an army of 2,000 men, Croft staged a successful show of force in Munster, accepting the submission of MacCarthy Mór and establishing a commission of the peace headed by the earl of Desmond. In September 1551 he marched into Ulster to deal with two main problems: a succession dispute which had plunged the O'Neill lordship into civil war, and the settlement along the north-east coast of growing numbers of Scots, seen as a potential bridgehead for England's closest enemy. Croft succeeded in obtaining the nominal support of most of the Ulster Gaelic lords, but was unable to inflict any serious damage on the Scots; instead a raiding party dispatched to Rathlin Island had to be humiliatingly ransomed. By arresting Conn Bacach O'Neill, equally, Croft asserted royal authority but did nothing to end the fighting between the old chief's would-be heirs. A second expedition to Ulster in summer 1552 ended in military defeat near Belfast.[81]

In addition to a new level of military activity, the succession of short administrations during the reign of Edward VI also saw a further important innovation: the beginnings of the first attempt to follow up the military subjugation of a Gaelic area by its plantation with English settlers. The initial

[80] White, 'The Reign of Edward VI', 205.

[81] J. Michael Hill, *Fire and Sword: Sorley Boy MacDonnell and the Rise of Clan Ian Mor 1538–90* (London, 1993), 35–40.

proposal was a limited and pragmatic one: soldiers from Fort Protector and Fort Governor were to be granted farms in the surrounding countryside, thus making the two garrisons self-sufficient in food. In 1550, however, the English council ordered a more general distribution of land to tenants of English stock. Grantees were to be required to keep sufficient weapons to defend themselves, and were not to sublet to any of the O'Mores or O'Connors. Around the same time a consortium of twenty-three Anglo-Irish and English soldiers applied to be assigned the whole territory in exchange for a rent of £600 per year—the first example of a plan for plantation as a corporate venture undertaken on commercial grounds. The council ignored this offer but ordered Croft to proceed with the settling of tenants. In the event he made little progress: plans became bogged down in a debate over whether to settle large numbers of colonists on small holdings, or to encourage investment by granting a few large estates. Nevertheless, when Sir William Herbert, a spokesman for the much more radical Munster plantation of a later era, wrote a plea for further colonization in 1591, he paid tribute to what he saw as a predecessor by entitling the work *Croftus*.

All this makes clear the contrast between the last years of Henry VIII and the short reign of his son. Yet the discontinuity in policy should not be overstated. St Leger, in the first place, had never relied on conciliation alone. In his very first campaign in Wicklow, in his dealing with Conn O'Neill, and at other crucial points, he had been ready where necessary to reinforce the offer of tenure under the crown with firm military action. By the same token, neither Bellingham nor Croft relied solely on force. Instead, as the most recent account of their administrations makes clear, both men combined their military venture with sustained attempts to continue St Leger's policy of seeking to draw Gaelic lords into a relationship with the crown. These included both formal surrender and regrant agreements, such as that Croft concluded with MacCarthy Mór, and a willingness to arbitrate in disputes with a combination of firmness and flexibility.[82] It is also important to recognize that Croft's and Bellingham's military campaigns, for all their vigour, were primarily defensive in aim. Croft's expeditions to Ulster in 1551–2 were in response to the threat of foreign intervention, and in particular to Scottish infiltration along the east coast. Otherwise both men concentrated their efforts on the traditional task of securing the frontier beween English and Gaelic Ireland. The eclipse of the Kildares had widened the area under direct English rule. But Forts Governor and Protector in the midlands, Newry and Lecale to the north, Leighlinbridge and elsewhere to the south, were essentially a chain of fortifications encircling a somewhat enlarged Pale (see Map 3).

Even what is superficially the most dramatic new development of the period, the plantation of settlers on confiscated Gaelic land, was less radical than it

[82] Brady, *Chief Governors*, 45–52.

appears at first sight. The selective establishment of colonies of English settlers had been a fairly regular feature of the plans for the strengthening of the lordship put forward over the previous half-century or more. The emphasis, however, was on introducing small, concentrated groupings of settlers, who would help to secure strategic points and at the same time disseminate English manners and economic practices among the surrounding Gaelic population. In the case of Leix and Offaly, Croft's orders reflected a new ruthlessness towards troublesome Gaelic populations. The first survey of the territory, carried out in 1549, had assumed that most of the area would be regranted to the native population. By 1552, on the other hand, it appears to have been assumed that the whole territory was to be granted to settlers. But the overall aim remained limited and defensive: to solve the specific problem of the O'More and O'Connor lordships, and so secure the new western frontier of the Pale.

The other area in which the years after Henry VIII's death saw distinct changes of policy was religion.[83] The Henrician Reformation had seen only modest innovations in liturgy and doctrine, with a sharp move towards the restatement of Catholic orthodoxy in the last years of the reign. Under Edward VI, on the other hand, Ireland's chief governors had to implement the directives of a regime that moved steadily towards an unambiguously Protestant doctrine and liturgy. Bellingham made the first moves in 1548, when he suppressed surviving houses of mendicants during a tour of the south-west. In November the government produced a 'Book of Reformation', now lost but presumably following the main liturgical innovations, notably the use of a vernacular liturgy and the banning of surviving symbolic elements such as holy water and candles, that had already been introduced in England. In June 1549, following the introduction in the English parliament of an act of uniformity applying to all the king's dominions, Bellingham and his council ordered the use of the English Book of Common Prayer.

In thus dutifully implementing the crown's religious programme, Bellingham received little cooperation from either clergy or laity. In Dublin George Browne, the equivocal agent of the Henrician reformation, cooperated in drawing up the Book of Reformations. Bishop Staples of Meath, the other previous supporter of reform, came out openly to declare that the mass was a commemoration rather than a sacrifice, and in consequence found himself denounced as a heretic and boycotted by the local gentry. Elsewhere, however, there was little enthusiasm for the new liturgy or the doctrines on which it rested. In Armagh George Dowdall, a former regular who had resisted the suppression of his priory but had subsequently been rewarded for his acceptance of the royal supremacy by his appointment as archbishop, flatly refused to implement the required changes. Bellingham went through the motions of requiring those appointed

[83] Brendan Bradshaw, 'The Edwardian Reformation in Ireland 1547–53', *Archivium Hibernicum*, 34 (1977), 83–99.

to benefices in the crown's gift to undertake that they would promote the new liturgy. But in practice he could do nothing to enforce such covenants. It is also significant that the government made no attempt to suppress the numerous guilds and chantries that existed in Dublin and elsewhere. Their continuance, resting on the belief both in purgatory and in salvation by the works of oneself and others, was a blatant contradiction of reformed principles. But these central institutions of the old corporate religious culture were clearly too widely and determinedly supported for Bellingham to consider tampering with them.

In this respect, as in others, St Leger's restoration in September 1550 marked a change in emphasis rather than direction. St Leger approached the task of managing change with his customary attention to vested interests. His diplomacy was particularly evident in appointments to bishoprics. One opponent of the reformation, Bishop Coyne of Limerick, was persuaded to resign, but the earl of Desmond was permitted to nominate a successor, William Casey, who is reported to have been an active reformer. When a second bishop, Nicholas Comyn of Waterford, also resigned, the choice of his successor was left to the dean and chapter. In the more distant Kilmore St Leger even recommended appointing the papal nominee, who had surrendered his bull of appointment. (The papally-appointed bishop of Dromore had already been accepted on this basis during Brabazon's brief period as Bellingham's successor.)[84] In Kildare and Leighlin, closer to the Pale, St Leger appointed English reformers, but guaranteed security of tenure to the local Gaelic clergy by admitting them to hold benefices as Englishmen. He also tried unsuccessfully to win over Dowdall, using his old supporter, Sir Thomas Cusack, now lord chancellor, who was the archbishop's cousin. As in other areas, however, St Leger's conciliatory approach was a means to an end. Hostile contemporaries, including Archbishop Browne, maintained that St Leger had indicated his dislike of the new liturgy, and lamented its disruptive effects.[85] But if so his private preferences did not prevent him from promoting the long-term goal of religious uniformity between Ireland and England. It was St Leger who initiated the printing in Dublin of the English Book of Common Prayer, which appeared during 1551. He had also secured authority to produce a Latin version, which though never printed circulated in manuscript in some areas. Ostensibly a gesture to those who could not read English, this could also be seen as an astute packaging of the new liturgy in the language of the old. In January and February 1551 Cusack and another royal official, Patrick Barnewall, the king's serjeant at law, made another tour through the south-west to demand conformity to the new ecclesiastical order.

During Crofts's period as lord deputy the English reformation became more radical. The second Book of Common Prayer, introduced in 1552, broke

[84] Edwards, *Church and State in Tudor Ireland*, 141–5.
[85] See in particular Jefferies, *Priests and Prelates of Armagh*, 159.

decisively with the outward appearance of the mass. Croft's orders had emphasized the promotion of religious reform, and he duly incorporated an undertaking to promote the new liturgy into the instructions of the Munster commission of the peace. Dowdall responded to the new climate by leaving Ireland, apparently in some haste, to take refuge in Italy. The attitude of Ireland's other senior ecclesiastic, Archbishop Browne of Dublin, is less clear-cut. Browne had lobbied energetically against the religious unsoundness of both St Leger and Dowdall. But his campaign was at least partly motivated by personal hostility in the first case, and in the second by his ambition to have Dublin supplant Armagh as the primatial see. He had possibly shown more of his true preferences when he joined in the refusal to consecrate a newly appointed bishop, John Bale, according to the revised rubric, in which he would hand his new episcopal colleague a bible rather than a pastoral staff. Certainly Bale, while praising Lord Chancellor Cusack as 'our special good lord and earnest aid in all our proceedings', denounced Browne as wholly lacking in commitment to reform.

Bale was one of two English reformers whom the privy council in London, ignoring Croft's recommendation of local clerics, had nominated to vacant sees. (The other was Hugh Goodacre, archbishop of Armagh, who died before he could take up his duties—poisoned, according to Bale, by the clergy of his new diocese.) He went on to have a dramatic, though short, career as an Irish bishop. His memoir, written immediately after his withdrawal in 1553, makes clear just how little impact the reformed liturgy had made on religious practice even within the English shires. Landing in Waterford, he was scandalized to find that 'the communion or supper of the lord was there altogether used like a popish mass, with the old apish toys of antichrist, in bowings and beckings, kneelings and knockings'. In Kilkenny he launched immediately into a head-on attack:

> Much ado I had with the priests; for that I said among other, that the white gods of their making, such as they offered to the people to be worshipped, were no gods, but idols; and that their prayers for the dead procured no redemption to the souls departed; redemption of souls being only in Christ, of Christ, and by Christ. I added that their office, by Christ's strict commandment, was chiefly to preach, and instruct the people in the doctrine and ways of God; and not to occupy so much of the time in chanting, piping and singing.

Here all attempts at gradual change had been abandoned. Instead the central tenets of the traditional religion, with its stress on salvation through the accumulated merit of prayer and good works, was directly challenged by an uncompromising emphasis on the sole efficacy of redemption by God's grace, and on a preaching rather than a ritual ministry.

What might have happened next remains unclear. Neither Croft nor any other deputy, conscious of their limited coercive resources and already struggling to maintain order in Ulster and the midlands, would have wanted to push the otherwise loyal inhabitants of the Pale and the cities beyond passive resistance into actual revolt. On the other hand the Edwardian regime could hardly have ignored indefinitely the increasingly clear rejection of its religious policies. In the event Edward VI died on 6 July 1553. The Protestant pretender Lady Jane Grey was proclaimed queen in Ireland on 27 July, but by that time supporters of Henry VIII's Catholic daughter Mary had already established her on the English throne. In Kilkenny Bale's clerical colleagues left no doubt as to their response:

They rung all the bells . . . they flung up their caps to the battlement of the great temple with smilings and laughings most dissolutely . . . they brought forth their copes, candlesticks, holy water stock, cross and censers, they mustered forth in general procession most gorgeously, all the town over, with *sancta Maria, ora pro nobis* [holy Mary, pray for us] and the rest of the Latin litany; they cattered it, they chanted it, with great noise and devotion, they banquetted all the day after, for that they were delivered from the grace of God into a warm sun.[86]

By the time the priests of Kilkenny celebrated the anticipated return of the true faith, the sword of state had changed hands yet again. The aggressive policy pursued by Edward VI's councils had from the start been expensive. In the last years of Henry VIII subventions from England, to bridge the gap between Irish revenue and government expenditure, had run at around £8,000 a year. In 1546–7 this rose to over £12,000; by 1548–9 the figure was more than £24,000 and in 1550–1 it was almost £40,000. As in England itself, the government sought to solve the problem by issuing increased quantities of coin with a sharply reduced silver content. The inevitable inflation devastated the economy of the Pale: at the end of 1551 Croft reported that over the year prices there had become between four and six times higher. Yet the public deficit remained enormous. Altogether it was claimed that Edward's government spent £250,000 on Ireland, of which £150,000 came from England. At a time when economic hardship had brought widespread popular revolt in England itself, this burden could not be sustained. Croft left Ireland at the end of 1552 and already before Edward's death the decision had been taken to restore St Leger yet again as chief governor.[87]

St Leger's third term of office was to be his last. Shortly after his reinstatement the English privy council appointed two commissioners to inquire into the management of the public finances. The immediate result was the dismissal and imprisonment of Brabazon's son-in-law, Andrew Wise, who had succeeded as

[86] John Bale, *The Vocacyon of Johan Bale to the Bishoprick of Ossorie in Ireland, his Persecucions in the Same, and finall delyveraunce* (1553), printed in *Harleian Miscellany*, ed. William Oldys (London, 1810), vi. 447, 446, 448, 452. For the poisoning of Goodacre see p. 449, and for Browne's stance on Bale's consecration p. 447.

[87] White, 'Reign of Edward VI', 208–10; Ellis, *Ireland in the Age of the Tudors*, 269; Brady, *Chief Governors*, 62–4.

undertreasurer two years earlier. St Leger's response to the threat of a wider-ranging inquiry was both characteristic and effective: the senior of the two commissioners promptly succeeded to Wise's office, and was drawn into other potentially profitable schemes. In October 1554, however, the government dispatched a new commissioner, Sir William Fitzwilliam, who proved less easy to deflect, most probably because his brother-in-law, Thomas Radcliffe, Lord Fitzwalter, another ambitious young courtier, coveted St Leger's office for himself. Over the next year and a half a number of St Leger's associates were dismissed in disgrace and some, including Lord Chancellor Cusack, were imprisoned. Meanwhile Fitzwilliam attacked, not only St Leger's financial malpractice, but his failure to deal with disorders in the midlands, Ulster, and elsewhere. Fitzwilliam had the backing of the powerful Howard faction at court, as well as of St Leger's long-standing opponents—and by this time also Howard clients—the Butlers. In May 1556 the queen dismissed St Leger; a subsequent inquiry was to conclude that he owed the crown £5,000 in unpaid rents and misappropriated moneys. Fitzwalter, who in 1557 was to succeed to his more familiar title of earl of Sussex, replaced him as deputy, with Fitzwilliam as Keeper of the Great Seal and another brother-in-law, Sir Henry Sidney, as undertreasurer.[88]

What was the state of Ireland at the time of St Leger's final departure? The traditional view, that the years after 1558 saw a shift towards a more militaristic policy of conquest and colonization, turns out on inspection to be an oversimplification. Projects like the fortification and settlement of Leix and Offaly represented improvisation rather than a new strategy, and the long-term commitment to the extension of English law by means of the assimilation of the Gaelic elite remained in place. Sir Thomas Cusack, St Leger's trusted adviser and the putative inspiration for his strategy of conciliation, continued in office as chancellor under both Bellingham and Croft. In 1552 he submitted a highly positive account of a tour he had undertaken through all four provinces. 'Irishmen are now soon brought to obedience . . . And the gentleness that my Lord Deputy doth devise among the people with wisdom and indifference doth profit and make sure the former civility.'[89] The deputy in question, it should be noted, was Croft, not St Leger, who did not resume the office until September of the following year. On the other hand the English ambassador to Paris, in 1550, quoted the agents of those Gaelic chiefs seeking French assistance as saying that unless they fought back 'they looked for none other but to be driven out of their ancient possessions . . . as had lately been served to O'More and O'Connor'.[90] This, of course, was both hearsay and the sort of rhetoric that might have accompanied an expedient alliance; the years that followed were

[88] This account follows Brady, *Chief Governors*, 65–71.

[89] *Carew MSS 1515–1574*, 245–6. Cusack's report is there dated 1553, but White ('Reign of Edward VI', 207) corrects this to 1552.

[90] Quoted Ellis, *Ireland in the Age of the Tudors*, 266–7.

to present many examples of continued pragmatic cooperation between Gaelic lords and the English authorities. Yet it stands as a reminder that political change does not have to be either planned or sudden. Edward VI's Irish servants may primarily have responded to immediate problems. But the nature of their response had implications for the future behaviour of English and Irish alike. What was happening was event rather than process; but events, even if only in hindsight, can be seen to have had their own momentum.

4

Expansion and Resistance

A MAP OF IRELAND

AROUND 1567 an English cartographer, John Goghe, produced one of the first detailed and reasonably accurate maps of the whole island of Ireland (see Map 8). A striking feature of his work, to modern eyes, is its failure to use the conventional north–south axis. Instead the map depicts Ireland with west at the top and east at the bottom. The image is also subtly tilted, and the lettering positioned, so that the province of Leinster is to the front, with Munster, Connacht, and Ulster arranged in a line behind it. From the point of view of its immediate purpose—annotations suggest that the map was used intensively by Elizabeth I's chief minister, William Cecil—the perspective adopted in Goghe's map is a logical one: we look outwards from Dublin and the Pale to the Gaelic hinterland beyond, whose control or subjugation was becoming increasingly a priority. For the historian, too, such a perspective provides one possible line of approach: a narrative that takes as its starting point the political structures of the English lordship, and whose focus is divided between the government of the lordship itself and its relations with the various powers beyond its frontiers. Nor is such a focus necessarily illegitimate. The transformation of a geographically circumscribed English lordship into a kingdom embracing the whole island is not only a coherent organizing theme. It is also a development of central importance, determining the legal and institutional framework within which the destinies of all sections of the population were to be worked out over the next two centuries or more.

For all this, however, any such account, adopting the standpoint of a slowly but inexorably expanding English state, remains inescapably a sectional perspective. To see this we have only to turn Goghe's map upside down. The former hinterland is now at the centre of our picture: an extensive region, twice as large as the east coast lordship, though perhaps containing somewhat fewer inhabitants. It is a region dominated by a distinctive system of political and social organization, an elaborate code of laws, and an ancient and sophisticated literary culture. If its links with the English lordship cast it in the role of a periphery, it had its own separate connections, economic, cultural, ecclesiastical, and diplomatic, with a wider European world. It also had its own political history. The Irish annals of the period depict a hierarchy of greater and lesser powers bound together in networks of dominance and subordination, alliance and conflict, in which the English of the east coast for long make only intermittent appearances, as one participant among many. There is also evidence of a capacity, over time, to adapt political, economic, and legal structures to changing circumstances.[1] Holding the map this way up, the story of the sixteenth century thus becomes one of a potential path of development truncated by military conquest and forcible dispossession.

Alternative geographical perspectives thus bring into focus two very different narratives to which any account of sixteenth-century Ireland must seek to do justice: on the one hand, the growth from small beginnings of an English-ruled kingdom of Ireland; on the other the closing off of alternative possibilities of development in a complex and by no means static Gaelic society. Yet these polar opposites do not exhaust the possibilities. A third and final look at Goghe's map makes clear that the initial impression it conveys, an east coast English enclave and beyond it a Gaelic hinterland, is in fact misleading. Just to the south (or left) of Dublin, separating the capital from the anglicized south-east county of Wexford, lay the Gaelic sept of O'Byrne. Further inland, the lands of the earls of Kildare and Ormond, familiar figures at the court of Elizabeth I, adjoined a variety of Gaelic lordships in differing degrees of accommodation with the crown, from the still hostile O'Carrolls and O'Molloys to the MacGillpatricks, now the 'Fitzpatrick' barons of Upper Ossory and Leinster's premier Gaelic loyalists.[2] Beyond the Gaelic lordships of the midlands lay the territories of three other earldoms: the Fitzgeralds of Desmond, at this time yielding an uneasy allegiance with the crown; the Burkes of Clanricard, former 'English rebels' now halfway on a journey towards full loyalty; and the O'Briens of Thomond, another Gaelic lordship transmuted by an English title of nobility. Well back from the English Pale, meanwhile, stood the cities of Cork, on the south coast, and Limerick and Galway on the west, all clearly identifying themselves with the king's government, but nevertheless depending for their existence on trade with the surrounding Gaelic countryside. What Goghe's map reveals, in other words, is not a simple dividing line between two cultural and political zones. Rather it depicts a land of multiple frontiers, political, cultural, and environmental. Behind its contours can be detected a whole range of interactions, from accommodation and exchange to bloody and destructive conflict. It is a snapshot of a particular moment in what has come to be considered the Tudor conquest of Ireland. But in itself, viewed without the benefit of hindsight, it provides the basis for no one clear narrative of the kind that label would imply.

[1] See Ch. 1 above.

[2] *MacGiollapadraig* means, literally, 'the son of the servant of Patrick'. In taking the surname Fitzpatrick the barons of Upper Ossory abandoned the Irish 'mac' for the French 'fitz' common among the English of Ireland. To avoid losing sight of the family's Gaelic origins, it seems better to retain the original surname, in anglicized form, in referring to the sept as a whole.

THE SWORD OF STATE

By the mid-sixteenth century English government in Ireland had begun to take on the shape it was to retain until the civil wars of the 1640s. In place of a local magnate to whom the English crown delegated control of the Irish lordship, a succession of English chief governors now acted as local administrators, directly answerable for their stewardship to the monarch and privy council. The geographical reach of the Dublin administration remained well short of the theoretical claim to a kingdom comprising the whole island. But the policies of Bellingham, Croft, and St Leger had created a moving frontier: the area under the control of crown officials expanded steadily from the 1550s onwards, first in the midlands, then in Munster and Connacht. Direct rule over an enlarged area in turn required a growth in the formal apparatus of government, both military and, to a lesser extent, civil.[3]

The gradually expanding role of government was reflected in its physical infrastructure. The earls of Kildare, as local magnates, had been able to maintain a reasonable level of display out of their own resources. In 1489 the eighth earl had impressed Dubliners when he equipped the men standing sentry outside his house at Thomas Court with six handguns recently sent to him from Germany. There was also the Fitzgerald castle at Maynooth, to which the ninth earl introduced a touch of Renaissance grandeur. By contrast Surrey, the first of the English governors, had complained that Dublin Castle, designated his residence and place of business, was in too ruinous a condition to occupy for either. Thirty years later incoming chief governors could still not rely on being provided with even the most basic necessities. Sir James Croft, rehearsing in old age his losses in royal service, complained that his sudden elevation to the deputyship in 1551 left him 'altogether unfurnished to supply such a place . . . altogether unprovided of horses, household stuff, plate meet for that place and all other necessaries whatever'.[4] In the late 1560s Sir Henry Sidney extensively refurbished the state

[3] For a general survey of the machinery of government see in particular J. G. Crawford, *Anglicising the Government of Ireland: The Irish Privy Council and the Expansion of Tudor Rule 1556–1578* (Dublin, 1993). S. G. Ellis, *Reform and Revival: English Government in Ireland 1470–1534* (Woodbridge, 1986) can be supplemented by the same author's *Ireland in the Age of the Tudors 1447–1603: English Expansion and the End of Gaelic Rule* (2nd edn., 1998), ch. 7, less detailed but covering a longer period. See also Ciaran Brady, 'Court, Castle and Country: The Framework of Government in Tudor Ireland' in Ciaran Brady and Raymond Gillespie (eds.), *Natives and Newcomers: The Making of Irish Colonial Society 1534–1641* (Dublin, 1986), 22–49. Ciaran Brady, *The Chief Governors: The Rise and Fall of Reform Government in Tudor Ireland 1536–1588* (Cambridge, 1994), though primarily a political analysis, contains much incidental information on administration. For the army see also Ciaran Brady, 'The Captain's Games: Army and Society in Elizabethan Ireland', in Thomas Bartlett and Keith Jeffery (eds.), *A Military History of Ireland* (Cambridge, 1996), 136–59.

[4] 'The Autobiography of Sir James Croft', *Bulletin of the Institute of Historical Resarch*, 50 (1977), 52.

rooms in Dublin Castle, to provide reception rooms, new premises for the courts of justice, and a room for meetings of the privy council. By this time a residence had been provided for chief governors, in the premises of the former priory of Kilmainham, west of the city. Here too Sidney contributed to the physical development of the site, erecting a stone bridge of nine arches across the River Liffey.

The council thus provided with a regular venue in Dublin Castle was itself a testimony to the changing character of English government in Ireland. An advisory body consisting of ministers and magnates had from the start been part of the structure of government. In 1479 Edward IV ordered that the lord deputy was to act on the advice of a majority among seven key officials, including the chancellor, the lord treasurer, and three senior judges, the nomination of whom had already in all cases been reserved to the king. The aim was clearly to impose some limits on Kildare's management of the lordship. In practice the local power of the eighth and ninth earls was sufficient to ensure that councils were no real check on their activities. From 1520, the point where Surrey's appointment inaugurated a new era in government, there are references to a privy council. From this point too both the new inner body and the larger council began to take a more active role in administration. In the short term this change was masked by the continuing power struggle between Kildare, his local rivals, and the crown. After 1534, on the other hand, the council emerged as an active organ of government. Larger assemblies, a great or afforced council, comprising all the lords spiritual and temporal, still met for certain important functions: to authorize exceptional taxation or to declare a state of war. But it was the privy council, meeting on average once a week, that managed the regular business of government, including both finance and military affairs. Instructions from England came addressed to the lord deputy and council. Proclamations and other orders likewise went out in the name of both; on the frequent occasions when military or other concerns took the lord deputy away from Dublin, they were issued in the name of the council alone. The council was also responsible for the overall supervision of the legal system. This included hearing individual cases, especially those concerning treason, public order, or the proper administration of justice, or where the persons involved were peers or other men of substance. From 1571, after an earlier false start in 1563–6, this judicial business was transferred to a separate Court of Castle Chamber, whose membership largely overlapped with that of the council.

The average number of active council members rose from eleven or twelve under Mary Tudor to twenty-two under Elizabeth. In addition to the judges and senior office holders who had made up the nucleus of the old council, these now included the archbishop of Dublin and the bishop of Meath, as well as senior military commanders. With them sat the two leading Anglo-Irish magnates, the earl of Ormond and the recently rehabilitated earl of Kildare. This made the privy council a sectional body in a divided society: St Leger's experiment of giving places on the council to the ennobled Gaelic lords of Tyrone and Thomond had been quietly dropped, and the heads of the third great Anglo-Irish dynasty, the earls of Desmond, were likewise excluded. Within these self-imposed limits, the council's effectiveness as an organ of government remains the subject of debate. A study of the men who held the office of viceroy between the 1550s and the 1580s takes as its starting point the assertion that the council was invariably subordinate to the chief governor. By contrast the fullest study of the council itself presents a more nuanced picture, in which the council consistently served as an active partner in government, its precise degree of influence varying from one chief governor to the next.[5]

The same evolution of new structures evident in the inner decision-making core of government can be seen, though less clearly, in the legal system. In the late fifteenth century the jurisdiction of the two main courts of law was poorly defined, with King's Bench dealing with many civil actions of a kind that in England were by this time confined to Common Pleas. By the early sixteenth century a clearer demarcation had emerged, partly because King's Bench had now ceased to itinerate round the Pale and had joined Common Pleas at a fixed location, generally the castle, in Dublin. Up to 1494 parliament had had an important role as court as well as legislature, particularly in cases where normal legal forms or procedures were inadequate. Poynings's Law, drastically reducing the frequency of meetings, largely put an end to this function. Already before this date, however, chancery, presided over by the lord chancellor, had established itself as a court as well as an administrative department, offering a similar equitable jurisdiction. During the sixteenth century its judicial business was to expand significantly, and chancery acquired a temporarily important role as a forum in which English and Gaelic law could in some respects interact. The fourth of what was to become Ireland's four courts, the Exchequer, had a specific role in relation to the king's rights, in terms both of seigneurial entitlements and of the fines levied for breaches of the law. By the late fifteenth century, however, it also catered for a substantial number of civil litigants, attracted by its more rapid procedures.[6]

The Dublin courts, like other branches of central government, operated within a geographically restricted area. In the early sixteenth century cases came mainly from Counties Dublin, Meath, and Louth, with smaller numbers from Wexford, Waterford, and Kilkenny. But centralized justice was also carried to the outlying counties by the fairly regular appointment of itinerant commissioners. The abolition in 1534 of the liberty of Kildare brought the fourth of the Pale counties more fully under the jurisdiction of the Dublin courts. In the second half of the century judges from the three courts of King's Bench, Common Pleas, and Exchequer, began to travel regularly on circuit to preside over assizes, both in

[5] Brady, *Chief Governors*, p. xi; Crawford, *Anglicizing the Government of Ireland*, 28–37.
[6] Ellis, *Reform and Revival*, ch. 4.

the Pale and further afield. As early as 1570 assizes took place not only in the four Pale counties, Carlow, and Kilkenny, but also in Westmeath and in the new shires of King's County and Longford. In the 1590s assizes began to be held in the Ulster counties of Cavan, Monaghan, Down, and Antrim. However, it was not until after 1603 that regular assizes circuits were established for the whole country.[7]

The expanding competence of the central courts was matched by a growth in the number of lawyers. No precise statistics exist, but the lord deputy commented in 1557 that there were three times as many Irish in the universities, 'and at the study of the law of the realm', as there had been in an earlier generation.[8] In 1541 a group of judges, law officers, and lawyers received a lease on the house and gardens of a former Dominican friary on the north bank of the Liffey, where they had already been meeting for two years and which they had named the King's Inn. The new body gave the Irish legal profession a meeting place and a corporate identity, but it offered no systematic legal instruction. Instead an Irish statute of 1542 required all those wishing to plead at the Irish bar to qualify by attending one of the English Inns of Court for a period, later specified as five years.

Contemporary accounts of the Irish legal profession at all levels were generally unfavourable. There were complaints that Irish lawyers, required to attend an English Inn but not necessarily to be called to the English bar, returned home inadequately trained, and that the lawyers and judges alike were ignorant, partial, and corrupt. Such charges are to some extent supported by anecdotal evidence. In 1582, to cite one famous example, Sir Robert Dillon, chief justice of the Queen's Bench, paid off a score against a fellow judge, Nicholas Nugent, by securing his conviction and execution on a transparently bogus charge of treason. The antagonism between the two men appears to have begun when Nugent had earlier defeated Dillon in the competition to become chief justice of the Common Pleas by the simple expedient of paying the lord chancellor, Sir William Gerrard, £100.[9] Yet it is also necessary to be cautious. Neither corruption nor faction, after all, were rarities in the English legal system of the period. Allegations that Irish lawyers fell short of English standards may in part at least have reflected political antagonisms, at a time when the professional classes and gentry of the Pale were becoming both openly resistant to the state religion and vocal in the defence of their political rights against the encroachments of central government. Most important of all, it might be argued that the quality of the justice administered by the Irish courts was, in the Irish context, less important than their slowly expanding presence. The real task, for most if not all of the sixteenth century, was to persuade the Irish gentry and aristocracy to prefer litigation to private

[7] See below, Ch. 7, 'The Clock of Civil Government'.

[8] Quoted in Colum Kenny, *King's Inns and the Kingdom of Ireland: The Irish Inns of Court 1541–1800* (Dublin, 1992), 50.

[9] Brady, 'The Framework of Government', 36.

violence, and to associate them formally with the workings, however imperfect, of a centralized legal system.

Where the Irish state more clearly failed to develop structures adequate to its needs was in the management of the royal finances. The Irish civil administration was tiny in comparison to its English counterpart: the thirty-four salaried positions listed in 1534 have been contrasted with the 450 that existed at Westminster thirty years earlier. This modest establishment seems to have dealt reasonably effectively with the administrative needs of the truncated Irish lordship inherited by Henry VIII, in the sense that costs remained low and salaries and other payments were made as required.[10] When both revenues and expenditure grew rapidly after 1534, on the other hand, the Irish exchequer proved unable to adapt. Yet despite repeated complaints of corruption, poor record keeping, laxity, and incompetence, there was no overhaul of increasingly antiquated structures and procedures. Crown lands were let with no attempt to evaluate receipts against market value. The customs and other imposts were farmed out for sums well below their nominal value. There was no systematic attempt, as there was in England, to exploit the financial potential of the crown's feudal rights.[11] In the period 1565–85 the nominal rental of crown lands alone stood at over £8,000. The earl of Sussex, outlining his programme for government in the early 1560s, offered optimistic estimates of a potential Irish revenue of £12,000 or even £18,000. Yet actual revenues in the same period averaged only £4,500.

Inadequate administrative structures were of course only part of the problem. The massive underletting of confiscated lands uncovered by the commissioners of inquiry in 1554–6 was part of St Leger's strategy both for building up a lord deputy's party and for oiling the wheels of his policy of gradual reform. Undercollection of taxes, and the otherwise unprofitable farming out of imposts at a fixed rate, must likewise be seen in the context of a government which was only gradually establishing a presence in areas formerly beyond its reach and which continued, even after St Leger's departure, to rely on persuasion as well as force. Most of all it must be recognized that the full nominal, or even the alleged full potential, revenue of the kingdom would still have come nowhere near meeting the new commitments, primarily military, of the crown in Ireland. The £43,000 raised from Irish revenues during 1556–65 fell so far short of total expenditure of more than £322,000 that administrative reform in itself could never have been seen as a feasible solution or even a priority.[12] An antiquated and inadequate financial bureaucracy was thus both a symptom and a partial cause of the chronic financial weakness that lay at the heart of the problems of English government in sixteenth-century Ireland.

[10] Ellis, *Ireland in the Age of the Tudors*, 178–9; *Reform and Renewal*, 105.

[11] Brady, 'The Framework of Government', 33–5.

[12] Brady, *Chief Governors*, 85. These figures, like others for spending within Ireland, are in Irish pounds, worth roughly two-thirds of a pound sterling.

The increasing insolvency of the Irish government was due to the creation, and then the expansion, of the standing army. At the beginning of the sixteenth century the earl of Kildare, drawing partly on his own resources and partly on crown revenues, had maintained a retinue of 120 galloglass and 120 kern. For larger-scale operations, such as the expedition that culminated at Knockdoe, this force could be supplemented by levies raised within the Pale, and by soldiers provided by Gaelic allies. The destruction of the Leinster Fitzgeralds created the need for a more substantial investment. During the 1530s and 1540s chief governors, even during quiet intervals, found it necessary to maintain a force of some hundreds of English troops, as well as locally raised galloglass and kern. Thereafter expanding military commitments pushed troop levels up substantially. Between the 1550s and the 1580s the army generally stood at between 1,000 and 2,500 men, with peaks of around 3,000 in the mid-1560s, and 6,000 at the time of the Desmond rebellion. There were also small forces of kern, falling from around 300 to around 135 after 1575. Overall military spending accounted for some two-thirds of the annual budget.

Although the military establishment thus expanded to a scale that dwarfed the stunted civilian and legal bureaucracy, there was no corresponding development of administrative procedures. Neither Sir Nicholas Bagenal, who became knight marshal in 1547, nor his son, who succeeded him around 1590, made any sustained attempt to discharge their ostensible duties as overall head of the Irish armed forces. The first two occupants of the next most important position, head of the office of ordnance, responsible for training and equipping soldiers, held office for life and were grossly negligent. In the absence of centralized control, responsibility for every aspect of the raising, fitting out, paying, and organizing of soldiers devolved almost entirely on the captains of individual military units. With no effective mechanism for auditing of accounts or regular inspection, captains routinely claimed for dead, missing, or non-existent soldiers, while skimping on uniforms and equipment. Meanwhile successive attempts to reform the system of provisioning the army by entrusting victualling to contractors paid out of public revenues collapsed. Instead soldiers continued to be fed and sheltered through the practice of cess, requisitioning food and lodging from the inhabitants of the area in which they were quartered. Since these were paid for at a fixed rate well below market value, cess became an increasingly contentious issue as army numbers rose. But poor administrative structures made a bad system worse. In this case the failure of bureaucratic reform was to carry a heavy political price.[13]

The most important changes to take place in the framework of Irish government during the sixteenth century were in the management of the localities. In the late fifteenth and early sixteenth centuries a system of local government based on the county already existed in Louth, Meath, Dublin, and Kildare. In the

[13] Brady, 'The Captain's Games'. See below, Ch. 5.

other, more distant shires created during the high point of English expansion, Kilkenny, Tipperary, Waterford, Cork, and Limerick, the outlines of the same system operated under much looser central control.[14] After 1534 the shiring of new areas provided a rough guide to the gradually expanding reach of the Dublin government (see Map 4). The western part of County Meath led the way in 1542, when it became Westmeath. The lordships of O'More and O'Connor Faly, now being planted with settlers of English stock, became Queen's and King's County in 1556. In 1570 the whole of Connacht was shired as the counties of Galway, Mayo, Roscommon, and Sligo. Thomond, which had already had a sheriff for some years, was also annexed to Connacht as County Clare. In the same year Annaly, the lordship of the O'Farrells, became County Longford, while the north-east was shired as Antrim and Down. The rest of Ulster followed, on paper at least, between 1579 and 1591. The last Irish county to be created was Wicklow, where a county created in 1577 had withered away, and was re-established in 1606.[15]

The speed with which government acted to impose boundaries and county names on the landscape beyond the traditional shires reflects its commitment to replicating in Ireland the structures of English society. Yet the gesture can hardly be taken at face value. Even within the Pale the institutions of county government were at times no more than vestigial. The lord chancellor, Sir William Gerrard, arriving at Trim in County Meath for the assizes in 1577, 'found the hall where the sessions had been kept all open, full of dung and cattle in it'. Next day he opened the sessions in hastily arranged alternative premises, but 'I neither found bailiff, crier nor sheriff'.[16] In England, moreover, the central figure in local government was by this time the justice of the peace, recruited from an increasingly wide cross section of the county gentry, and charged with a growing range of functions that made him the effective link between central government and locality. In Ireland justices of the peace were mentioned from the fifteenth century onwards. However, the term was initially no more than an alternative title for the medieval keeper of the peace, whose role was primarily military. By the mid-sixteenth century there appears to have been some clearer concept of a justice on the English model, whose duties included the trial as well as the prosecution of offenders. Yet the office remained of secondary importance, with the sheriff still regarded as the official primarily responsible for local administration. Even where the upper layer of English-style local government existed, in other words, there had been little progress towards extending the system downwards, by recruiting men of property as the collective embodiment of state power. In the newer shires, meanwhile, even the major structures of county government had in many

[14] See above, Ch. 2.

[15] The dates given here follow map 45 and commentary by K. W. Nicholls in *NHI*, ix. Other accounts give somewhat different dates for a number of counties.

[16] Charles McNeill (ed.), 'Lord Chancellor Gerrard's Notes on his Report on Ireland', *Analecta Hibernica*, 2 (1931), 114.

cases little meaning. Where sheriffs were outsiders imposed from the centre, such as military commanders or even men drawn from collateral branches of the dominant Gaelic sept, their intrusion frequently met with resistance. Where they were members of the local elite, they were rarely willing to pay much attention to the commands of a distant crown. In either case taxes remained uncollected, writs ignored, and the forms of the common law for practical purposes unknown.

For the substance as opposed to the form of effective local government it is necessary to look beyond the county to other structures. The first of these was the constable or seneschal. Commencing in a small way from the 1530s, and more systematically from the 1550s, chief governors appointed their own nominees, mainly army commanders, to the traditional feudal offices of constable of a particular castle or seneschal or chief administrator of a district. Officials designated as seneschals were appointed as far afield as Westmeath, Clare, and Galway. In Ulster the constable of Carrickfergus became a central figure in dealing both with the Clandeboye O'Neills and with the Scots of the north-east coast. However, the institution was most important in south Leinster, in intermediate zones such as the Dublin and Wicklow mountains and parts of Counties Carlow and Wexford, where control of a sort had been imposed over Gaelic septs such as the O'Byrnes, the O'Tooles, and the Kavanaghs, but the normal institutions of county government could not be expected to operate. Commanding small bodies of soldiers, and with power to levy others among compliant Gaelic septs, the constables and seneschals were expected to organize local defence, keep forts and other strongholds in repair, and suppress and punish disorder. They were also to compile registers listing or 'booking' the kern and other followers of local lords, who could then be held accountable for any depredations these committed, and to ensure the collection of rents and other dues and services. They discharged these responsibilities largely free of legal restraints, in some cases employing Gaelic principles of collective responsibility and compensation, in others punishing resistance by punitive raids and summary executions. In one incident in 1580 the seneschal of Wexford, Thomas Masterson, killed some sixty of the Kavanaghs in a single ambush.

Military commanders invested with a free hand were hardly likely to be the ideal ambassadors for a new social and political order. The constable of Dungarvan, it was claimed in 1569, surrounded himself with men who enjoyed the company of 'a hawk, a whore, and a hound'.[17] A further problem was the tendency for these agents of central government to become absorbed into the society they were intended to police. Required to establish and maintain their local power, seneschals, like the English colonists of an earlier era, commonly took over many of the prerogatives of a local Gaelic chief. 'The seneschal,'

[17] Quoted in Brady, *Chief Governors*, 274. For seneschals in general see ibid. 271–86; Nicholas Canny, *The Elizabethan Conquest of Ireland: A Pattern Established 1565–76* (Hassocks, 1976), 307–23.

Gerrard explained to the English privy council in 1577, 'although he be English, and tied to govern according to English laws, yet useth he all Irish customs, taking exactings, spendings, impositions and conies, as the Irish captain useth and taketh'.[18] Like their medieval predecessors, moreover, they quickly discovered the importance of forming alliances with local Gaelic lords. One, Robert Pipho in west Wicklow, went so far as to marry an O'Byrne. Before long there were complaints that the judicial and military powers of the office were being abused, as seneschals ignored or even colluded in the depredations of allies while unleashing unjustified violence against others. A further problem was the efforts of seneschals and constables, like other landless adventurers of the period, to establish their own fortunes, spreading alarm and resentment as they uncovered long-defunct royal or monastic titles or otherwise invented legal challenges to the rights of local proprietors. In all of these respects the modicum of central control achieved by the seneschal system came at a substantial political price.

The other major instrument for the transformation of local government was the provincial president and council. The model here came from earlier experiments in Great Britain: the council of the north, re-established in 1525, which had brought a degree of central control to the northern shires and the Scottish border, and the Council for Wales in the Marches, created in 1543. Its extension to Ireland was first proposed in 1562 by the then lord deputy, the earl of Sussex. Sussex had recommended three provincial presidents, for Ulster, Munster, and Connacht. In the event only two were appointed, for Connacht in 1569 and for Munster in 1571. In the case of Ulster Sussex's proposal had been for a more elaborate version of the seneschal scheme that already operated in Gaelic parts of Leinster. The president would have been in effect a military governor, supported by an army of 800 men. In Munster and Connacht, on the other hand, both Sussex's original plan and the scheme eventually adopted envisaged a primarily political and administrative office. The presidents were to have a retinue of only fifty men each. They were to govern as far as possible according to common law, and were to operate in cooperation with a council made up of the lords and bishops of the province. Sussex had even suggested, although unsuccessfully, that there should be an initial period in which the presidency courts would recognize elements of Gaelic law, and allow brehons to plead before them.[19]

This vision of provincial presidents acting as firm but peaceful agents of political and social transformation was not realized. In Munster the presidency was established in the shadow of revolts by members of the houses of both Ormond and Desmond, and continued in an environment transformed by confiscation and plantation. In Connacht, after a period of initial resistance, presidents gained a greater degree of acquiescence from local lords, but continued

[18] McNeill, 'Gerrard's Notes', 116. 'Conies' was presumably another version of 'coyne'.

[19] Canny, *Elizabethan Conquest*, ch. 5; Brady, *Chief Governors*, 137–43; Crawford, *Anglicizing the Government of Ireland*, 307–23.

to make widespread use both of military force and of the summary powers of life and death conferred by martial law.[20] The creation of this new office nevertheless marked an important stage in bringing the two provinces of the south and west more firmly under the control of central government, and in introducing a degree of bureaucratic regulation to their affairs. In particular the courts attached to the two presidencies brought the common law to both regions. Presided over by a chief justice and second justice, and served by a crown attorney and other specialized staff, the presidency courts had authority to try both civil and criminal cases. They were permitted to deal summarily with misdemeanours, but in cases of treason and felony were required to use the full procedure of indictment and trial by jury. Moreover all capital sentences were subject to ratification by the lord deputy. In practice the justice they dealt out was often harsh. The first president of Munster, Sir John Perrot, reported that he had held court sessions 'and at some of them there have been executed for treasons and felonies 28 or 30 at the time'. By April 1573 he claimed to have hanged about 800 persons, 'both by the laws of this realm, and also by martial law'. His successor, Sir William Drury, appointed in July 1576, by which time the excuse of suppressing armed rebellion no longer applied, reported that he had hanged 400 in twenty months.[21] Despite this judicial ruthlessness, however, the surviving records of the Munster court reveal a significant number of Gaelic surnames among the litigants. This implies that some at least of the indigenous population found in the presidency courts—cheaper, procedurally more straightforward, and possibly less open to abuse by the rich and powerful than their common law rivals—an attractive means of resolving disputes or seeking redress of grievances.[22]

*

The greater importance of the privy council, the expanding competence of the courts, the erection of new shires, the appearance of seneschals and provincial councils: all these contributed to the gradual development of a more elaborate machinery of government. Yet the single most important figure in the maintenance of English rule in Ireland, at the century's end as at its beginning, was the chief governor or viceroy. The transition to direct rule had inevitably brought changes. The Kildares, in their heyday, had managed the lordship largely without reference to London, to the extent of raising and spending the king's revenue along with their own. After 1534 chief governors were required to account in detail for both income and expenditure, and to submit to constant scrutiny of their performance by the queen and her advisers. By this time, too, the crown had abandoned the legal fiction of appointing a royal prince as the king's lieutenant, with the real chief governor acting as his deputy. Chief

[20] See below, Ch. 5.

[21] For Perrot, see Canny, *Elizabethan Conquest of Ireland*, 102, and for Drury Ellis, *Ireland in the Age of the Tudors*, 306.

[22] Liam Irwin, 'The Irish Presidency Courts 1569–72', *Irish Jurist*, 12 (1977), 113.

governors after 1534 were deputies directly of the king or queen, although the earl of Sussex in 1560–4, and Essex in 1599, held the more exalted title of lieutenant, as Surrey had done in 1520–2. In other respects, however, what is striking is how little was done to redefine the formal powers of the office in the light of a wholly new political context. Instead the chief governor, regardless of title, continued to be the representative of the absent monarch. He thus had full powers to pardon offences and confirm death sentences, raise troops, declare war, and make peace. If he had now to act under closer supervision from England, moreover, the steadily expanding geographical reach and military commitments of the English administration brought a corresponding expansion in the resources he disposed of, and therefore of the patronage he controlled. 'And verily', William Camden wrote in 1610, 'there is not (look through all Christendom again) any other viceroy that cometh nearer the majesty of a king, whether you respect his jurisdiction or authority or his train, furniture and provision'.[23]

These far-reaching powers made the office of chief governor both attractive and dangerous. It offered extensive opportunities for the display of both administrative and military prowess, for the enrichment of oneself and one's dependants, and for the exercise of patronage. But the holder became personally responsible for every turn of events both within and beyond a frequently contested frontier. In addition the power and resources of the office made it the object of ruthless competition, both among ambitious individuals and between rival factions at court. Individual incumbents, isolated in Ireland, had thus to accept the likelihood of constant unfriendly scrutiny. They had also to cope with the built-in conflict between the demand of successive monarchs and their advisers that Ireland should be kept secure and orderly, and their reluctance to provide the money and troops required to achieve this end. For all of these reasons the Irish viceroyalty proved to be a seductive trap. None of the well-connected and skilful political operators who served as lord deputy or lieutenant between the 1550s and the 1590s emerged with their credit enhanced. Indeed two, Sir John Perrot in 1592 and the earl of Essex in 1601, were to follow their predecessor Lord Leonard Grey in ending their lives as condemned traitors.

In response to these pressures, it has been suggested, the period from the mid-1550s onwards saw a marked change in the style and tactics of Irish chief governors. Aware of their exposed position, Sussex and his successors committed themselves to detailed programmes of reform, precisely costed and to be achieved within a specified time. Such a programme, approved in advance, provided at least some guarantee of continued support, and a degree of autonomy while it was being implemented. But 'programmatic government' also produced a dangerous inflexibility, leaving its advocates ill placed to respond effectively to

[23] Hiram Morgan, 'Overmighty Officers: The Irish Lord Deputyship in the Early Modern British State', *History Ireland*, 7/4 (1999), 17.

anything that lay outside their preconceived plan of action.[24] Equally important, the new style of governor made no attempt to create a local power base. Grey and, much more successfully, St Leger had each sought to rest their administration on a network of allies, clients, and dependants. Their successors, by contrast, relied solely on their credit at court. By doing so they not only cut themselves off from informed experience and advice; they also contributed to a developing estrangement between the representatives of the English crown and those who had formerly been its most loyal local supporters.

All of these points are illustrated in the careers of the two most important chief governors of the mid-sixteenth century. The earl of Sussex had displaced St Leger in 1556 by mobilizing the resources of faction: a grandson of the second duke of Norfolk, he could employ both the influence of the powerful Howard affinity at court and the long-standing hostility between St Leger and Norfolk's Irish associates, the Butlers. As lord deputy he committed himself to a series of campaigns whose guiding principle seemed to be the forceful assertion of royal authority as an end in itself. Continuing the policy of his predecessors, he pushed ahead with plans to settle the territory of the O'Mores and the O'Connors, and launched a new offensive against the Scots of the north-east coast. He also intervened in the Gaelic lordship of Thomond, to uphold the claims of Conor O'Brien, whose claim to succeed to the earldom, as eldest son of the deceased second earl, was challenged by his formidable uncle Sir Donnell. Sussex's insistence that the English law of succession must now override the Gaelic preference for the strongest eligible candidate contrasts with the willingness of his predecessors, in Thomond and elsewhere, to depart from the principle of strict primogeniture; on the other hand, the fact that it was Sir Donnell who had killed his rival's father soon after his installation as second earl makes Sussex's stand rather less dogmatic than has been implied.[25] In Ulster Sussex launched a similarly determined campaign to overthrow Shane O'Neill, who had likewise challenged the recognized successor to the lordship. The crushing tax burden created by these military ventures led him into conflict with representatives of the Pale. But in the end what brought him down was what had earlier brought him to power, the workings of court faction. The queen's favourite Robert Dudley, rival to Sussex's patron Norfolk, secured an inquiry into Irish finances. Its findings, along with the failure of a last campaign against O'Neill in 1563, led to Sussex's recall the following year. Unlike others he was to recover from his Irish setback. From 1568 he was president of the Council of the North, and from 1572 lord chamberlain, his revived credit at court even allowing him to exert an intermittent influence on Irish affairs.

Sussex's immediate successor was Sir Nicholas Arnold, a Dudley client who had headed the enquiry that was the instrument of his predecessor's downfall.

[24] This is the central thesis of Brady, *Chief Governors.*

[25] See the criticisms of 'Sussex's folly' in Brady, *Chief Governors*, 98–9.

In 1565 Arnold was replaced by another ambitious courtier, Sir Henry Sidney, who had come to Ireland with his brother-in-law Sussex but had subsequently transferred his allegiance to another brother-in-law, Dudley. Despite this adroit shift in loyalties, Sidney in practice took over much of the agenda of his temporarily discredited predecessor.[26] In particular he continued to devote a considerable proportion of his energy and resources to the campaigns against Shane O'Neill and against the Ulster Scots. In addition the central element in his policy for reform, the establishment of provincial councils on the model of those that had brought order to Wales and the north of England, echoed ideas put forward by Sussex in 1562. All such plans were overthrown when first Munster then Connacht rose in separate revolts. Sidney was recalled in 1571. His replacement, Sir William Fitzwilliam, ordered to reduce expenditure, pursued a cautious policy, avoiding confrontation with either Gaelic lords or feudal magnates. In 1575 Sidney returned as chief governor. His reappointment came at his own request, apparently inspired by the arguments of his former secretary, Edmund Tremayne, that the provincial presidencies could be made to work, and the finances of the Pale reformed, by converting coyne and livery and other military exactions into cash rents. But his attempts to implement this strategy provoked open revolt in Connacht and a taxpayers' strike in the Pale, leading to his second recall in 1578.

THE DEATH OF SHANE O'NEILL, 2 JUNE 1567

On 31 May 1567 Seán O'Neill, the most important Gaelic warlord of his day, crossed from Tyrone to the east side of the River Bann and made his way, accompanied by a small entourage, to Cushendun on the north-east coast. For the previous fifteen years Shane, as he was generally known to English contemporaries, had dominated the politics of Ulster as ruler of the O'Neills of Tyrone, as well as extending his power south into Connacht and intermittently threatening the northern Pale. A few weeks earlier, however, an ill-planned invasion of the north-west had ended with his catastrophic defeat at Farsetmore, where the O'Donnells and the MacSweenys had shattered his army, killing some 600 men and driving a further 1,300 to their deaths in the rising tidal waters of the River Swilly. In the wake of this disaster O'Neill first considered a theatrical surrender, with a halter round his neck, to the lord deputy, Sir Henry Sidney. His eventual choice, however, was to seek an alliance with the Scottish MacDonnells on the Antrim coast, former allies but most recently his enemies. At Cushendun he engaged in intensive negotiation with the MacDonnell leader, Alasdair Óg.

[26] This is the argument developed by Brady, ibid. 117–19. The alternative view, that Sidney's term of office marked the transition to a radical new policy of aggressive colonization, provides the central theme of Canny, *Elizabethan Conquest of Ireland*.

On the second day, 2 June, talks temporarily broke down. However O'Neill insisted on trying again, and the two leaders, each accompanied by five followers, moved away from the remainder of their forces. But O'Neill had miscalculated. 'Alexander Óg, instead of sweet words, cut his throat with a scian [knife], and the five that was with him went not back to tell no tales'.[27]

Shane O'Neill was in many respects a typical product of the Gaelic political system. He had been born about 1530, the youngest son of Conn Bacach O'Neill, the strong leader of the most powerful of the Ulster lordships. Conn O'Neill's chosen successor was his favourite, Feardorcha, also known as Matthew, the illegitimate product of a liaison with Alison Kelly, wife of a blacksmith in Dundalk. This choice put him at odds with his *tánaiste*, Niall Connallach, and after Niall's death with the *tánaiste*'s son Turlough Luineach O'Neill. It also caused conflict with Conn's own older sons Conn, Turlough, and Brian. In 1551 Conn, finding his authority within the lordship under threat, went to war against Turlough Luineach, against his sons, and even against Matthew. In the vicious civil war that followed, Shane, the obscure younger son, was able to become his father's leading supporter, and to establish his own authority among the O'Neills by his military success. By the end of 1552 Shane's brother Conn was apparently dead, Brian had become his prisoner or dependant, Turlough had sought the protection of the English, and Matthew was in hiding with a handful of followers. As in other cases, and indeed as the succession system was intended to permit, a militarily competent and determined claimant had asserted himself over better placed but less forceful candidates.

All this, however, was only part of the background. The Gaelic political system had a built-in potential for internal conflict of the kind that brought Shane to power. But that potential had been significantly increased by the way in which the English crown had, over the past two decades, encroached on the internal affairs even of the northern Gaelic heartland. The difficulties in maintaining his authority which eventually drove Conn Bacach O'Neill to plunge his lordship into civil war can in part be traced back to one of the great set pieces of St Leger's deputyship: Conn's appearance at Greenwich on 1 October 1542 to pay homage to Henry VIII and accept from his hands a grant of lands and title. It was at this point that Matthew, now styled baron of Dungannon, was recognized as Conn's heir, with all the consequences that were to follow. But there were also other problems, connected with the O'Neill claim to the status of provincial overlord. Conn had initially demanded the title of earl of Ulster, a settlement of his claims to territory bordering the rival O'Donnell lordship, and a recognition of his right to exact tribute from lesser lords like the O'Hanlons and the O'Neills of the Fews. Faced with Henry VIII's refusal to surrender a title long attached to the English crown, he settled for the lesser dignity of earl of Tyrone. But

[27] Ciaran Brady, 'The Killing of Shane O'Neill: Some New Evidence', *Irish Sword*, 15 (1982–3), 123. For an overview of Shane's career see Brady's short study *Shane O'Neill* (Dublin, 1996).

his territorial disputes and claims to overlordship were left to later adjudication by royal commissioners. In the years that followed, Conn found himself caught between incompatible pressures. The Dublin government refused to uphold his claims against O'Donnell and the lesser lords, and regarded his attempts to assert his rights by the traditional methods of punitive raiding as a violation of his new status as the king's loyal servant. At the same time his perceived inability to uphold the traditional dominance of the O'Neill left him open to challenge from within the dynasty. It was against this background that Conn resorted, in 1551, to unilateral military action, and included in his attack Matthew, whose stake in the 1542 settlement aligned him with the English government. And when the lord deputy, Croft, retaliated by imprisoning Conn, it further opened the way to Shane's rise to power as the champion of the O'Neills.

Another important part of the background to Shane's rise to power was the intrusion into Ulster of a second disruptive external influence, the Scots. The Scottish presence on the north-east coast had begun around 1400, when Ian Mór MacDonnell, younger son of the lord of the Isles, married Marjory, daughter of Hugh Bisset, and through her inherited the Glens area of present day County Antrim. By the early sixteenth century the family still retained lands in Kintyre and the southern Hebrides. But its Scottish base had been much eroded, following the forfeiture in 1493 of the lordship of the Isles at the hands of a strengthening Scottish monarchy, and the rising power in the west Highlands of the rival Campbells. In Ulster, on the other hand, the MacDonnells extended their power westwards into the Route, territory of another Scottish family, the MacQuillans, and also south, at the expense of the O'Neills of Clandeboye.[28] The appearance of this new, ruthlessly expansionist force contributed in three ways to the growing instability of Gaelic Ulster. By undermining existing lords it upset the balance of power. Secondly it meant the further introduction of professional fighting men recruited among the surplus population of the western Highlands and Islands. In contrast to the long-serving galloglass the new 'redshanks', so called from the state of their bare legs in the northern climate, were a mobile resource, serving on short-term contracts and transferred quickly from lord to lord. Thirdly the Scottish presence led successive English governments, alarmed at the risk of encirclement, to intervene in the affairs of Ulster with a level of force, and a degree of ruthless violence, well beyond what it normally employed to uphold its authority in Ireland.

The O'Neills had traditionally regarded the Scottish interlopers with hostility. But to Shane, engaged in a fight to the death against multiple better placed rivals, they became a crucial weapon of war. In 1551 and 1552 he joined the

[28] Simon Kingston, 'Delusions of Dal Riada: The Co-ordinates of MacDonnell Power 1461–1550', in P. J. Duffy, David Edwards, and Elizabeth Fitzpatrick (eds.), *Gaelic Ireland: Land, Lordship and Settlement c.1250–c.1650* (Dublin, 2001), 98–114; J. Michael Hill, *Fire and Sword: Sorley Boy MacDonnell and the Rise of Clan Ian Mor 1538–90* (London, 1993).

MacDonnells and also the O'Neills of Clandeboye, traditionally seen by the main branch of the O'Neills as rebellious vassals, in resisting Croft's expeditions to dislodge the Scots from their north eastern strongholds. From this alliance, later reinforced by his marriage to Catherine, daughter of James MacDonnell, came the supply of Scottish mercenaries which Shane, as a landless contender, needed to hold his own in the wars of mid-Ulster. In May 1553, as part of a new round of peace initiatives following Croft's departure, the Dublin government concluded peace with Shane, subsequently offering him tacit recognition by the grant of a royal pension. In 1554, still in alliance with the Scots, he fought off a new attack, this time by Conn Bacach, who had joined with Matthew in an attempt to reassert his authority. In 1558 Shane consolidated his hold on the lordship by arranging Matthew's assassination. Meanwhile he raided smaller lordships to the south to enforce the traditional O'Neill claim to tribute. When Conn Bacach died the following year, a powerless exile in the Pale, Shane was inaugurated in his place as the O'Neill.

Shane's rise to formal control of the lordship posed obvious problems for the English government. Mathew had left two sons, Brian and Hugh, who under the settlement of 1542 were now heirs to the earldom and lands of Tyrone. However, his illegitimate birth provided an adequate pretext for disregarding that part of the 1542 settlement, especially since Shane consistently asserted that Conn had not in fact been the father of Alison Kelly's child. And indeed the English privy council, in 1559, gave orders for Shane, as 'the person legitimate in blood' and now in what it somewhat fancifully described as 'quiet possession' of his father's estates, to be recognized as his father's successor and earl of Tyrone.[29] The lord deputy, Sussex, on the other hand, insisted the crown must uphold the claims of Mathew's heirs against the disloyal Shane. As in the case of Thomond, this insistence was not necessarily as self-destructively obstinate as has been claimed: there was a good case to be made for the view that to ratify Shane's blood-soaked ascent made nonsense of the idea of converting Gaelic warlords into law-abiding nobles. But the result was a damaging inconsistency. Sussex campaigned unsuccessfully against Shane during 1557–8, engaged unwillingly in negotiation in September 1559, and made war again, with equal lack of success, during 1560–1. In January 1562, following detailed negotiations conducted through the earl of Kildare, Shane travelled to London under safe conduct to make his submission to the queen and present his case.

Shane's appearance at the court of Elizabeth I was, superficially, an encounter between wholly different worlds. Arriving with his escort of axe-wielding galloglass, their shirts dyed with saffron fixed with urine, the barbarian warlord prostrated himself at the queen's feet while he delivered a long wailing lament in Irish for his crimes against her. Modern accounts, however, suggest a more sober assessment. Contemporary reports of Shane's extravagant behaviour—his

[29] Brady, *Chief Governors*, 99.

prodigious drinking, his ravenous sexual appetite, and his bestial cruelty—may or may not have had a foundation in fact.[30] But his challenge to English interests depended, not on any supposed role as the embodiment of a rebellious Gaelic culture, but rather on a capacity to modernize and adapt his Ulster inheritance. His heavy reliance on Scottish mercenaries, itself significant as a professionalization of warfare, was financed by systematic efforts to develop the economic resources of his territory. These had included encouraging farmers to migrate from the Pale to Ulster, bringing with them the skills of a tillage-based economy, and drawing on contacts with a County Meath family, the Flemings, to introduce ploughs and other equipment.[31] Shane further increased his military manpower by another break with tradition, looking beyond the traditional classes of fighting men to recruit and train the peasantry of the region, the despised churls, as soldiers. Nor did he himself conform to the stereotype of the reckless warrior: reports of his performance ('the last that would give the charge upon his foes, and the first that would flee') suggest that his victories rested on his qualities as a tactician rather than a swordsman.[32]

Shane, moreover, did not look to warfare alone. He also opened negotiations in 1566 with Charles IX of France, offering to give his allegiance to the French crown if Charles would assist him in driving out the English heretics and restoring the Catholic faith. Shane's credentials as a Counter-Reformation warrior were, to say the least, dubious: in the very same year he showed his disapproval of a sermon by Richard Creagh, Catholic archbishop of Armagh, on the duty of loyalty to the crown, by burning the cathedral at Armagh, an act that led to his double excommunication, by Creagh and by his Protestant counterpart. It is in any case possible that his letter to Charles IX was intended more to impress the English, who intercepted it, than the French themselves. But even this tactic confirms Shane's political sophistication, and his awareness of a larger diplomatic context.

Alternative accounts of Shane's London visit likewise suggest a more nuanced picture. Whatever the extravagant display he indulged in at his first appearance, in the negotiations that followed he presented a precise and carefully argued defence of his rights under the 1542 settlement. He also appears to have impressed contemporaries by the facility with which, aided by a generous loan from the queen, he adopted the dress and manners of a courtier.[33] Nor was this necessarily the only occasion on which he did so. An inventory of clothing seized by the lord deputy after his death lists gowns, doublets, and trousers, comprising some twenty items in all, including such garments as 'one night gown of black velvet

[30] Brady, *Shane O'Neill*, 3–7, carefully sifts the limited evidence available.

[31] N. P. Canny, 'Hugh O'Neill and the Changing Face of Gaelic Ulster', *Studia Hibernica*, 10 (1970), 28–9.

[32] Sir George Carew, quoted in Hill, *Fire and Sword*, 80.

[33] Ciaran Brady, 'Shane O'Neill Departs from the Court of Queen Elizabeth', in S. J. Connolly (ed.), *Kingdoms United? Great Britain and Ireland since 1500* (Dublin, 1999), 13–28.

laid with parchment lace of gold and buttons of gold and furred with black connye [rabbit fur]', as well as 'one parliament robe with a coat belonging to the same' and a 'Spanish jerkin edged with parchment lace of gold'.[34] All this would suggest that Shane, no less than other Gaelic lords, was able to hold his own at the level of aristocratic display as well as in the ambushes and skirmishes by which political power was acquired and retained. Indeed it must raise the possibility that Shane's dramatic performance at the feet of the queen was less a meeting of widely separated cultures than an artfully contrived piece of theatre.

The most direct indication of Shane's outlook and ambitions is provided by his letters to the Dublin administration, written by his secretary in both Latin and Irish, but signed in his own hand 'mise [I am] O'Neill'.[35] Here he expressed an uncompromising commitment to the defence of his dynastic rights and what he considered his territory. 'Even if the best of the Clan O'Neill were dead together with myself', he told Baron Slane, head of his allies the Fleming family, 'such of them as remained alive would not be enroached upon, for it was often attempted to take possession of their country, but it was never yet accomplished.' There was also a clear sense of ethnic distinctions. Slane, a Pale nobleman, was addressed as one of 'the chiefs of the foreigners of Ireland [*maithibh Gall na h-Eirinn*]', while Sussex was ordered to withdraw his soldiers from Armagh, 'for as long as there shall be one son of a Saxon in my territory against my will' he would offer no settlement. Yet all of this went along with Shane's extravagant professions of devotion to 'my mistress the queen', and assertions of his burning desire 'to present my person before her serene highness'. There was even the promise 'that I might bring the wild countries which are under me to civilization and to goodness, and that I myself, and those who should come after me, might devote our time to the honour and service of the queen, and of the servant who should be appointed in Ireland by her'. Such decorative flourishes need not necessarily be taken at face value. But Shane's ability to appropriate the language of both courtly deference and English cultural superiority for his own purposes is further evidence of his political sophistication. At the same time the letters as a whole, with their superficially contradictory mixture of defiance and submission, make clear that his ambitions were framed wholly within the traditional assumptions of the Gaelic political world, where territorial self-aggrandizement, and a strong sense of Gaelic ethnic identity, coincided with a pragmatic acceptance of the English crown and its representatives as legitimate, and even potentially dominant, participants in a system of competing lordships.

Against this revised background it becomes much easier to see how negotiation with Shane as putative earl of Tyrone could seem a credible alternative to fighting him on his home ground. But his London mission quickly became entangled

[34] HMC, *De L'Isle and Dudley MSS*, ii. 6.

[35] John O'Donovan (ed.), 'Original Letters in the Irish and Latin Languages by Shane O'Neill, Prince of Tyrone', *Ulster Journal of Archaeology*, 5 (1857), 262–73.

in the politics of not two, but three kingdoms. Shane's appearance had been sponsored by the earl of Kildare, the Irish client of Lord Robert Dudley. Dudley's rival at court, William Cecil, therefore worked behind the scenes to sabotage the negotiations. Instead he proposed taking advantage of recent divisions in Scotland, where the Protestant earl of Argyll had appealed for support against the pro-French party: Argyll was to detach the MacDonnells, whose Scottish head was married to Argyll's sister, from their alliance with Shane, who could then be crushed. In May Shane returned to Ireland unsatisfied, and was soon plundering the lands of his Ulster rivals and rampaging along the northern borders of the Pale. Within a few months, however, signs that the MacDonnells were instead moving towards the pro-French party round Mary Stewart, along with further shifts in the balance of power at court, dictated another abrupt reversal. Now Shane was to be appeased to clear the way for a campaign to drive the Scots completely from the north-east. On 11 September 1563 Kildare and the former lord chancellor Thomas Cusack concluded a treaty with Shane at Drumcree, by which the government undertook to secure legislation which would extinguish the Dungannon title and clear the way for his recognition as earl of Tyrone. On this basis Shane, in 1564, launched a campaign against his former MacDonnell allies, and after some reversals inflicted a devastating defeat at Glenshesk on 2 May 1565. The very scale of his victory, however, meant that he himself once again became the main threat to English interests in Ulster. Dudley and Kildare, in a shameless reversal, now campaigned for Shane's destruction, to be accomplished by the new deputy, Sir Henry Sidney. Sidney established a fort at Derry, and boasted of having shortened O'Neill's Christmas by a surprise midwinter raid into the heart of Tyrone. But he was still vainly pursuing significant military advantage when Shane came to grief at the hands of the O'Donnells at Farsetmore.

What emerges from this complicated narrative of alliances made and broken is more than anything else the dominance on all sides of pragmatic and short-term objectives. Shane O'Neill's ambition was clearly a limited one: to be the O'Neill, and to exercise his dynasty's traditional authority over the lesser lords of Ulster. He also demanded his father's title of earl, though how far he saw this as valuable in its own right, and how far simply as a guarantee of English recognition, remains uncertain. To achieve these aims Shane was willing to make war on his own family and fellow Gaels, to ally himself with the Scottish intruders along the north-east coast, to become a pensioner of the English crown, and even to become England's instrument against his former Scottish allies. Nor did other Gaelic lords behave any differently. None of the wars waged in Ulster during the 1550s and 1560s were fought by English soldiers alone. Croft, in his campaigns against the Scots in 1551 and 1552, demanded and got contributions of men from most of the Ulster chiefs. Later campaigns against Shane, by Sussex and Sidney, likewise involved cooperation with lesser figures such as Maguire and O'Reilly, as well as support from the main provincial rivals of the O'Neills, the

O'Donnells. English policy in the region thus consisted of a constant juggling of friends and enemies: the abrupt transitions of 1563–5, when Shane was first an opponent, then an ally against the Scots, then once again the main threat to English interests, were just the most extreme example.

Against this background the fatal encounter at Cushendun in 1567 can also be better understood. The bloody damage they had suffered at Shane's hands at Glenflesk had left the MacDonnells with good reason to seek revenge. Meanwhile there were clear though imprecise signals that the English government might be willing to reward their assistance in his downfall. Yet when Shane, his army shattered by the defeat at Farsetmore, turned to them in desperation with offers of a new alliance, their reaction was level-headed. The two days of negotiation indicate that they considered carefully what he had to offer. Only then, when they had decided it was not enough, did they decide to safeguard themselves against any possible revival in his fortunes, and perhaps gain some favour in English eyes, by cutting his throat.

FRONTIER WARS

'If Shane settle', Sussex told the queen's principal secretary in 1561, 'all be overthrown; if Shane be overthrown, all is settled.'[36] In fact, Shane's death settled almost nothing. William Piers, the constable of Carrickfergus, arrived on the scene four days after the killing to exhume the hastily buried body and send the head, preserved in salt, to Dublin, where it was exhibited on a pole at the castle. Almost immediately, however, Turlough Luineach O'Neill, son of Conn Bacach's discarded *tánaiste*, was proclaimed O'Neill in succession to Shane. Meanwhile the leader of the MacDonnells, Somhairle Buidhe ('Yellow [haired] Sorley', widely but misleadingly anglicized as Sorley Boy), had begun to reoccupy the family's east coast strongholds and to rebuild their armed forces. Exactly what promises had been made to encourage the MacDonnells to act against Shane remains unclear. But it seems to have stopped short of an undertaking to legitimize their presence in Ireland. The queen, two months after the killing, told Sidney that they were to be 'well rewarded according to such promises as you made', and then forcibly expelled from Ulster.[37] Faced with this continued hostility Sorley Boy looked for allies. In 1568 Turlough Luineach O'Neill married Agnes

[36] Quoted in Brady, *Chief Governors*, 78.

[37] Hill, *Fire and Sword*, 121. Hill's detailed review of what can be reconstructed of the negotiations (pp. 111–13) concludes that the government carefully stopped short of any definite promise to accept the Scots presence. Brady, 'Killing of Shane O'Neill', 120, suggests that Piers may have given some such assurance. Brady also speculates that the claim that Shane had provoked his own death by drunkenly boasting of how he would handle Mary queen of Scots in bed, bizarrely enshrined in the parliamentary statute posthumously declaring him a traitor, was intended to cover up whatever English involvement there had been in the killing.

Campbell, daughter of the third earl of Argyll and widow of James MacDonnell. Around the same time Agnes's daughter, Finola MacDonnell, nicknamed 'Inion Dubh' or dark daughter, married Hugh O'Donnell, lord of Tyrconnell. The MacDonnells were thus linked to the two leading Gaelic dynasties in Ulster. In addition Agnes Campbell and Finola MacDonnell, both formidable political operators in their own right, considerably strengthened the military resources of their new husbands by each bringing with them a substantial dowry of redshanks.

These were alliances based on expediency, and over the next few years all parties, English, Scottish, and Irish, manoeuvred to improve their position. Sorley Boy's aim seems to have been to make Turlough Luineach a problem for the English without allowing him to become too dangerous a rival. He gave limited support to O'Neill's attacks on the Pale during 1569–70, but then cut off his supply of redshanks, forcing him to make peace in 1571. The English for their part had fixed on the idea of establishing colonies along the east coast, thus driving a wedge between Gaelic Ulster and Gaelic Scotland. In 1572 Sir Thomas Smith, Queen Elizabeth's principal secretary, received a grant of land in Clandeboye and the Ards peninsula. In August his son arrived in the Ards with an advance party of 100 men. The problem with this choice of location, however, was that the territory concerned was held, neither by the Scots nor by Turlough Luineach, but by Sir Brian MacPhelim, head of the Clandeboye O'Neills, whose past record was mainly that of a supporter of English interests. When he protested, the queen gave instructions that he should be allowed to retain his land, while Smith promised to be a good neighbour. These responses, often written off as empty promises, may simply have rested on the assumption that there was enough land to go round, given the low density of population in the region as a whole. But if so Sir Brian refused to be reassured. Allied to Turlough Luineach he made open war both on Smith's colony and on the English in general, burning part of Carrickfergus in spring 1573 and striking south to Dundalk and beyond. Faced with this onslaught, as well as obstruction from the lord deputy, Fitzwilliam, who resented this intrusion on his authority, the colony wilted. In October 1573 an Irish servant shot and killed the younger Smith; his body was subsequently boiled and fed to the dogs. Two further expeditions, one in 1574 of 200 men, failed to rescue the project.

The immediate response of the crown to the resistance of Sir Brian and Turlough Luineach was to seek an alliance with the third regional power. In April 1573 Sorley Boy received a patent granting him the rights of a subject, in exchange for a promise to assist in asserting the crown's rights over the Irish of Ulster. The following month, however, the earl of Essex received a grant of lands comprising Clandeboye, the Glynns, the Route, and Rathlin Island. His instructions, by his own account, were to remove the Scots but to leave the native Irish in peace. This grant added further to the already conflicting claims within the region. It took in not only lands held by Sorley Boy and the MacDonnells, but also some already granted to Smith, and at the same time guaranteed to Sir

Brian. However, Smith was willing to cede some of his theoretical holding in exchange for progress towards bringing the region under control. There was also the possibility that one of the three local interests involved, Sir Brian, Turlough Luineach, and the Scots, might be willing to support a colonization at the expense of the others. During 1574 Essex negotiated intermittently with all three.[38]

Essex had assured the queen that he 'would not willingly imbrue his hands with more blood than the necessity of the cause requireth'.[39] It was in retrospect an ominous undertaking. In November 1574 he apparently came to terms with Sir Brian, only to stage a surprise attack at the end of a celebratory feast, slaughtering between one and two hundred of the Clandeboye O'Neills. Sir Brian himself, with his wife and his brother, were sent to Dublin and later executed as traitors. The following spring, aided by troops from the Pale, Essex mounted an expedition into the Blackwater valley, forcing Turlough O'Neill to offer his submission. He then turned towards the Glynns, but Sorley Boy avoided giving battle. Essex withdrew his main force to Drogheda, but then launched a surprise attack on Rathlin Island. Three ships commanded by the naval adventurer Francis Drake set out from Carrickfergus on 20 July, carrying around 380 men under Captain John Norris. The castle on the island was garrisoned by only fifty soldiers. However, the MacDonnells had also moved their women and children there for safety. After the castle wall had been breached, the constable surrendered on the promise that his life and that of his wife and child would be spared, 'the lives of all the rest within to stand upon the courtesy of the soldiers'. According to Essex his men, 'being moved and much stirred with the loss of their fellows who were slain, and desirous of revenge, made request or rather pressed to have the killing of them'. Given that the attackers had lost a total of three men, this reads like a rather thin attempt at justification. Yet Essex's account of what happened next shows no apparent trace of discomfort: 'There were slain that came out of the castle of all sorts 200 and presently news is brought me out of Tyrone that they be occupied still in killing and have slain that they have found in caves and in the cliffs of the sea to the number of 300 or 400 more.' A spy subsequently reported that Sorley Boy, watching from the mainland, 'was likely to run mad for sorrow . . . tearing and tormenting himself and saying that he then lost all that ever he had'.[40]

Neither these atrocities, nor the military campaigns that accompanied them, brought any significant gains. With support for his project rapidly disappearing, Essex returned to Ireland in March 1576 with the new title earl marshal, but died there six months later. By this time Sidney was attempting to negotiate

[38] For general accounts of these Ulster ventures see Hiram Morgan, 'The Colonial Venture of Sir Thomas Smith in Ulster 1571–1575', *Historical Journal*, 28 (1985), 261–78; Hill, *Fire and Sword*, chs. 7, 8.

[39] Quoted in Richard Bagwell, *Ireland under the Tudors*, 3 vols. (London 1885–90), ii. 243.

[40] Essex to the queen, 31 July 1575, *CSPI* 1571–1575, rev. Mary O'Dowd (Dublin and Kew, 2000), 881–2; Essex to Walsingham, 31 July 1575, ibid. 883.

new agreements with both Sorley Boy and Turlough Luineach. Over the next ten years Sorley Boy, aided by a ready supply of redshanks, continued to defend the MacDonnell territories against every attempt to dislodge him. Eventually, in 1586, he received a grant from the English crown of the greater part of the Route, with the constableship of Dunluce Castle; his nephew Angus MacDonnell, eighth lord of Dunyveg and overall head of the family, received a grant of the Glynns. Meanwhile Turlough Luineach retained his position as the leading power in Ulster. Sidney's memoirs present him as a drunken buffoon, visiting Dublin to spend £400 on a three-day debauch and protesting his devotion to the queen 'as reverently (as his little good manners did instruct him)'. The deputy was far more impressed by Agnes Campbell, 'a grave, wise and well-spoken lady, both in Scots-English and French, and very well mannered'.[41] Turlough Luineach may well have benefited from his wife's greater sophistication, although it is also important to remember that her interests, given her MacDonnell links, did not always exactly coincide with his. Whatever the precise means, however, he steered a skilful course, adroitly exploiting the shifts in both Irish and Scottish politics to move in and out of peace and war with the English administration. The English, for their part, having failed to force an entry into the province, had no choice but to accept, for what they were worth, his repeated short-term submissions.

The other region which saw a similar clash between English and Gaelic forces in the 1560s and 1570s was the midland territory of the O'Connors of Offaly and the O'Mores. Bellingham, Croft, and St Leger had made grants of land, on various terms, to soldiers and to some civilians; however, there had been no progress, up to the mid-1550s, towards the more general plantation that had been projected. An Irish act of parliament in 1557 provided what was in effect a new start, dividing the land into two shires, to be called the Queen's and King's Counties, after Mary and her husband, Philip II of Spain, and declaring both to be entirely in the possession of the crown. The two military settlements were likewise renamed, Fort Governor becoming Philipstown, and Fort Protector Maryborough. Sussex had already proposed a plantation of two-thirds of the area, leaving the western one-third to the native proprietors. However, negotiations broke down and the O'Mores and O'Connors rose in arms. One settler reported that he had lost seventeen men in defending his property. Order of a sort had been restored by the end of the year, but repeated commissions of martial law testified to continuing tension. During 1563–4 Sussex began systematically to issue leases to settlers. The O'Mores and O'Connors attacked again, provoking a campaign of ruthless repression. According to one account at least ninety O'Connors and thirty-five O'Mores had been killed or executed by crown forces.

As in Ulster, this was no simple war of English against Irish. Twenty-nine out of a total of eighty-eight grants of land in King's and Queen's Counties were

[41] Ciaran Brady (ed.), *A Viceroy's Vindication: Sir Henry Sidney's Memoir of Service in Ireland 1556–78* (Cork, 2002), 98–9, 76.

to Gaelic Irishmen. Most of these were to members of smaller septs formerly subordinate to the O'Mores and O'Connors, such as the O'Dempseys, O'Kellys, and MacEvoys. This conversion of former clients into independent freeholders was a logical means towards the end of transforming a society of feudal warlords into an orderly hierarchy under the crown; from another point of view, it constituted a classic strategy of divide and rule. Its most spectacular beneficiary was Owen MacHugh O'Dempsey, rewarded for his service as commander of kern under Sussex with an estate of over 3,000 acres. He continued to serve the crown until killed by an O'More in 1578; a son, Terence, was to serve as sheriff of King's County, and to be knighted by the earl of Essex for his service during Elizabeth's last great Irish war, during 1594–1603. Nor were the O'Mores and O'Connors wholly excluded. One of the three main branches of the O'Mores received a substantial grant. Members of a second, having submitted to Sidney in 1566, received a token portion, and their descendants were later employed in suppressing continued resistance in the area. In Offaly, likewise, some O'Connors received land and fought on the side of the government against their dispossessed kinsmen.

The next major challenge to the midlands settlement arose from something of a special case. Rory 'Caoch' O'More had been the recognized lord of the Leix until his brother Gilpatrick MacConaill killed him in 1546. It was Gilpatrick who had died as an imprisoned rebel in 1548, leading to the confiscation of the family lands. To be dispossessed for the offences of a usurper was clearly an anomaly. Two of Rory Caoch's sons chose to pursue their case in England. Their mother, Rory Caoch's second wife, had been a Butler, and they thus had the patronage of the earl of Ormond. Rory Óg, a son of Rory Caoch's first marriage, took a different course. Fostered by the O'Byrnes of Wicklow, he was for a time a soldier in the service of the local seneschal, Francis Cosby. In 1571, however, he assembled supporters and proclaimed himself chief of the O'Mores. By 1573, after unsuccessful attempts at negotiation, he had launched an all-out assault on the settlers, in concert with the O'Connors and his fosterers, the O'Byrnes. After two years of destructive fighting, Rory submitted to Sidney in November 1575, but in March 1577 he joined Cormac O'Connor in a new offensive, dramatically raising the stakes by advancing into the Pale, where he burnt the town of Naas. Rory Óg was hunted down and killed in June 1578, but the cycle of raids and reprisals continued for several years.

The midlands war was a particularly vicious episode. This was in part inherent in the nature of the conflict, where settler and native populations did not merely confront one another militarily, but occupied the same limited territory. It also reflected the crown's strategy of allocating land to soldier colonists, who were then left to organize their own defence by whatever means they chose. Men like Francis Cosby, credited with killing between thirty and forty Irishmen in hand to hand combat during the siege of Maryborough, were hardly likely to show restraint in the face of armed attack, and the repeated issue to them of commissions of martial law largely removed any legal control on their actions. A petition submitted in 1559, probably by Cormac O'Connor, complained that 'if it were once spoken of a soldier or captain's mother, it was a sufficient quarrel for the captain to rob, prey, and kill the person accused and all his tenants without other authority or commission than the captain's allegation'. A particularly notorious episode of arbitrary violence took place in March 1578, when the settler leaders Sir Francis Cosby and Robert Hartpole, accompanied by their ally O'Dempsey, agreed to meet a party of O'Mores and O'Connors at Mullaghmast in County Kildare. As the Irishmen arrived 'they were surrounded on every side by four lines of soldiers and cavalry, who proceeded to shoot and slaughter without mercy, so that not a single individual escaped, by flight or force'. The number killed was put by one set of annals at seventy-four. Another Gaelic source recorded the killing during the hunt for Rory Óg of Rory's wife, 'and with her have been killed women and boys, and humble folk, and people young and old, who according to all seeming deserved not to be put to the sword'.[42]

With the benefit of hindsight these local wars, in Ulster and the midlands, can be seen as part of a downward progression, as the strategy of gradual assimilation adopted in the 1540s was slowly undermined, and the way was prepared for the descent into total war that took place in the 1590s. Episodes like Essex's massacre of the Clandeboye O'Neills, the slaughter on Rathlin Island, and the ambush at Mullaghmast, recorded in the Gaelic annals as outstanding instances of cruelty and bad faith, created a widespread distrust of Englishmen and English government. For their part English audiences became habituated to tales of Irish rebellion and murder. In this respect *Image of Ireland*, the volume of woodcuts produced in 1581 by the English engraver John Derrick, may well have been of particular importance. Published to celebrate the exploits of Sir Henry Sidney, Derrick's images of orderly ranks of breastplated pikemen in combat with long-haired, mantled raiders provided a vivid depiction of Ireland as a battleground between English civility and native barbarism and treachery.[43] From a longer historical perspective, likewise, the resistance of the midland Irish can be seen as the first in what was to be a long series of similar conflicts. Rory Óg O'More, the vengeful figure haunting his lost ancestral lands, is a forerunner of the wood kern who terrorized early seventeenth-century Ulster settlers, and of the tories and rapparees of Restoration Ireland.

For all their contemporary and later resonances, however, the Ulster and midland campaign must be placed in a wider context. Both regions were for specific reasons zones of direct confrontation: the midlands because they bordered on the Pale, and Ulster because of its proximity to Scotland. As such they must be

[42] Vincent Carey, 'The End of the Gaelic Political Order: The O'More Lordship of Laois 1536–1603', in P. G. Lane and William Nolan (eds.), *Laois: History and Society* (Dublin, 1999), 225–6, 246.

[43] Vincent Carey, 'John Derricke's *Image of Irelande*, Sir Henry Sidney, and the Massacre at Mullaghmast, 1578', *IHS* 31 (1999), 305–27.

contrasted with other regions, in which relations between English and Gaelic Irish were quite different. To see this it is only necessary to look at the memoirs of Derrick's hero, Sir Henry Sidney. Side by side with an account of the hunting down of Rory Óg occur a variety of other comments. The chief of the O'Haras, whom he met in 1566, 'fell in such love and liking of Englishmen and English government as he vowed to go into England to behold the majesty of our sovereign, which he performed'. Elsewhere Sidney praised 'the good knight Sir Hugh O'Donnell', lord of Tir Conaill, whom he himself had knighted. In the Dublin and Wicklow mountains, where St Leger had begun his programme twenty-five years earlier, the Kavanaghs, MacMurroughs, and Kinsellas 'lived as loyally as any people in the shire ground . . . obedient, quiet and rich'. Meeting the nobility and gentry of Munster at Cork, where he celebrated Christmas in 1575, he 'found such humbleness in them, and willingness to become English, and accordingly to live under English law, and by the same be defended, each weaker from his stronger neighbour'. On another occasion he launched a punitive raid against Art MacMahon, who had killed the son of Sir Hugh Magennis, 'as towardly a young gentleman as ever I knew of the Irishry'. In this case Sidney's enthusiasm was echoed in another account, written more than a decade later, in which Sir Hugh was reported to be the most civil of all the Irish of east Ulster, having abolished the custom of tanistry and wearing English dress on every festival day.[44]

Such glowing accounts need not necessarily be taken at face value. Sidney was concerned to talk up his successes as diplomat as well as soldier. Hence it suited him to ignore the motives of expediency that might lie behind the compliance he valued so highly. To a lesser lord like O'Hara or Magennis, the forces of the English crown were a welcome counterweight to the overlordship claimed by the O'Donnells or the O'Neills. But the point remains that the violent clashes in Ulster and the midlands represented only one extreme form of the relationship that could exist between Gaelic Ireland and a slowly expanding English state.

Another Gaelic lord singled out for praise in Sidney's account was Sir Barnaby Fitzpatrick, baron of Upper Ossory, 'my particular sworn brother, and the faithfullest man for the queen's service for martial action that ever I found of that country'. The MacGillpatricks had traditionally been allies of the Kildares.[45] But in 1532 their lord, Brian, had astutely transferred his allegiance to the crown. In return he became the first Irish chief to be ennobled and took his seat, as baron, in the parliament of 1541. Two years later he sent his son Barnaby, then aged about 8, to the English court, where he was raised alongside the future Edward VI. The young Barnaby graduated from the position of whipping boy, the playmate appointed to receive the corporal punishment that could not properly be inflicted on the juvenile royal himself, to the place of gentleman of the young king's privy chamber, and then to that of diplomat (and spy) on a mission to Paris in 1552.

44 Brady, *Viceroy's Vindication*, 46–7, 48, 91–2, 85, 101; *Carew MSS 1575–1588*, 436–7.

45 For the names Fitzpatrick and MacGillpatrick see above, p. 125 n. 2.

In 1554 he returned to Ireland to effectively seize control of Upper Ossory from his father. He subsequently served in Scotland, where he was knighted in 1560 for his services, campaigned against Shane O'Neill in Ulster, and waged merciless war against the O'Connors and O'Mores. It was his men who killed Rory Óg O'More in 1578. Yet for all his court upbringing and pro-English loyalties, Sir Barnaby's local power remained that of a Gaelic lord. He continued to draw his wealth primarily from large-scale cattle rearing, administered his territory under brehon law, and maintained kern and galloglass by means of coyne and livery. He also pursued his family's long-standing feud with the Butlers of Ormond by the traditional methods of raiding and plunder. Queen Elizabeth responded by asking how one 'who hath been so civilly brought up here within our realm from his young years' could have been guilty of such 'barbarous acts'. Her officials in Ireland, on the other hand, were unwilling to question the doings of such a valuable ally.[46]

MacGillpatrick's active collaboration, like that of the O'Dempseys and of the pro-government O'Mores and O'Connors, was the survival strategy of a Gaelic lord who found himself in close proximity to an expanding English state. Those further away from the centres of English power could get away with a much more limited level of accommodation. Donal McCarthy Mór, favoured by Sussex, was knighted in 1558 and in 1565 travelled to Westminster to pass the formalities of surrender and regrant and receive the title of earl of Clancare. A mere four years later he joined in the rebellion launched by members of the Butler family, but was pardoned and confirmed in his title and estates. Predictably, lesser branches of the McCarthys, McCarthy Reagh and McCarthy of Muskerry, over whom McCarthy Mór claimed to be overlord, more consistently aligned themselves with the crown. In 1577 Sidney wrote to his son in England, and to the privy council, asking them to assist Sir Cormac MacTadhg MacCarthy, the sheriff of County Cork, who a few years earlier had distinguished himself in the crown's service during the first Desmond rebellion. MacCarthy, Sidney warned, 'is not the best courtier, for his bringing up has been somewhat homely', but he was a firm supporter of English government, 'my good friend and a special man'.[47]

The O'Briens of Thomond, like MacCarthy Mór, trod an uneven path. Conor O'Brien had succeeded his murdered father as third earl in 1558 only with English support. Yet in 1570 he staged a brief rebellion against the demands of the president of Connacht, before submitting and receiving a pardon. A Gaelic poet, around 1574, wrote a satirical piece berating Thomond for his withdrawal of patronage, and threatening to report to the authorities the earl's continued

[46] Brady (ed.), *A Viceroy's Vindication*, 100. For Elizabeth's comment see David Edwards, 'The MacgiollaPadraigs (Fitzpatricks) of Upper Ossory 1532–1641', in Lane and Nolan, *Laois*, 92. See also idem, 'Collaboration without Anglicisation: The MacGiollapadraig Lordship and Tudor Reform', in Duffy etal., *Gaelic Ireland*, 77–97.

[47] HMC, *De L'Isle and Dudley MSS*, ii. 53. For McCarthy as sheriff of County Cork, and his role in the Desmond rebellion, see below, p. 269.

adherence to Catholicism and to the levying of prohibited Gaelic exactions. It was left to the fourth earl, Donough, a court-educated Protestant who succeeded his father in 1581, to complete the family's journey to unqualified loyalism. Both Clancare and the third earl of Thomond were present, along with others, at the parliaments held during the reign of Elizabeth. Sidney recalled how Clancare, appearing at the parliament of 1569–71 to make a public submission, first spoke 'in English in far other and better terms than I thought he could', but then asked leave to repeat his speech in Irish 'for that he saw many in the chamber in Irish mantles'.[48]

The response of the Gaelic political elite to pressures for political and cultural conformity may also be glimpsed, to a limited extent, in the poetry of the period. A striking poem, *Fúbún fúibh, a shluagh Gaoidheal* [shame on you, O Gaels], apparently dating from the 1540s, offers clear evidence of early opposition to the whole process initiated by St Leger's policy of surrender and regrant.[49] In quick succession it denounces the most prominent of those who have come to terms with the crown: the MacCarthys, the O'Briens, Manus O'Donnell, and O'Neill, who 'has exchanged in foolish submission his kingship for the Ulster earldom'. A penultimate stanza links submission to foreign authority, changes in culture, and the Reformation:

> Shame on the grey foreign gun
> Shame on the golden chain
> Shame on the court without the language of the poets,[50]
> Shameful is the denial of Mary's son.

However, it is important to recognize that these multiple betrayals are contrasted with the virtues of O'Carroll, to whom the poet declares himself bound by oaths, apart from whom 'there is not in all Ireland at the present time one person worthy to be called a man'. During the 1540s Calvach O'Carroll was struggling to defend his position in Offaly against the English-backed Tadhg, created Baron of Ely in 1551–2. There is thus at least the possibility that the ringing denunciation of national betrayal represented the sort of expedient use of national rhetoric

[48] Brady, *Viceroy's Vindication*, 80.

[49] Brian Ó Cuív, 'A Sixteenth-Century Political Poem', *Éigse*, 15 (1973–4), 261–76. The poem survives in a seventeenth-century manuscript; the case of dating it to the 1540s rests on the wealth of contemporary references. Nicholas Canny, *Making Ireland British 1580–1650* (Oxford, 2001), 421, argues that its sentiments are so out of line with those of other sixteenth-century texts that it is more likely to be a seventeenth-century composition, projecting the political sentiments of the Counter-reformation backwards onto the events of the 1540s. But would any Catholic propagandist, writing in the aftermath of the Nine Years War, have felt able to denounce O'Neill and O'Donnell in these terms?

[50] This adopts the suggestion that *béarla*, by the seventeenth century used to mean the English language, is here used in its earlier sense of meaning simply 'speech', and is furthermore a shorthand for *Béarla na bhFileadh*: see Marc Caball, *Poets and Politics: Reaction and Continuity in Irish Poetry 1558–1625* (Cork, 1998), 163 n. 7. Ó Cuív's alternative reading, that the verse condemns those who attended the English court without knowing its language, seems somewhat convoluted.

on which Geoffrey Fionn O'Daly had commented two centuries earlier.[51] In any case the poem remains an isolated instance. There are a small number of other pieces more clearly tied to particular events, such as Turlough O'Neill's intermittent wars against English intruders and Brian O'Neill's conflict with Smith and Essex. However, it is not until later, in the 1580s and 1590s, that an appreciable number of poems can be found on the theme of resistance to English intrusion. Even then they remain a mere handful beside the much larger number of pieces that concentrate on the traditional eulogies of ruling lords and their families.[52] The idea of a crusade against the foreign enemy clearly had a certain inherent appeal, as it had done for centuries. But the indications are that nothing that had so far happened had seriously disturbed the preoccupation with local and dynastic politics.

One further episode which casts a certain light on the transitional relationship between Gaelic lords and English state power took place in 1583, when two of the O'Connors of Offaly appeared before the lords justices and council. Connor McCormac O'Connor accused Tadhg McGilpatrick O'Connor of killing some of his followers; Tadhg responded that the dead men had been in league with a noted 'rebel'. At the suggestion of Sir Nicholas Whyte, master of the rolls, the council agreed to let the matter be settled in single combat in the inner yard of Dublin Castle. Armed with swords and shields, the two confronted each other with 'great valour and resolution'. Eventually Connor, wounded in the leg and eye, sought to take his opponent with him in a last all-out attack, only to be thrown to the ground, clubbed repeatedly with a sword hilt, then beheaded with his own weapon. At first sight the spectacle of two Irishmen fighting to the death, before an audience of councillors and officials, suggests savagery on one hand and a callous indifference to the brutality of lesser beings on the other. Yet the contrast between cultures is less acute than might at first sight appear. If trial by combat had been abandoned in England by the end of the fifteenth century, the duel remained a common way of settling disputes between gentlemen. It was against this background that the council imposed a degree of formality on the proceeding, by assigning 'patrons to them both to bring them into the lists, and all other officers of the field to grace the action so well as might be'. (It also had both men searched for additional weapons before the fight began.) A second important point is that the two men had submitted their differences to the council in the first place. Tadhg had earlier been known as a raider of the Pale. A few weeks after the combat, however, Whyte reported that he had taken a farm on which he hoped to settle with the favour of the lords justices.[53] The

[51] See above, pp. 49–50.

[52] The fullest survey is Caball, *Poets and Politics*, 40–82. For a fuller discussion of the debate on the political content of the Gaelic poetry of the period see below, pp. 236–7.

[53] Lord Walter Fitzgerald, 'The Duel between Two of the O'Connors of Offaly in Dublin Castle on the 12th of September 1583', *JRSAI*, 40 (1910), 1–5. The quotations are from the account of the combat sent to the earls of Warwick and Leicester by Sir Geoffrey Fenton.

whole episode, with its mixture of brutality and legal forms, ethnic separateness and pragmatic accommodation, is perhaps as good a metaphor as any for the interaction in this period of English and Gaelic Ireland.

FEUDAL REVOLT

The wars of east Ulster and the midlands arose from the confrontation of English with Gaelic Irish. A second set of episodes of violence arose from conflicts between representatives of the crown and the lords of English descent who controlled large parts of the island outside Ulster. The term 'feudal' is a dangerous one. It is often loosely used, it has pejorative overtones, and in this context it may potentially prejudge the issue, by implying a straightforward opposition between a modernizing state and the obstinate defenders of an outdated system. Employed with more precision, however, it retains a point. The essence of feudalism was the use of landed estates to maintain bodies of armed retainers. These private armies allowed magnates to trade military support to the crown for legal privilege and substantial local autonomy, while at the same time extorting a variety of dues and services from the local population in exchange for their protection. This was the the system that the crown and its servants sought to eliminate from Ireland. Their efforts to do so introduced a further element to the overlapping conflicts of the 1560s and 1570s.[54]

The leading aristocrats of English Ireland, with whom the crown thus came into collision, were very different in character and background.[55] The head of the Ormond Butlers, following the mysterious death of the ninth earl in 1546, was Thomas, tenth earl of Ormond. Born in 1531, and in active charge of the dynasty's affairs until his death in 1614, 'Black Tom' had been educated at the English court and remained an important figure there throughout his life. Tall, good-looking, and a master of both intrigue and flattery, he established himself as a favourite of Queen Elizabeth, who regarded him, through the Boleyn connection, as her cousin. He introduced something of the style of the same court

[54] The fullest account of this aspect of crown policy is Brady, *Chief Governors*, ch. 5. For feudalism see in particular David Edwards, *The Ormond Lordship in County Kilkenny 1515–1642: The Rise and Fall of Butler Feudal Power* (Dublin, 2003).

[55] Unless otherwise stated, what follows draws on the following sources: for Ormond, Edwards, *Ormond Lordship*; idem, 'The Butler Revolt of 1569', *IHS* 28 (1993), 228–55; for Kildare, Vincent Carey, *Surviving the Tudors: The 'Wizard' Earl of Kildare and English Rule in Ireland 1537–1586* (Dublin, 2002); for Desmond, Ciaran Brady, 'Faction and the Origins of the Desmond Rebellion of 1579', *IHS* 22/88 (1981), 289–312; Anthony M. McCormack, *The Earldom of Desmond 1463–1583: The Decline and Crisis of a Feudal Lordship* (Dublin, 2005); for the Burkes, Bernadette Cunningham, 'From Warlords to Landlords: Political and Social Change in Galway 1540–1640', in Gerard Moran and Raymond Gillespie (eds.), *Galway: History and Society* (Dublin, 1996), 97–129. For general political narratives see Brady, *Chief Governors*, ch. 5; Canny, *Elizabethan Conquest*, ch. 7.

to his Irish estates. While his contemporaries continued to live in tower houses and heavily fortified castles, he had his main residence at Carrick-on-Suir largely rebuilt in the 1560s and 1570s as a splendid mansion in the latest style, with fine interior plasterwork and Italianite fireplaces, and also added a modern mansion house to the family castle at Kilkenny. Gerald Fitzgerald, eleventh earl of Kildare, also had a court background, though of a very different kind. A son of the ninth earl by his second wife, Elizabeth Grey, he had been spirited away following the collapse of the Kildare revolt, first to the protection of Manus O'Donnell, then to the Continent. There he had spent time both with the exiled English ecclesiastic Cardinal Pole at Florence and at the royal court in France. Allowed to return to England in 1549, he was restored to his title and to the family's Irish lands in 1554, but was never wholly to shake off the shadow of his family's rebellious past.

Both the Kildares and the Ormonds had a long history of participation in the government of English Ireland. By contrast the Burkes of Connacht were the leading examples of degenerate English, largely cut off from both their cultural roots and their political allegiance. However, the evocatively named Ulick na gCeann (Ulick of the [presumably severed] heads) had accepted the title of earl of Clanricard in 1543. When he died the following year his son Richard was able to succeed him and maintain his position against local rivals only with the help of the English. In response he was generally willing to cooperate with the government, and to go at least some way towards an acceptance of English law and manners; his nickname, significantly, was 'Richard Sassenach'. Instead it was to be the fourth of the great English Irish dynasties, the earls of Desmond, that was to come most destructively into collision with the crown. Following his family's long estrangement after the execution of the seventh earl in 1468, James Fitzjohn Fitzgerald, the thirteenth earl, took advantage of the benign climate of St Leger's administration to re-establish links with the crown, and thereafter worked for the most part harmoniously with a series of administrations. However, his son Gerald Fitzjames, who succeeded in1558, was ill equipped to cope with the more challenging world in which a magnate family had by that time to operate. Educated, unlike his peers, in the family's south-western stronghold, and fostered among the O'Moriartys, the new earl had neither courtly skills nor political connections, and was further hindered by poor judgement and an apparent emotional instability. Summoned to England in 1562 to answer complaints regarding his raids on Ormond's land, he provoked the privy council into placing him in confinement for over a year.

Despite these differences in culture and circumstances, the four main lords of English Ireland shared a common dependence on the maintenance of private bodies of armed men. Desmond and Clanricard kept their forces of kern and galloglass in much the same manner as the Gaelic chiefs with whom they feuded and allied themselves. The newly restored Kildare, commencing in the mid-1550s to rebuild his family's estates, devoted himself not just to recovering title to land and reinstituting rents and other dues, but also to reconstructing his father's and grandfather's military resources. Like other landowners in both England and Ireland his leases required tenants to provide both military service and labour in the construction and upkeep of fortifications. But Kildare also maintained a force of galloglass and kern, which he quartered on the countryside by the traditional method of coyne and livery. He was able to do this because the government continued to rely on him and other lords to defend English Ireland. On several occasions, as in the conflict with Shane O'Neill in 1558–9 and during the midland disturbances of 1563–4, Kildare was entrusted with military commands, and on these occasions it seems to have been accepted that he could billet his troops as required. In the case of Ormond the tenth earl, unlike his predecessors, no longer maintained substantial forces in the settled inner core of his lordship. In 1564 he issued a proclamation abolishing coyne and livery throughout the liberty of Tipperary, and instead instituting a county militia. On the borders of the lordship, however, where its territory adjoined that of the MacGillpatricks and other Gaelic lords, and where intermittent localized warfare between Butler and Desmond had gone on for decades, very different arrangements were necessary. Here junior members of the Butler family held castles and lands which they defended by bodies of men supported by coyne and livery in the traditional fashion.

The practical results of this continued militarization were vividly demonstrated in 1565, when Ormond and Desmond confronted one another in a full-scale battle at Affane in County Waterford. The two magnates, already heirs to a long-standing feud, were in dispute over ownership of various lands, over the tax levied on wine imports in certain southern ports, and over the return of the dowry which Joan Fitzgerald, now Desmond's wife, had brought to her first husband, the ninth earl of Ormond. In February 1565 Desmond, whose men had already been raiding Ormond's lands, marched into County Waterford to assert his overlordship, possibly in the form of a demand for rents or an imposition of coyne and livery, on the lands of Sir Maurice Fitzgerald, lord of Decies. However, Fitzgerald had sought Ormond's assistance. It is possible that Desmond walked into a trap: certainly Ormond's men were in better order when they confronted Desmond's straggling column, which they scattered with heavy losses. Desmond himself, wounded in the thigh by a pistol ball, was carried off to be paraded in chains through Waterford city. Ormond subsequently claimed that his force had amounted to 100 horse and 300 galloglass and kern, while Desmond put his numbers at 56 horse, 60 galloglass, and 60 unmounted kern. Since this was at a time when both men were anxious to deny that they had come seeking a battle, both figures may well be significantly below the truth.[56]

[56] George Butler, 'The Battle of Affane', *Irish Sword*, 8 (1967–8), 33–47. Butler uses a complaint concerning the number of cattle Desmond had taken to feed his army to calculate that he might have had as many as 1,000 followers, while suggesting that Ormond might have had as many as 4,000 men. However, Edwards (*Ormond Lordship*, 186) points out that the earldom's forces, at

The first attempt to deal with the problems posed by this combination of landed and military power came in the early 1530s. The indentures proffered to Ormond and probably to Kildare would have required the lords concerned to dismantle their armed forces, sever their links with Gaelic clients, and accept the operation within their territories of the courts and other institutions of central government. By the 1560s both Sussex and Sidney saw the solution as lying in provincial councils, which would deprive local magnates of their independent power while offering them an alternative role as partners in local government under the crown. How far these proposals, with their mixture of carrot and stick, might have succeeded in peacefully taming magnate power remains unclear. In the event their implementation was blighted by a mixture of bad luck and mismanagement. Up to mid-1567 the war against Shane O'Neill distracted attention from the affairs of the other three provinces. The first attempt to create a presidency for Munster, in 1566, came to grief when Ormond successfully lobbied against Sidney's choice of Sir Warham St Leger. The issue was factional: Sidney and Kildare were both linked to the court party headed by Robert Dudley, now earl of Leicester; Ormond, whose ties were to the rival Norfolk faction, saw the appointment of Sir Warham, son of his father's old adversary Sir Anthony, as part of a strategy to favour the Fitzgerald over the Butler interest. In response to his protests the queen not only countermanded St Leger's appointment, but ordered Sidney to favour Ormond 'as reason shall require'. Meanwhile she delayed further progress towards establishing the Munster presidency, apparently in order to avoid the expenditure involved.

Trapped between factional antagonisms and royal favouritism, Sidney proceeded piecemeal. After Affane both Ormond and Desmond had been forced to enter into recognizances in the huge sum of £20,000 each to keep the peace. In 1567, confronted by evidence that Desmond was once again pursuing the feud by raids on Ormond's land, Sidney arrested him and declared his bond forfeited. The earl was to remain in confinement in England until 1573. At the same time Sidney sought to curb the military power of the Butlers. During 1566–7 he had three of Ormond's brothers prosecuted for acts of violence and lawlessness, along with a large number of their followers, some of whom were hanged. Meanwhile Sidney courted further controversy by pursuing another of his proposed instruments of Irish reform, the introduction of colonies of English settlers. His protégé St Leger established one such settlement at Kerrycurrihy, west of Cork. This was on land legitimately obtained from Desmond in exchange for £10,000. But St Leger and a consortium of associates also petitioned government for further grants of land in Munster, to be confiscated from the Gaelic inhabitants. Meanwhile a Devon gentleman, Sir Peter Carew, had come forward

their peak in the 1530s, numbered between 800 and 1,000, and that not all of Ormond's soldiers were present at Affane. The often-quoted figure of 300 dead on Desmond's side derives from an account written in 1745 (Butler, 'Affane', 45).

to claim lands in Meath and Carlow, on the basis of grants made to ancestors in the medieval colony. The ancient titles Carew unearthed seem to have been genuine enough; but their revival cut across a whole series of subsequent changes of ownership, including later royal grants and modern purchases. In Meath the modern occupier, Sir Christopher Cheevers, came to terms with Carew. Carew's main claim, however, related to the barony of Idrone in County Carlow. Here Sidney, having earlier facilitated Carew in his trawl through official records, now issued an order of the Irish council confirming his ownership. Most of the lands concerned were occupied by Gaelic Kavanaghs. But Carew's new acquisitions also included an estate belonging to Ormond's brother, Sir Edmund Butler.

By the late 1560s the crown had thus managed to antagonize both of the major Munster dynasties. Sidney had initially sought to balance his arrest of Desmond by knighting the earl's brother, Sir John of Desmond, and putting him in charge of a commission of the peace covering the Desmond lordship. The following year, however, the queen had Sir John arrested too. This permitted James Fitzmaurice Fitzgerald, the earl's cousin and leading military retainer, to establish control over the lordship and then, at the beginning of 1569, to launch an armed revolt. His rising had the support of Clancare, who resumed his former title of MacCarthy Mór, and of a number of other Gaelic lords. Meanwhile Sir Edmund Butler had attended the parliament in Dublin in January, but had failed to halt Carew's annexation of Idrone. In June he too rose in arms, along with his brothers. The two revolts, ominously for an English government which had always been able to balance one faction against another, were linked. In mid-July the Butlers, Fitzmaurice, and MacCarthy Mór joined forces to mount an unsuccessful siege of Kilkenny. In addition the rebel Butlers entered into a pact with Turlough Luineach O'Neill, who undertook to support the southern revolt by raiding the Pale from the north.

The revolt of 1569 was clearly a response to the recent aggressive intrusions of the crown and the Dublin administration. Fitzmaurice and his allies ravaged the settlement at Kerrycurrihy and pursued the inhabitants to Cork, which they besieged. The Butlers, likewise, destroyed Carew's property at Idrone and Leighlin. Not all of the victims of the revolt, however, were English newcomers. The Butlers also launched an all-out assault on the MacGillpatricks, and also attacked the property and followers of Ormond himself. The Fitzgeralds and their Gaelic allies, likewise, attacked MacCarthy of Muskerry, Sir Maurice Fitzgerald of Decies (who had helped to bring Desmond to grief at Affane), and others identified as supporters of Sidney's attempts to introduce a Munster presidency. In this sense the Butler and Fitzgerald revolts were not just a war of resistance against English colonization, but also a local vendetta against those who had seen it in their interest to become supporters of a new social and political order.[57]

[57] This aspect of the revolt is emphasized in Edwards, 'Butler Revolt'.

As the former tenant of Kerrycurrihy, which Desmond had leased to St Leger, Fitzmaurice had a direct personal grievance. Yet explanations of his revolt as the protest of an abandoned and desperate retainer appear to be misconceived: he had in fact been reasonably compensated by grants of other lands. Instead his main motive was a deeply felt hostility to the Protestant Reformation. At the beginning of 1569 a poorly documented assembly, apparently involving the Catholic archbishop of Cashel and bishop of Ross, as well as Fitzmaurice, MacCarthy Mór, and possibly other bishops and Gaelic lords, produced a document declaring that Queen Elizabeth had, through her heresy, forfeited the title to Ireland conferred on her ancestors by the bull *Laudabiliter*, and inviting Philip II of Spain to provide them with a new ruler. Some of the language used has been seen as reflecting the influence on Fitzmaurice of events in France, where Catholic nobles were at that time mobilizing against the Huguenots. Once again, as in Offaly's revolt of 1534, Ireland threatened to become a theatre for the wider European conflict between Catholic and Protestant.[58]

The southern revolt, uniting Gaelic Irish and English Irish, and driven by the threat both to religion and land, was at first sight a formidable challenge: the combined force besieging Kilkenny was estimated at 4,500 men. However, their failure to capture the city left the rebels without a regional stronghold. Meanwhile Turlough Luineach, awaiting his Scottish dowry of redshanks, delayed his promised offensive until August. By then it was too late. At the end of July Sidney had marched south with some 600 men, later joined by 400 reinforcements from England, and started to regain control of Counties Cork and Limerick. Meanwhile royal forces had relieved Kilkenny and begun to encircle the rebel Butlers. Ormond landed at Rosslare, County Wexford, in mid-August, and on 1 September accepted the surrender of his brothers. Resistance in the south-west continued longer. In September Sidney appointed a new governor of Munster, Sir Humphrey Gilbert, a partner in St Leger's colonization scheme who had earlier campaigned in Ulster against Shane O'Neill. Armed with martial law powers, Gilbert conducted a ruthless campaign of pacification, wasting the lands of rebel leaders and summarily executing men found in arms. To reinforce the message he set up a grisly charade whereby those coming to offer their surrender had to approach his tent by walking between two lines of severed heads. By the end of the year Clancare and most of the Fitzgeralds had submitted. However Fitzmaurice remained in arms. When a president was at last appointed for Munster, in December 1569, the first incumbent, Sir John Perrot, was in practice forced to continue Gilbert's tactics of harsh repression. It was not until February 1573 that Fitzmaurice surrendered on terms.

By the time Munster had thus been brought under control the crown faced a new series of revolts, this time in the west. In February 1570 the earl of

[58] For this reading of Fitzmaurice's motives see McCormack, *The Earldom of Desmond*, 110–17, 160–2.

Thomond drove Sir Edward Fitton, president of Connacht, out of County Clare, by denying him supplies, and arrested Tadhg MacMurrough O'Brien, a local rival whom Fitton had appointed sheriff. The immediate cause of his protest was Fitton's high-handed and authoritarian behaviour. Appointed in December 1569, he had launched an immediate attack on the independent military and political power of the regional magnates, requiring provincial lords to enter into bonds for the good behaviour of their retainers, and deliberately promoting lesser figures, like Tadhg MacMurrough, to positions of local power. He had also linked political obedience to cultural surrender, demanding that those who submitted to him should 'cut their glibs, which we do think the first token of obedience', and launched an aggressively Protestant religious policy, dispersing communities of friars and destroying religious images. At the same time the O'Briens, as well as the Burkes of Clanricard, were also long-standing allies of the house of Ormond, and there is at least the suspicion that Thomond and others were reacting to the recent Butler revolt. Thomond himself linked his stand to recent events in England. In November 1569 two northern earls, Northumberland and Westmorland, had risen, demanding a return to Catholicism and invoking the names of Mary queen of Scots and of the duke of Norfolk. Thomond, four months later, declared that 'he would do nothing with the lord deputy nor lord president, but as the duke of Norfolk would say'.[59]

Thomond's revolt was short-lived. Ormond, having pacified his own rebellious brothers, went to Connacht and accepted the earl's submission in April 1570. Thomond subsequently fled to France, but then negotiated his submission and pardon through the English ambassador at Paris. However, his example had provoked O'Rourke, the Burkes of Mayo, and a variety of others, into joining the revolt against Fitton. As the president struggled to regain control of the region, his continued resort to martial law, along with the exactions required to support the royal army, alienated hitherto compliant local lords. Clanricard, indebted to the English government for his succession to the earldom, had initially cooperated with the president, but became increasingly resentful. Moreover his sons, Ulick and John, known as the 'Mac an Iarlas' (earl's sons), had joined the revolt initiated by Thomond. By 1572 relations had deteriorated to the point where Fitton arrested Clanricard for alleged complicity in the actions of his sons. This precipitate action did nothing to stem the revolt. In the summer of 1572 Fitton largely lost control of the province, after the Mac an Iarlas had burnt Athenry and Athlone and threatened Galway. By this time Sir William Fitzwilliam, a follower of Sussex and friend of Ormond, had succeeded Sidney as lord deputy. There followed a rapid change of policy. In August Clanricard was sent back to Connacht, with powers to grant pardons at his discretion, and in November his sons submitted to Fitzwilliam.

59 Quoted in Ellis, *Ireland in the Age of the Tudors*, 298.

The relative peace thus established did not last long. The trouble began when Sidney, restored for a final term as lord deputy, made a progress through Connacht in spring 1576 during which he spurned offers of submission on the part of the Clanricard Burkes, and arrested the Mac an Iarlas, who had come to him under safe conduct. Sidney's motives are not wholly clear. He may have genuinely concluded that the Burkes could be brought to heel only by force. But there is also the suggestion that he sought to punish them for their earlier part in derailing his reform programme, or to strike at Ormond, whom he saw as his most bitter enemy, by attacking his western allies. In either case, the result was a new round of rebellion. In June the brothers escaped from their Dublin gaol, retreated across the Shannon, and launched a new campaign of devastation, aided by a force of 2,000 Scottish mercenaries. Sidney retaliated by arresting Clanricard, charging him with complicity in the treason of his sons and making real efforts over the next few months to have him condemned and executed. Meanwhile he appointed Captain Nicholas Malby as military governor of Connacht. Malby drove the Scots back into Ulster, then launched a savage campaign of pacification in which, in his own words, he 'spared neither old nor young'.[60] By early 1577 Connacht was once again beaten into a state of relative peace.

Two main points emerge from this series of collisions between the crown and the leading Irish aristocrats. The first is that there was no campaign to destroy the provincial magnates. Instead the underlying assumption, the only possible one in terms of the resources available to the Tudor state in either England or Ireland, was that the maintenance of social and political order depended on a hierarchy of authority that would extend downwards from the aristocracy to the greater and lesser gentry, and then through the further multiple gradations of society, down to the master of the household disciplining and responsible for his family and servants. At the same time it was essential that the supremacy of the crown was acknowledged at every level of this hierarchy: hence successive reform initiatives sought to curb the independent military power of the great lords, to reduce their control over lesser proprietors, and to make them accept the intrusion into their territory of agencies of crown government which they would help to operate but would not control. Such a transformation unavoidably involved a degree of coercion. Direct resistance, where offered, could in the short term lead to drastic reprisals. But along with this ruthlessness went a striking willingness to accept the subsequent submissions of even the most recalcitrant and bloodstained. In the case of the Butler revolt, for example, there was a price to be paid for the devastation of Kerrycurrihy and the acts of violence that had followed. But it was paid by the armed retainers of the delinquent Butler brothers, whom Ormond and Gilbert joined in hunting down with ruthless efficiency. Ormond's brothers, on the other hand, retained their lives and liberty, although all the earl's lobbying

[60] Quoted in Lennon, *Sixteenth-Century Ireland*, 246.

could not prevent an act of attainder which stripped them of their property and rights of inheritance. In the same way Sidney found his vendetta against Clanricard vetoed by the queen and her advisers, just as Fitton's had earlier been; by 1579 the charges of treason had been abandoned. The earl's sons remained in arms for some time longer. But when Clanricard died in 1583 Ulick, by now reconciled with the crown, succeeded him without difficulty.

The pardoning of the Butlers and Burkes can in part be attributed to the influence at court of Ormond, the queen's favourite. But the crown's attitude to the other two aristocratic families of English Ireland was equally indulgent. In Munster it offered pardons, not just to Clancare and other secondary figures, but even to James Fitzmaurice Fitzgerald. Meanwhile the queen had sent Desmond back to Ireland, after six years in England, in March 1573. Initially confined in Dublin Castle, he escaped in November, but in September 1574 was allowed to make his submission from the security of his earldom. Over the next few years he was given a central role in the government's plans for the reform of the province. In Leinster the crown had already acknowledged its continuing dependence on major regional lords as agents of stability by summoning the earl of Kildare home from exile and restoring him to his family's forfeited estates and titles. In 1575 the earl was arrested and sent to the Tower. The charge was that Kildare, echoing the conduct of his father and grandfather, had incited the midland Gaels, the O'Mores and O'Connors, to revolt, with the aim of undermining the administration of the unsympathetic Fitzwilliam, and of settling scores against local rivals. The evidence against him was damning: Kildare's steward confessed that, on the earl's orders, he had murdered three key witnesses, the earl's falconer and the two leaders of his band of kern. Yet in 1578, as the Leix and Offaly revolt wound down, he was released from custody and once again charged with the task of maintaining the stability of the midlands.

The second point to emerge from this series of revolts was the ease with which a clash between central government and local magnates could take on other meanings for those involved. The Kildare revolt, forty years before, had already demonstrated how a breakdown of relations could bring to the surface what was clearly a widespread and deep-rooted dislike of religious change. In the same way James Fitzmaurice Fitzgerald denounced the newfangled doctrine and ceremonies of the Elizabethan religious compromise; Thomond declared his solidarity with the northern earls. In the longer term this linking of attachment to traditional Catholicism with resistance to an encroaching English state was to be central to Ireland's future, both political and religious. Fitzmaurice's appeal to Spain, champion of the Counter-Reformation, was likewise an ominous pointer towards a future in which Ireland would become a theatre for international conflict between England and its enemies. But it is important to avoid the undue influence of hindsight. Individuals, like Fitzmaurice, were in some cases already inspired by a militant commitment to the Counter-Reformation. For most of those involved in the Butler, Desmond, and western revolts, however, religion seems to have been at best a subsidiary concern, at times perhaps an opportunistic rallying cry. What is equally important, the crown and its servants showed no inclination to overemphasize the religious element in the revolts. Instead their assumption seems to have been that resistance to the reformed faith was part of a more general recalcitrance, to be overcome by a mixture of repression and judicious mercy.

More significant than appeals to religion, in the short term at least, was the extent to which protest against pressure from central government was linked to a rejection of enforced anglicization. Thus Donal MacCarthy, joining in Fitzmaurice's revolt, renounced his title of earl of Clancare and instead proclaimed himself once again MacCarthy Mór. The earl of Desmond and his wife, escaping from custody in Dublin, having earlier endured an enforced six-year stay in England, ostentatiously donned Gaelic dress as they headed back to the security of their south-western territories. The sons of Clanricard, making their own escape two years later, likewise publicly discarded their English dress as they withdrew across the Shannon to set themselves up in defiance of the crown. Sir Edmund Butler, meanwhile, took the rejection of English clothing one step further. According to Sir Henry Sidney, 'he would cause English dead men's bodies to be stripped out of their English garments and their hose and doublets (being stuffed and trussed) he would set up as marks for his kerns to throw their darts at.'[61] Not all such gestures can be interpreted in the same way. MacCarthy, a Gaelic chief, was merely reverting to a status he had surrendered four years earlier. Desmond and the Mac an Iarlas were Anglo-Irish lords, but only recently recalled to their English allegiance. Sir Edmund Butler, by contrast, was the brother of the courtier earl of Ormond. The implications also differed. The doffing of English dress by Desmond and Kildare may have been partly opportunistic, as they prepared to rally support in their western strongholds, and partly a symbolic gesture of protest. (There are echoes perhaps of the declaration of Kildare and his supporters to Sir Richard Edgecombe that they would 'become Irish' rather than accept the king's unreasonable demands.[62]) The more outrageous actions attributed to the rebel Butlers, meanwhile, can be seen as primarily a response to the intrusion of buccaneering English newcomers. Yet the recurrence of the issue was hardly a coincidence. The state's attempts to promote the anglicization of the Irish elite were clearly resented, a resentment that linked, if it did not quite unite, the Gaelic Irish and some at least among the descendants of the medieval colonists.

PROJECTS AND POLICIES

The twenty years after 1558, continuing a trend already established over the preceding decade, were thus marked by a series of episodes of violence: the bloody

[61] Brady, *Viceroy's Vindication*, 62. [62] Above, p. 63.

attempts to colonize Antrim and Down, the campaigns against Shane O'Neill, the continuing conflict in Leix and Offaly, the suppression of revolts in the south and west. Each of these incidents had its own specific context: the war of conquest in the midlands became necessary because the Kildares were no longer available to defend the western frontier of the Pale; the Rathlin and Clandeboye massacres came about through the conjunction of the licensed ambitions of two well-connected courtiers and the real anxieties created when Scottish aliens established a presence in the north-east. At the same time the contrast between these episodes and the optimistic and conciliatory policies that had prevailed for most of the 1540s makes it necessary to ask how far the rise in overall levels of aggression reflected a change in underlying attitudes. And indeed it has been suggested that it was precisely these years, the 1560s and 1570s, that saw a decisive change in the way in which English statesman looked on Ireland and the problems it presented.

The evidence for such a change lies partly in the new tone of pessimism evident in contemporary comment. Edmund Tremayne, the main inspiration behind Sidney's policy of provincial presidencies funded by composition, openly declared in 1571 that neither religious nor legal reform would be sufficient to bring civility to Ireland, without the application of military force:

> But here it may be justly said that make what bishops you list, bring what lawyers you list, plant as many presidents as you can, and all is to no purpose to reform the wickedness of those stubborn, rude and most barbarous people. It is indeed very true, for there must come with it a third minister that will give effect to the other two, and without that both the others shall quickly come in contempt. And this minister must be indeed her Majesty's army.[63]

What was significant about this and similar comments was that they went beyond the traditional denigration of the Gaelic Irish to include as equally irredeemable those who had formerly been regarded as the main upholders of the crown's interest in Ireland, the English of the Pale and beyond. The growing distrust was largely due to the stubborn adherence of these English of Ireland to their traditional religion. But in the rhetoric of frustrated reformers it grew into a more general condemnation of the Old English as having been corrupted by the Irish environment they had so long inhabited. Thus Tremayne went on to argue that the only sure way to reform was to exclude these natives of English blood from office, replacing them with 'good men, new and new, out of England'. The same twin themes—the shared degeneracy of Gaelic Irish and Old English, and the necessity to promote reform by coercion rather than persuasion—can be detected in other writings of the period.

[63] Quoted in Nicholas Canny, 'Revising the Revisionist', *IHS* 30 (1996), 248. The argument that the 1570s, and more specifically the viceroyalty of Sir Henry Sidney, saw a decisive shift in policy towards Ireland, forms the main theme of Canny, *Elizabethan Conquest.* It is subjected to systematic critique in Brady, *Chief Governors,* to which 'Revising the Revisionist' constitutes Canny's reply.

The change in official attitudes is also evident in the growth of interest in large-scale colonization. As with the period 1547–58 it is necessary to distinguish between different types of scheme. Proposals to plant colonies in Gaelic areas had been part of Irish reformist thinking for decades. The aim in such cases was not the wholesale expropriation of the Gaelic Irish but their eventual assimilation. Small, strategically placed settlements populated by Englishmen (whether of birth or blood) would help to preserve order and protect the main English territories from attack. At the same time they would serve as agents of cultural and economic change, disseminating English language and manners, spreading knowledge of agricultural techniques, and drawing the natives into new commercial relationships.[64] The progress of plans for the territories of the O'Connors and O'Mores had shown how such long-standing strategies could merge imperceptibly into something more, the confiscation of whole territories and their allocation to English proprietors and settlers who would replace the existing population. The same drift towards expropriation rather than reform is evident in two proposals made during the 1560s. A document headed 'The Ulster Project', probably presented to the English Privy Council in 1565, sought support for an expedition to overthrow Shane O'Neill and give the projectors title to all lands east of the River Bann, on which they would settle 4,000 of the queen's subjects. In February 1569, during the Munster revolt of the Butlers and Desmonds, a consortium headed by Sir Warham St Leger petitioned for confiscation of the lands of MacCarthy and other Gaelic Irish now in arms in a large area of Cork and Kerry, and the settlement there of 3,000 English colonists. Although neither of these proposals was implemented, the next major project, Smith's scheme for a plantation in eastern Ulster, was. The main aim was once again a limited one: to secure this vulnerable region from Scottish intrusion, and to create a barrier between the Ulster Gaelic lords and their allies and suppliers of mercenary troops in the Highlands and Islands. Yet the grant to Smith included not just Clandeboye and the Ards, but also Tyrone. This appropriation of the whole of central Ulster rested partly on the act of the Irish parliament declaring Shane O'Neill a traitor whose lands were forfeit to the crown, and partly on a revival of the crown's claim to the lands once vested in the defunct earldom of Ulster.

These early advocates of a policy of colonization did not in general refer to what were still the relatively insignificant English settlements being established on the other side of the Atlantic. Instead their references were overwhelmingly to the precedent of ancient Rome. Here they could draw both on the writings of the ancient historians themselves and on the works of Machiavelli, whose manuals of Renaissance statecraft had laid strong emphasis on Rome's practice of securing newly acquired territories, in Italy and beyond, by planting colonies

[64] Brady, *Chief Governors*, 248–54 emphasizes the conservative and limited nature of colonization schemes, extending his argument even to the plans of Smith and Essex in the 1570s.

of its citizens. Such references are important as a reminder that the concept of colonization did not yet have the connotations of expropriation and exploitation on racial grounds that it was to develop in the age of extra-European empire. Yet they should not be taken wholly at face value. An appeal to classical precedent could also be used to lend respectability to what were in fact schemes for conquest and self-enrichment. There is also the possibility that behind these projects lay an alternative, unacknowledged model, the profitable empire that Spain had created in southern and central America. This is not a source of inspiration that Protestant Englishmen would have rushed to acknowledge, at a time when the Spanish plunder of the New World was already becoming the subject of a black legend to rival the Inquisition. Hence the evidence remains at best conjectural.[65] But Smith's outline of his proposed colony, whether consciously or not, was of a society that would not have been very different from that of Spanish Peru or Mexico. He did, it is true, envisage a teacher in every parish 'of the Irish children . . . to speak English'. Moreover the native lower classes, 'which commonly be called churls', were to be 'gently entertained, and for their ploughing and labour shall be well rewarded'. But in all other respects his vision was of a two-tier society, where a colonial elite ruled over a subordinate native population. Any Englishman wearing Irish dress was to lose his lands and freedom and suffer banishment. Meanwhile

> Every Irishman shall be forbidden to wear English apparel or weapon upon pain of death; that no Irishman born of Irish race and brought up Irish shall purchase land, bear office, be chosen of any jury, or admitted witness in any real or personal action, nor be bound apprentice to any science or art that may damage the queen's majesty's subjects hereafter.[66]

In the same way the plans of St Leger and his associates in Munster envisaged the survival of a class of propertied Irishmen, of whom those enjoying annual incomes of more than £40 would be required to demonstrate their loyalty by appearing every two years before the lord deputy. Where the majority were concerned, however, their proposal was chillingly casual. The 'obedience and civility' introduced by the plantation 'will work in the wildest and idlest, a means to imitate and follow the like. Or else through idleness offend to die.'[67]

That official attitudes to all sections of the Irish population should to some extent have hardened over time is hardly surprising. St Leger's original scheme

[65] D. B. Quinn, 'Ireland and Sixteenth-Century European Expansion', in T. D. Williams (ed.), *Historical Studies* (London, 1958), 25–7. Quinn points out, for example, that Richard Eden, author of one of the first books in English on the Spanish conquest, was a friend both of Sidney and of Sir Thomas Smith, and that Sidney had been in Spain in 1554. But this image of Sidney as the key figure in the emergence of a new ideology of colonization has since been challenged. See in particular Brady, *A Viceroy's Vindication*, 22.

[66] Petition of Thomas Smith and associates, *c.*1570 (HMC, *De L'Isle and Dudley MSS*, ii. 14).

[67] Petition addressed to Sidney, 12 Feb. 1569 (D. B. Quinn (ed.), *The Voyages and Colonizing Enterprises of Sir Humphrey Gilbert* (London, 1940), ii. 491–2). See aso Peter J. Piveronus, 'Sir Warham St Leger and the First Munster Plantation', *Eire–Ireland*, 14 (1979), 15–36.

for the assimilation of Gaelic Ireland through surrender and regrant had clearly envisaged a gradual, incremental process of change. But as years went by the resilience of the Gaelic system, and the hard-headed pragmatism of the Gaelic lords, experienced by the English as intransigence, backsliding, and bad faith, inevitably eroded confidence in the whole process. Whether the undoubted frustration that resulted had, by the 1560s and 1570s, given rise to a decisive transition from a policy of reform to one of coercion is more difficult to say. Sir Henry Sidney, the longest-serving viceroy of this period, openly stated in 1575 that 'forcible subjection' was his preferred method of dealing with Ulster, with the reform of the O'Neill lordship as a second best, if the queen insisted on a peaceable solution. But this was in relation to what was by now the last frontier with untamed Gaeldom. In relation to the island as a whole Sidney's retrospective account of his Irish service, with its list of Gaelic lords whom he counted as supporters of reform, provides little support for the notion that he had abandoned reform in favour of conquest.[68]

A different perspective again is suggested by the papers presented to the English privy council in 1577–8 by Sir William Gerrard, the English-born lord chancellor. Gerrard distinguished sharply between two separate groups responsible for the disorders of Ireland. The first was the Irish, who were to be dealt with either by the sword or by keeping them quiet with the smallest force possible, and the second was the degenerate English. Gerrard's dismissal of the Gaelic Irish, who 'mortally hateth the English' and '(whatsoever he say or profess) liketh of no superior' is striking in its starkness. Taken together with the proposals advanced by Smith and Warham St Leger it serves to emphasize how little the declaration of an Irish kingdom in 1541 had done to remove the assumption of a fundamental ethnic divide. At the same time Gerrard explicitly rejected the views of those who claimed 'that the curse of God is light upon that soil, and therefore not to be reformed . . . That the sword must subdue all sorts.' For those English actually in rebellion against the crown, 'the sword must also be the instrument'. But for the rest, whose degeneracy consisted in having adopted Irish ways, different methods must be used:

> Such as affirm that the sword must go before to subdue these, greatly err. For can the sword teach them to speak English, to use English apparel, to restrain them from Irish exactions and extortions, and to shun all the manners and orders of the Irish? No, it is the rod of justice that must scour out those blots.

Such language seems to point, less to a decisive shift in government policy, than to a continuing debate between advocates of different strategies. Certainly Gerrard's conclusion, that the best way forward was to work with the earls of Ormond and Kildare to restore the workings of justice, was in sharp contrast

[68] Sidney to English Council, 15 Nov. 1575 (HMC, *De L'Isle and Dudley MSS*, ii. 28); above, p. 151.

to Tremayne's call to exclude natives of English blood from any share in the government.[69]

Any analysis of the changing nature of crown policy in Ireland must also take account of the way in which that policy was made. Much of the discussion has centred on the chief governor, whether on Sidney's role as the putative architect of a radical new policy, or on the 'programmatic governors' as a group. Yet no chief governor could make policy in isolation. Each was required to work with other officials in the Dublin administration—and the case has been made for the view that the privy council was a real partner in the direction of Irish affairs.[70] Secondly, there was the influence of central government. The issue was not just that all chief governors were answerable to the crown, and needed to tailor their policies so as to gain and keep support at court. There were also the discontinuities and changes of direction imposed from the centre. During the reigns of Edward VI and Mary, St Leger had been replaced by the more military-minded Bellingham and later by Croft, only to return to Ireland twice more, the first time in response to a temporary shift of power in the Edwardian court, the second when it became clear that the cost of a more aggressive military policy could not be sustained. After 1558 policy was no longer vulnerable to upset by sudden changes of regime. But the long reign of Elizabeth I brought its own constraints. Her rule was marked by financial prudence bordering on parsimony, caution lapsing into chronic indecision, and an openness to the attentions of favourites. The discontinuities thus continued. If Sussex was the first programmatic governor, his immediate successor, Sir Nicholas Arnold, returned to a less ambitious policy of cooperation with local interests. Reform-minded Palesmen like Thomas Cusack came back into office, while the earl of Kildare was given a central role in directing affairs. In the same way Sidney's replacement on his second recall, in 1578, was a caretaker administration composed of senior officials, with no clear programme beyond reducing costs and maintaining order. Later still Sir John Perrot, another advocate of aggressive intervention, was to give way to the minimalist and pragmatic Sir William Fitzwilliam. Such alternations, and the interludes of largely reactive government to which they gave rise, must count strongly against any attempt to chart the emergence of a conscious policy of conquest.

Looking beyond the details of individual chief governorships, it is possible to see in these sudden, centrally imposed changes of direction a clue to the underlying reason for the disastrous outcome of Ireland's first half-century as a kingdom. The logic of this new status, and of the associated policy of surrender and regrant, was clear. Over time Ireland, both its Gaelic territories and the English-ruled lands beyond the Pale, was to be transformed into a society like that which England had itself become over the preceding century: an orderly,

[69] McNeill, 'Lords Chancellor Gerrard's Notes', 96–8.
[70] Crawford, *Anglicising the Government of Ireland*, 28–37. See above, p. 128.

hierarchical world in which all power came downwards from the crown. To this end the rulers of autonomous lordships had to be converted into magnates answerable to their monarch for their exercise of local power; reliance on private military force had to give way to acceptance of a rule of law. Such a transformation would require a mixture of coercion and persuasion: St Leger and Sidney would have been agreed on this point, even if they differed on the balance between the two. But it also required the creation of a reliable, consistent, and effective central authority. Only in this way could a lord be sure that the boundaries of his territory could be preserved without the constant low intensity warfare of raid and counter-raid, and that disputes could be settled satisfactorily without a resort to private warfare of the kind seen at Affane, or in the Ulster civil war that determined the O'Neill succession in 1551–2.

It was this part of the implicit bargain that the crown was unwilling or unable to keep. Elizabeth I financed short-term assertions of royal authority, such as those of Sussex. But she was unwilling to spend the money needed to make obsolete the traditional methods by which Gaelic and Anglo-Irish lords protected their property and dependants. By not doing so she rendered demands for the demilitarization of the Irish lordships simply unrealistic. Instead even loyalists like Ormond and Fitzpatrick of Upper Ossory had no choice but to accept their role as local warlords, relying on their favour at court, and the value to government itself of their military resources, to deflect the inevitable recriminations. Failure to establish and support effective authority also encouraged, and indeed required, the crown's own servants to rely on their own resources, and pursue their private advantage. Hence English-born newcomers, such as the seneschals and the midlands settlers, came to rely for the maintenance of their position on much the same combination of clientalism and private violence employed by local lords, and to pursue their own enrichment at the expense of any wider policy of reform. It was against this background that men like Shane O'Neill and the earl of Desmond found themselves denounced for defying royal authority, while at the same time being denied the framework within which they could be expected to behave otherwise. Meanwhile their most immediate encounters were in many cases with crown servants whose behaviour was at times as arbitrary and partial as anything done by those they claimed to discipline.

5

The Wars of Ireland

THE 1560s and 1570s saw a variety of military confrontations, with Gaelic Irish, Scots, and Anglo-Irish provincial lords. Yet successive conflicts were local in character. Despite the undoubted savagery sometimes displayed on both sides, moreover, the queen and her ministers showed what in retrospect seems like a remarkable unwillingness to see revolt as final. Again and again former rebels, both Gaelic and Anglo-Irish, were allowed to appeal for pardon and resume their property and social position. The years after 1580, by contrast, saw fresh revolts in Leinster and Munster put down with unprecedented severity, followed in the case of Munster by the plantation of thousands of English settlers on land seized from the defeated rebels. The same decade saw a crisis in relations between the crown and the inhabitants of the Pale, reflected in a new awareness of the long-standing distinction between these Irish-born of English blood and those they were coming to regard as English-born intruders. In the 1590s attempts to extend crown government into the Gaelic lordships of Ulster were to provoke a fresh war which by 1598 had escalated into a nationwide conflict, resolved by a campaign of repression even more brutal than the earlier pacification of Munster. It is this continued descent into new levels of savagery that has led historians to search back through the chief governorships of the years before 1580, in quest of the origins of a new strategy of conquest and colonization. If the evidence for such a coherent development remains elusive, moreover, it seems clear that faith in the earlier vision of a gradual process of cultural and political assimilation had indeed been gradually eroded by repeated disappointments, as local magnates clung stubbornly to their traditional way of life and from time to time lapsed into open rebellion.

Having said this, it is also important to consider the wider context within which Elizabeth I and her servants decided on the management of her second kingdom. Here too, both in international affairs and in the politics of the Tudor court, the years around 1580 marked an important transition. The most important development was the drift towards war with Spain. From 1585 Irish policy was made against the background of what was seen as a continuing struggle for English survival against an enemy possessed of a worldwide empire and avowedly determined to wipe out the Protestant heresy. War-time taxation, combined with poor harvests, several times provoked popular revolt within

England itself, to which an insecure elite responded with draconian reprisals. The Anglican religious compromise was also under attack, not only from Counter-Reformation Catholicism but from radical Protestants, whom an embattled establishment condemned as 'puritans'. The circle surrounding the queen had also changed. Sir William Cecil, Lord Burghley, lived until 1598, and the rise to influence of his younger son, Sir Robert, ensured an element of continuity. But the other men who had shaped policy in the first half of the reign were disappearing one by one, leaving a new generation of courtiers to compete for the favour of the ageing queen. If Irish policy took a new direction from the 1580s, this should perhaps be seen in the context of a 'second reign of Elizabeth', characterized by an unstable and faction-ridden court, new levels of xenophobia and anti-Catholicism, and a harsh and authoritarian response to internal opposition.[1] There were also discontinuities relating more specifically to Ireland. Men whose views had taken shape at a time when St Leger's initiatives were still a recent memory were giving way to a new generation whose starting point was the more recent succession of revolts and border wars, and which was perhaps from the start impatient with the half measures its elders had accepted as unavoidable.

'LIKE WELL TEMPERED WAX': THE CONQUEST AND PLANTATION OF MUNSTER

The interaction of domestic and international circumstances is illustrated in the opening phase in what was to develop into the final reduction of Ireland, the Munster revolt of 1579–84.[2] Relations between the earl of Desmond and the crown had reached a low point in 1574. Following his escape from Dublin, the earl had not only replaced his English clothes with the dress of a Gaelic lord. He had also forcibly retaken control of fortresses held by crown forces, as well as seizing the Butler castle of Derrinlaur on the River Suir. Ormond, supported by the lord deputy, Sir William Fitzwilliam, had replied in kind, recapturing Derrinlaur in August and summarily executing the entire garrison. By this time, however, the queen and her council had become concerned at the consequences of driving Desmond to extremes. Working partly through the earl of Kildare, as well as the earl of Essex, they negotiated his submission in September. Fitzwilliam, now under attack for having treated Desmond too harshly, was

[1] John Guy, 'Introduction: The Second Reign of Elizabeth I?', in John Guy (ed.), *The Reign of Elizabeth I: Court and Culture in the Last Decade* (Cambridge, 1995), 1–19.

[2] The most detailed study is now Anthony M. McCormack, *The Earldom of Desmond 1463–1583: The Decline and Crisis of a Feudal Lordship* (Dublin, 2005). See also Ciaran Brady, 'Faction and the Origins of the Desmond Rebellion of 1579', *IHS* 22/88 (1981); Brady, *The Chief Governors: The Rise and Fall of Reform Government in Tudor Ireland 1536–1588* (Cambridge, 1994), 193–201.

recalled the following year. In his place Sir Henry Sidney began a second period as lord deputy.

Sidney returned to Ireland with a new strategy, apparently based on a series of papers drawn up by his one-time private secretary, Edmund Tremayne.[3] What he proposed was to sweep away the whole tangled and indeterminate web of exactions which greater men, in both Gaelic and Anglo-Irish Ireland, imposed on lesser. In place of these rights—the tribute in food and goods, the compulsory hospitality for the lord and his entourage, the billetting of armed retainers, the forced labour, and the quotas of fighting men—lords were to receive fixed payments in cash or in kind. At the same time the traditional levies, cess and purveyance, by which the crown had raised men and resources as military necessity required, would be replaced by a fixed tax.[4] A society based on extortion by private military force would thus be transformed into a stable hierarchy, in which status was reflected in income rather than military power, and men of all degrees contributed to the costs of effective government in the name of the crown. In the case of Munster responsibility for negotiating this 'composition' rested with the new president, Sir William Drury, appointed in June 1576. Relations with Desmond were initially tense; in July 1577 the earl, outraged at Drury's plans to hold court sessions within the area covered by his palatine liberty, seemed on the point of declaring open war. By 1578, however, the two men were on good terms. Desmond had agreed to reduce his armed retinue to a token twenty men, and to commute all dues and services owed to him to a cash rental of £2,000 per year.

To Desmond, heir to an extended territory ravaged by a long sequence of internal and external conflicts, and with a personal authority weakened by his extended absence, composition on these terms was in many ways an attractive option. Others in Munster had less reason to welcome the new arrangements. The generous terms offered to the earl reflected the crown's conservative vision, in which powerful territorial magnates comprised the top layer of an orderly social pyramid. Just a few years earlier, on the other hand, when the aim had been to contain Desmond rather than to co-opt him into the business of government, the queen and her servants had proceeded on very different principles, encouraging lesser landowners, and the leading citizens of the Munster towns, to cast off their dependence on the earl. Now this sanctioned autonomy came to an end, and those concerned found themselves forced to pay composition rents both to a rehabilitated Desmond and to the provincial presidency. Secondly there were the professional fighting men and their captains, for whom the new order promised only the loss of employment and status. Desmond and other lords were required to register or 'book' the small personal retinues they retained,

[3] Tremayne's role as the author of the composition scheme is identified by Brady, *Chief Governors*, 140–3. Nicholas Canny, 'Revising the Revisionist', *IHS* 30 (1997), 249, insists that Tremayne was merely 'a mouthpiece of Sidney'.

[4] For these levies see below, p. 203.

and take responsibility for their actions. Those not so accounted for, and unwilling to abandon their traditional way of life, were liable to discover the other side of Sidney's new strategy for imposing civility. Masterless men figured prominently among those hanged under martial law, or by the courts of the new provincial presidencies.[5] Two important figures in Desmond's household, meanwhile, had their own grievances. James Fitzmaurice Fitzgerald had been permitted to surrender in 1573. But Desmond had subsequently repossessed the land he had given his cousin to replace his lost tenancy at Kerricurihy, and in 1575 Fitzmaurice left for France. Sir John of Desmond had been both his brother's legal heir and, for a time, the man favoured by government as a possible alternative to the defiant earl. But the birth of a son to the earl's wife in 1571, and Desmond's subsequent rehabiliation, had left Sir John isolated and without prospects.

Fitzmaurice, in exile on the Continent, made the first moves. Aided by Maurice Fitzgibbon, the papally appointed archbishop of Cashel, he applied first to France and then to Spain. At this stage, however, both continental powers still saw England as a potential ally against the other. It was left to the pope, Gregory XIII, to provide an expeditionary force of 1,000 Italian soldiers. Their commander was Thomas Stukeley, an Englishman who had once served as seneschal in County Wexford, but who since 1570 had been on the Continent seeking a patron. Having got as far as Lisbon, however, Stukeley opted for an alternative version of holy war, joining King Sebastian of Portugal in an expedition to Morocco, where both men were killed at the battle of Alcazar on 4 August. Back in Spain Fitzmaurice, aided by the archbishop of Compostela, with the king ostensibly neutral but sufficiently irritated by Elizabeth's first overtures to the Dutch rebels to allow him to proceed, put together a contingent of some 600 soldiers of different nationalities, including survivors of Stukeley's force. His fleet of four ships landed at Smerwick harbour, near Dingle, on 18 July 1579.

The Smerwick landing marked the arrival, in uncompromising military form, of the European Counter-Reformation. Accompanied by Nicholas Sanders, an English priest who had been named as Gregory XIII's commissary, Fitzmaurice came ashore under a papal banner and issued a proclamation declaring that he was engaged in a war in defence of the Catholic religion, against a queen who had forfeited her throne through her adherence to heresy. His personal commitment to such a religious crusade appears to have been genuine. Yet the response to his proclamation within the wider Munster community was apparently muted. Instead what seems to have converted Fitmaurice's incursion into a major revolt was a gesture of a more traditional kind. On learning of the landing Drury, now governing Ireland as lord justice following Sidney's recall, had dispatched Henry Davells, constable of Dungarvan, to enlist Desmond's support against the rebels.

[5] Nicholas Canny, *The Elizabethan Conquest of Ireland: A Pattern Imposed 1565–76* (Hassocks, 1976), 106. See also below, pp. 265–6.

On 1 August Sir John of Desmond and another of the earl's brothers, Sir James, killed Davells, along with another English official, Arthur Carter, provost marshal of Munster, and eighteen of their companions, as they slept at an inn in Tralee. Sir John now assumed command of the revolt, his position confirmed when Fitzmaurice was killed on 18 August while attempting to push across the Shannon. By the following month he commanded an army of 2,000 to 3,000 men.

It was at this point that the weakness of the crown's demilitarization policy became clear. Desmond had assured the lord justice, with apparent sincerity, that he would deal with his brother's rebellion. But in the event he found himself able to raise no more than sixty men. His problems worsened when the reasonably sympathetic Drury fell fatally ill. Nicholas Malby, who as governor of Connacht had already confirmed his capacity for ruthless repression, took command of operations in Munster. He scored an early success when he defeated John of Desmond's army, outnumbering his own by two to one, at Monasternenagh on 3 October. But his treatment of Desmond was less productive. Denouncing the earl as a rebel sympathizer, he ravaged his lands and demanded that he surrender all local authority. Given his precarious position Desmond may well have been in some sort of contact, as Malby alleged, with the rebel forces. But it appears to have been the governor's confrontational tactics that forced him into open revolt. When Malby demanded admittance to Desmond's castle at Askeaton, the earl drove him away with a musket shot. Malby had the new lord deputy, Sir William Pelham, proclaim Desmond a traitor on 2 November. Ten days later the earl confirmed his break with the crown by leading rebel forces in the brutal sacking of the town of Youghal.

With a large part of the south-west now in revolt, the crown turned back to its traditional reliance on Irish factional antagonisms, appointing Ormond to command the army in Munster. During the spring and early summer of 1580, Ormond and Pelham staged a ruthless campaign of repression: a Gaelic annalist reported the slaughter of 'blind and feeble men, women, boys and girls, sick persons, idiots and old people'.[6] Before long Gaelic and Anglo-Irish lords were hurrying to make their submissions. At this point, however, unforeseen events gave the crisis a new twist. James Eustace, Viscount Baltinglass, was a member of a County Kildare family that had supported the crown against the Kildares in the 1530s. However, a period in Rome had turned him into a committed supporter, like Fitzmaurice, of the Counter-Reformation, and he had been briefly imprisoned in 1578 for refusing to pay the fine imposed on those attending Catholic rather than Protestant services. In addition there were marriage alliances, through his father's sisters, with the O'Byrnes and O'Tooles. Over the previous forty years the main branches of these once fearsome raiders from the mountains south of the capital, the pioneers of surrender and regrant, had reached a largely successful accommodation with the Dublin administration.

[6] S. G. Ellis, *Ireland in the Age of the Tudors 1447–1603* (Harlow, 1998), 313.

However one sub-branch of the O'Byrnes, the Gabhal Raghnaill, smaller and more geographically isolated, had benefited less from the new order, while their mountain stronghold had also become a refuge for some of those displaced by the colonization of Leix and Offaly. The appointment in 1577 of a new and more aggressive seneschal, Sir Henry Harrington, further added to their alienation. In June 1580 Fiach MacHugh, son of the Gabhal Raghnaill chief, seized the opportunity presented by the Munster rebellion to rise in arms, supported by the O'Tooles. Baltinglass, in an unprecedented move for a member of the Pale elite, chose to join them, in what he saw as part of a Catholic crusade to overthrow a heretical queen. In response the newly appointed lord deputy, Baron Grey de Wilton, led an expedition into the Wicklow mountains. But on 25 August his force of several thousand, consisting mainly of raw English levies and Irish kern, came under ambush at Glenmalure and were driven back in disarray.[7]

Glenmalure, a defensive victory achieved in the heart of the insurgents' territory, was in military terms of limited significance. An English official reported six officers and twenty-five men killed, although this might not have included Irish kern employed by the crown. Nevertheless the ignominious routing of a government expedition so close to Dublin was a blow to prestige and morale. News of Fiach MacHugh's victory encouraged opportunistic declarations of support from Turlough Luineach O'Neill, O'Donnell, and Brian O'Rourke, and a new rising by the O'Connors of Offaly. The government's problems further multiplied on 10 September, when a further continental expedition comprising some 600 Spanish and Italian troops, commanded by Bastiano di San Giuseppi, landed at Smerwick harbour.

The crisis proved to be relatively short-lived. By mid-October reinforcements from England had given Grey an army of almost 6,500 men, allowing him to suppress resistance in the Pale while at the same time leading an army into the south-west. The Spanish and Italian invaders were not an advance guard for any of the European powers but an indifferently equipped collection of men that San Giuseppi, one of Stukeley's former captains, had raised on his own initiative. At Smerwick they had occupied a fort originally constructed by Fitzmaurice, where Grey laid siege to them in early November. On 10 November the defenders surrendered. Grey disarmed the prisoners, set aside twelve officers for ransom, then had all of the remainder, numbering around 600, killed. This ruthless action may in part have reflected his militant Protestantism: he had been involved in suppressing Norfolk's conspiracy in 1571 and had been one of the party that called for Mary, queen of Scots, to be executed for her involvement. But the massacre is perhaps best seen as a deliberate act of exemplary terror, designed to discourage further incursions, in the same way that the Spanish and Portuguese

[7] Christopher Maginn, 'The Baltinglass Rebellion 1580: English Dissent or Gaelic Uprising?', *Historical Journal*, 47 (2004), 205–32. For the Gabhal Raghnaill see idem, *'Civilizing' Gaelic Leinster: The Extension of Tudor Rule in the O'Byrne and O'Toole Lordships* (Dublin, 2005), 100–39.

responded to French attempts to establish colonies in Florida and on the Amazon by the indiscriminate slaughter of whole populations of men, women, and children.[8] What is certain is that Grey's action was widely approved. The queen added a note to a dispatch commending him as the chosen instrument of God's glory. Ten years later the master of the ordnance, awaiting another anticipated Spanish attack, expressed his hope of being able 'to make the like reckoning of them as my Lord Grey did in his government'. Grey's former secretary, Edmund Spenser, writing around 1597, allowed one of the speakers in his famous dialogue to question 'that sharp execution of the Spaniards, at the fort of Smerwick'. But the point being raised was one of honour rather than cruelty. Spenser's other speaker responds immediately that the invaders had surrendered unconditionally, with no promise of mercy. Moreover they could produce no commission from any foreign prince, 'but were only adventurers that came to seek fortune abroad'.[9]

By the end of 1580 the backs of both the Munster and Leinster risings had been broken. Yet the war continued for a further three years. Its prolongation was at least partly the result of divisions among the crown's servants, along with premature attempts to reduce spending. In late 1580 and early 1581 the queen and privy council received a series of letters from English army officers and officials alleging that Ormond, as military commander in Munster, was delaying the suppression of the rebellion, partly through his unwillingness to deal decisively with his countrymen, and partly from a desire to boost his own emoluments and postpone settlement of his debts to the crown. These complaints need not have been wholly unjustified: Ormond gave clear proof of his willingness to further his own interest rather than the crown's when he used the military emergency to justify the arrest of his old enemy, the unswervingly loyalist Barnaby Fitzpatrick, baron of Upper Ossory, who died in prison in November 1581. But the tone of the attacks also reflected the division that was emerging between the English of Ireland and a growing body of English-born newcomers. In May 1581 the queen ended Ormond's appointment as lord lieutenant of Munster. At the same time she announced a general pardon for all except Desmond, Sir John of Desmond, and Baltinglass, as well as a reduction in troop numbers. However, few of the Munster rebels offered their surrender. This may have been the fault of Grey, who added further names to the list exempted from pardon; but there was also a report that rebel leaders had taken the proclamation as a sign that they too would soon be rehabilitated, and were promising to take revenge on those who deserted or opposed them.[10]

Ormond's removal left Grey free to pursue his preferred policy of severe repression. Faced with an enemy that avoided pitched battles, and with his

[8] Bruce Lenman, *England's Colonial Wars 1550–1688* (London, 2001), 76, 285.

[9] Edmund Spenser, *A View of the State of Ireland*, ed. Andrew Hadfield and Willy Maley (Oxford, 1997), 105. For the queen's annotation see Richard Bagwell, *Ireland under the Tudors* (3 vols.; London, 1885–90), iii. 75.

[10] Compare Bagwell, *Ireland under the Tudors*, iii. 88, 91.

own forces reduced to under 2,000, he resorted to a strategy of indiscriminate slaughter and destruction of property across five counties of the south-west. He was later to report that during his two years of government he had killed almost 1,500 persons 'of note . . . not accounting those of meaner sort, nor yet executions by law and killing of churls, which were innumerable'. By spring 1582 these ravages, along with the counter-attacks of the rebels, had reduced much of Munster to famine. Sir Warham St Leger reported in March that at least 30,000 had died of starvation within the past six months. Two decades later Spenser, while holding up Grey's policy as a model for how Ireland could be finally reduced to obedience, made no attempt to conceal the horrors he had witnessed:

> they were brought to such wretchedness as that any stony heart would have rued the same. Out of every corner of the woods and glens they came creeping forth upon their hands, for their legs could not bear them; they looked like anatomies of death, they spoke like ghosts crying out of their graves; they did eat the dead carrions, happy where they could find them, yea, and one another soon after, insomuch as the very carcasses they spared not to scrape out of their graves; and, if they found a plot of water-cresses or shamrocks, there they flocked as to a feast for the time.[11]

By this time many of the rebel leaders were no longer active. Sir James of Desmond had been captured in 1580 and was hanged, drawn, and quartered in Cork. Sanders died of dysentery in April 1581. Early the same month Sir John of Desmond was killed and his head sent to Grey as a new year's gift. However, Desmond remained at large. By August 1582 the queen had lost patience with Grey's lack of progress, and ordered his recall. In December she reappointed Ormond as general of Munster, with an army of 1,000 men. In place of Grey's indiscriminate repression, he set about isolating Desmond by offering pardons freely to his supporters: one dispatch at the end of May reported 134 rebels killed, and a further 247 granted protection. By this time Desmond was effectively confined to his south-western stronghold of Kerry and west Cork. On 11 November he was hunted down and killed by a party from a minor sept, the Moriarties, whose property his men had plundered.

Well before Desmond's death, the queen's advisers had begun to debate the disposal of his lands.[12] The scale of the rebellion, and the exclusion from pardon of Desmond, opened up the possibility of radical change. Lord Justice Pelham, in 1580, had expressed the hope that after the rebellion Munster would be 'like well tempered wax, apt to take such form and point as her majesty will put upon it'.[13] But the nature of that form and point was less clear. The writings of Smith and others had made ideas of systematic colonization, justified by references to

[11] *Carew MSS 1589–1600*, 17; Ellis, *Ireland in the Age of the Tudors*, 317; Bagwell, *Ireland under the Tudors*, iii. 98; Spenser, *View of the State of Ireland*, 102–3.

[12] The following account of the plantation of Munster draws mainly on Michael MacCarthy-Morrogh, *The Munster Plantation: English Migration to Southern Ireland 1583–1641* (Oxford, 1986), and Nicholas Canny, *Making Ireland British 1580–1650* (Oxford, 2001), ch. 3.

[13] Quoted in MacCarthy-Murrough, *Munster Plantation*, 19.

Roman practice, part of the debate on Irish policy. Yet the outcome of Smith's own project, or of Essex's similar venture, had hardly been encouraging. The queen and her advisers had already shown themselves temperamentally averse to radical and potentially expensive policies. There were also pragmatic reasons for not provoking further resistance. Thomas Cecil, Burghley's son, wrote of the need 'to take away the fear of conquest of late deeply grafted in the hearts of the wild Irish'.[14] In Leinster the crown had already seized the lands of Baltinglass and other rebels, and sold them off to purchasers drawn mainly from the Pale—the same outcome, a redistribution among existing interests, that had earlier followed the Kildare revolt. In the case of Munster, however, a powerful lobby of English soldiers and officials pressed for the proceeds of confiscation to be granted to those, referred to as 'servitors', who had suppressed the rebellion. Such a settlement would follow the precedent already established in Leix and Offaly. It would have the advantage of clearing arrears of pay owed by the crown, while at the same time placing the region in loyal and militarily competent hands. On the other hand Ormond, deeply hostile to the pretensions of the servitors, could point to another lesson from Leix and Offaly: that military adventurers, though undoubtedly eager for land, rarely had the financial resources required to establish a secure and well populated settlement.

In choosing between these alternatives, the English privy council seems to have been particularly influenced by reports of the depopulated state of the territory concerned. Sir Valentine Browne, who had headed the group commissioned to survey the lands liable to confiscation, reported in October 1584 that 'not one of thirty persons' remained alive.[15] This was wild exaggeration, though modern calculations suggest that as much as one-third of the population of Munster may have died through fighting, famine, or disease. But reports of devastation on this scale made it seem both necessary and legitimate to restock the region with imported settlers. During 1585–6 the English privy council agreed a detailed plantation scheme, confirmed in letters patent issued on 27 June 1586. Confiscated land was to be allocated in 'seignories' of between 4,000 and 12,000 acres. The grantees, known as 'undertakers', were to be Englishmen of substance, and committed themselves to settling their land with fixed numbers of families from England. For a full seignory of 12,000 acres the quota was 90 families, of whom six were to be headed by freeholders each farming 300 acres, six by farmers each holding 400 acres, and 42 by copyholders each holding 100 acres. Each seignory was also to include a village of at least 26 families, with a mill and a clergyman's residence, while each nine seignories were to support a market town. There was also to be a militia, with 15 horsemen and 48 footsoldiers for each 12,000 acres. The scheme was thus for an orderly and hierarchically

[14] Quoted in Canny, *Making Ireland British*, 124.

[15] Browne quoted in Canny, *Making Ireland British*, 133. The modern calculation is that of A. M. McCormack, 'The Social and Economic Consequences of the Desmond Rebellion of 1579–83', *IHS* 34/133 (2004), 1–15.

organized rural society, an idealized version of contemporary England, devoted to a commercial, market-oriented agriculture, and providing for its own defence. In addition undertakers were to pay a rent to the crown of between £66 and £200 for a full seignory of 12,000 acres. They were to enjoy three years' exemption from rent, and three years at half-rent, as well as exemption from customs duties until 1595. But they were expected to have completed the settlement of their lands within seven years, by 1593.

That was the theory. In practice social engineering on this scale proved to be beyond the resources of the Tudor state. During 1585–6 the Irish parliament passed a bill for the attainder of 136 rebels, though only on condition that some individuals allegedly named in error were to be restored to their estates. Ninety-eight of those attainted were Old English, including Desmond, whose estates accounted for an estimated 70 per cent of the total amount forfeited. Thanks to the liberal use of pardons in Ormond's last campaign, those attainted were mainly men who had died, been executed, or been killed in rebellion: of eighty-four whose property was subsequently surveyed as forfeited, only nine were still alive. Meanwhile, in February 1586, the privy council wrote to the justices of the peace for Cornwall, Somerset, Devon, Dorset, and Cheshire asking them to publicize the scheme among potential undertakers. The initial assumption was thus that settlers would come mainly from places contiguous to Ireland, although in the event only a quarter of those eventually granted seignories were to be from these counties. By summer 1586 the privy council had applications from eighty-six potential undertakers. But progress then faltered owing to delays in the huge task of surveying and measuring the confiscated lands. As the work progressed, meanwhile, it became clear that the amount of land to be allocated was much less than had originally been claimed. Despite this the crown, to the dismay of the volunteer undertakers, began to accept petitions for grants of land in Munster from military commanders and officials in Ireland, as well as from its own courtiers. In February 1587 the privy council, tacitly accepting the reality of what had become a scramble to lay hands on a share of finite spoils, authorized grantees to divide the land by agreement among themselves. Between 1587 and 1595 a total of 35 undertakers, only 15 of whom had been among the original 86, received letters patent under the articles of plantation. A detailed analysis has categorized them as comprising (with some overlap) 12 military men, 8 officials, 4 courtiers, 4 merchants, and 13 English country gentlemen.[16] Between them they received just under 300,000 acres, not much more than half the 577,000 acres suggested in Browne's original survey.

Even the issue of letters patent provided the basis for no more than an interim settlement. Well before 1587 it had been clear that Browne's hasty survey of confiscated land was open to multiple challenges. The principle was clear enough: a person judged guilty of treason forfeited his property to the crown. But in

[16] MacCarthy-Murrough, *Munster Plantation*, 69.

Ireland, where lordship was linked more to power than to property titles, its application was less straightforward. Browne and his colleagues had included in Desmond's estates a variety of lands from which the earl had exacted, or claimed, payments in cash or in kind. The inhabitants of these 'chargeable lands', however, denied that such customary exactions constituted a rent, especially if they were extorted by threat or force, and that they were in fact freeholders rather than tenants. Others claimed possession of forfeited land under a lease from the attainted occupier, or through holding a mortgage of the type still common in Ireland, where the lender took possession of the mortgaged property, the borrower retaining only an option to repurchase. Others again offered proof that they rather than the attainted persons were the real owners of the land, or alternatively that the forfeiting proprietor had been innocent of rebellion, or had been pardoned.

In 1588 the volume of litigation forced the crown to appoint a commission headed by the lord chief justice of England, Sir Edmund Anderson. Commencing with the principle that the crown's rights were to be defended wherever possible, Anderson and his colleagues rejected all but one of the seventy-four cases brought before them by Irish-born claimants, the fortunate exception gaining only permission to pursue his suit at common law. This blatantly unjust outcome did nothing to secure the plantation. A procession of claimants continued to take their cases to the English privy council, in many cases successfully. In 1592 the crown appointed a second commission, headed by Sir Thomas Norris. Norris was himself an undertaker, but he and his colleagues appear to have recognized that only some measure of compromise could hope to resolve the Munster land question. Of 98 suits against settlers, 28 succeeded, 43 failed, and 27 remained unresolved. Yet even this more balanced outcome did not put an end to litigation. Numerous further lawsuits are recorded in the 1590s and after, once again often ending in success. A survey in 1611 indicates that a total of some 94,000 acres originally granted to undertakers had since been restored to local claimants.[17]

Behind these judicial decisions lay deep and continuing inconsistencies in official thinking on the way in which different groups within Ireland were to be dealt with. The original design of the plantation had been explicitly discriminatory. The undertakers were to be English-born. Indeed initial drafts had suggested that their tenants too should be exclusively 'of the birth of England'. This was subsequently changed to stipulate that plantation land could be let or sold only to those 'descended of an English name and ancestor': the New English, after all, had to consider the possibility that they might have Irish-born children, and there was also the necessity of providing for Old English Protestant conformists. The 'mere Irish', however, remained explicitly excluded both from

[17] Anthony Sheehan, 'Official Reaction to Native Land Claims in the Plantation of Munster', *IHS* 23 (1983), 303–5, 311–13. MacCarthy-Murrough, *Munster Plantation*, 97–106, presents a broadly similar picture, though with different figures.

tenancies and from any future purchase of plantation land. All this made clear once again that the 'constitutional revolution' of the 1540s, whatever else it had achieved, had not put an end to the practice of enshrining ethnic divisions in law and policy. At the same time this reassertion of ethnic inequality must be set against the treatment accorded to appeals against the disposal of forfeited land. Anderson's commission in 1588 offered claimants a summary dismissal. But this was on the principle that the queen's rights took precedence over all others. Other judgments, by Norris's commission and by the privy council, were more even-handed, reducing the planted area by very nearly one-third. Most of the successful claimants, like most of those originally deprived of their lands, were from the English of Ireland. But the government also accepted the claim of the earl of Clancare to lands granted to Valentine Browne, on the grounds that various rents and services he had extracted as MacCathy Mór made him the legal owner, and the forfeiting occupiers only his tenants. Sir Owen MacCarthy, lord of Muskerry, likewise recovered lands which he claimed had not belonged to any forfeiting proprietor but had been granted to his family in 1577. In this latter case crown advisers chose not to exploit the argument that Sir Owen's claim to be the heir to the lands in question was under Gaelic rather than English law. They also chose not to pursue a second potential line of defence: that since the greater part of Munster had at one time been under English control, true title to these lands lay with the descendants of the medieval colonists, or with the queen. The 1592 commissioners, asked to rule on crown title to certain fishing rights, replied that though the ports concerned had once been in English hands, 'the Irishry prevailed . . . and now are become dutiful subjects . . . very conformable to all obedience'.[18] It would be naive to see such judgments as an exercise in abstract justice: there were sound pragmatic reasons for not creating alarm about land titles among the natives of the newly pacified province, and for paying particular attention to the demands of a magnate like Clancare. But it remains the case that the explicit ethnic distinctions built into the plantation scheme had not become part of government policy in general.

English settlement in Munster fell short of the ambitious scheme originally envisaged. Twenty-five full seignories, each with ninety settler families, would have amounted to a population of over 11,000 English emigrants. In fact surviving records suggest a plantation population rising from 3,000 in 1592 to about 4,000 in 1598. The impact of English settlement was further reduced by the piecemeal nature of the confiscations, which left seignories scattered across a wide area rather than concentrated in a compact block of plantation territory. Some undertakers sought conscientiously to fulfil their obligations by importing English tenants. In 1589 Warham St Leger and Richard Grenville claimed to have 145 'persons of natural English birth' on their joint seignory in County Cork; Henry Billingsley, on his full seignory in County Limerick, reported

[18] MacCarthy-Murrough, *Munster Plantation*, 85.

forty households of freeholders, farmers and copyholders of English birth, with between four and seventeen persons per household.[19] Yet successive surveys made clear that even these model planters continued to rely for the development of their estates on large numbers of Irish labourers and smallholders, remaining within the terms of their covenants by keeping them as tenants at will rather than leaseholders. Meanwhile other undertakers, in particular those who had acquired grants through their service as officials or army officers, lacked the resources for investment on the scale envisaged; instead they let out their land at the best rate possible to locally recruited tenants, or sought to realize a short-term profit from the felling of woods. Surveys also made clear that most undertakers, even those most committed to the plantation scheme, concentrated on pasture rather than tillage, in many cases using improved breeds of sheep and cattle brought with them from England. As on other occasions ecological and economic realities triumphed over the ideological preference for manuring and ploughing as the basis of a civil agriculture.

None of this is to deny that the Munster plantation had an important effect: 4,000 English settlers, however short of the official target, represented a significant addition to the population of the southern counties. The total investment of the incomers has been estimated at some £18,000 from undertakers and a further £10,000 from the freeholders who accompanied them. As well as new breeds of livestock, the settlers brought with them new styles of house building, and a variety of other techniques: St Leger and Grenville, for example, noted that they had lent another undertaker the services of an artisan 'to make a mill'. In terms of political and social relationships, the impact of the newcomers varied enormously. Some undertakers became bitter critics of their new environment. Edmund Spenser, deputy clerk of the council of Munster and undertaker for the 3,000-acre seignory of Kilcolman in County Cork, has been taken as typical of this group. His *Faerie Queen* offered a grim allegory of the necessary employment of merciless justice, while his *View of the State of Ireland* argued more explicitly that only extreme violence could bring order to Ireland.[20] Others too argued that Munster could never be civilized until the remaining native proprietors were dispossessed, and until rigorous government, if necessary untrammelled by legal constraints, had put an end to both popery and lawlessness.[21] But this was only one response. In other cases undertakers and other settlers, like the seneschals and midlands planters of the preceding decades, sought to establish and strengthen their position by establishing connections with local families, not just as tenants, but as clients, partners, or allies. There were claims, for example, that settlers colluded with natives making claims for the restitution of confiscated lands, by offering only a weak defence, but then compounded with the successful claimant

[19] Canny, *Making Ireland British*, 147–8. [20] See below, Ch. 6.

[21] For these different responses, contrast Canny, *Making Ireland British*, 157–9, with MacCarthy-Morrogh, *Munster Plantation*, 274–84.

so as to regain all or part of the lands free of crown rents. There were also marriage alliances. The son of Sir Valentine Browne, one of the architects of the plantation, married a daughter of O'Sullivan Beare, while other members of the family subsequently married into various branches of the MacCarthys. Such local marriages provide one reason why, by 1641, the descendants of no fewer than five of the original undertakers, including both the Brownes and the grandsons of Edmund Spenser, had become Catholic. Not for the first or the last time the interactions resulting from English intrusions into Ireland were to prove more complex and varied than any official programme could have provided for.

NEW WINE IN OLD BOTTLES: ELIZABETH'S REFORMATION

The death of Edward VI on 6 July 1553, and the accession after a brief tussle of his Catholic half-sister Mary, brought a temporary end to the Irish Reformation. Northumberland and his advisers, alarmed at the rising cost of Croft's more aggressive policies, had already decided to restore St Leger as lord deputy. But when he returned in October 1553 he now had instructions to restore 'the same order in divine service and administration of the sacraments . . . as near as they may that hath been of old time used, and is now begun again within this our realm of England'.[22] In the same month the queen, anomalously employing the authority of a supreme governorship she was about to renounce, appointed an archbishop to Cashel, vacant since 1550, and a bishop to Ossory, deemed vacant following Bale's flight to England. Meanwhile Archbishop Dowdall returned from exile to resume control of Armagh. By the time the earl of Sussex replaced St Leger in 1556 Mary had renounced her uncomfortably inherited title of supreme head of the church. An Irish parliament summoned for June 1557 opened with a theatrical display of national repentance. Kneeling before the assembled Lords and Commons, the lord chancellor read aloud the papal bull acknowledging Ireland's return to obedience. The members of the two houses, 'hearing the same read, embraced and right reverently and humbly kneeling on our knees, being repentant, for declaration of our repentance, immediately attending upon the said lord deputy, resorted to the cathedral church, yielding thanks, had *Te Deum* solemnly sung'.[23] These formalities being concluded, the parliament went on to repeal the Henrician act of succession, recognize Mary's legitimate birth, and repeal all statutes of the previous thirty years directed against papal authority.

[22] E. P. Shirley (ed.), *Original Letters and Papers in Illustration of the History of the Church in Ireland during the Reigns of Edward VI, Mary and Elizabeth* (London, 1851), 75.

[23] These details are given in the preamble to the act restoring the pope's spiritual authority: Irish Statutes, 3&4 Philip and Mary, c. 8 (1556).

The reversal of two decades of religious innovation was, in contrast to what took place in England, a wholly bloodless affair. Sussex's instructions as lord deputy required him to cooperate with the papal authorities in punishing heresy, and the legislation of 1557 duly restored the English statutes for trying and executing heretics. However, these were never applied: there was no Irish equivalent to the 300 English men and women burned to death under Mary. The absence of Protestant martyrs was hardly surprising, given the very limited local support there had been for either the jurisdictional or the liturgical aspects of what had taken place under Henry and Edward. What is more striking is the limited scope of the purge of bishops and clergy. In April 1554 Dowdall and others received a commission to hunt out married bishops and clergy and deprive them of their sees and benefices. On this basis they deprived the two main supporters of the Henrician and Edwardian Reformations, Browne in Dublin and Staples in Meath. They also removed the bishops of Kildare and of Leighlin, both of them Edwardian appointees, as well as an unknown number of the lower clergy. William Casey, appointed to Limerick in 1551 and reportedly a strong supporter of the reformed religion, was deprived somewhat later, in 1556. However, the remaining bishops, including one Edwardian appointment and several who had submitted to the royal supremacy, were left undisturbed. Staples was later to complain that he was 'driven almost to begging, thrust out of my house, cast from estimation, and made a jesting stock amongst monks and friars, nor any cause why was laid against me, but for that I did marry a wife'.[24] On the other hand Browne, who had already disposed of his wife in the dangerous atmosphere of Henry VIII's last years, and who now accepted a pardon from the papal legate, was permitted to take up the reasonably congenial office of prebendary of St Patrick's cathedral, which he held until his death in 1556.

For the laity the impact of the Marian restoration was limited. In areas where the Edwardian liturgical reforms had been imposed, such as Dublin and Kilkenny, the new regime brought a generally welcomed return to traditional ways. Across the much larger area where compliance with successive stages of the Reformation had never been more than superficial, the external signs of the return to orthodoxy would have been correspondingly less. In the case of England recent studies argue that Mary's reign saw, not just a brutal campaign to suppress Protestantism, but a significant effort to improve the organization and pastoral efficiency of the restored Catholic church. The proposed legatine visitation that might have extended this to Ireland as a whole never took place. However, the actions of Archbishop Dowdall, immediately on his return to Armagh, provide at least some evidence of a similar recognition of the need not just to restore but to reform. A provincial synod meeting at Droghdea in 1553 laid down new regulations on preaching and clerical dress, and imposed restrictions on

[24] Staples to Cecil, 16 December 1558 (Shirley, *Original Letters and Papers*, 87–8).

the fees charged for religious services. In December 1557 the crown appointed commissioners in every county to seek out and recover ornaments, bells, and other church property that had passed into lay hands under Henry VIII and Edward VI. However, there was no attempt to recover the much more extensive, and for that reason potentially more contentious, lands that had been granted or sold off following the dissolution of the religious orders. On the contrary, the legislation of 1557 explicitly guaranteed property rights arising from grants of former monastic lands. The single most important social consequence of the early Irish Reformation thus survived the brief Catholic restoration intact.

The return of England and Ireland to the papal fold was short-lived. Queen Mary died on 17 November 1558. By April 1559 her successor, Elizabeth I, had taken the title of supreme governor (rather than, as with her father, supreme head) of the Church of England, and had re-established a liturgy close to, though not identical with, that of the Edwardian Reformation. When, in July, the queen reappointed Sussex as lord deputy in Ireland, she ordered that he and his English-born councillors should, in their houses at least, observe the ceremonies just enacted for the English church. In January 1560 the Irish parliament met to bring the kingdom once again into line with England. An act of supremacy recognized the queen's title as supreme governor, and required office holders to take an oath acknowledging that supremacy. An act of uniformity prescribed a new liturgy, and imposed a fine of one shilling on persons failing to attend service in their parish church. As in England, the new order of service was that set out in the prayer book of 1552 but modified in two important respects: minor changes to the communion service made it possible to retain some notion of a real presence within the elements of the body and blood of Christ, as opposed to a purely commemorative ceremony, while church ornaments, and the dress of officiating ministers, were to be those used in 1549. A further clause, specific to Ireland, provided that in areas where the minister did not speak English he could perform the prescribed services in Latin. This proviso may not have been a direct concession to Irish conservatism; rather, it is suggested, members of the parliament opted for Latin as an alternative to legalizing services in Irish.[25] But taken together with the ornaments rubric the clause made it possible to maintain much of the external appearance of traditional worship while remaining nominally within the requirements of the established church—especially since the text of the Latin prayer book published in England in 1560 was more conservative than the English-language service. As such it played its part in the ambiguity that continued to characterize religious loyalties for at least the first two decades of the new reign.

[25] Henry Jefferies, 'The Irish Parliament of 1560: The Anglican Reforms Authorized', *Irish Historical* Studies, 26 (1988), 133. Later the same year, a Latin prayer book was published in England. It was intended mainly for use in college chapels and for private prayer; but there are signs of last-minute amendments intended to facilitate its use in Irish parishes: William Haugaard, *Elizabeth and the English Reformation* (Cambridge, 1970), 112–13.

The acts of supremacy and uniformity, reversing the ecclesiastical order adopted only two and a half years earlier, appear to have passed through both houses of the Irish parliament without serious opposition. Before Sussex returned to Ireland, he and others had discussed the possibility of summoning two of the Marian bishops, and three leading office holders, to England, where they could be detained while parliament sat. But no such drastic tactics proved necessary. Immediately after the session concluded the two suspect bishops, William Walsh who had replaced Staples in Meath, and Thomas Leverous of Kildare, refused to take the oath of supremacy and were removed from their sees. However, the majority of their colleagues conformed without protest to the new order. This was true both of the men who had already remained in office during the previous ecclesiastical revolution of 1553–7, and of the more recent appointees chosen ostensibly as the leaders of a restored Catholic church. Indeed two Marian appointees, Hugh Curwin, who had replaced the deposed George Browne in Dublin and as lord chancellor had introduced the papal bull in 1557, and Thomas O'Fihilly of Ferns, emerged from an early stage as public supporters of the Elizabethan settlement. All this was in sharp contrast to England, where all but one of Queen Mary's bishops chose to forfeit their sees rather than conform to her half-sister's moderate Protestant establishment.

This tame acceptance, on the part of clergy and laity alike, of successive religious innovations is an essential part of what is now recognized as the puzzle surrounding the almost complete failure of the Irish Reformation. That changes in the state religion should have had almost no impact on Gaelic Ireland is not entirely surprising, given the differences in language and culture, and the virtual autonomy of the Irish lordships. Yet even here the examples of Wales and Highland Scotland make clear that such obstacles to the spread of Protestant doctrine and liturgy were not insurmountable. In the case of English Ireland, moreover, there are real difficulties in explaining why the inhabitants, at all social levels, so obstinately refused to accept religious changes that were successfully carried through within the wider cultural and political community to which they belonged. The first academic historian of the Irish Reformation, writing in the early 1930s, suggested that 'a fundamental Catholic disposition' had kept both ethnic groups within Ireland loyal to their traditional faith.[26] Once detailed investigation made clear just how little real opposition there was to the royal supremacy, the suppression of the monasteries, or even the Elizabethan act of uniformity, that assumption quickly became untenable.[27]

[26] R. Dudley Edwards, *Church and State in Tudor Ireland: A History of Penal Laws against Irish Catholics 1534–1603* (Dublin, 1935), 244. See James Murray, 'Historical Revisit: R. Dudley Edwards, *Church and State in Tudor Ireland*', *IHS* 30 (1996).

[27] The key figure in this reassessment was Brendan Bradshaw. For his starting point, the discovery of the limited resistance offered to the Henrician Reformation, see the works cited above, Ch. 3 nn. 38, 40. His alternative analysis, emphasizing the conflict between alternative strategies

Instead, and partly perhaps in reaction against the simplistic pieties of a bygone era, more recent historians have concentrated instead on an essentially political explanation for the failure of an Irish Reformation. Protestantism, it is suggested, was unacceptable to the people of Ireland, both English and Irish, because it seemed to be inextricably linked to a series of unpalatable developments: the remorseless extension of English state power, the resulting loss of cherished rights and liberties, and the intrusion of a new and predatory class of English-born officials and adventurers.[28]

The political background thus emphasized in most recent accounts of the failure of the Irish Reformation was undoubtedly important to the long-term outcome. Yet the idea that the Irish, of both ethnic backgrounds, would be more resistant than the English to religious change should not perhaps be rejected out of hand. Ireland, sitting on the western fringe of Europe, was less open than England to the new religious ideas beginning to circulate in Germany and elsewhere; where it did have trading links with the Continent, these tended to be with the south rather than the north. There was no tradition of native heresy, comparable to English Lollardy. Nor are there indications of significant popular anti-clericalism, of the kind that has sometimes been seen as preparing the way for the Reformation in sections of English society. There was no university to act as a nursery of advanced or subversive ideas. To this lack of foundations on which an Irish Reformation could build can possibly be added a more positive influence: the special position which it was claimed circumstances had given, in both Gaelic and English Ireland, to the concept of papal authority.[29]

An initial lack of enthusiasm for religious change does not in itself mean that the Irish Reformation was doomed. Recent studies of England have emphasized that there too it was only a minority that actively supported the introduction of a reformed doctrine and liturgy. That England was nevertheless transformed, over several decades, into a Protestant society was due, not to popular demand, but rather to efficient regimentation: the low-key but persistent use of church courts, commissions, and visitations to chivvy ministers, churchwardens, and

of persuasion and coercion (see below, n. 54), the growing association of Protestantism with an aggressive colonizing policy, and the reconstruction of a Catholic church from the reign of Mary Tudor onwards, is set out in 'Sword, Word and Strategy in the Reformation in Ireland', *Historical Journal*, 21 (1978), 475–502; 'The Edwardian Reformation in Ireland 1547–53', in *Archivium Hibernicum*, 34 (1977), 83–99; 'The Reformation in the Cities: Cork, Lismore, and Galway 1534–1603', in J. Bradley (ed.), *Settlement and Society in Medieval Ireland* (Kilkenny, 1988), 445–76.

[28] Bradshaw's argument along these lines was echoed by Karl S. Bottigheimer, 'The Failure of the Reformation in Ireland: Une Question Bien Posée', *Journal of Ecclesiastical History*, 36 (1985), 196–207, although Bottigheimer saw the turning point as coming in the late rather than the mid-sixteenth century. It is most impressively developed in Colm Lennon, *The Lords of Dublin in the Age of the Reformation* (Dublin, 1989).

[29] Above, Ch. 3.

congregations into implementing, little by little, changes for which they had no particular inclination.[30] In Ireland, by contrast, it was only in the inner Pale that the institutional framework existed for anything like the same detailed regulation of local communities. It would be wrong, within that area, to understate the power of the state. The speed with which long-established communities of monks and friars were dispersed in 1539, and the apparently general acceptance of the ban on pilgrimages and images, indicate a considerable willingness to comply with firm orders from above. At the same time it seems clear that obedience did not run quite as deep as in England. To see this we have only to look at the northern protest against religious change known as the Pilgrimage of Grace of 1536–7. The third duke of Norfolk, commander of the king's troops, was himself deeply hostile to religious innovation. His soldiers, he reported, thought the Pilgrims' cause 'good and godly'.[31] Yet the rebellion against royal authority was pitilessly suppressed. The contrast with the conditional loyalties repeatedly displayed on the other side of the Irish Sea, most notably during the near-contemporary Kildare rebellion, is evident.

Even a determined drive by the state to impose religious change on an unenthusiastic population would thus probably have enjoyed less success in Ireland than in England. In reality, no such effort was made. Instead the enforcement of religious policy, even within the limits of what could realistically be attempted, consistently took second place to other considerations. The dissolution of religious houses in the Pale and Ormond during 1539–40, and the simultaneous suppression of shrines and images, were exceptional bursts of concentrated activity, directed at specific ends. Where the wider goal of enforcing general religious conformity was concerned, Grey's failure to support Archbishop Browne against the recalcitrant Canon Humphrey was an early indication that even an assertive lord deputy saw little point in creating unnecessary resentment.[32] Under Grey's successor St Leger a willingness to look for no more than a token compliance in religious matters was an essential part of the strategy of bringing both Gaelic and Anglo-Irish lords gradually into a new relationship with the crown.

To the absence of machinery for effective enforcement can be added the lack of resources to persuade. Late medieval religion had balanced the terrors of eternal damnation with the promise that good works, the prayers of others, and the intercession of the Virgin and saints could all help the sinner to escape the wrath of God. The Reformation, by contrast, offered only a single, austere road to salvation, by means of a Bible-based faith in the saving merits of Christ's

[30] On the nature of the process see in particular Ronald Hutton, 'The Local Impact of the Tudor Reformations', in Christopher Haigh (ed.), *The English Reformation Revised* (Cambridge, 1987). For the wider context, Eamon Duffy, *The Stripping of the Altars: Traditional Religion in England 1400–1580* (New Haven, 1992).

[31] D. M. Palliser, 'Popular Reactions to the Reformation', in Haigh, *English Reformation Revised*, 97.

[32] See above, Ch. 3.

atonement. For so demanding a creed to have any chance of taking hold, it was necessary that it should be preached with conviction by a theologically sophisticated—in practice university-trained—clergy. Ireland, however, was by no means well placed to recruit such a graduate ministry. There was no local university; and for those trained elsewhere the Irish church offered few attractive postings. In 1538–9 85 per cent of all livings in English Ireland were valued at less than £10 per annum, compared to 70 per cent in Wales and only 50 per cent in England.[33] One possible solution would have been to use some of the assets acquired from the dissolution of the religious houses to provide for a well-endowed clergy. But the lands and goods of the monasteries were instead employed, partly to balance the royal budget, and partly to secure the good will of the urban elites, gentry, and aristocracy to whom they were disposed of on easy terms. In 1547 Archbishop Browne argued for the establishment of a university, and of grammar schools, to be funded by a further round of confiscations directed at chantries. But his plea went unanswered, and Ireland waited more than forty years for a university. Meanwhile the now Protestant Church of Ireland continued to be staffed mainly by what concerned contemporaries categorized as reading ministers: incumbents or curates who lacked the education to preach, confining themselves instead to reading the prescribed prayers and exhortations.

The Elizabethan settlement brought no great improvement. The acquiescence of most of the Marian bishops was recognized from the start as largely pragmatic. Two ecclesiastical commissioners sent from England in 1564 praised the archbishop of Armagh, Adam Loftus, and the bishop of Meath, Hugh Brady, both Elizabethan appointments. They also described Curwin as 'civil and conformable, and will do as he seemeth, what authority shall command'. The rest of the bishops, however, 'as we hear be all Irish, we need say no more'. Other assessments of Curwin were less favourable. Brady considered him an 'old, unprofitable workman', and included him in a strong denunciation of the clergy of St Patrick's cathedral: 'from bishop to petty canon, none but disguised dissemblers; they say themselves they be old bottles, and cannot a way with this new wine'.[34] Another Leinster bishop, Patrick Walsh of Waterford, originally an Edwardian appointment, appears to have been secretly reconverted to Rome by a papal bishop who had been committed to his custody, although he continued to hold the see in nominal obedience to the crown until his death in 1578. Outside the Pale ambivalence was more open. Hugh Lacy, bishop of Limerick, another Marian appointee who had taken the oath of supremacy, received Sidney, when the lord deputy visited Limerick in 1567, wearing a full set of vestments and with all the ceremonies of the traditional mass. Despite his apostasy, he was

[33] S. G. Ellis, 'Economic Problems of the Church: Why the Reformation Failed in Ireland', *Journal of Ecclesiastical History*, 41 (1990), 248–9.

[34] Shirley, *Original Letters and Papers*, 139, 201, 162.

recommended to Rome in 1563 as a possible candidate for the archbishopric of Armagh.[35]

Lacy was finally deprived of his diocese in 1571. On the other hand Christopher Bodkin in far away Tuam, who had held his archbishopric through three religious revolutions since 1536, remained in office until his death nine years later. Roland de Burgo, similarly, had held Clonfert from the pope since 1534, and from the crown since 1541. In 1551 he had also accepted Elphin from the crown. Under Mary he had continued in Clonfert, though not Elphin, where the queen recognized the papal appointee. Under Elizabeth he once again enjoyed both dioceses. The Jesuit emissary David Wolfe, reporting to Rome in 1561, noted resignedly that both men had submitted to Elizabeth, and that Bodkin had displaced a papally appointed predecessor 'by force of arms and the royal authority'. Yet both were 'worthy men according to the standard of the world'. Bodkin in particular, 'by force and at great personal risk', had restored the long-secularized cathedral at Tuam, and now daily attended in the choir while mass was sung there.[36]

If the bishops inherited from the Marian regime had little real enthusiasm for the new liturgy, or the doctrines on which it rested, the same must have been even more the case with the lower clergy. Trained in the traditional prayers and rites by apprenticeship to a predecessor, the great majority of priests were from the start unlikely advocates of the austere doctrine of justification by faith, or of a liturgy pared of unscriptural accretions. 'The ragged clergy', Bishop Brady lamented in 1564, 'are stubborn and ignorantly blind, so as there is left little hope of their amendment.'[37] The ambivalence of most bishops left such men under no pressure to embrace uncongenial new ways. Even where the bishop was a committed reformer, like Loftus or Brady, moreover, he enjoyed only limited control over incumbents at parish level. A substantial proportion of pre-Reformation parishes had been annexed to religious houses, which provided pastoral services while receiving the parochial revenues. When, after 1539, the property of the dissolved houses was sold or leased, the rights of patronage went with them. Figures from 1615 indicate that no less than 60 per cent of Irish parishes were thus impropriate, in the possession of a lay patron who received the tithes and was responsible for providing a curate. What this meant in practice was that, in more than half of all cases, the appointment and maintenance of a local minister was the reponsibility of a mainly recusant laity. In Meath, Sidney reported in 1576, only 18 out of 105 impropriated parishes were served by a curate able to speak English, 'the rest

[35] Edwards, *Church and State*, 220, 210; Bagwell, *Tudors*, ii. 114.

[36] *CSP Rome*, i. 49. For De Burgo see F. X. Martin, 'Confusion Abounding: Bernard O'Higgin, O.S.A., Bishop of Elphin 1542–61', in Art Cosgrove and Donal Macartney (eds.), *Studies in Irish History* (Dublin, 1979), 40, 65–9, and for De Burgo's seizure of Clonfert, above, p. 109.

[37] Brady to Cecil, 14 March 1564, in Shirley, *Original Letters and Papers*, 135.

Irish priests, or rather Irish rogues, having very little Latin, less learning and civility'.[38]

Against this background what is perhaps surprising is less the weakness of the Irish Reformation than its relative success. For, despite the obstacles, the new faith found significant numbers of local adherents.[39] In Ossory Bale came into sharp conflict with a diocesan clergy clearly hostile to his uncompromising brand of Protestantism. But he also found supporters among the laity. These included the sovereign of Kilkenny, Robert Shea, 'a man sober, wise and godly'. When Bale's household came under attack following the death of Edward VI, Shea led a party of horse and foot to bring him safely into the city, 'the young men singing psalms and others godly songs all the way, in rejoice of my deliverance'.[40] In Limerick the reformed religion found an active supporter in Edmund Sexton, a leading merchant who had been mayor during 1535–6. Another early Protestant, prominent at national level, was Sir Thomas Cusack, a close associate of St Leger, who served as lord chancellor from 1550, but was excluded from office under Mary.

After 1558 native-born Protestants could once again expect favour. In Dublin a group of six or so Protestant families emerged among the civic elite, of which the most prominent were the Usshers, the Balls, and the Challoners. The Challoners were recent arrivals from London. The Usshers, on the other hand, were a long-established Dublin patrician family. John Ussher, an alderman from 1562 until 1585 and the most prominent native Protestant of his generation, sponsored the publication in 1571 of a Protestant primer and catechism, the first ever book printed using a Gaelic typeface. A separate branch of the family was to produce two early seventeenth-century archbishops of Armagh, Henry (1595–1613) and James (1624–55). The Balls were a divided family. The eldest son, Walter, was a strong Protestant whose will, drawn up in 1579, directed that he was to be buried 'without any superstitious charges'; instead his soul was 'to be saved by the precious death and blood shedding of my dear saviour Jesus Christ without any worthiness or merit of mine own'.[41] However, his mother, Margaret, the widow of Alderman Bartholomew Ball, who had died in 1567, was a committed Catholic, as was her younger son Nicholas, lord mayor 1583–4. In 1581, while serving his turn as lord mayor, Walter arrested Margaret as a recusant, and she remained in prison until her death some three years later.

[38] Sidney to the queen, 1576, printed in John Healy, *History of the Diocese of Meath* (Dublin, 1908), i. 198.

[39] What follows is deeply indebted to Alan Ford's superb account of the rise and fall of a native Irish Protestantism in the late sixteenth and early seventeenth centuries: *The Protestant Reformation in Ireland 1590–1641* (2nd edn.; Dublin 1997).

[40] John Bale, *The Vocacyon of John Bale to the Bishoprick of Ossorie in Irlande, His Persecucions in the Same, and Finall Delyveraunce*, in *Harleian Miscellany*, ed. William Oldys (London, 1810), vi. 451, 453.

[41] Lennon, *Lords of Dublin*, 136.

Elsewhere too local circumstances could provide the basis for a significant Protestant presence. In Thomond the conformity of the fourth earl, who succeeded in 1581, provided encouragement to a scattering of local adherents to the reformed religion. In the city of Galway the opposite process may have been at work, in that townsmen looked to the newly instituted presidency of Connacht as a counterweight, in religion as in other matters, to the dominance of the regional magnate, Clanricard. The citizens, Sir Richard Bingham reported in 1586, were 'very well affected in religion . . . and more given to embrace the doctrines of the gospel generally than any people in Ireland'.[42] In both cases conformity was rewarded by the rapid advancement of local men. In Thomond Murtagh O'Brien, second son of the head of a lesser sept, studied at Cambridge and returned to serve as Protestant bishop of Killaloe. In Galway two other Cambridge graduates, Roland Lynch and Nehemiah Donellan, became respectively bishop of Kilmacduagh (1587–1625) and archbishop of Tuam (1595–1609). Elsewhere too locally born churchmen, where available, found favour. Hugh Brady replaced William Walsh in Meath from 1563, while Robert Daly became bishop of Kildare in 1564; both men were zealous supporters of Protestant reform, Daly in fact being regarded as an extreme puritan. In Leighlin, in 1567, the crown succeeded in co-opting a member of the dominant local sept with the appointment of Daniel Kavanagh. In Ossory it appointed Nicholas Walsh in 1577. Walsh's father had clearly been a pragmatist in religious matters, continuing as bishop of Waterford throughout the shifting ecclesiastical regimes of Edward, Mary, and Elizabeth. Nicholas, by contrast, was a convinced Protestant, who was named as a contributor to the Irish-language New Testament eventually published in 1603.[43]

These different examples make clear how unwise it would be to assume that the attempt to bring the Reformation to the inhabitants of Ireland, whether English or Gaelic by descent, was foredoomed to failure. At the same time it must be recognized that native-born Protestants, even in the most favoured circumstances, remained a minority within their local communities. In the case of Limerick, for example, it is probably significant that Edmund Sexton, the local leader of the Edwardian Reformation, was an outsider, marked out from the civic elite by his Gaelic descent. The depth of hostility he had aroused by his conformity was vividly demonstrated following his death, when his body was removed from its tomb in the city's cathedral, leaving behind only the severed right arm. When in 1574 the Jesuit and papal agent David Wolfe reported to Rome on the state of religion in Ireland, he counted only seven or eight Protestant households in Limerick, and about fifteen in Galway. Cusack, according to the Protestant bishop of Meath, was the only native lawyer to support the reformed church.

[42] Ford, *Protestant Reformation*, 42–4. For this explanation of Galway's conformity, Nicholas Canny, 'Galway: From the Reformation to the Penal Laws', in Diarmaid Ó Cearbhaill, *Galway: Town and Gown 1484–1984* (Dublin, 1984), 13–16.

[43] Coslett Quinn, 'Nicholas Walsh and his Friends: A Forgotten Chapter in the Irish Reformation', *Journal of the Butler Society*, 2/3 (1984), 294–8.

Even in Thomond and Galway the commitment of some ostensible adherents of the Reformation was soon called into question.[44]

Rejection of the Reformation did not at this stage necessarily mean open defiance of official religious policy. Wolfe's report suggests that in the towns at least attendance at the services of the state church was in fact the norm. In Dublin, for example, the citizens, though all Catholics, 'go perforce to the communion and sermons of the heretics'.[45] Those who aspired to office had no choice but to go further. James Stanihurst, a merchant and lawyer, held office as recorder of Dublin. He was also speaker of the House of Commons, in 1557, in 1560, and again in 1569–71, an office which would have required him to take an active part both in the restoration of Catholicism under Mary and in the return to a Protestant establishment under Elizabeth. Yet his household clearly remained a Catholic one, and his son Richard was to emerge, in the very different climate of the 1580s and after, as the spokesman for a more assertive Catholic nonconformity. Sir John Plunkett, Chief Justice of the Queen's Bench until his death in 1582, was likewise an outward Protestant who maintained a Catholic private chapel in his mansion. Where political and economic duty thus required men to make outward shows of conformity, women emerge as having played an important role in preserving religious continuity. Their domestic obscurity placed them under less pressure to compromise their beliefs, while their position within the household allowed them to transmit their commitment to others. Margaret Ball, for example, maintained a priest as chaplain and was praised for her devotion to the religious instruction, not only of her own children, but of a succession of young males and females whom she trained for employment as servants in other recusant houses.[46]

A widespread passive rejection of the Elizabethan religious settlement cannot be identified with the Catholicism of the Counter-Reformation. The Council of Trent, planning the religious reconquest of Europe, had prescribed a uniform and strictly hierarchical territorial organization of parish and diocese. The loose network of priests sheltering within a lax establishment, or supported by the private resources of lay patrons, that sustained the first generation of Irish recusants came nowhere near this ideal. Nor could the church papistry of so many laymen, or the willingness of both priests and bishops to be even nominally part of a church with the queen as its spiritual head, be easily reconciled with the militant rejection of heresy intrinsic to the Catholic counter-attack. On the other hand this was not, as in England or Wales, the resistance of a minority

[44] For Sexton, Colm Lennon, *An Irish Prisoner of Conscience of the Tudor Era: Archbishop Richard Creagh of Armagh 1523–86* (Dublin, 2000), 28–31; Wolfe, in *CSP Rome*, ii. 159, 161; for Cusack, Edwards, *Church and State*, 237–8. For doubts about Thomond and Galway, see below, Ch. 8.

[45] *CSP Rome*, ii. 152, 154, 159.

[46] Lennon, *The Lords of Dublin*, 213–15; Mary O'Dowd, *A History of Women in Ireland 1500–1800* (Harlow, 2005), 159–64.

of dissenters. Almost the entire community of English Ireland, including the merchants and gentry who constituted the natural leaders of urban and rural society, were united in their opposition to religious change. Their resistance was facilitated not only by their control both of the machinery of local government and of law enforcement, but also by their having in their possession a large part of the resources of the established church itself. In the longer term this control was to be important in permitting a distinctively Catholic laity to support a network of clergy and an alternative system of religious services. However, the records of the best-documented of the chantries, the Guild of St Anne in Dublin, suggest that it was not until the 1590s or later that the guild's leaders began to use the substantial wealth at their disposal in this way.[47] Before that, in the first half of Elizabeth's reign, what the state church confronted was something still distinctly less than a rival establishment, but already more formidable than mere survivalism.

In the face of this challenge two possible responses were available, though neither, on the basis of experience elsewhere, was likely to be sufficient on its own. The first was evangelization: to develop the pastoral resources of the Church of Ireland so as to equip it for the task of educating the people in the doctrines of the reformed faith. The leading exponent of this strategy was Hugh Brady, who served as bishop of Meath from 1563 to 1583. A petition on his behalf by the Irish lords justices in 1567 commended his 'sincere preaching of God's most holy gospel, as well in the English, and the Irish tongue'. It also noted that he had set up at his own expense a school for the education of the youth of his diocese, and supported a learned preacher who assisted him in its management.[48] Looking beyond his own diocese, Brady revived Archbishop Browne's proposal for the establishment of a university, both as a general agent of civilization and as a training school for a godly ministry, calling on the crown to divert to this purpose the buildings and revenues of Dublin's second cathedral, St Patrick's. However, the crown, initially favourable, vetoed the plan, apparently in deference to what was by this time widespread unease about the conversion of ecclesiastical property to secular purposes. Three years later, in 1569, initially promising discussions in the Irish parliament likewise came to nothing, this time because the proposal to fund the college by private endowments would place it under the control of the largely recusant gentry and aristocracy from whom these would come.[49] Parliament did agree to an act for the erection in each diocese of a free school, but this requirement does not appear to have been enforced with any rigour.

47 Colm Lennon, 'The Chantries in the Irish Reformation: The Case of St Anne's Guild, Dublin, 1550–1630', in R. V. Comerford et al. (eds.), *Religion, Conflict and Coexistence* (Dublin, 1990), 11–16, 24–5.

48 Shirley, *Original Letters and Papers*, 318. See Helen Coburn Walshe, 'Enforcing the Elizabethan Settlement: The Vicissitudes of Hugh Brady, Bishop of Meath 1568–84', *IHS* 26 (1989), 352–76.

49 James Murray, 'St Patrick's Cathedral and the University Question in Ireland, *c*.1547–1585', in Helga Robinson-Hammerstein (ed.), *European Universities in the Age of the Reformation and Counter-Reformation* (Dublin, 1998), 11–21.

The act of 1570 stipulated that diocesan schools were to be run by an English speaking master. Yet policymakers did not wholly ignore the potential barrier represented by language differences. Recommendations written for locally born clergymen like Brady and Daly noted specifically their ability to preach in Irish as well as English. In 1563 the queen granted funds for the printing of a Gaelic New Testament. The project was long delayed, leading her to threaten to demand her money back. But in 1571 the type acquired was used to print the short catechism and articles of religion sponsored by John Ussher, the text being prepared by John Kearney, treasurer of St Patrick's cathedral. Work was also done on a translation of the New Testament, although this was not published until 1603. These steps, however halting, suggest that language was in the long run less of a problem than the continuing inability to provide an adequate supply of qualified pastors. Here the failure to establish schools and a college was a serious blow to hopes for the evangelization of Ireland by a godly and learned clergy. Yet even if a better educational infrastructure had been provided, it is difficult to see how the new graduate clergy would have been supported, given the small number of livings that provided a reasonable income, and the small proprtion of these in the hands of the bishops.

The other possible approach to the task of furthering the Irish Reformation was coercion: the use of ecclesiastical censures and civil penalties against nonconforming clergy and laity. But here policy at the upper levels of government remained markedly inconsistent. The queen's initial instructions to her lord deputy, in 1559, having ordered her English-born councillors to use the new Protestant liturgy in their private houses, had originally added that 'it shall be well done' if the Irish-born councillors had done the same. The councillors concerned were assured that if their consciences did not so move them, the queen did not 'mean to judge otherwise of them than well'. Yet even this cautious hint disappeared from the final version, deleted in the hand of Elizabeth's secretary, Sir William Cecil.[50] The Irish act of uniformity followed the English in introducing fines for non-attendance at Protestant services. In May 1561 the queen went further still, issuing a letter ordering that those absent from church, or encouraging others to absent themselves, should be imprisoned. Yet in practice there is no evidence of arrests, or even of the levying of fines.

In October 1564 the queen authorized a court of high commission to search out and punish religious offences. Headed by Loftus, this set to work vigorously the following summer, summoning local juries throughout the Pale to present offenders. However, it quickly came up against the practical difficulties of seeking to enforce laws opposed by almost the whole local elite. The juries presented a variety of offences, but returned no charges against the nobility and leading gentry. When the commissioners themselves summoned local notables and questioned them on oath, they confessed to regularly attending mass, and

[50] Shirley, *Original Letters and Papers*, 90.

to ignoring the services of the state church. Loftus's first instinct was to impose heavy fines, and require the offenders to enter into bonds guaranteeing their future conformity. However, having taken into account 'that they be the nobility and chief gentlemen of the English Pale, and the greatest number too', he decided prudently to await direct instructions before attempting such a frontal assault.[51]

Faced with these difficulties, action against both recusants and dissident clergy remained sporadic. In 1565 the commission arrested and imprisoned the deprived Marian bishop of Meath, William Walshe, who had remained in the diocese, openly proclaiming his opposition to the new religious settlement. Two years later a local military commander arrested Richard Creagh, whom the pope, a year before, had consecrated as archbishop of Armagh. Yet Creagh's subsequent interrogation in London indicates that the authorities were more concerned by his recent arrival from Rome, and the possible diplomatic or political dimensions of his mission, than by his status as a papal rival to the queen's nominee as primate.[52] In Connacht the newly appointed president, Sir Edward Fitton, reported in 1570 that he had visited 'sundry and many of the idols and images in their churches and committed them to the fire, and expulsed and discharged sundry of the friars of Athenry and Kilconnel'.[53] Within two years this aggressive policy, along with Fitton's cavalier treatment of local magnates like Thomond, had plunged the province into full-scale revolt. But Fitton's religious zeal was very much the exception. More commonly the crown and its local representatives allowed issues of conformity to take second place to pragmatic political considerations. In 1568, for example, the surrender and regrant that began a long alliance between the crown and the lordship of O'Connor Sligo was facilitated by an agreement that the Dominican house at Sligo founded by the family should remain, as long as the friars were replaced by (or more probably assumed the guise of) secular canons.

Supporters of the Irish Reformation could thus choose between two alternative strategies, persuasion and coercion, 'word' and 'sword'. That dichotomy, it has been suggested, was itself part of the reason for the failure of Irish Protestantism, dividing committed reformers into rival camps and diverting their energies into factional struggle. The division, moreover, had an apparent ethnic dimension, with support for a strategy of reform by persuasion coming mainly from Irish-born churchmen and officials, such as Bishop Brady of Meath and the veteran administrator Sir Thomas Cusack, while the case for coercion was most vigorously pressed by newcomers like the Yorkshire-born Adam Loftus.[54] Yet it is important not to oversimplify complex issues. Treatments of the debate have tended to present two contrasting figures: Brady, the conscientious pastor putting

[51] Loftus to the queen, 17 May 1565, in Shirley, *Original Letters and Papers*, 194–6.

[52] Lennon, *Richard Creagh*, 62–5.

[53] T. S. Flynn, *The Irish Dominicans 1536–1641* (Dublin, 1993), 76.

[54] This argument, first put forward in Bradshaw, 'Sword, Word and Strategy in the Reformation in Ireland', is echoed in Ellis, *Ireland in the Age of the Tudors*, 236–8.

his faith in persuasion, and Loftus, the ecclesiastical careerist and advocate of coercion. Yet the most recent work on Loftus offers a rather different picture. Around 1566 he can indeed be found demanding a more aggressive role for the court of high commission, and complaining of the lack of support from Brady and other local men. Over the next few years, however, he himself turned to a different approach. Working with the lord chancellor, the English-born Robert Weston, he sought to encourage popular acceptance of the new diocesan institutions by a deliberately lenient approach to ecclesiastical justice combined with the cultivation of an element of traditional ceremonial. His acceptance of the deanery of St Patrick's was a further blow to Brady's scheme for a university funded from that cathedral's endowments. But Loftus made his control of the office an alternative means to the same end, using the livings it placed in his hands to establish a body of graduate clergy at the heart of his diocese.[55] All this would suggest that the interaction between sword and word should be seen less in terms of stark ideological opposites than of a shifting balance between strategies that were as much complementary as alternative.

It is also important, in considering religious policy, to recognize the geograpical limits of official thinking. Whether the emphasis was on coercion or on persuasion, discussion was concerned almost exclusively with the Pale. The lord deputy and privy council, reporting to London in 1566, noted that in the dioceses of Dublin, Armagh (by which they would have meant Armagh *inter anglicos*), and Meath religious reform proceeded only slowly, for which they blamed both the hold which traditional religion had on people's minds, and the want of livings for suitable pastors. But they nevertheless distinguished sharply between this region and what lay beyond

> and out of their said dioceses, the remote parts of Munster, Connacht and other the Irish countries and borders thereof (saving the commissioners for the ecclesiastical causes have travelled with some of the bishops and other their ministers residing in the civil and nearer parts), order cannot yet so well be taken with the residue until the countries be first brought into more civil and dutiful obedience.[56]

The sense of different priorities was evident in the approach to episcopal appointments. In 1566, for example, Adam Loftus recommended James MacCaghwell for the archbishopric of Cashel: 'It is meet for none but one of the Irish birth, and I do not know where a fitter man might be provided.' A few months earlier he had recommended what turned out to be the crypto-Catholic Christopher Gaffney for Ossory, in very similar terms: 'for that the place is Irish, and none of his country birth (that I know) more meeter than he'. Even in the case of Leighlin, on the borders of the Pale, Sidney's recommendation of Daniel Kavanagh—'a

[55] James Murray, 'The Diocese of Dublin in the Sixteenth Century: Clerical Opposition and the Failure of the Reformation', in James Kelly and Dáire Keogh (eds.), *History of the Catholic Diocese of Dublin* (Dublin, 2000), 107–9; Murray, 'St Patrick's Cathedral', 30.

[56] Shirley, *Original Letters and Papers*, 234.

gentleman of those parts, and a professor of divinity... enabled by the wealth and strength of his friends... to be a good servant to the queen'—seemed to give at least as much weight to his potential political as to his pastoral services.[57]

For the 1560s, and much of the 1570s, then, relationships between the crown and its Irish Catholic subjects remained in a state of suspended hostility. Despite occasional bursts of repression, such as Fitton's Connacht offensive, the court in London, and its local representatives, tolerated church papistry among leading Irish officials, and made no systematic effort to suppress even open recusancy. The willingness of authority to overlook religious dissent was evident in the career of the English Catholic scholar Edmund Campion, who in 1570 came to Ireland, where he hoped to become involved in plans for the establishment of a university. Lodging in the house of James Stanihurst, whose son he had tutored at Oxford, Campion came to know, among others, the lord deputy, Sir Henry Sidney, and it was Sidney who after some months warned him to go into hiding to escape arrest. The appointment of men like Brady and Loftus was clearly an attempt to install convinced reformers in the key dioceses of the Pale. But elsewhere officials remained eager to accept defectors from the papal camp. Richard Creagh, while being held prisoner in London in 1565, was offered royal confirmation of his bishopric if he would renounce the pope's authority. In 1570 the queen appointed Miler Magrath, a Franciscan who five years earlier had become papal bishop of Down, to the see of Clogher, from where he moved on almost immediately to become archbishop of Cashel. Nor was this desire for compromise all on one side. Sidney, visiting Limerick in 1575, received the submission of the leading gentry of the region.

> Likewise there came three or four bishops of the provinces of Cashel and Tuam which bishops (albeit they were papists) submitted themselves unto the queen's majesty, and unto me her deputy, acknowledging that they held all their temporal patrimony of the queen's majesty, and desired humbly that they might (by her highness) be inducted into their ecclesiastical prelacy.

In the end the talks came to nothing, because the bishops maintained that their submission did not extend to their holy orders, while Sidney insisted on 'the queen's absolute authority'.[58] Yet what is interesting, five years after the pope had declared Elizabeth excommunicate and deserving to be deposed by force, is that the approach should even have been made. It is a further reminder that Irish recusancy, however widespread and determined, was still far removed from the militant spirit of the European Counter-Reformation.

[57] Loftus to Cecil, 7 November, 17 June 1566, ibid., 281, 259; Sidney to privy council, 18 May 1566, ibid. 246.

[58] Ciaran Brady (ed.), *A Viceroy's Vindication: Sir Henry Sidney's Memoir of Service in Ireland 1556–78* (Cork, 2002), 86.

What is more difficult to estimate is what this incomplete process of reform meant for the religious beliefs and practices of ordinary men and women. Francisco de Cuéllar, a survivor of the Armada passing through Breifne, described a young woman he encountered as 'a Christian . . . as much as Mohammed'. His comment has often been quoted. But then the woman concerned had just joined with her father and another in stripping de Cuéllar of most of his possessions. In a subsequent general description of manners, his tone is more neutral: 'These people call themselves Christians: mass is said among them and they observe the rules of the Roman church.'[59] By this time, 1588, de Cuéllar could also see evidence of violent religious repression, in the form of burnt and pillaged monasteries and churches. But such intrusions were a recent and initially only sporadic development. For most of the second half of the sixteenth century crown servants had neither the ability nor the will to engage in systematic religious repression in Gaelic Ireland. Hence it is likely that the pattern of popular religious observance continued much as before, closely integrated with the needs of civil society, but with the essentials of Christian doctrine and practice perhaps better preserved than has often been realized.[60] Conditions in the English areas are less easy to guess at. On the one hand the closure of religious houses, the removal of images, the suppression of traditional observances, and the partial breakdown of ecclesiastical control must to some extent have disrupted the maintenance and transmission of religious ideas and practices. Against that, the reading clergy so despaired of by Sidney and Bishop Brady, preserving as much as possible of the old ways under cover of conformity, would have helped to ensure an element of continuity, on which the Counter Reformation Catholicism of a later generation would be able to build.

OLD AND NEW ENGLISH

In 1577 Edmund Campion's former Oxford pupil Richard Stanihurst contributed a description of Ireland, and a narrative of its recent history, to the English literary entrepreneur Raphael Holinshed's *Chronicles of England, Scotland and Ireland*.[61] His account was clearly written out of a strong degree of local pride. He offered a long and detailed account of his native Dublin, 'the beauty and eye of Ireland', and a catalogue of the island's other urban centres, such as Waterford, wealthy and industrious, and Limerick, with its 'sumptuous and substantial' buildings. He also devoted several pages to refuting the slanders of

[59] Francisco de Cuéllar, 'A Letter From One who Sailed with the Spanish Armada', in Patrick Gallagher and D. W. Cruickshank (eds.), *God's Obvious Design* (London, 1990), 232–3, 239.

[60] Above, Ch. 2, 'The Talking Crucifix'.

[61] Stanihurst, 'The Description of Ireland', in *Holinshed's Chronicles of England, Scotland and Ireland*, vi, *Ireland* (London, 1808), 1–38, 66–9. For an analysis see Colm Lennon, *Richard Stanihurst, The Dubliner* (Dublin, 1981), 70–81.

Alan Cope, an English writer who had poured scorn on the patriotic legend that St Patrick had banished snakes from Ireland, and had added gratuitously that the only venomous thing there was the people. All this, however, was in the context set by an introductory chapter that had emphasized the clear division between English and Irish Ireland. The inhabitants of the Pale and the cities and towns, Stanihurst insisted, 'differ little or nothing from the ancient customs and dispositions of their progenitors, the English and Welsh men'. With a frustration that was to be shared by later inhabitants of Anglo-Ireland, he complained of the tendency of Englishmen to lump all the inhabitants of the island together, so that they assumed that a visitor even from the Pale would have arrived unable to speak English. Stanihurst's account of 'The Manners of the Wild Irish', on the other hand, emphasized the rude style of living that prevailed among the Gaelic population, their inferior culture, their lack of law and good government, and their loose approach to marriage, as well as their hatred of the English of Ireland. He noted the permanent state of alert which the citizens of Cork maintained against their Gaelic neighbours, and commented proudly on the fear inspired among the Irish by the black standard which the inhabitants of his own city used in their military expeditions.

In all of this Stanihurst made no apology for the colonial origins of the community for which he spoke. The English of Ireland had planted themselves as conquerors. Like Finglas and other commentators from earlier in the century, he lamented the decline of the lordship from its medieval peak. Like them, equally, he saw this contraction in terms, not just of military failure, but of cultural contamination. So long as the English had kept themselves wholly apart from Gaelic Ireland, civility had spread, rebellion was suppressed, 'and in fine the coin of a young England was like to shoot in Ireland'. Classical precedent made clear that it was for the conquered to adopt the language, law, and dress of the conqueror. But in Ireland Gaelic customs and language had been allowed to creep into English areas: 'this canker took such deep root, as the body that before was whole and sound, was by little and little festered, and in manner wholly putrified'.[62]

The Englishness insisted on in Stanihurst's description was not only cultural, but also political. His 'Description' of 1577 noted the unfailing loyalty of the Pale, and of urban communities like Waterford, to the crown of England. In 1571 he had become tutor to the son of the restored earl of Kildare, and his 'History' included a lengthy and favourable account of the long service to the crown of the eighth and ninth earls. Its composition led him unavoidably to a treatment of the fatal events of 1534. Here Stanihurst blatantly suppressed the real nature of the dynasty's rebellion, creating instead the legend of malicious provocation that was to remain current for over four centuries.[63] The work as

[62] For Stanihurst's dubious status as a witness in these matters, see above, Ch. 2.
[63] Above, Ch. 3 n. 24.

a whole was dedicated to the lord deputy, Sir Henry Sidney, and it concluded with a prayer that government policy, combined with the grace of God, would lead the savage Irish to 'amend their lives [and] frame themselves pliable to the laws and ordinances of her majesty'.

The author of these reflections, then aged 30, was a member of a wealthy Dublin family. A grandfather and great grandfather had been mayors of the city; his father, James, was recorder of Dublin and three times speaker of the Irish parliament. The 'Description', combining an intense local patriotism with an equally intense insistence on ethnic separateness, has been taken as a particularly full and eloquent expression of the distinctive cultural and political identity that had emerged among those who considered themselves the English of Ireland. Yet his views, even on his own showing, were not universally shared. On the one hand, his complaints of cultural degeneracy imply that there were others who had a more relaxed attitude to Gaelic language and ways. On the other, Stanihurst found it necessary to distance himself from those whose rejection of any sense of Irishness went even further than his own. 'Some of the ruder sort', he noted, sought to reject the name of Irishmen in favour of 'Ireland men', an affectation Stanihurst indignantly rejected: who 'will grate upon such nice diversities, in respect that he is ashamed of his country, truly (in my opinion) his country may be ashamed of him'.

Tensions and ambiguities of this kind were nothing new. The notion of the descendants of the early colonists as a middle nation, caught between their English blood and Irish birth, is a commonplace of Irish medieval history.[64] In the second half of the sixteenth century, however, this middle position was coming under new types of strain. By the late 1590s Stanihurst himself, now an ordained Catholic priest, was living in exile in Spain and actively supporting Hugh O'Neill, earl of Tyrone, in the last great Gaelic rising against the spreading power of the English crown. Only a minority of his fellow Irishmen of English blood were to make so complete a journey from loyalism to rebellion. But by the end of the century the relationship between the crown and what by this time was beginning to be described as its Old English subjects had begun to change significantly.

One reason for this change was the involvement of the Pale elite in a series of constitutional clashes arising from the financial demands of successive viceroys. Traditionally the costs of government had been met from a combination of customs duties, the income from crown lands, the profits of justice, and the feudal entitlements of the crown, supplemented by a modest parliamentary subsidy. After 1534 the transition to rule by an English chief governor, along with the expansion of the area over which the crown aspired to exercise direct control, pushed costs beyond the limits of these established sources of income. In response chief governors dramatically redefined certain customary entitlements.

[64] Above, Ch. 2.

In particular they began to take up large quantities of wheat, oats, and other goods, levied at a fixed rate per ploughland and paid for at valuations well below market prices, for the use of the army. The practice began under St Leger and Bellingham, who justified the exactions as a commutation of the obligation to attend in arms, and to provide transport and provisions, for a general hosting. Under Sussex and Sidney, however, what had begun as an occasional levy for specific military purposes became a regular tax. There were general impositions of this kind in every year between 1556 and 1563, and again in 1566, 1569, 1575, and 1576. Sussex and Sidney also expanded purveyance, the traditional right of the governor to take up provisions for his household, again at a fixed rate independent of the prevailing market, disposing of what they did not use at full price. Meanwhile the sharp rise in military numbers created a further grievance, as soldiers were billeted on households throughout the Pale, paying for their board at a fixed and once again inadequate rate. Each man, it has been estimated, cost the country not less than 29*s.* per month, and the real burden was often considerably greater, as irregularly paid and poorly provisioned soldiers, unsupervised and largely unaccountable, extorted what they could from the civilians placed at their mercy.[65] As resentment of these different impositions grew, they came to be referred to collectively as 'the cess', the term used for the various levies which military lords like Desmond or Kildare imposed on those under their control.

Resentment of the cess first became evident in 1557. Archbishop Dowdall of Armagh and the earl of Desmond went to court to complain of Sussex's exactions. At home Sussex imprisoned a lawyer MP who had attacked his use of the prerogative, and dismissed the attorney general Barnaby Scurlock for his support of the opposition. Meanwhile a number of soldiers died in clashes with hostile civilians. In 1562 a group of law students complained to the privy council of the ravages inflicted by the military on the people of the Pale. When the council imprisoned them for their presumption, the gentry and aristocracy of the Pale sent one of their number, William Bermingham, to London to present a letter repeating the complaints. Their protest was reinforced by a widespread refusal to comply with the latest cess, and by renewed affrays between soldiers and civilians. The court favourite Robert Dudley exploited the incident for his own purposes, bringing about Sussex's recall. But the underlying issue remained unresolved. From 1574 Sussex's successors Fitzwilliam and Sidney faced a new series of protests. Once again the aristocracy and gentry of the Pale raised funds to send three delegates, among them Barnaby Scurlock, to present their case in London, while covertly organizing resistance to the levying of provisions and other goods. By now the leaders of this assertive and highly organized protest had begun to refer to themselves as 'commonwealth men' and as defenders of 'the

[65] The cess issue, and the protests to which it gave rise, are discussed in detail in Brady, *Chief Governors*, 215–44. For the administrative background see also Ch. 4 above.

country cause', language which made clear their sense of upholding traditional rights against the unwarranted extension of prerogative government.

In other circumstances this issue of how far the crown's English subjects of Ireland could be expected to finance the expansion of effective royal government might have been confronted, and perhaps even resolved, in the forum of parliament. In England, Henry VIII's use of statute to implement his ecclesiastical revolution during 1529–34 inaugurated what was to be, despite various tensions, a long-lasting and for the most part effective partnership between parliament and crown. For a time a similar evolution seemed possible in Ireland. Its parliament dated back to the late thirteenth century, initially as an assembly of nobles but coming over time to include two elected representatives from counties and from urban centres whose charters gave them the status of a parliamentary borough. Despite the physical contraction of the lordship, membership was never confined to the Pale: regular enactments on purely local concerns suggest the participation of representatives from Counties Wexford, Waterford, Limerick, and Tipperary, as well as coastal towns such as Carrickfergus and Galway. Lists from 1499 indicate a House of Commons of 46 and a House of Lords of 34, of whom 32 and 29 respectively attended the first session. It was to this body that the king and his servants turned to implement the momentous changes of the 1530s and 1540s. The parliament of 1536–7 saw potentially divisive religious innovations achieved by means of a negotiated compromise, while in 1541–2 St Leger not only used parliament to announce Ireland's new status as a kingdom, but also made it part of his strategy of drawing Gaelic and Anglo-Irish lords into the business of government under the crown. Over the next few decades the extending reach of central government was to permit a widening representation, through the creation of new shires and the incorporation of new boroughs. Ten counties and twenty-eight boroughs sent members to the parliament of 1560. By 1585 membership of the Commons had risen to 128, which by now included a sprinkling of Gaelic Irish. By this time, however, it had become clear that a broadening of membership was not to be matched by a recognized role as a regular partner in government. The meeting in 1585–6 was the first since 1569–71, and an Irish parliament was not to sit again until 1613.[66]

The failure of successive viceroys to follow St Leger in exploiting the potential of parliament as a means of managing consent is understandable. There were, in the first place, the restrictions on its potential imposed by the act of 1494.[67] It has long been recognized that what came to be known as Poynings's Law was not introduced for the purpose of circumscribing Irish legislative initiative; rather the aim was to prevent any future lord deputy making Ireland an independent power base,

[66] For the fullest account of parliament in Tudor Ireland see S. G. Ellis, *Reform and Revival: English Government in Ireland 1470–1534* (Woodbridge, 1986), 143–54. For the parliaments of 1536–7 and 1541–2 see above, Ch. 3. For that of 1585–6 see Victor Treadwell, 'Sir John Perrot and the Irish Parliament of 1585–6', *PRIA*, C, 85 (1985).

[67] See above, p. 65.

as the duke of York had done in 1460, and Kildare had subsequently threatened to do. But the effect on the actual workings of the Irish parliament were nevertheless considerable. Where before parliament had met almost yearly, the formal preliminaries now required meant that it came to be summoned only every five or six years. Less frequent sittings in turn meant that parliament no longer served, as it had earlier done, as an administrative and judicial agency as well as a legislative body; St Leger's use in 1541–3 of a peripatetic parliament as a superior court of arbitration was a short-lived attempt to reverse this narrowing of functions.

Even leaving aside Poynings's Law, moreover, there was the inescapable political reality of Ireland's dependent status. Its consent to the first stages of the Reformation in 1536–7, and to a redefinition of Ireland's own status in 1541, clearly had a certain propaganda value. In 1557–8, and again in 1560, on the other hand, its role was clearly to acquiesce in changes already decided in England; under Mary, in fact, the restoration of Catholic doctrine and worship took place before parliament even met. Against this background it is hardly surprising that successive chief governors, committed to ambitious programmes of reform, should have seen no need to expose themselves to the added uncertainties of bargaining with an assembly of questionable status. To complete the picture it must be recognized that even when the crown showed some willingness to cooperate with an Irish parliament, as in 1536–7 and in 1541–3, the members showed little disposition to address the widening gap between government revenue and expenditure. Instead the parliamentary subsidy remained a fraction of the overall requirement, rising from an annual £500 or so in the 1530s to £750 in the late 1540s, but then declining to barely £300 per year by 1560. In this sense the Palesmen, however sincere their outrage at what they saw as arbitrary taxation, had contributed to their own misfortune.[68] But it remains the case that the bypassing of parliament closed off one route by which conflict could have been managed, if not averted.

This is not to suggest that disputes over cess were in themselves sufficient to call into question the political allegiance of the English of Ireland. Their use of the term 'commonwealth' reflected their determination to present themselves as upholding traditional relationships. Their direct opposition to the cess was forceful, in many cases violent. But their formal statements of grievance were presented in suitably deferential petitions to the queen. They also carefully disassociated themselves from any suggestion that their protest was intended to promote a return to the pre-1534 practice of rule through one of the great Irish nobles, such as Ormond or Kildare. The crown, for its part, responded to these ostentatiously conservative appeals. The student petitioners of 1562 were briefly imprisoned for their presumption; but in the end the complaints they

[68] For this point, and the role of parliament generally, see S. G. Ellis, 'Parliament and Community in Yorkist and Tudor Ireland', in Art Cosgrove and J. I. McGuire (eds.), *Parliament and Community* (Belfast, 1983), 55–63.

initiated brought down Sussex. Later delegates from the Pale likewise received a sympathetic hearing. Yet, for all the moderation shown on both sides, the issue was an important one. It gave those who had up to now seen themselves as the English of Ireland a clearer sense of collective identity, tied both to an expression of their rights as a political community and to a sense of having to defend those rights against the high-handed action of successive English viceroys. Taken in isolation, disputes over the cess were a political irritant; interacting with other developments, they became the occasion for a shift in fundamental assumptions and allegiances.

One such development was the addition to the long-standing division between the English of Ireland and the Gaelic Irish of a third group of more recent settlers from England, what were in time to be referred to as the New English. There was in itself nothing new about such fresh arrivals: if the core of the English population of Ireland had been created in the twelfth and thirteenth centuries, its numbers had been continuously reinforced by further small-scale movement. What made the New English of the Elizabethan era different, to the point of requiring a new name to refer to them by, was two things. First, their arrival in Ireland was not part of the random movement to be expected between two culturally linked and geographically proximate regions, but rather a result of the progressive imposition of tighter English control over the crown's Irish possessions. Secondly, coming from a post-Reformation England, they differed from the English already established in Ireland in being Protestant, and in some cases aggressively so.

The New English presence in Ireland in the second half of the sixteenth century is difficult to quantify with any precision. Moreover it is important to avoid imposing a misleading uniformity: as with the Old English, a group identity was something that developed over time, and in response to the pressure of circumstances. However, several elements can be identified. First, there was the growing number of office holders of English birth. After 1556 the men appointed to serve as lords justices, lord chancellors, and undertreasurers were all English-born, while growing numbers of Englishmen also appeared in lesser offices. The number of what could be considered career officials of English birth rose from 60 in 1556 to 200 by 1603.[69] In the church, the crown was clearly willing to promote native-born Protestants where these could be found. Nevertheless there were three English-born bishops in 1570 and seven by 1590. At parish level too, the drive to create a university-trained preaching ministry inescapably meant the allocation of a high proportion of the best livings to English-born clergymen. Finally there was the growing number of soldiers drawn to Ireland by the opportunities for employment, profit, and glory created by a much enlarged military establishment and a succession of local wars. Though

[69] J. G. Crawford, *Anglicising the Government of Ireland: The Irish Privy Council and the Expansion of Tudor Rule, 1556–1578* (Dublin, 1993), 106.

some were mere transients, others acquired a significant local role through their appointment as seneschals or constables, with administrative and judicial as well as military functions.

Officials, clerics, and soldiers were all figures of influence. But what made the New English presence in Ireland of particular significance was the opportunities that had arisen for members of this group to acquire, not just salaries, but land. English-born grantees made up the largest group of beneficiaries from the dissolution of the monasteries, with seventeen individuals sharing some 40 per cent of the total proceeds. Others profited from the distribution on favourable terms of the huge Kildare estate. Later came the plantation of Leix and Offaly, where about one-third of the eighty-eight grantees were New English. In other cases New English military men benefited from the policy of offering land to those who would secure strategic areas. The most striking example was Nicholas Bagenal, whom Bellingham established at Newry on the border between the Pale and Gaelic Ulster. By 1575 his estate consisted of the town of Newry, containing fourteen substantial freemen, most of whom were English, thirteen small tenants with English surnames, probably soldiers, and eighty-three mainly Irish small occupiers, probably artisans or petty traders. He also drew rents from an overwhelmingly Irish tenantry on three adjacent estates. In the same way Thomas Le Strange, installed as captain of Athlone in 1578, built a house and castle nearby and established a settlement of 'artisans and English merchants'. Captain William Piers, the constable of Carrickfergus who had paid the MacDonnells for the head of Shane O'Neill, was eventually rewarded for his long years of service with a grant of land in County Westmeath, laying the foundations for what became a prominent landed family.[70]

Hints of the tensions that were to develop between these newcomers and the long-established English of Ireland were already apparent in the parliament which Lord Deputy Sidney summoned in 1569. Before the last meeting of parliament, in 1560, Sidney's predecessor, Sussex, had spoken explicitly of the need to build 'a strong party'. In practice this had in many cases meant the return of reliable Englishmen: eight out of nine members of the Irish council elected to parliament in 1560 were English-born, along with four other officials, making up a total of twelve New English in a Commons of seventy-six members.[71] There is no direct evidence that Sidney did the same. But it is probably significant that among the first issues raised in the parliament was the validity of the electoral returns. The administration gave way to opposition demands that mayors and sheriffs who had returned themselves as MPs should be excluded, along with members

[70] For Bagenal and Piers, see Canny, *Making Ireland British*, 79–81, 88. For English settlement generally see Rolf Loeber, *The Geography and Practice of English Colonization in Ireland from 1534 to 1609* (Athlone, 1991); for L'Estrange, ibid. 24–5.

[71] Henry Jefferies, 'The Irish Parliament of 1560: The Anglican Reforms Authorized', *IHS* 26 (1988), 129–31. For Sidney's parliament see V. Treadwell, 'The Irish Parliament of 1569–71', *PRIA*, C, 65 (1966), 55–89.

claiming to represent unincorporated towns. However, it refused to exclude members not resident in the constituencies they represented. (This ignored an Irish act against non-residents from as recently as 1542, but was in line with contemporary English practice, where the statutory ban on non-resident MPs had long been a dead letter.) A main reason for the touchiness of local members seems to have been Sir Peter Carew's attempt to invade long established property rights by exploiting ancient titles. The developing hostility between the two groups of English was evident when John Hooker, MP for Athenry and Carew's solicitor, was alleged to have referred to the Irish-born members of the house as 'kern'.

A further noteworthy feature of the parliamentary session of 1569 was the debate over Poynings's Law. Strictly interpreted, the act of 1494 meant that an Irish parliament could discuss only those bills that had been sent to England for approval, and had been returned under the great seal, as part of the preliminaries to its being summoned. The compromises over specific issues that had eventually permitted the enactment of the crown's legislative programme in 1536–7 had been possible only because an early measure of that parliament had been the temporary suspension of the law, allowing additional bills to be considered. An amending act of 1557 modified the requirements of the law, permitting the Irish council to submit further draft bills to England for approval while parliament was in session. Despite this concession, the administration in 1569 once again sought approval for a bill that would suspend the operation of Poynings's Law. The Commons, however, initially rejected the proposal, and later allowed it to pass only on an undertaking that no future bills of this kind would be transmitted to England for approval without the agreement of both houses of the Irish parliament. The episode confirms the limited place which parliament occupied in the political aspirations of the English-Irish elite. Later generations of patriots were to see Poynings's Law as a fatal check on Ireland's capacity for self-government. To Elizabeth's Irish subjects of English blood it clearly represented a valued safeguard against legislative ambush by a distrusted executive.

Another development central to the changing political outlook of the English of Ireland was a hardening of religious policy. Early hopes that the queen might somehow reach an accommodation with Catholicism at home and abroad had not survived the 1560s: during 1569–71 the duke of Norfolk and other leading Catholic peers were discovered to be plotting to replace her with her Catholic cousin, Mary queen of Scots, while in 1570 Pope Pius V declared her excommunicated and her crown forfeit. For more than a decade longer, however, Spain, the only power in a position to implement the pope's judgment, held back, preferring to see Elizabeth as a potential ally against France. But in a religiously divided Europe it was increasingly difficult to avoid taking sides. By 1585 Elizabeth's support for the Dutch Protestant revolt had brought the long avoided Spanish war, and the mid-1580s also saw three further Catholic plots against Elizabeth's life. External aggression and conspiracy at home in turn legitimized religious repression. An English act of 1585 increased the fines levied on recusants and also made Catholic priests liable to execution if found in the kingdom. Against this background the predominant recusancy of the Pale was increasingly at odds with the claim to be loyal subjects. Nor was the new suspicion with which they were regarded wholly groundless. As early as 1534 Thomas Lord Offaly had looked to religion as a rallying cry to revolt, and his example had more recently been followed by the leaders of the revolts of 1569–73 and 1579–83. Calls to followers to join in a crusade against heresy may in many cases have been opportunistic.[72] But there were also some, like Fitzmaurice and Baltinglass, who found in the new spirit of militant religious commitment spreading through Catholic continental Europe a reason to take arms against the crown whose service their ancestors had placed at the centre of their political creed.

Baltinglass's revolt in turn inspired a further rising in the Pale, this time centred on the Nugent family. If Stanihurst, with his vehement rejection of all things Gaelic, represented one aspect of the culture of English Ireland, the Nugents of Westmeath represented the other, moving freely between two elite cultures, Gaelic and English. Christopher Nugent, ninth Baron Devlin, educated at Cambridge, had presented the queen with a primer of the Irish language. His brother William, an Oxford graduate who had spent time at court, was himself a well regarded composer of poetry in the Gaelic tradition. At the same time the Nugents had long been accepted as key figures in the defence of the west Meath border. A poem on the death of the eighth baron in 1559 had praised him, with typical Gaelic pragmatism, as 'the protecting tree of the *Gall*'.[73] In December 1580, however, the Irish council arrested the ninth baron, along with his brother-in-law the earl of Kildare, on charges of complicity in Baltinglass's revolt. In reality it seems that both men, though aware of Baltinglass's plans, had held back from committing themselves. Their arrest was thus an overreaction, and it provoked William Nugent to raise an armed force to demand their release. At this point the family's Gaelic connections ceased to be a mere cultural curiosity. Nugent's revolt drew on the support of the MacGeoghegans, the O'Connors, and other Gaelic septs. When the government sent troops against him he withdrew into the O'Reilly territory in East Breifne. In July 1581 he returned to raid County Longford, this time with the backing of O'Rourke of West Breifne, as well as Scots mercenaries supplied by Turlough Luineach O'Neill. Nugent

[72] See in particular the well-documented critique of Desmond's invocation of the Catholic cause in McCormack, *Earldom of Desmond*, 181–90.

[73] For the Nugents and Gaelic culture, see Vincent Carey, '"Neither Good English nor Good Irish": Bi-lingualism and Identity Formation in Sixteenth-Century Ireland', in Hiram Morgan (ed.), *Political Ideology in Ireland 1541–1641* (Dublin, 1999), 52–7. For the events of 1580–1, Helen Coburn Walshe, 'The Rebellion of William Nugent, 1581', in Comerford et al., *Religion, Conflict and Coexistence*, 26–52.

also remained in contact with the Pale, where another gentleman, John Cusack, had begun to gather support for a rising. By the autumn, however, a military expedition against Turlough Luineach had disposed of the immediate threat, and the Pale conspiracy began to unravel. Nugent fled to France in January 1582; Baltinglass had already sailed the previous November.

Baltinglass, like Fitzmaurice, was an untypical figure. His revolt received the support of only a handful of mainly younger men. More were involved in the Nugent–Cusack conspiracy. But since this never came to fruition their motives, and the extent to which individuals actually committed themselves, remain harder to document. Religious commitment was once again a motive. But there are also suggestions of resentment at the diminishing share of official employment going to members of the Pale community; kinship and clientage also probably played a part. From the government's point of view, however, the spread of religious revolt from the half-tamed Munster frontier to the heart of the Pale was enough to confirm its worst suspicions. The willingness of those involved to join with the traditional enemies of their class and nation, the Gaelic Irish just beyond the Pale frontier, could likewise be seen as undermining the claims to unswerving loyalty central to the political self-image of the English of Ireland. It was also the case that some of those involved, including the Nugents, had earlier been prominent in the agitation against cess.

Against this background the government responded with an unprecedented harshness. Dozens of alleged conspirators, including members of prominent landowning and legal families, were arrested on charges of treason. In the event nine gentlemen were executed for their part in the Baltinglass revolt, and a further eight on charges arising out of Cusack's conspiracy. There was also an unknown number of lesser men summarily executed under martial law. Large numbers of others paid substantial fines in exchange for pardons. If some of those executed proclaimed themselves martyrs for the Catholic faith, others were caught up in a witch-hunt. Chief Justice Nicholas Nugent was hanged, through the machinations of a rival, on what was clearly false evidence,[74] while others were accused or convicted on the malicious or self-serving evidence of informers. Some cases, such as the execution of two sons of Barnaby Scurlock, smacked of retaliation for earlier opposition on the issue of the cess. That the overall death toll was not higher was due to the English privy council, which recognized the damage being done and intervened to call a halt to the trials. But the experience of the Pale community had been a traumatic one. Even after the main bloodletting had finished, moreover, the conspiracy claimed one more victim. In 1583 the authorities arrested Dermot O'Hurley, just returned from Rome, where he had been appointed papal archbishop of Cashel. On orders from London O'Hurley

[74] Ciaran Brady, 'Court, Castle and Country: The Framework of Government in Tudor Ireland', in Ciaran Brady & Raymond Gillespie (eds.), *Natives and Newcomers: The Making of Irish Colonial Society 1534–1641* (Dublin 1986), 36.

was tortured to extract evidence of his involvement in the Baltinglass and Nugent conspiracies; the method used was 'to toast his feet against the fire with hot boots'. When this failed to extract evidence for a regular trial for treason, the archbishop was convicted under martial law and hanged outside Dublin in June 1584. He was not the first priest to die: others had been killed or executed in the course of various conflicts over the previous fifteen years. But what was becoming Catholic Ireland now had its first prominent martyr on unequivocally religious grounds.[75]

Already before these events in the Pale, the widening split between the English by blood and the English by birth had found expression in another context, through the campaign by New English officials and army officers to have Ormond removed from command of the Munster campaign. There followed another power struggle, once again pitting Ormond against a lobby of New English 'servitors', over how the lands of the defeated rebels should be disposed of.[76] The eventual solution, that the confiscated lands should go to well-funded undertakers, rejected the claims of the servitors. But the stipulation that the undertakers were to be of English birth institutionalized for the first time the distinction between two kinds of English.

The alienation of the Pale community was confirmed in a final confrontation, the parliament summoned by a new lord deputy, Sir John Perrot, in April 1585. Perrot's main aim was to reach a final settlement on cess. The agitation of 1574–8 had ended with an agreement that the government would accept an annual payment of £2,000 in lieu of other exactions, and subsequent negotiations had reduced the amount to £1,500 or £1,600. Perrot's plan was for a single national settlement, in which the government's claims on the Pale, and all payments and services demanded by lords elsewhere, would be replaced by a cash rent payable to the crown and levied according to a uniform unit of assessment. At the same time he also made clear from the beginning that he intended to take a tougher line than his predecessors towards religious dissent. Soon after his arrival he reported to London his discovery of 'a great nest . . . of massmongers', including leading lawyers, merchants, and gentry. In December he gave orders for the oath of supremacy to be administered to all adults. Having been persuaded to abandon this measure as impractical, he nevertheless proceeded with attempts to impose the oath on justices of the peace and other holders of local office, while at the same time insisting to London that he had been 'more politiquely slack than religiously forwards'. The bills drawn up for his proposed parliament included one to extend to Ireland twenty-seven English statutes, among them the most recent anti-Catholic laws.[77]

Perrot's proposals encountered determined resistance from representatives of the Pale, once again taking the name 'commonwealthmen'. As before, their

[75] Dudley Edwards, *Church and State*, 268–70.

[76] See above, 'Like Well Tempered Wax'.

[77] Charles McNeill (ed.), 'The Perrot Papers', *Analecta Hibernica*, 12 (1943), 11, 30.

most effective tactic was to block a proposal to suspend Poynings's Law, an essential step if Perrot was to have the flexibility to negotiate and then implement a composition. The suspension bill was rejected by thirty-five votes. Perrot sought to intimidate the opposition by a series of hostile interrogations, and by imprisoning one prominent Palesman, Richard Netterville, but their resistance remained firm. Parliament met for two further sessions, in November 1585 and April 1586. Once Perrot had abandoned all plans to legislate on religious matters, its other business, including an act for the attainder of Desmond and other rebels, went ahead with reasonable efficiency. But there was no agreement to a revised taxation system. Instead a delegation met Perrot once the sessions were over and negotiated a new composition in lieu of cess.

As Perrot's parliament closed the speaker, Nicholas Walsh, chief justice of Munster, delivered a concluding address which emphasized the idea of Ireland as a body politic in which all subjects were equal under the crown, and in which the balance of crown, Lords, and Commons acted as a safeguard against the assumption of arbitrary power by any one of the three. Walsh, though native-born, was a Protestant, and had been the government candidate for the speakership. Nevertheless his address has been seen as evidence of the well-defined sense of their constitutional liberties that the disputes of the past three decades had nurtured among the leaders of the English of Ireland.[78] Yet their victory on this occasion was a costly one. Failure to agree on the central issue of financing government at an appropriate level could only be taken to mean that the traditional concept of a community of interest between the crown's representatives and the English of Ireland no longer had real meaning. Perrot's failure had in part been due to divisions within his own administration: his short temper and high-handed ways had alienated many and there were claims that Archbishop Loftus and others had exploited the issues of cess and anti-Catholic legislation to undermine him. But the Irish parliament had also rejected what was possibly its last chance to earn a role in the government of the kingdom by assuming responsibility for the costs that went with it.

It is important not to overstate the change in the political position and outlook of the English of Ireland. Their long-standing cooperation with the crown in the business of government did not end all at once. In 1580 the holders of half the offices in the civil establishment were still Irish-born, just as, two years earlier, were eight of the eighteen members of the Irish council. The response of the queen and council to Perrot's attempt to impose rigid uniformity makes clear that there was no desire on the crown's side to see a breakdown in relations; and it would in any case have been impractical to proceed on that basis, so long as

[78] Brendan Bradshaw, 'The Beginnings of Modern Ireland', in Brian Farrell (ed.), *The Irish Parliamentary Tradition* (Dublin, 1973), 85–7. For the influence of Bradshaw's rather extravagantly worded claims see e.g. Colm Lennon, *Sixteenth-Century Ireland: The Incomplete Conquest* (Dublin, 1994), 206–7; Ellis, *Ireland under the Tudors*, 322.

the New English newcomers remained a small minority, and the bulk of both land and mercantile wealth remained in the hands of the English by blood. The Irish-born, for their part, were slow to abandon a long-standing identification with England and its people. Sir Edmund Butler, even after his revolt in 1569, insisted that 'I do not make war against the queen, but against those that banish Ireland and mean conquest'. James Fitzmaurice Fitzgerald, raising the papal standard ten years later, went out of his way to emphasize that his rebellion was not a repudiation of long-standing political allegiances: 'Therefore now we fight not against the lawful sceptre and honourable throne of England, but against a tyrant which refuseth to hear Christ speaking by his vicar.'[79]

The perceptible but gradual reassessment of allegiances and identity taking place among the English by birth found a more extended, if still indirect, expression in a second work by their main literary spokesman. *De Rebus in Hibernia Gestis*, published by Richard Stanihurst in 1584, gave a new account of 'the English province of Ireland', cultured, prosperous, and holding itself wholly aloof from its less developed neighbour. Yet Stanihurst, himself now an exile in Holland, was writing in a context quite different from that of his earlier work. Where before he had sought to justify the English of Ireland to an English audience, he now wrote to offer continental Europe a positive portrait of Ireland as a whole. In addition his growing commitment to the Counter-Reformation meant that the Gaelic Irish, still less civilized neighbours, were also fellow Catholics. Against this background, his account of Gaelic culture, though critical, was perceptibly softer than in 1577. His very first step, in fact, was to reject as 'insulting defamation' claims that the Irish lived a nomadic and barbarous life. 'For while the Irish do not approach the standards of refinement and urbanity to be found in the English province, nevertheless they have not abandoned civilised living as they are alleged to have done.' He still believed that it was not in the interest of the English of Ireland that the Irish language should spread among them. But he was now prepared to accept that it was nevertheless an ancient tongue, 'rich in vocabulary, elegance and wit'. Where his own community was concerned, meanwhile, Stanihurst introduced a new claim: that the English spoken in Ireland, based on that of Chaucer, was superior to the 'strange and florid English', laced with foreign words, that had now become fashionable in England itself.[80]

In addition to tempering his earlier hostility to Gaelic Ireland, and hinting perhaps at a new sense of separateness from an unsympathetic England, Stanihurst's second book introduced a new ethnic label for his own community. He called them *Anglo-Hiberni*. His coinage, translating as 'English Irish' rather than

[79] Butler, quoted in Bagwell, *Ireland under the Tudors*, iii. 158; Fitzmaurice's proclamation printed in Grenfell Morton, *Elizabethan Ireland* (London, 1971), 126.

[80] Stanihurst's text is translated in Lennon, *Richard Stanihurst*, 131–60; for analysis, ibid. 88–98.

the misleadingly modern 'Anglo-Irish', did not become common usage. At the same time it appears that his sense that a new term was needed was widely shared. A petition of 1568 referred to the Palesmen as the queen's 'old ancient faithful English subjects'. Thirty years later the term, in a less cumbersome form, was clearly entering common usage. A tract of 1598 referred to what it called 'the extract of the English nation' in Ireland as 'the Old English'.[81] Spenser, writing about the same time, likewise referred to 'the old English' (although he also used 'English-Irish'). He also noted the complaint among these long established colonists 'that they are wronged by the new Englishmen's entering thereunto'.[82]

'ALL CONNACHT UNDER BONDAGE'

In July 1584 the new lord deputy, Sir John Perrot, reported that he had sent to England the sons of the earls of Desmond and Clancare. There he hoped that the provision which the English council would make for the education of the two boys 'may work in them that fear of God and duty to their prince that their parents wanted'.[83] Even in the aftermath of two major Munster rebellions, in other words, an Irish chief governor was still willing to talk in terms of training a new generation of Irish lords, of both Gaelic and English blood, to assume their proper place in the social hierarchy. Yet his optimism proved in both cases to be misplaced. Tadhg McCarthy returned to Dublin, where he was to have continued his education in English ways, but he escaped and took refuge in France, where he died some time before 1588. Young James Fitzgerald had a longer life, but probably a bleaker one. Born in 1571, he had been in government hands since 1579, when his mother had been persuaded to surrender him as a guarantee of the loyalty which his father was just about to abandon. He spent the next two decades in the Tower of London, in liberal but firm confinement, a pawn held in reserve for any unexpected twist in Irish politics. His moment came in 1600, when Sir George Carew brought him to Munster to rally support for the crown at the height of a renewed war. However, it was a brief one. Initially welcomed, he lost support rapidly after being seen to attend the services of the Church of Ireland, and returned to England where he died the following year.

By this time Perrot himself had also died, in 1592, a prisoner in the same Tower and under sentence of death for treason. His governorship of Ireland, between 1584 and 1588, can be seen in retrospect as the last attempt to implement the reformist strategy that had shaped English policy towards Ireland, intermittently at least, since the early 1520s. Some of the influences that had undermined

[81] Nicholas Canny, *The Formation of the Old English Elite in Ireland* (Dublin, 1971), 31; Ciaran Brady, 'Conservative Subversives: The Community of the Pale and the Dublin Administration', in P. J. Corish (ed.), *Radicals, Rebels and Establishments* (Belfast, 1985), 30, 32.

[82] Spenser, *View*, 26, 59, 66, 143.

[83] McNeill, 'Perrot Papers', 2.

that strategy had already been apparent well before Perrot took office. There was the disillusionment that developed with repeated setbacks, as local lords resorted to yet another opportunistic revolt, disregarding solemn pledges of allegiance and the abject declarations of submission that had followed earlier revolts. There were the new dangers presented by a background of war to the death against the Spanish empire—an element reinforced by the destruction along Ireland's western coastline of the remains of the Great Armada in October 1588. There were the first serious intrusions into Irish domestic politics of the religious divisions of Counter Reformation Europe. But to these military and religious pressures, disruptive enough in their own right, there was now to be added another disastrous development: the commencement of a phase of ruthless profiteering by New English adventurers, facilitated in their fortune-hunting by a collapse of political initiative at the centre of government in Ireland.

Perrot was an extravagant, contradictory figure. Reputedly an illegitimate son of Henry VIII, he was noted for his quarrelsome temper and violent rages. At a council meeting in 1587 he was alleged to have beaten the 79-year-old Sir Nicholas Bagenal to the ground. Reports of his public rantings at the failure of the queen to support his policies ('Ah, now, silly woman, now she shall not curb me, she shall not rule me now') helped to bring about his eventual downfall.[84] He was also no stranger to the harsher side of Irish government. As president of Munster during 1571–3 he had directed the suppression of the first Desmond rebellion, and the beginnings of a policy of mass executions as a means of ridding the country of masterless men and unacknowledged retainers. Yet he commenced his lord deputyship, a post he had actively solicited, with an explicit affirmation of the principle of assimilation that had been proclaimed, in theory at least, when Ireland became a kingdom four decades earlier. The queen's will, he told his audience in an early address, was that they should be 'governed, cherished and corrected with equal care and without distinction of nation, English or Irish, as being equally by right of both crowns interested in them'.[85]

These were reassuring words—if they were taken seriously. But Perrot also made clear that his promises of equal treatment were made in the context of a far-reaching programme of social change. One of his aims, he proclaimed, was to emancipate the peasantry: his aim was to abolish 'the name of churl and the crushing of a churl', and to replace it with 'the titles used in England, namely husbandmen, franklins or yeomen'. He pressed for a new programme of surrender and regrant, arguing that the uncertain Gaelic system of inheritance, giving no man an incentive to preserve what he held for his posterity, lay at the root of the kingdom's backwardness. More directly still he called for the

[84] Hiram Morgan, 'The Fall of Sir John Perrot' in Guy, *The Reign of Elizabeth I*, 121. The fullest account of Perrot's governership is now Hiram Morgan, *Tyrone's Rebellion: The Outbreak of the Nine Years War in Tudor Ireland* (Woodbridge, 1993), ch. 3.

[85] McNeill, 'Perrot Papers', 6–7.

continued extension of the institutions of country government, so that, in the words of his biographer:

> the poor people might have more ready and less chargeable trial of small causes at home, the ignorant might be instructed in the law, and the wilful might be made subject to the law, the great lords might be brought from tyrannising of their tenants, and they on the other side might learn to support themselves by lawful means from unlawful usurpations and exactions.

The rhetoric of assimilation looked back to the era of St Leger. But it also stated openly what in the 1540s had been only implicit: that assimilation must imply a complete restructuring of Gaelic society, including the powers and privileges of local lords, in accordance with English norms.[86]

Perrot's first attempt to implement this revived, if toughened, strategy of reform was in Ulster. The northern province had initially not been a priority, but the arrival in summer 1584 of up to 2,000 redshanks, imported to support the sons of Shane O'Neill in an assault on Turlough Luineach, led Perrot to mount an expedition. The redshanks had already withdrawn, and an attack on the other Scottish bridgehead, the MacDonnells on the north-east coast, ended inconclusively. However, his presence in Ulster, backed by a substantial army, allowed Perrot to negotiate an agreement with the Ulster lords. His initial plans for Ulster were elaborate. He proposed a garrison of 2,000 foot and 400 horse, along with a network of seven towns, seven forts, and seven bridges at strategic points. But expenditure on this scale was no more acceptable to the queen than it had been a quarter of a century earlier, when Sussex had suggested a similar programme of garrisons and fortifications. Instead Perrot was left to reach a less ambitious local settlement, whereby the principal Ulster lords agreed to provide billets for 1,100 English soldiers. In addition Perrot designated three lieutenancies. Sir Nicholas Bagenal, the military strongman long established at Newry, took charge of the counties of Antrim and Down, Turlough Luineach O'Neill became responsible for a large western region, while Hugh O'Neill, the son of Shane O'Neill's rival Matthew and his successor as baron of Dungannon, was entrusted with what were shortly to become the counties of Armagh and Monaghan. Meanwhile Perrot also resumed the negotiation of surrenders and regrants, eventually concluding agreements with almost all of the remaining lords of Connacht, Ulster, and the north midlands.

After not much more than a year in office, Perrot could thus claim to have imposed order on Ulster, the last major region of Gaelic autonomy. But without the substantial military investment he had originally envisaged, his achievement was less substantial than it appeared. In one region, East Breifne, the lord deputy was able to further his ambition of dismantling the power

[86] Morgan, *Tyrone's Rebellion*, 42; *The History of that Most Eminent Statesman, Sir John Perrott* (London, 1728), 177, 193–4.

structures of Gaelic Ireland. Under a settlement negotiated in late 1584, Sir John O'Reilly—recognized as lord of the whole territory as recently as the previous year—received four out of seven baronies; the remaining three went to other members of the sept, to be held under the crown independently of any overlordship of Sir John's. East Breifne, however, was close to the Pale. Moreover Perrot was able to exploit internal divisions, imprisoning the most recalcitrant senior member of the sept, Philip O'Reilly, while dividing the lordship among other claimants. In Ulster as a whole the tripartite division between Bagenal, Turlough Luineach, and Dungannon was in practice an acceptance of existing spheres of influence, rather than an extension of royal authority. Attempts to give Ulster the institutions of shire government were likewise largely nominal. When an English soldier, Captain William Mostian, tried to take up his office as sheriff of Donegal, O'Donnell promptly ran him out of the newly established county.

The remainder of Perrot's period of office saw further concessions to political reality. In March 1586, following a new treaty with Scotland and moves towards open war with Spain, he received orders to make his peace with the MacDonnells; Sorley Boy and his nephew Angus duly submitted to the deputy in June and were granted patents to hold their lands on the north-east coast under the crown. By this time the number of troops to be maintained by the Ulster lords had been reduced to 550, and among these local recruits were said to have largely displaced the original English. Later the obligation to maintain even this reduced force was commuted to rents in cash and cattle, which in practice remained unpaid. In 1587 Perrot lobbied vigorously to have the O'Neill lordship dismantled as East Breifne had been. This would have involved balancing the earldom of Tyrone, already bestowed on Hugh O'Neill, with a separate earldom of Omagh for Turlough Luineach, and dividing the territory between them. However, the court was unwilling to override the claims of the increasingly powerful and, so far, loyal Tyrone. Instead Perrot was forced to resort to lesser measures to contain his rising power. He promoted surrender and regrant agreements for the south Ulster lords MacMahon and O'Hanlon, and encouraged them to resist Tyrone's claims to overlordship. When Tyrone negotiated a marriage alliance with his hereditary rivals the O'Donnells, the lord deputy resorted to more direct action. The prospective bridegroom, Hugh Roe O'Donnell, was lured on board a ship in Lough Swilly for a drinking party, captured, and imprisoned in Dublin Castle.

Perrot's other major area of operation was Connacht. Between 1577 and 1584 Sir Nicholas Malby, as president, had successfully operated a financial settlement, collecting a rent in lieu both of the exactions of local lords and the cess demanded by the English garrison. In 1585 Perrot initiated a revised and more systematic composition. Commissioners, including leading landowners as well as the new president, Sir Richard Bingham, supervised a survey to determine the number of chargeable units of inhabited land ('ploughlands') in each barony. This formed the basis of a series of tripartite agreements between the crown, the ruling lords, and the freeholders and inhabitants of each district. The crown was to receive a rent of 10 shillings per quarter of inhabited land. In addition freeholders were required to attend military hostings within the province. These new obligations were to replace all previous rents and services demanded by local lords in exchange for their protection. Instead the provincial president, supported by the new crown rent, would be responsible for the defence of the region, the security of life and property, and the remedying of just grievances.[87]

This principle of commuting the multiple exactions of Gaelic society to a rent payable to the crown looked back to Sidney's earlier strategy for reform, and was a central part of Perrot's own plans to replace indigenous power structures with an extension of England's social and political hierarchy. Yet the details of the scheme represented an important modification of the original policy. As before, the composition required lords and chiefs to give up their Gaelic titles and to hold their lands under English law, including succession by primogeniture. But in compensation for this loss of status, a certain part of their land was defined as 'freedoms', exempt from composition charges. In addition former regional overlords were to receive a rent, separate from that payable to the crown, from all lands over which they had formerly claimed supremacy. The principal beneficiaries were the earls of Thomond and Clanricard. In Thomond Perrot and Bingham had the advantage of working with the court-educated fourth earl, who had succeeded in 1581. Ulick Burke, who had succeeded as earl of Clanricard in 1582, had a less reassuring history. As one of the 'Mac an Iarlas' he had been in sporadic rebellion since 1572, exploiting local dislike both of the Reformation and of his father's dependence on the English. By 1582, however, he had turned to the government to support him against his brother's rival claim to the earldom. Like Thomond he now became a strong supporter of the composition. Both magnates, moreover, found the new arrangement highly advantageous. They were required to give up the right to maintain private armies by coyne and livery; but this had always been as much a burden as a privilege. Instead they now received a reliable and substantial cash rent. The areas granted to them as 'freedoms' were also substantial, and this turned out to be a particular advantage as the highly mobile peasantry of an underpopulated Connacht showed a definite preference for settling on lands thus exempted from composition tax.

In the southern half of Connacht the composition thus secured a relative political stability, but it did so by consolidating rather than undermining the power of the great regional lords. One suggested reason for this outcome is that Perrot, at odds with senior New English officials like Bagenal and Archbishop Loftus, was open to the alternative influence of a continuing tradition of reformist thinking represented by Irish-born officials like Sir Nicholas White, the master of the rolls.[88] But it is also possible that Perrot himself, with his

[87] Bernadette Cunningham, 'The Composition of Connacht in the Lordships of Clanricard and Thomond, 1577–1641', *IHS* 24 (1984), 1–14.

[88] Ibid. 8.

genuine if often heavy-handed belief in assimilation, responded to what were for once good prospects for magnate cooperation. In either case the composition in south Connacht contrasts sharply with the outcome further north, where Perrot's tactics came closer to those employed in East Breifne. In 1576 Shane MacOliverus Burke, elected head of the Lower MacWilliam or Mayo Burkes in 1571, had submitted to Sidney, agreeing to hold his lands from the queen for an annual rent of £200 and the service of 200 soldiers for two months each year.[89] When Shane died in 1580, however, Malby had tacitly accepted the claim of the *tánaiste*, Richard-an-iarainn Burke, to succeed to the supposedly defunct title of MacWilliam. (This was even though Richard-an-iarainn had just submitted after rising in support of Desmond, and had shown every sign of being ready to assert his claim in arms.) Shane's brother Richard MacOliverus, his heir by English law, had to be content with the title of sheriff of County Mayo, succeeding as MacWilliam only when Richard-an-iarainn died in 1583. When Richard MacOliverus died in his turn in 1586, on the other hand, Perrot abandoned the pragmatic policies of his predecessors. Instead he sought to break up the lordship, allocating the deceased chief's lands to his son William, and dividing the remainder of the territory between six other proprietors. The result was a revolt engulfing the whole of north Connacht. The crisis deepened when two of Sorley Boy MacDonnell's nephews, in a last military outing for the Scots of the north-east, led a force of over 2,000 mercenaries into Connacht. Bingham, at the head of only 600 men, ambushed the invaders as they tried to cross the River Moy, killing over half of them. But although the immediate danger had passed, the region remained seriously unstable.[90]

By 1588 Perrot's reform policy had run its largely unsuccessful course. He had fallen out catastrophically with key New English office holders, and had failed to secure the agreement of the English by blood to a new framework for financing the government of the kingdom, while his vision of a restructured Gaelic Ireland had achieved at best uneven results. In any case the times had quickly become unsuited to a reforming chief governor. From August 1585, when the queen agreed to commit troops in support of the Dutch Protestant revolt, London's priority was to keep Ireland quiet so as to free resources both for the Netherlands themselves and for the wider war with Spain that must inevitably follow. To achieve this the crown now turned to one of its longest-serving Irish ministers. Sir William Fitzwilliam had come to Ireland in 1554 to head the investigation that had brought down St Leger, and had remained there as undertreasurer under his brother-in-law Sussex. Having already served as deputy in the interval between Sidney's two deputyships, during 1571–5, he now replaced Perrot in June 1588.

[89] For the division between the two Burke dynasties see above, Ch. 2 n. 75.

[90] Most accounts attribute the MacWilliam revolt to Bingham's authoritarian behaviour. However Morgan (*Tyrone's Rebellion*, 50) makes clear that the trouble began with Perrot's determination to break up the lordship.

Fitzwilliam's age, experience, and temperament may have suited him for the role of a retrenching, caretaker governor. But in other ways he was far from suitable. He was heavily indebted to the crown for shortfalls in his account as undertreasurer. Possibly as a response to these pressures, he had acquired a reputation for shameless corruption. His only desire, one contemporary complained, was 'to fill his own bags daily and hourly'.[91] His first step on attaining office was to head off the threat that Perrot would either return or use his influence in London to discredit him. To this end Fitzwilliam procured a renegade priest, Sir Denis O'Roughan, who testified, among other things, that he had said mass for Perrot, and that he had transmitted a letter from the deputy to Philip II of Spain, offering to help him conquer Ireland in exchange for a grant to himself of the principality of Wales. The charges were so extravagant as to be ridiculous, but Fitzwilliam had the support of Lord Burghley, a relative by marriage, while Perrot's patron at court, Sir Francis Walsingham, had just died. It was in these circumstances that Perrot was convicted of treason in April 1592. The queen refused to sanction his execution, but he remained in the Tower, where he died in September.

Fitzwilliam's reported corruption was manifold. He was alleged to retain crown rents and other payments, to sell both government offices and livings in the church, to appropriate to himself the profits of wardship and other royal prerogatives, and to traffic in pardons and licences. The most startling allegations concerned the partition in 1590 of the MacMahon lordship in Monaghan. The MacMahon chief, Sir Ross, died in 1589. Fitzwilliam initially supported the claims of his brother, Hugh Roe, to succeed him as lord of the territory. Later, however, he withdrew his support, and had Hugh Roe tried and executed for the crimes of resisting the queen's sheriff, maintaining Scottish mercenaries, and extorting from his neighbours the traditional but now prohibited exactions of Gaelic lordship. The charges were well enough founded, but Hugh Roe had hardly behaved differently from other lords; indeed one of the beneficiaries of his fall was Hugh Óg MacMahon, Sir Ross's *tánaiste*, who had fought and defeated the troops Fitzwilliam sent to support his rival. The real reason for Fitzwilliam's transfer of his support, it was alleged, was that Hugh Roe had failed to deliver the 800 cows he had promised in exchange for the deputy's support. The final settlement was more radical even than Perrot's intrusion in East Breifne. As with the O'Reillys, the lordship was broken up, with seven leading MacMahons each receiving a demesne, on which they were to pay rents to the crown. In addition 287 lesser men were established as freeholders, paying rents to the principal lords but holding their lands from (and paying a second rent to) the crown. The church lands in the lordship were bestowed on a range of outsiders, including Bagenal. Once again there were claims that Fitzwilliam himself had profited substantially from these dealings.

[91] Morgan, *Tyrone's Rebellion*, 59. For Morgan's detailed account of Perrot's fall see n. 78 above.

In addition to Fitzwilliam's own depredations, the presence of a passive, and bribable, governor created a profitable hunting ground for other predators. From the late 1590s the crown made increasing use, in both England and Ireland, of a new means of raising revenue: by issuing suitable individuals with speculative grants entitling them to a lease on any royal property that they discovered to have improperly passed into private hands, it gained both an immediate rent and eventual complete possession of the lands concerned. In England the hasty secularization of the property of monasteries and religious guilds, as well as numerous more routine transactions, had given rise to enough irregularities to make such proceedings reasonably lucrative. But in Ireland, with its rudimentary record-keeping, fluid and poorly defined land boundaries, and a history in which possession had consistently counted for more than legal title, the scope for both real and fraudulent discoveries was even greater. The scramble for gain was epitomized in the figure of Richard Boyle, a younger son from an obscure Kent family who had come to Ireland in 1588 and obtained an appointment to the post of deputy escheator. This gave him responsibility for establishing royal title to concealed lands before a local jury, and for issuing a certificate assessing their value. In this role he made free use of bribes, intimidation, and the manipulation of legal processes to obtain verdicts in the crown's favour. His master-stroke, however, was to force those holding grants of concealed lands to sell all or part of their interest to him, by obstructing their attempts to establish royal title on their own behalf. He then used these grants to secure leases for himself at absurdly low valuations. By 1614 he had built a fortune of £4,000 a year. Yet he was only one of many, and indeed his spectacular success was in part achieved by exploiting his official position to fleece those who had come to fleece others. Lord Chief Justice Gardiner, in 1595, complained of 'underhand and nimble officers, most of them lately come from England to make their better provision'.[92] However Burghley, whether from loyalty to Fitzwilliam, a desire to protect a profitable source of revenue, or both, ignored the complaints of corruption and warnings of growing resentment.

At local level the consequences of Fitzwilliam's permissive regime were particularly evident in the case of Connacht. The president, Sir Richard Bingham, was a hardened military man. A veteran of campaigns in Scotland, France, and the Netherlands, he had reportedly served under Don John of Austria against the Turks in the Mediterranean, and had also, closer to home, taken part in the massacre at Smerwick. His hardline tactics had brought him into conflict with Perrot. In 1587, as the McWilliam Burke revolt continued, he was transferred to service in the Netherlands while Perrot sought to conciliate the disaffected local lords. Bingham returned in 1588 in time to confront a new threat: the shipwreck during September and October of vessels from the Grand Armada that had just

[92] Terence Ranger, 'Richard Boyle and the Making of an Irish Fortune, 1588–1614', *IHS* 39 (1957), 261 n. 1.

failed to invade southern England. He dealt quickly with the immediate threat, killing those castaways that came into his hands, then launching punitive raids against Irish lords accused of having sheltered survivors. In response the Lower McWilliam Burkes and their allies once again rose in revolt. The new eruption alarmed the queen and council, which ordered Bingham to withdraw from the province while Fitzwilliam investigated his rule. By the end of the year, however, the Irish council had dismissed the charges.

Returning to Connacht with his authority confirmed, Bingham resumed his campaign to subdue the lords of north Connacht. In spring 1590 he occupied West Breifne, where Sir Brian O'Rourke had long defied him. O'Rourke fled to Scotland, but James VI sent him to London, where he was hanged, drawn, and quartered. The lordship was partitioned among the chief lords of the region. However, Bingham blocked plans for a restructuring of landholding along the lines followed in Monaghan. His concern was with the maintenance of effective power rather than with any broader strategy of reshaping the Gaelic social and political order, and he had no desire either to destabilize the region or to see his own wide powers as president undermined by the introduction of regular tenancies under English law. Elsewhere in north Connacht, meanwhile, Bingham, deploying a substantial military force backed by the steady flow of composition rents, continued his campaign of suppression. The complaints of arbitrary violence made against him must be read against a background of intense factional conflict. But Bingham's own dispatches leave no doubt as to his ruthlessness. In spring 1590, for example, he reported casually that he had spent sixteen days in Tyrawley, 'spoiling the country and putting the people to the sword'. Soon after he was at Burrishoole, further south, where he found that the main body of the O'Malleys had fled by boat, but was able to seize 100 cows 'and slew all the churls, women and children'.[93]

At the same time that he established the military supremacy of the president in north Connacht, Bingham also established himself and his relatives and allies in positions of power throughout the region. In particular he took advantage of the death in 1588 of Sir Donal O'Connor Sligo. Sir Donal had concluded a surrender and regrant agreement in 1568, and the 1585 composition had acknowledged his claim to overlordship by allocating him a rent charge from lesser lords in the region. In 1588, however, Bingham refused to accept Sir Donal's nephew, Donogh, as his legal heir, alleging that he was illegitimate. Instead he took possession of the estate for himself, not only receiving the rents but also levying troops on the area and demanding entertainment for his retinue in the style of a Gaelic chief. Meanwhile he installed his brother George in Sligo Castle, strategically important as it controlled the main corridor linking Ulster to Connacht. George Bingham also received land seized from the MacDonaghs.

[93] *CSPI 1588–92*, 329; Anne Chambers, *Granuaile: The Life and Times of Grace O'Malley c.1530–1603* (Dublin, 1998), 121.

George's son Henry became constable of another fortress, Ballymote Castle; his wife's nephew Nicholas Martin later held the same position, and was also sheriff of County Sligo. Another of Richard's brothers, John, established a residence at Castlebar, while a cousin, Captain George Bingham, was in command of Sligo Castle when he was killed in 1595. Some allowance can be made for Sir Richard's concern to have reliable allies in places of strategic importance. But the ruthless establishment of the president's authority was clearly intertwined with a campaign of family aggrandizement.

The Binghams, moreover, were only one of a growing number of outsiders who established themselves in north Connacht during this period. Already by 1585 there were some two dozen new landed proprietors in the province. Initial settlement, as might be expected, had been heaviest in the area just west of the Shannon. Malby had acquired a grant of 17,000 acres round Roscommon, and had established several dozen settlers on the land. In 1593 Bingham reported that the whole area between Roscommon and Athlone was 'well peopled with English'. In the south of the province, the powerful position of Thomond and Clanricard, bolstered by the 1585 composition, left relatively few opportunities for interlopers. In northern Connacht, on the other hand, a fragmented local elite at odds with an authoritarian presidency created the conditions for what amounted to a piecemeal but extensive process of informal colonization. In Mayo, John Browne, sheriff of the county, acquired a substantial estate at the Neale. Theobald Dillon, collector of composition rents, persuaded the MacCostellos to accept him as their lord, then converted what they took as a relationship of clientship into what in English law became a title to their lands.[94] In Sligo there were a dozen new proprietors by around 1595 and a further twelve outsiders who had acquired land on leases. Some of these newcomers were New English, like Malby and Browne. However, others, like Dillon, were Palesmen attracted by the speculative gains to be made in the west. Members of Galway merchant families also seized opportunities to acquire land in the city's hinterland. In some cases, as with Neale and the Binghams, newcomers made their gains by force, or, as with Dillon, by chicanery. Others used political connections to gain leases to crown or former church lands. Others again acquired land by lending money on mortgages which the proprietors concerned then failed to redeem.

What was the response of Gaelic Ireland to this final phase of reform government, followed by a descent into localized freebooting? Perrot used the parliament he summoned in April 1585 to advertise the progress he had made in drawing the native Irish lords into the body politic. Delegates from no fewer than forty-two septs attended the formal opening, among them Turlough Luineach, who walked in procession before the lord deputy carrying the sword of state. The following year Perrot applied (unsuccessfully) for permission to bring

[94] Bernadette Cunningham and Raymond Gillespie (eds.), *Stories from Gaelic Ireland: Microhistories from the Sixteenth-Century Irish Annals* (Dublin, 2003), ch. 2.

Turlough, Hugh O'Neill, Clancare, and others with him to court once parliament was dissolved. There is no reason to assume that the Gaelic chiefs concerned appreciated these patronizing gestures of inclusion. As in Munster a decade earlier, Perrot had insisted that they attend him wearing English dress which, one observer commented, they embraced 'like fetters'. Yet not all Gaelic participation in the proceedings of parliament was of this theatrical character. There were also twenty-one ordinary members, six peers, and fifteen MPs, with Gaelic Irish names. In County Clare, for example, one of the two knights of the shire returned was Baothghalach MagFhlannchadha, from a bardic family, described by a later annalist as 'a man fluent in the Latin, Irish and English languages'. Such men presumably represented a more wholehearted accommodation to the structures of the English kingdom than the passive observers summoned to represent their septs. Even these latter, moreover, bore testimony—as was the intention—to Perrot's success in imposing on the greater part of the island both the substance and the symbolism of an extended royal authority.[95]

Even in the case of the military and proprietorial intrusions that took place in Connacht and elsewhere, it is important not to jump to conclusions. The Gaelic sources suggest that the imposition of military dominance, leading to loose political control, was not in itself seen as illegitimate. When McWilliam Burke submitted to the queen in 1576, agreeing to pay her an annual rent and provide a fixed military service, the terms were not very different from those that an overlord like O'Neill or O'Donnell would have imposed on a subordinate chief. The composition of Connacht, likewise, appears in the work of a local annalist in traditional terms, as the levying of a tribute. A similar willingness to fit English newcomers into an existing framework of social and political relationships is evident in the same annalist's obituary of Sir Nicholas Malby, who died in 1584:

> Sir Nicholas Malby who had been captain over Connacht died the 3rd day of March, and there came not to Éirinn his own time nor often before a better gentleman of the foreigners than he, and he placed all Connacht under bondage. And it is not possible to count or reckon all that this man destroyed throughout Éirinn, and he executed many works especially on the courts of the towns of Athlone and Roscommon.

In this account Malby's ferocity in war, and his imposition of English rule, became the attributes of a powerful lord, to be praised rather than resented. Nor is such an attitude surprising. A similar pragmatic acceptance of the rise of new lords at the expense of old ones had earlier permitted newcomers like the Butlers and the Fitzgeralds to establish themselves as recognized overlords. It was an approach characteristic of a political system in which the fact of effective power

[95] McNeill, 'Perrot Papers', 52. For attendance at Perrot's parliament see Victor Treadwell, 'Sir John Perrot and the Irish Parliament of 1585–6', *PRIA*, C, 85 (1985), 281. For 'fetters', *NHI*, iii. 112. For MagFhlannchadha, Katherine Simms, 'The Brehons of Later Medieval Ireland', in Daire Hogan and W. N. Osborough (eds.), *Brehons, Serjeants and Attorneys: Studies in the History of the Irish Legal Profession* (Dublin, 1990), 75.

had always counted for more than any abstract notion of legitimacy. It was also wholly in tune with a tradition of historical and genealogical writing in which the whole of Irish history was characterized as a succession of successful invasions.[96]

It is also important to recognize that the conflicts of the period, even if they arose in the context of what can in retrospect be seen as a progressive extension of English state power, did not at the time assume the form of a simple opposition of English and Irish interests. The search for concealed lands, for example, undoubtedly caused resentment and insecurity. But the profiteering grantees were not all English; they included numerous Old English speculators, as well as a few of Gaelic Irish origin, such as Patrick 'Crosby', an anglicized member of the bardic family of Mac Uí Crosain, who acted as Fitzwilliam's agent. Their victims, equally, were New English settlers and officials as well as local-born proprietors. As newcomers sought to establish themselves, moreover, they frequently intermarried or formed other connections with local families. In Sligo, for example, the former soldier Roger Jones joined in ventures with the local merchant family of Crean, reinforcing the connection through the marriage of his niece to one of their number. A substantial proportion of the soldiers maintained by the president were Gaelic, as were some of the captains under whom they served.[97] Where local lords were concerned, English intervention produced both losers and winners. Recognition of their status as territorial magnates made Clanricard and Thomond into firm supporters of the 1585 composition, and ultimately of government in general. Lesser lords too could look to the crown as ally as well as threat. For O'Connor Sligo, for example, submission to the queen was a price worth paying to escape the demands of O'Donnell's overlordship.

The patchwork of varying allegiances that characterized Gaelic Ireland was evident in the fate of the Armada survivors. During September and October 1588 a total of twenty-six ships were lost in violent storms along the western and northern coasts of Ireland as they tried to make their way out into the Atlantic and home to Spain. Of the 6,000 men they carried, more than half died in the wrecks. But the estimated 2,250, most of them trained soldiers, who came ashore alive outnumbered the Irish standing army. Faced with this threat the provincial authorities reacted ruthlessly. In County Clare Boethius Clancy, the Gaelic Irish sheriff, captured the sixty-four survivors from two vessels and hanged them on the spot. In Galway Bingham similarly hanged every one of the 300 to 350 Spaniards brought to the county gaol, while his lieutenants dispatched other groups of survivors up and down the coast. Some Gaelic lords, such as O'Rourke, risked the crown's displeasure by harbouring Spaniards. Others, however, cooperated

[96] Bernadette Cunningham and Raymond Gillespie, 'Englishmen in Sixteenth-Century Irish Annals', *IESH* 17 (1990), 5–21; *Stories from Gaelic Ireland*, ch. 7.

[97] These points are emphasized in Canny, *Making Ireland British*, 92–103. For those involved in the discovery of concealed lands, see Ranger, 'Richard Boyle', 273–4.

in their destruction. Some of the prisoners executed at Galway had been turned in by the O'Flahertys. On Clew Bay the O'Malleys initially sheltered some sixty-eight survivors, but killed them all following an attempt at escape. In Ulster Hugh O'Neill, earl of Tyrone, sent 150 men, commanded by two of his Old English servants, the Hovenden brothers, to intercept a much larger party of 350 survivors from a wreck near Malin Head. Having persuaded the Spaniards to surrender on terms, they stripped the whole group naked, separated out the officers, and then scattered the rest with a volley followed by a cavalry charge, killing more than half their number. In other cases again coastal populations simply plundered the defenceless survivors, equally indifferent to both sides of the political and religious conflict that had brought them into their hands.

There was no question, then, of Gaelic Ireland at the end of the sixteenth century being united in resistance to English rule. But the potential for conflict had undoubtedly increased. There were those who benefited from successive extensions of English power. But projects such as the invasion of the O'Rourke lordship, or the suppression of the Lower MacWilliam title, nevertheless created a reserve of the disaffected and dispossessed. Submission to the queen could still be accepted pragmatically as the tribute required by a powerful overlord. But the signs were multiplying that it would come to mean more. Crown servants, and the queen herself, might still opt for expedient compromise. But where circumstances permitted they had begun to demand that formerly nominal agreements to abandon the military role of an Irish chief, and the prerequisites of Irish lordship, for the life of an English-style landlord, should actually be honoured. One official commented that the fate of Hugh Roe McMahon would do more than the slaughter of 1,000 rebels in battle to teach Gaelic lords to respect their articles with the state.[98] Against this background local lords, in Connacht and elsewhere, had once again to decide where their interest or safety lay as a new conflict developed in Ulster and spread to engulf almost the whole island.

[98] *CSPI 1588–92*, 369.

6

Wild Fruit from Savage Soil: The Crisis of the 1590s

FROM DUNGANNON TO TULLYHOGUE: THE RISE OF HUGH O'NEILL

IN October 1584 Perrot, reporting to the English privy council on his dealings with various Ulster lords, noted that the baron of Dungannon had been the subject of 'jealous conceits'. But Perrot himself had no such reservations. 'Truly I find no such thing in him, but that he maketh his whole dependence of the state, yielding to be made great and small at her Majesty's pleasure.'[1] Events were to prove the judgement spectacularly wrong. Yet the deputy's assessment is nevertheless significant. Hugh O'Neill, then baron of Dungannon and soon after earl of Tyrone, was to deal the last, fatal blow to the hope that the warrior lords of Gaelic Ireland could be transformed as a group into a gentry and aristocracy owing fealty to the English crown. Yet if O'Neill was to be the gravedigger of the Tudor policy of reform by assimilation, he was also very much its product.[2]

He had been born around 1550, the second son of Shane O'Neill's unfortunate rival Matthew. He became Matthew's heir after Turlough Luineach killed his older brother, Brian, in 1562. By this time Hugh had become the ward of Giles Hovenden, an Englishman who had settled in Queen's County. He came of age in 1567, the same year that the MacDonnels killed Shane and Turlough Luineach took the title of O'Neill. In 1568 Sidney established the young baron of Dungannon in Oneilland, east of the River Blackwater, with an allowance to enable him to maintain a detachment of cavalry. Over the next few years he built up his local power, using the traditional methods of imposing tribute and settling his followers on neighbouring lands, including church lands belonging

[1] Charles McNeill (ed.). 'The Perrot Papers', *Analecta Hibernica*, 12 (1947), 10.

[2] The fullest modern account of O'Neill's career is Hiram Morgan, *Tyrone's Rebellion: The Outbreak of the Nine Years War in Tudor Ireland* (Woodbridge, 1993). See also H. A. Jefferies, 'Hugh O'Neill, Earl of Tyrone, *c.*1550–1616', in Charles Dillon and Henry A. Jefferies (eds.), *Tyrone: History and Society* (Dublin, 2000), 181–232; Nicholas Canny, 'Taking Sides in Early Modern Ireland: The Case of Hugh O'Neill, Earl of Tyrone', in Vincent Carey and Ute Lotz-Heumann, *Taking Sides? Colonial and Confessional Mentalités in Early Modern Ireland* (Dublin, 2003), 94–115.

to the see of Armagh. At the same time he established a network of connections. Of particular importance here was his alliance with the O'Donnells, traditional rivals of the O'Neills, a connection reinforced by Dungannon's marriage to Siobhan O'Donnell and later by the marriage of one of his daughters to the O'Donnell heir, Hugh Roe. He used his visits to court in 1567–8 and 1587 to cultivate potential supporters, notably Sidney's brother-in-law, the earl of Leicester. He also enjoyed a degree of support from the earl of Ormond, whose influence straddled the Irish Sea. Where English Ireland was concerned, Tyrone's upbringing with the Hovendens gave him links with a number of prominent New English families. There are also recurrent reports, unverifiable but persistent, that he further increased his influence in government circles by extensive bribes, including payments to Fitzwilliam.

In Ulster too Dungannon's rise to power was achieved by skilfully playing a complex political game. In his early years in Oneilland he allied himself with Sir Nicholas Bagenal, whose Newry colony remained the only significant English settlement in Ulster. During 1573–5 he actively supported the bloody colonizing venture of the earl of Essex, who paid him £2,876 for his military services. In 1579 he briefly showed something of the true nature of his ambitions, when he suddenly repudiated the O'Donnell alliance, sending Siobhan back to her father so that he could marry a daughter of Turlough Luineach and become his *tánaiste*. This reconciliation with his main local rival quickly collapsed, and Dungannon redeemed himself in the eyes of the English by going south to serve briefly in the suppression of the Desmond revolt; Grey praised him as the only Irish nobleman who had drawn blood under his command. In 1582 he received a commission, jointly with Bagenal, to protect the Pale against raids from the north, with command over government troops and authorization to use martial law at his discretion.

Having recovered from his momentary lapse of judgement, Dungannon proceeded over the next five years to consolidate his power in central Ulster. During 1583–4 Turlough Luineach, now in failing health, came under renewed attack from the allied forces of Dungannon to the east and O'Donnell to the west. His problems multiplied with the arrival in August 1584 of an army of redshanks sent to support his other regional rivals, the MacShanes or sons of Shane O'Neill, five brothers by three different mothers who continued to regard themselves as the rightful candidates for the title of O'Neill.[3] It was against this background that Perrot imposed his tripartite division of Ulster into spheres of influence for Turlough Luineach, Dungannon, and Bagenal. In 1585, however, Dungannon, using the MacShane threat as an excuse and exploiting a temporary alliance with Turlough's son Art, took over central Tyrone. He now controlled two-thirds of the O'Neill lordship. Earlier in the year he had attended parliament in Dublin, and had taken his seat as second earl of Tyrone. In spring 1587 he

[3] For their parentage and status see Morgan, *Tyrone's Rebellion*, 92.

visited the court and negotiated a new settlement, under which he was to succeed to the entire lordship on Turlough Luineach's death. Art was to succeed to the lands formerly held by his grandfather Niall Connallach, owing the same services to Tyrone that Niall had owed to Conn Bacach.

The English government's support for Dungannon/Tyrone had from the start been governed by expediency. He was the son of the man whose claims Sussex had upheld at such cost against Shane O'Neill. But the crown, when it suited, could play as fast and loose with the rules of primogeniture as any Gaelic lord. (Years later, when Tyrone was in open rebellion, an official proclamation was brazenly to assert that the sons of Shane O'Neill, one of whom Tyrone had hanged, were men of more noble parentage than the earl himself.[4]) The young Dungannon had been established in east Ulster as a counterweight to the unreliable Turlough Luineach, and had subsequently been supported as an alternative to the MacShanes. By 1587, however, his power had grown to the point where he seemed to represent a threat rather than an asset. Perrot's agreements with MacMahon and O'Hanlon, and his kidnapping of Tyrone's son-in-law Hugh Roe O'Donnell, were all designed to curb this new over-mighty subject.[5] When Turlough Luineach, responding to a new offensive, defeated Tyrone in battle at Carricklea in April 1588, Perrot was elated, and added to the earl's discomfiture by forcing him to provide a bond of £1,000 for his future good behaviour. When the Armada shipwrecks demanded that he demonstrate his allegiance, Tyrone took the pragmatic course, sending the Hovenden brothers to enact their own minor Smerwick.[6] However, the government, in an indication of changing times, took seriously allegations that he had treasonably assisted the Spanish castaways, and there is evidence that he did in fact hedge his bets by protecting a number of individuals. In 1590 Tyrone was summoned to London, and for a time placed under house arrest, after he had defied the government's direct order by his hanging of Hugh Gavelach O'Neill, one of the MacShanes, who had by now allied with Turlough Luineach against him.

The following year Tyrone faced a new threat to his power, when the government created a commission charged with enforcing the rulings of the recently established northern assizes circuit, with Sir Henry Bagenal, who had succeeded his father as marshal of the army, as chief commissioner. The Bagenals had long since become rivals rather than allies, and Tyrone protested vigorously at being placed in the hands of what he claimed was a 'malicious enemy'. In the long run he resolved the problem by having his territories exempted from the new commission's jurisdiction. Before this, however, he had attempted quite a different solution to the problem of the marshal's rising power. Having already buried one wife and divorced a second, he proposed a marriage to Bagenal's

4 *Carew MSS 1589–1600*, 111, Proclamation of 28 June 1595.

5 Above, Ch. 5.

6 See above, p. 226.

20-year-old sister, Mabel. When Bagenal refused indignantly, Tyrone seduced the young woman and carried her off to a marriage ceremony performed by no less a person than Thomas Jones, Church of Ireland bishop of Meath. (The embarrassed prelate subsequently explained that he had acted to safeguard the young lady's honour.) The episode intensified rather than softened the antagonism between the two men. The marshal tried vainly to prove the marriage invalid, and intensified his vendetta against the earl. Tyrone, for his part, added to his list of grievances Bagenal's failure to hand over Mabel's marriage portion. Later, in 1599, he was even to insist to a new lord lieutenant that the elopement had been the sole cause of his having been outlawed and driven into rebellion.

Tyrone's elopement with Mabel Bagenal brings into focus his position as an inhabitant of two cultural worlds. He had been brought up in an English gentry family in Leinster, with periods spent in England.[7] As he established himself in Ulster he provided evidence of his metropolitan tastes by importing furniture from London for his castle at Dungannon. His seduction of Mabel, likewise, was possible only because he possessed the status and social graces to insinuate himself as a guest at the north County Dublin manor to which her brother had sent her for protection. On the other hand a report that after his marriage 'he did somewhat reform his household according to the English manner, appointed officers Englishlike, had cooks, his meat well-dressed and decently served' would suggest that up to that point his lifestyle in his Ulster base did not wholly conform to English concepts of civility. Moreover, it was claimed, 'this good order continued not long'. Sir John Harrington, visiting Tyrone in 1599, offered a similarly mixed account. The earl's sons, aged around 13 and 15, were dressed 'in English clothes, like a nobleman's sons, with velvet jerkins and gold lace'. But Harrington also referred to the earl's 'fern table, fern forms spread under the stately canopy of heaven', as well as his bodyguard of 'beardless boys without shirts'. A drawing of Dungannon a few years later shows a stone wall enclosing a solid keep. But the larger earthwork enclosure contains a collection of round huts of the traditional Irish type, with wattle and daub walls of thatched roofs.[8] Later still, when Tyrone had fled into continental exile, the Irish attorney general gleefully predicted that 'his train of barbarous men, women, and children . . . will be taken for a company of gypsies and be

[7] Morgan (*Tyrone's Rebellion*, 92–3) rejects as a legend of later origin the claim that Tyrone spent his early years in the household of Sir Henry Sidney in England, arguing that a reference to his having been educated 'amongst the English' referred instead to his upbringing by the Hovendens, who had a residence near Dublin. A contemporary description does, however, state that Tyrone was 'well brought up, partly in the court of Engl[and]': *The Description of Ireland . . . in Anno 1598*, ed. Edmund Hogan (Dublin, 1878), 33.

[8] Sir James Perrott, *The Chronicle of Ireland 1584–1608*, ed. Herbert Wood (Dublin, 1933), 73; 'Report of a Journey into the North of Ireland', in Sir John Harington, *Nugae Antiquae*, 3 vols. (London 1779), ii. 3–4; Caoimhín Ó Danachair, 'Representations of Houses on Some Irish Maps of *c*.1600', in Geraint Jenkins (ed.), *Studies in Folk Life* (London, 1969).

exceedingly scorned', and that 'the formal Spanish courtiers' would be struck by the 'heavy aspect and blunt behaviour' of the earl himself.[9]

As for Mabel Bagenal, her transition to this hybrid world does not appear to have been a happy one. Within a short time she had retreated to her brother's house and lodged a complaint against her husband with the privy council. The main problem, it appears, did not lie with the style of housekeeping at Dungannon, but rather with cultural differences of another kind. Her complaint was that Tyrone, in his own delicate phrase, 'affected two other gentlewomen'. She appears to have returned to her husband, since she died at Dungannon in 1595. A deposition in the state papers relating to an episode two years earlier describes in passing her apparent distress on realizing that her husband's foster-brothers had just butchered a disloyal subordinate barely out of her sight, and the way in which her protest was sharply silenced by her husband.[10]

Meanwhile the military struggle within Gaelic Ulster continued. Tyrone's greatest weakness at this stage was the collapse of his allies in the O'Donnell lordship of Tirconnell, where the imprisonment of Hugh Roe had left his father, Sir Hugh O'Donnell, unable to hold his own against would-be successors backed by Turlough Luineach. Hugh Roe had a fierce defender in his mother, the Scottish noblewoman Inion Dubh.[11] In 1588 she had her bodyguard kill Hugh MacCalvach, a member of the O'Gallagher family, favoured by the Dublin government, who had pursued the lordship of Tirconnell in alliance with Turlough Luineach, whose forces he had led to victory at Carricklea. In September 1590 she defeated and killed the family's leading rival, Donnell O'Donnell. The real turning point, however, came at Christmas 1591, when Hugh Roe escaped from Dublin Castle. As soon as he was back in Ulster Sir Hugh resigned the O'Donnell title in his favour, and by early 1593 the new O'Donnell had beaten his two main rivals, Niall Garbh O'Donnell and Hugh Dubh O'Donnell, into submission. Turlough Luineach was now once again caught between the forces of Tyrone to the east and O'Donnell to the west. In May 1593 he agreed to surrender the government of the O'Neill lordship to Tyrone, retaining only his demesne lands round Strabane and a pension of £2,000 per annum.

At the same time that he was deploying the traditional methods of a Gaelic warlord to reduce his rival Turlough Luineach, Tyrone had also to deal with an increasingly suspicious English establishment. Early in 1593 Captain Humphrey Willis launched an aggressive expedition into Fermanagh, where he had obtained

[9] Quoted in Micheline Kerney Walsh, *An Exile of Ireland: Hugh O'Neill, Prince of Ulster* (Dublin, 1996), 67. Davies's comments were, of course, highly partisan, and Walsh points out that the Spanish ambassador in Rome in fact acknowledged Tyrone as 'a great nobleman'. That, however, does not necessarily tell us what he thought of the earl's manners.

[10] *Trevelyan Papers*, part 2, *1446–1643*, ed. J. P. Collier, Camden Society (London, 1863), 102; *CSPI 1592–6*, 107–9.

[11] See above, Ch. 4.

a commission as sheriff. Hugh Maguire drove him out of the county, then followed up his victory by a raid into Connacht, in retaliation for what he claimed were Bingham's repeated incursions. Maguire was supported by galloglass from Tirconnell, as well as forces under the command of Tyrone's brother Cormac MacBaron and his foster-brothers the O'Hagans. Tyrone himself remained nominally neutral, but twice refused a summons to Dublin, correctly fearing that the council would have him arrested. Instead he met members of the council at Dundalk between 14 and 28 June. Acutely aware that Tyrone's army was encamped just a few miles away, the councillors chose to avoid confrontation. They considered allegations that Tyrone had encouraged Maguire and engaged in treasonable correspondence with Spain, but rejected the evidence before them as inadequate. Instead they ratified the earl's settlement with Turlough Luineach, and commissioned him to return Maguire to obedience. When Maguire remained defiant, Tyrone joined his rival Bagenal in uneasy joint command of a punitive expedition. They defeated Maguire in battle at Belleek in October. A spear wound in the thigh allowed Tyrone to boast of his proven loyalty. But there were claims that he had met secretly with Maguire, and had allowed him to move large numbers of his cattle into his own territory for safekeeping while hostilities continued. By the end of the year, the earl had once again become openly defiant. He dismissed the English soldiers who had been assigned to him for the campaign, and instead began raising additional troops among his own followers. When the queen, in February 1594, sent orders that he should either persuade or force O'Donnell to submit, he explicitly refused to act, citing lack of reward for his past services.

The response of the crown and council to the earl's renewed truculence made clear that neither had any stomach for a confrontation. In March Tyrone again met government commissioners at Dundalk, and delivered a statement of grievances singling out what he presented as the hostility of Fitzwilliam and Bagenal, as well as the crown's failure to acknowledge his services. In response, the queen ordered an inquiry into his complaints, and forbade Bagenal to interfere with him. She also recalled Fitzwilliam, now seriously ill. His successor, Sir William Russell, arrived on 1 August, to be almost immediately confronted by a new crisis. A force sent to relieve the besieged English garrison at Enniskillen was ambushed at a river crossing on 7 August, losing fifty-six men; the provisions scattered by the fleeing soldiers gave the engagement its lasting name as 'the Ford of the Biscuits'. Joining Maguire in command of the attacking force was once again Cormac MacBaron. Later intelligence was to reveal that the earl himself had appeared soon after to claim his share of the booty. In the immediate aftermath, however, Tyrone was able once again to exploit the government's desperate anxiety to avoid a confrontation. Ten days after the battle he appeared in Dublin to offer his submission to Russell. Bagenal called for his arrest, but other council members, supported by Russell, overruled him. Instead the deputy and council accepted the earl's promise to call off his brother, restrain

O'Donnell, and cooperate in the extension to his lordship of English law and local government.

The respite earned by this latest retreat from confrontation was a brief one. During the winter of 1594–5 O'Donnell and the other Ulster lords in open rebellion commenced negotiations with the government. They demanded a general pardon, the restoration of the O'Rourke and MacMahon lords, and a measure of practical autonomy, under which they would pay rents to the crown but be left free from the intrusion of royal officials. In the spring, however, they resumed their offensive. In February, another of Tyrone's brothers, Art MacBaron, seized the fort on the River Blackwater, while in May Maguire recaptured Enniskillen. In June Tyrone himself openly took the field against the crown. As Henry Bagenal marched from Newry with 1,750 men to relieve the besieged garrison at Monaghan, Tyrone appeared to tell one of his officers that by 10 next morning 'it should be seen whether the queen or they should be masters of the field and owners of Ulster'.[12] The next day, as Bagenal returned towards Newry, the earl openly directed a series of frontal attacks. By the end of the day he had also personally drawn blood, when a Palesman named Seagrave, charging him at the head of forty men, managed to bring him to the ground. A son of the O'Cahan chief intervened to slice off Seagrave's arm, and Tyrone finished him off with his dagger. On 23 June, ten days after Bagenal's battered force had straggled back to Newry, the deputy and council declared the earl a traitor. In September, following the death of Turlough Luineach, Tyrone had himself installed as the O'Neill at the traditional inauguration site at Tullyhogue.

TYRONE'S REBELLION

The origins of what became the most destructive military conflict in Tudor Ireland are at first sight puzzling. How did a government so clearly anxious to avoid going to war nevertheless find itself committed to an all-out struggle against Tyrone and the other Ulster lords? The answer lies partly in the contradictions built into the strategies pursued over the preceding decade. After 1585 the demands of the escalating conflict with Spain left the crown's Irish servants in no position to pursue an aggressive policy. This was particularly the case in relation to Ulster, still almost wholly controlled by Gaelic lords who maintained a social organization designed to support formidable numbers of fighting men. The desperate attempts of the lord deputy and council, first to secure Tyrone's support against the other Ulster chiefs, then to avoid confrontation by ignoring his blatant misconduct, were due primarily to an acute awareness of their military weakness. Yet inactivity at the centre also unleashed the rapacity of those who were the

[12] G. A. Hayes-McCoy, *Irish Battles: A Military History of Ireland* (Belfast, 1990), 96.

crown's nominal servants at local level. Bingham's consolidation of his Connacht empire brought him into direct conflict with O'Donnell, whose dynasty had long claimed supremacy over the northern part of the region. Tyrone's hostility to the Bagenals, father and son, was rooted in a recognition that they aspired to achieve a similar place for themselves in Ulster. Captain Willis's violent intrusion into Fermanagh, which provided the occasion for the start of serious hostilities, seems likewise to have been a piece of legalized freebooting. Most important of all, it appears, there was Fitzwilliam's own opportunistic intervention in Monaghan. The commissioners who met Tyrone in March 1594 reported to London that the central issue which had united the Ulster lords was 'the example and precedent of Monaghan (whereat they all do grudge), fearing it is meant and intended that now shortly Fermanagh, and consequently both Tirconnell and Tyrone will be reduced to the same estate'.[13]

Despite its military weakness, then, the actions of the Irish administration and its local representatives had convinced the Ulster lords that they were under immediate threat from the same aggressive extension of central control, accompanied by unbridled profiteering, that had already taken place in Munster and Connacht. Against this background it is possible to begin to make sense of Tyrone's conduct. His aim, it seems clear, was to prevent or minimize the intrusion into Tyrone of sheriffs, royal judges, and other officials. He was fiercely opposed to the establishment in Ulster of a presidency of the kind that had already imposed a new order on Connacht and Munster. He was equally determined to maintain his family's traditional hegemony over subordinate chiefs like the O'Hanlons and the Magennises. What is more difficult to explain are the lengths to which he carried his intransigence. His power as a regional magnate, combined with the military weakness of the government, makes it hard to see why he could not have followed Thomond and Clanricard, in negotiating an advantageous accommodation with an expanding central state. His upbringing in English Ireland, and his early successes at court, suggest that it might even have been possible for him to emulate Ormond in establishing himself as a figure of substance on both sides of the Irish Sea. Yet he chose instead a path of increasing confrontation. On occasion, when tactically necessary, he promised his cooperation in the introduction of English laws and institutions. But his behaviour made it increasingly clear that he was in reality unwilling to accept any degree of central government control.

At this stage it becomes difficult to offer more than speculation and inference. The circumstances of the earl's rise to power permit some assessment of his personality. He was clearly ruthless, calculating, and devious. At the same time his two successful visits to court, as well as his seduction of Mabel Bagenal, suggest a man capable, when he chose, of considerable charm. There are occasionally glimpses of what might be the inner man, vulnerable to doubt and anxiety.

[13] Morgan, *Tyrone's Rebellion*, 164.

Sir Robert Gardiner, chief justice of the Queen's Bench, left an account of the extraordinary scenes at the end of the earl's meeting with himself and other commissioners outside Dundalk in March 1594: 'Then he, much lamenting with tears, said, I pray you let me not lose you, that hath been my dear friend. Then, said I, you have not lost me until you first lost yourself. And so did take him by the hand.'[14] Tom Lee, an English army officer sympathetic to the earl who was allowed to visit him in August 1596, reported that he was depressed and fearful. Yet these are momentary observations, and it is in both cases possible that even here Tyrone was playing a part. At other times, his real ambitions, and the source of his relentless drive for power, remain concealed behind an apparently infinite capacity for duplicity. It has been suggested that his uncompromising pursuit of virtual autonomy drew on the claims of the O'Neill dynasty to a unique sovereign status, reflected in its inauguration ceremony and in its long history of primacy among the Irish lordships. The suggestion gains some weight from the way in which the earl inaugurated his open rebellion by taking the title O'Neill, and by his readiness thereafter to use this title rather than 'Tyrone'.[15] But it remains unclear how far the earl, given his anglicized upbringing, was really influenced by this aspect of his Gaelic inheritance.

Moreover, the opposite case has also been put. Shane O'Neill, the crown's previous Ulster-based arch enemy, had claimed the O'Neill title according to Gaelic law and sought only the tributes customarily due to its holder. Tyrone, by contrast, had bypassed the traditional process of election, establishing his dominance by force of arms, and with substantial help from the English government. Once in power, moreover, he ruthlessly expanded his own land and power and that of his immediate relatives, disregarding the traditional entitlements of other branches of the O'Neill dynasty. In this perspective Tyrone was the product, not of Gaelic Ulster, but of a breakup of traditional political values that had been initiated by Conn O'Neill's ill-judged attempt to impose the questionable Matthew as his heir.[16]

To these conflicting hypotheses two other points should be added. The first is that some at least of what seems like Tyrone's unnecessary intransigence was in fact forced on him by the type of power he had chosen to pursue. A world in which authority depended on the constant, effective use of violence was one in which every sign of weakness invited attack from rivals and rebellion from subordinates. An overlord like Tyrone—or like his distant kinsman Kildare six decades earlier—might thus find that he had no choice but repeatedly to increase the stakes, regardless of risk. If Thomond and Clanricard were models for a successful transition from warlord to aristocrat, the earl of Desmond was

14 *CSPI 1592–6*, 225.

15 Morgan, *Tyrone's Rebellion*, 85–8. On the use of the title O'Neill see ibid. 188.

16 Nicholas Canny, 'Hugh O'Neill, Earl of Tyrone, and the Changing Face of Gaelic Ulster', *Studia Hibernica*, 10 (1970), 19–23.

an equally significant warning of what could befall a magnate who allowed himself to fall between the twin stools of personalized military lordship and an encroaching but unreliable state. Secondly, there is the need to include an element of pragmatic response to specific circumstances. Tyrone was clearly shrewd enough to have recognized what the experience of Munster and Connacht made clear: that the extension of central government power was an incremental process, so that to agree to even limited intrusions was to open the way to a progressive loss of independence. Meanwhile repeated attempts at appeasement by an administration desperate to avoid conflict gave the clear message that boldness pushed to extremes could yield major gains.

To discuss the origins of the war of 1594–1603 in terms of Tyrone's ambitions takes us only so far. Contemporaries, it is true, talked of 'Tyrone's rebellion'. But what of the other Ulster lords with whom he cooperated? One potential source of information on the political outlook of Gaelic society, or rather of its elite, is the bardic poetry of the period. Yet its evidence is at best ambiguous. A number of studies have emphasized the evidence, in poems from the 1580s and 1590s, of a new awareness of unwelcome political and cultural change. Discussion, however, has tended to centre on a relatively small number of texts, selected from a corpus of verse in which the dominant theme remains the celebration of individual patrons in terms of their genealogy, their courtly virtues, and their real or imagined pre-eminence within what was still seen as a world of competing lordships. Even those texts that reflect awareness of an encroaching English state, moreover, do so within the limits of a traditional vocabulary and conventions. A poem addressed to Cormac O'Hara by Tadhg Dall O'Higgin in the mid-1580s, for example, provides a glimpse of the grim reality behind the policy of requiring local lords to register or 'book' their dependants: 'They require that everyone under heaven have a guarantor, or else . . . die forthwith.' But O'Higgin's reference to these new laws as imposed 'by the noble, bright-handed Engish host' highlights once again the difficulty of determining what real political content was concealed behind a stylized poetic vocabulary.[17] In another poem Fergal Óg MacWard lamented the captivity of Hugh O'Donnell, but took as his central conceit the idea that the English had made him a prisoner for his own good, so that the discipline of imprisonment would enable him to be a better ruler.[18] Against this background it is hard to assess even a more straightforwardly political text. An ode to O'Rourke, again by Tadhg Dall O'Higgin, concludes with a vision of the Gael uniting under his leadership to drive 'the Saxon tribe' out of Ireland. But was this anything more than a literary flourish, inspired by the highly specific circumstances of O'Rourke's feud with Bingham?[19] In the same

[17] Joep Leerssen, *Mere Irish and Fíor-Ghael* (Cork, 1996), 184–5.

[18] Padraig Breathnach, 'An Address to Hugh Roe Ó Domhnaill in Captivity, 1590', *IHS* 25 (1986), 198–213.

[19] Leerssen, *Mere Irish and Fíor-Ghael*, 189.

way poems lamenting the spread of English manners and the resulting decline of patronage for the traditional arts can be read as evidence of a real sense of cultural crisis. But they can equally be seen as reflecting the narrow preoccupations of the poets themselves, as a conservative caste whose privileges were threatened by social change.[20]

The rigidity of the poets might at first sight confirm the conventional image of an inward looking, tradition-bound Gaelic society, incapable of a coherent political response to developments that threatened its very existence. But this would be to assume that the writings of a closed group, working according to long-established and inflexible formulae, reflected the outlook of the elite as a whole. As early as the Geraldine League of 1539 there had been signs of a willingness by long-standing rivals to unite against a suddenly more aggressive English presence. Shane O'Neill's brief but spectacular career had been based on both military and economic innovation, and on a flexible diplomacy, as well as on the traditional skills of an Ulster warlord. By the late sixteenth century fragmentary evidence indicates that other Ulster lords were beginning to adopt styles of dress and manners closer to the generally accepted norms of European civility, and to pursue new types of commercial as well as military activity.[21] Against this background it would be unwise to dismiss Maguire and O'Donnell as mere followers of the more politically sophisticated Tyrone. They were clearly men of more local cultural and political horizons. O'Donnell, for example, despite more than four years' imprisonment in Dublin Castle, could understand English, but could hardly speak it.[22] On the other hand both men were able, using Ulster Catholic bishops as intermediaries, to establish diplomatic contact with Spain; later, after defeat in 1601, O'Donnell went in person to negotiate with the Spanish court. If they generally took their lead from Tyrone, it would be wrong to assume that they and others did not also have their own understanding of the issues at stake.

The aim of preserving Ulster's autonomy could be achieved only through effective military force. Here Tyrone built on existing foundations. Late medieval Ulster may already have been more militarized than other parts of Gaelic Ireland, in terms of supporting a large population of professional soldiers. During the sixteenth century redshanks imported from Scotland had become an increasingly important resource. There was also an increase in the use of firearms. But military tactics remained traditional. In continental Europe the systematic deployment

[20] For differing views see T. J. Dunne, 'The Gaelic Response to Conquest and Colonization: The Evidence of the Poetry', *Studia Hibernica*, 20 (1980), 7–30; Leerssen, *Mere Irish and Fíor-Ghael*, 177–90; Michelle O'Riordan, *The Gaelic Mind and the Collapse of the Gaelic World* (Cork, 1990), ch. 2; Marc Caball, *Poets and Politics: Reaction and Continuity in Irish Poetry 1558–1625* (Cork, 1998), 14–81.

[21] Hiram Morgan, 'The End of Gaelic Ulster: A Thematic Interpretation of Events between 1534 and 1610', *IHS* 26 (1988).

[22] Patricia Palmer, *Language and Conquest in Early Modern Ireland: English Renaissance Literature and Elizabethan Imperial Expansion* (Cambridge, 2001), 45.

of formations of shot and pikemen, along with the use of artillery and new styles of fortification, had begun to transform warfare. Military conflict in Gaelic Ireland, by contrast, continued to be dominated by the hit and run tactics of the ambush and the raid. Where set-piece battles occurred, as at Glenshesk in 1565, they took the traditional form: bows and guns would be used to harass the enemy, but the decisive event was a massed charge by opposing forces of infantry who engaged one another with axe and sword. In this respect Tyrone was to be a major innovator. In place of the traditional conglomeration of galloglass, redshanks, and kern, with their swords, axes, and darts, Tyrone was reported in February 1595 to have 4,000 musketeers, 1,000 cavalry, and 1,000 pikemen. The Irish military establishment around the same time consisted of 1,500 infantry and 250 horse—a balance that does much to explain the frantic efforts of the Dublin administration to avoid pushing him into rebellion. Tyrone's other innovation lay in the composition of his modernized army. The armed forces of Irish lords had traditionally consisted of two elements: a 'rising out' of principal tenants, either as horse or foot, and a mercenary element, including some kern but composed mainly of galloglass and redshanks. Shane O'Neill had attracted comment as the first man to arm the ordinary peasantry. Tyrone greatly extended the same practice. His army included both Scottish mercenaries and the rising out of those bound to serve him. But its backbone consisted of native Irish, recruited from both Ulster and further afield, who served for regular pay and were trained in the new arts of the pike and the gun.

The introduction to Gaelic Ulster of the new technology of gunfire systematically deployed required careful preparation. There were claims that the nucleus of Tyrone's army consisted of soldiers trained by captains supplied for that purpose by the crown during his period of loyal service. Thereafter other accounts testified to the earl's close attention to the training of men; one even spoke of children being drilled with wooden muskets. By 1600, when Lord Mountjoy took over as chief governor, he found the rebels 'so far from being naked people, as before times, that they were generally better armed than we, [and] knew better the use of their weapons than our men'. Cavalry remained the weakest element in the Ulster army, mounted on slight animals, only lightly armed, and still riding in the traditional fashion without stirrups on which to brace the rider's body during combat.[23] At Clontibret, however, O'Neill's horsemen moved forward in formation, supported by musketeers, to charge the English lines. An alarmed council reported to London that the Ulster lords were 'wonderfully altered from their Irish manner of arms and weapons, and the use thereof, besides their order and discipline in governing their men'. Tyrone's status as a crown servant also permitted him initially to build up stocks of gunpowder purchased in Dublin. Later he imported powder, weapons, armour, and other supplies from Scotland.

[23] Hiram Morgan, 'Disaster at Kinsale', in Hiram Morgan (ed.), *The Battle of Kinsale* (Bray, 2004), 131.

These purchases, as well as the payment of a growing army, involved substantial expenditure. In 1598 it was claimed that the war was costing Tyrone £500 a day. Although the evidence is fragmentary, it seems clear that his military innovations were sustained by an intensive exploitation of the full economic resources of his lordship, through the sale or barter of cattle, hides, tallow, yarn, and fish, as well as through the promotion of tillage as a means of feeding the thousands of men under arms.[24]

All this, however, was in the future. In the immediate aftermath of his outlawry Tyrone skirmished with an expeditionary force under Sir John Norris which Russell had sent into Tyrone. By 18 October 1595, however, he had offered his submission and concluded a new truce with the crown. Protracted negotiations continued over the winter, with O'Neill, backed up by O'Donnell, now openly acting as leader of the Ulster lords. By April 1596 the two sides had agreed terms of peace. The crown asserted its sovereignty over Ulster, and refused to withdraw its garrison at Armagh unless Tyrone agreed to the shiring of his lordship. In practical terms, however, the Ulster lords were to control their territories without interference. Government negotiators rejected a demand for formal liberty of conscience, but the articles agreed specifically accepted that the lords would not be expected to proceed against Catholic clergymen within their jurisdiction. Tyrone was required to surrender the title O'Neill but retained control over the lesser lords formerly subject to Turlough Luineach. Within a month of agreeing these apparently generous terms, however, Tyrone and O'Donnell had received a Spanish army officer, Alonso Cobos, dispatched to Ireland by Philip II. In the talks that followed the Ulster lords undertook to abandon the peace they had just concluded. Instead they offered to become vassals of the king of Spain, and asked for an army of 6,000 soldiers to assist them in liberating Ireland from English rule.

Cobos's mission was in response to messages which Tyrone had sent to Spain around September 1595, appealing for support to liberate Catholic Ireland from Protestant rule.[25] This was not the first such overture; the earl's first emissary may have arrived in Spain as early as 1589. When two Catholic archbishops, Edmund Magauran of Armagh and James O'Hely of Tuam, approached the Spanish court in 1592–3 to solicit military assistance on behalf of a confederacy of Ulster lords headed by O'Donnell and Maguire, Tyrone was once again discreetly involved. However, it seems likely that these early ventures were primarily an insurance policy. Tyrone's tactics over the next two years, and in particular his willingness to take the field against Maguire, suggest that he still believed that his best chance

[24] For the organization and financing of Tyrone's war effort see G. A. Hayes-McCoy, 'Strategy and Tactics in Irish Warfare, 1593–1601', *IHS* 2 (1941), 255–79; idem, 'The Army of Ulster 1593–1601', *Irish Sword*, 1 (1950), 105–17; Morgan, *Tyrone's Rebellion*, 179–83. For Mountjoy's report see Fynes Moryson, *An Itinerary*, 4 vols. (Glasgow 1907), iii. 152.

[25] The fullest account of contacts between the Ulster lords and Spain is J. J. Silke, *Kinsale: The Spanish Intervention in Ireland at the End of the Elizabethan Wars* (Dublin, 2000).

of achieving the regional autonomy he desired was to convince the queen and her servants that Ulster could not be ruled without his cooperation. For his part, Philip II had shown some interest in the mission of 1592–3, but remained too preoccupied with campaigns in the Netherlands and France to divert resources to Ireland. By 1596, however, he and his advisers had been sufficiently impressed by the military successes of the Ulster lords to see intervention there as a worthwhile investment. Within weeks of Cobos's landing, two further Spanish missions had arrived in Ulster, charged with surveying possible landing sites and collecting other topographical information.

Why did the Ulster lords abandon the apparently satisfactory settlement they had just negotiated with the English crown? The most likely answer is that the new peace, however attractive in the short term, provided no long-term security. The Ulster lords had been promised de facto regional autonomy and liberty of conscience. But they had no guarantee that the crown might not at some later date, when circumstances were more favourable, resume its attempts to make its sovereignty over Ulster a reality, or to impose religious uniformity. Even as things stood the fortress at Armagh, and Bagenal's presence in the east, remained a check on Tyrone's independence. It is also important to avoid hindsight. The option of a Spanish-backed military revolt may eventually have proved to be the wrong one. But it was hardly foredoomed to failure. England was suffering badly from the strains of war. And if Dutch Protestants backed by England could cast off an oppressive ruler, there was no obvious reason why Irish Catholics backed by Spain could not hope to do the same.

Tyrone's short-term thinking thus seems clear enough. What is more difficult to decide is how far he had now committed himself to the all or nothing strategy of open revolt in alliance with a foreign power. The Spanish alliance was reflected in an immediate change in rhetoric. Up to this point Tyrone and others had presented themselves as defending their territories against the unwarranted intrusions of oppressive officials like Bagenal and Willis. In July 1596, however, they issued a circular letter calling on the Catholics of Munster and elsewhere to join them in a war on behalf of 'Christ's Catholic religion'. The language echoed the terms of the previous year's appeal to Spain. But Tyrone made no attempt to make it a reality by carrying the war beyond Ulster. It is possible that he was holding his forces in reserve while awaiting the promised Spanish force. An invasion fleet of 100 ships left Lisbon in October, but was scattered by a storm, with the loss of an estimated 2,000 lives. However, it is equally possible that Tyrone even now preferred to avoid action that would completely close off the option of a settlement with the English crown.

The other point that must be remembered in assessing Tyrone's strategy is the imminence of radical political change in England. Elizabeth I, at 63, was clearly coming to the end of her life. Her death would provide the opportunity for Spain to impose its candidate, Philip II's daughter Isabella, on the English throne. Alternatively the throne might pass to James VI of Scotland. Gaelic lords had in the past found in the Scottish crown a potential ally against English interests. This ceased to be the case after 1586, when Elizabeth acknowledged James as her lawful successor, as Sir Brian O'Rourke found to his cost in 1591. But it was still by no means clear how James's accession might affect the nature of the monarchy, or the structures of power within the British Isles. At the very least it was expected to bring about the fall of the dominant Cecil faction, whose leader had been largely responsible for the death of James's mother, Mary queen of Scots. In these circumstances it made sense for Tyrone to bide his time, rather than committing himself more than was necessary, or risking his painstakingly assembled forces in a premature military confrontation.

Regardless of Tyrone's hesitations, however, the state of Ireland was now, from the crown's point of view, deeply alarming. It had almost completely lost control of Ulster, its only remaining footholds being the controversial garrison at Armagh, now dangerously exposed, and another at Carrickfergus. It also faced disaster in Connacht, where the war had given O'Donnell an opportunity to assert his dynasty's long-standing claims to overlordship. In June 1595 Ulick Burke, a relative of Clanricard who commanded the garrison at Sligo Castle, killed the constable Captain George Bingham, a cousin of the Connacht president, and handed the fortress over to O'Donnell. Control of this vital stronghold, dominating the main route from Ulster into Connacht, allowed O'Donnell to overrun the greater part of the province, taking hostages from local chiefs and installing his own candidate as chief of the MacWilliam Burkes. Only Clare and Galway, defended by Thomond and Clanricard, remained secure. Meanwhile the government had received intelligence that the Wicklow chief Fiach MacHugh O'Byrne, Baltinglass's former ally and the victor of Glenmalure, was in touch with both Tyrone and Spain, and was collecting materials of war. A pre-emptive attack in February 1595 failed to capture O'Byrne, and the administration now faced a further guerrilla war on its very doorstep. In addition there remained the ever-present threat that a further Spanish expedition would appear to support Tyrone's challenge.

This combination of threats made a major increase in the crown's Irish army unavoidable. Between October 1594 and May 1597 the privy council ordered the levying of more than 7,000 recruits from the counties of England and Wales. It also transferred 1,400 seasoned troops from France in April 1595. This brought the army in Ireland up to a theoretical strength of around 8,000.[26] Meanwhile Lord Thomas Burgh, who had earlier served in the Netherlands, replaced Russell in May 1597. Connacht was also in new hands. Bingham, widely blamed for the collapse of order in the province, was suspended in September 1596 and subsequently imprisoned on charges of abusing his martial law powers. His replacement, Sir Conyers Clifford, another veteran of the Dutch war, abandoned

[26] Statistics on the recruitment and deployment of government troops during the war are taken from John McGurk, *The Elizabethan Conquest of Ireland: The 1590s Crisis* (Manchester, 1997).

Bingham's dictatorial methods in favour of diplomacy. Having recaptured Sligo Castle in March 1597, he handed it over to Donogh O'Connor Sligo, whom Bingham had dispossessed a decade earlier. He also gained the support of Tibbot Burke, son of Richard an Iarainn, whom he agreed to recognize as heir to the MacWilliam Burke estates. In July Burgh led 3,500 men towards the Blackwater, while Clifford with 1,200 marched north towards Tirconnell. The two-pronged assault had limited success. Clifford crossed the River Erne at Belleek but failed to take O'Donnell's fortress at Ballyshannon and had to retreat into Connacht. Burgh regarrisoned Armagh and retook the Blackwater fort, but was unable to proceed beyond the river. However, his advance was sufficiently impressive for Tyrone to destroy his own fortress at Dungannon, for fear that it might become an English stronghold. In mid-October, at a time when the military balance was already moving towards stalemate, Burgh died of typhus at Newry. Shortly afterwards another Spanish invasion fleet came to grief in the autumn storms. Against this background Ormond, appointed as the crown's stopgap military commander, agreed a new truce with Tyrone in December.

Tyrone's willingness to negotiate a new truce raises once again the question of how far he was still open to a compromise agreement with the crown. He may have been merely biding his time. Once the truce expired, in June 1598, he resumed the offensive by besieging Cavan and the Blackwater fort. He also sent forces into Leinster, where the government's difficulties had encouraged fresh revolts among the O'Connors, the O'Mores, and other victims of the midlands plantation. But it is also the case that the dramatic escalation of Tyrone's revolt that took place during 1598 came about through a catastrophic misjudgement on the opposing side. Ormond had advised abandoning the Blackwater fort, as both a strategic liability and an unnecessary provocation to Tyrone. Instead the council agreed to Bagenal's proposal to lead a major relief expedition. On 24 August 1598, as his 4,000 infantry and 300 horse crossed the River Callan at a place known as the Yellow Ford, it encountered the forces of Tyrone, O'Donnell, and Maguire. What followed was part ambush and part set-piece battle. The Irish troops, deployed behind a ditch and protective hedge, held the road against the advancing crown forces, while musketeers raked Bagenal's column from the cover of the woods. Bagenal was killed, as were 1,000 to 1,300 of his men; 300 Irish troops deserted to Tyrone, leaving not much more than half the original force to retreat to Armagh.

Tyrone's immediate response to his victory was restrained. In exchange for the surrender of the Blackwater fort, he agreed not to wipe out the broken remnant huddled in Armagh. But his victory nevertheless transformed the character of the war. O'Donnell swept back into Connacht, forcing Clifford to retreat to Athlone and re-establishing his client as the MacWilliam. Even Thomond was overrun for a time, as a brother of the earl took up arms, proclaiming himself 'the O'Brien'. In Wicklow the crown had scored an apparent early victory in May 1597, when soldiers ran down and killed Fiach MacHugh O'Byrne. But the O'Byrnes remained in arms under Fiach's son Phelim. By the end of the year raiders from the Dublin and Wicklow mountains, acting in conjunction with rebels from the midlands, were able repeatedly to pillage the southern suburbs of Dublin. In the midlands themselves the revolt once again built on the grievances created by the Leix and Offaly plantations. But the assassination in King's County of Calvach O'Carroll, a government supporter knighted in 1585 with the title 'Sir Charles', indicates that there was also a conflict within the local septs, between those who had reached an accommodation with the new order and those who remained dispossessed and unreconciled. Among the O'Mores, Tyrone's instrument was Owny MacRory, son of the Rory Óg who had been the scourge of the midlands plantation in the 1570s. To assist him Tyrone sent Captain Richard Tyrrell, a Westmeath man and former officer in the queen's army, who had emerged as one of his most competent military commanders.

From the midlands the revolt spread to Munster. In early October Owny MacRory O'More and Tyrrell, responding to an appeal for aid though having apparently waited for Tyrone's permission, marched into Tipperary and then Limerick with around 800 men. They remained only until 19 October. However, attacks on the plantation had been increasing since the killing of the first English settler in 1596, and the incursion of the Leinstermen inspired a general revolt. Contemporary English observers complained that the minority of undertakers actually resident fled in panic, making no attempt to mount a defence. 'The meaner sort (the rebellion having overtaken them) were slain man, woman and child; and such as escaped came all naked to the towns.'[27] Other accounts relayed horrific accounts of severed tongues and noses, and infant children casually battered to death. The revolt had a figurehead in James Fitzgerald, a grandson of the fourteenth earl, who had set himself up as heir to the Desmond title, although some ridiculed his pretensions by dubbing him the *sugán* or 'straw rope' earl. The crisis deepened when members of several Old English landed families, including the heads of two branches of the Butler family, Viscount Mountgarrett (a son-in-law of Tyrone) and Lord Cahir, joined in the revolt.

Disaster on this scale required a desperate response. During 1598–9 the privy council issued orders for the levying of just under 8,900 men in England and Wales. It also transferred some 600 experienced troops from France, and 2,000 more from the Netherlands. When the earl of Essex, the queen's favourite and the hero of a spectacular raid on Cadiz in 1596, took office as lord lieutenant in March 1599, he had an official army establishment of 1,300 horse and 16,000 foot, twice the size of England's forces in the Low Countries. The initial plan was for Essex to drive a wedge between the two main Ulster lords, by establishing a base at Lough Foyle. However, the Irish council persuaded him to begin by pacifying the other three provinces. Aided by Ormond he succeeded in

[27] A. J. Sheehan, 'The Overthrow of the Plantation of Munster in October 1598', *Irish Sword*, 15 (1982–3), 11–22.

securing Leinster and most of Munster, his successes including the submission of Mountgarret and Cahir. But there were also two important defeats. In May Phelim MacFiach O'Byrne routed an army in the Wicklow mountains. On 5 August Sir Conyers Clifford died when a force of nearly 1,500 troops he was leading to assist O'Connor Sligo was heavily defeated in the Curlew mountains of Roscommon. The following month Essex eventually marched on Ulster, only to be halted on the Louth–Monaghan border by Tyrone's army. After a parley, the two earls agreed a truce. Essex's decision to negotiate rather than fight has been defended as a responsible and indeed self-sacrificing move to ensure the safety of the Pale rather than protecting his personal reputation by a risky battle in which he was outnumbered roughly two to one.[28] To contemporaries, however, it represented abject failure. There were also allegations that he had entered into treasonable discussions with Tyrone as to possible joint action in the power struggle that was to be expected once the queen died. Essex returned to England two weeks later, to face disgrace and later execution after a half-hearted attempt to regain his position there by a show of force.

Tyrone was by now the leader of something close to a nationwide insurrection. How far this had come about through a long-term strategy, and how far through the misjudgements of others, remains unclear. But both his actions and his rhetoric took on a conspicuously new dimension. On a triumphant progress through Munster in February and March 1600 his behaviour, as one local settler noted, was that of a ruler: 'he makes viceroys, creates earls, bestows baronies, sets up and pulls down'.[29] In particular he endorsed the claims of Florence MacCarthy Reagh, like himself an anglicized Irishman and former client of the crown, to the title of MacCarthy Mór. Subsequently he appointed this MacCarthy and the pretended earl of Desmond as commanders over, respectively, the Irish and the Old English of the province.[30] However, Tyrone explicitly disavowed any intention of making himself king of Ireland. Instead he pursued two alternative visions of Ireland's future. One was a new accommodation with the English crown. In late 1599 Tyrone drew up a set of twenty-two articles. These contained just enough concessons to English interests to suggest that they were seriously

[28] Bruce Lenman, *England's Colonial Wars 1550–1688* (London, 2001), 134. See also John McCavitt, *The Flight of the Earls* (Dublin, 2002), 26–7.

[29] Hiram Morgan, 'Hugh O'Neill and the Nine Years' War in Tudor Ireland', *Historical Journal*, 36 (1993), 35.

[30] Finian MacCarthy Reagh (1562–*c*.1640) had a career as convoluted, if less dramatic in its wider effects, than that of Tyrone himself. Born into the second most important branch of the MacCarthys, he had been raised as a ward of Sir William Drury, president of Munster. Having distinguished himself in the suppression of the Desmond rebellion, he had spent time at court, where he anglicized his christian name. He had fallen out of favour in 1588, when his quest to succeed to the senior MacCarthy title led him to elope with the daughter of MacCarthy Mór, whom the crown had already destined, along with her father's lands, for the son of the Munster planter, Sir Valentine Browne. The crisis of the late 1590s allowed him for a time to offer his support to whichever side would back his claims, but these equivocations were to end in his being consigned for the rest of his long life to the Tower of London.

meant. Ireland was to be governed by a noble member of the English privy council, and half the army was (by implication) to be English. On the other hand the lord chancellor and other major officers of state, the judiciary, and council were to be Irish, as were the provincial governors and the other half of the army. The inhabitants of Ireland were to have full freedom to travel and trade with foreign countries, all statutes against their preferment were to be repealed, they were not to be subject to impressment into the royal army, and heirs inheriting as minors were no longer to be handed over to the crown as royal wards. There was also to be a Catholic church establishment owing allegiance to the pope. The queen's principal adviser, Sir Robert Cecil, dismissed the document with the single word 'Ewtopia'.[31] This left the alternative that Tyrone and others had first proposed in 1596: that the inhabitants of Ireland should transfer their allegiance to the Spanish king, who would then provide a suitable ruler. One early candidate was the Archduke Albert, married to Philip II's half-sister and ruler of the Spanish Netherlands.

To cast off the rule of an established monarch required justification. The basis of the initial appeal to Spain by the Ulster lords had been the defence of their Catholic religion against a heretic prince. Within Ireland, too, Tyrone had presented himself as a Catholic champion as early as July 1596, in his letter to the gentlemen of Munster. But from 1599, as he sought to extend the revolt to all parts of Ireland, his propaganda became more insistent. In November 1599 he addressed a proclamation to the lords and gentry of the Pale, calling on them to support him in a war for 'the extirpation of heresy, the planting of the Catholic religion', and pointing to the example of the French Catholics who had made war on their natural prince, Henry IV, until he was reconciled to the papacy. Writing to the loyalist David Barry, Lord Buttevant, in March 1600, he accused him of having 'separated yourself from the unity of Christ's mystical body, the Catholic church', and called on him to join with others 'to shake off the cruel yoke of heresy and tyranny'.[32] Tyrone's private sentiments, here as in so much else, remain unclear. He was undoubtedly a religious conservative: as early as 1584 the government had noted with concern that he had celebrated Easter according to the newly introduced papal calendar. But he had also been willing to attend Protestant services in Dublin. When, in 1599, he accused loyalist Catholics of failing in their religious duty, one of their number responded sharply that he and others in the Pale 'are Catholics and were when he [Tyrone] was not thought to be one'. By this time, however, Tyrone had begun to demonstrate his own piety, attending daily mass, and also promoting the reform of the Catholic church in the territories under his control, notably by banning priests from keeping wives.

[31] O'Neill's articles are printed in Edmund Curtis and R. B. McDowell (eds.), *Irish Historical Documents 1172–1922* (London, 1943), 119–20. See also Hiram Morgan, 'Faith and Fatherland in Sixteenth-Century Ireland', *History Ireland*, 3/2 (1995), 13–20.

[32] *Pacata Hibernica, or A History of the Wars in Ireland*, ed. Standish O'Grady, 2 vols. (London, 1896, i. 10–11.

Lombard noted as a special point in his favour that this drive to enforce clerical celibacy involved no unwarranted lay intrusion on the rights of the church. Instead Tyrone proceeded against the women involved, having repeat offenders whipped or branded, or alternatively ordering that their faces should be slashed.[33]

To the religious justification for a repudiation of the English crown, Tyrone added secular grievances. His proclamation of November 1599 declared his aims to be not just the defence of Catholicism, but also 'the delivery of our country of infinite murders, wicked and detestable policies by which this kingdom was hitherto governed'. Writing to a wavering Anglo-Irish loyalist, James Fitzpiers, sheriff of County Kildare, likewise, he argued that 'it is lawful to die in the quarrel and defence of the native soil, and that we Irishmen are exiled and made bond slaves and servitors to a strange and foreign prince'. What was new about such manifestos was their appeal to an inclusive Irish identity. In place of the traditional emphasis on the ethnic division between Gaelic Irish and Old English, Tyrone's language assumed a common interest as Irish victims of English misgovernment. The same emphasis was evident in his 'utopian' articles, which referred simply to the rights of 'Irishmen'. This important break with earlier traditions of self-definition may in part have reflected Tyrone's own upbringing. Alternatively it might be seen as reflecting the influence on Gaelic Ireland of the Renaissance rediscovery, via classical political theory, of the idea of patriotism or attachment to one's native land. More immediately it is possible that Tyrone's rhetoric borrowed something from the notions of good government and the corporate rights of subjects that had underpinned the commonwealth movement in the Pale.[34]

The new ideology of 'faith and fatherland' received its fullest expression in an elaborate work, *De Regno Hiberniae*, written during 1599–1600 by Peter Lombard, then professor of theology at the University of Louvain. Tyrone had commissioned the work to counter opposition at Rome to his requests for papal backing. Lombard, significantly in terms of the alliance Tyrone was trying to create, was not a Gaelic Ulsterman, but an Old English native of Waterford. His account duly described the attempts of Protestant England to stamp out Catholicism in Ireland, the steadfast fidelity of the people to the true religion, and the armed resistance in defence of religion that had begun with James Fitzmaurice Fitzgerald and now continued with Tyrone. However, he prefaced all this with an account of Ireland's earlier glorious history as a bastion of Christianity, 'the island of saints', followed by a description of its seizure by England on the basis of the false accusations against the Irish church enshrined

[33] Thomas O'Connor, 'Hugh O'Neill: Free Spirit, Religious Chameleon, or Ardent Catholic?', in Morgan, *The Battle of Kinsale*, 60–6. O'Connor concludes that O'Neill had by the end of the 1590s experienced a genuine conversion to the Catholic cause, but the evidence remains circumstantial.

[34] For these points, and the statements quoted, see Morgan, 'Hugh O'Neill and the Nine Years' War', 1–17; idem, 'Faith and Fatherland in Sixteenth-Century Ireland', 13–20.

in *Laudabiliter*, and the subsequent oppression of its natives. In addition to acknowledging the achievements of pre-conquest Irish Christianity, Lombard also offered a qualifed but significant defence of the Irish character against the allegations of barbarism levelled by writers from Gerald of Wales onwards. In all these respects his book, circulated initially in manuscript but published in 1632, represents the beginnings of a break with the tradition of Old English exclusivism that had only recently found such clear expression in the work of Stanihurst.[35]

Where the clergy of the emerging Irish Catholic church were concerned, Tyrone's call to arms deepened already existing divisions. Some priests and bishops had from the start assumed that their allegiance to the papacy implied a commitment to the military as well as the spiritual arm of the Counter-Reformation. The most conspicuous example was Maurice MacGibbon, archbishop of Cashel from 1567 until 1578, who had served as Fitzmaurice's emissary to Philip II. Others, however, tried to separate political and religious allegiance. The best-documented example is Richard Creagh, a Limerick man of Old English cultural background (though distant Gaelic ancestry) who became papal archbishop of Armagh in 1564, and who consistently protested his loyalty to 'my natural prince and country'.[36] In the 1590s Tyrone and his allies were actively supported by Gaelic ecclesiastics. The central intermediaries in the first contact between the Ulster lords and Spain were Edmund Magauran, archbishop of Armagh, and James O'Hely, archbishop of Tuam, drowned as he returned to Ireland with a Spanish mission in 1593. In the south Dermot McCreagh, who had returned to Ireland with Fitzmaurice and become bishop of Cork and Cloyne, preached in support of the war and offered those who fought in it a general absolution. Some Old English clergy, especially those based or trained in the continental centres of the Counter-Reformation, were also active supporters. Henry Fitzsimons, a prominent Old English Jesuit in Dublin, initially opposed Tyrone, but by the end of 1599 had come to believe that his victory would open up the possibility of recapturing Ireland for Catholicism. James Archer, also a Jesuit, actively promoted the rebellion in the south, and travelled to Rome in 1600 to put Tyrone's case for unreserved papal backing. Others, however, remained firmly opposed to the revolt, insisting to Rome that they continued to enjoy de facto religious freedom under the crown, and that Tyrone was concerned to establish only his own ascendancy.

Among the Old English laity, Tyrone's appeal for an alliance of Old English and Gaelic Irish on the basis of religious solidarity achieved even less. Individual

[35] The fullest modern analysis of Lombard's text is in Morgan, 'Hugh O'Neill and the Nine Years' War', 29–31.

[36] Colm Lennon, *An Irish Prisoner of Conscience of the Tudor Era: Archbishop Richard Creagh of Armagh 1523–86* (Dublin, 2000), 112. There is, however, the possibility that Creagh was temporarily converted to the idea of a Spanish invasion at the time of the excommunication of Elizabeth, once again on the grounds that the English crown had failed to live up to the conditions on which it had been granted custody of Ireland. Ibid. 101–2.

Palesmen like Tyrrell and the Hovenden brothers appear as supporters or associates of the earl. Indeed it has been suggested that the prominence of Old Englishmen in his immediate entourage was a further indication of Tyrone's distance from the Gaelic Ulster of which he had become leader. Some merchants in Dublin and other centres were accused of supplying the rebel army, whether for ideology or profit, with munitions and other supplies. For the most part, however, the aristocracy and gentry of the Pale, and the citizens of Dublin and other towns, ignored Tyrone's calls to join him. In Munster, similarly, some junior members of landed families joined the revolt. But the majority of the gentry and aristocracy supported the crown. In County Cork Lord Buttevant flatly rejected Tyrone's appeal:

> I am undoubtedly persuaded in my conscience, that by the law of God and His true religion, I am bound to hold with her Majesty. Her highness has never restrained me for matter of religion; and, as I felt her Majesty's indifference and clemency therein, I have not spared to relieve poor Catholics with dutiful succour. . . . You shall further understand that I hold my lordships and lands, immediately under God, of her Majesty and her most noble progenitors by corporal service, and of none other, by very ancient tenure, which service and tenure none may dispense withal, but the true possessor of the crown of England, being now our sovereign lady Queen Elizabeth.[37]

All this was a little too good to be true—and with reason. Buttevant's brother had joined the Munster rebels, and he himself was under suspicion for having undermined attempts to organize a defence of the plantation with defeatist warnings. Nevertheless he did in fact remain loyal to the crown throughout the war. This being the case his declaration, with its quasi-feudal language and pragmatic acknowledgement of de facto toleration, may stand as a valid if somewhat flowery statement of Old English loyalism.

A second revealing exchange, though again one dressed up for government eyes, took place early in 1600, involving Edward Fitzharries, a loyalist who visited the camp of the *sugán* earl of Desmond, and engaged in debate with the Jesuit James Archer. Where Buttevant had cited feudal loyalties, Fitzharries, reproaching Archer for betraying his English descent, appealed instead to long-standing ethnic divisions. If Tyrone were to prevail, 'the Irish nation should enjoy the whole as before the conquest'. This would mean that 'the Irish, who had neither learning nor any way inclined to civility, [would] rule as superiors', and that 'we, descended of the English, not able to defend our own, should in time be banished'. In response Archer was able to argue that such an outcome was unlikely, 'considering the ancient English were so many', and that the long period that had elapsed since the conquest had in any case 'removed all the claims of the Irish, [it] being not possible to know who had those places upon the conquest'.[38] But the response from the Pale and the towns makes clear that

[37] *Pacata Hibernica*, ed. O'Grady, i. 12; *CSPI 1599–1600*, 494.
[38] *CSPI 1599–1600*, 500.

it was Fitzharries who more accurately reflected the prevailing view among the Old English of what remained a predominantly Gaelic Irish revolt.

The stand taken by these Catholic loyalists, clerical and lay, was facilitated by the cautious pragmatism of the papacy. As a self-proclaimed champion in the war against heresy Tyrone appealed to Rome, not just for military and financial support, but also for spiritual armament. Through Lombard the earl demanded to be allowed to nominate to all important ecclesiastical vacancies, that his supporters should receive the indulgence granted to those who participated in the crusades, and, most important, that the pope should issue a sentence of excommunication against Catholics who supported the queen. Yet things had changed since the 1570s, when Pius V had declared Elizabeth excommunicate and his successor had provided men for Fitzmaurice's holy war. Already in 1580 Pope Gregory XIII, in response to the appeals of English Catholics horrified by the predicament in which the bull of 1570 had placed them, had offered the appropriately casuistic declaration that they were not bound to act on the call for Elizabeth's removal until such time as it became practical to do so. His successor, Clement VIII, was in addition unwilling, for diplomatic reasons, to align the papacy too closely with Spanish interests. Instead he steered a middle course. He accepted O'Neill's recommendation of Matteo de Oviedo, a Spanish Franciscan who had been in Ireland with Fitzmaurice and had subsequently supported Tyrone at the Spanish court, as archbishop of Dublin in 1599. He also appointed Lombard as archbishop of Armagh (although in this case Tyrone had wanted Edmund MacDonnell, his agent at the Spanish court). In 1600 he recognized Tyrone as 'captain general of the Catholic army in Ireland', and granted him and his followers a plenary indulgence. At the same time he refused to declare Catholics who remained loyal to the queen excommunicate. And when, in 1601, he appointed a papal legate for Ireland, he ignored Tyrone's nomination of Oviedo, choosing instead an Italian Jesuit, Ludovico Mansoni.

Tyrone's progress through Munster in the first weeks of 1600 was in retrospect the high point in his military fortunes. (Even then the venture ended badly, with the death of his son-in-law and valued ally Maguire in a skirmish in County Cork on 1 March.) On 28 February Charles Blount, Lord Mountjoy, was sworn in as lord deputy. Mountjoy was a follower of Essex, and lover of the earl's sister Penelope Rich, and for a time he allowed himself to be drawn into a plan to divert his army to England for a showdown with the Cecil faction, court rivals of the increasingly desperate Essex. Before long, however, Mountjoy had decided that his future lay instead in succeeding where his patron had failed. In Munster he had a hostile but competent subordinate in Sir George Carew, a cousin of the land-grabbing Sir Peter, who took up office as president in March. Judiciously combining military force with offers of pardon to waverers like Florence MacCarthy, Carew quickly began to regain territory. Meanwhile another English commander, Sir Arthur Savage, joined with Clanricard to secure the southern half of Connacht, although the north remained under O'Donnell's control. The deputy himself campaigned successfully against the O'Mores of Offaly in July and August.

As crown forces regained control of the rest of the island, Mountjoy began to tighten the noose on Ulster and north Connacht. In May he revived Essex's original plan to exploit the one area where English forces enjoyed undoubted superiority, control of the sea, by sending Sir Henry Docwra, with 3,000 men, to land at Lough Foyle and establish a camp at Derry. His own first serious campaign, in late September, ended unpromisingly. At the Moyry pass between Dundalk and Newry Tyrone's troops, fighting behind an elaborate system of ditches, earthen banks, and stonework, held up Mountjoy's 4,000 men for two weeks of hard fighting. Tyrone's sudden withdrawal allowed Mountjoy to march north, only to find himself trapped when the Irish reoccupied the pass; in the end his army escaped only by crossing Carlingford Lough in boats, in effect a humiliating retreat. Shortly afterwards, however, Docwra's force, which had remained on the defensive in Derry, suffering badly from disease and shortage of supplies, gained a vital advantage when they were joined by Hugh Roe O'Donnell's long-standing rival Niall Garbh. Mountjoy then chose to keep up the pressure on the Ulster lords when he broke with tradition by continuing his campaign during the winter of 1600–1. By the summer of 1601 he had regarrisoned Armagh and established a new fort on the Blackwater. From controlling more than three-quarters of Ireland, Tyrone had by now been forced back into his Ulster heartland, and even there faced the threat of Docwra's force to his rear. Supported by Niall Garbh and also by Cahir O'Doherty, lord of Inishowen, Docwra was able to raid into northern Tirconnell and north Tyrone. In August Niall Garbh captured Donegal Castle. Meanwhile another capable soldier, Sir Arthur Chichester, commanding the garrison at Carrickfergus, had also begun to strike at Tyrone's territory, by a series of amphibious raids across Lough Neagh.

At this desperate moment in the fortunes of the Ulster lords the long-awaited Spanish expedition suddenly materialized. The settlement of a dispute with France over Savoy meant that 2,000 men awaiting embarkation at Lisbon suddenly became available as the nucleus of a new Irish expedition. A fleet of 33 ships carrying 4,464 soldiers under the command of Don Juan del Águila sailed on 3 September. The ships were separated in a storm near the Irish coast, so that Águila landed at Kinsale on 2 October with only 1,700 men. Within a week, however, the arrival of stragglers had brought his force up to around 3,700. The choice of landing site followed the original advice of the Ulster lords, that a substantial invasion force should disembark in the south, where it would be fed more easily than from the already overstretched resources of Ulster. A subsequent injunction, in the wake of Carew's pacification of Munster, to land no further south than Limerick had reached Spain only after Águila's departure. And indeed the Spanish landing provoked only a limited response from a recently pacified Munster. The lords from whom Águila expected support, such as Florence

MacCarthy, were under arrest. Others, headed by Donal O'Sullivan Beare, lord of Bantry, offered support, but Águila, uncertain whom to trust, rejected them. Meanwhile Mountjoy marched with the bulk of his army to join Carew. By the end of October, he had laid siege to Kinsale with a force of around 7,000 men.

Tyrone and his allies now faced a cruel strategic dilemma. Their decision, after a short hesitation, to march south, leaving their Ulster base dangerously unprotected, has been seen as a departure from Tyrone's characteristic caution. They had, in Mountjoy's words, 'quit their own countries, to recover them here, or else to lose all'.[39] But Tyrone could presumably foresee the alternative: that Carew and Mountjoy would first crush the Spaniards, then resume the remorseless reduction of Ulster which the invasion had interrupted. O'Donnell set out on 23 October, eluding an intercepting force under Carew by a night-time march across the frozen Slievephelim mountains in Tipperary. Tyrone moved south a week later, but paused to ravage the Pale. When this tactic failed to draw Mountjoy away from Kinsale, he moved on to rendezvous with O'Donnell at Bandon in County Cork on 5 December. A few days earlier a further six ships, carrying 650 soldiers, had landed to the west of Kinsale and taken possession of the ports of Castlehaven, Baltimore, and Bantry. This time the commander, Don Pedro Zubiaur, willingly accepted the support offered by O'Sullivan Beare, various branches of the MacCarthys, and other local lords, although he was able to provide arms for only 1,000 of the 3,000 followers they brought forward.

The English forces besieging Kinsale were now in their turn trapped between the Spaniards and the Ulster army. O'Neill and O'Donnell had an estimated 6,000 infantry and 800 horse, reinforced by 200 Spaniards and 1,200 Irish sent by Zubiaur. The Spanish force had fallen to around 2,500 men fit for combat, while Mountjoy and the earl of Thomond had perhaps 7,000 out of an original force of over 12,000.[40] Águila, desperately short of supplies, persuaded Tyrone to agree to a joint attack. On Christmas Eve (according to the English calendar—3 January 1602 by the papal reckoning favoured by Tyrone and his allies) the Ulster army moved forward. Descriptions of the battle that followed vary greatly. Later Gaelic accounts told of a battle plan sold by a MacMahon for a bottle of whiskey, and disrupted by the jostling rivalry of the O'Neill and O'Donnell forces. But these, it has been suggested, were inventions to explain the simpler fact of ignominious defeat. Tyrone had made significant progress in introducing

[39] Moryson, *Itinerary*, iii. 71.

[40] Estimates of both troop numbers and casualties once again vary widely. The figures given here are from Silke, *Kinsale*, 127, 134–5, 140. Morgan estimates that the Ulster lords had 400 Leinstermen under Tyrrell, 200 Spaniards from Zubiaur's force along with 1,000 Munstermen who had rallied to them, 2,500 men and 500 horse under Tyrone, and 1,500 men and 300 horse under O'Donnell and O'Rourke ('Disaster at Kinsale', in Morgan, *The Battle of Kinsale*, 118). Other reports presented them as bringing with them around 11,000 men, but Silke (p. 126) regards these as misleading.

his Ulster army to new techniques of fighting. But the Spanish naval commander at Kinsale was unimpressed by the Irish forces as a whole, commenting that they relied on raids and ambushes, making war 'as the outlaws and bandits of Catalonia and Calabria do'. The cavalry, in particular, remained fit mainly for light skirmishing.[41]

In a real set-piece battle, as opposed to glorified ambushes like Clontibret and the Yellow Ford, these limitations of Tyrone's military revolution were pitilessly exposed.[42] His vanguard reached a position before the English lines while the remainder of the army under O'Donnell lagged far behind. Tyrone still had a numerical superiority of five to one, but nevertheless chose to withdraw rather than risk combat. The English, however, seized the opportunity to charge their normally elusive enemy across open ground. The Irish line withstood a first charge by the English horse. But the Irish cavalry, ordered to counter-attack, broke and fled, and an English charge then scattered the Irish infantry. Meanwhile the Spaniards, having missed the prearranged signal, ventured out of Kinsale only when it was too late, and hastily withdrew. In a devastating rout, completed within two hours, the Irish lost up to 1,200 dead, as against a handful of English casualties. There were also reports of the summary execution of around 200 Irish prisoners.[43]

The battle of Kinsale broke the military challenge of the Ulster lords, but it did not end the war. Águila surrendered to Mountjoy on 2 January 1602, and was allowed to sail back to Spain with his army. Zubiaur had already sailed, bringing with him Hugh Roe O'Donnell. Tyrone retreated into Ulster. O'Sullivan Beare, refused pardon and still in command of 3,000 men, seized his castle of Dunboy from the capitulating Spaniards, and embarked on a desperate rearguard action. In June, however, Carew captured Dunboy and hanged the defenders. Earlier crown forces had taken a secondary O'Sullivan fortress on Dursey Island, where they had re-enacted the tragedy of Rathlin, butchering not only the small garrison but the women and children sent there for safety. On the last day of the year O'Sullivan Beare, accompanied by 400 soldiers and 600 other followers, embarked on a 300-mile forced march across the frozen countryside, reaching O'Rourke's territory in Leitrim two weeks later with only 35 survivors. By this time Mountjoy had struck deep into Tyrone. In June the earl once again destroyed his own castle at Dungannon and retired into the woods north of Lough Neagh. In July O'Cahan, his son-in-law and the most important of his subordinate lords, submitted to Mountjoy. By this time Mountjoy had

[41] For the Spanish commander's comment, see Morgan, *Battle of Kinsale*, 96. For cavalry see ibid. 131.

[42] Different accounts of the battle are to be found in Hayes-McCoy, *Irish Battles*, 162, 170; Silke, *Kinsale*, ch. 10; and Hiram Morgan, 'Disaster at Kinsale'.

[43] Silke, *Kinsale*, 145, puts the Irish dead at between 500 and 1,000. McGurk (*Elizabethan Conquest of Ireland*, 244) suggests 1,200 Irish dead and 800 wounded, and Morgan likewise suggests 1,200 dead ('Disaster at Kinsale', 129–30).

encircled Tyrone's shrunken stronghold by a ring of more than twenty forts extending from Derry round to Carrickfergus. At the beginning of September he struck a powerful symbolic blow by seizing Tullyhogue, north of Dungannon, and smashing the stone chair on which O'Neill lords had for centuries been inaugurated. About the same time O'Donnell died in Spain. In December his brother Rory submitted to the crown, as did most of the Connacht chiefs still in arms.

The war now coming to a close had been waged at an enormous cost, human and financial, to the English crown and people. Between 1594 and 1601 the privy council had levied some 33,000 men from the shires of England and Wales for service in Ireland. (A further 4,000 were to be raised during 1602.) Although the call was for the sons of freeholders and husbandmen, local authorities struggling to meet their quota were more likely to impress criminals, vagrants, and similar marginal individuals. The commissioners for muster at Bristol described one levy as 'small weak starved bodies taken up in fairs, markets and highways to supply the places of better men kept at home'. Recruitment specifically for Ireland meant that most of the English troops sent there were raw recruits with no previous experience of warfare. The system whereby officers received a lump sum out of which they clothed and armed their companies left many soldiers inadequately equipped. (The even less efficient requirement that each soldier pay for the gunpowder he used in battle was abandoned only in 1601.) Deaths in combat, with the exception of the Yellow Ford, were not numerous: one attempted tabulation of major engagements between 1593 and 1602 gives a total of 2,631 English killed and 1,158 wounded, with the Yellow Ford accounting for half of all the fatalities.[44] Sickness and exposure, on the other hand, devoured whole armies. During the siege of Kinsale Mountjoy reportedly lost 6,000 men, of whom only a handful died fighting. A Gaelic account described how 'the entrails of the horses and the corpses of the dead men lay among the living throughout the tents'.[45] It is little wonder that a common saying in Chester, the focal point of much recruiting, was that it was better to be hanged at home than to die like a dog in Ireland. In financial terms, meanwhile, Cecil estimated that the war had cost just under £2 million, as compared to £255,000 spent suppressing the Desmond rebellion of 1579–83.[46]

To the sufferings of the miserable conscripts must be added the even greater horrors inflicted on the civilian population, especially in Ulster. Part of Mountjoy's strategy for wearing down Tyrone and the other rebel lords was a relentless onslaught on the peasantry who gave their power its economic base. As his men

[44] McGurk, *Elizabethan Conquest of Ireland*, 244. For the comment of the Bristol commissioners, see ibid. 33.

[45] Ó Cléirigh's life of O'Donnell, quoted in McCavitt, *Flight of the Earls*, 39.

[46] McGurk, *Elizabethan Conquest of Ireland*, 264.

moved into Tyrone's territory, they systematically cut down standing corn, seized or burnt harvested crops, and butchered or carried off livestock. They also killed anyone they came across. The dispatches of Mounjoy's commanders make no attempt to conceal either the scale or the indiscriminate nature of the slaughter. Chichester, describing one raid across Lough Neagh in May 1601, boasted that he had struck within four miles of Dungannon, 'where we killed man, woman, child, horse, beast, and whatsoever we found'. Docwra, a year later, reported that one of his captains, on a raid into O'Cahan's territory, had killed a hundred people, including three men of importance, 'many kern, the rest churls, women and children (for he spared none) and brought away only 20 cows'.[47] O'Hagan, a government supporter, complained in September 1602 that a thousand people lay dead between Tullahogue and Toome, and that 3,000 in all had starved since the English offensive began. Mountjoy's secretary, writing after the war, drew a similar picture: 'no spectacle was more frequent in the ditches of towns, and especially in wasted countries, than to see multitudes of these poor people dead with their mouths all coloured green by eating nettles, docks, and all things they could rend up above ground'.[48]

Yet even this ruthlessness was not sufficient to procure either Tyrone's surrender or—as Mountjoy admitted—his betrayal by his own people. Meanwhile pressure to end the war continued. The cost remained ruinous. 'In short time', Cecil told Mountjoy, 'the sword cannot end the war, and in long time the state of England cannot well endure it.'[49] There was also the recognition that if Tyrone decided to flee the country he would find a refuge with one of England's enemies and become a permanent threat to security. In addition, both Mountjoy and Carew, with a new reign imminent, were anxious to resume their political careers in England. A first round of negotiations in early 1602 broke down, but Cecil encouraged Mountjoy to keep lines of communication open. At the beginning of March 1603 Mountjoy received Elizabeth's permission to offer Tyrone a pardon. Three weeks later, spurred into action by news of the queen's illness, he invited the earl to come before him under safe conduct. On 30 March Tyrone appeared at Sir Garrett Moore's mansion at Mellifont, County Louth, kneeling for an hour before the deputy to make his submission. Following this ritual self-abasement, however, the two men proceeded to work out what was in effect a surrender on terms. Mountjoy's sudden eagerness to negotiate reflected what he had just learned but Tyrone did not yet know: that Queen Elizabeth was dead, and that the future for both himself and the earl now lay in the hands of a new monarch whose intentions remained to be disclosed.

[47] John McCavitt, *Sir Arthur Chichester, Lord Deputy of Ireland 1605–16* (Dublin, 1998), 12; Docwra to English privy council, 11 March 1602 (*CSPI 1601–1603*, 323).

[48] Moryson, *Itinerary*, iii. 208, 281.

[49] Frederick M. Jones, *Mountjoy: Last Elizabethan Deputy* (Dublin, 1958), 151.

THE FLAIL OF TALUS

In 1596 Edmund Spenser published the second instalment of his ambitious work *The Faerie Queene*.[50] The son of a London merchant, Spenser had come to Ireland as secretary to Lord Grey, and the poem was written on the 3,000-acre estate at Ballycolman, County Cork, which he had received as an undertaker in the Munster plantation. A dedicatory sonnet described the volume, revealingly, as 'the wild fruit which savage soil had bred'. What it offered was a work of moral education, and at the same time an epic allegory of English identity. The twelve knights, each embodying a different virtue, who journey across a landscape of monsters and sorcerers are dispatched from the court of the eponymous queen, explicitly identified with Elizabeth, and their paths repeatedly cross with that of her future consort, Prince Arthur. In the fifth of the six completed books, ancient myth and broad allegory give way to more specific contemporary references, as the knight Artegall sets out to assist the lady Irena in recovering her kingdom from the giant Grantorto (great wrong).

The significance of this fifth book lies not just in the way in which recent events in Ireland are presented, but in the wider context within which they are set. For the controlling theme of the Fifth Book is justice. More specifically, its concern is with the relationship between justice, mercy, and the necessary use of violence.[51] Artegall has been trained by the nymph Astraea 'in all the skill of deeming right and wrong'. Her teaching allows him to deliver perfect judgments in disputed cases, and unflinchingly to uphold right by force of arms. But Artegall, like Spenser's other heroes, also strays for a time from the true path, in his case when he shrinks from beheading the Amazon queen Radigund. For this moment of weakness he is punished by being enslaved, condemned to wear female dress and perform the womanly labour of spinning. His failure contrasts with the conduct of two others, both fictional representations of Elizabeth. His lover Britomart defeats and kills Radigund, while Queen Mercilla resists the twin temptations of pity and anger and reluctantly but firmly condemns the witch Duessa, representing Mary, queen of Scots, to death.

By the end of the fifth book Artegall too has learned from his earlier mistake. He not only slays Grantorto and liberates Irena's kingdom, but sets about restoring it to proper discipline and social order:

50 Nicholas Canny, *Making Ireland British 1580–1650* (Oxford, 2001), ch. 1, provides a useful introduction to the very extensive literature on Spenser and Ireland.

51 Particularly useful discussions of this theme are Brendan Bradshaw, 'Edmund Spenser on Justice and Mercy', in Tom Dunne (ed.), *The Writer as Witness* (Cork, 1987), 76–89; John D. Staines, 'Elizabeth, Mercilla, and the Rhetoric of Propaganda in Spenser's *Faerie Queene*', *Journal of Medieval and Early Modern Studies*, 31 (2001), 283–312.

During which time, that he did there remain,
His study was true justice how to deal,
And day and night employed his busy pain
How to reform that ragged commonweale.

His instrument, here as throughout the book, is Talus, an iron man armed with a metal flail whom Astraea has sent to serve him.

And that same iron man which could reveal
All hidden crimes, through all that realm he sent.
To search out those, that used to rob and steale,
Or did rebel gainst lawful government;
On whom he did inflict most grievous punishment.

His reign of justice, however, is short-lived. Artegall is summoned back to the Faerie Court, against his will, leaving Irena's kingdom 'ere he could reform it thoroughly'. On the way he finds himself assailed by the figures of envy and detraction, who accuse him of having stained his sword 'in guiltless blood of many an innocent', and present even Grantorto as the victim of treachery. The final outcome is unclear, since the twelfth book, with the return of Artegall and other knights to the Faerie Court, was never written. But the parallel is clearly with Spenser's former patron, Grey, condemned as 'a bloody man' and recalled to England before he could complete his work of reducing Ireland to obedience.[52]

It is important, given the place that historians of the Irish sixteenth century now accord to Spenser's poem, to emphasize that the Irish sections of the *Faerie Queene* cannot be taken in isolation. Spenser himself sets the defeat of rebellion in Ireland firmly in a wider European context. This includes English intervention in the Netherlands, as Arthur helps the lady Belge to defeat the tyrant who has devoured twelve of her seventeen sons. There is also the defection to Catholicism of Henry IV of France, represented by the knight Burbon, who has cravenly cast away his shield on the pretence that 'to temporize is not from truth to swerve', while his love Flourdelis is seduced by the same tyrant Grantorto who has seized Irena's kingdom. It is also important to remember, in reading the vividly rendered scenes of violence, that the poem as a whole is a strikingly bloody one. From the graphically described killing of a dragon in the first canto of Book I, Spenser's knights wade through seas of gore. The rationale for this relentless, and meticulously rendered, bloodletting, likewise, is the same throughout: evil is powerful and all-pervasive, and must be ruthlessly confronted in direct and violent conflict.[53] Having said this, however, Spenser's choice of Ireland as the location for his argument that true justice must at times involve the suppression of pity remains striking. Taken against the background of the actual events of

[52] *Faerie Queene*, V. xii. xxvi, xl. For Grey as a 'good Lord blotted with the name of a bloody man', see Edmund Spenser, *A View of the State of Ireland*, ed. Andrew Hadfield and Willy Maley (Oxford, 1997), 103.

[53] These points are emphasized in Canny, *Making Ireland British*, 9–23.

Grey's government, his tale of beheadings and dismemberment, and the slaughter not just of individual monsters and tyrants but of whole armies of their deluded followers, takes on a new significance. Much of the actual killing is done by the iron man Talus. 'Immovable, resistless, without end', he represents a key figure in Spenser's vision: the provost marshal, seneschal, or other officer of military government reimagined as a perfect killing machine.

It is precisely these resonances that have made Spenser's writings a key, if much debated, text among historians of late Elizabethan Ireland. How far did his murderous fantasies reflect the development of a new and harsher attitude to Ireland and its people? How far, in turn, does such a development help to explain why earlier programmes for political and cultural assimilation gave way to an increasing reliance on force, culminating in the war of extermination which Mountjoy and his subordinates mounted against central Ulster? To explore these issues it will be necessary, first to look more closely at what Spenser actually said about Ireland, and secondly to enquire how his ideas, in so far as they can be ascertained, compared with those of his New English peers.

The suggestion that Spenser should be seen as the spokesman for a new colonizing mentality does not depend solely on a decoding of the complex allegories of the *Faerie Queene*. Instead the poem is normally read side by side with a second, and more direct expression of Spenser's views, the dialogue entitled 'A View of the Present State of Ireland'. In doing so, however, it is important to recognize that virtually everything that is said about the relationship between the two texts is guesswork. All that is known for certain is that one of Spenser's London publishers registered the *View* with the Stationers' Company (the normal preliminary to publication) in April 1598, that the text nevertheless remained unprinted, and that it circulated quite widely in manuscript before finally reaching print, in edited form, in 1633. The book may have been suppressed by the government—not necessarily because of its content, but because the authorities opposed any public discussion of Irish matters of state. Alternatively, it may have fallen victim to a quarrel between publishers. Or again the planned publication may have lapsed with Spenser's death in London, a refugee from the collapse of the Munster colony, in 1599.[54] A passage in Book VI of the *Faerie Queene* can be read as indicating that Spenser decided, in response to events in Ireland, to abandon the whole idea of promoting moral education through allegory, and turned instead to direct political prescription in the form of the *View*.[55] But it has also been suggested that the first versions of the *View* were already written by the time Book VI appeared.[56] One scholar has even questioned

[54] Andew Hadfield, 'Was Spenser's *View of the Present State of Ireland* Censored? A Review of the Evidence', *Notes & Queries*, 41 (1994), 459–63.

[55] Canny, *Making Ireland British*, 27.

[56] David Edwards, 'Ideology and Experience: Spenser's *View* and Martial Law in Ireland', in Hiram Morgan (ed.), *Political Ideology in Ireland 1541–1641* (Dublin, 1999), 143.

whether Spenser was in fact the author of the *View*, although this doubt is not widely shared.[57]

The *View* is presented as a dialogue in which Irenius, lately returned from Ireland, begins by explaining to an enquiring companion, Eudoxus, the three great evils affecting the kingdom. These are that the common law fails to function, because it was imposed prematurely on a land not yet reduced to obedience; that the customs of the inhabitants, including both 'the wild Irish' and the 'Old English', are barbarous; and that the entire population are not only papists but for the most part too 'blindly and brutishly informed' to know the basis of their religion. Problems so deep-rooted, Irenaeus goes on to argue, cannot be dealt with by making new laws, for these would simply not be obeyed. Instead reform must be by the sword. Specifically his vision was of a determined military campaign to stamp out rebellion once and for all. An army of 10,000 foot and 1,000 horse would continually harass the enemy, in winter as well as summer, systematically destroying his livestock until 'he shall have no heart nor ability to endure his wretchedness'. The defeat of the rebellion would leave the way open for a major campaign of social engineering. The natives of the two main centres of rebellion, Ulster and the Leinster mountains, would be transplanted to each other's territories, to live as tenants of new English proprietors. The population as a whole would be organized, along lines borrowed from the England of Alfred the Great, into 'tithings' and 'hundreds', to be held collectively responsible for delivering up to the authorities any offenders from among their number. All those with inadequate land to support them would be assigned a trade, which for able bodied men was not to include the classic idle Gaelic pursuit of cattle herding. This reformed social order was to be upheld by a continuing military garrison of 6,000 men. There was also to be in each shire a provost marshal, supported by some horsemen, with power to impose summary justice on 'loose persons' and on any former rebels that might relapse into their old ways. To all this Spenser added a somewhat perfunctory provision for religious reform, to be achieved not by terror but by 'mildness' and 'gentleness', using clergy recruited from the native population.[58]

If the background to the composition of the *View* invites speculation rather than certainty, so too, in many ways, does its interpretation. Spenser's opening identification of the premature introduction of the common law as one of the great evils affecting Ireland represents a definite break with conventional thinking, where the spread of English law had been seen as central to the progressive reform of the country. A second notable feature was his refusal to offer even a token

[57] Jean Brink, 'Constructing the *View of the Present State of Ireland*', *Spenser Studies*, 11 (1992), 203–28.

[58] Spenser, *A View of the Present State of Ireland*, ed. Hadfield and Maley. The main text of this edition, it should be noted, is the version published by Sir James Ware in 1633 (see below, pp. 402–3). However, an appendix (pp. 170–6) includes the passages Ware omitted as too harsh for Ireland's changed condition.

acknowledgement of the distinction between the Gaelic Irish and those who continued to see themselves as the English of Ireland. The Old English, in Spenser's account, were in many cases more lawless, and more hostile to true English interests, than the 'wild Irish', and they were clearly to be subjected to the same process of military pacification and enforced reform. When it comes to the reform process itself, on the other hand, Spenser's proposals are, on the face of it, less drastic than is often claimed. He did, it is true, advocate starvation as the principal means by which rebellion should be extirpated. But Irenius had already argued that the rebels would respond to the call for surrender by sending in 'old men, women, children and hinds (which they call churls)'. In theory, then, the victims of the man-made famine would be fighting men rather than civilians. Elsewhere Spenser insisted that his aim was not to extirpate the Irish but to reform them. By 'the sword' he did not mean 'the cutting off all that nation with the sword, which far be it from me, that I should ever think so desperately, or wish so uncharitably', but simply the use of the royal power to root out evil. He also rejected the idea of creating a permanent separation between the English and the conquered Irish: 'since Ireland is full of her own nation, that ought not to be rooted out . . . I think it best by an union of manners, and conformity of minds, to bring them to be one people.' In the same way Spenser advocated confiscating the lands of rebels in Ulster and Leinster, as well as a commission to discover intrusions on royal land. But he insisted that there should be no general confiscation, or even 'the utmost advantages enforced against them'.[59]

At first sight, then, a reading of Spenser's text might suggest that his rhetorical bark was somewhat worse than the bite represented by his actual prescriptions. Certainly there is nothing to justify loose suggestions that the *View* explicitly advocated a policy of genocide. On the other hand the vision he set forth was undoubtedly a harsh one. When Eudoxus talks of 'these rueful spectacles of so many wretched carcasses starving, goodly countries wasted, so huge desolation and confusion', the purpose is to allow Irenius to develop the theme that once the 'course of reformation' has commenced there must be 'no remorse nor drawing back'.[60] The word 'remorse', in particular, takes us back to the philosophical landscape of the *Faerie Queene*, where justice requires not just firmness of purpose but the repression of natural human emotions. The real problem with the *View*, however, is whether even this explicit vision can be taken at face value. The holocaust being described is in theory confined to those still in obstinate rebellion. Yet Spenser's model for the proper government of Ireland was his former master, Lord Grey. To illustrate how effectively the tactics he advocated would defeat rebellion once and for all, he offered a graphic and presumably first-hand account of the famine that accompanied the suppression of the Desmond revolt.[61] And he must without question have been aware that both this famine, and the other

[59] Ibid. 100, 93, 144, 142. [60] Ibid. 102, 106. [61] Above, p. 178.

forms of bloodletting over which Grey had presided, had engulfed far more than the rebellious lords and their armed followers.

It is also important to note the extent to which both Spenser's most extreme statements, and the qualifications that accompany them, must be read as part of a systematic rhetoric of bad faith. The dialogue format is central to this process. Eudoxius's questions, raising issues of justice and morality in a not very challenging manner, are in reality repeated opportunities for Irenius to recast his proposals in an acceptable form before proceeding to the next stage of the argument. The overall result has been well described as a process of 'assertion, qualification, assertion and reaffirmation'.[62] What remains impossible to say with certainty is how, in personal terms, this rhetorical tactic is to be interpreted. Was the *View* simply a work of propaganda, dressing up brutal but expedient solutions in acceptable form? Alternatively, can Spenser's evasions and inconsistencies be seen as evidence of an inner crisis, as he struggled to reconcile deeply held moral beliefs with the desperate realities of the Ireland of Tyrone's rebellion?[63]

To these uncertainties as to Spenser's purpose and outlook can be added another level of ambivalence. This relates to the characteristic dilemma of the colonist, caught between an alien but increasingly familiar homeland and a native but increasingly unfamiliar mother country. Side by side with the numerous references to Irish savagery, both literal and metaphorical, that litter Spenser's writings, there are moments when Ireland appears in another guise: as a known landscape to be named, described, and even at times idealized. Contradictory responses are particularly evident in Book IV of the *Faerie Queene*, where the Irish rivers take their place at the wedding of the Thames and the Medway. They include 'the pleasant Boyne, the fishy, fruitful Bann', 'the gentle Suir, that making way' | By sweet Clonmel, adorns rich Waterford', and—nearer to Spenser's home at Kilcolman—'the pleasant Bandon, crowned with many a wood'. But there is also 'the baleful Oure'—the river that gave Glenmalure its name—'late stained with English blood'. The completed fragment of the projected Book VII expresses the same mixed emotions. Ireland, Spenser maintains, was once in fact the richest and most fertile 'of all that bear the British Islands name'. However, it has been abandoned and cursed by the insulted goddess Diana, so that its 'fair forests' and fertile plains 'doth to this day with wolves and thieves abound'.[64] In other respects too there are faint signs that Spenser's hostility to Gaelic culture was tempered by a reluctant fascination with certain of its elements. In particular he interrupted his denunciatory account to acknowledge the status accorded to bardic learning. And his introduction in Book IV of the

[62] Ciaran Brady, 'Debate: Spenser's Irish Crisis, Humanism and Experience in the 1590s', *Past & Present*, 120 (1988), 214.

[63] See in particular the exchange between Canny, who sees Spenser as articulating views common among the New English, and Brady, who stresses instead Spenser's personal crisis, in *Past & Present*, 120 (1988), 201–15.

[64] *Faerie Queen*, IV. xi. 40–4, VII. vi. 38, 55.

Faerie Queene of the wizard Merlin has been seen as a representation of his own developing self-image as a prophetic voice, speaking in allegory, from a base in the Celtic periphery.[65]

The weight to be given to such occasional references and speculative readings will remain a matter of judgement. What can be detected much more clearly in Spenser's poetic texts is his estrangement from the reality of the England whose glorious destiny he has set out to celebrate in allegorical form. The ambivalence is already evident in 1591 when Spenser, newly returned from Elizabeth's court, wrote *Colin Clout's Come Home Again*. The shepherd Colin, travelling to the kingdom of Cynthia, encounters a fruitful, tranquil landscape:

> No wailing there nor wretchedness is heard,
> No bloody issues nor no leprosies,
> No grisly famines, nor no raging sword
> No nightly bodrags [raids], nor no hue and cries.

Yet the corruption and deceit which he encounters at Cynthia's court leads him to abandon this 'contented bliss' and return instead to his own 'barren soil, where cold and care and penury do dwell'. The *Faerie Queene* openly attacks the weakness and inconsistency of royal policy towards Ireland, particularly in the transparent parallel between Sir Artegall and Lord Grey. An episode in the final completed book, where Spenser indulges in a gloating, if not near-pornographic, description of the naked and helpless Lady Serena, rescued from human sacrifice only by the armed intervention of Sir Calidore, can likewise be read as an expression of his possibly unconscious hostility to a queen he had earlier represented in a succession of resolute and independent heroines. If Spenser's writings provide an insight into the thinking of the New English of his own day, they may also be seen as providing early pointers towards the conflicts that were to complicate the allegiances of later generations.

*

But how far can Spenser in fact be taken as the voice of the New English elite in late sixteenth-century Ireland? The evidence of manuscript copies indicates that the *View* circulated widely. Traces of its arguments have been detected in the writings of other leading commentators, and there is also the likelihood that its central depiction of a merciless war against rebellion struck a chord with many who had little time for the wider philosophical concerns that preoccupied the author. In 1589 another Munster undertaker, Sir Edward Denny, anticipated Spenser's central argument when he insisted in a letter to government that 'persuasion' would never bring the Irish 'to God or to her majesty, but justice

[65] Christopher Highley, *Shakespeare, Spenser and the Crisis in Ireland* (Cambridge, 1997), 15–23, 39, 127–31; Andrew Hadfield, *Edmund Spenser's Irish Experience: Wilde Fruit and Salvage Soyl* (Oxford, 1997), 66–71, 178–81. For Spenser's use of the Irish landscape see also Patricia Coughlan (ed.), *Spenser and Ireland: An Interdisciplinary Perspective* (Cork, 1989), 53–9.

without mercy must first tame and command them'.[66] But all this was one side of a continuing argument. Denny's comments were part of an attack on another undertaker, Sir William Herbert, and on Richard Beacon, attorney general to the Munster provincial council, both of whom he saw as unduly lenient in their treatment of the Irish. Both men in turn left their own assessments of what was needed to reduce Ireland to a more orderly state. In 1591 Herbert composed a Latin tract, *Croftus*, urging the government to undertake a continuing programme of colonization, using the confiscated lands of traitors and the Ulster lands granted to the first earl of Essex. His argument remained uneasily balanced between a traditional concern with the assimilation of the native Irish to English civility, and a harsher coercive approach. On the one hand he made clear that the common people were to be excluded from office and from bearing arms. He also referred indirectly but menacingly to the likelihood that some future prince would act to disperse or exterminate any who had refused to embrace the civility offered to them. At the same time the settlers were enjoined to treat the natives with 'kindness and affability', setting them an example 'of all that is best'. Herbert also called for the establishment of universities at Dublin and Limerick to foster 'virtue, learning and civilization', and for the production of prayer books and other religious texts in Irish.[67]

Three years later Beacon published his own contribution to the debate. *Solon his Follie* is a dense text primarily concerned to use a complex web of parallels from classical literature to attack the administration of Fitzwilliam, which had dismissed Beacon from his Munster office. It placed greater emphasis than Herbert had done on ruthless military action, echoing Spenser's admiration for the strict government of Lord Grey, and also praising 'that famous knight Sir R. Byngham [who] by his singular art and skill in military discipline as another Caesar suppressed at the last Vercingetorix and the rebelling Gauls'. But Beacon nevertheless drew a clear distinction between periods of rebellion, when it was legitimate to proceed against offenders without the normal legal forms, and other times, when government should operate within the law.[68] His prescriptions, like those of Herbert, marked a clear departure from the traditional emphasis on the progressive extension to Ireland of English laws, manners, and institutions. Both men also agreed with Spenser in paying little attention to the distinction between Old English and Gaelic Irish. Neither, however, shared his exclusive reliance on the sword as the instrument by which society was to be reshaped.

[66] Quoted in Clare Carroll and Vincent Carey, introduction to Richard Beacon, *Solon his Follie* (Brighampton, 1996), p. xxi.

[67] Herbert, William, *Croftus sive de Hibernia Liber*, ed. A. Keaveney and J. A. Madden (Dublin, 1992). For a useful discussion see S. G. Ellis, '"Civilizing" Tudor Ireland: A Review Article', *North Munster Antiquarian Journal*, 34 (1992), 44–7.

[68] Beacon, *Solon his Follie*, ed. Carroll and Carey; Vincent Carey, 'The Irish Face of Machiavelli: Richard Beacon's *Solon his Follie* and Republican Ideology in the Conquest of Ireland', in Morgan, *Political Ideology*, 83–109.

By the time these tracts by Spenser, Herbert, and Beacon were written, western Europe was coming to the end of its first century of exploitative subjugation of the indigenous population of the New World. However, this background left no overt trace in the arguments advanced by any one of the three. Instead, as with Smith's first proposals for an Ulster colony two decades before, their references were to the European past. Spenser and Beacon made passing reference to Machiavelli's prescriptions for government. Herbert, more systematically, drew on Machiavelli's account of how the Romans had used colonies to establish their control over newly acquired and peripheral territories. He also dwelt at length on Wales as an example of the successful assimilation of an uncivilized outlying territory, achieved by a combination of military conquest and cultural assimilation. As with Smith's self-justificatory writings, it would be unwise to take the citation of respectable classical precedents at face value.[69] But it remains significant that Ireland continued to be presented, formally at least, as a problem of government, the reduction to order of an unruly periphery, rather than as a theatre of colonial expansion.

This is not to suggest that there were no links between the final reduction and partial colonization of Ireland on the one hand, and the beginnings of English empire in North America on the other. There was in fact considerable overlap in terms of individual careers. Humphrey Gilbert, transferred from Ulster to Munster to suppress the first Desmond revolt, was a pioneer of transatlantic exploration, who seems to have turned his full attention westwards only after failing to secure sufficient backing for colonizing ventures in Ulster or Munster. Walter Ralegh and Richard Grenville, both undertakers in the Munster plantation, were also the sponsors of the first English settlement in what became Virginia, at Roanoke in 1585; indeed it has been suggested that their preoccupation with securing their share of the Munster pickings was one reason for the neglect that led to the colony's collapse. Ralph Lane, first military commander at Roanoke, had earlier served in the Munster campaign, and had with him what he called 'mine Irish boy' (whom he trusted sufficiently to allow him to use his pistol to shoot the local chief, Pemisapan, 'thwart the buttocks').[70]

These biographical details remind us that the recurrent wars of late sixteenth-century Ireland, and the confiscations that followed them, attracted the same sort of ruthless and ambitious man of action as did the beginnings of settlement in North America. In that sense they throw a certain light on the character and mentality of the New English. Beyond this, however, too much should not be read into a mere overlap in personnel. It would, after all, be equally easy to demonstrate the close links between involvement in Ireland and service in England's other major theatre of war, the Netherlands. It is also necessary to remember the different character of the two colonial ventures. Englishmen were

69 See above, Ch. 4, for the evidence that Smith was in fact partly influenced by Spanish precedent.

70 Lenman, *England's Colonial Wars*, 94.

attracted to America by the hope of finding precious metals, as the Spaniards had done further south, or alternatively, like Humphrey Gilbert, by the dream of a north-west passage to the Pacific. It was only gradually that they resigned themselves to the second best of colonies of settlement supported by trade and agriculture, of the kind that had from the start been the focus of Irish projects. At that point it was, if anything, Ireland that provided a model for American ventures, rather than the other way round.

Any assessment of the interconnections between the expansion of English power in Ireland and the beginnings of transatlantic colonization must further take account of the growing body of work that makes clear that the New World was not in fact the universal presence once assumed in the consciousness of Tudor Englishmen. The eyes of statesmen and military commanders, it now appears, remained firmly fixed on continental Europe and the Mediterranean, while even the educated seem often to have been only dimly aware of what are now seen as the beginnings of a transatlantic empire.[71] It is hardly surprising, as Englishmen followed Spaniards in establishing themselves in parts of the New World, that parallels should from time to time be drawn between the indigenous peoples they found there and the Gaelic society they or others had encountered in Ireland. But it would be unwise to interpret casual comments as evidence of a coherent colonizing mentality. Around the same time, after all, a supercilious Spanish official in Milan pronounced that the Italians, 'although they are not Indians, have to be treated as such'. The earl of Tyrone, meanwhile, developed an American parallel of a rather different nature, when he warned that the Spaniards could not expect to win himself and the other Ulster lords over with 'hallowed beads and poor counterfeit jewels, as if we had been petty Indian kings'.[72]

To question the significance of parallels between Gaelic Ireland and native America is not in any sense to deny that the former was seen as lying outside the boundaries of civilized society. The point is rather that there was nothing new about that perception. From the twelfth century onwards both the English of Ireland and the English of England had been agreed that the native Irish, dedicated to pastoral agriculture, lacking towns and commercial networks, and governed by what to outsiders seemed to be an irrational legal and political system, stood on a lower rung on the ladder of cultural development. The main influence on Tudor writing on the Gaelic Irish, in fact, continued to be the writings of Gerald of Wales, compiled in the 1180s and widely circulated throughout the intervening centuries as the core document of the English presence in Ireland.

[71] Lenman, *England's Colonial Wars*, 284–5; David Armitage, 'Literature and Empire', in Nicholas Canny (ed.), *Oxford History of the British Empire*, i. *The Origins of Empire* (Oxford, 1998), 99–123.

[72] Henry Kamen, *Spain's Road to Empire: The Making of a World Power 1492–1763* (London, 2002), 347; McCavitt, *The Flight of the Earls*, 16–17. For contemporary comment on parallels between Ireland and America see D. B. Quinn, *The Elizabethans and the Irish* (New York, 1996), ch. 9.

What was involved was thus essentially an assessment of conditions on the periphery based on the criteria of civility that prevailed within the European heartland. Against this background, occasional comparisons between the Gaelic Irish and the indigenous population of the New World were at best a superficial addition to a long-established tradition. Sir Francis Bacon, writing to Essex in 1599, reminded him that the forthcoming campaign was 'no ambitious war against foreigners, but a recovery of subjects . . . not only to obedience, but to humanity and policy, from more than Indian barbarism'.[73] The passing reference to the native Americans was less significant than two other points: the assertion that the Gaelic Irish were part of the same political community, and the assumption that they could be civilized, even if by military means.

The extent to which attitudes to Gaelic Ireland were or were not affected by contact with the New World is important because an influential line of argument suggests that it is precisely to such contact, encouraging a new anthropological perspective, that the growing ruthlessness of Tudor policy in the second half of the sixteenth century can be attributed. Parallels with native Americans, it has been argued, encouraged a perception of the Gaelic Irish as an inferior race, whose savagery justified their violent subjugation. Episodes such as Essex's essays in frightfulness at Belfast and Rathlin, the massacre at Mullaghmast, the severed heads lining the path to Sir Humphrey Gilbert's tent, or the mass starvation imposed on Ulster in the last stages of Tyrone's war, can thus be seen as evidence of a new colonial context, in which the agents of the expanding English state felt themselves to be released, in their handling of recalcitrant natives, 'from all normal ethical restraints'.[74] To these deliberately planned instances of exemplary terror must be added the remorseless use of summary justice. Casual references to the uncounted numbers executed under the repeated commissions of martial law issued during the 1570s and 1580s suggest something close to a campaign

73 Canny, *Making Ireland British*, 76. For the continuity of English perceptions of the Gaelic Irish from the middle ages into the Renaissance period see John Gillingham, 'The English Invasion of Ireland', in Brendan Bradshaw, Andrew Hadfield, and Willy Maley (eds.), *Representing Ireland: Literature and the Origins of Conflict 1534–1660* (Cambridge, 1993), 24–42. For Gerald of Wales see Hiram Morgan, 'Giraldus Cambrensis and the Tudor Conquest of Ireland', in Morgan, *Political Ideology*.

74 Canny, *Elizabethan Conquest of Ireland*, 127–34. The notion of a shift towards extraordinary levels of state violence as the century continued is also central to the work of Brendan Bradshaw, who differed from Canny in seeing the eclipse of reform by coercion as coming earlier, and as having its roots in Protestant theology. See Brendan Bradshaw, 'The Elizabethans and the Irish', *Studies*, 61 (1977), 38–50. By the mid-1980s historians of the period were moving away from this debate towards a more empirical analysis of the workings of government and society, a change clearly signalled in the introduction to Ciaran Brady and Raymond Gillespie (eds.), *Natives and Newcomers: The Making of Irish Colonial Society 1534–1641* (Dublin, 1986), 14–16. More recently, however, an emphasis on what is presented as the exceptionally brutal nature of late Tudor government in Ireland has once again become prominent, notably in the work of David Edwards cited below. Meanwhile Canny's *Making Ireland British* has restated the case for the primary influence of an ideology of ruthless conquest, though without the earlier emphasis on the influence of European expansion overseas.

of social cleansing, in which the swordsmen and other retainers retained by local lords, along with vagrants, itinerant bards or musicians, and other undesirables, were consigned in batches to the gallows.[75] Robert Gardiner, the chief justice of the Queen's Bench, provided an even more startling perspective on the use of martial law when he complained in 1589 of the bounties paid to those who brought in severed heads, 'never examining or knowing whose heads, whether of the best or worst, so no safety for any man to travel: a strange course in a Christian Commonwealth'.[76]

The rising tempo of violence in the second half of the sixteenth century is undeniable. The reasons have already been explored. The moving frontier created by attempts to secure the Pale following the destruction of the Kildares, the inability of the crown to manage the Anglo-Irish feudal lords, the real or imagined threat of Spanish intervention, the provocative activities of licensed New English freebooters, all help to explain why military conflict became more frequent, extensive, and protracted. What is less clear is that the methods employed in these conflicts represented a departure from accepted contemporary norms. The wholesale use of martial law, for example, was an extension to Ireland of a practice already adopted in England under Edward VI and Mary, where new powers of summary justice introduced against a background of political instability and economic depression were used indiscriminately against the wandering poor.[77] By the same token gruesome executions, like the half-hanging, castration, and disembowelment of Sir Brian O'Rourke, or the sentence of burning alive passed on Rose Toole, wife of Fiach McHugh O'Byrne, were the standard penalties inflicted on traitors, English or Irish. The repressive tactics used in Ireland also have parallels in Scotland. Confronted with what he considered the barbarous Highlands, and the even more barbarous Islands, James VI, like his predecessors, repeatedly issued commissions of fire and sword executed to their own profit by predatory lords on the fringes of the troublesome region. Later the union of crowns permitted him to set up an Anglo-Scottish commission to terrorize the Border counties into submission by dispensing very much the same sort of summary justice as that meted out by the Munster and Connacht presidencies.

If ruthless action against rebels and peripheral regions can hardly be seen as peculiar to Elizabethan Ireland, the same is true of such celebrated individual episodes of brutality as the Rathlin or Mullaghmast massacres. The same decade, after all, saw the killing of 6,000 citizens of Antwerp by mutinying soldiers in the 'Spanish fury' of 1576. Three years later, following the fall of Maastricht, Spanish and German troops slaughtered 10,000 men, women, and children, one-third of the city's population. In France an estimated 70,000 Huguenots died in the massacres that began on St Bartholomew's day 1572. Once again it

[75] David Edwards, 'Ideology and Experience: Spenser's *View* and Martial Law in Ireland', Morgan, *Political Ideology*, 133–6.

[76] Canny, *Making Ireland British*, 91

[77] Edwards, 'Ideology and Experience', 130–1.

is difficult to sustain the view that England's Irish policy in the late sixteenth century involved a departure from accepted ethical restraints so radical as to require an extra-European framework of explanation.

The violence of the English state and of the colonial entrepreneurs it sanctioned must also be set against the norms of warfare that prevailed among their native opponents. Irish kern employed in France and Scotland during the honeymoon period following St Leger's agreements with the Irish lords horrified all concerned by their refusal to take prisoners, instead beheading all who came into their hands. The French, having protested in vain, retaliated in a manner which once again puts the atrocity stories of Elizabethan Ireland in perspective: 'the Frenchmen ever after, if they could take any of the Irish scattering from the company, used first to cut off their genitals, and after to torment them with as great and as lingering pain as they could devise'.[78] The butchery at Belfast and on Rathlin can be set against Shane O'Neill's punitive raid on Tyrconnell in 1564, which caused the deaths of an estimated 4,500 inhabitants. In the same way the devastation of Munster during the second Desmond rebellion, which so appalled and fascinated Spenser, was only a more extreme version of Desmond's own earlier depredations, as described to the queen by Sidney on his return from an extended tour of the south in 1567: 'Yea, the view of the bones and skulls of your dead subjects who, partly by murder, partly by famine, have died in the fields, is such that hardly any Christian with dry eyes could behold.' Two years later members of the other great Anglo-Irish magnate family demonstrated their capacity for indiscriminate savagery when Sir Edmund Butler's followers attacked the Lady Day fair at Enniscorthy, killing large numbers of the citizens by stabbing or drowning while 'divers young maidens and wives' were raped 'before their parents' and husbands' faces'. In the same way Butler's ally James Fitzmaurice Fitzgerald burned the town of Kilmallock in 1571, 'hanged the sovereign of that town, and others of the townsmen (as many as he could take) at the high cross in the market place, and carried all the plate and wealth of the town with him'.[79]

Even the most brutal episodes in the late Elizabethan wars, the use of famine first in Munster then in Ulster, must not be taken out of context. The destruction of crops and livestock was a well established tactic of war. Surrey, in 1521, reported that he had marched through the O'Connor lordship in Connacht, 'burning all his towns and houses, and destroying a marvellous deal of corn', so that 'his people shall be enforced either to forsake the country, or die for hunger this winter coming'.[80] Its use was encouraged, in the case of Ireland, by the nature of Irish military tactics, combined with the dispersed character of settlement, which made it impossible to secure a decisive victory by

[78] *Holinshed's Chronicles of England, Scotland and Ireland*, vi. *Ireland*, 315.

[79] Ciaran Brady, *Shane O'Neill* (Dublin, 1996), 55; Sidney to the queen, 20 April 1567 (*CSPI 1509–73*, 330); David Edwards, 'The Butler Revolt of 1569', *IHS* 28 (1993), 250; *The History of that Most Eminent Statesman, Sir John Perrott* (London, 1728), 50.

[80] Surrey to Henry VIII, 29 July 1521 (*SP Henry VIII*, ii. 75–6).

conventional means. After Russell had fought off an ambush at the Moyry Pass in the summer of 1595, a member of his entourage complained that a similar retreat by Spanish troops in France or Flanders would of necessity have led to the capture of towns or territory. 'But these rascals, although they run away and be dispersed into so many parts as they are heads, yet till they be all killed, or the fastness of their countries garrisoned upon, and their cows, which is their revenues, and their very lives, taken from them, will cloak themselves together.'[81] It is also important to note that Mountjoy, before unleashing the third horseman upon central Ulster, made some attempt to separate out committed rebels from uncommitted civilians. In August 1602 he announced his intention to clear Tyrone of inhabitants, 'enjoining such of them as would become subjects, to live on the south side of the Blackwater'. By the following month he had established two sons of Shane O'Neill on these wastelands to the south, with instructions to settle as many followers as came to them and plant the next year's corn. In the same way his instructions to the governor of Kerry, in the event of a further Spanish landing, were not only to burn all the corn he could not secure, but to 'remove the Irish inhabitants with their goods to a country near Limerick'.[82] None of this alters the reality, openly acknowledged in Mountjoy's dispatches and in the subsequent narrative of his secretary, Fynes Moryson, that English tactics would involve the death by starvation of non-combatant males, women, and children. But, as with Spenser's *View*, it makes clear the distinction between famine as a weapon of war and famine as an instrument of genocide.

It is also important to remember that none of the conflicts that contributed to the growing violence of late sixteenth-century Ireland was a straightforward war of the Irish, or even the Irish and Old English, against the English of England. Essex's bloody incursion into Ulster was supported by the young baron of Dungannon. The long drawn out and cruel reconquest of Munster during 1580–3 was the work not just of Gray but of Ormond. The war against Tyrone was no exception. An account of the ambush of Russell in the Moyry Pass in summer 1595 notes in passing that the only casualty was O'Hanlon, who was that day taking his turn as the queen's standard bearer.[83] At a later stage Moryson paid tribute to Connor Roe Maguire, recalling how in the expedition of autumn 1600 'the father had his horse killed under him and the son killed three rebels with his own hand'.[84] Clifford, in Connacht, depended heavily on alliances with O'Connor Sligo, Tibbot Burke, and others. Docwra, similarly, was able to make progress only with the support of Niall Garbh and other allies. A major expedition in pursuit of Tyrone in December 1602 consisted of 50 English horse, 450 English foot, 200 of O'Cahan's kern, and 100 of O'Doherty's.[85] Irish

[81] *Carew MSS 1589–1600*, 117.
[82] Moryson, *Itinerary*, iii. 202, 207–8, 286.
[83] *Carew MSS 1589–1600*, 117.
[84] Moryson, *Itinerary*, ii. 348–9.
[85] *Docwra's Derry: A Narration of Events in North-West Ulster 1600–1604*, ed. William Kelly (Belfast 2003), 68.

natives also served in the rank and file. In August 1601, for example, Mountjoy reported that he had placed 'certain Irish companies' in a fort near MacMahon's country, 'as fittest to spoil and waste the country thereabouts'. At one point, indeed, the deputy claimed that more than half of his soldiers were Irish, while Moryson put the proportion in the army at Kinsale at one-third.[86]

To the modern historian the inclusion of such large numbers of native Irish in Mountjoy's army is a further reason to avoid simplistic models based on an opposition between a victimized 'native Ireland' and a colonizing England. Mountjoy himself, on the other hand, mentioned their presence to emphasize his military weakness. He and other commanders made no secret of their view that native soldiers were unreliable fighters and potentially treacherous followers. Even consistently loyal local lords like Tibbot Burke and O'Connor Sligo, in his view, 'do all somewhat juggle and play on both hands, to serve their own turns'.[87] Docwra, while acknowledging a few of his local allies as 'faithful and honest', offered repeated accounts of chiefs who had joined him only to lead his men into ambushes or betray his fortresses, or who at best had kept a foot in both camps while the conflict continued.[88] But none of this was new. Sir Henry Sidney, and before him St Leger, had presumably been fully aware of the pragmatic motives that might lead a lesser lord like O'Hanlon or Maguire to ally with the crown against a domineering regional potentate such as O'Neill. Yet both wrote positively and with apparent warmth of those who were their allies. By the end of the sixteenth century, on the other hand, the prevailing attitude towards even the most loyal native was suspicious and grudging. John Hooker, having acknowledged the services of Sir Cormac MacTadhg MacCarthy, sheriff of County Cork, including the capture of Sir James of Desmond, felt it necessary to proceed immediately to the story of Jupiter's cat, transformed by the god into a beautiful lady but unable to refrain from snatching a passing mouse, 'as the ape, though he be never so richly attired in purple, yet he will still be an ape'.[89] Mountjoy, meanwhile, repeatedly assured correspondents that the death of Irish troops serving in the queen's army 'was rather gain than loss to the commonwealth'. These 'unpeaceable swordsmen' were rebels themselves, 'or would have been upon any slight occasion. And therefore we hold it a very good piece of policy to make them cut one another's throats, without which this kingdom will be never in quiet.'[90]

Mountjoy's casually ruthless calculation of advantage provides what is perhaps one key to the real nature of the changes taking place in the Irish policy of the late Elizabethan state. What we see is not the development of a radically

86 Moryson, *Itinerary*, ii. 348–9, 437, 425; iii. 39. See also McGurk, *Elizabethan Conquest of Ireland*, 41–3.

87 Moryson, *Itinerary*, iii. 215.

88 *Docwra's Derry*, 47–9, 52, 58, 61.

89 *Holinshed's Chronicles*, vi. 433.

90 Moryson, *Itinerary*, ii. 410; Mountjoy to English privy council, 19 July 1601 (*CSPI 1600–1601*, 441).

new anthropological perspective on the Gaelic Irish, but rather the results of a long-term process of corrosive dillusionment. Henry VIII had dispatched Surrey to Ireland in the belief that all that would be needed to reduce the whole island to obedience would be to demonstrate to its inhabitants the benefits of English-style agriculture and of life in an orderly commonwealth. Eighty years later his daughter's servants were openly contemptuous of what they saw as the invariably self-interested cooperation of Gaelic lords. That transition, from a vague benevolence born of the assumption of effortless cultural superiority to a weary cynicism, no doubt explains part at least of the growing willingness, not just to see unreliable allies die in combat, but to unleash indiscriminate violence against the native population.

Even at this point, however, it is important to distinguish between a new impatience with the recalcitrance of the Gaelic Irish and an abandonment of the underlying aim of converting them into reliable and civil subjects. To see this, we have only to look at the views of the two men most closely identified with the reduction of Ulster by sword and famine. Mountjoy, drawing up his recommendations for the post-war order, specified as 'one of the best medicines of that estate' what he called 'the keeping of the principal persons Irish in terms of contentment and without just particular of complaint, and generally the carrying of an even course between the English and the Irish, whether it be in competition or controversy, as if they were one nation'. Chichester, likewise, argued strongly that plans for a restructuring of Ulster society must include a reasonable provision for the Gaelic Irish.[91] The settlement that actually took place was largely to ignore the views of both men. But that was a result of subsequent events, rather than any direct consequence of the undoubtedly brutal confrontation with Tyrone and his allies.

THE END OF GAELIC ULSTER

When Tyrone learned that Queen Elizabeth was dead he wept. Characteristically, he claimed that the tears were from 'a tender sorrow for the loss of his sovereign mistress'. Mountjoy's secretary believed that in fact he wept from rage. If he had not been tricked into a premature submission, he might have sought better terms from the new monarch, or possibly taken advantage of whatever internal political upheavals accompanied a change of dynasty.[92] In practical terms, however, it is difficult to see how Tyrone could have improved significantly on what he had

[91] Memorandum dating probably from late 1602, printed in Jones, *Mountjoy*, 191. For Chichester, see McCavitt, *Sir Arthur Chichester*, 1–4, 149–52.

[92] Moryson, *Itinerary*, iii. 303. Moryson, it should be pointed out, claimed the credit for having advocated withholding news of the queen's death until after Tyrone's submission. He thus had every reason to talk up the value of that stratagem. See Nicholas Canny, 'The Treaty of Mellifont and the Reorganization of Ulster', *Irish Sword*, 9 (1970), 249–51.

in fact achieved. Under the terms agreed at Mellifont, confirmed by a detailed settlement worked out during a visit to court in the summer of 1603, Tyrone secured both his lands and his earldom. In September he received a formal pardon. His tenacity after Kinsale, as well as his willingness to sacrifice the thousands who had died by famine and the sword in the last terrible year of the war, thus received its reward.

There was, of course, a price to pay for defeat. Tyrone's agreements with the crown required him to renounce the title of O'Neill, to abjure all dependency on foreign potentates, and to agree that he would abolish 'barbarous customs' contrary to law. He also had to accept some encroachments on his territory. Grants of land to two of his former subordinates, Turlough McHenry, lord of the Fews, and Henry Óg O'Neill in the south-east corner of County Tyrone, created independent lordships on his southern border. In addition the crown retained two military outposts, Fort Charlemont on the Blackwater and Fort Mountjoy on Lough Neagh, each with 300 acres of land attached. As against this, the terms of Tyrone's surrender guaranteed not only his life, his lands, and his earldom, but his position as a regional magnate. In other cases, such as the composition of Connacht, the crown had translated Gaelic overlordship into a rent charge, while recognizing the rights of lesser proprietors. Tyrone, however, was acknowledged as absolute owner of the lands formerly granted to Conn Bacach O'Neill. This concession was at the expense of lesser local lords who had seized the opportunity to escape from O'Neill domination by allying with the English in the recent war. A particular loser was Donal O'Cahan, lord of a fertile region extending north from Tyrone to the sea between the rivers Foyle and Bann, who had supported Dowcra in exchange for a promise of crown title to his lands, but now found himself categorized as a dependant of the earl.

Tyrone's main allies, the O'Donnells, were initially set to fare less well. Hugh Roe had died in Spain in 1602, and Mountjoy initially planned to divide his lordship among freeholders, on the lines of the earlier partition of Monaghan. Towards the end of 1602, however, Docwra's ally Niall Garbh had himself inaugurated as the O'Donnell, and tried to assassinate Hugh Roe's brother and heir Rory, who had surrendered to the crown. Niall Garbh was quickly subdued, but his attempted coup appears to have convinced the government to prefer stability to social reform. It not only restored Rory O'Donnell to his brother's estates, but created him earl of Tyrconnell. However, he lost all jurisdiction over the O'Connor Sligos and the O'Dohertys, both of whom he had claimed as subordinate lords, and the crown also reserved the right to dispose of Niall Garbh's lands.

With title and property came political rehabilitation. In Wales, which along with western England had borne the brunt of wartime recruiting, Tyrone was pelted with mud and stones as he accompanied Mountjoy along the road to London in the early summer of 1603. Once at court, however, he was well received, even joining the new king on the hunting field. Having successfully opposed plans to create a provincial president for Ulster, he himself became lieutenant of the counties of Armagh and Tyrone. Back in Ireland he set about rebuilding his economic position, imposing tough bargains on O'Cahan and other subordinates and calling on government to require his tenants to return to their lands. He also mounted a vigorous campaign to restore law and order, even boasting that he had hanged his own nephew as an outlaw. Later there were to be claims that he had in fact used his powers of martial law and summary execution to take revenge on those who had supported the crown in the recent war.

All this, however, was under the administration of Mountjoy's immediate successor, Sir George Carey, 68 years old at the time of his appoinment and reported to be concerned primarily with enriching himself. At the beginning of 1605, Tyrone's old military opponent Sir Arthur Chichester replaced Carey as lord deputy. Along with Sir John Davies, a Wiltshire-born lawyer appointed solicitor general in 1603 and attorney general in 1606, Chichester initiated what became a concerted legal offensive against Tyrone and the other Ulster lords.[93] They began by persuading the king to issue a proclamation, in March 1605, declaring all inhabitants of Ireland to be 'free, natural and immediate' subjects of the crown, rather than dependants of any lord. The proclamation also stated that the patents granted to Tyrone and others after the war had not extinguished the pre-existing rights of freeholders. Next Davies secured a commission to determine the rights and obligations of different classes of proprietor. During 1605 the commissioners imposed a settlement on Donegal, forcing Tyrconnell to grant freeholds to several lesser families. In addition Niall Garbh, forgiven for his offences, received almost 13,000 acres near the town of Lifford, which Tyrconnell complained was 'the only jewel' he possessed. The following year the commissioners turned to south Ulster. In Monaghan they confirmed, with some modifications, the division of lands imposed in 1591. In Fermanagh they divided the demesne lands of the Maguires between two rival claimants, while finding that all remaining land, as well as the whole of County Cavan, should be divided among freeholders. By these means Davies congratulated himself and his colleagues on having 'cut off three heads of that hydra of the north, namely McMahon, McGuire, and O'Reilly'.[94]

At the same time that it thus began to encircle Tyrone, picking off his local allies one by one, Chichester's administration had launched an aggressive new policy of fining and imprisoning prominent recusants for their failure to attend the state church.[95] Already during his visit to court in 1603 Tyrone had taken the lead in presenting a petition requesting toleration for Catholics. Now, in

[93] For different assessments of the relative importance of Davies and Chichester in the formulation and execution of policy, see Hans S. Pawlisch, *Sir John Davies and the Conquest of Ireland: A Study in Legal Imperialism* (Cambridge, 1985), and McCavitt, *Chichester*, 88–9.

[94] *The Works in Verse and Prose of Sir John Davies*, ed. A. B. Grosart (privately printed, 1869–76), iii. 161

[95] See below, Ch. 8.

late 1605, he was reported to have quarrelled violently with Chichester over the assault on recusancy. How far Tyrone had by this time come genuinely to feel the religious commitment he had professed during his revolt, and how far he simply felt it expedient, in his new circumstances, to court Old English support, is impossible to say. (The prominence of religious grievances in the petitions he was later to submit following his flight to the Continent is equally uninformative, since he was by this time under the protection of Counter-Reformation Spain.) But at the very least Chichester's drive to impose conformity was another sign that the autonomy Tyrone had apparently secured in 1603 was now under concerted attack.

The commissioners of 1605 and 1606 had avoided direct confrontation with Tyrone: when he had responded to the 1605 visitation with a transparently meaningless proposal to confer freeholds on some close relatives, the matter had simply been dropped. Behind the scenes, however, Davies had begun to probe weaknesses in the earl's patent, in particular his claim to overlordship of the economically and strategically important O'Cahan lands. His eventual conclusion was that neither Tyrone nor O'Cahan had valid title to the lands in question; instead, under the sweeping terms of the attainder of Shane O'Neill, they and most of the rest of Ulster belonged to the crown, with Tyrone's patent entitling him only to the demesne lands once held by Conn Bacach. From the end of 1606, meanwhile, a new opponent appeared. George Montgomery, the newly arrived bishop of Derry, Clogher, and Raphoe, began a series of legal actions against local proprietors, including both Tyrone and Tyrconnell, for the recovery of former church lands in their possession. In the first half of 1607 these different lines of attack converged. Montgomery, concerned either to assist O'Cahan in breaking with his father-in-law or to put him under further pressure to do so, issued an ecclesiastical judgment requiring him to set aside Tyrone's daughter and return to his wife by an earlier marriage. Meanwhile Davies accepted a petition from O'Cahan to represent him in his lawsuit against the earl. By this time, moreover, O'Cahan's suit was being openly presented as a test case, whose success would encourage other lesser proprietors to challenge Tyrone's claims to be their overlord.

In the face of these multiple attacks, Tyrone was not politically defenceless. Claims that Mountjoy, now back in England as earl of Devonshire but still a figure of influence as lord lieutenant of Ireland, felt himself bound in honour to uphold the Mellifont settlement are unfounded: Devonshire was aware of, and supported, Chichester's aim of reducing Tyrone from regional magnate to local lord.[96] However, he was also conscious of the danger of provoking disorder, and hence did indeed act as a curb to Chichester's aggression. Even after Devonshire's death in April 1606, moreover, the arguments for not pushing Tyrone into a corner remained strong. Retrenchment following peace with Spain in 1603 had

96 McCavitt, *Chichester*, 24–5.

reduced the Irish garrison to skeleton levels: in 1606 there were 900 infantry and 200 or so horse. In the summer of 1606 the earl petitioned successfully against a new attempt to establish a presidency for Ulster, and had also secured permission to submit his legal disputes for adjudication in London. When the Irish privy council heard O'Cahan's case against Tyrone in late June 1607 and found that neither man had title to the land, Tyrone immediately sought permission to travel to court. He was encouraged in this strategy by a recent promise of the king's favourable consideration, as well as by the council's own acknowledgement that its decision required royal approval.

By this time, however, two other sets of events had begun seriously to affect Tyrone's position. The first concerned the plans of his fellow Ulster lords. Both Tyrconnell and Cúchonnacht Maguire were by this time in desperate circumstances. Harassed by the authorities and unable to support themselves adequately from their shrunken patrimonies, they had come to see exile on the Continent, as aristocratic soldiers of fortune or pensionaries of one of the Catholic powers, as preferable to poverty and humiliation at home. In 1607 Maguire left Ireland secretly to make arrangements for their flight, arriving in Brussels in June. Meanwhile the government had received reports, in February of the same year, that Tyrone's son Henry, commander of the Irish regiment in Spanish service stationed in Flanders, along with a Pale nobleman Sir Christopher St Lawrence, soon to become Lord Howth, were planning a new invasion of Ireland. In May St Lawrence himself began to feed Chichester information of an alleged plot involving both the Old English and the Gaelic Irish. The main figures he named were Tyrconnell and Richard Nugent, fifteenth baron Delvin, whose father's imprisonment two decades earlier had provoked the rebellion of his uncle William Nugent.[97] Although Howth accused Tyrone of also being party to the plot, his evidence was less specific and based on hearsay.

There is no reason to think that at this stage Tyrone was contemplating desperate measures. He and the other Ulster lords had been in clandestine contact with Spain since 1604, and he was also later to admit to 'secret dealings', including discussion of armed action, with some of the Old English.[98] But there is no reason to see such contacts as more than a prudent insurance against unexpected turns of events, as well—in the case of Spain—as a means of obtaining financial support. Tyrone's eagerness to take his case to London indicates that he still hoped to secure his position by peaceful means. Moreover he was on the point of giving himself a new foothold at court by the marriage of his son to a daughter of a leading Scottish nobleman, the earl of Argyll. When the king's summons to England duly arrived in mid-July, however, it had a distinctly menacing tone, most probably the result of Howth's allegations

[97] Above, Ch. 5. Delvin was subsequently to escape from prison and was for a brief period on the run with an armed band, before negotiating a pardon in exchange for his surrender.
[98] McCavitt, *Flight of the Earls*, 61.

of treason. Soon after, Tyrone began to hear rumours that once in England he would be imprisoned or even executed. These may have been genuine warnings. Tyrone had long been famous for the web of contacts he maintained within Pale society, and even within the administration. But there were also recurrent suggestions that Chichester and other members of the administration deliberately sought to panic Tyrone into precipitate action.[99] In either case the arrival in August of a secret message that Maguire was about to return with a French vessel to transport himself and others overseas could not have come at a worse time for Tyrone. Already compromised, he could hardly hope to survive the hostile inquiries into possible treasonable conspiracies that would follow such high-profile departures.[100] On 4 September 1607 he sailed from Lough Swilly along with Tyrconnell, Maguire, and a group of dependants and followers, numbering in all around 37.[101] That Tyrone's decision was taken at short notice is confirmed by accounts of a desperate attempt in the last days before his departure to gather up scattered members of his family. In the event he left behind Conn, his youngest son by his fourth wife, Catherine Magennis, who was aged 6 or 7. Tyrconnell likewise had to abandon his wife, Bridget Fitzgerald, inconveniently located at her family's mansion in Maynooth.

The flight of the northern lords provided the opportunity to move beyond the piecemeal tactics of the past four years to a radical restructuring of Ulster society. Tyrone, Tyrconnell, and Maguire could now be condemned as traitors and their lands confiscated. Tyrconnell's wife had the advantage of being not only a daughter of the twelfth earl of Kildare but also a granddaughter of the earl of Nottingham, currently lord high admiral of England. Following the flight she made her way to court, where she charmed James I and received a modest annuity out of her husband's lands. Young Conn O'Neill was, like his father half a century earlier, dispatched to receive a proper anglicized upbringing, first at the fort at Charlemont and then, from 1615, at Eton College. Possible immediate successors to Tyrone, by contrast, fared less well. His nephew Brian MacArt, already in custody on a charge of murder, was tried in Dublin, convicted, and hanged. His brother Cormac was imprisoned for what turned out to be life, despite evidence that he had been on poor terms with the earl and had refused

[99] Ibid. 132–3. Two of those reported to have alerted Tyrone to his peril played particularly ambiguous roles. Sir Garrett More was a long-standing friend of Tyrone: it was at his house in Melifont that the earl submitted to Mountjoy, and it was from the same location that he set off for Lough Swilly, taking with him a child that Moore had been fostering. But Moore was also close to Chichester. Howth, erratic and possibly mentally unstable, was now refusing to cooperate in incriminating the men he had betrayed. Hence his reported warnings to Tyrone might be seen as the work either of a divided conscience or of a double agent.

[100] The above is a composite of the reasons given for Tyrone's flight. McCavitt (*Flight of the Earls*, 86–91) emphasizes the king's change in attitude and the rumours of impending arrest or worse; Nicholas Canny, 'Historical Revision, XVI: The Flight of the Earls 1607', *IHS* 17 (1971), 396–7, emphasizes the crisis precipitated by Maguire's return.

[101] McCavitt, *Flight of the Earls*, 98, gives the reasons for rejecting the more common figure of around 100.

to join in his flight. And indeed Conn O'Neill, about the time he reached full adulthood in 1622, was to vanish forever into the Tower of London.

All this cleared the way for a settlement of Tyrone, Donegal, Fermanagh, and Cavan. Initially, however, what Chichester and others envisaged was that this would consist primarily of the establishment of native freeholders. Land was to be provided for 'servitors'—current or former military commanders deserving of reward for their services in the recent war—as well as for colonies of English and Scottish settlers. But this was to be done after 'every man of note' among the Irish had received what he and his followers could stock and cultivate. Indeed Chichester even advocated offering land to some of the leaders of the Irish regiment in Flanders, as a means of detaching them from their allegiance to Tyrone and Spain.[102]

What transformed government thinking on the restructuring of Ulster society was another outbreak of revolt, this time from an unexpected quarter. Sir Cahir O'Doherty was in many respects the epitome of the loyal native. During the war he had seized the opportunity to cast off his family's traditional dependence on the O'Donnells, and had fought alongside Docwra, who had knighted him for his bravery. More recently he had served as foreman of the jury which, in January 1608, indicted Tyrconnell for treason. He was also engaged in lobbying, with the support of Bishop Montgomery, for a place in the household of the prince of Wales. However, he was on bad terms with the governor of Derry, Sir George Paulet. The problem lay partly with Paulet's personality: Chichester was later to admit that he was so detested that if rebels had not killed him his own men might have done so once the opportunity arose. But O'Doherty was also a victim of the climate of intense suspicion that prevailed following the flight of the Ulster lords. His problems had begun in autumn 1607 when Paulet had insisted on treating what O'Doherty claimed was a simple woodcutting expedition as an armed rising. When O'Doherty appealed to Chichester, the lord deputy—in what he later admitted was a misjudgement—had not only refused him redress but imposed punitive securities for his good behaviour. Matters came to a head in April 1608. Following an incident in which Paulet had insulted and assaulted him, O'Doherty raided the small English settlement at Derry, killing Paulet and burning all eighty-five houses. He went on to broaden the basis of his revolt, proclaiming that he had acted in defence of the Catholic religion. Chichester's response was to send north the greater part of the shrunken English garrison, between 800 and 900 men, to face what was by now a rebel army of around 1,000. After some weeks of campaigning the crown forces captured O'Doherty's castle at Burt, then engaged him in a pitched battle at Kilmacrennan on 5 July, where O'Doherty was killed.

Already rattled by the flight of the Ulster lords, and the unknown plans for invasion or rebellion that might lie behind it, the Dublin administration reacted

[102] McCavitt, *Chichester*, 150–1.

violently to O'Doherty's short-lived revolt. It gave explicit orders that captured rebels were not to be hanged under martial law but instead kept alive for trial, so that the public could witness the more elaborate butchery of hanging, drawing, and quartering. Over the next few months Chichester directed a campaign to track down surviving bands, or alternatively to persuade them, with promises of selective pardons, to destroy one another. In summer 1609 residents of County Armagh, crippled by punitive fines, proposed that surviving rebels should be permitted to leave the kingdom. Chichester, after some hesitation, agreed, although he insisted that the destination was to be the distant and Protestant Baltic, rather than dangerously close, and Spanish-controlled, Flanders. A first detachment of 240 men, destined for the armies of the king of Sweden, left in July, followed by 1,000 more at the end of the year and 600 in the summer of 1610. Details of later shipments are unclear, but in all Chichester claimed to have sent 6,000 men 'to the wars in Sweden'. The deported, taken from all provinces but predominantly drawn from Ulster, included not just participants in O'Doherty's revolt but convicted criminals, vagrants, and others regarded as a threat to social order. As early as September 1609 the attorney general reported that Chichester had 'taken in all the woodkern and loose people in every county', leaving Ulster 'in more complete peace and obedience than has ever been since the conquest'.[103] Already by this time, however, it was becoming clear that the long-standing project of clearing the countryside of 'idle swordsmen' was to be only a small part of the radical structuring of Ulster society that an unexpected turn of events had suddenly made possible.

[103] Gráinne Henry, 'Ulster Exiles in Europe 1605–41', in Brian MacCuarta (ed.), *Ulster 1641: Aspects of the Rising* (Belfast, 1993), 41–3. See also McCavitt, *Flight of the Earls*, 156–61.

7

The Third Kingdom

THE death of Elizabeth I on 24 March 1603 meant more than a change of ruler and dynasty. In James the Sixth and First Ireland now had a Scottish king who aspired to rule an integrated multinational state. As a Christian monarch wedded to the whole island, the new king told the English Commons in 1604, he did not wish to be the husband of two wives. In practice, however, Ireland's transition from dependency of the English crown to component of a multiple monarchy meant less than might have been expected. English political opinion flatly rejected the invitation to take on a British identity; even James's new title 'king of Great Britain' was initially challenged, as implying the dissolution of England's laws and constitution. Ireland, moreover, had not even figured in the debate. James was prepared at times to make use of the rhetoric of a supra-national Britishness: addressing a Catholic delegation in 1613, he claimed to have a special concern for Ireland, both as a long-standing possession of the English crown and because he himself, as ruler of Scotland, was descended from Irish kings.[1] But he had made no attempt to include Ireland in his thwarted plans for political union. His complaint was of being the husband of two wives, not three.

Ireland, then, remained an appendage, not a partner. But the union of crowns did nevertheless make a difference. To the New English, who had since the mid-sixteenth century been taking over the offices and profits of government in Ireland, was now added a smaller number of Scots. In addition Scots were to have a major share in the single most significant Irish innovation of the new king's reign, the plantation scheme for Ulster introduced in the wake of the flight in 1607 of Tyrone and other northern lords. These settlers brought with them not only a distinctive culture but also—much against the wishes of their monarch—a new brand of Protestantism. A whole new layer was thus added to the already complex pattern of ethnic, religious, and political division that existed within Irish society.

Other developments likewise necessitated a reassessment of traditional lines of division and association. Fears of foreign invasion and native revolt did not disappear after 1603. But the defeat of Tyrone's rebellion meant that, for the first time, the government of Ireland was not carried on in the shadow of a constant border warfare sporadically escalating into military crisis. Internal ethnic

[1] *Carew MSS 1603–1623*, 291.

divisions also became somewhat less clear-cut, as the native population became both less self-evidently distinctive in their customs and physical appearance and more fully integrated into the economic structures of English Ireland. Religious divisions, on the other hand, were becoming more acute. In part this was due to changes in the character of both Irish Catholicism and Irish Protestantism. In part it reflected the cruelly altered position of the Old English, as the final reduction of Gaeldom made their role as a loyal alternative to the wild Irish less important, and their recusancy correspondingly more so. It was against this background that the early seventeenth century saw the beginnings of what was to be a transformation of alignments, redefining the relationship between political allegiance, religion, and, ultimately, national identity.

CATTLE AND IRON

In its politics and government, the Ireland of 1603 was a very different place from the island across which, almost exactly a century earlier, the earl of Kildare had led his diverse forces to battle at Knockdoe. In economic terms too there had been change, though on a much lesser scale. The growth of population in England, from perhaps 2.5 million in 1500 to just over 4 million a century later, increased demand from Ireland's main trading partner. The uneven but progressive extension of state control in areas such as the midlands and south Ulster opened the way to more sustained and highly organized economic activity. English settlers, whether arriving as part of a formal plantation, as in Munster, Leix, and Offaly, or in the less structured penetration seen in areas like Sligo, brought with them capital, trading contacts, and improved agricultural and manufacturing techniques. The country's main exports were still unfinished raw materials, in particular fish and hides. However, the port books recording goods arriving at different English centres, while too unsystematic to permit precise statistical analysis, and capturing only one part of Ireland's foreign trade, suggest that the later decades of the century saw a significant rise in exports of wool, linen yarn, tallow, and timber. There was also a more limited growth in tanning, while exports of pork and live cattle had commenced on a small scale by the 1590s.[2] Population also seems to have risen, from perhaps 750,000 in 1500 to a million or slightly above a century later: a significant increase, given the demographic havoc wreaked in the last three decades of the century by war and famine, first in Munster and then in Ulster.[3]

If rising exports suggest a quickening of economic activity in English Ireland, the implications for Gaelic Ireland are of a more far-reaching change: the

[2] A. K. Longfield, *Anglo-Irish Trade in the Sixteenth Century* (London, 1929), 71–80, 87–93, 108–9, 118–24.

[3] For population figures see Appendix.

beginnings of a shift from a society based on consumption, where a lord's status was measured in the number of his followers rather than his wealth, to a market economy. The change was a gradual one. The Gaelic magnates who attended Perrot's parliament in 1585 had to be supplied with suitable robes for the occasion. Later, when the deputy sought permission to bring Clanricard, Clancare, Turlough Luineach, and others with him to London, he asked the queen to provide £3,000 against cattle they would deliver to the garrison, explaining that 'most of them be lords of cattle, but not of much money'. Seven years earlier, however, the same Turlough Luineach, coming to meet a previous lord deputy at Newry, had brought with him £400 sterling, which he proceeded to spend in a three-day drinking bout, 'as he thought, much to his glory'.[4] Over time, such demands for money, whether to cut an appropriate figure on state and social occasions, or to pay the fees and charges that came with integration into the English legal and administrative framework, became more frequent. In the case of south Ulster the process of commercialization is clearly indicated in the rise during the last decades of the sixteenth century of the ports of Drogheda, Dundalk, Carlingford, and Carrickfergus, as they exported growing quantities of linen yarn, wool fells, and tallow collected from their still overwhelmingly Gaelic hinterland. Something similar may perhaps have been taking place in the Gaelic areas of Offaly, where Mountjoy's secretary, in the summer of 1600, found it 'incredible, that by so barbarous inhabitants, the ground should be so manured, the fields so orderly fenced, the towns so frequently inhabited, and the highways and paths so well beaten'.[5]

In the decades after 1600 these trends towards a more developed market economy, and a more systematic exploitation of resources, continued at an accelerated pace.[6] The military defeat of Gaelic Ulster commenced a prolonged period of internal peace, and also made possible the final extension across the whole island of a single political and legal framework. Scots and English newcomers were settled in six counties of Ulster, and informally colonized two more. The Munster plantation was reconstructed, and there were lesser plantation ventures in the south and midlands. All these schemes involved a further importation of personnel, capital, and skills. In addition James I's

[4] Charles McNeill (ed.), 'The Perrot Papers', *Analecta Hibernica*, 12 (1943), 52; Ciaran Brady (ed.), *A Viceroy's Vindication: Sir Henry Sidney's Memoir of Service in Ireland 1556–78* (Cork, 2002), 98.

[5] Fynes Moryson, *An Itinerary*, 4 vols. (Glasgow, 1907), ii. 330. For the rise of the north eastern ports, see Longfield, *Anglo-Irish Trade*, 39–40.

[6] For general accounts of economic development see the contributions by Butler and Clarke in *NHI*, iii. chs. 5, 6; Raymond Gillespie, *The Transformation of the Irish Economy 1550–1700* (Dundalk, 1991). Two important regional studies are: Michael MacCarthy-Morrogh, *The Munster Plantation: English Migration to Southern Ireland 1583–1641* (Oxford, 1986), esp. 223–43; Raymond Gillespie, *Colonial Ulster: The Settlement of East Ulster 1600–1641* (Cork, 1985). There is also a wealth of detail on economic matters in Nicholas Canny, *Making Ireland British 1580–1650* (Oxford, 2001), esp. ch. 6.

government restored stability to the Irish monetary system. Conditions for trade with France also improved, as its economy strengthened, and as the transfer of economic dynamism from its Mediterranean to its Atlantic ports became increasingly evident.

Once again the scale of the transformation is most easily seen in the volume and range of goods exported. Exports of fish continued, despite an apparent decline in the industry as herring shoals moved to new feeding grounds. The trade in Ireland's other traditional export, hides, expanded rapidly. In Chester imports of Irish hides in 1639 were twenty times or more what they had been in the late 1580s. Imports of Irish wool had risen more than thirty-fold in the same period. To this traditional export of unfinished raw materials, moreover, was added a new trade in processed agricultural products, butter and barrelled beef. Timber exports, mainly in the form of the narrow staves used in making barrels, also grew rapidly. Most important of all, there was a huge expansion in the export of live cattle. English port books suggest the import each year by the late 1630s and early 1640s of somewhere below 20,000 cattle and 10,000 sheep. Other evidence indicates that these records failed to capture a significant proportion of the trade from Ireland. Official estimates showed cattle exports rising from fewer than 7,000 in 1616–17 to over 30,000 by 1626 and to more than 45,000 by 1640–1, while exports of sheep rose from just over 7,000 annually in 1626 to nearly 35,000 by 1640–1.[7] The apparent increase may largely reflect the extended range of an improved customs administration. But the later figures nevertheless indicate the scale of a trade that four decades earlier had been of marginal significance. Another development, less significant economically but reflecting a notable shift towards intensive cultivation, was the appearance in good years of an export trade in grain, mainly wheat and oats, from both Ulster and Munster.

In non-agricultural activity the most spectacular, if short-lived, development was in iron smelting. Ireland's main asset was plentiful supplies of timber (for the making of charcoal), at a time when English iron production was running up against a shortage of suitable fuel. Iron ore could either be imported, particularly where coastal locations facilitated transport, or produced locally, from deposits occurring on or close to the surface. The largest proprietor was apparently Sir Charles Coote, whose three ironworks in counties Roscommon and Leitrim were reported to have employed over 2,500 men between wood cutting, mining, transport, and the actual operation of the furnaces. Richard Boyle set up ironworks on several parts of his huge Munster estates, while others operated in King's and Queen's counties and in Fermanagh. A further venture, in County Clare, was apparently owned by a consortium of London merchants. Iron manufacturing declined in the 1630s, as timber became scarcer

[7] Donald Woodward, 'The Anglo-Irish Livestock Trade of the Seventeenth Century', *IHS* 18 (1973), 493.

and more expensive, and as Irish iron failed to compete in international markets with Swedish and other rivals. But its brief flowering was to be remembered as evidence of what was assumed to be Ireland's untapped industrial potential. The profits for those involved had also been substantial. It was sales of iron that in 1629 allowed Boyle, at short notice, to provide Charles I with a loan of £15,000.[8]

Other forms of manufacturing also grew. Exports of linen yarn, mainly to the Lancashire textile industry, continued to expand. The wife of a Church of Ireland bishop, newly arrived in Derry in 1606, found the local flax and thread of high enough quality to recommend it to correspondents in England: 'it is very good and the price not dear'.[9] There was a continued trade in woollen cloth from Munster, although the market for coarse frieze mantles had contracted as English clothing fashions became more sophisticated, and the overall volume of exports was probably lower than in the sixteenth century. A further industrial venture, on a smaller scale, was the manufacture of glass. The main attraction of Ireland, as with iron, was the abundant supply of timber, the other main raw material, sand, being imported from England. An account from the early 1620s describes a substantial enterprise in south County Waterford, possibly controlled by the earl of Cork, for producing window glass. By the 1630s the most important glassworks were at Birr, in King's County, owned by the Parsons family, from where 'Dublin was furnished with all sorts of window and drinking glasses, and such other as commonly are in use'.[10]

Economic expansion was reflected in the growing size and prosperity of towns and cities. Dublin, in particular, experienced the first stages of what were to be two centuries of spectacular growth. Part of the initial impetus for expansion came from short-term disaster. In March 1597 an accident with barrels of gunpowder standing on the city's quay caused a devastating explosion, killing 126 people, wholly demolishing up to forty houses, and severely damaging many more. The rebuilding work that followed spread beyond the city walls onto newly reclaimed land to the east, laying the foundations for what was to become the new city centre, between the Castle and the recently established Trinity College. Much of this new building was in brick, rather than in the timber that had predominated in medieval and Tudor Dublin. To the English lawyer Luke Gernon, writing in 1620, Dublin was still a modest centre. It 'is resembled to Bristol, but falleth short'. Sir William Brereton, fifteen years later, was torn between a similar provincial scale of

[8] H. F. Kearney, 'Richard Boyle, Ironmaster', *JRSAI* 83 (1953), 156–62. For Coote's ironworks see Gerard Boate, *Ireland's Naturall History Being a True and Ample Description of its Situation, Greatness, Shape, and Nature* (London, 1657), 134–5. Comparison with Boyle's records leads Kearney to reject Boate's total of 2,500 men employed by Coote as too high ('Richard Boyle', 160). But Boate's figure refers, not just to direct employees of the ironworks, but to woodcutters, boatmen, and other ancillary occupations.

[9] Susan Montgomery to John Willoughby, received 8 October 1606 (*Trevelyan Papers*, ed. W. C. Trevelyan and C. E. Trevelyan (London, 1872), iii. 101).

[10] Boate, *Ireland's Natural History*, 162; M. S. D. Westropp, *Irish Glass: An Account of Glassmaking in Ireland from the Sixteenth Century to the Present Day* (London, [1927]), 21–30.

comparison, and what were clearly intimations of something more impressive. Dublin was 'the fairest, richest, best built city' he had met on his journey through Ireland, Scotland, and the north of England—with the significant exceptions of York and Newcastle. It was 'far beyond Edinburgh', but nevertheless had nothing to compare with Edinburgh's 'great long street'. He also noted the 'divers commodities cried in Dublin as in London, which it doth more resemble than any town I have seen in the king of England's dominions'.[11] Best estimates suggest that the population of the city rose from around 10,000 in 1600 to 20,000 or more by the early 1640s. This expansion reflected Dublin's role as Ireland's leading port. Its share of total customs receipts rose from 21 per cent in 1616–17 to 33 per cent by 1630. In 1626 it exported more than half of all Irish beef and tallow, more than a third of all cattle, hides, sheep, and linen yarn, and a quarter of all wool.

From another point of view, of course, this dominance of a whole island's overseas trade by its capital city was evidence of the low level of overall economic development. However, the first half of the seventeenth century saw some progress towards the creation of a more finely graduated urban hierarchy. Galway, with its well developed trading contacts with Spain and France, was still regarded in the 1640s as Ireland's second city, followed by Limerick and Waterford. All three seem to have shared in the general expansion of overseas trade: Waterford in 1626 was Ireland's leading exporter of butter, while in 1640–1 Limerick and Galway between them accounted for a quarter of Ireland's exports of hides. However, the most spectacular growth was in the towns of the south coast, where the reconstruction of the Munster plantation had opened up the way to the exploitation of a fertile hinterland. The population of Cork rose from around 2,400 in 1600 to 5,500 by 1641.[12] Youghal and Kinsale, though smaller, grew even more rapidly. Already by 1626 Youghal accounted for more than half of all exports of Irish sheep, and almost half of all exports of wool.[13]

Such evidence of urban development in favoured and mainly coastal locations contrasts sharply with conditions in much of the Irish interior, where population remained thin and settlement dispersed. A party of officials arriving at the town of Monaghan in 1606 found that it 'doth not deserve the name of a good village, consisting of divers scattered cabins or cottages', most of which in fact were occupied by soldiers discharged from the nearby fort. In County Cavan the son

[11] Gernon, 'A Discourse of Ireland', printed in C. Litton Falkiner, *Illustrations of Irish History and Topography, Mainly of the Seventeenth Century* (London, 1904), 350; Sir William Brereton, *Travels in Holland, the United Provinces, England, Scotland and Ireland*, ed. Edward Hawkins (London, 1844), 137, 144.

[12] This is Gillespie's figure (*Transformation of the Irish Economy*, 28). Cullen (*NHI*, iii. 390–1) suggests a much slower growth in the first half of the century of only around 50 per cent, but Gillespie's figure fits better with the 6,000 or so estimated by Dickson, on somewhat stronger evidence, for *c.*1660: David Dickson, *Old World Colony: Cork and South Munster 1630–1830* (Cork, 2005), 114.

[13] For exports in 1626 and 1641 see Donald Woodward, 'Irish Trade and Customs Statistics 1614–41', *IESH* 26 (1999), 54–80.

of the Church of Ireland bishop left a vivid account of conditions at the end of the 1630s:

The only considerable town in the whole county was Belturbet, which yet was but as one of our ordinary market-towns here in England . . . The town of Cavan itself, being the county town, was nearer . . . but not so big by one half as Belturbet. Excepting these two towns there was nothing considerable in the county. Kilmore [the bishop's residence] itself was but a mere country village, of good large bounds, but so thinly inhabited that no where in the whole parish any street or part of a street was to be found.[14]

Even in less favoured regions, however, new venues for economic exchange were beginning to appear. Between 1600 and 1641 licences were issued for 223 markets, most of them held weekly in a town or village, and for 321 fairs, larger gatherings held once or twice each year. A high proportion of the markets, 153 in all, were for sites in Ulster, but the fairs were more evenly distributed, with 93 for Leinster, 80 for Munster, 63 for Connacht, and 85 for Ulster. Not all the new ventures were successful—only around 200, in fact, were still in operation in the second half of the century—and in some cases the extended reach of central government may have led proprietors to seek official sanction for what were in fact long-established trading ventures. The earl of Thomond, for example, took out a patent in 1609 for a weekly market and twice yearly fair at Ennis, where a regular market had in fact existed since the fifteeenth century. But the overall picture is nevertheless of a more commercialized agriculture and expanding manufactures. A growing export trade brought small-scale local producers into a wider if not yet national network, as merchants and agents from port towns toured the hinterland buying up livestock, grain, and cloth. Domestic demand, in a poor economy, was of less significance. But it was presumably at the same fairs and markets that households acquired the small items of hardware and clothing, along with the tobacco, reported as beginning to circulate more widely in the early decades of the seventeenth century.[15]

One development which clearly helped to promote the expansion of Ireland's export trade, and the intensified exploitation of the island's resources that lay behind it, was the re-establishment of a stable currency. Reckless debasement in the last years of the war against Tyrone had created economic chaos. After 1603, however, James I's ministers took decisive action, reducing the face value

[14] *The Works in Verse and Prose of Sir John Davies*, ed. A. B. Grosart (privately printed, 1869–76), iii. 128; *Two Biographies of William Bedell, Bishop of Kilmore*, ed. E. S. Shuckburgh (Cambridge, 1902), 57.

[15] Patrick O'Flanagan, 'Markets and Fairs in Ireland 1600–1800: Index of Economic Development and Regional Growth', *Journal of Historical Geography*, 11 (1985), 364–78. For Ennis see Brian Ó Dálaigh, 'The Origins, Rise and Decline of the Ennis Fairs and Markets', in D. A. Cronin, J. Gilligan, and K. Holton (eds.), *Irish Fairs and Markets: Studies in Local History* (Dublin, 2001), 46, 48. For statistics on patents see Anthony Sheehan, 'Irish Towns in a Period of Change, 1558–1625', in Ciaran Brady and Raymond Gillespie (eds.), *Natives and Newcomers: The Making of Irish Colonial Society 1534–1641* (Dublin, 1986), 116.

of the substandard coin, and issuing new shillings and sixpences valued at slightly below their silver content as a means of restoring confidence and stability. This in turn made it possible once again to allow sterling to circulate freely, at a premium of 9*d*. to an Irish shilling. The actual money in use in Ireland remained a medley of English, Irish, and foreign coins, of different ages and values, and there were continued complaints that the volume in circulation was too small to facilitate transactions. But already by the early seventeenth century payment in cash rather than in kind or by barter seems to have been the norm for commercial dealings. For long-distance transactions, merchants were willing to accept cash in exchange for bills drawn on trading partners in other centres, although such bills were still personal arrangements rather than institutionalized financial instruments.[16] When Christopher Lowther, representing a family of gentlemen merchants based in Cumberland and Westmorland, arrived in Dublin in 1632 to arrange a shipment of wheat to the Canaries, the financial system he encountered combined the sophisticated and the precarious. Lowther was to receive £315 from three local merchants in return for bills drawn on one of his partners in London, and to raise more by sales of cloth and letters of credit. In the event, however, one of the local merchants was unable to pay up. Others were too heavily in debt to existing trading partners to consider Lowther's cloth. Moreover there was 'scarcely £1,000 stirring in all this city' until accounts were settled at the end of the legal term.[17]

Evidence regarding other developments in the kingdom's infrastructure is more patchy. An act of 1613 required each parish to provide labour annually for the repair of roads with stones and gravel. Accounts from Ulster in the 1630s, still to be considered a zone of recent British settlement, suggest that roads were poor and bridges infrequent, and it is likely that much the same was true in Connacht. In Munster and Leinster, on the other hand, communications appear to have been considerably better. The English gentleman Sir William Brereton, visiting in 1635, was able to lodge in specialized inns, rather than private houses: Mrs Vesey's, 'reported one of the best inns in [the] north of Ireland', at Dundalk, the sign of the Boot, at Swords, north of Dublin, where he and his companions 'were well used', the sign of the Windmill in Wexford, the King's Head at Waterford, 'a good house, and a very complete gentlemanlike host', the Three Cups at Carrick-on-Suir. About the same time the earl of Cork was able regularly to make the journey from his Munster estate to Dublin by coach, with three overnight stops along the way.[18] On the other hand the routes into Kerry in the

[16] Michael MacCarthy-Murrough, 'Credit and Remittance: Monetary Problems in Early Seventeenth-Century Munster', *IESH* 14 (1987), 5–19.

[17] D. R. Hainsworth, 'Christopher Lowther's Canary Adventure: A Merchant Venturer in Dublin 1632–3', *IESH* 2 (1975), 26–8.

[18] Brereton, *Travels*, 128, 132, 134, 136, 154, 159, 160. For Cork see Michael MacCarthy-Murrough, 'The English Presence in Early Seventeenth-Century Munster', in Brady and Gillespie (eds.), *Natives and Newcomers*, 176.

south-west were so poor that it alone of the thirty-two Irish counties had only one visit each year by the judges of assizes, in summer.[19]

Rising prosperity, along with the closer political and social integration of Ireland and Great Britain, influenced the character of Irish elite society. Already in the sixteenth century the ninth earl of Kildare, and a few decades later the tenth earl of Ormond, had returned from a boyhood spent at the English court, bringing with them something of its tastes and habits. The trend continued with the fourth earl of Thomond, who built himself an English-style manor house on his County Clare estate, although in the event popular dislike of his commitment to anglicization forced him to live instead in his castle at Bunratty. Randal MacDonnell, grandson of the Scottish warrior Sorley Boy but now earl of Antrim, returned to Ulster in 1638 not only with the manners of a polished nobleman but as husband to one of the great prizes of the English court, Katherine, widow of the assassinated royal favourite, the duke of Buckingham. Their castle at Dunluce was lavishly equipped in the best contemporary style, with silk- and velvet upholstered furniture, carpets and tapestries, ornamented cabinets and screens, although members of the household dressed in Irish clothing, and a retinue included an Irish harper. The spread of metropolitan fashions was also furthered by the continued influx of Englishmen and Scots. In 1627 the newly appointed provost of Trinity College, himself a man of distinctly austere tastes, complained of 'newfangledness in apparel, and long hair and ruffles, wherein this city, and the very greatest of the clergy are, methinks, very exorbitant'. In many cases, however, the newcomers had risen, in favourable Irish conditions, to a station for which their upbringing had not necessarily prepared them. Richard Boyle, son of a Kent yeoman, was painfully aware that he lacked the social accomplishments that might have been expected of the earl of Cork. Among the indigenous population, too, the penetration of new standards of gentility was inevitably uneven. Sir William Brereton, visiting Wexford in 1635, found the mayor to be 'a well bred gentleman' who had studied at the English Inns of Court. His wife, on the other hand, oddly dressed in a threadbare short coat, 'knew not how to carve, look, entertain, or demean herself'.[20]

The evidence for a more developed literary culture to match new standards of gentility is likewise patchy. The second Viscount Conway had a celebrated library, amounting to 8,000 volumes or more, on his estate in County Antrim. Bishop Montgomery had 2,000 volumes in his house in Derry, destroyed in

[19] See the comments in *Wadding Papers 1614–38*, ed. Brendan Jennings (Dublin, 1953), 287.

[20] Bedell to Ussher, 10 Sept. 1627 (*The Whole Works of the Most Rev. James Ussher D.D. . . . with A life of the Author and An Account of his Writings*, ed. Charles Richard Elrington (16 vols; Dublin, 1847), xvi. 458); Brereton, *Travels*, 155. For MacDonnell see Jane Ohlmeyer, *Civil War and Restoration in the Three Stuart Kindgoms: The Career of Randal MacDonnell, Marquis of Antrim, 1609–83* (Cambridge, 1993), 74–5, and for Boyle Nicholas Canny, *The Upstart Earl: A Study of the Social and Mental World of Richard Boyle, first Earl of Cork* (Cambridge, 1982), 70–4.

Doherty's rebellion. Other collections, however, were more modest. Thomond, in 1639, had around 200 volumes in his house in County Clare. A landlord at Castleisland in County Kerry had 100 'great and little books'.[21] There was clearly a reading public for religious polemic. The legal monopoly of printing in Ireland enjoyed first by an officially designated king's printer and then, from 1618, by the London Stationers' Company gave Protestants exclusive access to printing in Ireland. But controversial works aimed at the Old English were answered in books printed abroad and illegally imported, with some texts going into second editions. In other respects, however, there is little to suggest a lively print culture. The total output of the Dublin presses between 1603 and 1641 amounted to only 96 titles. A list from around 1620 shows that it was necessary to import even such basic texts as schoolbooks and bibles. Richard Hadsor, writing in 1623, noted that Ireland had only one printer, who was barely employed, 'which argues the general defect of learning there and the little affection that is carried to the art of good letters'.[22]

What, finally, did the changes taking place in the Irish economy mean for the great majority of the population, who did not stay in inns, wear wigs, or read books? In the years after 1603 the inroads that the market economy had already made into Gaelic Ireland became deeper and wider. The pace of change inevitably varied. In the south-east, where the medieval manorial economy had already provided a commercial framework, traditional practices continued, so that Brereton, in 1635, found most tenants operating as sharecroppers, allowing their landlord every third sheaf of the harvested crop. In Ulster, on the other hand, English and Scottish colonization brought what must have been for most the novel demands of a money economy. A new proprietor in Londonderry, writing in June 1616, reported that he had been forced to accept 'pawns' from his tenants, because 'the Irish have no moneys till their cows be fat'.[23] Induction into the money economy in turn meant access to marketed commodities. Already by the second decade of the century, it has been pointed out, the volume of hats, stockings, household implements, and other small wares being imported into a town like Coleraine was too large to be destined for the settler population alone.[24] The change was perhaps most evident in dress. Gernon, in 1620, found that 'the better sort are apparelled at

[21] Raymond Gillespie, *Reading Ireland: Print, Reading and Social Change in Early Modern Ireland* (Manchester, 2005), 68. For Montgomery's library see John McCavitt, *The Flight of the Earls* (Dublin, 2002), 141

[22] Declan Gaffney, 'The Practice of Religious Controversy in Dublin 1600–1641', in W. J. Sheils and Diana Wood (eds.), *The Churches, Ireland and the Irish* (Woodbridge, 1989), 147–51; Raymond Gillespie, 'Irish Printing in the Early Seventeenth Century', *IESH* 15 (1988), 81–8; George O'Brien (ed.), *Advertisements for Ireland* (Dublin, 1923), 42. For Hadsor's authorship of this text, see below, n. 104.

[23] T. W.Moody, *The Londonderry Plantation 1609–41: The City of London and the Plantation in Ulster* (Belfast, 1939), 352. For sharecropping see Brereton, *Travels*, 149, 162.

[24] Raymond Gillespie, *Conspiracy: Ulster Plots and Plotters in 1615* (Belfast, 1987), 47.

all points like the English', except that they continued to wear the traditional Irish mantle over their doublets and knee-length breeches, and along with their hats. In the decades that followed their social inferiors seem increasingly to have followed suit. By the 1650s Sir James Ware reported that 'the Irish universally conform to the English dress in the general'. 'Some few of the meaner sort of people' still wore mantles, but the tight-fitting trews had everywhere given way to loose hanging trousers. The other external marks of ethnic distinctiveness, heavy moustaches and 'glibs' of hair hanging forward over the face, seem to have died out around the same time: in 1635 the Irish parliament thought it safe to repeal the statute banning the wearing of a moustache without a beard. Meanwhile the first half of the century also saw the emergence of Ireland's first widely marketed luxury, in the form of tobacco, imported in substantial quantities and quickly becoming a familiar product in Gaelic as well as English Ireland.[25]

What is impossible to quantify is the price that had to be paid for this modest introduction to the new world of commercial goods. Contemporary English writers wrote proudly of the liberation of the Irish peasantry from the oppressive rule of their traditional lords, as arbitrary 'cuttings' gave way to the fixed payments and duties of legal tenancy. But new forms of economic activity were necessary to meet those payments. Labour discipline too almost certainly became tighter. Contemporary stereotypes of the Gaelic economy as consisting solely of an effort-free pastoralism were wild exaggeration. But the move towards more intensive exploitation of resources, oriented towards export markets, created demands on a new scale. There was ground to be tilled and harvested, forests to be cleared, roads, bridges and buildings to be erected. Rising exports of linen yarn, equally, were possible only through the lengthy and repetitive labour of women and children. A precise balance of exploitation between the old system and the new is impossible to calculate. The most that can be said is that the continued growth of population, from a million or slightly above in 1600 to as much as 1.5 million forty years later, suggests some improvement in living standards, at least at the level of basic subsistence. As yet, however, any such gains remained distinctly fragile. This became clear between 1627 and 1629, when a series of bad harvets brought both starvation and disease. By early summer 1629 survivors were eating dogs and horses, and the government had ordered an extraordinary assizes and gaol delivery, for fear that prisoners awaiting trial would otherwise starve to death. The mayor of Wexford reported in July 1629 that there had been many deaths from famine, while a report from Cavan spoke of 'the look of death set in the face of every man'.[26]

[25] Mairead Dunlevy, *Dress in Ireland: A History* (Cork, 1999), 78–81. For Gernon, see Falkiner, *Illustrations*, 356–9.

[26] Bedell to Ward, 24 May 1629, in *Tanner Letters*, ed. C. McNeill (Dublin, 1943), 89; Raymond Gillespie, 'Harvest Crises in Early Seventeenth-Century Ireland', *IESH* 11 (1984), 12.

BUILDERS AND PLANTERS

The new Irish opportunities which the accession of James I had opened up to certain Scots became apparent almost as soon as Tyrone's rebellion had been crushed. In April 1605 the king issued a letter granting the lands of southern Clandeboye and the Ards to James Hamilton, with provision for him to divide the territory with Hugh Montgomery and with the Gaelic lord of the region, Conn O'Neill. The letter had a complex history. Hugh Montgomery was an ambitious Scottish laird who, in the tense period leading up to Elizabeth's death, had established a claim on the gratitude of the future James I by passing on to him intelligence received from his brother George, a clergyman with a living in southern England. George received his reward when he became bishop of Derry, Raphoe, and Clogher, and subsequently played a central part in the downfall of Tyrone. Hugh Montgomery laid the foundations for his own fortune when he organized the escape of Conn O'Neill, lord of Upper Clandeboye and the Great Ards, from Carrickfergus Castle, where he had been imprisoned since taking up arms in 1601, and then accompanied him to court to secure his pardon. For this O'Neill apparently promised Montgomery one-half of his lands. At court, however, Montgomery encountered an even better connected predator. James Hamilton, a Scot who had settled in Dublin as a schoolmaster, and subsequently a fellow of the newly founded Trinity College, had acted as James's agent in both Ireland and England. He was thus well placed to induce the king to convert Montgomery's profitable arrangement into the tripartite division agreed in April 1605. Meanwhile Hamilton had laid the basis for further acquisitions by purchasing from a London merchant, Thomas Ireland, a grant of lands in Ireland worth £100 per year.

To realize these gains, however, and in particular to make effective use of Ireland's letter, Hamilton required the cooperation of the Dublin administration. Sir Arthur Chichester, the lord deputy, was initially hostile. Hamilton's grants, he protested, gave him more land than the greatest lords in the kingdom, by a form of tenure, socage, which deprived the crown of future revenue.[27] Hamilton's solution was to smooth the path by agreeing to transfer a substantial part of his gains to the deputy himself. Chichester had already been rewarded for his services to the crown with a grant of Belfast Castle and surrounding lands, extending as far north as Carrickfergus. To this he now added, in two transfers from Hamilton in 1605 and 1606, a further block of land extending west as far as Lough Neagh, the east coast peninsula of Islandmagee, and an augmentation of his existing

[27] Socage was a form of tenure in which the tenant's main obligation was the payment of rent. Knight service, by contrast, was derived from the military tenure of the feudal past, and subjected the tenant to a range of other burdens, of which the most important was the crown's right of wardship (see below, p. 321).

fishing rights on the River Bann. In return Hamilton was allowed to follow the example of Richard Boyle and others by using his single king's letter to obtain no fewer than five separate grants of land between 1605 and 1608, to a value many times the £100 stated.[28]

All this is at first sight little short of piracy. Yet public policy also played a part in the transactions. The grant to Hamilton and Montgomery required them to plant the territory they received with Englishmen and Scots, and barred them from disposing of land to any native other than Conn O'Neill. O'Neill, for his part, was also bound to settle one-third of his diminished estate with Scots or English tenants, to be provided by Hamilton and Montgomery, with a proviso that he would forfeit his land if these tenants were not willing to remain with him. Chichester too could claim that his dealings served a wider interest. He had repeatedly argued that Ulster and other potentially troublesome areas could be secured only by establishing reliable Englishmen in strategic locations. He himself was to let out much of his newly acquired land to former soldiers or other English tenants, and there are indications that his arrangement with Hamilton included an understanding that the Scot would pass a proportion of his gains on to others of the same class.[29] But it remains the case that the murky transactions arising from Conn O'Neill's misfortunes began the process by which Chichester, the landless second son of a minor Devonshire gentleman, acquired one of the largest landed estates in the kingdom.

Hamilton's and Montgomery's acquisitions, providing the basis for what was to become a very successful settlement of Scots and English in counties Antrim and Down, created a reassuring barrier separating Gaelic Ulster from Gaelic Scotland. Within a few years, however, the flight of Tyrone and others, followed by O'Doherty's revolt, had opened up the possibility of extending the colonizing enterprise into the Gaelic heartland itself. Chichester's own vision of how this situation was to be exploited was modest. In the immediate aftermath of O'Doherty's revolt he had briefly taken up the idea of clearing the whole area bounded by the Rivers Erne, Blackwater, and Bann of its native inhabitants. Before long he reverted to his earlier proposal for a limited plantation of servitors and others who would coexist with native freeholders. By this time, however, other officials, notably the attorney general, Davies, had come to favour setting aside all or most of the province for British or English settlers, and it was this view that quickly prevailed.[30]

[28] M. Perceval-Maxwell, *The Scottish Migration to Ulster in the Reign of James I* (Belfast, 1990), 1–2, 49–55; Peter Roebuck, 'The Making of an Ulster Great Estate: The Chichesters, Barons of Belfast and Viscounts of Carrickfergus 1599–1648', *PRIA*, C, 79 (1979), 6–12.

[29] Perceval-Maxwell, *Scottish Migration*, 54–5.

[30] For general accounts of the plantation of Ulster see Moody, *Londonderry Plantation*; Philip Robinson, *The Plantation of Ulster: British Settlement in an Irish Landscape 1600–1670* (Belfast, 1994); Canny, *Making Ireland British*, ch. 4. James Stevens Curl, *The Londonderry Plantation 1609–1914* (Chichester, 1986) contains vivid material on the material infrastructure of the

What seems to have tipped the balance in favour of the more comprehensive plantation scheme was, at least in part, the close personal interest which the king, up to this point largely indifferent to Irish affairs, now began to take in the settlement of Ulster. As ruler of Scotland James had had almost two decades of experience in the problems of governing what he considered barbarous peripheries. In the Highlands he had promoted repeated schemes for the plantation of Lewis and Kintyre with loyal subjects. On the Anglo-Scottish border, after 1603, he had not only created a new governing council, but had sanctioned the forcible transportation of members of the unruly Graham clan, sending some to military service on the Continent, and attempting to make others settle in County Roscommon. In Ulster the way was now open for similar experiments on a much larger scale. The two enterprises were in fact complementary. Gaelic Ulster and Gaelic Scotland represented a single ungovernable hinterland. The passage back and forth across the narrow waters of the North Channel of mercenary fighting men had long sustained the rebelliousness of one and the militarized disorder of the other. Plantation in Ulster, along with continued efforts to discipline the clan chiefs of the Highlands and Islands, would fracture this zone of Gaelic barbarism, removing a major threat to the security of all three British kingdoms.[31]

Between 1608 and 1610 a committee sitting in London, but composed mainly of Irish privy councillors and other officials, worked out detailed plans for a plantation of Ulster. The scheme, published in January 1609 and confirmed in revised form in May 1610, proposed that confiscated land should be allocated to three main groups, undertakers, servitors, and natives. Of these the undertakers were central to the scheme for large-scale colonization. They were to hold portions of 1,000, 1,500, or 2,000 acres of profitable land, with a chief undertaker in each district whose holding could be up to 3,000 acres. No part of this land was to be let, under any terms, to the native Irish. Instead each undertaker was required to settle at least ten English or Scottish families, containing twenty-four able-bodied

plantation. There are useful shorter accounts in John McCavitt, *Sir Arthur Chichester, Lord Deputy of Ireland 1605–16* (Belfast, 1998), ch. 9; idem, *The Flight of the Earls* (Dublin, 2002), ch. 8. For settlement in the non-plantation counties of Antrim and Down see Perceval-Maxwell, *Scottish Migration*; Gillespie, *Colonial Ulster*.

31 The question of how exactly the shape of the plantation was decided remains curiously obscure. McCavitt (*Sir Arthur Chichester*, ch. 9) suggests that the lord deputy lost the initiative by failing to submit a detailed proposal in good time. The same author's *The Flight of the Earls*, 171–2, emphasizes the king's role in determining the outcome, as does Perceval-Maxwell, *Scottish Migration*, 74–5, and Maurice Lee, *Great Britain's Solomon: James VI and I in his Three Kingdoms* (Urbana, Ill., 1990), 215. Canny (*Making Ulster British*, 189–92), preoccupied with demonstrating the extent to which policy was shaped by a coherent colonial ideology shared by what he considers a unitary 'servitor' class, plays down the differences between Chichester and Davies, on the not strictly relevant grounds that the lord deputy's arguments for allocating a substantial share to the native Irish were motivated by pragmatism rather than ideology. He also suggests, though with no direct evidence, that it was possibly Chichester who aroused the king's interest in the project by proposing to include Scots as well as English in the plantation.

men, on every 1,000 acres held. As in the Munster plantation thirty years earlier, these settlers were to be organized into a predetermined social hierarchy. For each 1,000 acres there were to be two tenants holding fee farm grants—perpetual tenure at a fixed rent—of 120 acres each. Three others were to hold leases, to run for three named lives or for twenty-one years, of 100 acres each. The remaining four families (besides that of the principal undertaker) would be 'husbandmen, artificers or cottagers'. Undertakers were also to build a stone house surrounded by a defensive wall or bawn. The other settler families were to take up residence near this centre, both for security and to provide the nucleus for towns and villages. Servitors, soldiers or officials granted land in acknowledgement for their services, were to hold similar portions of 2,000, 1,500, or 1,000 acres, and were likewise required to build houses and bawns. Unlike the undertakers, they were allowed to let their land to Irish tenants, and there was no obligation to import British tenants. But servitors who did observe the same conditions as undertakers would pay rent to the crown at the same lower rate. Native grantees faced no restrictions on who was to inhabit their lands. However, they were required to give their tenants fixed rents and conditions, with no Irish exactions, and to 'use tillage and husbandry after the manner of the English'. They also paid a higher rent than either undertakers or servitors.[32]

This was the scheme adopted, from 1610, in the counties of Armagh, Cavan, Donegal, Fermanagh, and Tyrone. In 1609, however, at a time when the project seemed to be losing momentum, the crown had brought pressure to bear on the City of London to assume responsibility for part of the plantation. The territory assigned to the Londoners comprised the county of Coleraine, the towns of Derry and Coleraine, and in addition a substantial territory of woodland, the barony of Loughinsholin, formerly part of County Tyrone. A charter issued in 1613 brought these territories together in a new county and city, both named Londonderry. The same charter created a new corporate body, in effect a committee of the Common Council of London, which was eventually to become known as the Irish Society. The Society undertook to fortify the two towns, building 200 houses in Londonderry and 100 in Coleraine, with room for expansion in both cases. Almost a quarter of the profitable land in the new county was recognized as church land, while some 10 per cent was allocated to thirteen native Irish freeholders. In addition Sir Thomas Phillips received lands at Limavady, which he held as a servitor, in compensation for surrendering his acquisitions at Coleraine. The remainder of County Londonderry, just under two-thirds of the whole, was divided into twelve portions, each of which was allocated to a group of those guilds or companies, fifty-five in all, that had contributed to the £40,000 which the City had been required to invest in the

[32] Edmund Curtis and R. B. McDowell, *Irish Historical Documents 1172–1922* (London, 1943), 133. Undertakers were to pay an annual rent of £5 6*s*. 8*d*. for every 1,000 acres, servitors £8, and natives £10 13*s*. 4*d*.

plantation. In practice, however, each group was headed by one of the city's main companies, which took over the direct management of the portion and became in effect the proprietor.

In the other five counties the plantation was implemented during the summer of 1610. The original settlement scheme had proposed a random distribution of land throughout the province by the casting of lots. Instead the final scheme divided the five counties into precincts, of which nine were set aside for Scottish and seven for English undertakers, with another nine being shared by servitors and natives. The chief undertakers in each county drew lots to decide which precinct they would take charge of, then allocated land within their assigned precinct to the lesser undertakers grouped under them. Chichester had objected to the original plan on the grounds that random distribution throughout the region would prevent men settling close to their associates. However, it has been plausibly inferred that security was also a consideration. The precincts scheme gave the colonists sole possession of consolidated blocks of territory, in a way that had not been achieved in Munster three decades earlier. It also removed native Irish grantees from their existing territorial base, where they might retain the support due to traditional lords, and relocated them under the supervision of hardened military men established in the same precincts as servitors.

In seeking to establish how this neat formal structure worked out in practice, it is necessary to choose between two not entirely satisfactory sets of data. Figures derived from the grants made by the commissioners in charge of the plantation provide an indication of the intended outcome. However, the stated acreages, in a thinly populated landscape, excluded land classified as bog or woodland. More important, the commissioners did not attempt a measured survey of the lands concerned, but instead employed existing territorial units, variously termed ballyboes, quarters, and polls, which were in fact measurements, not of area, but of agricultural potential. Where the commissioners made grants stated as totalling 459,000 acres, the total area of the six escheated counties was in fact more than seven times larger. Estimates by the historical geographer Philip Robinson, by contrast, are based on precise modern measurements of area. Robinson's figures, however, relate only to the 64 per cent of all pre-plantation units, unevenly distributed between counties, that he has been able to match with modern townland names.

In practice the correspondence between the two sets of figures is, given these circumstances, remarkably close (see Table 7.1.). Taken together they suggest that fifty-one English and fifty-nine Scottish undertakers acquired between them just over a third of the planted area, with roughly equal shares going to the two ethnic groups. The next largest share of land, though far below their previous holdings, went to the native Irish. Twenty-six major grantees and a variety of lesser occupiers holding individually or collectively received between them around one-fifth of the land allocated. The established church was a major beneficiary. The commission set up in 1609 to investigate issues of title firmly

Table 7.1. *Distribution of Land in the Ulster Plantation (%)*

	A	B	C
English undertakers	18	17	21
Scottish undertakers	18	17	5
Servitors	12	14	9
Native Irish	20	18	25
London companies	8	8	n/a
Irish Society	2	2	n/a
Church	16	18	30
Trinity College, Dublin	3	2	7
Schools, towns, and forts	3	4	0.5

A: Proportions as given in the plantation grants.
B: Proportions as calculated by Dr Philip Robinson for the 64% of units disposed of in the plantation which he was able to identify with a modern townland.
C: Percentages for County Armagh, worked out on the same basis, for over 98% of the land area, by Mr R.J. Hunter.

Source: A and B—P. S. Robinson, *The Plantation of Ulster* (Dublin, 1984), 86; C—R. J. Hunter, 'County Armagh: A Map of Plantation *c*.1610', in A. J. Hughes and W. Nolan (eds.), *Armagh: History and Society* (Dublin, 2001), 276.

rejected attempts by Bishop Montgomery to claim land formerly held by coarbs and erenaghs for the church, insisting instead that these were the property of the occupiers (and so liable to forfeiture), with bishops being entitled only to a rent charge. Having established the point of principle, however, the crown went on to bestow on the church nearly a sixth of the redistributed acreage in the six escheated counties. This was to give the Ulster dioceses a significant advantage over those in other provinces, the greater part of whose inheritance had been lost through alienation to laymen. The servitors, despite Chichester's advocacy, did less well. Chichester himself received a special grant, to add to his already extensive possessions, of the entire barony of Inishowen. But the servitors as a class, numbering fifty-five grantees, received between them only one-eighth of the land distributed. This was only slightly more than the one-tenth share of the total forfeited land accounted for by the holdings of the London Companies.

Who were the undertakers? Sir Francis Bacon, James I's lord chancellor, had counselled that the plantation 'must rather be an adventure for such as are full, than a setting up of those that are low of means'. He did not expect men of great substance personally to transplant to Ulster; rather he hoped that they would use the opportunity to make provision for younger sons and other kin.[33]

[33] 'Certain Considerations Touching the Plantation in Ireland . . .' (1606), in *The Letters and Life of Francis Bacon*, ed. James Spedding (London, 1868), iv. 120, 124.

Such hopes were only partially realized. The crown managed to find men of some substance, including five Scottish and one English noble, to act as chief undertakers. The ordinary undertakers, however, included many who were men of modest means seeking to better themselves. The Scots were for the most part landowners, with a sprinkling of townsmen. But a detailed survey suggests that around half had incomes that were at or below the average for the Scottish gentry of around £150 per annum. This modest figure must be set against estimates that put the cost of erecting even a modest house and bawn of the kind required at £500 to £600, to which had to be added the cost of livestock and equipment, the travelling expenses of tenants, and a range of other expenses. A sample of thirteen English undertakers, possibly biased towards the less affluent among them, reveals a somewhat higher average income of just over £200. But even this would have left many with little realistic chance of meeting the obligations they now assumed.[34] This pessimistic assessment is confirmed by the high turnover in estate ownership in the early years of the plantation. Already by 1619, 32 of the 51 estates granted to English undertakers, and 33 of the 59 granted to Scottish undertakers, had changed hands.

The fifty-five servitors were a mixed group. The majority were army officers, professional soldiers for whom the happy accident of having served in Ireland at just the right time provided a once-in-a-lifetime opportunity to convert the precarious gentility of a military commission into the more solid status of a landowner. Ralph Bingley, for example, had been born into a obscure Cheshire family and had served with Drake and Hawkins in the Caribbean and Pacific before joining Docwra's Lough Foyle expedition. In the lean years following the defeat of Tyrone he had coped with the loss of his colonel's pay by returning to sea in a venture that briefly landed him in gaol on charges of piracy. Now, however, he became the owner of 1,000 acres at Kilmacrenan in County Donegal, to which he was later to add further land acquired from native Irish grantees and from two English undertakers.[35] A smaller group of servitors consisted of leading office holders, among them Chichester and Davies, of whom most (though not Chichester) also took land as undertakers. Finally there were some Palesmen who were allowed to retain, as servitors, lands they had purchased in the escheated counties, in the process adding a Catholic element to what was otherwise a solidly Protestant body of grantees.

The main losers from the plantation were, by any calculation, the native Irish. For the best part of a century crown policy had centred on the idea of replacing the Gaelic tenurial system, with its uncertain boundaries, overlapping claims, and fluid laws of succession, with the English system of ownership and inheritance.

[34] For the incomes of Scottish undertakers see Perceval-Maxwell, *Scottish Migration*, 106–13, and for the English sample ibid. 111, 362. For start-up costs see ibid. 132–7.

[35] R. J. Hunter, 'Sir Ralph Bingley *c.*1570–1627: Ulster Planter', in Peter Roebuck (ed.), *Plantation to Partition: Essays in Ulster History* (Belfast, 1981), 15–19.

Henry VIII had characteristically asserted that he enjoyed an absolute power, independent of all law, over land and people; he had also stubbornly refused to abandon completely the crown's right to the huge territories once vested in the earldom of Ulster. In practice, however, he had endorsed the strategy of surrender and regrant. Under this successors continued attempts to promote a consensual transformation of tenure coincided or alternated with episodes of confiscation and plantation. Yet here too the crown and its servants held back from any open assertion of arbitrary power. Elizabeth's grants of Ulster lands to Essex and Sir Thomas Smith rested mainly on the sweeping terms of the act of attainder against Shane O'Neill passed by the Irish parliament in 1569. The Munster plantation, similarly, took the unsatisfactory form of a patchwork of scattered holdings precisely because it could be implemented only on those lands whose proprietors it had been possible to have attainted in the wake of the Desmond rebellion.

All this, of course, was in the context of the expanding but still limited power of the Tudor state. Sir John Davies, who as attorney general became the architect of the new legal framework for the government of Ireland after 1603, took as his starting point the claim that with the defeat of Tyrone and his allies the conquest of Ireland was now complete, so that James I enjoyed sovereign authority throughout the island. On this principle he procured, in 1606, a judicial resolution stating that titles to land under gavelkind, the Gaelic system of inheritance by division among multiple male heirs, had no standing in English law. At the same time Davies drew a distinction between conquest by a despot, which deprived the conquered of all rights, and conquest by an English monarch, whereby the inhabitants would retain their existing rights, though as subjects under English law. Hence he offered assurances that those holding by gavelkind since before the accession of James I would not be disturbed in their possession. Instead the emphasis in crown policy in the years up to 1607 was on undermining the power of magnates like O'Neill and O'Donnell, first by upholding the rights of lesser lords like O'Cahan, and secondly by establishing in each lordship an intermediate class of freeholders who would pay rent but would otherwise be economically and politically independent of their lords.

As soon as the advocates of large-scale plantation had won the argument, however, this aspect of crown policy underwent a dramatic change. Where previously the crown's policy had been to minimize the personal estates of great lords like Tyrone and Tyrconnell, it now became convenient to treat them as sole proprietors of the whole territory over which they had claimed authority, which could then be treated as forfeited. During the summers of 1608 and 1609 commissions headed by Chichester and Davies toured Ulster, holding sittings in each county for the purpose of establishing the crown's title to the proposed plantation lands. These judged the whole of County Tyrone, along with the barony of Oneilland in County Armagh, to be forfeit to the crown by Tyrone's attainder. Donegal, similarly, was forfeit through the attainders of Tyrconnell and Sir Cahir O'Doherty, and Cavan by that of Sir John O'Reilly, who had died while in rebellion in 1596. For other parts of Armagh, as well as for coarb and erenagh lands in Tyrone not included in Hugh O'Neill's patent and for O'Cahan's territory of Coleraine, the crown fell back on the older claim arising from the attainder of Shane O'Neill.[36]

This opportunistic endorsement of the claims of attainted overlords in order to justify the confiscation of whole counties involved a cynical abandonment of the lesser men whose claims the crown had only recently promoted. In County Monaghan, the policy of creating native freeholders had gone too far to be abandoned; the county, as a result, was not part of the plantation. In Cavan, on the other hand, native proprietors who sought the protection of the courts against the plantation scheme, pleading the freeholds they had been granted only five years earlier, now got short shrift. In 1608 Davies had engineered the transfer of a case involving a surrender and regrant in County Cork from the Munster presidency court to King's Bench. Judgment was duly given that the proprietor concerned, holding land as a *tánaiste* rather than an heir in English law, had in fact had nothing to surrender, so that the whole transaction was void. This ruling, extending the invalidity of Gaelic titles backwards beyond the previous starting date of 1603, allowed Davies to argue that the titles of the Cavan freeholders, deriving from gavelkind or tanistry, were similarly invalid in English law. Yet when three native Irish women in County Donegal claimed that certain lands should be exempted from forfeiture as representing their dowries and jointures under English marriage law, Davies rejected their suits on the grounds that Gaelic law gave widows no right in their husbands' property.

Even with the use of such blatant double standards, obstacles remained to the policy of wholesale legal appropriation. In Fermanagh, the sixth county earmarked for plantation, Cúchonnacht Maguire, attainted after joining Tyrone in his flight, had held four of the seven baronies. The other three, however, had been held by his nephew Conor Roe Maguire, who had in fact been granted letters patent for the whole county in 1601. In addition, as Chichester noted, Cúchonnacht's father had 'died a subject', and he too had already held letters patent for the whole territory. This meant that his second wife, still living, could claim one-third of it as her jointure under common law. The lady, however, was old (she was a daughter of Shane O'Neill), and unfit for travel or lawsuits, so that a pension for life would be enough to settle her claim.[37] The unoffending

[36] For a detailed account of the commissions see F. W. Harris, 'The Reblion of Sir Cahir O'Doherty and its Legal Aftermath', *Irish Jurist*, 15 (1980), 298–325; idem, 'The Commission of 1609: Legal Aspects', *Studia Hibernica*, 20 (1980), 31–55. For the wider legal background, Hans S. Pawlisch, *Sir John Davies and the Conquest of Ireland: A Study in Legal Imperialism* (Cambridge, 1985) 55–81.

[37] R. Dudley Edwards (ed.), 'Letter Book of Sir Arthur Chichester 1612–14', *Analecta Hibernica*, 8 (1938), 158–9; T. W. Moody (ed.), 'Ulster Plantation Papers 1608–13', *Analecta Hibernica*, 8 (1939), 297.

Conor Roe, meanwhile, was pressurized into surrendering his claims to the whole county in exchange for a regrant of just one barony.

Two other claimants, Sir Niall Garbh O'Donnell and Sir Donal O'Cahan, were unlikely to prove so tractable. Both had at one time been important instruments in the campaign to contain Tyrone and Tyrconnell. Now, however, the claims to independent proprietorship they had been encouraged to pursue became an obstacle to the goal of wholesale confiscation. The commissions of 1608–9 had already struck out both men's claims, declaring that O'Cahan's land had been forfeit by the attainder of Shane O'Neill and that Niall Garbh had never received a patent for the lands excluded from Tyrconnell's grant. But they nevertheless remained a potential embarrassment. Sir Donal was already in custody before O'Doherty's rebellion, having been accused of treasonable activity by his brother, who had himself gone on to join the revolt. Sir Niall was arrested soon after the outbreak. The evidence against him came mainly from Sir Cahir's widow, who accused him of inciting her husband on his destructive course for his own purposes, and also from Finola O'Donnell, mother both of Tyrconnell and of Hugh Roe, whom Niall Garbh had betrayed by joining Docwra. A local jury, despite being confined for several days without food, refused to bring in a guilty verdict, forcing Davies to withdraw the indictment. Instead both Niall Garbh and Sir Donal were consigned unconvicted to the Tower, where they remained until they died, in 1626 and 1627 respectively. Their experience confirms what is already evident from other parts of the Ulster settlement, and indeed from the whole management of early seventeenth-century Ireland. If a point is to be identified at which reasons of state openly took priority over considerations of legality and justice, it is to be found, not in the violent later years of Elizabeth, but in the less bloody reign of her successor.

Having said this, it is important to recognize that the plantation did not wholly ignore the native Irish. Nor, indeed, would it have been possible to do so. Sir John O'Reilly might be held to have forfeited the county by dying in rebellion. But his son Mulmory had later died fighting on the English side. Mulmory's son, Mulmory Óg, duly received 3,000 acres in County Cavan. Sir Henry Óg O'Neill, similarly, had died fighting against O'Doherty and his allies. His family received 5,000 acres in Tyrone and Armagh. Sir Turlough McHenry O'Neill of the Fews, and Turlough MacArt O'Neill of Strabane, two more of the lesser lords earlier patronized as a counter to Tyrone's dominance, received respectively 9,900 and 3,300 acres. Other natives who received grants, either as the reward of loyalty or in recognition of their prominence in the pre-plantation order, included Tyrone's brother Art McBaron O'Neill, as well as two sons of Shane O'Neill. Overall about one-third of the land granted to natives went to members of one branch or other of the O'Neills, while just over a quarter was divided between O'Reillys and Maguires. The O'Cahans, despite Sir Donal's misfortune, obtained six grants for a total of over 5,000 acres in the former county of Coleraine, while the MacSweenys, former galloglass and vassals of the O'Donnells, retained just over 7,000 acres in Donegal. The O'Donnells themselves were by contrast spectacular losers, receiving five grants for a total of less than 1,500 acres in a county which they had previously dominated as Ulster's second most important lordship.

Although the plantation had native as well as British beneficiaries, however, few among them had much cause to be grateful. The long-established belief that native grantees were deliberately consigned to poorer and more remote lands has been shown to be without foundation. Calculations based on modern valuations, which in turn correlate closely with the pre-plantation pattern of profitability as measured by the density of ballyboes, show no significant difference between the lands granted to Irish and to British settlers.[38] The problem, instead, lay not with the quality of land, but rather with the quantity. Of 280 Irish grantees, only 26 received grants of more than 1,000 acres. The remainder received on average less than 150 acres each. Even the small minority of larger beneficiaries, moreover, received far less than they felt entitled to. Turlough McHenry, for example, got roughly half his former territory in the Fews; Mulmory Óg O'Reilly received a modest estate, where his grandfather and father had been, as Chichester himself admitted, 'both chiefs of their name in their times and possessors of the County of Cavan or Country Breifne O'Reilly not only by custom of the country, but also by virtue of a custodiam from the late queen'.[39] In some cases, as with Art McBaron O'Neill, the native proprietor was to hold only for life, with the land then passing to a British grantee. A further grievance was that natives, in a deliberate attempt to break up traditional ties of dependency and clientage, almost invariably received land at a distance from their existing place of residence.

To the rough justice thus meted out to the native Irish upper classes must be added the arbitrary treatment intended for the ordinary Gaelic population. The Munster plantation, two decades earlier, had required grantees to take only tenants of English descent. The articles of the Ulster plantation went further, binding undertakers to clear the lands allocated to them of all native Irish inhabitants. Native settlement was permitted only on the land assigned to native grantees, to servitors, or to the church—and even there servitors had a financial incentive to prefer British tenants, while holders of church lands, under an agreement negotiated by Bishop Montgomery, were to be obliged to plant British tenants at one-third the level required of the undertakers. The reason for the policy of segregation was concern for the security of the areas of British settlement. Sir John Davies, citing as evidence the downfall of the Munster settlements, argued that the 'civil persons' had to be numerically superior in the planted areas, since otherwise the natives 'will quickly overgrow them, as weeds overgrow the good corn'.[40] Such an approach, defensive rather than punitive,

[38] Robinson, *Plantation of Ulster*, 14, 87–9.
[39] Edwards, 'Letter Book of Sir Arthur Chichester', 28.
[40] McCavitt, *Flight of the Earls*, 171.

was not incompatible with the belief, expressed elsewhere by Davies, that the natives could in the long run be assimilated to the society of the civil persons. But the proposal forcibly to transplant one-third of the existing inhabitants of six counties, regardless of behaviour or disposition, nevertheless represents a further hardening of attitudes. And the terms in which the whole plantation scheme was formulated make clear that Ireland's incorporation into a multinational polity had done nothing to rule out the continued use of ethnic origin as the basis of both thinking and policy.

Intention and execution were, however, two different things. The plantation scheme required undertakers to be present in Ireland to receive their grants by 24 June 1610, to take up residence before 29 September, and to have completed their buildings, and settled the required number of tenants, by Easter 1613. But this left the question of how colonists arriving only in the summer and autumn were to feed themselves through the winter that was to follow. A proclamation issued in August 1610 allowed natives in the precincts assigned to undertakers to remain, as rent-paying occupiers, until the following May. The privy council subsequently extended this deadline to 1 May 1612. But this date too passed with no evidence of any serious attempt to clear the affected territories. Instead a detailed survey conducted during 1613–14 by Sir Josias Bodley, overseer of fortifications, revealed that everywhere in the escheated counties the native Irish remained numerically dominant. The problem was in part an inadequate inflow of settlers. If undertakers and the London companies were to establish twenty-four adult male settlers on every 1,000 of the 120,000 acres nominally granted to them, then their estates alone should have had a population of some 2,800 men. In fact Bodley's survey showed a total of between 1,900 and 2,200 British males in the whole of the escheated counties. Even the full complement of British tenants, however, would hardly have been adequate to settle an area that was in fact seven times that nominally assigned to grantees. From another point of view such calculations are beside the point. The real problem, contemporary critics repeatedly alleged, was that undertakers anxious for an early return on their investment found English and Scottish settlers, even where available, less attractive as tenants than the natives, who would pay high rents to be left undisturbed and did not have to be wooed with favourable terms of occupancy.

The king responded indignantly to Bodley's survey, giving the undertakers until 31 August 1616 to meet their obligations or forfeit their grants. A new survey by Bodley sometime that year confirmed that they continued almost universally to default. In October 1618 a royal proclamation ordered the native Irish inhabitants of all precincts reserved for undertakers to leave by 1 May 1619, or face a fine of 10 shillings for every native adult, male or female. Behind this apparent toughening of policy, however, private interests were once again coming to the fore. In February 1619, three months before the deadline, the crown farmed out the collection of these Ulster fines for seven years at a rent of £100 per annum. The ultimate beneficiary of this lucrative perk was James I's favourite George Villiers, duke of Buckingham, who was at this time extending his relentless quest for profit into all aspects of the Irish administration. How far Buckingham's intervention was decisive, and how far the king's active interest in his disappointing Ulster venture was already fading, remains unclear. But in either case occasional further proposals to hold the undertakers to their commitments made no headway. Instead their estates yielded a steady flow of income from fines, in many cases paid by the undertakers themselves as a reasonable price for the freedom to retain compliant and profitable tenants. It was not until 1624, at a time when impending war with Spain left the crown in need of money, that the question was reopened, this time by the undertakers themselves. By 1628 the crown had agreed to grant them new patents, doubling their rents and other charges, and in return allowing them to settle natives legally on one-quarter of their lands. Even then the settlement became possible only because Buckingham had earlier, at a point where the farm of fines on native occupiers had just six months to run, accepted £4,000 in compensation for its withdrawal. The new agreement stipulated that the native inhabitants of the other three-quarters of the undertakers' lands were to leave by the following May Day. But this formulaic rider was ignored as completely as its predecessors had been.[41]

The plantation, then, never came near fulfilling the dream of an Ulster dominated by large tracts of exclusively British settlement. At the same time it is important to recognize the extent to which it nevertheless transformed irreversibly the face of what had previously been the last stronghold of Gaelic Ireland. The modest flow of English and Scottish settlers indicated by Bodley's total of around 2,000 adult British males in 1613 strengthened notably in the years after 1615. Further surveys in 1619 and 1622 suggested that the figure was now 6,000 or more. Outside the planted counties, meanwhile, both Hamilton and Montgomery proved highly successful in attracting tenants to their newly acquired estates in Antrim and Down. Another leading County Antrim proprietor, Randal MacDonnell, son and heir to the formidable Sorley Boy and son-in-law to Tyrone, was initially bitterly hostile to Hamilton's intrusion. After 1607, however, he made his peace with the new dispensation, and began encouraging Scottish settlement on his own lands. The inward movement of Scots and English settlers to both planted and unplanted areas slowed down after about 1620. But in 1630 muster lists drawn up to record those available for local military service nevertheless listed around 6,500 adult British males in the six escheated counties, and a further 5,600 in Antrim and Down. Allowing for evident deficiencies in the muster roll, we thus have a rough total of perhaps

[41] T. W. Moody, 'The Treatment of the Native Population under the Scheme for the Plantation in Ulster', *IHS* 1 (1938), 59–63; Robinson, *Plantation of Ulster*, 97–108. For Buckingham's involvement, Victor Treadwell, *Buckingham and Ireland 1616–28* (Dublin, 1998), 137–8, 270–1.

15,000 adult British males in Ulster by 1630.[42] From about 1633 there was a further wave of migration from Scotland, apparently in response to poor harvests there. All in all it is likely that by 1641 the British population of Ulster stood at 40,000 or more. This would still have accounted for no more than one-fifth at most of the total inhabitants of the nine counties of Ulster. But it represented a new element too substantial to ignore.[43]

Within this growing British population Scots made up a clear majority. In the 1620s they accounted for around 60 per cent of the British males listed in the six escheated counties, and for 75–80 per cent of those in Antrim and Down. Further Scottish immigration in the 1630s would have reinforced this numerical advantage. Close links between Ulster and Scotland were not of course new. The narrow sea passage had encouraged a continuous trade in goods and mercenaries, and the MacDonnells had for two centuries held land on both coastlines. These long-standing links, however, were with the Gaelic society of the Highlands and islands. The settlers imported into Ulster by the plantation scheme, on the other hand, came mainly from the Border counties and the south-west. The less structured migration into Antrim and Down encouraged by improving landlords (including the MacDonnells) was likewise mainly from the south west. What they brought them was thus a Lowland rather than a Gaelic Scottish culture. But they nevertheless represented a distinctive new element in appearance, customs, and language. A ship arriving in Derry in 1615 carried essential items of dress: 'plaids' and 'Scotch cloth', as well as 27 'Scots daggers'. Surviving correspondence indicates that upper-class settlers as well as their social inferiors continued throughout the first half of the seventeenth century to use a characteristically Scottish spelling and orthography. In 1624 a group representing undertakers and other prominent figures petitioned for the appointment of a Scottish clerk to the Irish council, on the grounds that their petitions, 'being written in the Scotch hand', were not read or understood.[44]

The less numerous English participants in the formal and informal plantation were more diverse in their origins. Some undertakers and servitors recruited

[42] Figures from the 1630 muster roll for the six escheated counties, along with the results of a succession of earlier surveys, are tabulated in Robinson, *Plantation of Ulster*, 212–24 and reviewed in ibid. 104–6. For Antrim see Perceval-Maxwell, *Scottish Migration*, 232–3, 250, and for Down Gillespie, *Colonial Ulster*, 55.

[43] Any attempt to move beyond the total of 15,000 adult males in 1630 to estimates of population is inescapably speculative. Perceval-Maxwell (*Scottish Migration*, 126) provides reasonably solid evidence of a ratio of three women to every four men, permitting an estimate of 26,000 British adults. An alternative approach is to assume an average of two males per family, and a family size of between four and five, to give a total population in 1630 of between 30,000 and 37,000. There is no way of calculating the population of Ulster at this time. But it is hard to see how it can have amounted to more than the 20 per cent of Ireland's total population indicated in the more reliable data for the second half of the century, and its share of the national total (an estimated 1.5 million in 1641) may well have been substantially less.

[44] Perceval-Maxwell, *Scottish Migration*, 301; Philip Robinson, 'The Scots Language in Seventeenth-Century Ulster', *Ulster Folklife*, 35 (1989), 86–99; *CSPI 1615–25*, 502.

tenants in their home area. However, surname analysis suggests that the largest group of settlers was drawn from the hinterland of the main ports of embarkation, Chester and London. In 1622 English and Scottish settlers were still for the most part found on the estates of landlords of their own nationality. Thereafter, however, the artificial ethnic pigeonholing of the plantation scheme became gradually less relevant, as existing settlers redistributed themselves across the Ulster landscape and newcomers followed paths dictated by geography and economic advantage rather than by the formal plantation scheme.

In addition to a new demographic mix, the plantation brought change to the physical environment. The survey of 1619 counted 149 defensive enclosures or bawns in the six plantation counties, 26 of earth or timber and earth, the rest of stone or brick. There were also 43 tower houses or castles. These were mainly the work of leading undertakers from Scotland, where the fortified tower house was still current. Some English servitors and undertakers were content to erect a simple timber dwelling, or even to live in a thatched earthen-walled house of the local Irish design. Others, however, sought to transplant to their new environment the full topography of English civility. At Dungiven Sir Edward Doddington, chief tenant and administrator on the estate of the Skinners' Company, built a two-and-a-half storey manor, with symmetrical facades and casement windows, beside a formal garden in the best English Renaissance style. At Limavady Sir Thomas Phillips, having added a second tower and drawbridge to the tower house formerly occupied by O'Cahan, laid out a formal garden enclosed by a wall, with a tree-lined walk and a second geometrically designed pleasure garden adjoining the nearby River Roe. Meanwhile Chichester had erected a 'very stately house' at Carrickfergus, as well as 'another dainty stately house' at Belfast, with 'dainty orchard, gardens and walks planted'. Writing in 1610, he noted the contrast between these works and his own earlier activities in the same region. 'We are now all of us become builders and planters here, and not wasters and destroyers as in our younger years'.[45]

More humble settlers also contributed to the introduction of new styles and standards of building. The 1619 survey counted 1,897 English-style dwelling houses. Englishness, in these cases, seems to have consisted primarily of the existence of chimneys, and of internal subdivision into rooms. Some 'English houses' had stone walls. Others were of cagework, a timber frame filled in with wattle and clay, while roofs could be tile, slate, wooden shingle, or thatch. Even by this loose criterion, however, the number of 'English' houses falls well short of the more than 3,000 British families in the six escheated counties by this time. A substantial minority of the poorer British settlers seem instead to have drawn on local skills and labour to erect houses of the kind already in use. This was the case, for example, in the plantation village of Movanagher in County

[45] Curl, *Londonderry Plantation*, 286–91, 431–2. For Chichester's house see Brereton, *Travels*, 129, and for his comment of 1610 McCavitt, *Chichester*, 151.

Londonderry, where excavation has revealed a settler living in a simple rectangular structure with mass walls of turf or clay held up by posts lightly driven into the ground. Such a preference for indigenous building techniques, however, may have owed less to indolence or lack of resources than to a pragmatic adaptation to environment. George Canning, chief tenant of the Ironmongers' estate, noted ruefully in 1615 that Irish cabins, 'built low that a man may reach the top with his hand', and roofed with turf and straw tied down with wattles, had survived a storm that stripped the slates from his own newly built English houses.[46]

In other respects, too, the plantation brought real but nevertheless limited changes to the physical environment. The amount of land under tillage undoubtedly increased. This was due in particular to the Scots, who found a soil and climate similar to their own and well adapted to their existing staple crop, oats. By 1618, in fact, Ulster's exports of grain were so large that the Scottish council imposed a penal import duty to exclude them. Despite this setback, Ulster in the 1620s produced 18 per cent of Ireland's grain exports. Yet the goal of a landscape recast wholly into the neat patterns of a settled, tillage-based agriculture remained elusive. Instead much Scottish, and even more English, land, as well as the large proportion of the planted counties still occupied by native Irish, continued to be devoted primarily to stock rearing. Improvements in communications were likewise limited. By 1640 there were two bridges across the River Lagan, at Lisburn and Dromore, as well as others at Downpatrick, Newcastle, and Newry, and across the Foyle at Strabane. The more formidable Bann, on the other hand, slicing Ulster in two all the way from Lough Neagh to the sea, could still be crossed only by ferry, or on the sort of precarious structure by which Thomas Phillips passed from Antrim into County Londonderry in 1632: 'without rails or any thing for succour on the sides, the coach of each side had but four inches spare'. Roads, too, were in many cases no more than rough tracks. Sir William Brereton, landing at Islandmagee in July 1635, found that the road from Carrickfergus to Belfast was 'most base way, and deep in winter and wet weather'. From Dromore to Newry, equally, was 'a most difficult way for a stranger to find out', and he and his party needed a guide after losing the path.[47]

The plantation scheme of 1609–10 assumed that the settler population would live congregated in groups. The freeholders, leaseholders, and cottagers on each portion were to build their houses round the undertaker's bawn and residence, and there were also to be twenty-five incorporated towns. This preference for village and urban settlement arose partly from a concern for defence, but also from a desire to see what was conceived of as the nomadic barbarism of Gaelic

[46] Audrey Horning, '"Dwelling Houses in the Old Irish Barbarous Manner"', in Patrick J. Duffy, David Edwards, and Elizabeth FitzPatrick (eds.), *Gaelic Ireland: Land, Lordship and Settlement c.1250–c.1650* (Dublin, 2001), 375–96; Canning, quoted in Canny, *Making Ireland British*, 218.

[47] Brereton, *Travels*, 128, 132. For bridges see Gillespie, *Colonial Ulster*, 22–3, and for Phillips's crossing Moody, *Londonderry Plantation*, 346.

Ireland replaced by stable and ordered communities. It was, however, only imperfectly realized. With estates many times larger than the plantation scheme had envisaged, the majority of rural settlers found it more convenient to live on their individual holdings, in isolated farmsteads rather than in a central location. Canning, in 1616, noting that two of his tenants were in fact building close to one another, added sardonically that this would mean 'a town of six houses, which is a great town in this country'.[48] Where larger settlements were concerned, the plantation promoted the beginnings of an urban network. The most important new centre was Londonderry, erected on the nucleus of Docwra's fortified settlement at the base of Lough Foyle and entrusted to the Irish Society. By 1619 the town was encircled by a defensive wall 24 feet high and 6 feet thick, reinforced by an earthen rampart, and by 1622 its streets were fully paved. Within the walls there were 102 houses built by the Irish Society (as compared to the 200 specified in the Society's charter), and 38 other dwellings. The muster roll of 1630 listed 599 British males, implying a population of perhaps 1,500. In Coleraine the Society had built 70 houses and contributed to the cost of 21 more, and had paved the two main streets. The return of 357 British males in 1630 suggests a population of between 700 and 800.[49] However, the infrastructure was poor. The rampart surrounding the town enclosed too large an area, so that there were men available to defend only one-sixth of its length, and the clay and sod of which it was constructed had already begun to collapse in the rain-sodden climate. The market place was so choked with refuse that it could not be crossed.

Outside the planted area, the most important new town was Belfast, which developed in a small way as a social centre, through the residence there of the long-serving lord deputy, Sir Arthur Chichester. But its population remained well under 1,000. Surviving lists of freemen confirm the narrow range of economic activity, listing only 20 occupations where an English provincial centre like Norwich would have had over 100. One contemporary observer, writing in the early 1640s, dismissed both Belfast and Coleraine as places 'of small moment . . . hardly comparable to any of those fair market towns which are to be found in all parts of England'.[50]

There was also a range of smaller urban centres. Strabane, strategically placed on the River Foyle and benefiting from the patronage of an exceptionally active Scottish undertaker, the earl of Abercorn, had about 100 houses by 1622, and some 200 British male inhabitants by 1630. Other towns, like Lurgan in County Armagh or Lisburn in County Antrim, emerged as modest but stable marketing centres for the surrounding countryside. By 1625 a total of 18 towns in the six escheated counties, along with a further five in Antrim and Down and one,

[48] Quoted Moody, *Londonderry Plantation*, 317.

[49] Cf. n. 43 above. These estimates assume two males in each household of four or five persons.

[50] Boate, *Ireland's Natural History*, 9. For Belfast occupations, and the comparison with Norwich, see Gillespie, *Colonial Ulster*, 181. For Coleraine and Londonderry see Curl, *The Londonderry Plantation*, 72–84.

Monaghan, elsewhere in Ulster, had received a charter of incorporation. These creations, however, owed more to the need to create boroughs that could be counted on to return Protestant members to parliament than to a thriving urban life.[51] Even the larger centres, in fact, were unable to sustain a strong resident merchant class; instead the same traders appear as freemen of a range of towns, dividing their time between them. The shortage of residents of appropriate status frequently made it difficult to maintain the routines of corporate governance. A further problem was that only Carrickfergus and Derry were endowed with any lands, so that corporations lacked the funds to make provision for the poor or to provide other amenities and services.[52]

At the same time that the Ulster plantation was getting under way its most important precursor, the Munster colony, was coming back to life. The collapse of the English settlement in the 1590s had been so complete that the government briefly considered reverting to an older formula for stability by re-establishing the earldom of Desmond. In the event, the undertakers were allowed to retain their holdings, although between 1598 and 1611 eleven of the original seignories passed into new hands. More important, the restoration of peace in 1603 permitted a new wave of English settlement, involving both soldiers from the disbanded army and fresh immigrants, the latter drawn mainly from the same south-western counties that had provided the personnel for the original plantation. A survey of 1622 counted a total of 2,744 English households, suggesting a total population of about 14,000, possibly rising to around 22,000 by 1641. This renewed influx was not by any means confined to the patchwork of plantation seignories. Even landlords not bound by plantation conditions had begun to see English tenants as attractive, both as agents of economic improvement and as a means of strengthening the Protestant interest. This was true not just of New English proprietors but of the indigenous if anglicized earls of Thomond and Clanricard. Settlers themselves looked beyond the planted estates to areas of greater opportunity, such as the chain of English fishing towns, at Baltimore, Crookhaven, and elsewhere, that developed along the south-west coast. As in Ulster, but to a much greater extent, English settlement in Munster thus grew out of the interaction between a formal plantation scheme and a natural process of migration into an adjacent region in which new possibilities of economic and social advancement had suddenly opened up.

The Munster plantation enjoyed a number of advantages over its Ulster counterpart. In addition to being longer established, it was located in a region better suited to trade both with southern England and with continental Europe. There is also the possibility that migrants from south-west England brought with

[51] Below Ch. 8.

[52] Raymond Gillespie, 'The Origins and Development of an Ulster Urban Network', *IHS* 24 (1984), 15–29; R. J. Hunter, 'Ulster Plantation Towns 1609–41', in David Harkness and Mary O'Dowd (eds.), *The Town in Ireland* (Belfast, 1981), 55–80.

them a higher level of technical and commercial skills than those from northern England or Scotland. How far these circumstances gave early seventeenth-century Munster a clear-cut economic superiority remains a matter for debate. An ambitious analysis of the economic activities reflected in the depositions detailing Protestant losses in the rising of 1641 suggests a sharp contrast. In Munster artisans and specialized agriculturalists employed imported skills and techniques in a well-developed commercial economy aligned to external markets; in Ulster, by contrast, production remained within the framework of pre-existing economic activity, dominated by stock-rearing.[53] The problem with any such analysis, however, is that the distribution of 1641 depositions is the product, first of the timing and location of the revolt, and secondly of the survival rate of those under attack: in the case of Ulster more than two-thirds of all surviving statements come from what were almost certainly the poorer and less commercialized counties of Cavan and Fermanagh. Other evidence, meanwhile, indicates clearly that in Ulster too the plantation brought with it new techniques of production. Successive surveys, despite their recurrent criticism of the overall performance of the undertakers, detailed the appearance of new agricultural and manufacturing technology and practice. These included vertical water wheels (replacing the simple horizontal wheel formerly in use) for the grinding of corn, wind- and watermills for the finishing of cloth, heavier and more effective ploughs, improved breeds of livestock, stabling for the accommodation of cattle and horses, and the use of salt to preserve butter.[54]

In the case of Munster, meanwhile, the evidence does indeed indicate that the settler community had a reasonably broad economic base. In particular the first half of the seventeenth century saw substantial exports of fish and timber, and the establishment at different sites of ironworks. All three activities, however, had begun to falter by 1641, as the natural resources on which they depended appoached exhaustion. There was also some manufacture of woollen cloth, but mainly on a part-time basis, with most of the product being sent to the Netherlands for finishing; the greater part of the province's wool was exported. The main economic activity, for settlers as for natives, continued to be agriculture. Here there are some indications of the introduction of improved breeds of cattle and sheep, of more sophisticated ploughs and other implements, and of the hedging and ditching associated with enclosure. Tillage, where it existed, was for wheat as well as oats. For the most part, however, settlers followed native practice, and the imperatives of soil and climate, by concentrating on livestock. The commercial fisheries along the coast, and the charcoal furnaces

[53] This argument was first put forward in Nicholas Canny, 'Migration and Opportunity: Britain, Ireland and the New World', *IESH* 12 (1985), 7–32, and elaborated in Canny, *Making Ireland British*, ch. 6. For a critique see Raymond Gillespie, 'Migration and Opportunity: A Comment', *IESH* 13 (1986), 90–5 and Canny's reply, ibid. See also Perceval-Maxwell, *Scottish Migration*, pp. xxvi–xxviii.

[54] Robinson, *Plantation of Ulster*, 144–9, 178–82.

for iron-smelting that blazed in wooded parts of its interior, were evidence of a new and dynamic element working within the province's economy. But its most important exports continued to be cattle and wool.[55] All this would confirm the suspicion that the differences in economic development between Munster and Ulster were ones of degree rather than of kind.

Where Munster did demonstrate a clear superiority was in the sophistication of its physical and commercial infrastructure. The 1641 depositions reveal an intricate network of debt and credit linking Munster merchants and artisans to trading partners across the southern half of Ireland. Sir John Davies, visiting the province for the first time in 1604, noted that it had three cities, Cork, Waterford, and Limerick, 'besides divers fair corporate towns, not inferior to the better sort of market towns in England'.[56] In most of these centres, including Cork and Limerick, Old English oligarchies resolutely excluded English newcomers from acquiring property or setting up in business. The main exception was Youghal, where by 1641 more than half the town's freemen were New English, and where the influx of capital and entrepreneurship promoted rapid growth. Meanwhile the New English had developed their own towns. The most substantial, Bandonbridge, was Munster's answer to Londonderry: like it, a newly built town surrounded by a defensive wall, but with a population by 1641 of around 2,300. Coleraine had its equivalents in Mallow, with a population of around 800, and Tallow, with 750. In the countryside, too, anecdotal evidence suggests a landscape far more extensively tamed by the construction of roads and bridges, and the creation of manor houses, orchards, and walled gardens. Where Phillips's Limavady and Doddington's Dungiven were islands of English civility in what remained for the most part a crudely developed frontier, early seventeenth-century Munster, it has been suggested, more closely resembled 'a slightly raffish county on the English borders'.[57]

THE CLOCK OF THE CIVIL GOVERNMENT

In 1612 Sir John Davies, fresh from his triumphs in constructing the legal basis for the Ulster plantation, published *A Discovery of the True Causes Why Ireland was Never Entirely Subdued.* Here he identified two central reasons why Ireland, after four centuries of English rule, had never been reduced to obedience. The first was 'the faint prosecution of the war'. Successive monarchs had failed to commit sufficient military resources to establish their authority over the whole island. The second was 'the looseness of civil government': the crown had refused to accept the native inhabitants of Ireland as subjects, instead leaving them under

[55] MacCarthy-Morrough, *The Plantation of Munster*, 223–43. [56] *CSPI 1603–6*, 463.

[57] The phrase is MacCarthy-Morrough's: 'The English Presence in Early Seventeenth-Century Munster', in Brady and Gillespie, *Natives and Newcomers*, 190.

the rule of their own lords. It had also permitted the English of Ireland to abandon their laws and customs for those of the Gaelic Irish. Since the accession of James I, however, all this had changed. A uniform code of justice was in force throughout the country. The ownership of estates and possessions, for both Irish and English, had been definitively settled. Towns had been granted renewed charters and increased liberties. The common people, liberated from the tyranny of their lords, enjoyed comfort and security under the laws, and had begun to adopt English dress and manners. 'The clock of the civil government is now well set, and all the wheels thereof do move in order. The strings of this Irish harp, which the civil magistrate doth finger, are all in tune.'[58]

Davies's *Discovery* was the latest in a long line of treatises on the problems of governing Ireland, extending from the work of Darcy and Finglas in the reign of Henry VIII to that of Spenser only some fifteen years before. The continuity with the work of these predecessors is evident, particularly in his frequent citations of Finglas's 'breviate'. What is most obviously new is the change of tone: instead of appeals for action to remedy desperate problems, Davies's *Discovery* is a proclamation of unqualified success. The benefits of the conquest that he celebrated, moreover, were to be shared in, not just by the victorious English, but by the Gaelic Irish themselves. Davies frankly admitted the need for violence: 'a barbarous country must be first broken by a war, before it will be capable of good government'. Once rebellion had been defeated, however, a comprehensive act of oblivion had received the whole population into the king's protection, thus liberating them from the tyranny that their lords and chiefs had up to then exercised over them. This was hardly an adequate summary of the process by which three years of massacre and starvation had battered Gaelic Ulster into submission. By the same token the claim that the crown's victory had allowed it to achieve 'the settling of all the estates and possessions, as well of Irish as English, thoughout the kingdom', hardly conveyed the rough justice that had characterized the plantation settlement. But Davies's tract, for all its mendacity and evasions, presents a significant contrast to the vision outlined less than two decades earlier in Spenser's *View of the State of Ireland*. Where Spenser had prescribed a ruthless military regime to keep the native population in apparently permanent subjection, Davies saw the abolition of the customs of gavelkind and tanistry as opening the way to the spread of civility and order:

> all the possessions shall descend and be conveyed according to the course of the common law: every man shall have a certain home, and know the extent of his estate; whereby the people will be encouraged to manure their land with better industry than heretofore

[58] John Davies, *Discovery of the True Causes Why Ireland was never Entirely Subdued* (London, 1612). Quotations in the text are from pp. 284, 259, 5, 273, 272. For Bodin and the nature of sovereignty, see pp. 14–15. For a full treatment of Davies's thought, see Pawlisch, *Sir John Davies*. This should be balanced by the cautionary remarks on the extent of Davies's influence on policy in McCavitt, *Chichester*, 88–9

hath been used, to bring up their children more civilly, to provide for their posterity more carefully; these will cause them to build better houses for their safety, and to love neighbourhood; thence will arise villages and towns, which will draw tradesmen and artificers; so as we conceive a hope, that these countries, in a short time, will not only be quiet neighbours to the Pale, but be made as rich and as civil as the Pale itself.[59]

It is a vision of cultural assimilation, achieved through the self-evident superiority of English over Irish ways, that finds its closest parallel, not in Spenser's gloomy imaginings, but in the confident optimisim with which Henry VIII had set out, almost a century earlier, to reform his Irish lordship.

If Davies's positive vision of a reconstructed Irish society had echoes of the era of surrender and regrant, however, his prescription for how that reconstruction was to be achieved was based on an explicit rejection of all such schemes of gradual reform. His starting point was the work of the sixteenth-century French political theorist Jean Bodin, who had identified 'the true marks of sovereignty' as the power to make laws, to appoint magistrates and other officials, and to punish offences. English kings from Henry II onwards had failed to achieve this end. Instead they had been satisfied with superficial submissions and the payment of tribute from Gaelic lords who continued to govern their own territories as they chose. They had likewise allowed the English conquerors too great a degree of independence. The celebrated battle of Knockdoe, Davies pointed out, had been fought on a private quarrel, with no warrant from the king. In the same vein he recognized the achievements of later Tudor viceroys, from St Leger to Perrot, in extending the power of English government. However, they had not attempted to execute the law within the territories of the Irish chiefs. Instead they had left the common Irish under the rule of their lords, 'utterly ignorant of their duties to God and the king'. In this they had resembled the rulers of ancient Israel, who had been good kings but had failed to destroy the groves and high places of idolatory.[60]

For Davies, then, the long-term aspiration to see the native Irish themselves come to appreciate the benefits of English law and custom took second place to the immediate imperative of reducing them to absolute obedience. His willingness to promote the interests of the crown over those of the subject had been amply demonstrated in the singleminded manner in which he had provided a legal basis for the Ulster plantation. In other cases, relating to the currency, the levying of feudal dues, the fiscal privileges of the towns, and the coercing of recusants, he was equally consistent in his determination to uphold the royal prerogative. To do so he was willing to draw, as it suited, not just on the principles of English common law, but also on the civil law of continental Europe. He

[59] *The Works in Verse and Prose of Sir John Davies*, ed. A. B. Grossart (privately printed, 1869–76), iii. 161. See also his claims regarding popular enthusiasm for assizes justice, ibid. 195; *CSPI 1603–6*, 464, 469.

[60] See Davies, *Discovery*, 258–9.

also pioneered the practice of having judges collectively decide points of legal principle in a manner then accepted as binding: in effect, the making of law by crown-appointed judges rather than parliament.[61]

How far does Davies's tract reflect a change in the theory as well as the practice of government in Ireland? His record of unswerving support for royal claims, combined with the invocation of French political theory and legal principle, could be seen as marking him out as a representative of the new commitment to the principle of absolute royal power that some have seen as coming to the fore in early Stuart England. Yet attempts to demonstrate the growth of a coherent ideology of absolutism, as opposed to a vigorous assertion of the monarch's prerogative authority, have not won general acceptance. Conflict, it appears, was less about a choice between royal authority and constitutional restraints than about the balance that should exist between them. In the case of Davies, similarly, a vigorous campaign to extend the limits of the crown's legal rights made sense only on the assumption that such limits did in fact exist. In any case Henry VIII, almost a century earlier, had had no hesitation in proclaiming that, as Ireland's sovereign prince, he was, by his absolute power, above the law.[62] What had changed by 1612, it seems likely, was less the ideology of monarchy than the practical opportunities that now seemed open to the crown and its servants.

The most prominent symbol of the new regularity and order celebrated by Davies was the extension throughout the kingdom of a regular assizes system. Tipperary, the last surviving area of Palatine jurisdiction under the earls of Ormond, remained exempt from the visitations of the royal judges. County Kerry and, for a time, County Leitrim had only one assizes each year. In the other counties, however, people became accustomed to the regular appearance, in spring and summer, of two senior judges. Their main function was to hear major civil and criminal cases, or, as Davies put it, 'like good planets in their several spheres or circles, [to] carry the light and influence of justice round about the kingdom'. They were also expected to supervise the operations of local government. In addition they provided an important channel of communication, formal and informal, between the central administration and the localities. To assist in maintaining regular circuits the number of judges in each of the three central courts, King's Bench, Exchequer, and Common Pleas, was increased to three by 1607 and to four by 1612. The assizes did not replace the presidency courts that had operated since the 1570s in Munster and Connacht, but over time they took over a growing proportion of the business that these had formerly handled.[63]

[61] For a full discussion of Davies's legal thought, and its sources, see Pawlisch, *Sir John Davies*.

[62] Above, p. 78.

[63] John McCavitt, '"Good Planets in their Several Spheres: The Establishment of the Assizes Circuits in Early Seventeenth-Century Ireland', *Irish Jurist*, 24 (1989), 248–78. For assizes before 1603 see above, Ch. 4, 'The Sword of State'.

Below the assizes were the lower courts. Within each county the justices of the peace met four times a year, somtimes more frequently, in quarter sessions, under the supervision of the sheriff, to try less serious offences. In addition landholders holding their land by a royal patent giving the estate the legal status of one or more manors were thereby empowered to hold manor courts (also known as courts leet and courts baron).[64] Presided over by the landlord's own official, these settled disputes among tenants on issues such as trespass or small debts, as well as recording transactions between landlord and tenant. They also had jurisdiction over minor criminal offences, with power to fine and inflict corporal punishment, though not to imprison or execute. The distribution of manor courts was uneven. They seem to have been relatively rare in the long-settled counties of the Pale. On the other hand authority to hold manor courts was a standard feature of the patents granted to undertakers in the Ulster plantation and to other new proprietors in the early seventeenth century, and the beneficiaries seem generally to have responded enthusiastically to the opportunity to profit from fees and fines and to consolidate their authority. The flavour of the new style of social discipline that thus accompanied the spread of plantation is suggested by the regulations drawn up around 1620 for the newly acquired estate of Sir Laurence Parsons at Birr in King's County. There were to be fines for throwing dung or rubbish into the street. Anyone lighting a fire other than in a stone chimney was to be banished from the estate. Any woman who took it on herself to sell beer was to be put in the stocks for three market days. A set of stocks is likewise a prominent feature on the map of Sir Thomas Phillips's carefully laid out settlement at Newtownlimavady in County Londonderry.[65]

The other outward symbol of the extension across Ireland of a uniform administrative system was the consolidation of county government.[66] During 1605–6 the administration put the final touches to the formal structure, re-establishing a county of Wicklow in the mountainous region south of Dublin, incorporating the shadowy county of Desmond, created in 1571, into County Kerry, and tidying up a variety of minor anomalies. In addition what had earlier been purely nominal creations now became functioning administrative units. One of the aims of the commissioners who toured Ulster in 1606 was to provide for the erection in each county of a gaol and a session house. The resulting structures were not always impressive. In Enniskillen in 1625 witnesses being kept in protective custody could not be lodged in the county gaol because its

[64] Courts leet had originally dealt with criminal offences, courts baron with civil actions, but the distinction had been largely lost over time: Gillespie, *Colonial Ulster*, 156–7. See also Raymond Gillespie, 'A Manor Court in Seventeenth-Century Ireland', *IESH* 25 (1998), 81–7.

[65] A. P. W. Malcomson, 'A Variety of Perspectives on Lawrence Parsons, Second Earl of Rosse', in William Nolan and Timothy P. O'Neill (eds.), *Offaly: History and Society* (Dublin, 1998), 441. For the relative absence of manor courts in the Pale see Gillespie, *Colonial Ulster*, 213.

[66] For good general accounts see McCavitt, *Chichester*, ch. 6; Gillespie, *Colonial Ulster*, ch. 5, ; Mary O'Dowd, *Power, Politics and Land: Early Modern Sligo 1568–1688* (Belfast, 1991), 45–61.

single room already housed those against whom they had testified. In Armagh, on the other hand, the grand jury claimed in 1632 to have spent £800 erecting a gaol and sessions house. In Ennis, County Clare, similarly, the grand jury some time before 1641 built a stone courthouse on the market square, with an arcaded ground floor to accommodate traders.[67]

With buildings went personnel. The principle, as in England, was to co-opt men of property as the unpaid local agents of the state. The key figure in county administration was the sheriff, expected to receive and implement the directions of central government, to oversee the collection of taxes, and to supervise the work of local courts. In this he was assisted by four deputy sheriffs. Justices of the peace, chosen from among local landowners or their agents, were responsible for law enforcement in their immediate area, and for trying offences at quarter sessions. There are also references to other officials: a coroner in each county, to inquire into unnatural deaths, and constables and bailiffs, charged with executing writs and warrants. How far these latter two officials overlapped remains unclear. Nor is it possible to say how far either were lesser householders playing their part in local administration at a level appropriate to their social standing, or how far, as at a later period, they were paid substitutes, or employees of the county. Another proposal, to have in each county a clerk of the peace, was never implemented. Instead there continued to be a clerk for each of the four provinces.

The failure to provide each county with a clerk of the peace, essential to the maintenance of orderly procedures and the keeping of adequate records, is a reminder of how far the new apparatus of local government, though much extended, fell short of the English model on which it was based. The appointment of sheriffs and justices of the peace was no longer a mere formality, as it had been at the time when the administration was attempting to win the voluntary cooperation of Tyrone and other local lords. But it was still necessary to respect the realities of local power. The pool of men qualified to serve was at best a limited one. It became even more so on those occasions when shifts in official policy dictated that Catholics should be excluded. In the mid-1620s, for example, there were only thirteen members of the commission of the peace for each of the counties of Antrim and Down, and officials were able to identify no more than nine possible additions.[68] The shortage of suitable alternatives explains why sheriffs and justices were so often able simply to ignore writs against relatives, friends, or associates (or, in the case of Catholics, against their co-religionists), and why some could retain their positions despite clear evidence of abuse of power or other misdemeanours.

Circumspection was also required in dealing with leading magnates. The case of the Ormond estate, subjected to a sustained attack on its privileges after it had passed from Elizabeth's favourite 'Black Tom' to an active Catholic dissident

67 *CSPI 1625–32*, 35, 644; Cronin et al., *Irish Fairs and Markets*, 49–50.
68 Gillespie, *Colonial Ulster*, 103.

in 1614, was an exception.[69] By contrast the earls of Thomond and Clanricard continued to enjoy the substantial practical autonomy conferred, not just by their broad acres, but by the continued existence of the Munster and Connacht presidencies. Other regional notables were likewise able either to ignore or to dominate the new institutions of centralized government. In 1627 there were complaints that the earl of Antrim had refused to allow the sheriff onto his lands to requisition horses, that he fined and imprisoned those who initiated any legal process in the royal courts rather than in his own manor courts, and that he had put a bailiff in the stocks for arresting a man without first obtaining his permission. The following year an ironmaster involved in a legal dispute with the earl of Cork was arrested as he landed at Youghal, despite the fact that he had a pass as an accredited king's messenger. One of Cork's servants allegedly told him that he had been a silly fool to think he could escape the earl's clutches with a scurvy warrant, and that Cork had never yet come into conflict with any man without bringing him to his knees.[70]

For all this, the extension to the whole island of a regular assizes system brought the inhabitants of previously remote counties into sudden contact with a wholly new concept of centralized order. The assizes held in Monaghan, Cavan, and Fermanagh in the summer of 1606 were arranged to coincide with sittings of the commission, headed by Lord Deputy Chichester, for inquiring into the titles of landed proprietors.[71] The combined expedition was an impressive one, with an escort of 120 to 140 footsoldiers and 50 to 60 horse. At Monaghan two notorious cattle thieves were convicted and executed. Two leading gentry of the county had also been indicted for receiving stolen cattle, but these were pardoned after confessing on their knees before the lord deputy. The proceedings at Fermanagh were less successful. Men taken up as idle persons were bound over to find masters or give sureties for good behaviour, but the failure of inexperienced native justices to bind accusers to prosecute meant that none of those indicted for felonies could be convicted. At Wicklow later the same year, on the other hand, the judges once again hanged two notable thieves, 'in the nature of rebels'. However, they dealt more leniently with a series of indictments for minor thefts. The offences dated from the period before the recent shiring of the region, when the local seneschal had been in the habit of dealing with such cases under Gaelic custom, by restitution and fine rather than the hangman's noose. Accordingly the judges substituted charges of trespass, allowing the offenders to escape with a fine.[72]

Davies's reports from the 1606 circuits thus present an image of measured severity, with a careful balancing of justice and mercy and strict attention to the

[69] Below, Ch. 8, 'Half Subjects'. [70] *CSPI 1625–32*, 277–8, 314.

[71] Above, p. 272.

[72] Davies's letters to Salisbury describing the Ulster, Munster, and Leinster circuits are printed in full in *The Works in Prose and Verse of Sir John Davies*, iii. 119–98. For Munster see also *CSPI 1603–6*, 463–77.

need to adhere to legal forms. However, this flattering self-image must be set against two other considerations. The first is that the legal convictions so proudly reported were achieved only through a degree of duress. At Monaghan jurors had initially acquitted all those brought before them. It was only after one jury had been punished 'with good round fines and imprisonment, for acquitting some prisoners contrary to direct and pregnant evidence' that the two thieves were convicted. In Waterford, similarly, juries had sometimes to be threatened with penalties to make them find a verdict for the crown. Later, in the aftermath of O'Doherty's rebellion, two men referred to the court of Castle Chamber for acquitting supposed traitors contrary to the evidence were each fined £100, pilloried at Dublin and Derry, and had an ear cut off.[73] Davies justified such tactics by citing both the reluctance of jurors, in a society still dominated by a limited number of surnames, to convict those they regarded as kinsmen, and the evidence of potential jurors themselves that they feared reprisals from the families of anyone they convicted. But the definition of 'direct and pregnant evidence' was not always necessarily clear-cut. Within a few years, moreover, events in Wexford and Connacht were to show how easily the punishment of juridicial delinquency could expand into naked intimidation.

The other hint of a darker picture concealed behind Davies's positive report is provided by one of the cases tried at Limerick. This concerned Captain John Downing, a provost marshal who had arrested two simpletons kept as fools by the earl of Thomond and another County Clare gentleman, Sir John MacNamara, when they passed through his village one Sunday. They were on their way to visit the sister of Thomond's man, and had passes, but Downing had nevertheless hanged them both. Following a protest from Thomond, he was tried for murder and convicted, despite the blatant attempts of the lord president of Munster, Sir Henry Brouncker, who presided, to secure his acquittal. Davies, one of the judges, applauded the verdict, not only because 'the fact was foul' but also because 'our provost marshals are oftentimes too nimble and too rash in executing their commissions, so that it were not amiss that one or other of them did smart for it'. Yet the prosecution had gone ahead only on the understanding that Downing's authority to carry out summary executions was not in question. Instead the grounds for his capital conviction were that he had known Thomond's man, and his condition, and had acted out of malice. Even then, moreover, because Downing had served well in the war against Tyrone, 'and because we would not utterly discountenance the martial law, which at that time and that place had been necessary', the judges recommended him to the lord deputy for a pardon, which was duly granted.[74]

[73] *The Works in Prose and Verse of Sir John Davies*, iii. 136–7; *CSPI 1603–6*, 464–5; Gillespie, *Colonial Ulster*, 37.

[74] Davies's less than frank report of the trial (*CSPI 1603–6*, 470–1) is supplemented, and in places corrected, in David Edwards, 'Two Fools and a Martial Law Commissioner: Cultural Conflict

The sad end of Lord Thomond's fool was not an isolated incident. At the same time that he reported the dispatch of assizes judges on the newly established circuits in 1606, Chichester also noted that it remained necessary to use martial law, administered by provost marshals, to deal with the problem of 'idle vagabonds, thieves, lawless and masterless men' in several counties.[75] The wording makes clear that the programme of indiscriminate social cleansing launched in the 1570s and 1580s was still in progress in the reign of James I. The class-based nature of the system was openly acknowledged in 1613, when Chichester dismissed complaints about the arbitrary powers vested in provost marshals by pointing out that they could not execute by martial law anyone owning £10 worth of goods or freehold property worth £2 per year. The scandal created by the Downing affair appears to have made government somewhat more cautious, for a time at least, in their use of martial law.[76] But complaints of the arbitrary behaviour of provost marshals and their followers continued.[77] In 1628, when Catholic representatives were negotiating with the crown a package of reforms in exchange for new taxation, one of their demands was that there should not be more than one provost marshal for each province, and that they should have no power to execute outside times of war or rebellion. The clock of civil government may have been set, as Davies claimed. But the flail of Talus had all too clearly not been laid aside.

The provost martial, with his arbitrary powers of life and death, over men of no property at least, was only the most visible aspect of a general feature of the government of James I's Irish kingdom: the close interconnection of civil and military functions. The Irish army, reduced to a mere 880 men in the aftermath of Tyrone's submission, had to be hastily expanded to meet the challenge of O'Doherty's revolt. Even after the emergency had passed, its numbers were fixed at a new peacetime level of 2,100 men. In addition this latest revolt had pushed the crown into financing a further round of investment in a programme of fortification that had been in progress since the late sixteenth century. The most important works were at Duncannon and Castle Park, commanding the approaches to Waterford and Kinsale harbours, at Haulbowline Island in Cork harbour, and the cities of Limerick and Galway. Here government engineers constructed or renovated citadels according to the most up-to-date continental models, with low thick walls designed both to withstand cannon and to provide a solid base for heavy artillery, protected from scaling by projecting bastions giving defenders a field of fire along their length. These formidable defences, located along the vulnerable south and south-west coast, were primarily intended to repel

at the Limerick Assize of 1606', in David Edwards (ed.), *Regions and Rulers in Ireland 1100–1650* (Dublin, 2004), 237–65, which draws on Thomond's alternative account.

[75] McCavitt, *Chichester,* 102–3.

[76] Edwards, 'Two Fools and a Martial Law Commissioner', 258–60.

[77] *CSPI 1611–14,* 415; *CSPI 1615–25,* 38.

invaders. But they also had an internal security function, explicitly acknowledged in the case of Limerick and Waterford, where the citadels were provided with gun platforms facing inland as well as out to sea.[78]

In 1611 Sir George Carew, an old Irish hand dispatched by the English privy council to impose a round of economies, cut the size of the Irish army to 1,450 foot and 212 horse. Yet this still left Ireland with a permanent standing army of a kind seen in no other part of the Stuart dominions. Although overall numbers were reduced by one-third, moreover, the officer corps remained largely intact. Men who had formerly commanded companies or regiments remained in pay as governors of forts, provost marshals, or constables maintaining 'petty wards' from which strategic areas could be policed. In this way a network of minor outposts across the interior came to supplement the major citadels at Limerick, Galway, and elsewhere. In addition a corps of experienced military men remained available to discharge a range of executive functions in both central and local government. In 1618, for example, the English privy council, in an important act of centralization, transferred the collection of fines and other revenues out of the unreliable hands of county sheriffs and other locally based officials, and into those of specially appointed collectors working on commission. Of twenty-two such collectors identified in one list, fourteen were army officers. At the very centre of government, equally, soldiers were heavily represented; in the long lord deputyship of Chichester they made up almost half the members of the Irish privy council. Chichester, himself an ex-soldier, was a particular champion of the military servitor interest, and he was to be succeeded by another of the same background, Oliver St John, who had seen service on the Continent before coming to Ireland with Mountjoy.[79]

The prominence thus given to army officers as agents of an expanding Irish state also allowed some of their number to acquire a new status as landowners. Most commonly this happened when the crown leased or granted adjacent lands to commanders of forts or garrisons, using for this purpose land formerly attached to religious houses. By this means Thomas Phillips acquired the lands at Coleraine which he later exchanged for what became his permanent settlement at Newtownlimavady. In the same way Sir Toby Caulfield, a veteran of both the Netherlands and Tyrone's rebellion and ancestor of the earls of Charlemont, gained land round the fort of that name, of which he was now commander, while Sir Basil Brooke, forerunner of another Ulster political dynasty, acquired

[78] Rolf Loeber and Geoffrey Parker, 'The Military Revolution in Seventeenth-Century Ireland', in Jane Ohlmeyer (ed.), *Ireland from Independence to Occupation 1641–1660* (Cambridge, 1995), 67–70. For the context for this concern with internal security, the urban recusant 'revolt' of 1603, see below, Ch. 8.

[79] The role of the military in the government of Jacobean Ireland is a central theme of Joseph McLaughlin, 'The Making of the Irish Leviathan 1603–25: Statebuilding in Ireland during the Reign of James VI and I' (Ph.D. thesis, National University of Ireland, Galway 1999), to which this and the next paragraph are heavily indebted. See in particular pp. 145–7, 307–10, 276–86, 357–8. For the prominence of military men in Chichester's council see McCavitt, *Chichester*, 76–7.

a small estate in Donegal. These grants were subsequently augmented by the more substantial grants made to military servitors in the plantation that followed Tyrone's departure. Soldiers who had for the most part begun life as fortuneless younger sons thus joined strategically placed officials in forming the nucleus of a New English landed elite, and eventually, after mid-century, a new Irish ruling class.[80]

The extended authority of central government in the counties and provinces was not matched by any spectacular accession of resources or prestige at the centre itself. Dublin Castle, the home of the lord deputy and headquarters of his government, remained a ramshackle jumble of buildings surrounded by partly outmoded defensive structures. Sir Henry Sidney had made improvements in the 1560s, including a room for meetings of the Irish council. In 1620, however, the roof of this chamber collapsed, taking with it several rooms above. Four years later what was described as the principal tower of the castle crashed to the ground, along with the artillery mounted on it. Sir Thomas Wentworth, appointed lord deputy in 1631, found the castle 'in great decay', with one tower requiring immediate demolition and the rest 'so crazy as we are still in fear part of it may drop down upon our heads'. The accommodation was also poor, with a bakery directly below the deputy's study 'and the woodreek just full before the gallery windows, which I take not to be so courtly, nor to suit well with the dignity of the king's deputy'. The chief governor's horses, meanwhile, essential if he was to ride out properly attended, were stabled in the nearby church of St Andrew.[81]

By the time Sir William Brereton visited Dublin in 1635 there had been some improvements. The council chamber had been rebuilt, and the recently departed lord deputy, Viscount Falkland, had added 'a pretty neat short gallery . . . the lower part of it is built arch-wise and very gracefully, so as it is a great ornament to the castle'. Wentworth, Falkland's successor, had added 'a gallant, stately stable as any I have seen in the king's dominions', with large stalls capable of accommodating up to sixty horses. On the other hand, Brereton found the two houses of parliament, at that time located within the castle, 'much less and meaner than ours'. The Lords met in 'a room of no great state or receipt', while 'the Commons House is but a mean and ordinary place; a plain and not very convenient seat for the speaker, nor officers'. Luke Gernon, eight years earlier, judiciously summed up the public face of government in Ireland as 'not very magnificent, nor to be disregarded'. On ordinary occasions the lord deputy had a guard of fifty tall men, dressed as soldiers rather than in red livery, and carrying halberds. For formal meetings he sat under a cloth of state, while all others present stood with their heads uncovered, and he dined with 'of men of quality as many

[80] See the last section of this chapter.

[81] *CSPI 1615–25*, 294, 311, 489, 503–4; *The Earl of Strafford's Letters and Dispatches*, ed. William Knowler, 3 vols. (Dublin, 1740), i. 68, 131.

as the table will contain'. Falkland's installation as lord deputy in 1622, likewise, had been attended by a decent but modest level of ceremony. Having landed at Howth, seven miles north of the city, he was met halfway on the road to Dublin by members of the nobility and privy council. Next day he went in procession to Christ Church cathedral, attended by the council and the gentlemen pensioners and with the sword of state carried before him, to take his oath of office.[82]

To members of the Dublin administration, and to their masters in London, the extension of effective royal authority into the Irish provinces was a substantial good, to be pursued for its own sake. But there was also a financial imperative behind these new attempts to extend the reach of the central state.[83] During the period 1603–11 the cost of the Irish civil establishment almost doubled, to around £18,000 per annum. The rise was due partly to the increased cost of a much expanded judicial system, but even more to a sharp rise in the number of pensions paid from Irish revenues. The military establishment, on the other hand, had been brought down to around a quarter of its wartime levels. However, there was still the cost of maintaining a reduced but still sizeable standing army, as well as a substantial investment in new fortifications. Military spending in the period 1611–21 averaged around £54,000 per annum, roughly three times the non-military budget. The Irish revenues available to meet these demands rose from around £20,000 per year in the early years of the reign to between £30,000 and £35,000 annually from 1612, owing mainly to the additional income received from Ulster plantation rents. The gap was filled by subventions from the English exchequer, in the form of silver coin shipped regularly across the Irish Sea. In the period 1604–19 this flow of 'treasure' amounted to a total of £708,000 sterling, or an average of £47,000 sterling per year.[84] This drain on English resources added substantially to what were in any case the acute political difficulties arising from James I's unwillingness to continue his predecessor's cautious spending habits, combined with the English parliament's firm refusal to offer more than the traditional modest supplements to the crown's permanent revenue. Subsidies to the Irish government, in fact, consistently represented the single largest item of crown spending in England, in some years amounting to two-thirds or more of the royal deficit.

One reason for the dire state of the Irish public finances was the derisory yield from customs revenue. Traditionally the king was entitled to poundage, amounting to a levy of 5 per cent on all exports and imports, as well as the

[82] Brereton, *Travels*, 140–1; Luke Gernon's account, printed in Falkiner, *Illustrations*, 351; *CSPI 1615–25*, 345–6.

[83] The fullest published account of Irish finances in this period is McCavitt, *Chichester*, ch. 3. The most detailed analysis is in McLaughlin, 'The Making of the Irish Leviathan 1603–25', to which this section is once again much indebted. Unless otherwise stated, the figures are in Irish pounds, which by this time were worth three-quarters of a pound sterling (IR1*s*. = 9*d*. stg).

[84] This is the figure, based on a variety of accounts relating to the supply of 'treasure', offered by McLaughlin, 'Irish Leviathan', 122–5. The total cost of governing Ireland, including payments for Irish-related purposes made in England, was significantly higher. See McCavitt, *Chichester*, 41.

great custom, payable on wool, woodfells, and hides, and the petty custom, an additional levy of *3d.* in the pound on exports and imports by aliens. During the sixteenth century, however, the crown had largely surrendered these entitlements. The freemen of Dublin, Drogheda, Waterford, and Galway were exempt from payment of poundage. Most of the major Irish ports had gained control over the appointment of local revenue officers, ensuring that collection was lax or non-existent. Where money was collected many towns had acquired the right to retain the revenue for themselves, applying it to the upkeep of walls and to other public works. The only significant royal levy on the profits of trade was thus a separate impost on imports of wine procured in 1569 by Sir Henry Sidney. Farmed out from 1583, this brought in a significant sum, amounting to £1,866 out of a total revenue of £28,000 in 1614–15.

The concessions so long enjoyed by the Irish port towns reflected their standing as islands of English civility and loyalty in an otherwise alien land. After 1603 that role had lost much of its meaning. The Old English elites that dominated the main cities and towns were now less to be prized for their loyalty than suspected for their Catholicism. Robert Cecil, now earl of Salisbury and James I's chief minister, singled out customs as the area in which crown revenue in England could most readily be increased, so it is hardly surprising that the Irish urban communities soon came under similar pressure. In 1606 two speculators, one of them, Thomas Hibbots, a close associate of Chichester, acquired the exclusive right to export wheat, wool, hides, and other products, so that all other traders would have to pay them for export licences. The following year the Dublin administration began legal proceedings against Waterford and other towns claiming exemption from customs duties. The case came before one of the special assemblies of judges and law officers, English and Irish, that had become Davies's favoured method of settling controverted legal questions. The outcome was not entirely onesided. The judges confirmed the exemption from poundage of the Dublin, Waterford, and Drogheda freemen, as well as some minor exemptions. However, they also found that these and other towns had illegally retained revenues due to the crown. The prospect of arrears being exacted, combined with the threat of other sanctions, allowed the crown to resume control of local collection through its own officials. When the three towns continued to insist on the exemption of their freemen from poundage, letters patent under the great seal imposed a special duty of equivalent amount on all persons so exempt. By 1612 receipts, which in 1606 had been estimated at only £200 sterling, had risen to £1,500 sterling. The following year the crown farmed out the right to collect customs duties throughout Ireland to a consortium of English entrepreneurs, for a period of nine and a half years, at an annual rent of £6,000 sterling.[85]

[85] Victor Treadwell, 'The Establishment of the Farm of the Irish Customs 1603–13', *English Historical Review*, 93 (1978), 580–602.

The second major resource available to ministers seeking to increase royal revenue without recourse to parliament was the rights of the crown as a feudal lord, from whom all landed proprietors in theory held their estates as tenants in chief. The most burdensome of these feudal exactions was wardship. Minors succeeding to a property held by what had once been the military tenure of knight service became royal wards, committed to the care of guardians who would pay a substantial fine to the crown for the lucrative prospect of administering the estate, as well as having a hand in the disposal of a prime asset on the marriage market.[86] Later the heir would pay further substantial sums when he sued out his livery on coming of age, and when he married. In the early years of the new reign the management of this potentially lucrative royal perquisite remained a minor, and not very rigorously exploited, perk of the serving lord deputy. From 1616 the wardships of non-nobles became the responsibility of a commission, enlarged in 1617 and given greater powers and resources from 1619 onwards. Through its work revenue from wardships, which in 1614–15 had amounted to less than £300, rose to an average of £3,365 in the five years to 1622. The creation of a fully developed court of wards in 1623, with its jurisdiction extended a year later to include nobles as well as commoners, more than doubled average receipts, to around £7,200 per year.[87]

These reforms and innovations significantly strengthened the financial position of the Irish administration. In 1621 overall revenue stood at £47,000, as compared to £33,000 in 1617. The increase was mainly accounted for by the yield of the customs farm (£9,484 as compared to £1,616) and of wardships (£3,719 as compared to £855). But income still fell well short of a civil and military establishment that stood at over £71,000. In 1618 the English privy council had taken advantage of the improvement in revenue to convert the fluctuating annual subsidy from England into a fixed contribution of £20,000 sterling, which still represented well over a third of state spending. The partial success of these fiscal innovations, moreover, had political consequences. Even Protestant proprietors were likely to find the closer scrutiny of land titles and feudal obligations, the more rigorous collection of taxes, and the intrusions into local areas of the crown's law officers, an irritant. Those most affected, however, were the Catholic elite. The withdrawal of the exemptions previously granted to the port towns was a practical demonstration of the estrangement of the crown from its Old English subjects. The new regime of wardship too had a particular relevance to Catholics, since recusants were barred from becoming guardians, and even more because an heir suing out his livery was required to take the oath of supremacy. To hunt through the 1610s and 1620s for the beginnings of later conflicts would be to fall into the classic pit of teleological history. But the reordering of the state

[86] For knight service and other tenures, see above, n. 27.

[87] Victor Treadwell, 'The Irish Court of Wards under James I', *IHS* 12 (1960–1), 1–27; idem, *Buckingham and Ireland*, 223–4.

apparatus that took place in the reign of James I can nevertheless be seen as the first stage of a process that was increasingly to set the crown at odds with both its older and its newer Irish subjects.

'THEIR OWN PRIVATES ALTOGETHER THEIR STUDY'

In August 1633 Thomas Viscount Wentworth, just sworn in as lord deputy of Ireland, wrote to an English correspondent describing the New English establishment he had encountered. 'I find myself in the society of a strange people, their own privates altogether their study without any regard at all to the public.'[88] The comment reflected what was to remain Wentworth's consistent stance as a viceroy determined to uphold the claims of crown and state against all vested interests, old and new. But it also highlighted the apparent contradiction at the heart of the workings of the early modern state: the extent to which the growth of new and more elaborate institutional structures was achieved through a fusion of public and private interests. Practices such as the sale of public offices, the routine payments made for assistance or support at every level of the administrative system, or the open regard shown for networks of kinship and clientelism, can all be viewed, from a modern standpoint, as a failure to progress towards bureaucratic rationality. And, taken to extremes, they could indeed become an obstacle to the effective functioning of government. From another point of view, however, vertical ties of patronage and family connection were a substitute for more impersonal notions, not yet developed, of loyalty and obligation. Fees and other payments provided an alternative to a public payroll beyond the scope of any early modern taxation regime to finance. Vested interest created a growing class committed to upholding the existing political and administrative system. What was once dismissed as mere 'corruption' has now come to be recognized as in fact an essential part of the oil that kept the machinery of government working—if not in fact the engine that drove it.[89]

In the case of Ireland, the interaction of public and private ends was already an issue well before 1603. The Munster plantation had been a pioneering venture in harnessing private capital in the service of public policy. Later, in the 1590s, a loss of direction at the centre had allowed individual profiteering to rise to new levels. The resulting feeding frenzy, reflected in the legal chicanery of officials like Boyle, and the blatant self-aggrandizement of local military strongmen like Bingham, had been a major reason why the Gaelic lords of the north came to believe that they must go to any lengths to preserve their local autonomy. After 1603, however, total victory in the resulting war opened the way for a restructuring of Irish society more radical than anything previously attempted. 'Ireland', Fynes

[88] H. F. Kearney, *Strafford in Ireland 1633–41: A Study in Absolutism* (Manchester, 1959), 172.
[89] Linda Levy Peck, *Court Patronage and Corruption in Early Stuart England* (London, 1991).

Moryson wrote, 'was left as a pair of clear tables, wherein the state might write laws at pleasure'.[90] This happened, moreover, at just the same time that the tight-fisted caution of Elizabeth's reign gave way to a very different dispensation, as her indolent and free-spending successor allowed well placed courtiers to convert the business of government into a means of enriching themselves and others. Taken together these developments meant that the state whose tentacles were being extended across the newly accessible breadth of early Stuart Ireland was also, to a degree not previously seen, a machine for private profit.

The method of self-enrichment that had flourished most conspicuously in the last years of Elizabeth had been the hunting out of concealed lands. By the start of the new reign Salisbury had come to see the encouragement earlier given to this trade as a threat to political stability. In 1606 the king created a commission empowered to give new letters patent to any subjects who had held land under the crown since the reign of Henry VIII and now wished to obtain a more secure title. Security, however, came at a price. Those who took advantage of the new commission incurred substantial costs in fees and fines. In addition the process of scrutinizing and confirming title provided an opportunity for the state to uncover liability to crown rents, or to feudal obligations such as wardship, which might previously have been quietly evaded.[91] The uncertainty created over the previous twenty years by the state's indulgence of legalized piracy thus gave the crown another means of improving its income, at the expense of a large cross-section of the older landed class. Meanwhile the hunt for concealed lands, though no longer officially encouraged, continued at the level of private enterprise, with a further sixty grants being issued between 1603 and 1624.

Where the Commission for Defective Titles did prove attractive was to those new proprietors who had built their fortunes on precisely that scramble for concealed lands. The royal grants they had used so effectively rewarded discoverers only with leases for a period of up to twenty-one years. However, well placed members of the establishment, or those willing to purchase the assistance of officials, were now able to use the commission to exchange such leases for new letters patent, in which temporary tenure was converted into permanent possession. Most commonly the new titles were in fee simple and by common soccage, which meant that the holder neither paid rent to the crown nor incurred such burdensome feudal obligations as wardship. Prominent among those involved in this lucrative trade in grants and patents were Richard Boyle, Adam Loftus, Francis Annesley, and William Parsons. Annesley, created Lord Mountnorris in 1628, was a member of the Irish Council from 1616 and

[90] Graham Kew (ed.), *The Irish Sections of Fynes Moryson's Unpublished Itinerary* (Dublin, 1998), 61.

[91] The frequent claim that the Commissioners systematically altered tenures to more burdensome varieties seems, however, to be unfounded. See Mary O'Dowd, '"Irish Concealed Lands Papers" in the Hastings Manuscripts in the Huntington Library, San Marino, California', *Analecta Hibernica*, 31 (1984), 78–9.

vice treasurer from 1625. Parsons, surveyor general and master of the Court of Wards, rounded off his fortune by acquiring an estate of his own in the Wexford plantation, while his brother Sir Laurence was one of the chief beneficiaries of a plantation in Ely O'Carroll in what was now King's County. Loftus, a nephew of the archbishop of Dublin, was lord chancellor from 1619 and became first viscount Ely in 1622. Between 1629 and 1632 he and Boyle, now earl of Cork, were to govern as lords justices in the absence of a viceroy. By the 1620s the murky transactions of earlier decades, laundered through the Commission for Defective Titles, had thus provided the basis for the creation of what was in effect a new ruling elite.[92]

By this time, however, such Irish-based profiteers found themselves in competition with a new and very formidable predator. Chichester's long service as lord deputy had depended on the support, first of Salisbury and then of the Howard faction who succeeded him as the dominant interest at the English court. By 1616, however, power had passed into the hands of a new royal favourite, George Villiers, soon created earl, marquess, and eventually duke of Buckingham, a young Leicestershire gentleman of limited fortune but considerable political and administrative ability whose striking male beauty won him the slavish devotion of the ageing James I. The precise course of events is complicated by the circumstance that Buckingham initially allied himself with opponents of the blatant profiteering of the Howards. Hence Chichester's recall, and his replacement by Oliver St John, had the support of reformist elements within the English administration, although the king firmly vetoed any suggestion that the outgoing deputy should be subjected to personal censure. But St John, a former master of the ordnance and as such a senior but not particularly prominent member of the establishment, was also a relative by marriage of Buckingham and quickly emerged as his willing agent.[93] Soon afterwards another Buckingham client, Sir Francis Blundell, took over the key post of king's secretary for Irish business. Over the next few years Buckingham, through these and other agents, ruthlessly colonized all aspects of Irish public life. He himself acquired some plums, notably the farm of the Irish customs, which he took over in 1619 on terms good enough to allow him to leave the actual management to others while still receiving a pure rentier's income of £ 3,000 a year. In other cases his role was as broker, claiming a commission on grants or other favours obtained through his intervention. Meanwhile his allies, relatives, and dependants, including significant numbers

[92] T. O. Ranger, 'Richard Boyle and the Making of an Irish Fortune 1588–1641', *IHS* 10 (1957), 282–95. O'Dowd, however, emphasizes that not all New English grantees were treated as indulgently as Ranger claimed: ' "Concealed Lands Papers" ', 79.

[93] This seems to be the best way of reconciling the account in Treadwell, *Buckingham and Ireland*, ch. 1, with those of McCavitt (*Chichester*, ch. 12) and Vera L. Rutledge, 'Court-Castle Faction and the Irish Viceroyalty: The Appointment of Oliver St John as Lord Deputy of Ireland in 1616', *IHS* 26 (1989), 233–49, both of whom are inclined to take St John's reformist credentials at face value.

from St John's extended family, filled Irish offices at every level. Members of the existing Irish establishment had either to accept co-option into the Villiers connection, as Annesley, Loftus, and Parsons all chose to do, or find themselves excluded and possibly victimized. Even the devious and by now very powerful earl of Cork was first pressurized to pay heavily for a marriage alliance with the Villiers clan, and then, when he proved insufficiently compliant, obstructed and harassed in his affairs.[94]

One method of converting political influence or royal favour into profit, widely used in both England and Ireland, was through letters patent giving the holder exclusive control of some branch of trade, or some profitable administrative activity. Thus Blundell, in 1619, procured a patent authorizing Edward Wray, in return for a crown rent of £100 per year, to collect the fines from native Irish remaining on the lands of Ulster undertakers. The real beneficiary of the patent, estimated to have brought in well over £1,000 a year, was Buckingham. Wray's reward was £310 a year, and even this was paid, not as a share of Buckingham's profits, but as three pensions from royal funds. Other grants likewise reveal both the long reach of the Buckingham connection and its relentless thirst for profit. A restriction on the timber trade, introduced in 1612 to conserve supplies for the royal navy, became the basis for a patent giving the holder the sole right to license exports, issued in 1618 to Henry Mitton, but in fact covertly assigned by him, possibly under duress, to Buckingham. In 1619 Sir Thomas Roper, a distant Villiers relative, received a monopoly on the licensing of ale houses. When representatives of the Irish lords and gentry protested at this encroachment on what in England was a matter for local regulation, Roper surrendered his patent for an annuity of £1,000, a quarter of which, in a private arrangement, was to go to Buckingham's half brother. Later it was agreed that Roper could receive his annuity as part of the profits from a new patent to collect the crown's revenue from a revised licensing system.

A second area in which the Buckingham stranglehold on Irish affairs was clearly demonstrated was the dramatic and blatantly mercenary expansion of the Irish peerage. At the time of the accession of James I there had been twenty-five Irish peers. By 1616 he had created only three more: a nephew of Ormond's who became Viscount Butler, Chichester, who became Baron Chichester of Belfast, and Rory O'Donnell, unconvincingly transformed in the postwar settlement of Ulster into a British earl. Between 1616 and 1619, by contrast, James created fourteen Irish peers, and between 1620 and 1629 a further sixty-one. The explosion of honours was not entirely Buckingham's doing. The initial impulse, in fact, came from the contentious parliament of 1613–15, which had demonstrated the dangerously high proportion of recusants in the House of Lords. Other creations were a reasonable enough acknowledgement of the

[94] Unless otherwise stated, the material that follows is derived from Treadwell's exhaustive account of the Buckingham ascendancy.

enhanced status of the most successful planters, such as James Hamilton, who became Viscount Clandeboye in 1622, or Hugh Montgomery, who became Viscount Montgomery of Ards in the same year. Even where those ennobled owned no land in Ireland, as was the case with thirty or so of James I's creations, it has been argued that their elevation to an Irish peerage, by promoting interchange between the elites of three nations, furthered the aim of bringing the three Stuart kingdoms into a closer union.[95] Yet the aura of commerce hanging over the whole business remains inescapable. And much of the profit went to Buckingham. An account drawn up by Blundell for his master's information, covering just the five years 1618–22, listed a total of £24,750. This represented the price of nine peerages, eleven baronetcies, and four knighthoods, as well as Loftus's appointment as lord chancellor of Ireland and the inclusion in the Irish council of Sir Charles Coote, another local Villiers client whom St John had already advanced from the modest position of provost marshal to the vice-presidency of Connacht. Of this sum Buckingham himself had taken £13,100, while the rest had been paid to other members of the connection. Richard Boyle, for example, had paid £4,000 to Sir Edward Villiers for the earldom of Cork he received in 1620. As for the argument that these transactions served a wider purpose of integration, this was not a perception shared by contemporaries. On the contrary there were bitter disputes over precedence, where English lords found themselves outranked by men bearing technically superior, but in their eyes suspect, Irish titles. The newly created Irish lords, for their part, felt hard done by when they found themselves taxed as peers in both kingdoms, while at the same time still being required to attend compulsory military musters in England in the rank of commoners.

Customs farms, patents granting monopolies, and the sale of honours were all valuable assets. The best prospect for permanent gains, however, remained the acquisition of land. The quest for further plantations predated Buckingham's arrival in Ireland. It had the active support of Chichester, who remained convinced that the Ulster settlement had done nothing like justice to the claims of the servitors, and that the establishment elsewhere of colonies of planters and ex-soldiers remained the best way to safeguard and further the establishment of English law and government. The first major opportunity came in 1610, when Thomas Masterson, a long-established seneschal in north County Wexford who had become embroiled in a dispute with the local Kavanaghs, initiated a claim that the whole territory was in fact crown property. Government law officers quickly took over the management of the case. Vigorous legal opposition by local proprietors, linked to a wider campaign of opposition to government policy during and after the parliament of 1613, caused the king briefly to waver. By

[95] This is the uncharacteristically charitable verdict of Treadwell, *Buckingham and Ireland*, 112–14. For the other points made above see C. R. Mayes, 'The Early Stuarts and the Irish Peerage', *English Historical Review*, 73 (1958), 227–51.

1618, however, the plantation had been completed, with grants to eighteen New English undertakers and to seven servitors, all but one of whom was likewise New English. Four of the grantees were relatives of Chichester, while Chichester himself received land in the name of at least two proxies.[96]

The plantation of Wexford did not represent expropriation on the scale seen in Ulster. Instead it conformed to Chichester's preferred model, in which the claims of local occupiers were balanced against the aim of introducing a body of reliable settlers. The undertakers and servitors received a total of 31,000 acres, while the remaining 54,000 was reserved for existing proprietors. Among these about 150 of the most prominent among the native Irish received land in freehold. The main losers in the process were thus smaller occupiers, holding less than 100 acres, who were reduced to tenant status. But the overall proportion of land in north Wexford held by natives was nevertheless substantially reduced, from 60 per cent in 1600 to 36 per cent by 1620.[97] The legal basis of the process, moreover, remained distinctly questionable. The Kavanaghs had engaged in a series of surrender and regrant agreements going back to 1543, and there had been a further surrender as recently as 1609. The crown's case for overthrowing all such engagements rested on a purely strategic, and very temporary, act of submission by Art MacMurrough Kavanagh, in 1399, as part of which he had nominally surrendered his lands to Richard II. The king had then granted them to Sir John de Beaumont, from whom they had passed to Viscount Lovell, attainted for treason in the reign of Edward IV. This, of course, was a Yorkist monarch, on whose family's subsequent deposition the claims of the Tudors and Stuarts depended. But the crown had a second claim, in the act of 1494 by which the king had resumed the Irish lands of all non-resident English proprietors, which of course included any nominal possessions of the English-based Lovells.[98]

All this, along with the partial nature of the plantation, allowed Chichester to protest, and possibly even to believe, that no injustice was being done: 'the king has not a fairer title to any land in England or Ireland than to those into which those buggers have intruded'.[99] The truth was that to give credit to ancient grants, ignoring the moving frontiers and shifting alliances of the intervening centuries, was to favour opportunism at the expense of long possession. Hence it is not surprising that members of the Old English elite, aware that their own titles had roots in the same unstable past, were willing to join with the Kavanaghs and other native freeholders in challenging the plantation as a blatant injustice. Opposition, however, once again brought out the new capacity of the state for the arbitrary exercise of power. When the first jury to be impanelled, in 1611,

96 Henry Goff, 'Conquest of an Irish Barony: The Changing Pattern of Landownership in the Barony of Scarawalsh 1540–1640', in Kevin Whelan and William Nolan (eds.), *Wexford, History and Society* (Dublin, 1987), 122–49; McCavitt, *Chichester*, 162–7.

97 Goff, 'Scarawalsh', 135–8; *CSPI 1615–25*, 294.

98 *Carew MSS 1603–1623*, 251–2.

99 McCavitt, *Chichester*, 164.

refused to find title for the crown, its members were fined and imprisoned. Later St John and his council sought to present continuing opponents of the plantation as seditious troublemakers egged on by the Catholic clergy. These tactics paid off when some members of a deputation sent to London in 1620 as part of the continuing campaign for redress were set aside for transportation to Virginia.[100]

At the same time as he initiated the plantation of Wexford, Chichester began to explore the possibility of asserting crown claims in Longford and elsewhere. However, the protracted legal and political battle arising from that first venture delayed matters. Hence it was St John, and behind him Buckingham, who in 1619 initiated a further round of plantations. The most important, carried out during 1619–20, were in counties Longford and Leitrim, and in the territory of Ely O'Carroll, part of King's County, with lesser exercises in forced redistribution elsewhere in King's County, Queen's County, and Westmeath. In each case the method used, as earlier with Wexford, was a claim of crown title to the land concerned. By this time, however, the English privy council had become concerned at the unrest that might result from further plantations in Ireland. Hence Buckingham and his allies sought to present their proceedings as in effect a form of surrender and regrant, whereby holders of defective titles surrendered a part of their lands to the crown in exchange for secure titles to the rest.

What actually took place varied from county to county. In Longford the dominant family, the O'Farrells, had a long history of working through rather than against English law and political structures. They had successfully contested earlier plantation schemes in 1605 and 1611. But in 1619, faced with a claim of royal title to the whole territory, they appear to have bowed to the inevitable and negotiated a reasonably favourable settlement, whereby freeholders with more than 100 acres retained three quarters of their lands. The main branches of the O'Farrell family thus secured their position while the main losers, as in Wexford, were the smaller owner-occupiers. In Ely O'Carroll, the administration first undermined the position of the heir, John O'Carroll, by having him declared illegitimate, then secured his voluntary submission by allocating to him a total of more than 8,000 acres in the plantation that followed. In County Leitrim the O'Rourke lordship had passed to a minor, raised in England as a royal ward. In 1620, just as he came of age, he was detained in the Tower of London following his alleged involvement in a drunken brawl. These convenient circumstances permitted the architects of the plantation to deal more brutally than elsewhere with local opponents. When a lesser proprietor, Sir John MacCoghlan, organized a campaign of legal resistance, he and his associates were punished by losing a third rather than a quarter of their lands. Overall one-half of the county was thus declared available for distribution. Even then a later commission of enquiry

[100] *CSPI 1615–25*, 294–5, 306.

heard numerous complaints that native proprietors had received less land than they were entitled to, or land of poor quality, or in some cases nothing at all.[101]

The beneficiaries of the new round of plantations were a mixed group. Many of the lesser grantees were, as contemporaries complained, poor men, army officers and others who had either the connections or a record of service that made it convenient to pay them off at minimal expense to the crown, but none of the resources to enable them to become successful planters. More sizeable grants, on the other hand, went to English-based courtiers and office holders, and to members of the developing New English establishment within Ireland. Sir Laurence Parsons, attorney general in the Munster provincial administration, admiralty court judge, and brother of the surveyor general, acquired what became an estate of over 5,000 acres in King's County, where his descendants were to be earls of Rosse. Another major beneficiary of the Longford plantation, Sir Francis Aungier, master of the rolls, had taken the precaution of buying up land and an associated rent charge within the county. In return for surrendering these, he obtained a substantial regrant free of the obligations imposed on other planters. The price paid for this profitable subterfuge, however, was that he soon after quietly conferred the reversion of his mastership of the rolls on one of Buckingham's English clients. Meanwhile Buckingham himself acquired 6,500 acres in the heart of what had been O'Rourke's territory. The allocation was initially made to two compliant courtiers, then transferred to Buckingham's men of business, with the favourite himself accepting formal title only in 1627.

On paper the new round of plantations was a further stage in the long-term project of extending the regular administration of law and order, efficient exploitation of economic resources, and English language and culture beyond their existing frontiers into the Gaelic world. Grantees, unlike their counterparts in Ulster, were under no obligation to import British settlers. Instead tenants on the planted estates were to be required to adopt the hallmarks of British civility: they were to live in villages, build houses with chimneys and gardens, and enclose and hedge a proportion of their land. A commission of inquiry in 1622 reported that little effort had been made by the mainly absentee new proprietors to enforce these regulations. In this respect the plantations represented the clear triumph of private over public ends. Yet it would be wrong to conclude that they produced no results beyond the establishment of a predatory rentier class. If most grantees were either too poor or too rooted in the Dublin and London elites to do more than collect rent from native tenants, a minority established themselves more securely on their new estates, often buying up the holdings of less committed or less successful fellow planters. In Longford, for example, the Scottish Forbes

101 Raymond Gillespie, 'A Question of Survival: The O'Farrells and Longford in the Seventeenth Century', in Raymond Gillespie and Gerard Moran, *Longford: Essays in County History* (Dublin, 1991), 13–21; Treadwell, *Buckingham and Ireland*, chap 3, section 3; Brian MacCuarta, 'The Plantation of Leitrim 1620–41', *IHS* 32 (2001), 297–320.

family became resident proprietors and eventually earls of Granard in the Irish peerage—although it was not until 1670 that they disposed of their Scottish lands. In addition proprietors anxious to extract a profit from their new estates, whether absentee or not, found it necessary to import otherwise scarce technical skills or capital, through the introduction of English or Scottish tenants and craftsmen. Even in the absence of a formal colonization scheme, therefore, the midlands plantations further strengthened the British presence in Leinster. Rural settlement was most notable in Wexford, where the 1641 depositions reveal a scattering of English tenants on plantation estates. In Queen's and King's counties, Longford, and Leitrim, on the other hand, British deponents were mainly town dwellers, artisans attracted by new ventures such as the ironworks established by Coote and others.[102]

Buckingham's numerous profitable ventures in Ireland depended wholly on his political dominance in England. In 1621, however, a formidable challenger appeared. Lionel Cranfield, from 1622 first earl of Middlesex, was a former merchant who had risen as Buckingham's protégé but who now, as lord treasurer, embarked on a determined campaign to reform the royal finances. When opposition elements in the parliament of 1620–1 took up complaints of malpractice in Ireland, Cranfield supported the appointment of a commission of inquiry. Chaired by Sir William Jones, a former Irish judge now promoted to the English bench, its twenty-one members brought together a group of English MPs and other notables as well as the principal Irish office holders. This last group included both the outgoing lord deputy, Oliver St John, now Viscount Grandison, and his successor, Henry Cary, Viscount Falkland. Its work did not by any means represent a frontal assault on Buckingham's Irish empire. The private instructions accompanying the commission stressed that the aim was to reform procedures rather than to punish faults, and its members, aware of the favourite's continuing power at court, held back from inquiring too closely into anything connected to him. But their investigation, conducted between April and October 1622, nevertheless found much to complain of. In addition to commenting sharply on the failure of the Ulster undertakers to fulfil their obligations and dismissing the more recent southern plantations as a sham, they drew attention to a variety of abuses in the administration of justice and the handling of public funds.

The first response to the commissioners' report was an order to Falkland, on 19 January 1623, to pass no further grants of land. Over the next few months Middlesex pushed through a sweeping programme of reform. The subsidy from England was to end. Instead all expenses were to be met from Irish revenues, with army and central administration costs having first claim. Arrears owed by the army were cut by one-third, and arrears of pensions by one-half, the remainder

[102] For British settlement in Queen's County, see Canny, *Making Ireland British*, 372–84. For Leitrim see MacCuarta, 'The Plantation of Leitrim', 315–17.

to be paid only out of what was raised from existing debts to the crown. In May the crown created a standing commission, including four English judges and two officers of the English exchequer, to supervise all business relating to Ireland. The new regime continued for almost a year, seriously inhibiting the activities of the Buckingham connection. By May 1624, however, Middlesex was a broken man, impeached and disgraced after he had made the mistake of challenging Buckingham on the question of war with Spain. With his fall the regime of reduced expenditure, balanced accounts, and close supervision quickly came to a close. 'We say here', Falkland wrote from Dublin, 'that Michael and his angels hath overthrown the Dragon and his angels, and mightily rejoice that Lucifer is fallen, for during the time of his dominion all we here, who were friends to Michael, lived under a grievous oppression.'[103]

The triumphant restoration of the Villiers ascendancy did not have consequences only for Irish public finances. The new commissioners of Irish affairs had made clear that they regarded the reform of native Irish society as more important than further plantation schemes designed to benefit British proprietors. Meanwhile one member of the 1622 commission of inquiry had offered a more direct critique. Richard Hadsor, a Protestant from an Old English family, had served in England as an adviser on Irish affairs from the 1590s. What appears to have been his private report to Middlesex, presented on his return, lamented the exclusion from any share in government of 'the English Irish', who had for so long been the crown's chief supporters. Instead 'some sharks . . . of obscure fortunes, birth and quality' were permitted to monopolize office and enrich themselves. Hadsor, true to his Old English origins, was less favourable to the Gaelic Irish, complaining of large numbers of idle natives who should be put to work or transported to Virginia, and suggesting a modified form of plantation, in which chiefs might be required to let their land to British or English-Irish tenants, dispersing 'their rabble of Irish tenants and followers' to a more improving environment. But he also acknowledged that the existing plantations had been unjustly implemented, and argued that oppression at the hands of officials was the prime cause of Irish disaffection.[104]

With the destruction of Middlesex, all such voices of restraint became irrelevant. Buckingham's next venture was a plantation in Upper Ossory. An inquisition of 1621, disregarding a long history of bloodthirsty loyalty on the part of the MacGillpatricks, had found title for the crown. The basis of the finding was once again an ahistorical plunge into the records of centuries long past: in 1247, at the high point of the medieval colony, the lands concerned had passed by inheritance to the Mortimer earls of March, from whom they had subsequently

[103] Quoted in Treadwell, *Buckingham and Ireland*, 257–8.

[104] *Advertisements for Ireland*, ed. George O'Brien (Dublin, 1923). For Hadsor's authorship of this anonymous tract, and the link with the commission of 1622, see Victor Treadwell, 'Richard Hadsor and the Authorship of "Advertisements for Ireland" ', *IHS* 30 (1997), 305–36.

descended to the house of York, and thus to King Edward IV. The settlement, finalized in 1624–5, gave Buckingham a total of 11,000 acres, two-thirds of it classified as arable or pasture. The MacGillpatricks, fobbed off with 10,560 acres in place of the 25,000 or so they had previously held, resisted vigorously but to no avail. Meanwhile Buckingham and his associates had also begun to reconnoitre a much larger prize: a plantation of the province of Connacht, where the inadequacies of previous territorial settlements, in 1585 and 1616–18, seemed to hold out the prospect of rich pickings. A third project, in County Wicklow, took a more sinister form, with what appears to have been an attempt to dispose of leading members of the O'Byrne family by means of trumped up charges of treasonable conspiracy. The Connacht project was postponed when wartime pressures made it inexpedient to antagonize the powerful local interests that would be affected, while the assassination of Buckingham in August 1628 put a permanent end to the operations of his Irish connection. Falkland, under attack for a range of issues, including the O'Byrne scandal, was recalled a year later. By this time, however, a decade of blatantly predatory activity had left its mark on relations between the crown and a large section of what aspired to be its loyal subjects.

8

Religion and Nation

TRUE FAITH AND GOSPEL TRUTH

At an unknown date, probably in the 1580s, Slaney O'Brien, sister of the baron of Inchiquin, married Sir Turlough O'Brien. In doing so she became the wife of a leading native loyalist. Sir Turlough, a nephew of the second earl of Thomond, was a member of the provincial council for Connacht and MP for County Clare in the parliament of 1585–6. He was also a staunch Protestant. Here, however, husband and wife parted company. In 1591 Sir Turlough recalled indignantly how, a year before, Slaney 'stole from my said house into a wood four or five miles distant to meet [a] friar to participate of his idolatrous ministration and massmunging communion, refusing to associate with me the day before for the true communing of the supper of the lord'. This difference in religious commitment may or may not have contributed to the couple's divorce seven years later, in 1598. What is more significant, however, is Slaney's next choice of partner: she went on to marry Murrough O'Brien, Church of Ireland bishop of Killaloe. Her attachment to the rituals of her ancestors was clearly not incompatible with the double unorthodoxy of becoming wife to a heretic bishop. But then Murrough's ascent to the reformed episcopacy had itself been a dynastic matter: the second son of O'Brien of Arra, he had been sent to Oxford in 1570 specifically to be groomed for the bishopric, once his father made clear that he would tolerate no other appointee. It may well be that Slaney found him more tolerant in liturgical matters than her former husband had been. Certainly the censorious Sir Turlough, at a time when he had not yet lost his wife to Murrough, condemned the bishop both for his lack of interest in preaching the reformed faith and for the 'expert gaming, music and carousing' indulged in by him and his clergy.[1]

This brief glimpse of a well-born native woman is consistent with the general response of Gaelic Ireland to the first stages of the Reformation: a continuing preference for traditional liturgy and doctrine combined with a pragmatic

[1] For Slaney O'Brien, see the long document by Sir Turlough edited by Bernadette Cunningham, 'A View of Religious Affiliation and Practice in Thomond, 1591', *Archivium Hibernicum*, 48 (1994), 17, 24. For Murrough O'Brien see ibid. 16, and for his route to his bishopric R. D. Edwards, *Church and State in Tudor Ireland: A History of Penal Laws against Irish Catholics 1534–1603* (Dublin, 1935), 219.

acceptance of changes in institutional affiliation, encouraging a marked fluidity in formal religious allegiance. By the end of the sixteenth century, however, such fluidity was becoming more difficult to maintain. Changes taking place both in the Church of Ireland and in its Roman rival operated together to eliminate the scope for ambiguity, creating not just a society more clearly divided between Catholic and Protestant, but one in which religious lines of division coincided closely with those of ethnic origin and, increasingly, of power and wealth.

The earliest evidence of a hardening of previously blurred distinctions relates to developments among the Old English elite. The emergence in this group of a more distinctive Catholic identity can be explained in more than one way. Old English recusancy, thanks to the efforts of the Marian clergy and the support network provided by a close-knit and self-confident community, had from the start represented something more than mere survivalism.[2] But religious allegiances had also been reinforced by political pressures. Already in the late sixteenth century clashes with successive lords deputy, inside and outside parliament, as well as the experience of being shouldered aside by assertive New English newcomers whose main qualification for favour was their Protestantism, had between them sharpened a sense of Old English identity in which Catholicism was a central element. The unprecedented severity of the reprisals following the Baltinglass rebellion had further contributed to this identification, while also giving Old English Catholicism its first martyrs. After 1603 the coincidence between pressures for religious conformity and an assault on long-standing legal privileges and immunities was to become clearer still. The precise balance between reasons rooted in religious culture and those arising more from political pressures remains a matter for debate. The evidence for a transition towards a more assertive Catholic identity is, however, clear. By the end of the sixteenth century members of recusant families increasingly chose marriage partners from within their own religious circle, spurning alliances with both the minority of indigenous Protestants and the growing New English elite. There was also a change in educational preferences. Some sons of the Pale gentry and merchant oligarchy continued to travel to Oxford and less frequently Cambridge, along with the English Inns of Court, to complete their education. But a growing number now went instead to the universities of Catholic Europe. Thirdly, and most significant, there were the beginnings of a more systematic use of ecclesiastical assets under lay control, whether impropriate tithes or the revenue of the guilds, to support an alternative religious establishment. In 1597, for example, the guild of St Anne, which had appointed its last chantry priest to say masses for the souls of dead members in 1564, refurbished its chapel in St Audeon's parish, and later began to support six priests under the guise of 'singing men'.[3]

[2] See above, Ch.5.

[3] This account of an emerging Catholic identity is heavily indebted to the pioneering work of Colm Lennon. See *The Lords of Dublin in the Age of Reformation* (Dublin, 1989), 146–50, 157–63;

In Gaelic Ireland too religious and political conflict were interlinked. In the recurrent military conflicts of the late sixteenth century crown forces regularly destroyed religious houses and killed captured clergy. Thus Catholic sources recorded the mass execution of the prior and brethren of the Cistercian monasteries of Graiguenamanagh, County Kilkenny, in 1584 and Monasteranenagh, County Limerick in 1591, as well as of numerous other individuals, both secular and regular.[4] Yet these experiences seem not, at this stage at least, to have produced quite the same early hardening of denominational identity. Gaelic poets of the 1580s and 1590s were beginning to pay some attention to the remorseless extension of English state power and English language and culture. But religion does not figure, even at the end of the century, as a prominent cause of grievance.[5] The widespread mobilization that accompanied Tyrone's rebellion, equally, does not seem to have involved demonstrations of specifically anti-Protestant sentiment of the kind that were to be so horrifically evident fifty years later. Even among the clergy, allegiances remained blurred. An inquisition into the state of the church in County Monaghan in 1606 found the churches under the control of priests appointed by the Catholic bishops, 'but many of them, like other old priests of Queen Mary's time in England, ready to yield to conformity'. In Connacht in the same year a judge of assizes was reported to have administered the oath of supremacy to at least forty priests. In Derry the only bishop of the period to have made a serious effort to win over the native clergy, the short-lived Brutus Babington (1610–11), claimed to have converted three leading priests in his diocese. These had then prevailed successfully on 'the better half by odds' of their clerical colleagues to use the liturgy of the Church of England, with the assistance of the recently published Irish language version of the Book of Common Prayer.[6]

Over time, however, such flexibility in denominational allegiance was to become less common. As early as 1595 the Church of Ireland bishop of Cork, Cloyne, and Ross noted that many of the formerly conformist lower clergy of Irish birth 'forsake their benefices to become massing priests . . . by the persuasion of those seminaries [i.e. seminary educated priests] that come from beyond the

'The Chantries in the Irish Reformation: The Case of St Anne's Guild, Dublin, 1550–1630', in R. V. Comerford, Mary Cullen, J. R. Hill, and Colm Lennon (eds.), *Religion, Conflict and Coexistence in Ireland: Essays in Honour of Monsignor Patrick J. Corish* (Dublin, 1990), 6–25; 'The Rise of Recusancy among the Dublin Patricians', in W. J. Sheils and Diane Wood (eds.), *The Churches, Ireland and the Irish* (Oxford, 1989), 127–8.

4 Edwards, *Church and State*, 309–12. Two other mass killings, of 21 inmates of a Dominican house at Coleraine and of 32 members of the same order in Derry during the 1590s, are claimed but cannot be documented from contemporary sources. See Thomas Flynn, *The Irish Dominicans 1536–1641* (Dublin, 1993), 73–4.

5 Marc Caball, *Poets and Politics: Reaction and Continuity in Irish Poetry 1558–1625* (Cork, 1998), 77–81.

6 *The Works in Verse and Prose of Sir John Davies*, ed. A. B. Grossart (privately printed, 1869-76), iii. 138–9; *CSPI 1603–6*, 468; Alan Ford, *The Protestant Reformation in Ireland 1590–1641* (2nd edn.; Dublin 1997), 138–9; Babington to Salisbury, 20 January 1611 (*CSPI 1611–1614*, 4).

seas'. Others who remained loyal to their adopted faith found themselves isolated in their community, and even in their family. In 1614 the wife and children of Roland Lynch, once one of the brightest stars of the Connacht Reformation, were reported to be all Catholics. Sir Turlough O'Brien of Arra, who died in 1602, continued on his deathbed to insist that he was a Protestant, 'yet in his weakness languishing, his nearest friends and kinsfolk (being recusant papists) would not suffer any Protestant to come to him'. After his death they buried him 'in a superstitious island by the Shannon', dressed in a friar's habit, and with an alleged 100 to 120 priests and friars in attendance.[7] At this point his namesake, the abandoned husband of Slaney O'Brien, may well have come to feel that he had had a narrow escape.

This drawing of clearer lines of religious division took place against a wider European background. By the second half of the sixteenth century what was now the Roman Catholic church had begun to assume the shape it was to retain for the next two centuries or more. In response to the Protestant challenge the council of bishops and theologians that met in three sessions at Trent between 1545 and 1563 produced both a comprehensive restatement of religious doctrine and a new model of how popular belief and practice was to be structured and supervised. In place of the rich profusion that characterized late medieval religious culture, with its multiple organizations and overlapping jurisdictions, there was to be a uniform territorial system of parish and diocese, within which a theologically trained clergy, supervised by their bishops, would instruct the faithful and regulate their devotional life. The extension of these new structures to Ireland's part of the Atlantic periphery was a gradual process. The bishops of Achonry, Raphoe, and Ross, all Gaelic Irish, attended the third session of the Council of Trent, in 1562, and the decrees of the council were formally published by synods of the province of Tuam in 1566 and Armagh in 1568. In 1560 the pope dispatched David Wolfe, a Limerick-born Jesuit, to Ireland, charged with supervising the work of the clergy there and reporting on suitable candidates for appointment as bishops. In 1564 a papal bull authorized Wolfe and the newly appointed archbishop of Armagh, Richard Creagh, to use ecclesiastical funds to create schools and even a university. In the event an integrated educational system on Counter-Reformation lines was beyond what could be achieved in Elizabeth's Ireland. But the growing numbers of Irish students that were able to achieve entry to colleges in continental Europe over the decades that followed testify to the existence of a less ambitious but nevertheless essential level of educational provision, in the form of a network of grammar schools run by Catholic teachers.

Progress towards a more fully developed Irish mission on Tridentine lines had to wait on developments in European politics. The delay came, first, from Rome's hopes that Elizabeth might be won back to Catholicism, then by its commitment

[7] Ford, *Protestant Reformation*, 39, 45. For Sir Turlough, Raymond Gillespie, 'Catholic Religious Practice and Payments in Seventeenth-Century Ireland', *Archivium Hibernicum*, 47 (1993), 7–8.

to securing her overthrow by some combination of domestic treason and foreign invasion. By the 1590s, however, as the earl of Tyrone discovered to his cost, Rome no longer saw military action as the way to reclaim Ireland for the true faith. Instead there began the first steps towards a more coordinated missionary effort. The establishment in 1596 of a new Jesuit mission to Ireland, along with the arrival during the same decade of the first cohort of seminary-trained priests, is frequently taken as marking the start of the Irish Counter-Reformation. By this time, however, clear-cut confessional identities had already begun to take shape. Religious polarization, in other words, was a product of ethnic and political conflicts within Ireland, rather than of the importation to there of the competing religious ideologies of continental Europe. For that reason the Irish Counter-Reformation, as it got under way, was to be concerned less with combating the temptations of heresy than with reshaping indigenous religious traditions to conform to the new model laid down at Trent.

The first step was the establishment of a territorial framework of diocese and parish. Intelligence received by the government in 1606 listed fourteen Catholic bishops, of whom seven lived abroad and seven were in Ireland—four in Ulster, two in Munster, and one a prisoner in Dublin Castle.[8] In the years that followed, the extension of state power into more remote areas, and in particular the plantation of Ulster, sharply reduced the scope for a bishop to operate undetected. By 1618 there were no bishops resident in the island. The papacy, however, had partly filled the gap by appointing vicars apostolic to administer dioceses, commencing with three appointments in the 1590s. From 1618, encouraged by the absence over several years of any sustained attempt at religious repression, Rome resumed the appointment of bishops, making clear as it did so that these were now expected to reside in Ireland. By around 1630, there were seventeen bishops and archbishops, all resident, and thirteen vicars apostolic; each Irish diocese, and all four of the ecclesiastical provinces, was now in the charge of a clearly defined ecclesiastical superior. Meanwhile the legal foundations for a new system of diocesan and provincial administration were laid down in a series of seventeen provincial and three diocesan synods held between 1606 and 1640, at which bishops and clergy enacted formal statutes covering every aspect of ecclesiastical administration and religious life.[9]

In developing this new ecclesiastical framework, the reconstructed hierarchy could draw on a growing network of seminaries devoted to the training of priests for the Irish mission. The young Irishmen who in the late sixteenth century travelled in increasing numbers to continental Europe for their higher education had initially attended established universities, or the new colleges created to cater for English Catholic students, such as Douai, founded in 1568. In 1590, however, Irish Jesuits working with Portuguese sympathizers created a college

[8] *The Works in Verse and Prose of Sir John Davies*, iii. 196–8.

[9] Alison Forrestal, *Catholic Synods in Ireland 1600–1690* (Dublin, 1998), 35, 195.

specifically for Irish students at Lisbon. The Jesuit Thomas White created a second college, at Salamanca, in 1592, while an Irish college at Douai opened, again with Spanish support, in 1594. By 1611 there was a total of twelve Irish colleges in Spain, France, and the Netherlands. In addition to providing a stream of trained secular clergy, the new foundations permitted the religious orders, all but wiped out during the state's onslaught on formerly inaccessible regions during the war against Tyrone, to rebuild their Irish networks. By 1617 there were some 120 Franciscan friars in Ireland, of whom 33 had been judged fit to engage in preaching, as well as 40 students at Louvain, where the order had established a college in 1607. The Dominicans, whose last house, in a remote part of County Mayo, had closed in 1608, relaunched their mission from 1614. By 1626 there were twelve houses with 110 residents, of whom 51 were priests, as well as a further 32 priests and 33 students at colleges in Spain, Portugal, the Netherlands, France, and Italy. The total number of Catholic priests in Ireland remains elusive. Eugene MacMahon, archbishop of Dublin, reported to Rome in 1623 that there were 800 secular clergy and around 300 regulars, including 200 Franciscans, 40 Jesuits, and over 20 Dominicans. The figure for Dominicans, however, is only one-third of that revealed in the order's own records, suggesting that both the overall number and the proportion of regulars to seculars may be seriously understated.[10] Yet even a figure of 1,100 seculars and regulars would imply a ratio of better than one priest to every 900 people, a substantially higher figure than the Irish Catholic church was to achieve even in its late nineteenth-century heyday.[11]

If the number of priests available was not a major problem, their organization within the new territorial framework of parish and diocese was. The pattern established in the late Elizabethan period, whereby recusant merchants and gentry supported Catholic priests in a particular locality, often making use of their control of impropriated tithes or other resources, continued into the first half of the seventeenth century. Clergy in this position, receiving their support directly from a lay patron, had little incentive to allow a bishop or vicar apostolic to direct where or how they discharged their pastoral mission. The revival of the religious orders created further problems, as bishops insisted on their right to control all pastoral activities within their dioceses, while the regulars sought to preserve their autonomy under their own superiors. Abstract issues of jurisdiction had a financial edge, since seculars and regulars competed for the limited offerings available from the laity. The reports of different bishops suggest that by the 1630s

[10] Canice Mooney, 'The Golden Age of the Irish Franciscans 1615–50', in Sylvester O'Brien (ed.), *Measgra i gCuimhne Mhichíl Uí Chléirigh* (Dublin, 1944), 21–33; Flynn, *Irish Dominicans*, 158–61. For MacMahon's much quoted estimate see P. J. Corish, *The Catholic Community in the Seventeenth and Eighteenth Centuries* (Dublin, 1981), 26; Flynn, *Irish Dominicans*, 149–50.

[11] This is to take a total population of somewhere over a million in 1600 as still overwhelmingly Catholic. In 1871 there was a parish priest or curate for every 1,560 Catholics in Ireland: see S. J. Connolly, *Priests and People in Pre-Famine Ireland 1780–1845* (2nd edn.; Dublin, 2001), 57.

they had made significant progress in incoporating their clergy into a parochial system. But the establishment of a fully developed territorial framework on Tridentine lines, with each pastor assigned a clearly defined area, and directly responsible to a bishop for his care of the souls it contained, was both gradual and conflict-ridden.[12]

In other respects too the imposition of the new standards on the lower clergy was no easy task. A minority had gone through the rigorous theological and moral training provided in the continental seminaries: a speculative estimate relating to the clergy enumerated in 1623 puts the proportion at somewhere under 30 per cent of the seculars and somewhere over that proportion of the regulars.[13] The great majority, in other words, had had their training entirely within Ireland, most of them probably by apprenticeship to a serving priest. They had now to be brought into conformity with standards developed in a very different environment. This included what would, in some regions at least, have been the novel requirement that priests should not marry. Nor was this the only respect in which the conduct of a section of the clergy fell significantly short of the Tridentine ideal. In 1631 the bishop of Waterford offered a scathing depiction:

> most of our clergy are idle, contenting themselves to say mass in the morning, and until midnight to continue either playing or drinking or vagabonding; and as most of them are unlearned, they make a trade of being ecclesiasticals, thereby to live idle, sit among the best, go well clad, and if I would say it, swagger. . . . and alas very few spend one hour in a twelvemonth to teach the Christian doctrine, or instruct young children.

The decrees of a synod held at Drogheda in 1614 to lay down regulations for the province of Armagh included a lengthy section on the problem of clerical drunkenness, with a specific warning, backed up by the threat of suspension, that priests must not join in the common practice of challenging others to drinking competitions.[14]

Where the laity were concerned, the requirements of the new Tridentine discipline were likewise clear, in theory at least.[15] At its core was a transition from the collective devotional culture of late medieval Europe to a new emphasis

[12] The fullest account is Corish, *Catholic Community*, 27–9. [13] Ibid. 26.

[14] Patrick Comerford to Luke Wadding, 30 October 1631 (*Wadding Papers 1614–38*, ed. Brendan Jennings (Dublin, 1953), 609); Oliver Rafferty, *Catholicism in Ulster 1603–1983* (Dublin, 1984), 15.

[15] All subsequent work in this area has been strongly influenced by a pioneering essay by John Bossy: 'The Counter-Reformation and the People of Catholic Ireland', in T. D. Williams (ed.), *Historical Studies*, viii (Dublin, 1971), 155–70. This applies to Ireland ideas developed in Bossy's 'The Counter-Reformation and the People of Catholic Europe', *Past & Present*, 47 (1970), 51–70. Corish, *Catholic Community*, ch. 2, follows Bossy closely, but with much extra material. For more recent accounts see Tadhg Ó hAnnracháin, *Catholic Reformation in Ireland: The Mission of Rinuccini 1645–1649* (Oxford, 2002), ch. 2; Forrestal, *Catholic Synods*, chs. 1–3. Samantha Meigs, *The Reformations in Ireland: Tradition and Confessionalism 1400–1690* (Dublin, 1997), ch. 8, argues that there was less change, and more continuity, than Bossy and others suggest.

on personal faith and private devotion. The faithful were to attend Sunday mass regularly, and confess and receive communion at least once a year. The rites of passage—baptism, confirmation, marriage, and the last sacraments—were to be approached as moments in an individual's spiritual journey, rather than as occasions for reaffirming or creating social bonds. All this, once again, implied a sharp conflict with existing religious culture. Ecclesiastical legislation reveals a particular concern with wakes, where the passage of the recently dead was marked by feasting, drinking and ritual games, all with the aim of reasserting bonds of kinship and community and perhaps of placating the spirit of the deceased.[16] The explicitly sexual nature of some of the games played was another challenge to the new moral discipline. Marriage was a further area of difficulty. Communities for whom weddings were a means of creating or strengthening social bonds were not easily persuaded that the consent of two individuals given before witnesses was not adequate unless solemnized by the parish priest of one of the parties, that a close existing blood relationship could be an obstacle to union, or that a marriage contract remained binding even when the family or other alliances it had been created to secure had ceased to exist. As elsewhere in Europe, there was also a new concern to regulate devotional practices ancillary to the church's official liturgy. The Tridentine church reaffirmed the validity of a range of practices—the veneration of shrines and relics, acts of devotion to saints, and ritualized supplication for divine protection or assistance—denounced by Protestant reformers as superstitious accretions. But it also insisted that these must be purged of anything suggestive of the manipulation of the supernatural for human purposes. In Ireland the main focus of such concern was the veneration of holy wells, which were frequently credited with the power of healing or bestowing protection, and which on major feast days became the site of large gatherings that mixed acts of devotion with boisterous feasting and celebration.

Where orthodox religious practice was concerned, the most conspicuous clash of cultures related to the sacrament of penance. The decrees governing the province of Dublin enacted in 1614 complained that the principles were clear enough, but that 'with the backwardness of the people and the ignorance of some priests we have found it practically impossible to get them into people's heads'. The problem appears to have been that laity and clergy alike tended to interpret the whole business in terms of the procedures of negotiation and composition that lay at the heart of the Gaelic legal system. Penance, often in the form of a money payment to the clergy, became a compensation for the wrong done

[16] The nature of Irish wake games pushes even the most empirically-minded historian in the direction of playing the amateur anthropologist. For a discussion drawing on eighteenth- and nineteenth-century evidence see Connolly, *Priests and People*, 152–72. See also Gearóid Ó Crualaoich, 'The "Merry Wake"', in J. S. Donnelly and Kerby Miller (eds.), *Irish Popular Culture 1650–1850* (Dublin, 1998), 173–200. The classic folklorist's study, which also reprints the relevant ecclesiastical legislation from the early seventeenth century onwards, is Seán Ó Súilleabháin, *Irish Wake Amusements* (Cork, 1967).

rather than the overt expression of an acknowledgement of sin and a purpose of amendment. In other cases, the statutes added, indulgences were used both as an alternative to confession and as a licence to sin.[17]

Here, as elsewhere, what was required was not just a change in behaviour, but at least a basic grasp of quite complex theological propositions. This in turn implied provision for systematic religious instruction. The Drogheda decrees of 1614 distinguished between those qualified to preach and those whose role was only to teach the catechism, an approved summary of doctrine set out in question and answer form and designed to be learned by rote. Between the 1560s and the 1590s at least three Irish clergymen, including Richard Creagh, archbishop of Armagh, and Florence Conry, later archbishop of Tuam, compiled Irish-language catechisms, but none of these texts found its way into print. The first catechism in Irish, by Bonaventure O'Hussey, appeared only in 1611, produced with the help of the Irish Franciscans at Louvain, who had procured a specially cut Irish typeface. This, however, was intended for the instruction of the growing body of Irish soldiers serving in the Spanish army in the Low Countries, rather than for the Irish mission.[18] The ecclesiastical decrees of 1614 did not mention it, instead referring priests to standard Latin compilations of doctrine. Over the next few decades the Louvain Franciscans continued to publish devotional and theological works in Irish. Much of their output, however, was aimed at an audience assumed already to possess a significant level of theological knowledge.[19] The next Irish text aimed firmly at a popular audience, another catechism by Theobald Stapleton, did not appear until 1639. His preface came remarkably close to supporting the image of popular Catholicism propagated by the Protestant reformers, complaining of the sad spectacle of an Irish laity able to speak only their own language and so reduced to reciting their prayers 'in corrupt and unbecoming Latin speech, not knowing what they are saying'.[20]

If the religious instruction of the poor seems often to have been rudimentary, the Catholic elite were rather better provided for. The concern with advanced schooling evident in the premature commission to Wolfe and Creagh in 1564 remained. In the late 1620s, both the Franciscans and the Dominicans responded to an apparently improving political climate by setting up colleges that would

[17] Bossy, 'Counter-Reformation and Catholic Ireland', 166–7.

[18] Grainne Henry, *The Irish Military Community in Spanish Flanders 1586–1621* (Dublin, 1992), 102.

[19] See in particular Bernadette Cunningham, 'Geoffrey Keating's Eochair Sgiath An Aifrinn and the Catholic Reformation in Ireland', in Shiels and Wood, *The Churches, Ireland and the Irish*, 138–9.

[20] Quoted in J. T. Leerssen, *Mere Irish and Fíor-Ghael* (Cork, 1996), 261. For a systematic review of catechisms, both Protestant and Catholic, see Ian Green, '"The Necessary Knowledge of the Principles of Religion": Catechisms and Catechizing in Ireland *c.* 1560–1800', in Alan Ford, J. I. McGuire, and K. Milne (eds.), *As by Law Established: The Church of Ireland since the Reformation* (Dublin, 1995), 68–88.

provide teaching in philosophy, theology, and the liberal arts.[21] Their boldness quickly produced a clampdown by the authorities. But the biographies of the bishops appointed after 1618 suggest that urban dwellers had fairly easy access to a Catholic grammar school education, while those in the countryside, or at least the better-off among them, could hope to receive individual instruction from tutors or clergy.[22] Educated Catholics were also sustained by a growing religious literature produced by presses on the Continent. Of particular importance here were works of history and hagiography. Peter Lombard's *De Regno Hiberniae*, available in print from 1632, had already linked Irish resistance to the Reformation to the island's longer history as a stronghold of Christianity. Later works, notably the *Analecta Sacra* of David Rothe, bishop of Ossory, published at Cologne in 1616–19, and the *Florilegium Insulæ Sanctorum* (1624) of Thomas Messingham, rector of the Irish College at Paris, drew the same connection between distant and recent history. They also contributed to a steadily expanding list of Irish martyrs for the faith, retrospectively expanded to include not just undoubted victims of religious persecution such as Bishop O'Devany of Down and Connor, hanged in 1612, but participants in the Desmond and Baltinglass revolts. Tales of saints and martyrs thus provided the intellectual and emotional underpinnings for the Irish Catholic identity that had taken shape from the end of the sixteenth century.[23]

By the late 1630s, then, Catholic Ireland appears to have had the essentials of a diocesan and parochial system, within which a clergy containing a growing proportion of seminary-trained priests worked under the direction of resident bishops committed to enforcing the new discipline of the Counter-Reformation. The impact of these new structures on the character of popular religion is difficult to gauge with precision. The reports to Rome of different Irish bishops have been read as indicating a reasonable degree of satisfaction with the progress being made in what was now the all-important area of preaching and catechesis.[24] But conditions inevitably varied from place to place. In Dublin Sir William Brereton's account in 1633 of a recently confiscated Jesuit chapel indicates a creditable attempt to import the standards of baroque Catholicism:

> The pulpit in this church was richly adorned with pictures, and so was the high altar, which was advanced with steps, and railed out like cathedrals; upon either side thereof was there erected places for confession: no fastened seats were in the middle or body

[21] Mooney, 'Golden Age of the Irish Franciscans', 24–5; Flynn, *Irish Dominicans*, 151–4.

[22] Donald Cregan, 'The Social and Cultural Background of a Counter-Reformation Episcopate 1618–60', in Art Cosgrove and Donal Macartney (eds.), *Studies in Irish History* (Dublin, 1979), 105–6.

[23] Colm Lennon, 'Taking Sides: The Emergence of Irish Catholic Ideology', in Vincent Carey and Ute Lotz-Heumann (eds.), *Taking Sides? Colonial and Confessional Mentalités in Early Modern Ireland* (Dublin, 2003), 78–93.

[24] Corish, *Catholic Community*, 37.

hereof, nor was there any chancel; but that it might be more capacious, there was a gallery erected on both sides, and at the lower end.[25]

Elsewhere, by contrast, mass had to be said in the crude cabins referred to by Protestant observers as 'mass houses', in private residences, or even in the open air. How frequently the laity attended mass, in any of these venues, remains impossible to say, although evidence of a pattern of distinctly patchy church attendance in the eighteenth and early nineteenth centuries might be read as indicating that the Irish Counter-Reformation never in fact succeeded in making regular Sunday attendance part of the religious practice of a large section of the population. Later evidence likewise makes clear that the holy well and the wake, with their mixture of orthodox and unorthodox observance, their carnivalesque jollity and frequent sexual licence, remained a prominent part of popular culture.[26]

Attempts to assess the progress of Catholic reform are further complicated by continued divisions, affecting both clergy and laity, between Old English and Gaelic Irish Catholics. These were in part political. The many Gaelic Irish who had accepted Tyrone's revolt as a Catholic crusade resented the loyalism or passivity that had been displayed by the majority of the Old English. After 1603 the split continued between those, mainly Gaelic Irish, who believed that the future of Catholic Ireland was best secured by military action against a heretic ruler, and those, mainly Old English, who hoped instead for some form of accommodation with the crown. The conflict of allegiances was reinforced by competition for patronage and resources, as the growing body of Gaelic exiles challenged Old English dominance both in the continental colleges and in the Irish component of the Spanish army. Ethnic divisions also inflamed the conflict between secular and regular clergy. The mainly Old English Jesuits and Capuchins cooperated harmoniously with the bishops and secular clergy, whereas the mainly Gaelic Franciscans repeatedly clashed with them on issues of ecclesiastical jurisdiction. To all this was added the long-standing belief of the Old English in their own cultural superiority. The comments of David Rothe, bishop of Ossory, suggest that he interpreted the imposition across the whole island of the new Tridentine discipline in terms of the long-standing Old English preoccupation with the promotion of civility over Gaelic barbarism. The purpose of religion, he wrote in his *Analecta*, was to 'eliminate barbarous customs, abolish bestial rites and convert the detestable intercourse of savages into polite manners and a care for maintaining the commonwealth'. The remarks of John Roche, bishop of the south-eastern diocese of Ferns and himself the son of a New Ross lawyer, on the Gaelic Irish recently appointed to sees in Ulster and Connacht, are less hostile, but condescending: 'though simple

[25] William Brereton, *Travels in Holland, the United Provinces, England, Scotland and Ireland*, ed. Edward Hawkins (London, 1844), 141–2.
[26] Connolly, *Priests and People*, chs. 3, 4.

and inexperienced, they are good men, the best indeed that these provinces can offer.'[27]

Evidence of this kind has led some historians to argue that the Irish Counter-Reformation proceeded along lines determined largely by ethnicity. The Old English, led by a mainly secular clergy, responded willingly to the discipline of the post-Tridentine church, while in Gaelic Ireland, the religious orders, particularly the Franciscans, continued to minister to a fervent but unstructured popular piety of the traditional kind.[28] On closer examination, the model of two separate religious cultures becomes harder to sustain. Traditional religious practices were not confined to the Gaelic regions: holy wells and other shrines, for example, continued to flourish in and around the city of Dublin. Although the larger religious orders were dominated by Gaelic clergy, equally, their European-wide organization meant that their members were in fact more likely than the secular clergy to have been trained in continental seminaries. The theological writings of the Louvain Franciscans make clear that the Gaelic intelligentsia were in fact very much alive to the concepts and concerns of continental Catholicism. Nor were the efforts of this group confined to continental academies. Of the new generation of bishops appointed after 1618 with the task of furthering the restructuring of Irish Catholicism along Tridentine lines, a small majority, 19 out of 37, were in fact Gaelic rather than Old English in origin.[29] Recent work on a sample of these, notably Malachy O'Queely, archbishop of Tuam from 1630, makes clear that they were fully as active, in organizing synods, supervising and regulating the parish clergy, and promoting new standards of catechesis and pastoral service, as their Old English counterparts. A member of the papal mission that landed in a largely Gaelic region of County Kerry in 1645 reported his astonishment that 'among mountains and barren places', and in a population so desperately poor, 'there was not a man or woman or any little boy who could not recite the lord's prayer, the hail mary, and the precepts of the holy church'.[30] The progress of religious change was undoubtedly uneven. But it would be unwise to try to force the variations that resulted into a neat pattern of ethnic division.

At the same time that the Catholic church was assuming a new shape, the Church of Ireland was also changing its character. In the last decade of Elizabeth's reign it was still served primarily by native-born bishops and clergy. Some, like Roland Lynch and Nehemiah Donnellan, were committed converts to the reformed faith and, initially at least, zealous evangelists. There were others whose

[27] Rothe's frequently quoted remarks were first drawn attention to by Aidan Clarke in *NHI*, iii. 225. For Roche see Patrick Corish, 'An Irish Counter-Reformation Bishop: John Roche', *Irish Theological Quarterly*, 25 (1958), 114.

[28] The argument was first formulated by Aidan Clarke, 'Colonial Identity in Early Seventeenth-Century Ireland', in T. W. Moody (ed.), *Nationality and the Pursuit of National Independence* (Belfast, 1978), 66–71; cf. NHI, iii. 225–7. It is most fully developed in Brendan Fitzpatrick, *Seventeenth-Century Ireland: The War of Religions* (Dublin, 1998), 177–8.

[29] Cregan, 'Counter-Reformation Episcopate', 102.

[30] Ó hAnnracháin, *Catholic Reformation in Ireland*, 63. For O'Queely see ibid. 59–62.

real commitment to the new religious order was more open to question. Thus Sir Turlough O'Brien alleged in 1591 that William Laly, archbishop of Tuam, was head of a wholly Catholic household, and that one of his sons had become a Spanish subject.[31] In the same year there were claims that Miler Magrath, the former Franciscan friar and papal bishop of Down and Connor who had been archbishop of Cashel since 1570, had sheltered Catholic bishops in his house and engaged in treasonable correspondence with James Fitzmaurice Fitzgerald and the earl of Desmond. He had also allegedly been heard to proclaim that 'if there had been an alteration of the world he should get more at the pope's hand than most men as, forsaking the world, lived miserably for his sake'. Many of the lower clergy, likewise, were in many cases no more than nominal conformists, whom lack of supervision, physical remoteness, or simply the absence of an alternative incumbent permitted to maintain much of the traditional ritual. In 1606 Sir John Davies, relatively recently arrived from England, was shocked to find few churches without an incumbent, 'but the most part of them are full of the most miserable idols, so that we cannot think or speak of them but with grief or shame'.[32]

The charges against Archbishop Magrath remained unproven and his services during the war against Tyrone earned him the support of both William Cecil and Sir George Carew. On his performance as a churchman, however, there was less room for doubt. A commission of inquiry in 1607 uncovered what the archbishop of Dublin described as abuses so enormous as to give credence to the view that Protestants had no religion. A high proportion of livings—the lord deputy put the figure at about seventy—were in the hands of Magrath or members of his family, either directly or through an intermediary. In one case the archbishop's son had to supply the nominal incumbent of a benefice in his possession with a cloak, so that he could appear before the commissioners. Another clergyman, marginally more fortunate, admitted promising a different son two-thirds of the revenues of his vicarage in order to be appointed. The cathedral was in decay, and there were not more than six churches in the whole diocese in repair. Where cures were served by a clergyman these were unlearned, 'fitter to keep hogs than serve in the church'. In fact the commissioners did not find a single minister in the whole diocese whom they regarded as qualified to preach. The commission's report led to Magrath being required to surrender the diocese of Waterford and Lismore, which he had held since 1592. In compensation, however, he was granted the Connacht dioceses of Killala and Achonry, where he found livings for various clergy whom the commissioners had just ejected from Cashel and Emly. By 1610 he was reported to reside mainly on his family's lands in Ulster. Chichester, two years later, warned that he was best left alone, because

31 Cunningham, 'A View of Religious Affiliation', 19.

32 Lawrence Marron (ed.), 'Documents from the State Papers Concerning Miler McGrath', *Archivium Hibernicum*, 21 (1958), 113, 122–3; *Works in Verse and Prose of Sir John Davies*, iii. 196.

he was 'a powerful man among the Irish in Ulster and able to do much hurt by underground practices'. Accordingly he retained his archbishopric until his death, at an age apparently close to 100, in 1622.[33]

Magrath's personal and family influence permitted his survival as a bishop of the Jacobean church, but it was as an increasingly conspicuous archaism. Already in the early 1590s the Court of Faculties, commissioned by Archbishop Loftus to identify and remove unqualified, non-resident, and crypto-Catholic ministers, recorded 114 sentences of deprivation. In the two or three decades that followed, the pace of change picked up rapidly. Comparison of surviving records for two regal visitations, in 1615 and in 1633–4, suggests that across that period the number of clergy had risen by almost 30 per cent. In 1615, morever, only just over 30 per cent of resident ministers were graduates, who could be trusted to expound the complex theology of Protestantism in their own sermons. The remainder were reading ministers, considered competent only to read the prescribed service each Sunday. By 1633–4, the proportion of graduate preaching ministers had risen to over half.

The introduction of a properly learned clergy had been a central concern of Archbishop Loftus from the 1570s. Initially he had relied on English and Scottish graduates. By the late sixteenth century, however, the realization that Irish recusants, who had previously travelled to England for their university studies, were now increasingly going instead to Counter-Reformation Europe gave a new urgency to the long-standing debate on the creation of an Irish university. The way was smoothed by abandoning the earlier, divisive proposal to suppress St Patrick's cathedral. Instead the corporation of Dublin, recusant-dominated but anxious to demonstrate its loyalty, donated the dissolved Augustinian monastery of All Hallows to serve as a site, along with substantial funding. The new College of the Holy and Undivided Trinity received its charter in 1592. The Ulster plantation scheme helped to secure the instititution's finances, with grants of land totalling 12,400 acres in Armagh, Donegal, and Fermanagh. Student numbers rose from around 70 in the early 1600s to 100 or so by 1641. By the 1630s graduates of the college supplied around half of the clergy serving in the Pale dioceses of Meath, Kildare, and Dublin. This, however, was as much as a single college producing perhaps a dozen graduates a year, of whom about half went into the ministry, could be expected to provide. In other Irish dioceses the new graduate clergy were overwhelmingly products of English and Scottish universities. Even Trinity, moreover, only partially fulfilled its mission to produce a local educational elite. The proportion of students drawn from either the Gaelic Irish or English Irish has been estimated at just over one-third in 1605, falling to only 15 per cent by the eve of the civil wars. The remainder of its products were recruited either from England or from the sons

[33] *CSPI 1606–8*, 235–43; *CSPI 1608–10*, 501; *CSPI 1611–14*, 241. For Killala and Achonry, Ford, *Protestant Reformation*, 112.

of the New English. What this meant in practice was that the transition from a reading to a graduate clergy was also the replacement of a church staffed mainly by Irish-born ministers with one served principally by English and Scottish incomers.[34]

The recruitment of large numbers of English and Scottish graduates was a matter of supply as well as demand. By the early seventeenth century competition for clerical livings in England had increased with the number of university-trained candidates. At the same time the imposition of a new political and social order following the defeat of Tyrone had made Ireland a more attractive, or at least acceptable, alternative. The generous re-endowment of the church as part of the Ulster plantation created a concentration of well-paid positions, and it was in fact in Ulster that the number of Church of Ireland clergy grew most rapidly in the first decades of the seventeenth century. In many respects, in fact, the influx of clergy was simply part of the wider movement of British settlers promoted by the Ulster plantation, the rebuilding of the Munster colony, and the lesser plantation schemes of James I's reign. Leading settlers frequently brought ministers with them, or later recruited men to serve their growing colonies. Even in the absence of direct sponsorship, the presence of ready-made Protestant congregations in planted areas made the prospect of service in Ireland less daunting and potentially more rewarding. Once again, however, this meant that the recruitment of a better qualified ministry was achieved only at the price of giving Irish Protestantism a more clearly colonial character, as the church of the recently arrived Scottish and English settlers.

The change in ethnic composition was not confined to the lower clergy. On the death of Elizabeth in 1603 ten of the sixteen Irish bishops had been born in Ireland. Between 1600 and 1625, however, only four more Irish-born men were added to the Church of Ireland episcopate. How far this reduction reflected a shortage of suitable candidates, and how far a greater unwillingness on the part of government to consider native appointments, remains unclear. Two of the four Irish-born appointees, James Ussher, appointed to Meath in 1621 and to Armagh four years later, and William Daniel, archbishop of Tuam in 1609, were men of distinction too remarkable to ignore. The claims of the other two were less notable.[35] But the end result was in any case clear. Out of twenty-three bishops serving at the end of James I's reign in 1625, only three were Irish born: Daniel

34 Alan Ford, 'Who Went to Trinity? The Early Students of Dublin University', in Helga Robinson-Hammerstein (ed.), *European Universities in the Age of Reformation and Counter-Reformation* (Dublin, 1998), 62–7; Ford, *Protestant Reformation in Ireland*, 80, 96.

35 The other two were Robert Draper, bishop of Kilmore and Ardagh from 1603, and John Crosby, bishop of Ardfert in 1600. Davies reported in 1607 that the churches of Kilmore were for the most part in ruins and the clergy 'poor, ragged, ignorant creatures', and that Draper was diligent only 'in visiting his barbarous clergy, to make benefit out of their insufficiency': *The Works in Verse and Prose of Sir John Davies*, iii. 159. For Crosby, an anglicized Gael with good political connections, see below, p. 393. For numbers of Irish born bishops in 1603 and 1625 see Ford, *Protestant Reformation*, 46.

in Tuam, Ussher in Armagh, and Roland Lynch, in the last of his thirty-eight years as bishop of Kilmacduagh.

The increasing domination of newcomers did not in itself imply that the Church of Ireland should abandon a sense of mission to the native population. In the period following Tyrone's surrender both senior ecclesiastics and officials believed that the time had now come to impose conformity to the state religion on the population as a whole. In many cases the strategy they advocated looked no further than legal compulsion and repression. But this was mainly due to the prevailing assumption that the Catholicism of the masses was the product of superstition and custom rather than of deep-rooted conviction. If they could once be made to attend the services of the established church, and denied those of its Catholic rival, they would passively conform to their new religious environment. Some churchmen, moreover, looked beyond these purely negative tactics. In particular John Rider, bishop of Killaloe from 1612 to 1632, made a serious effort to appeal to the hearts and minds of those dragooned into his churches by the threat of recusancy fines or other penalties, by retaining native reading ministers to interpret for the graduate preaching clergy. By the beginning of the 1620s, however, it was becoming clear that the native population, whether Gaelic or Old English, remained stubbornly resistant to both force and persuasion. By this time, too, the state had shown that it could not be relied on to back up the latter with the consistent application of the former. It was against this unpromising background that ministers increasingly turned to the more rewarding task of meeting the religious needs of the settler population.

In addition to the ethnic exclusivity that was the inadvertent result of the professionalization of the clergy, it is also important to note other, more mundane problems that, in the seventeenth century as earlier, continued to limit the church's ability to win adherents, or even to retain all of those it already had. In Ulster plantation had provided the opportunity to re-endow dioceses and parishes with land for the support of their clergy. In the other three provinces, however, 60 per cent of livings were impropriate, with the tithes going to laymen who at best provided a small stipend for a curate. In the diocese of Dublin, for example, only £1,461 out of a total of £4,753 collected in tithes was devoted to the stipends of vicars and curates.[36] In addition a large part of the church's fixed endowment, in glebe lands attached to parishes and lands belonging to bishops' sees, had also been lost, whether through illegal alienation by earlier incumbents, through having been unprofitably leased out for the immediate gain of a substantial entry fine, or through lack of the systematic records needed to establish ownership. Poor endowments made it necessary to resort to large-scale pluralism, as the only means of providing a reasonable level of income, particularly for a graduate clergy. The combined effects of a non-resident clergy,

[36] M. V. Ronan, 'Archbishop Bulkeley's Visitation of Dublin, 1630', *Archivium Hibernicum*, 8 (1941), 57. For the national picture, see Ford, *Protestant Reformation*, 70–1, 86–7.

an indifferent laity, and often recusant patrons was likewise visible in the decay of the physical fabric, not itself particularly impressive, inherited from the pre-Reformation church. A royal visitation in 1615 found that only 43 per cent of churches in the three southern provinces were in a state of repair. In the diocese of Dublin the total was 123 churches in repair, as compared to 273 functioning places of worship in 1531. A later visitation, in 1630, moreover, found only 44 churches in a decent state, and later statistics for other areas also suggest that the 1615 commissioners had been distinctly generous in their classification.[37]

If the Church of Ireland was poorly endowed in terms of its mission, it was also, from the point of those it theoretically sought to win over, an irksome financial burden. Its most substantial exaction was the tithes levied on agricultural produce, objectionable both because they were imposed on a population to which the church did not minister and because, particularly in Ulster, they represented a novel conception of how a parish clergy should be supported. In addition it seems to have been widely expected that Catholics going to their own clergy for baptisms, marriages, or funerals should also pay fees to their nominal Protestant pastor or bishop. The main source of grievance, however, appears to have been proceedings in the diocesan courts, operating in the name of the bishop but normally run by a lay chancellor, which exercised jurisdiction over wills, marital matters, and a wide range of moral offences. The fines and charges levied in these courts were repeatedly cited as a major grievance. In 1630 a Catholic bishop, stung by allegations that he and his colleagues drained the country of large sums of money, insisted that the bishops' courts 'be more chargeable to the land than would the maintenance of an army be'. The midlands settler Matthew de Renzy, no friend to either Catholicism or the Gaelic Irish, confirmed that the clergy gathered 'great monies' by arbitrarily imposing fines for non-attendance at church, even though 'when a minister shall have 5 or 6 parishes under him, it is hard for people to know to what church to come'. William Bedell, the reformist Church of Ireland bishop of Kilmore, likewise complained of his own chancellor, whom the local people referred to as 'Pouke' (the pooka or bad fairy of Irish legend), whom they feared 'like the fiend of hell'.[38] There is no reason to assume that a more lenient policy in this area would have made much difference to popular religious allegiances. But it is nevertheless worth remembering, particularly in the light of events in 1641 and after, that the face which the Church of Ireland showed to the majority of the population was not only an increasingly alien but also a predatory one.

[37] Ronan, 'Archbishop Bulkeley's Visitation', 56; idem, 'Royal Visitation of Dublin, 1615', *Archivium Hibernicum*, 8 (1941), 3. For other regions see Ford, *Protestant Reformation*, 101–3.

[38] Roche to Wadding, 26 May 1630 (*Wadding Papers*, 370); Brian MacCuarta (ed.), 'Matthew De Renzy's Letters on Irish Affairs 1613–20', *Analecta Hibernica*, 34 (1987), 144–6; Bedell to Laud, 10 August 1630 (*Two Biographies of William Bedell, Bishop of Kilmore*, ed. E. S. Shuckburgh (Cambridge, 1902), 311).

The other major obstacle to pastoral work of any kind with the Gaelic part of the population was language. Here again the ambitions of the Elizabethan Reformation withered gradually rather than disappearing overnight. The provision of an Irish-speaking clergy recruited from conformist natives had been one of the original purposes for which Trinity College had been established. In 1605, at the same time that he was preparing to target prominent recusants in a campaign of enforced conformity, Chichester ordered the archbishop of Armagh to divert revenues from vacant benefices to the support of selected native students at Trinity. Out of 75 students listed in a college account for that year 16 were in fact native Irish, while another list in 1619 revealed 19 natives out of 82 students. Meanwhile the college had also provided the base for further progress towards the provision of an Irish language text of the scriptures. Around 1594 William Daniel, a Cambridge-educated native of County Kilkenny and now a fellow, resumed work on the translation of the New Testament that had been commenced by John Kearney and others in the 1570s. He went on with the project after leaving Trinity for Galway city in 1596, eventually publishing his New Testament in 1603 and an Irish version of the Book of Common Prayer in 1608. The following year he became archbishop of Tuam. Daniel, or Uilliam Ó Domnuill as he signed his work, was thus the latest in a line of native born Protestants entrusted with the evangelicization of the west. As a product of the strongly puritan Emmanuel College, however, he differed from predecessors like Lynch and Donnellan in being openly anti-Catholic. While sincerely committed to missionary work, he was more than willing to see his efforts reinforced by the banishment of the Catholic clergy, whom he identified as vassals of the Antichrist. In the end, however, he was no more successful than others in attracting significant numbers of adherents. As for Trinity, the reasonably healthy Gaelic presence seen in its early years was not sustained. By 1640 only 5 out of 102 student signatories in a volume dedicated to the lord lieutenant's son were native Irish, compared to 87 identifiable as either English or New English.[39]

The one significant attempt to challenge this progressive anglicization of the established church is remembered more for its inspirational qualities than its actual achievement. In 1627 William Bedell, the Cambridge-educated son of an Essex farmer and a leading scholar of classical and middle-eastern languages, came to Trinity as provost. As part of a wider programme of reform, he instituted Irish prayers in the college chapel on holy days, an Irish lecture delivered by a native speaker, and the reading of the Irish scriptures. He also began his own study of what he called 'the tongue of this country, which I see (although it be accounted otherwise) is a learned and exact language and

[39] Ford, 'Who Went to Trinity?', 53–74; John McCavitt, *Sir Arthur Chichester, Lord Deputy of Ireland 1605–16* (Belfast, 1998), 115.

full of difficulty'.[40] In 1631 he published *The A.B.C. or the Instruction of a Christian*, a collection of scriptural and other texts printed in parallel English and Irish versions. The previous year he had been appointed bishop of Kilmore. There he instituted services in Irish, sought to appoint clergy proficient in the language in preference to those who were not, and worked, with the assistance of two native convert clergy, on a translation into Irish of the Old Testament. Bedell's first biographers, his son and son-in-law, were to present these efforts as meeting with positive obstruction: one fellow bishop, commenting both on Bedell's plain style of dress and on his concern with the Irish language, was alleged to have asked him whether he wore brogues. But it is difficult to know what weight is to be put on frankly hagiographical narratives.[41] There were other reasons for hostility to Bedell: his determined preference for clergy capable of working through Irish, even over more academically qualified candidates, and his campaign against profiteering in the ecclesiastical courts. Moreover he did succeed, at the convocation of 1634, in persuading his colleagues to amend the church's canons to allow services in Irish. What is true is that his enthusiasm for a mission to the natives in their own language inspired few others. Nor did he succeed, for all his dedication, in making much impact on the Gaelic Irish themselves. He earned sufficient esteem to ensure that he was left largely unmolested at the outbreak of the rebellion of 1641, and even, supposedly, to have Catholic forces provide a firing party at his funeral the following year.[42] But he seems to have been no more successful than Daniel or others in winning more than a few isolated individuals to the reformed faith.

In the first half of the seventeenth century, then, the Church of Ireland was in practice becoming largely the church of the New English. Yet it was precisely in this same period that the first steps were taken towards asserting its roots in an ancient Irish past. The key figures were the two most distinguished Irish-born churchmen of the early seventeenth century. Archbishop Daniel, in 1608, gave his translation of the Book of Common Prayer a preface praising the flourishing state of Christianity in ancient Ireland, before it had been subjected to the corruptions of popery.[43] The point was developed in greater detail by James Ussher. Ussher, a graduate of Trinity College appointed bishop of Meath in 1621 and archbishop

40 Bedell to Ward, 16 July 1628 (*The Tanner Letters*, ed. Charles McNeill (Dublin, 1943), 86).

41 Note the rather different versions of the anecdote offered in the separate lives of Bedell written by his son and son-in-law: *Two Biographies of William Bedell*, 29, 131.

42 Ibid. 74–5, 205–6. Again the much quoted account by Bedell's son of the posthumous respect shown to his father needs to be contrasted with his brother-in-law's rather bleaker version, in which the presence of the armed rebels was sufficiently intimidating to prevent mourners taking up the invitation to conduct a full Anglican burial service, and the volley fired was in celebration of a prophecy that Bedell 'should be the last English man that should be put out of Ireland' (p. 205).

43 John McCafferty, '"God Bless your Free Church of Ireland": Wentworth, Laud, Bramhall and the Irish Convocation of 1634', in J. F. Merritt (ed.), *The Political World of Thomas Wentworth, Earl of Strafford* (Cambridge, 1996), 188–9.

of Armagh in 1625, belonged to one of the minority of Dublin patrician families that had accepted the Reformation. An uncle, Henry, had preceded him as archbishop of Armagh during 1595–1613. James's mother, on the other hand, was a sister of Richard Stanihurst. This did not prevent him becoming both a rigorous Calvinist and firmly anti-Catholic. A sermon at the installation in 1622 of Lord Deputy Falkland, calling for a stricter enforcement of the laws against recusancy, earned him a rebuke from his ecclesiastical superior, Archbishop Hampton of Armagh. Ussher's research and writing ranged far beyond Ireland, giving him a European-wide reputation in the fields of biblical scholarship, theology, and early church history. But he also took an interest in what, in an early letter to his uncle Richard, he described as 'the scattered antiquities of our nation'.[44] To this end he was willing to maintain contact with the same Catholic churchmen whose elimination he believed the state should undertake, offering the Rome-based Franciscan Luke Wadding materials from the diocesan registry at Armagh in return for transcripts from the Vatican archives, and even lending the volumes concerned to an Irish member of the order.[45]

The main fruit of this interest was *A Discourse on the Religion Anciently Professed by the Irish and British* (1622), a detailed historical treatise claiming to show that early Christianity in Ireland, England, and Scotland had been bibliocentric in its theology, preaching salvation through faith rather than works, recognizing the commemorative rather than transformative nature of the eucharist, and permitting a married clergy. This was an argument that potentially worked at several levels. It offered a local illustration of Ussher's wider thesis of a decline from the purity of the early Christian church to the corruptions against which the Protestant reformers had revolted. It gave the Irish, English, and Scottish churches a shared religious heritage. At the same time the depiction of the Church of Ireland as heir to a tradition of non-Roman Christianity traceable back to the days of St Patrick was a serviceable defence against two simultaneous threats: on the one hand claims to ecclesiastical primacy on the part of the Church of England, and on the other Catholic allegations that Irish Protestantism represented a mere foreign imposition. Indeed in Ussher's account it was in fact the English conquest of Ireland in the twelfth century that had brought about the final surrender of the true Irish Christian tradition to the corruptions of popery. By these means Ussher laid the foundations for what was to be an enduring origin legend underpinning the sense of a distinctively Irish Protestant identity.[46]

[44] Ussher to Richard Stanihurst, n.d. (*The Whole Works of the Most Rev. James Ussher D.D. . . . with A Life of the Author and An Account of his Writings*, ed. Charles Richard Elrington, 16 vols. (Dublin, 1847), xv. 2).

[45] *Wadding Papers*, 280, 349, 606.

[46] John McCaffery, 'St Patrick for the Church of Ireland: James Ussher's Discourse', *Bullán*, 3/2 (1998), 87–101; Alan Ford, 'James Ussher and the Creation of an Irish Protestant Identity', in B. I. Bradshaw and Peter Roberts (eds.) *British Consciousness and Identity* (Cambridge, 1998), 185–212.

All this, however, was primarily for the future. By the 1630s a Church of Ireland still weak in resources, and increasingly identified with the New English minority, confronted a rival Catholic organization that, for all its legal disabilities and internal divisions, was beginning to display both the organizational strengths and the ideological zeal of the Counter-Reformation. The record of a visitation in 1630 of the parish of Swords, just ten miles north of Dublin, vividly conveys both the disparity between the rival establishments and the sense, on the Protestant side, of earlier gains being lost:

> The church, by the neglect of the gents of that parish who are recusants, is lately fallen flat to the ground, and no part standing only some part of the bare walls. There is one Doyle, a mass priest who keeps school in the town of Swords, to whom many gents' sons do resort. This priest commonly sayeth mass in the house of Michael Taylor of Swords, gent, whereunto there is great concourse of people on Sundays and holydays. There used to come to church there about threescore to hear divine service and sermon.

Bishop Bedell, four years later, offered his own more general summary, acknowledging the strength of his church's Catholic rival, but at the same time not sparing his own colleagues. Because of the proliferation of pluralities, 'the Popish clergy is double to us in number, and having the advantage of the tongue, of the love of the people, of our extortions upon them, of the very inborn hatred of subdued people to their conquerors, they hold them still in blindness and superstition, ourselves being the chiefest impediments of the work that we pretend to set forward'.[47] His remarks, though gloomy, should not be taken as an epitaph. Bedell continued to believe that a determined campaign of evangelization could make Ireland a Protestant country. And there were to be others, at intervals over the next two centuries, whom the same vision was to inspire to sometimes heroic endeavours. But their enthusiasm was in each case to set them apart from a majority that accepted, with varying degrees of complacency or unease, the tension between the status of a national church and the reality of ministering to a privileged minority.

The new ethnic exclusiveness of the Church of Ireland can also be related, as both cause and effect, to its theological orientation. From the 1580s the leaders of the Church of England became increasingly intolerant of internal opponents of the compromise religious settlement worked out in the 1560s: 'puritans', who sought a church purged of what they saw as unacceptable vestiges of popish ritual and doctrine, and 'presbyterians', who wished to replace the authority of monarch and bishops with that of collective government by the godly, lay and clerical. The Irish church was more tolerant of both groups, partly because of its greater need for qualified recruits, but also because the more visible presence of popery in Ireland had given many of the existing clergy a strong puritan bias. Ireland thus

[47] Ronan, 'Archbishop Bulkeley's Visitation', 63; Bedell to Ward, 2 February 1634 (*Tanner Letters*, 104).

became a refuge for those who found themselves unable to conform to the tests of orthodoxy being imposed at home. The tendency towards a more rigorous Protestantism received a further boost with the foundation of Trinity College. The early staff of the college were recruited mainly from Cambridge, noted for its puritan leanings. They included Walter Travers, Trinity's first full-time provost, who had been a leading figure in the English presbyterian movement, as well as other exiled dissidents. The result was to give the theology taught there a decidedly Calvinist turn, emphasizing the total depravity of fallen man and the absolute division between those whom God had and had not predestined for salvation.[48]

The distinctive theological orientation which these different circumstances combined to give to the Church of Ireland were clearly revealed in the new articles of religion drawn up by the convocation of bishops and clergy that met in parallel to the Irish parliament during 1613–15. The 104 Irish articles drew heavily on the Thirty-Nine Articles of the Church of England, but there were also significant differences. The Irish articles were more strongly anti-Catholic in their language, particularly in identifying the pope as the Antichrist or 'man of sin' of biblical revelation. They bowed to puritan and presbyterian sensibilities in adding an article on the observance of the sabbath and in omitting an English article (the only one so omitted) relating to the consecration of bishops. They also offered a much more rigorous statement than the English articles of the doctrine of predestination. The idea that salvation depended exclusively on God's willingness to admit fallen human beings to a grace they had no claim to have earned had been central to the Reformation. In this sense all debates among Protestants on the question of salvation and election, in this period at least, were on matters of emphasis. But the differences insisted on by the Irish articles were nevertheless marked. In place of the formula used in the English articles, which had managed to allow some faint possibility of a belief in universal redemption, they offered an uncompromising statement of the doctrine of limited atonement. In doing so, they also gave explicit expression to the refinement known as 'double predestination': the insistence that just as God had chosen some to be saved so he had, from the beginning of time, destined others to inevitable damnation.

The relevance of all this to the self-image of the Church of Ireland, as it adapted to the political and demographic changes of the late sixteenth and early seventeenth centuries, is evident enough. The contrast between the Protestantism of the English and Scottish settlers and the stubborn Catholicism of the indigenous inhabitants, both Old English and Gaelic Irish, was all too easily identified, in the light of the doctrine of election, with the distinction

[48] The fullest discussion of the theology of the Church of Ireland, and of its implications for the church's sense of mission, is Ford, *Protestant Reformation*, ch. 8. See also idem, 'The Church of Ireland 1558–1634: A Puritan Church?', in Ford et al., *As by Law Established*, 52–68.

between those whom God had chosen for salvation and those, the reprobates, whom he had already irrevocably sentenced to a life of sin and spiritual darkness to be followed by eternal punishment. Contrasting stereotypes of settler industry, sobriety, and morality, and of native idleness, dishonesty, and vice, could be seen as further evidence of the same distinction. Even the losses suffered by the Irish in recent decades, and the gains made at their expense by the settlers, could be taken as evidence of, respectively, reprobation and election. Richard Boyle provides one clear-cut example of a New English adventurer buoyed up, throughout his long career, by an apparently genuine conviction that his ascent to wealth and power was a direct result of the workings of divine providence.[49] Representation of the pope as Antichrist, equally, was part of a wider apocalyptic theology, in which the Catholic Irish were identified as part of the forces of evil whose menace was destined to grow as the last days approached. In all of these ways the stricter predestinarian theology of the Church of Ireland reflected and, over time, helped to reinforce its identity as a church whose main roots were in a recently arrived settler population.

If Englishmen of a puritan bent found the Irish ecclesiastical establishment more flexible and accommodating than the one they had left behind, even greater latitude prevailed in what became, after 1603, a distinctive Scottish enclave within the Ulster church. James I's first Scottish bishop, George Montgomery, had begun his career in the Church of England. However others—in Clogher James Spottiswood (1621–44), in Raphoe Andrew Knox (1611–33) and John Leslie (1633–61), in Down and Connor Robert Echlin (1613–35)—came directly from Scotland. In addition some sixty-four Scottish ministers took up residence in Ulster during the reign of James I, forty-nine of them in the dioceses of these Scottish bishops. Clerical and lay settlers alike were the products of a hybrid ecclesiastical order. In a series of stages, between 1597 and 1610, James VI had reimposed government by bishops. However, these continued to preside over a system of kirk sessions and presbyteries closer to the corporate self-government of Presbyterianism than to the hierarchical structure of Anglicanism. The articles of Perth, in 1621, introduced further innovations, such as kneeling to receive communion, but these were widely disliked. Some of the ministers who came to Ulster in the 1620s, in fact, were in flight from unwelcome changes at home, or had been forced out of Scottish livings because of their refusal to conform to the new order.

In Ulster these refugees and others encountered a more permissive regime. When Lord Clandeboye invited Robert Blair, one such exile on theological principle, to minister at Bangor in 1624, he arranged for him to be ordained by Echlin. Echlin, having heard Blair's objections to episcopacy, offered to perform the ceremony in company with a group of clergymen, thus complying with the

[49] Nicholas Canny, *The Upstart Earl: A Study of the Social and Mental World of Richard Boyle, First Earl of Cork 1566–1643* (Cambridge, 1982), 19–29.

law of the land while allowing Blair to take it that the bishop was present 'in no other relation than a presbyter'. By the time another Clandeboye protégé, John Livingstone, came to Killinchy six years later Echlin, possibly due to pressure from more militantly conformist colleagues, had become less flexible. However, Livingstone was able to go instead to Bishop Knox in Donegal, who not only agreed to have a group of ministers perform the laying on of hands but invited Livingstone to mark in the service book any passages he wished to be omitted. On doing so Livingstone, by his own account, 'found it had been so marked by some others before that I needed not mark any thing'. Back in Killinchy Livingstone, despite Echlin's stricter stance, was able to institute what he described as 'the public worship free of any interventions of men'. Blair, similarly, administered communion to standing rather than kneeling worshippers, insisting on the point even with his patron Clandeboye. Both men also bypassed the ecclesiastical court, instituting their own system of parochial discipline on Scottish lines, joining with lay elders to pursue scandalous sinners whom they required to make a public confession of their offences or else face excommunication.[50]

From about 1625 Antrim and Down became the centre, not just of a Protestant liturgy and church organization that departed significantly from official norms, but of a dramatic explosion of popular religious enthusiasm. The initial inspiration came from the preaching of a young minister, James Glendinning, based in Carrickfergus. Glendinning himself was mentally unstable: his later teaching included the warning that those who, once in bed, turned on a different side could not be honest Christians, and he was eventually to leave Ulster to search for the seven churches of Asia named in the Book of Revelation. At Carrickfergus his vigorous preaching awakened hearers to the terrors of eternal damnation, but he proved unable or unwilling to lead them on to the next stage, a belief in salvation through Christ. The resulting confusion and distress led Blair and other ministers to initiate their own programme of preaching, coming together at Antrim on the first Friday of each month to deliver a programme of four sermons. Over the next few years these and similar gatherings developed into huge revivalist meetings, extending over two or three days, and reportedly capable of attracting up to 1,000 to 1,500 people. In addition to sermons and prayers those attending shared in communion, conducted as a ritual of collective solidarity, with the sacrament taken, not kneeling individually at an altar, but seated together at long tables.

To supporters of the traditional Protestant liturgy, these displays of enthusiasm were distasteful and alarming. Henry Leslie, dean of Down, reported in 1631:

> there is set abroad a new piece of divinity that no man can be converted unless he feels the pains of his new birth such as St Paul felt. So that every sermon, 40 or so people, for most

[50] *The Life of Mr Robert Blair, Containing his Autobiography*, ed. Thomas M'Crie (Edinburgh, 1848), 59, 61, 68–9; 'The Life of Mr John Livingstone . . . Written by Himself' in W. K. Tweedie (ed.), *Select Biographies* (Edinburgh, 1845), 140–2.

part women, fall down in the church in a trance, and are (as is supposed) senseless, but in their fits they are grievously afflicted with convulsions, trembling, unnatural motions.[51]

Leslie's description, so intriguingly close to the born-again conversionism of more recent periods, cannot be taken wholly at face value. Livingstone insisted that opponents had sought to discredit his colleagues and himself by exaggerating peripheral phenomena, such as 'a high breathing and panting, as those do who have run long', which they in fact discouraged. Blair, likewise, explicitly denied having taught 'the necessity of a new birth by bodily pangs and throes', and claimed that the convulsions affecting some worshippers were in fact a pernicious device of Satan, who 'did upon some ignorant persons counterfeit the work of the Lord'. Neither minister, however, denied that these physical manifestations had taken place. Blair, moreover, did in fact see his own preaching as divinely inspired. On one occasion he was horrified at being pressed to preach when already exhausted, only to find that 'the Lord so carried on that business' that the text he selected offered him only one proposition to elaborate. It was only as he was closing, 'in the very last comma of the sentence' that 'another edifying point' presented itself from the text, 'and so another still, till the glass was run. In all this I was but the voice of one crying.' Such exalted claims would suggest that the image of passionate preaching eliciting a dramatic emotional response was not wholly the fabrication of malicious opponents.[52]

The revival of the 1620s and early 1630s spread from Antrim and Down into parts of adjoining counties, and it seems also to have awakened echoes in adjacent parts of Scotland. Its heartland, however, remained the north-east. This geographical concentration reflected a strong though not exclusive ethnic base. One of the main instigators of the Antrim meetings was an English clergyman, John Ridge, a protégé of the retired lord deputy Chichester, while the gatherings also benefited from the patronage of the Clotworthies, another Devon family now established in the county. At the same time Livingstone, while acknowledging the involvement of 'some number of gracious English', confirmed that 'the greatest part' of those involved were Scots. The interaction of ethnic and religious identity was particularly evident in the large-scale communion services. The issue of tokens to those to be admitted to the sacrament permitted the exclusion of a handful of notorious offenders, but this was a sanction so dreaded that it had rarely to be invoked. Instead personal piety was subsumed into a manifestation of the godly community united round the sacred repast. Scottish settlement in Ulster, intended to strengthen the British Protestant interest, had

[51] *CSPI 1625–32*, 629. For general surveys of Scottish Protestantism in early seventeenth-century Ulster see M. J. Westerkamp, *Triumph of the Laity: Scots-Irish Piety and the Great Awakening 1625–1760* (New York, 1988), ch. 1; M. Perceval Maxwell, *The Scottish Migration to Ulster in the Reign of James I* (London, 1973), ch. 10; Alan Ford, 'The Origins of Irish Dissent', in Kevin Herlihy (ed.), *The Religion of Irish Dissent* (Dublin, 1996), 9–30.

[52] 'Life of Livingstone', 146; *Life of Blair*, 89–90, 85.

thus introduced a radically new element into the religion and culture of the region, one which in time was to force the question of what it actually meant to be Protestant, or for that matter British.

HALF SUBJECTS

In April 1606 Sir John Davies, returning from the assizes at Munster, stopped to pass Easter at the earl of Ormond's house at Carrick-on-Suir. Once there, however, he found that, since the feast day of St George was approaching, 'I was not suffered in anywise to depart until I had seen him do honour to that day'. Accordingly he remained to watch as the 74-year-old earl, too ill to sit up, had his attendants ceremonially spread his robes of state over him as he lay in bed. The whole performance was perhaps too ostentatious to be taken wholly at face value. Moreover Ormond, as the former Irish favourite of Elizabeth, had more fully than most been a part of the English as well as the Irish political world. But his gesture was nevertheless a fair enough reflection of the terms in which, throughout the sixteenth century and earlier, the English of Ireland had defined their political identity, if not always regulated their political behaviour. By the time of Davies's visit to Carrick-on-Suir, however, their claim to be the crown's loyal subjects, indeed their very status as the English of Ireland, was increasingly being called into question. Indeed it is possibly against this background that Ormond's little piece of theatre, by a man who was in fact far from being the decrepit relic of an earlier era, should be understood.[53]

The first clear indications of what was to become the crisis of the Old English came in the years 1595–1603, in the form of the cold, if not yet openly voiced, suspicion with which the queen's Irish representatives, in this period of acute crisis, regarded those who until quite recently had been seen as the principal representatives of the English interest in Ireland. The Old English of the Pale and of the towns and cities had for the most part resolutely ignored Tyrone's call to join him in a Catholic crusade. Yet they received no credit for their loyalty. Mountjoy's secretary later wrote explicitly that most of the 'English Irish' who were not in open rebellion had merely 'temporised with the state, openly professing obedience, that they might live under the protection thereof, but secretly relieving the rebels, and practising with them for their present and future safeties'. The controversies over cess in the 1570s and 1580s, and continuing wrangles over the raising of money and the billeting of troops, probably played their part in bringing about this alienation. The main cause, however, was clearly religion. 'The nobility, towns and people', Mountjoy himself reported in June

[53] *CSPI 1603–6*, 476–7. For the evidence that Earl Thomas was at this stage still a formidable political figure see David Edwards, *The Ormond Lordship in County Kilkenny 1515–1642* (Dublin, 2003), 106.

1601, 'are of so obstinate a contrariety in religion, that without question they are grown malicious to the government, and affect under the protection of the power of Spain to declare themselves.' Another comment, significantly, sought to blur what had once been the absolute distinction between Old English and native Irish: when the lords of the Pale faced criticism for their failure to support the war effort, it was claimed, they sent emissaries to England 'to make first complaint (after the Irish manner) of the wrongs done them by the army'. Even Ormond was not exempt. When he was taken prisoner by the O'Mores in 1600 'there wanted not others, who thought the earl was willingly surprised'.[54]

This deterioration in relationships was both reflected and furthered in what has become known as the recusancy revolt of April and May 1603. In Kilkenny, Wexford, and a number of leading Munster towns, news of the death of Elizabeth I inspired citizens and municipal authorities to join in a triumphant assertion of Catholic public worship, taking possession of cathedrals and churches, and resuming public mass and religious processions. In Cork they 'set up images and use the mass, saying that they did not know but that the king was of their religion, and use their discipline upon Good Friday by whipping themselves, and carry the cross about the streets and force men to reverence it'. In Cashel a Protestant goldsmith was tied to a tree, surrounded by torn-up copies of the Bible and the Book of Common Prayer, while a priest harangued him. These pent up religious grievances were reinforced by resentment at the burden of supporting a wartime army, particularly in the light of the economic dislocation brought about by a ruinous debasement of the currency and the ending of trade with Spain. A priest in Waterford told his listeners 'that now they might thank God that every man might freely enjoy the fruits of his own reward . . . where before all things were extorted from them by the rapine of the soldiers . . . for now Jezebell was dead'. The revolt was also an assertion of municipal liberties against an increasingly intrusive state. The citizens of Waterford sought to deny the lord deputy entrance on the basis of a charter from King John. In Cork, where the revolt went furthest, they took possession of the fort at Haulbowline, built against their wishes by the president of Munster, seized the arms stored there, then began to demolish another fort on the south side of the city. When troops sought to intervene the citizens exchanged gunfire with them, killing two soldiers and losing a man themselves.[55]

Faced with a challenge on this scale, just months after Tyrone's surrender, Mountjoy reacted with a characteristic mixture of firmness and conciliation. Marching south with 5,000 men, he quickly forced the submission of the rebel towns. His secretary was later to recount gleefully how his master had told the Waterford men that he was prepared to cut King John's charter with King

[54] Fynes Moryson, *An Itinerary*, 4 vols. (Glasgow, 1907), ii. 273, 397, 327, 301.

[55] *Carew MSS 1603–1623*, 7–12; Anthony Sheehan, 'The Recusancy Revolt of 1603: A Reinterpretation', *Archivium Hibernicum*, 38 (1983), 3–13.

James's sword, 'and to sow salt upon the soil of their destroyed city'. But in fact the deputy submitted to being met outside the walls by two priests in full vestments, and he entered the city only after he had made clear that he had no intention of prohibiting religious services in private houses.[56] At Cork, where blood had been shed, he had three men executed, but again made no attempt to forbid continued Catholic religious practice. Pragmatic accommodation had once again prevailed. But the potential for conflict between the crown and its English Irish subjects had been brought into the open in a way that seemed to validate all Mountjoy's suspicions.

Accommodation was, in any case, short-lived. After Mountjoy left Ireland in June 1603 his successors, Sir George Carey and, from 1605, Sir Arthur Chichester, embarked on a campaign of religious coercion. In November 1604 the incoming mayor of Dublin was excluded from office and fined for refusing to take the oath of supremacy. A proclamation in July 1605 banished priests from Ireland and ordered all persons to attend the services of the established church, on pain of the fine of one shilling provided for in the Elizabethan act of uniformity. Large numbers of fines were duly levied in the months that followed. Meanwhile, from November 1605, prominent Dublin recusants, including several aldermen, received 'mandates', letters in the name of the king ordering them to attend divine service, an exercise of the royal prerogative that left those who refused liable to unlimited fines and indefinite imprisonment. What was envisaged was thus a two-pronged strategy, driving the lower classes into church with recusancy fines, while breaking the resistance of their social superiors by heavier penalties. When the Catholic nobility and gentry of the Pale presented a petition challenging the legality of this use of the prerogative, Chichester imprisoned the two leaders, Viscount Gormanstown and Sir Patrick Barnewall, and placed others under house arrest.[57]

In January 1606 the London government, alarmed as ever by the prospect of disorders in Ireland, intervened to tell Chichester to act more cautiously. By agreeing that he could continue to make examples of notorious offenders, however, it left him room to continue his coercive policy in a somewhat less overt manner. Barnewall, transferred to the Tower of London, was given some liberty to act as spokesman for his co-religionists, but remained a prisoner until December 1606, when he was released after making a formal acknowledgement of his fault. Meanwhile the president of Munster, Sir Henry Brouncker, had launched his own campaign of mandates, as well as intervening to remove recusant mayors and sovereigns in towns throughout the province. In April 1607 reports of his activities led the English privy council to call again for moderation.

[56] Compare *The Irish Sections of Fynes Moryson's Unpublished Itinerary*, ed. Graham Kew (Dublin, 1988), 53 and F. M. Jones, *Mountjoy: Last Elizabethan Deputy 1563–1606* (London, 1958), 171–2.

[57] The fullest accounts of religious policy in this period are McCavitt, *Chichester*, ch. 7, 10; Lennon, *Lords of Dublin*, ch. 6. For Protestant thinking, see Ford, *Protestant Reformation*, ch. 3.

As before, however, it was not willing to go so far as to discountenance all action against recusants. It was only the crisis precipitated by the flight of Tyrone and his associates that put an end, for the moment, to the attempted enforcement of religious conformity.

Rather oddly, in the light of these transactions, the next attempt at a coercive religious policy, commencing in 1611, was at the instigation of the London government itself, which had by now taken fright at what it believed to be the international Catholic threat. Chichester, however, responded willingly. This time the chief instrument employed against the Catholic elite was the oath of supremacy. Its systematic administration was used to prevent recusants from being granted the wardship of minors, from practising at the bar, and from serving as mayors of towns or in other positions of local power. Meanwhile less prominent Catholics were once again prosecuted under the act of uniformity, and juries who refused to return verdicts against recusants were punished with heavy fines. The government had also taken prisoner two Catholic clerics, Conor O'Devany, bishop of Down and Connor, and a priest named Patrick O'Loughran. In January 1612 both men were convicted of treason, on the basis of their links with the exiled Tyrone. Their execution became a set piece in the theatre of martyrdom. The huge crowd that gathered to watch the spectacle kept up 'such a screeching, such a howling and such a hallowing, as if Saint Patrick himself had been going to the gallows'.[58] Afterwards people scrambled to take away pieces of the dead men's clothes and dip handkerchiefs in their blood, as well as rescuing the bishop's severed head. If the aim had been to intimidate, the outcome was a fervent display of recusant solidarity and an emotive addition to the list of Catholics venerated as having suffered for the faith.

The dubious use of the royal prerogative in the mandates campaign, and the resort to flimsy charges of treason against O'Devany and O'Loughran, had been necessary because Ireland had no equivalent to the laws criminalizing Catholic religious practice, and outlawing Catholic ecclesiastics, that had been introduced in Elizabethan England. By September 1612 the administration had decided that its programme for the forthcoming meeting of the Irish parliament should include bills against Jesuits and seminary-trained priests, as well as a ban on unapproved travelling abroad for purposes of education. The problem was to get such a programme through a parliament in which the Old English, by virtue of their extensive landholdings and dominance of all the major urban centres outside Ulster, would be the largest group. Suggestions included imposing the oath of supremacy on MPs, or at least threatening to do so in order to discourage Catholics from standing for election. Alternatively, potential troublemakers could be called over to England before parliament met. In the end, however, the solution adopted was to create some forty new boroughs, eighteen of them in Ulster, with charters placing the choice of members in reliable hands. The

[58] Barnaby Rich, quoted in John McCavitt, *The Flight of the Earls* (Dublin, 2002), 184.

80 Protestants thus returned were to give the government a majority of 32 in a Commons of 233 members. In the Lords the votes of the 20 bishops of the established church gave the government a guaranteed majority. To increase the embarrassingly meagre total of five lay peers on the Protestant side, however, the crown also issued writs to three major Irish landowners who held British rather than Irish titles, as well as to one holder of an Irish courtesy title of the kind normally granted to an eldest son.[59]

The elections of April–May 1613 took place in an atmosphere of open animosity. Alarm at the proposed penal legislation was heightened by Chichester's rejection of the claim that Catholic magnates were entitled, as part of a supposed 'grand council', to see the bills sent to England for approval under Poynings's Law. In Cavan recusants claimed to have been prevented from voting by armed soldiers. In Dublin the Protestant mayor disallowed the return of two Catholic candidates, provoking a riot in connection with which one man was later executed. Government supporters for their part alleged that recusant MPs arrived in Dublin to take their seats accompanied by armed retainers. Once parliament met on 18 May Catholic MPs challenged the legality of the new boroughs, refusing to take part in the election of a speaker until the issue had been resolved. When the Protestant MPs sought to force a vote, the Catholics placed their candidate, Sir John Everard, in the chair, only to have the other side force their choice, Sir John Davies, onto his lap.[60] After a farcical scuffle the Catholic MPs withdrew in a body, their continued abstention forcing the proroguing of parliament after less than three weeks.

Both sides now took their case to the king. James, at this point, was caught between contradictory impulses: his personal preference was for persuasion over coercion in religious matters, but he was also committed to an exalted view of monarchical authority. He gave the recusant delegation sent to him in the summer of 1613 an apparently gracious hearing, and conceded an inquiry into their complaints. However one delegate, Sir William Talbot, who was unwise enough to let himself be drawn into a debate on the doctrine that an excommunicated monarch could legitimately be deposed, found himself fined and committed to the Tower for his unsatisfactory answer. And when others of the party returned to Ireland in too obvious a mood of triumph, they provoked a harsh reaction. Summoned back to London in April 1614 to hear the king's judgment, they were taken aback to be subjected to a strongly worded rebuke, informing them that their complaints were without foundation, their petitions 'full of pride and arrogance', and their conduct in parliament 'rude, disorderly,

[59] Victor Treadwell, 'The House of Lords in the Irish Parliament of 1613–1615', *English Historical Review*, 80 (1965), 106–7.

[60] To appeciate this scene, it is necessary to recall contemporary descriptions of Davies, who 'goes waddling with his arse out behind him as though he were about to make every one that he meets a wall to piss against' (H. S. Pawlisch, *Sir John Davies and the Conquest of Ireland: A Study in Legal Imperialism* (Cambridge, 1985), 18).

unexcusable, and worthy of severe punishment'.[61] When delegates responded with a restatement of their case, the king had several imprisoned for their insolence. In June he instructed Chichester to reissue the 1605 proclamation against Catholic clerics, resume the levying of recusancy fines, and punish towns that consistently elected recusant officials by declaring their charters forfeit. This angry assertion of royal authority was, however, short-lived. A disastrous confrontation with the English parliament in the summer of 1614 brought the crown once again to the brink of financial collapse. Against this background the need for a grant of taxation in Ireland took precedence over all else. The imprisoned recusant delegates were released one by one, and in August James delivered a revised verdict, in which he met the main recusant complaint by ruling that the MPs for eight of the contested boroughs should be excluded, though only for the current parliament. When parliament resumed in October, the anti-Catholic legislation was no longer part of the legislative programme.

With the threat of penal legislation lifted, the second session of parliament passed off relatively peacefully. Indeed the sittings of 1614–15 seem to have seen MPs and members of the administration cooperating constructively on a range of measures of public concern, such as a bill to establish a system of road maintenance. There was also cautious progress towards circumventing the restrictions on Irish legislative initiatives imposed by Poynings's Law. In the second session the Commons confined itself to drawing up a list of measures it would like to see enacted, with a request that the deputy, in framing the relevant bills, should consult with particular named MPs; and it prefaced even this modest initiative with a formal acknowledgement that only the deputy and council were empowered to transmit bills to England for approval. By the end of the third session, however, MPs had progressed to drawing up full drafts of their favoured measures, engrossed on parchment, and asking that some of their number should be allowed to go to London to lay them before the council for approval and retransmission to Ireland as proper bills. The delays inherent in such cumbersome procedures, however, meant that the overall legislative output of the parliament was small. In particular the need to wait for a bill to be transmitted in proper form from London held up the preparation of the subsidy legislation, which was at this stage the administration's main purpose in keeping parliament in being. Meanwhile the Catholic MPs, initially quiescent, once again became vocal, raising in particular the exclusion of Catholics from legal practice, and the continued levying of recusancy fines under the act of uniformity. Chichester responded by proroguing parliament on 29 November, amid growing doubts whether the subsidy bill, even when available, would be passed. By the time parliament met again, in April 1615, however, Chichester had a new card to play: vague but alarming evidence pointing to a planned rebellion by the Irish

[61] James I's speech to the recusant lords and gentlemen, 18 May 1613 (*Carew MSS 1603–1623*, 288–92).

of Ulster. Against this background recusant MPs hurried to protest their loyalty, and to vote a subsidy of £25,000, before parliament was dissolved in October. [62]

For Catholics the parliament of 1613–15 represented a significant short-term victory. But their position had nevertheless worsened substantially in the twelve years since Tyrone's surrender. The last Catholic judge, Sir John Everard of the King's Bench, had been forced to resign in 1607. The previous year the deputy and council had imposed the oath of supremacy on all lawyers admitted to practise after 5 November 1605. In 1613, in retaliation for the prominent part played by lawyers in the Catholic parliamentary opposition, the oath was extended to all those seeking to practise law. Catholic merchants and professional men, likewise, continued to be excluded by the oath of supremacy from sharing in the government of the towns or cities in which they controlled the greater part of the commerical wealth, while at the same time facing fines or imprisonment because of their unwillingness to serve. When Chichester left office in 1616, his successor found more than eighty leading townsmen from Leinster and Munster in prison. In the counties the administration, which controlled the appointment of sheriffs, now nominated Protestants wherever possible. Fines for non-attendance at Protestant services continued to be widely levied, as were the fees and penalties dispensed by the church courts, the burden falling mainly on the Catholic poor, whom local officials found safer prey than men of property. Catholic landed estates were also under threat. In 1615 selected nobles and gentry in Munster and the Pale were ordered to send their eldest sons to England, where they would serve as hostages for good behaviour while being educated as Protestants. Shortly afterwards the crown began to enforce more rigorously the requirement that minors who became royal wards should take the oath of supremacy as a condition of entering into their inheritance. This closer regulation of wardship, culminating in the creation of the court of wards in 1622, posed a particularly serious threat to the large proportion of Catholics holding their lands by knight service.[63]

Aristocratic wardships were initially in a separate category being dealt with directly by the king. But here too developments in the two premier Old English dynasties gave James I the opportunity to demonstrate his determination both to undermine Catholic interests and to promote those of English intruders. When George Fitzgerald succeeded at the age of 9 years to the earldom of Kildare in 1620, James bestowed the wardship on a courtier, the duke

[62] For general accounts of the parliament and associated events see, again, McCavitt, *Chichester*, chs. 10–11; idem, *The Flight of the Earls*, chs. 9–10. For the more positive side of the parliament's legislative record, see T. W. Moody, 'The Irish Parliament under Elizabeth and James I: A General Survey', *PRIA*, C, 45 (1939), 62–71. For the role of the 1615 conspiracy, Raymond Gillespie, *Conspiracy: Ulster Plots and Plotters in 1615* (Belfast, 1987), 3–12.

[63] Colum Kenny, 'The Exclusion of Catholics from the Legal Profession in Ireland, 1537–1829', *IHS* 25 (1987), 343–7; Victor Treadwell, 'The Irish Court of Wards under James I', *IHS* 12 (1960), 1–27. For knight service and other forms of tenure, see above, Ch.7 n. 27.

of Lennox. Earlier, in a series of judgments taken into his own hands, he had already allowed Sir Robert Digby, a well connected Warwickshire gentleman, to claim a substantial part of the Kildare estate in right of his wife, Lettice, granddaughter of the eleventh earl. In the long run the main beneficiary was the earl of Cork, who in 1629 purchased the earl's wardship from Lennox's widow, and a year later arranged his marriage to Cork's own daughter. Meanwhile Cork had already acquired an interest in the other part of the Kildare inheritance by marrying another daughter, in 1626, to the heir to the Digby estate.

In the case of the Ormond estates, the tenth earl, having failed to produce a son, had secured the succession by marrying his daughter Elizabeth to his nephew and heir, Viscount Tulleophelim. When Tulleophelim died in 1613, Ormond's heir became a second nephew, Walter Butler of Kilcash. At this point, however, the king intervened to order the marriage of Tulleophelim's widow to a royal favourite, Richard Preston, Lord Dingwall. When the tenth earl died almost immediately after, Dingwall laid claim, in the right of his wife, to both the title and the estate. Walter Butler had served the crown loyally in the war against Tyrone. But he was also a committed Catholic, nicknamed 'Walter of the Beads and Rosaries'. Dingwall, by contrast, had further strengthened his position by becoming a client of Buckingham. In 1617 the king intervened to overturn a judge's verdict in favour of Walter, instead submitting the case to his own arbitration. His judgment, in 1618, had no choice but to allow Walter the title, firmly entailed in the male line, but allocated well over half of the Ormond estates to Dingwall. When Walter challenged the decision, he was imprisoned in London, where he remained until 1627, while his lands were handed over to his rivals. Meanwhile his grandson and heir, James Butler, was declared a ward of the crown and sent to England. The partition of the estate was reversed in 1629, when James married Elizabeth Preston, 13-year-old heiress to the Dingwall estate. But his upbringing in England, under the guardianship of the firmly Calvinist Archbishop Abbot of Canterbury, ensured that the head of Ireland's premier Old English family was to navigate the complex political waters of the next half century as a firm Protestant.[64]

Where Catholics as a body were concerned, policy in the decade after the conflicts of 1613–15 was inconsistent. Oliver St John, who replaced Chichester as lord deputy in August 1616, continued the campaign against recusants in the municipalities. When the aldermen of Waterford defiantly returned another Catholic mayor, the administration singled the city out for exemplary punishment, initiating proceedings that led to the forfeiture of its charter in 1618. A proclamation in 1617 announced the banishment of foreign-educated priests, but there was no apparent attempt to enforce the order. In the same year

[64] For a full account of these complex transactions see Victor Treadwell, *Buckingham and Ireland 1616–1628: A Study in Anglo-Irish Politics* (Dublin, 1998), 114–30; Edwards, *Ormond Lordship*, 103–28.

the crown transferred responsibility for collecting recusancy fees to the Church of Ireland, the proceeds to be used for ecclesiastical purposes. In the archdiocese of Armagh Archbishop Hampton agreed with recusants to suspend the fines for three years on condition that they paid for the refurbishment of parish churches. In the midlands, on the other hand, there were reports of Catholics who had already reached agreement with local Church of Ireland ministers regarding the fees for baptisms, marriages, and christenings performed by their own priests now facing retrospective demands from the bishops. When negotiations began in 1618 for a marriage alliance with Spain, the government largely suspended the collection of recusancy fines. Reports of a sharp corresponding drop in church attendance confirmed the existence of large numbers of unwilling conformists.[65] In 1621 there were reports that judges had once more been instructed to deal moderately with recusants, again in order to facilitate dealings with Catholic rulers. But the following year Middlesex's commission of inquiry found that some 40,000 recusants were either under sentence of excommunication or in danger of arrest on account of unpaid fines.[66]

In 1625 the demands of foreign policy brought the relationship between the crown and those it had branded half-subjects back to the centre of political debate.[67] War against Spain made it urgently necessary to provide for the defence of Ireland. The key figure in what followed was Sir John Bath, a Pale landowner and brother of the celebrated Jesuit scholar William Bath, who had earlier penetrated Irish circles in Spain as a spy for James I, his services apparently including the killing of the potentially dangerous émigré nobleman Donal O'Sullivan Beare.[68] This background leaves it unclear on whose behalf, the crown or the Old English, Bath now acted. In any case what emerged from secret discussions during the summer and autumn was a proposal that the Old English nobility and gentry should cooperate in raising a local militia, modelled on the 'trained bands' maintained in English counties and cities, in exchange for the replacement of the oath of supremacy by an oath of allegiance which loyal Catholics would feel free to take. As a first step the crown on 13 October ordered the suspension of recusancy fines. Over the next few months, however, the militia scheme collapsed, as it became clear that Falkland and other senior members of the Dublin administration were not prepared to cooperate in placing weapons in what they insisted were politically unreliable hands.

This left the question of defence unsolved. Already by late 1625 the Dublin government had had to revert to billeting an expanded army on the population,

[65] Treadwell, *Buckingham and Ireland*, 222.

[66] MacCuarta, 'De Renzy Letters', 11; Edward Brouncker to Ussher, 4 July 1621 (Ussher, *Works*, xvi. 377); Treadwell, *Buckingham and Ireland*, 221–3.

[67] The most detailed study of the crown's dealings with the Catholics in the years after 1625 remains Aidan Clarke, *The Old English in Ireland 1625–42* (London, 1966), chs. 2–3.

[68] Micheline Kerney Walsh, *An Exile of Ireland: Hugh O'Neill, Prince of Ulster* (Dublin, 1996), 102–6.

despite having already collected the annual 'composition' paid by the three southern provinces in lieu of that traditional right. In Waterford, unpaid soldiers had been driven to scavenging for food, 'a nutting and hunting of blackberries, like michers that run from school when they should be better occupied'.[69] Against this background, Bath travelled to England in summer 1626 to negotiate directly with Charles I, who had succeeded his father the previous year. He was accompanied by the earl of Westmeath, formerly, as Baron Delvin, involved in Tyrone's alleged conspiracy and even for a time out in arms as an outlaw, but now rehabilitated, in the eyes of the court at least.[70] What emerged was a new agreement: that the nobility of Ireland would be asked to pay for an expanded army of 5,500 men, in exchange for a series of concessions, described as 'matters of grace and bounty', which would include the oath of allegiance and the suspension of recusancy fines.

Back in Ireland, however, the leaders of the Old English landed elite proved unexpectedly uncooperative. To them the trained bands had been not just a bargaining chip, but an important symbolic gesture: a return to the traditional reliance on the Old English as the primary defenders of the crown's rights in Ireland. At a meeting of nobility in November 1626, and again at a 'great assembly' of elected delegates in April and May 1627, they made clear their unwillingness to be satisfied with the limited, impermanent concessions on offer. Meanwhile the bishops of the Church of Ireland also mobilized. At a meeting convened by Ussher in November 1626 they drew up a strongly worded protest insisting that to grant toleration to Catholics was to become an accessory to superstition, and that to do so for money was 'to set religion to sale, and with it the souls of the people'. They initially decided to withhold the document, hoping for a breakdown in the negotiations for which Catholics would take the blame. In April 1627, with an agreement apparently imminent, Ussher, Archbishop Hamilton of Cashel, and George Downham, bishop of Derry, all preached sermons attacking the proposal to condone popery in exchange for financial support, and Downham read out the text of the 1626 protest.[71] Falkland and other members of the Dublin administration likewise criticized the proposed concessions, suggesting that the money could be better raised by resuming recusancy fines on an increased scale.

By this time any dream of a reaffirmation of the bond between the crown and its loyal Catholic subjects, symbolized by the orderly ranks of a Pale militia

[69] David Rothe, RC bishop of Ossory, to Lombard, 17 September 1625 (*Wadding Papers*, 102–3).

[70] For Westmeath's earlier troubles see above, Ch. 6 n. 97, and McCavitt, *Flight of the Earls*, 121–3. For later allegations against him see below, 'The Contention of the Bards'.

[71] Alan Ford, 'James Ussher and the Godly Prince in Early Seventeenth-Century Ireland', in Hiram Morgan (ed.), *Political Ideology in Ireland 1541–1641* (Dublin, 1999), 203–28; Ford, 'Criticising the Godly Prince: Malcolm Hamilton's Passages and Consultations', in Carey and Lotz-Heumann, *Taking Sides*, 116–37. For the reasons for initially withholding the November protest see Ussher to Abbot, 9 February 1627 (Ussher, *Works*, xv. 366).

arrayed under the command of its natural superiors, had disappeared. But neither the crown, now at war with France as well as Spain, nor the Catholics, reminded yet again of the implacable hostility of the local administration and the established church, had any real alternative but to persevere with what were now hard-edged negotiations between mutually suspicious partners. In January 1628 a delegation of eight Catholics and three Protestants travelled to London for new talks. By May they had reached agreement on a total of 51 articles, known as 'his majesty's instructions and graces' or, more briefly, the Graces. These included some concessions relevant to all inhabitants of the kingdom, such as the curtailing of exploitative monopolies, and a reduction in official fees. The heart of the agreement, however, concerned Catholic grievances. Jurisdiction over offences to do with marriages, baptisms, and funerals was to be transferred from the ecclesiastical to the civil courts, thus curtailing the opportunities for predation by men like Kilmore's pooka.[72] Lawyers and heirs suing out their livery—though not office holders—were to be permitted to take an oath of allegiance rather than the oath of supremacy. In exchange Ireland was to provide three annual subsidies of £40,000 sterling each, to meet the cost of the army. The trained bands issue was partly resolved by a separate agreement that Old English officers would be placed in command of some of the new companies thus supported.

Two other items included in the articles of May 1628 had not previously been part of the negotiations, but from now on were to assume a central importance. The first undertook that the crown would, by means of an act to be passed in the next parliament, renounce all buried titles to land dating back more than sixty years. The second promised to resolve the special case of Connacht, where landholders had engaged in a general surrender of their lands during 1616–21 but the enrolment process for their new patents had never been properly completed. The unsuccessful attempt, not long after, to initiate a plantation in the province suggests that this omission may well have been deliberate, with Sir Charles Coote emerging as the most likely culprit.[73] The confirmation of the surrenders would remove the risk of any further attempts on the estates of Connacht proprietors, while the imposition of a time limit on the revival of royal claims would put an end both to grants of concealed lands and to larger-scale land-grabbing projects such as the Wexford and Leitrim plantations. Neither article related solely to Catholic property. But their inclusion, and the prominence they were hereafter to assume in Catholic demands, testifies to the extent to which the concerns of the Old English had shifted from reaffirming their claim to be accepted as loyal subjects to protecting themselves against what was assumed to be a hostile and predatory crown and government.

This background of suspicion and hostility was crucial to what happened next. Falkland, ordered to proceed with the legislation promised in the Graces, duly

[72] Above, p. 349. [73] Treadwell, *Buckingham and Ireland*, 265–7.

issued writs for a meeting of parliament. In doing so, however, he overlooked the strict terms of Poynings's Law, which required that a parliament could not be summoned until the bills to be laid before it had been approved in England. As a result the promised parliament had to be cancelled a fortnight before it was due to meet. This was even though the collection of the first of the promised subsidies had already begun. Old English leaders responded by staging a meeting in Dublin which lodged a protest against the failure to implement all of the Graces. However, their room for manoeuvre was limited. If some of the promised benefits had been withheld, others had been delivered. In particular Catholic lawyers had been readmitted to practise, from June 1628, on taking an oath of allegiance. Following the November protest, moreover, the court of wards ceased to require heirs reaching their majority to take the oath of supremacy, leading to an immediate rush of wards applying to sue out their livery. The cancelled parliament deprived the Old English of what had now become their two main objectives: the general confirmation of titles in Connacht, and a time limit on royal claims to land. But to go on the offensive, for example by refusing to continue paying the first subsidy, would jeopardize other substantial gains. There was also the question of whether, surrounded by an enlarged and needy army all too likely to turn to plunder, it was in fact safe to refuse the money needed for its pay. In this sense, it has been suggested, Falkland's procedural blunder had inadvertently called the Old English bluff.[74]

The Graces had included no explicit reference to Catholic religious practice. Clearly it made more sense to hope for a practical connivance than pointlessly to challenge a central assumption of the confessional state. During the 1620s the work of building up a Counter-Reformation church organization had continued. The new confidence encouraged by the negotiation of the Graces was evident in the ambitious schooling projects initiated from 1625 by both Franciscans and Dominicans.[75] By 1629, however, England's wars with both France and Spain were winding down. Against this background Falkland received permission to take action. A proclamation on 1 April complained of the insolence and presumption encouraged by 'the late intermission of legal proceedings'. It went on to forbid the exercise of ecclesiastical jurisdiction, the maintenance of religious communities, preaching, and the celebration of mass. Enforcement, however, proved difficult, in a kingdom where, despite two decades of New English advance, so much effective local power still lay in Catholic hands. In Drogheda, for example, Falkland complained that the reading of the proclamation was assigned to two soldiers, 'both being made, by too much drink, uncapable of that task, and perhaps purposely put to it, [who] made the same seem like a May-game'. In the kingdom as a whole mass houses and communities of

[74] This is the argument of Clarke, *Old English in Ireland*, 56.

[75] Mooney, 'Golden Age of the Irish Franciscans', 24–5; Flynn, *Irish Dominicans*, 151–4.

regulars, in Falkland's phrase, 'shut up the fore-doors', but continued with their business.[76]

By this time Falkland's deputyship was coming to an end. His administration had for some time been divided between two factions. One, headed by the earl of Cork, supported the lord deputy, while the other, headed by Lord Chancellor Loftus, opposed him. On Falkland's recall in October 1629, these two leaders took office jointly as lords justices. Loftus's faction had been accused of carrying their obstruction so far as opportunistically to encourage the Old English in their recent agitation. Now, however, the two joined in initiating a tightening of religious policy. On 26 December the mayor and archbishop of Dublin came under violent attack as they led a raid on the Franciscan friary in Cook Street.[77] In retaliation the government imprisoned a number of Catholic aldermen and others for failing to come to the mayor's assistance, and ordered a general closure of religious communities, enforced by the confiscation of any buildings in which they were found. In the towns and cities, though much less so in rural areas, the threat to property was for a time effective in making owners reluctant to rent to Catholic clergy, especially regulars. Meanwhile there were two further attempts during 1630–1 to initiate plantations on the basis of allegedly defective titles, one in the Ormond lands in Tipperary, the other in the counties of Mayo, Roscommon, and Sligo. Both quickly failed, but the effect can only have been to heighten the Old English sense of their continued vulnerability, despite the partial concessions of the Graces.

Ussher and his fellow bishops had condemned the toleration of Catholicism on the grounds that it made the state an accessory to heresy. For the state itself, however, the main argument both for excluding Catholics from its service, and for impeding or outlawing the practice of their religion, was that the obedience which their church required them to give to a foreign power, the pope, was in conflict with their loyalty to the crown. James I, lambasting the recusant delegates in May 1613, called them 'half subjects', entitled only to 'half privileges', 'you that have an eye to me one way and to the pope the other way'.[78] Others, continuing a line of argument that had already become clear during the war against Tyrone, made more direct allegations of disloyalty. Sir George Carew, in 1614, argued that the long-standing animosity of English Irish and Gael had now been laid aside, partly because of a new willingness to intermarry, partly because the native Irish themselves had become more civil in manner, and partly through a shared hostility to the New English. As a result 'the slaughters and rivers of blood shed between them is forgotten'. Indeed 'their union is such, as not only the Old English dispersed abroad in all parts of the realm, but the

[76] Falkland to Ussher, 14 April 1629 (Ussher, *Works*, xv. 438).

[77] *Wadding Papers*, 330, 333. See also F. X. Martin, *Friar Nugent: A Study of Francis Lavalin Nugent (1569–1635). Agent of the Counter Reformation* (London, 1962).

[78] *Carew MSS 1603–1623*, 290.

inhabitants of the Pale, cities, and towns, are as apt to take arms against us (which no precedent time has ever seen) as the ancient Irish'. Fynes Moryson, looking back around 1609 to his visit a decade earlier, fell back on the well-worn theme of the surrender of the older settlers to an inferior Irish culture:

> Our horses draw carts and like things with traces of ropes or leather, or with iron chains, but they fasten them by a withe to the tails of their horses, and to the rumps when the tails be pulled off. . . . We live in cleanly houses, they in cabins or smokey cottages. Our chief husbandry is in tillage, they despise the plough . . . to conclude they abhor from all things that agree with English civility. Would any man judge these to be born of English parents: or will any man blame us for not esteeming or employing them as English, who scorn to be so reputed.

To this familiar checklist of cultural degeneracy, however, he added a novel charge of conscious cultural renunciation: citizens of Waterford and Cork, 'having wives that could speak English as well as we', were displeased if they used the language with visitors.[79]

These suggestions of a new common interest between Old English and Irish were not wholly without foundation. Tyrone, from the safety of his continental exile, claimed that the mandates policy had driven some of the Old English to approach him and Tyrconnell, and even to propose an armed league to deliver the country from tyranny and heresy. There was further talk of a league when religious represssion resumed after 1611. A key figure on this occasion was William Meade, the former recorder of Cork, who had survived an attempt to have him convicted of treason following the Cork recusant revolt, and had retreated to exile in Spain.[80] Yet he and others like him remained a small minority. Self-interest had dictated that Old English lawyers should give their assistance to Irish proprietors threatened by the Wexford plantation, since the property of both ethnic groups was under attack. For other purposes, however, a renegotiated accommodation with the English crown, however loveless the union had by this time become, remained preferable to an alliance with Gaelic treason. Old English MPs in the parliament of 1613–15, accounting for all but 18 of the 100 Catholic members returned, unhesitatingly accepted the bill of attainder against Tyrone and the other Ulster fugitives, while in its final session the mere report of an Irish conspiracy was enough to induce them to pass the subsidy bill and allow the government to dissolve parliament.

For the Old English, then, the early decades of the seventeenth century were a difficult period, in which an increasingly unsympathetic Protestant state questioned or openly rejected their claim to be the true representatives in Ireland of the tradition of English civility. Their dilemma was neatly summed up, as early as 1598, by Sir Christopher St Lawrence, the Pale nobleman who was later

[79] 'A Discourse of the Present Estate of Ireland, 1614, per G.C.' (*Carew MSS 1603–1623*, 305); *Fynes Moryson's Unpublished Itinerary*, 50–1.

[80] McCavitt, *Flight of the Earls*, 61, 181, 198.

to play such an ambiguous part in Tyrone's flight from Ireland. Told by the English privy council that he should return to what he complained was a poor military command in Ireland because he was an Irishman, he responded with a vigorous protest: 'I am sorry that when I am in England I should be esteemed an Irish man, and in Ireland an English man. I have spent my blood, engaged and endangered my life often, to do her majesty service, and do beseech to have it so regarded.'[81] One of the clearest expressions of Old English political thinking, in this difficult period of transition, was an appeal to the king of Spain, submitted around 1623, asking him to have some provision for the Catholics of Ireland included in the treaty that was to accompany the expected marriage alliance with England. The issues on which the document concentrated were in many cases similar to those that were to figure in the negotiations that were soon after to result in the Graces: freedom of worship, the removal of the oath of supremacy from lawyers and office holders, an end to the subjection of Catholic families to religious interference from the court of wards. One article suggested a possible restoration to Catholic hands of church buildings and ecclesiastical lands, but also left open the possibility of a negotiated division of resources between Protestant and Catholic churches, and even of a continued collection of tithes by Protestant ministers. Two other articles called for the restoration of estates to those dispossessed following Tyrone's revolt, and for the removal of laws preventing the Old Irish ('los Irlandeses antiguos') from buying or renting plantation lands.

The inclusion of these last two elements confirms that Carew and others were not wholly incorrect in insisting that the Old English had begun to develop some sense of common interest linking them to their Gaelic co-religionists. A closing rhetorical flourish mentioning the Spanish descent of many of the ancient families of Ireland, introducing an origin legend enshrined in a succession of Gaelic sources, further highlights the hybrid nature of the document.[82] The main focus of the appeal, however, was on the practical ways in which Irish Catholics could be guaranteed acceptable conditions of life under the continued rule of the English crown. In framing their proposals, moreover, the authors appealed explicitly to a vision of constitutional rights seen as arising directly from the attachment of Ireland to the English crown. In order to ensure that what was now agreed would be adhered to for the future, 'all parliaments [are] henceforth to be held according to the ancient laws of England, particularly the instructions of Henry II, who ordered that all prelates, lords of baronies or the equivalent shall be entitled to speak and vote in parliament.'[83]

[81] Rowland Whyte to Sir Robert Sydney, 31 October 1599 (*Letters and Memorials of State*, ed. Arthur Collins, 2 vols. (London, 1746), ii. 138).

[82] For the supposed descent of the Irish from the Spanish 'Milesians' see the discussion of Keating's historical writing later in this chapter.

[83] Glyn Redworth, 'Beyond Faith and Fatherland: "The Appeal of the Catholics of Ireland" *c.* 1623', *Archivium Hibernicum*, 52 (1998), 3–23.

There remained the question of how continued loyalty to a Protestant English monarch was to be reconciled with the rival jurisdiction of the pope. Clement VIII had carefully avoided endorsing Tyrone's attempts to place himself at the head of a Catholic crusade. In doing so he had ignored the advice of, among others, the archbishop of Armagh, Peter Lombard, who had openly linked Tyrone's cause with that of the Catholic church. Since then, however, Lombard himself had had second thoughts. As early as 1604 he had dedicated a work to James I, and in 1613–14 he openly opposed Tyrone's attempts to promote a new invasion of Ireland, arguing that the interests of Catholics there were better served by encouraging them to accept James as their lawful ruler.[84] The decision soon after to resume appointing bishops to Irish sees was a consequence of this new pragmatism, and the men chosen, on Lombard's advice, were Old English clergy loyal to the crown. Thus David Rothe, appointed to Ossory in 1618, had dedicated the first part of his *Analecta* (1616) to the prince of Wales, the future Charles I, and had balanced his account of Catholic sufferings at the hands of Chichester with an unambiguous assertion of the subjection of Ireland to 'the dominion, crown and sceptre of the English'.[85]

Matters became more complex after Lombard's death in 1625. His successors Hugh MacCaughwell and Hugh O'Reilly were both Gaelic Irish Ulstermen, sponsored by the Spanish court and by the heirs of Tyrone and Tyrconnell. Thereafter popes followed a dual policy. In dioceses where Old English influence was strong they appointed Old English bishops, while in Gaelic areas they appointed Irishmen. The latter were not necessarily active opponents of the crown: the statutes introduced in 1631 by Archbishop O'Queely of Tuam, for example, contained an instruction to clergy to include the king and his family in public prayers. But the networks of influence to which they belonged nevertheless centred on the Spanish court, and on the Gaelic exile community. Similar divisions existed among the religious orders, separating the mainly Old English Jesuits and Capuchins from the mainly Gaelic Franciscans. When Lavallin Nugent, head of the Irish Capuchins, sought permission in 1624 to visit Ireland, he described himself as 'a vassal to his majesty, though I differ from him in points of religion'. Two years earlier he had complained to the papal nuncio of the damage likely to be done to the position of Catholics in Ireland by Philip O'Sullivan Beare's inflammatory history of the Desmond and Tyrone rebellions.[86] The ethnic division was not absolute. Among the Dominicans Old English and Gaelic Irish appear to have coexisted more harmoniously than

[84] Lombard's belated transfer of allegiance from Tyrone to the crown may have owed something to the predicament in which he was placed when it was discovered that his nephew, Robert Lombard, was apparently having an affair with the earl's much younger fourth wife (McCavitt, *Flight of the Earls*, 220).

[85] Colm Lennon, 'Political Thought of Irish Counter-Reformation Churchmen: The Testimony of the "Analecta" of Bishop David Rothe', in Morgan, *Political Ideology*, 189.

[86] Martin, *Friar Nugent*, 249–50. For O'Sullivan Beare, see the next section of this chapter.

elsewhere. The founder of the Franciscan college in Rome, and from 1625 the Vatican's main adviser on Irish affairs, was in fact an Old English friar, Luke Wadding. This anomalous position, however, merely exposed him to attack from both sides. Old English critics like Nugent criticized him as too close to the Gaelic Irish. Gaelic critics accused him of favouritism towards the Old English, and of insufficient enthusiasm for the Catholic cause, and in the years before his death in 1657 he was an isolated and disregarded figure.

The most significant effort, in this period, to create a bond between Old English and Gaelic Irish came in the field, not of politics, but of history and culture. Sometime between 1633 and 1635 Geoffrey Keating completed *Foras Feasa ar Éirinn* (Compendium of Wisdom about Ireland). Keating, born in County Tipperary around 1580, had studied or taught at the universities of Rheims and Bordeaux and by 1613 had returned to his native county to work as a priest. His *Foras Feasa* combined Gaelic sources, notably the eleventh-century *Lebor Gabála* (Book of Invasions), biblical chronology, and a selective use of other historical writings, to offer a comprehensive history of Ireland from the Flood to the twelfth century. Its aim was in part to rebut the stereotype of native Irish barbarity first offered by Giraldus Cambrensis and more recently continued by Spenser, Davies, and others. Instead the ancestry of the main Gaelic families was traced to the arrival around 1300 BC of Clann Mhíleadh, the Milesians or sons of Míl, who had come from Scythia via Egypt and Spain, thus bringing with them the advanced culture of the ancient Mediterranean. They had created a society firmly ruled by a monarchy and aristocracy, with an elaborate legal code and a well-developed literary culture.[87]

Yet Keating's careful itemization of the different peoples who had inhabited Ireland before the Milesians also contained another message: that Ireland had been the home of successive waves of conquering newcomers, of whom the English of the twelfth century were only the latest. Their intervention, moreover, had been a legitimate one, authorized by the pope's grant of Ireland to Henry II. To account for the undeniable warfare between Irish and English that had followed this intrusion, Keating distinguished between certain individual English lords who had abused their power, and whom God had punished by wiping out their posterity, and others, who had become the ancestors of the Old English lineages of his own day. For good measure Keating reminded his readers that James I and Charles I were also, through the long line of Scottish monarchs, descendants of Míl of Spain. In this way he combined a vindication of Gaelic civility with an origin legend capable of accommodating both Gaelic and English Irish. He likewise provided the historical underpinnings for the idea of an Irish kingdom, while unreservedly endorsing its attachment to the English crown. In addition his account of early Irish Christianity added a further element to the

[87] Bernadette Cunningham, *The World of Geoffrey Keating: History, Myth and Religion in Seventeenth-Century Ireland* (Dublin, 2000).

shared religious heritage of Gaelic and English Irish. Here Keating's account was strongly influenced by current preoccupations. In addition to recounting the lives of the celebrated saints of early Christian Ireland, he laid heavy emphasis on the reforms of the twelfth century as having established a diocesan church structured along proto-Tridentine lines.

Keating once again illustrates the variations concealed behind apparently clear-cut contemporary references to the English Irish or the 'Old English'. He was himself apparently a younger son of a propertied Old English family, clients of the Butlers of Cahir. But he also reputedly studied with the MacCraiths, a bardic family patronized by the Cahir Butlers. His own history was written in Irish, though in a modern prose rather than in the archaic dialect still used by the Gaelic literary elite, suggesting that it was addressed to an audience, whether Gaelic or English Irish, for whom this was their only, or at least an easily accessible language. The work was quickly absorbed into the Gaelic manuscript tradition, with copies circulating widely. An English translation, also in manuscript, was completed as early as 1635, addressed to an audience clearly expected to share the text's religious and political sympathies, and an interest in the Gaelic past, but unable to read its language. There were others, however, to whom the invitation to identify with Gaelic culture, whether in the original or in translation, had little appeal. The comments of Bishop Roche of Ferns, writing in 1631 and representing the voice of the urban elite rather than of the ethnically and culturally mixed rural hinterland, are at best dismissive:

> One Doctor Keating laboureth much, as I hear say, in compiling Irish notes towards a history in Irish. The man is very studious, and yet I fear that if his work come ever to light, it will need an amendment of ill-warranted narrations; he could help you to many curiosities of which you can make better use than himself. I have no interest in the man, for I never saw him, for he dwelleth in Munster.[88]

For Keating's family, or for their patrons the Cahir Butlers, *Foras Feasa* provided a sophisticated intellectual basis for a blending of language and tradition that was already well established. For others, it may have contributed to the gradual discovery of a shared Irish Catholic identity. For others again, however, the lines of division between Old English and Gaelic Irish, cultural as well as political and religious, were clearly still strong.

THE CONTENTION OF THE BARDS

Among the items of business proposed for the parliament of 1613 was the dismantling of what was still a formidable body of legislation founded on principles of ethnic exclusiveness. A royal proclamation in March 1605, issued

[88] Roche to Wadding, 19 July 1631 (*Wadding Papers*, 544).

as part of the strategy of reducing the territorial power of the Gaelic lords, had already declared all the inhabitants of Ireland to be 'free, natural and immediate' subjects of the crown. Sir John Davies, however, argued in 1611 that this needed to be confirmed by 'a common council of the whole realm'. (Significantly, he made no mention of the act of 1541.) Parliament duly repealed an act of 1432 permitting the arrest of 'Irish enemies' in time of peace, as well as three other statutes prohibiting trade, intermarriage, and fostering between Irish and English. It also repealed the act of 1557 making it a felony to introduce Scots into the kingdom. The act relating to natives of Irish blood also included a general statement that 'all the natives and inhabitants of this kingdom, without difference and distinction, are taken into his majesty's gracious protection, and do now live under one law as dutiful subjects of our sovereign lord and monarch'. To this it added a generous serving of three kingdoms rhetoric: by the removal of these barriers, the 'many worthy persons born in his majesty's said several kingdoms' would 'grow into one nation, whereby there may be an utter oblivion and extinguishment of all former differences and discord betwixt them'.[89]

In fact the legislation fell well short of this extravagant language. Scots were no longer technically outlaws, but they were still aliens. The original grantees in the Ulster plantation had received free patents of denization giving them full legal status in both England and Ireland. All others born in Scotland before James I's accession, however, had to pay heavily for similar patents before becoming eligible to own property. The anomaly continued until a general naturalization act was passed in 1634. In the case of Irish natives the repeal of a few specific measures in 1613–15 had left a formidable body of discriminatory legislation on the statute book, including the notorious Statute of Kilkenny. A bill initiated by the Commons to repeal this and other laws failed to pass through the multiple stages required by Poynings's Law. Instead the king promised a proclamation (never apparently issued) ordering that the Kilkenny enactments should be regarded as a dead letter until such time as they could be repealed. Charles I's parliament duly removed some further obsolete statutes. After 1635 it was no longer illegal to wear a moustache without a beard, or legal to kill out of hand members of any group entering County Meath for the purposes of robbery, even if they were not accompanied by someone in English apparel. In the end, however, most of the statutory legacy accumulated over centuries of frontier conditions was permitted to wither rather than being formally repealed.[90]

Declarations of equality under the law did not imply any softening of hostility towards Gaelic culture. James I, complaining in 1612 of the slow progress of the Ulster plantation, still presented the project in terms of 'the introducing of

[89] *Carew MSS 1603–1623*, 166; Irish Statutes, 13 James I, c. 5.

[90] Perceval Maxwell, *Scottish Migration to Ulster*, 156–7; Moody, 'The Irish Parliament under Elizabeth and James I', 63; Irish Statutes 10–11 Charles I, c. 6.

civility, order and government amongst a barbarous and unsubjected people'.[91] Legislation proposed, though not adopted, for the parliament of 1613 included not just acts to confirm the abolition of tanistry and brehon law, but new measures against Irish dress and language, and the outlawing of titles commencing with 'O' and 'Mac'. There was also to be an act against 'barbarous and rude customs; as howling and crying at the burial of the dead, drawing their plough-cattle only fastened by the tails, and blowing their milch cattle to make them give milk, etc, and pulling of sheep'. The parliament of 1634 did in fact ban both ploughing by the tail and pulling (rather than shearing) the wool from the bodies of live sheep. Earlier, in 1624, a proclamation authorized sheriffs encountering anyone wearing a mantle or trews in public to remove the offending garments and cut them to pieces. Recognition of the native Irish as full subjects was thus closely linked with measures for their coercive assimilation into English customs and economic practices.[92]

If contempt for the Gaelic way of life had not diminished, neither had the fear of Gaelic treachery. For more than two decades after the flight of the northern earls the Irish government remained preoccupied by the possibility of rebellion or conspiracy, particularly where it might link the Irish at home with their compatriots abroad and the Catholic powers who sheltered them. In 1615, opportunely in view of the difficulties being experienced in parliament, the chance arrest of a traveller in Ulster led to the discovery of a conspiracy involving some disgruntled members of the MacDonnell family, acting in concert with a number of the Gaelic Irish. Their plan was to seize control of towns in Ulster, massacre settlers, and rescue Tyrone's son Conn, still in custody at Charlemont Fort. Six of those involved were subsequently executed. In 1624 Falkland investigated reports from Leitrim and elsewhere of an imminent general massacre of the English. The aim was supposedly to make the recusant earl of Westmeath king of Ireland, and Falkland seemed disposed to pursue the earl until ordered by the king to drop the matter and punish the accusers. In 1625 members of the Maguire and MacGowran families were accused of plotting to seize castles in Cavan and Fermanagh in anticipation of a Spanish landing, with four supposed ringleaders being sentenced to death. In Tipperary five years later a report claimed that 'the dispossessed of the mere Irish, both civil and otherwise bred, are daily expectors of invasion, and that all the favours bestowed upon them will never quiet their disloyal and insatiable expectations'.[93]

None of these conspiracies, it should be noted, amounted to a very substantial threat. The 1615 plan was at best a sketchy one: the confederates planned to stay drinking in Coleraine until after the gates were closed, then seize the town,

[91] T. W. Moody (ed.), 'Ulster Plantation Papers 1608–13', *Analecta Hibernica*, 8 (1939), 277–8.

[92] *Carew MSS 1603–1623*, 157, 161, 163; R. R. Steele (ed.), *Tudor and Stuart Proclamations 1485–1714*, 2 vols. (Oxford, 1910), ii, pt. 1, *Ireland*, no. 252.

[93] Gillespie, *Conspiracy; CSPI 1615–25*, 477, 517–18; *CSPI 1625–32*, 75, 102, 35, 432, 436.

capture the weapons they optimistically assumed would be available there, and go on to attack other places. There was no attempt to secure foreign aid; but a fall-back was that, if things went badly, 'we can all go to Spain with the boy [Conn O'Neill] and be welcome'.[94] Later alleged plots are known only through the questionable evidence of informers. Yet if the spectre of organized conspiracy remained elusive, the threat of native violence was nevertheless real enough. In Ulster in the early years of the plantation British settlers suffered heavily from attacks. On the Drapers' portion at Moneymore in County Londonderry an agent spoke in 1615 of working 'as it were with the sword in one hand and the axe in the other'. A concerted drive in the winter of 1616–17 led to the execution of over forty reputed marauders, but frequent killings and robberies continued into at least the 1620s.[95] In Wexford, likewise, a party led by one of the Kavanaghs was reported in 1620 to have killed settlers and burned their towns and houses. In 1626 troops were deployed against raiders in Cavan, Longford, and Leitrim. The following year there were reports of disturbances elsewhere in Ulster, and in 1628 of a band of fourteen on the rampage in Galway and Roscommon.[96]

Violence of this sort must be seen in context. Banditry of one kind or another was endemic in all but the most well policed regions of early modern Europe. Ireland, with its substantial areas of surviving bog and woodland, its thin population, and its poor roads, provided an inviting field of operation. The very notion of an outlaw, moreover, depends on the existence of a recognized system of regulation beyond whose boundaries the outlaw, by certain actions, places himself or herself. In the Ireland of only a few decades earlier, with its numerous bands of armed retainers, its uncertain boundaries, and its acceptance of rights defined more by the successful assertion of control than by formal entitlement, the concept would have made only limited sense. By the reign of James I, on the other hand, the extension to the whole country of a uniform system of criminal justice had for the first time created a clear framework of legality which the individual could be categorized as either accepting or rejecting. At the same time there was not yet a system of law enforcement capable of dealing effectively with those who chose to take the latter path. In this sense early Stuart Ireland perfectly illustrates a more general point: that banditry is typically a product of an intermediate phase in the development of the law-enforcing state.[97]

[94] Gillespie, *Conspiracy*, 37.

[95] T. W. Moody, *The Londonderry Plantation 1609–41: The City of London and the Plantation in Ulster* (Belfast, 1939), 178, 329–31. Although Moody sees rebellion as 'smouldering . . . during the whole period' of his study, the examples he gives are no later than the 1620s. For contrasting views on the overall level of violence in post-plantation Ulster see Gillespie, *Conspiracy*, 35, and McCavitt, *Chichester*, 158. For the reasons for suggesting a change by the 1630s see below, Ch. 9.

[96] *CSPI 1615–25*, 295; *CSPI 1625–32*, 35,195, 217, 220, 248, 375–6.

[97] This is to apply an approach developed, in relation to Irish banditry in the late seventeenth century and after, in S. J. Connolly, *Religion, Law and Power: The Making of Protestant 1660–1760* (Oxford, 1992), 212, using a general model suggested in Brent D. Shaw, 'Bandits in the Roman Empire', *Past & Present*, 105 (1984), 3–52.

Having said this, banditry must also be seen in the context of a society torn apart by war and its aftermath. The last stages of the Tudor conquest had destroyed livelihoods, families, and communities. The armed retinues of the Gaelic and English lords had been disbanded. Large numbers—though never as large as government intended—had been driven from their lands to make way for settlers. Dislocation on this scale could hardly not have produced violence. It is equally safe to assume that ethnic and religious resentment would have played at least some part in legitimizing, if not actually inspiring, that violence. The distinction between those responding from choice to the opportunity to live by plunder and those driven or provoked to such a way of life remains impossible to draw precisely. The New English authorities, however, saw no reason even to try. Instead they referred routinely to outlaws of any kind as 'rebels'. The anomalies were noted by a fairly newly arrived Davies, when he presided over the assizes at Limerick in 1606, and heard of the depredations of 'two notorious thieves or, as they term them, rebels', operating on the borders of Clare and Tipperary. In Wexford, almost thirty years later, Sir William Brereton was told of woods that sheltered 'about sixteen stout rebels well appointed every of them with his pistols, skene, and darts; they also have four long pieces'. There is nothing to indicate, however, that what he described were more than highwaymen and housebreakers.[98]

For almost a decade after 1607 the main focus for both fears and hopes of a new upheaval in Ireland focused on the exiled Tyrone. The earl's flight had put him beyond the reach of James I, but had also made him the prisoner of European power politics. When bad weather forced him and his companions to land at the mouth of the Seine, rather than in Spain as planned, the French king had connived at the rapid removal of his embarrassing guests to the Spanish Netherlands. However, the Spanish, having concluded a long and destructive war with England only four years earlier, had no desire to reawaken hostilities. Accordingly they sent the Ulster lords and their entourage, not to Madrid, but to Rome, and thereafter made it a strict condition of continued financial support that they remained there, a threat against England to be held in reserve, but not an immediate provocation. Within months Tyrone, astute and tactically flexible as ever, was reported to be signalling his desire for a reconciliation with James I, talking openly of him as his sovereign, and of his many virtues. O'Doherty's revolt, on the other hand, led Tyrone to lobby vigorously for a new Spanish expedition to Ireland, arousing some interest but no concrete commitment. His hopes reawakened briefly, but again without result, when conflicts in the New World brought Spain and England close to war in 1612. In 1613 it was the turn of James I, alarmed at the strength of recusant discontent in Ireland, briefly to put out feelers for a reconciliation. By 1615 Tyrone, now insisting that he was

[98] *CSPI 1603–6*, 471; Brereton, *Travels*, 146, 155–6. A skene was a knife, a long piece a musket. For other references to 'rebels' see e.g. *CSPI 1625–32*, 195, 248, 375.

too near death to have anything to lose, was again agitating to lead an expedition to Ireland. Only his death on 20 July 1616 finally removed the possibility of one further twist in an already convoluted political career.[99]

By this time, however, Tyrone's household was only one part of a growing Irish population in continental Europe. The most prominent among these were soldiers. Companies of Irishmen in the service of France and Spain are recorded from the 1580s onwards. In 1605 Irish soldiers in the Spanish Netherlands were grouped in a regiment commanded by Tyrone's second son, Colonel Henry O'Neill. Between 1632 and 1636, in response to the continuing demands of the Thirty Years War, Spain created four further Irish regiments. Betwen 1635 and 1639, meanwhile, Spain's main rival in the conflict, France, raised six or seven regiments of infantry, comprising 5,000 men or more. To these must be added some 2,000 men recruited for Poland in 1621, and 200 or so for Denmark in 1628, as well as the 6,000 whom Chichester had earlier shipped to Sweden in preparation for the plantation of Ulster. Gaelic Ulstermen, headed by O'Neills and O'Donnells, comprised the largest and most influential section of the Irish contingent in Spanish service, giving rise to resentment from other groups. However eleven out of thirty captains serving in the Irish regiment between 1609 and 1622 were Old English, and two of the further regiments created in the 1630s had Old English commanders. In France, meanwhile, the regiments raised after 1635 were all commanded by Old Englishmen.

In later mythology these Spanish and other soldiers were the first of the 'wild geese', political and religious exiles driven to seek their fortunes on European battlefields. A more realistic perspective would start from the recognition that Ireland, peripherally located and economically underdeveloped, was in any case a natural recruiting ground for soldiers. There is no reason to assume that, even with a different political history, it would not have become one of those regions, like Scotland or Switzerland, whose surplus manpower helped to maintain the much expanded, and typically multinational, armies of the early modern military revolution. Expatriate Irish officers, equally, followed what would in any case have been one of the main careers open to the non-inheriting sons of noble or gentry families. Some of those who took service with Spain or other powers had earlier served the English crown in the war against Tyrone. Tyrone, at a time when he himself had as yet no intention of fleeing Ireland, had by his own account advised O'Donnell and Maguire that one way of escaping their financial difficulties would be to seek the king's licence to enter military service abroad. The English government, for its part, was generally willing to grant such applications, and to sanction the raising of soldiers in Ireland, on the grounds that idle or discontented men of military inclination were less dangerous abroad than at home.[100]

99 McCavitt, *Flight of the Earls*, 149, 187, 202, 213–17; Walsh, *Exile of Ireland*, 111–16, 121–8.

100 Henry, *The Irish Military Community in Spanish Flanders*; Roger Stradling, *The Spanish Monarchy and Irish Mercenaries: The Wild Geese in Spain 1618–1668* (Dublin, 1994); Harman

Military emigration, then, can in part be seen as no more than one part of a wider movement out of Ireland, inspired by the familiar duality of opportunity and need. The same period saw groups of Irish merchants, responding to the general expansion of foreign trade, take up permanent residence in ports on the western seaboards of Spain and France, and more particularly in the provinces of Galicia and Brittany; in the case of France the first naturalizations of Irishmen as French subjects were recorded in the 1610s. It also saw the beginnings of what was to be a recurrent feature of Irish life for most of the next three centuries: mass migration by the poor at times of economic crisis. Many went no further than England or Scotland. In 1605 the English exchequer had to compensate west coast ports for the extraordinary expenses involved in deporting large numbers of indigent Irish. Bishop Bedell, in 1629, was told that 1,000 had gone to England from County Cavan alone. But others, particularly from Munster, followed well-established trade routes to northern France, where the famines of 1603–5 and 1628–30 are reflected in reports of the arrival of large numbers of destitute Irish.[101]

This is not to suggest Irish military emigration did not also have a cultural and ideological dimension. Much of the recruitment, at least among the Gaelic Irish, drew on pre-existing attachments, with members of leading families raising men from among their traditional followers. Religious loyalties were also important. In 1587 a force of 600 Irishmen originally recruited to serve in the Netherlands under the English Catholic Sir William Stanley followed their commander when he defected to the Spanish. In the same way the men Chichester deported to Protestant Sweden subsequently deserted en masse to the army of Catholic Poland. In 1628 attempts to raise troops for Protestant Denmark seem to have met with objections on religious grounds, probably helping to account for the very small number recruited. If political and religious allegiances helped to inspire the Irish military diaspora, furthermore, it is also likely that the experience of foreign service in turn helped to shape Irish notions of identity. Exile, as always, brought a seductive clarity: aspirations and grievances could be rehearsed and elaborated with none of the qualifications and compromises imposed by day to day experience. Service in a multinational and polyglot army must have made its own contribution towards the emergence of a sense of Irishness, overlaying the still influential rivalries of competing septs and separate provinces. There was also, in the case of Spain, the close identification of military service with the cause of a Catholic reconquest of Europe.

Murtagh, 'Irish Soldiers Abroad', in Thomas Bartlett and Keith Jeffery (eds.), *A Military History of Ireland* (Cambridge, 1996), 294–7; Éamon Ó Ciosáin, 'A Hundred Years of Irish Migration to France, 1590–1688', in Thomas O'Connor (ed.), *The Irish in Europe 1580–1815* (Dublin, 2001), 98–102.

101 For migration to England see Treadwell, *Buckingham and Ireland*, 40–1; Bedell to Ward, 24 May 1629 (*Tanner Letters*, 89). For France, Ó Ciosáin, 'A Hundred Years of Irish Migration', 94–7.

If some Irishmen went abroad as professional soldiers with the approval of their king, then others continued to look to the day when they might return in arms to regain lost estates in an Ireland recaptured for the Counter-Reformation. Once again the distinction was largely on ethnic lines. In 1627 Owen Roe O'Neill, Tyrone's nephew, joined with the exiled archbishop of Tuam, Florence Conry, to draw up an elaborate plan to establish an independent Ireland with Spanish support. By contrast the Old English Thomas Preston, son of Viscount Gormanstown, openly clashed in 1608 with his commanding officer, Henry O'Neill, on the question of military action in Ireland, insisting that he would never bear arms against his sovereign. Later, in 1634, Preston had the active support of the lord deputy in recruiting men in Ireland for his own regiment in Spanish service. And when one of his officers defected to Owen Roe's rival regiment, he appealed to the deputy to take reprisals against the man's family in Ireland.

The second major group of Irish émigrés were the clergy. Again these were not new arrivals. Stanihurst, in 1584, began his second account of Ireland with a diatribe against the damage done to its reputation by low-born clergy, whose education went no further than 'learning to count the eggs in their mothers' chicken-coops', but who nevertheless made their way to Italy, where their shameless search for ecclesiastical preferment led Romans 'to ask all Irish beggars wryly, "Do you wish to become a bishop, my lord?"'.[102] By the early seventeenth century, however, Irish clerics on the continent had acquired their own expanding institutional base, as the colleges established in Spain, France, and elsewhere became home to teachers and scholars. Over time, too, a proportion of those educated in these institutions took benefices or administrative roles on the Continent, rather than returning to the Irish mission. There were close links between the clerical and military communities, with Irish priests serving as chaplains to Irish regiments and providing pastoral services to émigré families. Irish clergy also took an active political role, attaching themselves to the households of prominent exiles like the O'Neills, or serving as political advisers and intermediaries. Florence Conry (d. 1629), provincial of the Irish Franciscans and from 1609 archbishop of Tuam, who had served as O'Donnell's agent in Spain in the 1590s, remained particularly influential as an adviser to the Spanish council on Irish affairs, where he persistently advocated renewed military intervention in Ireland, and was openly critical of Old English attempts to reach an accommodation with the English crown. The same division between Old English and Gaelic Irish, partly institutionalized in the rivalry of Franciscans and Jesuits, was evident throughout the Irish church in exile. The Irish colleges, especially Douai, were also the site of bitter internal conflicts, as Gaelic ecclesiastics, their numbers and political influence growing rapidly after 1603, demanded their share of what had originally been Old English foundations.

102 Lennon, *Richard Stanihurst, the Dubliner 1547–1618* (Dublin, 1979), 132.

For Sir George Carew, writing in 1614, one reason for the dangerous new relationship between the Old English and Gaelic Irish was that 'the mere Irish (by their travel abroad) are civilized, grown to be disciplined soldiers, scholars, politicians, and further instructed in points of religion than accustomed'.[103] How far the Gaelic literary tradition of the early modern period had ever been wholly static and inward-looking remains open to debate. But it is undoubtedly the case that the multiple contacts with continental Europe imposed by circumstances from the end of the sixteenth century provided the basis for a new phase of creativity, in which traditional themes were reworked in the light of Renaissance and Counter-Reformation thinking.[104] A number of those prominent in bringing about this fusion of Gaelic and continental elements were themselves members of the hereditary bardic caste who, in changing circumstances, had opted instead for the training of a seminary priest. Thus Bonaventure Hussey (Giolla Brighde Ó hEodhasa), a Franciscan who lectured at Louvain, was a member of a bardic family who had in his youth composed an ode to Hugh Roe O'Donnell. His Irish-language catechism of 1611 made use of short passages in metrical verse as well as prose to provide the first printed manual of instruction in basic religious doctrine. Hugh MacCaughwell (Aodh MacAingil), again a Louvain Franciscan and later a short-lived archbishop of Armagh, was another seminary-trained poet. His *Sgáthán Shacramuinte na hAithridhe* (Mirror of the Sacrament of Confession) (1618) combined an exposition of the orthodox theology of repentance with explicit attacks both on the errors of Calvin and Luther and on the claims of Ussher and others to be the true heirs of early Irish Christianity. Florence Conry, founder of the Franciscan college at Louvain, whose family were scribes and historians to the O'Conors of Roscommon, translated a Catalan devotional text as *Sgáthán an Chrábhaidh* (Mirror of Faith) in 1616.[105]

This co-option of the traditional skills of the native literati to the service of the Counter-Reformation was not achieved painlessly. MacAingil anticipated objections to texts not written in a highly finished literary form, insisting that 'we are satisfied if we are understood even if we do not have correct Irish'. O'Hussey, similarly, wrote of using the 'wooden key' of ordinary spoken language, as opposed to the golden key of literary Irish.[106] In this sense Old English authors from Irish-speaking areas were possibly at an advantage. Keating's *Foras Feasa ar Éirinn*, as well as his two devotional tracts, *Eochair-sgiath an Aifrinn*, a defence of the mass, and *Trí Biorghaoithe an Bháis* (Three Shafts of Death), a meditation on mortality, were written in a clear and direct contemporary Irish, although

[103] *Carew MSS 1603–1623*, 305.

[104] The argument that the forced curtailment of 'insular bardic enforcement of outdated literary modes' opened the way for 'the golden age of Irish literature' is developed by Tadhg Ó Dúshláine, 'Devout Humanism Irish Style', in O'Connor, *The Irish in Europe*, 91–2.

[105] The role of priests from bardic families is particularly emphasized in Meigs, *Reformations in Ireland*, 81–9.

[106] Cunningham, *World of Geoffrey Keating*, 129; Meigs, *Reformations in Ireland*, 83.

the content of all three still assumed an educated audience. Theobald Stapleton, like Keating an Old English priest from County Tipperary, printed the text of his Irish catechism of 1639 in roman type, using a simplified spelling. His preface called on the Irish to join with other nations in preserving 'the native language of the fatherland', while at the same time denouncing 'the bad style of literary and poetical Irishmen, who have obfuscated it under a welter of overly obscure words'.[107]

Stapleton and others sought to develop a new form of written Irish, allied to the technology of print, as a means of disseminating the new doctrines of the Counter-Reformation within Ireland itself. By contrast the strongest statement of the political outlook of the expatriate Irish community, addressing a European audience and in particular the Spanish court, was in Latin. This was the *Historiae Catholicae Iberniae Compendium*, published in Lisbon in 1621, by Philip O'Sullivan Beare, a nephew of the defender of Dunboy. [108] O'Sullivan had gone to Spain in 1602, where he had been educated at the college of Santiago de Compostela before serving in the Spanish navy against Moors and Turks. The early parts of his compendium traced the ancestry of the Gaelic Irish to the Iberian prince Milesius, and countered the slanders of Gerald of Wales and his successors with an account of the high state of civilization, secular and religious, in early Ireland. His later writings, circulated only in manuscript, were to continue this theme, with detailed polemics against Stanihurst, for his dismissive account of Gaelic culture, against Thomas Dempster, who had recently claimed that the leading saints and scholars of the early Christian era had been Scottish rather than Irish, and against Ussher, for his attempt to present the Church of Ireland as the true heir to the church of St Patrick. In all this O'Sullivan Beare's concerns were close to those of Geoffrey Keating. Keating, however, sought to legitimize both the presence of the Old English in Ireland and the authority there of the English crown. O'Sullivan Beare, by contrast, presented the twelfth-century invasion as an unjust conquest, and the long succession of wars that had followed as an unbroken record of Irish resistance to tyranny, reaching a climax in the Munster and Ulster rebellions of the late sixteenth century. Where Keating sought to integrate Gaelic Irish and Old English into a single nation, O'Sullivan Beare's treatment was equivocal. He recognized that some of what he called the new Irish ('novi Iberni') had adopted Gaelic law and custom, and had supported the old Irish ('veteres Iberni') against the English. But he also commented bitterly on the failure of the Old English to support O'Neill and his allies, and his main emphasis was on an ancient Irish race defending its patrimony against unjust conquest.[109] O'Sullivan Beare himself had been expelled with others from the

[107] Leerssen, *Mere Irish and Fíor-Ghael*, 261–2. [108] Above, p. 252.

[109] Leerssen's conclusion that O'Sullivan Beare excluded the Old English from the Irish nation (*Mere Irish and Fíor-Ghael*, 273–4), is challenged by Clare Carroll, 'Cultural and Political Relations in the Work of O'Sullivan Beare', in Morgan, *Political Ideology*, 244–7. Carroll's analysis relies

college at Santiago in 1613 for opposing the Jesuit takeover of the institution, in one of the many clashes between Old English and Gaelic Irish that divided the émigré community.

O'Sullivan Beare's *Compendium* is noteworthy, not just for its uncompromising rejection of English rule over Ireland, but for the fusion of intellectual influences it represents. For his account of the Milesian origins of the Irish people, and of the advanced state of early Irish civilization, he drew on the rich corpus of pseudo-history and hagiography preserved in the Gaelic manuscript tradition. His critique of English rule in Ireland, on the other hand, appears to have drawn explicitly on the concepts of natural law, and of political legitimacy as founded in the customs of a community, that had been developed by the contemporary Jesuit theorist Francisco Suárez. His graphic depiction of the atrocities visited on the Irish by their English rulers may also have borrowed its imagery and rhetoric from the impassioned contemporary debate surrounding the treatment of the native population of the New World. In these ways O'Sullivan Beare, even more clearly than Keating or the Louvain Franciscans, created a new synthesis between the Gaelic literary tradition and the political thought of Counter-Reformation Europe. In addition, it has been pointed out, the very form of his compendium, in which the past both explains the present and provides political counsel, places him in the tradition of the new Renaissance historians such as Guicciardini, rather than of the Gaelic annalists of his homeland.[110]

In the first half of the seventeenth century, then, large numbers of Gaelic Irish found in emigration to continental Europe both a gateway to employment and status and a dramatic widening of intellectual horizons. By contrast the much larger body of Gaelic Irish who remained in Ireland confronted radical social and political change: the exile or dispossession of traditional lords, the extension to all regions of a new economic system and code of law, new pressures for religious conformity, and the imposition of a New English ruling class. These changes are clearly reflected in the substantial body of verse that continued to be produced, in the decades after 1603, by members of the hereditary bardic elite.[111]

less on the *Compendium* than on a separate manuscript, attributed to O'Sullivan Beare, which distinguishes more clearly between the 'ancient Irish', the 'English Irish' and what are referred to as 'mixed Irish', of English blood but culturally assimilated. Ó Buachalla draws attention to another text, *Zoilomastix*, in which O'Sullivan Beare challenges Stanihurst's description of the Old English as 'Anglo-Hiberni', insisting instead that there are only two groups within Ireland: Irishmen who are Catholic and Englishmen who are heretics: Ó Buachalla, 'James our True King: The Ideology of Irish Royalism in the Seventeenth Century', in G. D. Boyce, Robert Eccleshall, and Vincent Geoghegan (eds.), *Political Thought in Ireland since the Seventeenth Century* (London, 1993), 16. See also Lennon, *Richard Stanihurst*, 119.

110 This analysis of O'Sullivan Beare's difficult text is mainly based on Carroll, 'Cultural and Political Relations in the Work of O'Sullivan Beare', 229–53; eadem, 'Custom and Law in the Philosophy of Suárez and in the Histories of O'Sullivan Beare, Céitinn and Ó Cléirigh', in O'Connor, *The Irish in Europe*, 65–78.

111 For surveys, differing slightly in emphasis, see Bernadette Cunningham, 'Native Culture and Political Change in Ireland, 1580–1640', in Ciaran Brady and Raymond Gillespie (eds.), *Natives*

Poems survive lamenting the departure of the Ulster earls, and the death in exile of various of their number, presented as leaving Ireland grieving and desolate. Other texts comment disapprovingly on the abandonment of Irish for English fashions in dress. There are also frequent complaints of the decline of patronage for the bards themselves, with more than one poet theatrically expressing the wish that he had learned a useful trade in his youth. In the same spirit Connel MacGeoghegan, engaged in 1627 in translating into English the medieval *Annals of Clonmacnoise*, left a vivid image of the widespread lack of respect for ancient sources of this kind: 'some of them suffer tailors to cut the leaves of the said books (which their ancestors held in great account), and slice them into long pieces to make their measure of'.[112]

The Gaelic literati, then, were neither blind to what was happening around them, nor incapable of incorporating recent developments into the stylized language and formulaic structure of their verse. What is striking, however, is the absence of explicitly political comment. Poets lamented the decay of the traditional order. But they made no attempt to link the misfortunes they bemoaned to the policy of the crown and its servants, or even to the acquisitiveness of the New English. Instead they presented the downfall of Gaelic Ireland either as a natural catastrophe or as God's punishment on the Irish for their sinful ways. This fatalistic acceptance is evident even in one poem, much copied and therefore presumably widely circulated, which goes further than most to express the grievances of the dispossessed natives. The anonymous author, most probably writing in the aftermath of the Ulster plantation, noted the disappearance of the Gaels, replaced by 'an arrogant impure crowd, of foreigners' blood', 'Saxon' and 'Scottish', at whose hands the plain was converted into acres, 'the hillside is wrenched into fields'. But he went on explicitly to insist that the expulsion of the Gaels, 'although its vaunt is claimed for a foreign battalion', was due to the wrath of God. Nor was their fate to be seen as exceptional. 'They are not the only ones to have been destroyed; many's the race for whom there was decreed ill, as a result of the wrath of God in Heaven, whereat the shafts of his wrath burst.'[113]

Some of the most direct comment in the Gaelic literature on the effects of political and social change, and also some of the most revealing, is to be found in the prose satire *Pairlement Chloinne Tomáis* (The Parliament of Clan Thomas), written around 1615, probably somewhere in the south-west. Its subject is the rise above their proper station of the Irish peasantry, represented by the progeny of 'the surly and mis-shapen' Thomas, half human and half demon, and his wife, a daughter of Bernard the filthy. Ordered by St Patrick to devote themselves to

and Newcomers: The Making of Irish Colonial Society 1534–1641 (Dublin, 1986), 152–64; Michelle O'Riordan, *The Gaelic Mind and the Collapse of the Gaelic World* (Cork, 1990), chs. 3, 4; Caball, *Poets and Politics*, 81–142; Nicholas Canny, *Making Ireland British 1580–1650* (Oxford, 2001), 403–18.

[112] Connell Mageoghegan, *The Annals of Clonmacnoise*, ed. D. Murphy (Dublin, 1890), 8.

[113] William Gillies, 'A Poem on the Downfall of the Gaoidhil', *Éigse*, 13 (1969–70), 203–10.

'tillage and hard labour for the nobles and aristocracy of the Christian peoples', Clan Thomas had come into its own from the time of Hugh O'Neill. Wartime depopulation had allowed them to acquire land and marry well until, under James I, they could send their sons to study for the priesthood, 'and their daughters to learn silk-work and sampler making'. The text ends when Clan Thomas, assembled for a preposterous mock-parliament at which they had resolved to take noble surnames and draw up statutes to improve their condition, are interrupted by the arrival of a young English pedlar from whom one of them attempts to buy tobacco.

The young Englishman arrived and greeted them politely and said: 'God bless you, Thomas, and all your company.' Thomas answered him in no uncivilized fashion and said: 'Pleshy for you, pleshy, goodman Robin'. . . . Everybody gathered round him marvelling at Thomas's English. 'Ask him the price of the tabacco', said Bernard. Thomas spoke and said: 'What the bigg greate órdlach for the what so penny for is the la yourself for me?' Robin said: 'I know, Thomas, you ask how many inches is worth the penny', and he raised his two fingers as a sign and said, 'two penny an inch' . . . 'Act on our behalf', they all said. 'I will', replied Thomas, and he said: 'Is ta for myself the money for fart you all my brothers here.' Robin said, 'I thank you, honest Thomas, you shall command all my tobacco'. 'Begog, I thank you', said Thomas.

The social reality that lay behind this fantasy can only be guessed at. Taken at face value it would suggest that the rhetoric of the New English elite, from Perrot to Davies, was not wholly bogus: that some at least of the Irish poor did indeed benefit when they exchanged the crushing social subordination they had endured under the traditional Gaelic order for a new world of money wages and fixed rents and leases. But this may perhaps be too much to read into what is essentially a bitter comment on the loss of elite privilege. What is noteworthy, however, is that the author's resentment at the social changes taking place around him is directed firmly downwards: at the boorishness of the churls, their lack of proper respect for their superiors, and their ludicrous attempts to ape English speech and manners. To the historian, blessed with hindsight, Robin, the tobacco seller, might stand as a symbol both of the New English presence in early Stuart Ireland and of the commercial forces that were undermining the Gaelic social order. In the text, however, his role is to be the civil and tolerant foil to a bestial native underclass.[114]

If some Gaelic poems fatalistically lamented recent changes, furthermore, others show the bards concerned attempting, against all the odds and in radically

[114] *Pairliment Chloinne Tomáis*, ed. N. J. A. Williams (Dublin, 1981), 65, 67–8, 83, 97. For the suggested date see Williams's introduction (p. xxi). Raymond Gillespie, noting a reference to the poor emigrating to France (p. 96) suggests a date of 1629–31 ('Negotiating Order in Early Seventeenth-Century Ireland', in M. J. Braddick and John Walter (eds.), *Negotiating Power in Early Modern Society: Order, Hierarchy and Subordination in Britain and Ireland* (Cambridge, 2001), 294 n. 29). However, famine in 1603–5 had also led to a surge in migration to France: see Ó Ciosáin, 'A Hundred Years of Irish Migration', 94–5.

changed circumstances, to continue their traditional function of endorsing the social and political order. Two Ulster poets, Etach O'Hussey (Eochaidh Ó hEodhusa), poet to the Maguires of Fermanagh, and Fergal MacWard (Fearghal Óg Mac an Bhaird), also author of a noted elegy on Hugh Roe O'Donnell, celebrated the accession of James VI of Scotland. His sovereignty, O'Hussey wrote, would be a brilliance after the darkness of Elizabeth's death. 'Three crowns', MacWard proclaimed, 'shall be placed on James's head.' Both poets based their eulogies on a long-standing literary tradition that placed the Scottish royal line among the successors of Míl. These extravagant eulogies (MacWard's probably written before James took the throne) can in part be attributed to the same heightened expectations that inspired the 'recusancy revolt' in the southern towns.[115] Even after this initial, and in the event quite unrealistic, euphoria had passed, however, the same theme appeared in 'The Contention of the Bards', a sequence of poems written between around 1604 and 1624, in which Ulster and Munster poets debated the rival claims to primacy of the two 'halves', northern Leth Cuinn and southern Leth Moga, into which ancient Ireland had reputedly been divided. Taken as a whole this elaborate debate on a non-issue is a reminder of the preference for solipsistic artifice that continued into the last decades of the traditional Gaelic order. Florence Conry, passionately engaged in the work of furthering the Counter-Reformation, denounced those involved as 'hounds of great knowledge, wrangling over an empty dish'.[116] One significant feature, however, was that writers on both sides sought to buttress their case by tracing James I's descent to their half of the island.

In thus addressing James VI and I the two Ulster poets revealed an awareness of political change: where once they would have written exclusively for local lords, they now recognized that real power radiated outwards from the distant figure of the king. But their instinct was to invest this new source of authority with traditional marks of legitimacy and virtue. The same willingness to discharge the bard's traditional function of eulogy was evident in other cases. Owen Roe MacWard (Eoghan Ruadh Mac an Bhaird), who had earlier written a poem wishing Hugh Roe O'Donnell a safe journey to Spain, wrote in praise of Turlough Mac Airt Óg O'Neill, grandson of Turlough Luineach, who had fought with the English against Tyrone. He also wrote poems on the imprisonment in the Tower of another former ally of the English, Niall Garbh O'Donnell, sympathizing with his plight but advising him to trust in the wisdom of King James. In County Antrim Fear Flatha Ó Gnímh and his son Brian composed poems in favour of Sir Henry O'Neill, who as a surviving proprietor and head of the O'Neills of Clandeboye had become part of the county establishment. One poem specifically

115 Ó Buachalla, 'James Our True King', in Boyce et al., *Political Thought in Ireland*, 7–11.

116 Quoted in *NHI*, iii. 539. An alternative assessment suggests that two of the poets concerned had contrived the whole exchange as a means of attracting patronage: Robert Welch (ed.), *The Oxford Companion to Irish Literature* (Oxford, 1996), 261–2.

praised his learning, and his knowledge of English law. Sir Henry, possibly himself a Protestant, was married to Martha Stafford, daughter of a New English official. Fear Flatha addressed two praise poems to her, while Brian reminded Sir Henry of the long and honourable history of Gaelic lords taking English brides.[117] Most remarkable of all the County Cork poet Tadhg O'Daly, in 1618, addressed a poem to Sir George Carew, whose medieval ancestors had patronized O'Daly men of learning, requesting his support in resisting a rival O'Daly and in contesting the taxation of his lands. In exchange, he promised to continue his family's traditional function of glorifying the exploits of their Carew patrons. In this case, of course, Carew's military record was as the main agent of the brutal pacification of Munster during 1599–1602. O'Daly, however, had no problem in finding the appropriate language:

> It is right that I make it known, I am going to put in your 'battle roll' that no raider had raided Ireland since you were brought in.
> Until you left London with a large body of troops to help Ireland she had not succeeded in banishing her evils; the fame of doing it fell to you.
> You left this beautiful land of Ireland free, from end to end, from thieving, violence, evil and rapine in so far as it could be done.[118]

By the time that Tadhg O'Daly sought to remake Sir George Carew as the embodiment of the traditional warlike lord, and thus fit patron for a poet, the traditional bardic class within which he was trying to maintain his place had already begun to dissolve. Elite patronage did not disappear. But with the collapse of the Gaelic social order support no longer existed for the long years of training in bardic schools that had sustained the highly stylized craft of the traditional poets. Once again, however, the weakening of established cultural institutions brought with it liberation as well as loss. From the late sixteenth century new, less restrictive metrical forms began to appear in manuscripts alongside poems written according to the rigid conventions of syllabic verse. This in turn permitted the emergence, alongside the declining caste of bards, of a new group of non-professional poets, working in a language closer to spoken Irish and in simpler, more accessible patterns of metre and assonance. A poem written probably in the late 1630s by one such non-professional poet, Donnchadha Mac an Chaoilfhiaclaigh, illustrates the superior capacity of the new verse to offer a realistic response to contemporary events. Mixing English legal terminology into an Irish text, it denounces the oppression imposed by the court of wards, by

[117] Michelle O'Riordan, 'The Native Irish Mentality as Revealed in Gaelic Sources 1600–1650', in Brian MacCuarta (ed.), *Ulster 1641: Aspects of the Rising* (Belfast, 1993), 73–7; Bernadette Cunningham and Raymond Gillespie, 'The East Ulster Bardic Family of Ó Gnímh', *Éigse*, 20 (1984), 106–14.

[118] Anne O'Sullivan, 'Tadhg O'Daly and Sir George Carew', *Éigse*, 14 (1971–2), 27–38. The reference to Carew's ancestors was to the same thirteenth- and fourteenth-century predecessors whose holdings had formed the basis of the predatory ventures in the 1560s of Sir Peter Carew, Sir George's cousin.

amercements, rents, and exchequer fines ('meirse is cios is fis *Exchequer*'), and the imprisonment of juries who refused to convict on false charges. However, it was not to be until the transformative decade of the 1640s and beyond that poetry in this new style was to begin articulating a consistent political critique of English institutions and government.[119]

If the output of the Gaelic poets must in part be assessed in terms of the rigid stylistic and thematic framework within which they worked, it is also necessary to take into account the political background. The wars of the period 1579–1603, as well as earlier and later plantation schemes, had seen the dispossession of both large and small Gaelic families. But their losses—the basis of the new ideology of Irish Catholic grievance taking shape mainly in the émigré community—must be set against the experience of others who, with greater or lesser success, came to terms with the new political and economic order within Ireland. This was most clearly the case in Connacht, where the late Elizabethan settlement between leading proprietors and the crown remained intact. The leading western magnate family, the Burkes of Clanricarde, were of English rather than Irish descent, but their ancestors had become wholly gaelicized. The third earl (d. 1601), had been in arms against the crown in his youth, and Mountjoy and Moryson believed he secretly favoured Tyrone. However, his son Richard Burke (1572–1635), brought up mainly in England in the household of the earl of Essex, had the complete confidence of the deputy, who knighted him for his outstanding bravery at the battle of Kinsale.[120] Although resident mainly in England, and despite his open Catholicism, he remained influential in Irish affairs, serving as president of Connacht from 1604 to 1616 and then as governor of the city of Galway. The other main western dynasty, the O'Brien earls of Thomond, were by contrast wholly Gaelic in ancestry, but their accommodation to the new political order was even more complete. Sir George Carew confessed in 1600 that he found the court-educated Thomond 'as truly English as if he had been born in Middlesex'. The criteria on which Carew based this favourable judgement were characteristic: 'for he spares neither brother, uncle, kinsman or follower that is not obedient to the state, and hath drawn more blood of his own people than is to be believed'. Thomond was, unlike Clanricard, a Protestant, reported in 1613 to have incurred 'the high displeasure and hatred of the recusants generally', to which he remained indifferent. However, his unpopularity, which eventually forced him to move from his country house to the fortified tower of Bunratty, may have been due, not just to his choice of religion, but to his commitment to economic and social change. 'His course', an official commented approvingly in 1603, 'has been always English, striving to bring in English customs and to

[119] For stylistic change and the decline of the professional poets, see *NHI*, iii. 528–9, 537–8, 541. For Mac an Chaoilfhiaclaigh see Bernadette Cunningham, 'Native Culture and Political Change in Ireland, 1580–1640', in Brady and Gillespie, *Natives and Newcomers*, 165, and Canny, *Making Ireland British*, 428–9.

[120] Moryson, *Itinerary*, ii. 296–7.

beat down all Irish barbarous usages'. Both Clanricard and Thomond, moreover, sought to boost their rents, and by doing so underwrite their anglicized lifestyles, by actively promoting the settlement on their estates of English artisans and farmers.[121]

Clanricard and Thomond were unusual in the prominence they won for themselves in the new political order, but they were not unique in their willingness and ability to adapt. In the other branch of the Burkes, Tibbot-na-Long, son of the notorious Grace O'Malley and her husband Richard-an-Irainn Burke, supported the crown during the Nine Years War, as the best means of resisting O'Donnell pretensions to control north Connacht. Knighted in 1603, he made skilful use of both English and Gaelic law to consolidate his estate at the expense of other local families, and in 1627 became first Viscount Mayo. In the south-west, the earldom of Clancare conferred on the main MacCarthy line became extinct when the first earl died in 1597, leaving no male heir. The Muskerry branch of the MacCarthys, on the other hand, retained their status, and Charles MacCarthy was ennobled as Viscount Muskerry in 1628. In Sligo Tadhg O'Hara used the services of an Old English lawyer to obtain a regrant of his family's lands from the crown. On this basis his sons, reared as Protestants both after and possibly even before his death in 1616, were subsequently able to lay the foundations for a dynasty that was to be prominent in Sligo politics into the nineteenth century. In the midlands Terence O'Dempsey, sheriff of Queen's County in 1593, was knighted in 1599 for his military service under Essex, and became Viscount Clanmaliere in 1631. In Leitrim, similarly, the head of the McRannal family, under the name John Reynolds, was rewarded for his assistance in the plantation by receiving a regrant of his estate. His Protestant son Humphrey subsequently became auditor of the court of wards and married the daughter of the New English official and antiquary Sir James Ware.

Even in Ulster, there were winners as well as losers. Even if many of the native beneficiaries received less than they felt entitled to, the one-fifth or so of profitable land in the hands of Irish proprietors nevertheless created a substantial class who, whatever their grievances, had a place to maintain within the new political and social order. The overthrow of the great Ulster dynasts, moreover, had made it possible for a new group of lesser native proprietors, representing minor septs, or the cadet branches of leading families, to achieve the status and independence they had not previously enjoyed. This was the case, for example, with the Clandeboye O'Neills under the anglicized Sir Henry. In County Down, similarly, the decision of Art Roe Magennis to abandon his father-in-law Tyrone

[121] Carew to Cecil, 20 April 1600 (*CSPI 1600*, 111); Chichester to English privy council, 26 May 1613 (R. Dudley Edwards (ed.), 'Letter Book of Sir Arthur Chichester 1612–14', *Analecta Hibernica*, 8 (1938), 104); Sir Geoffrey Fenton to Cecil, 1 July 1603 (*CSPI 1603–6*, 65). See also Brian Ó Dálaigh, 'From Gaelic Warlords to English Country Gentlemen: The O'Briens of Thomond 1543–1741', *The Other Clare*, 25 (2001), 40–2. For the estate policy of Clanricard and Thomond see Canny, *Making Ireland British*, 329–31.

by coming to terms with Mountjoy in 1601 resumed a long-standing family strategy of looking to the crown as a means of escaping O'Neill overlordship. By sticking to his bargain after the Spanish landing at Kinsale, Art Roe helped to secure his family's future. He became Viscount Iveagh in 1623, while his son Hugh studied law in the Inner Temple and married a daughter of the prominent Pale family of Bellew.

Precisely what was involved in this assimilation of Gaelic notables into the upper levels of the new social and political order varied from case to case. The earl of Thomond became an aggressive and unpopular champion of English culture. Sir Henry O'Neill and Viscount Iveagh, on the other hand, continued to receive the homage of bardic poets. Nor did conformity in manners and behaviour necessarily guarantee wholehearted acceptance of a new political allegiance. Tibbot-na-Long Burke was twice detained, in 1607 and again in 1625, on charges of treasonable correspondence with Spanish-based exiles. The allegations may have been the work of malicious rivals; but it is also quite possible, given his numerous past shifts of allegiance, that he chose to maintain contact with representatives of the old as well as the new order. Sir John MacCoghlan, a leading native proprietor in County Leitrim, was another ambiguous figure, who reportedly reinforced his English knighthood and title deeds with a ceremonial inauguration as head of his sept. On the death of his father in 1590 he had assembled the inhabitants of his territory at a hill where a member of a client family placed a white wand in his hand, 'whereat the people gave a shout as if they said Vive le Roy gu maire tu thainim [may your name live]'.[122] How far did his actions betray a continuing attachment to the ways of his ancestors, and how far a pragamatic concern to benefit from all available sources of legitimacy? The answer is no clearer than in the case of that other accomplished straddler of two cultural worlds, Hugh O'Neill, earl of Tyrone.

Others, besides those fortunate enough to retain or acquire lands, likewise sought to accommodate themselves to the new political and social order. Chichester, reporting in 1610 on a tour of the northern counties, observed that the people of Tyrone, Armagh, and Coleraine, 'having reformed themselves in their habit and course of life beyond others and the common expectation held of them (for all that were able had put on English apparel and did promise to live in townreeds and to leave their creaghting), had assured themselves of better conditions from the King than those they lived in under their former landlords'.[123] Those expectations, as Chichester complained, were disappointed. But some nevertheless found ways of prospering under the new order. In County Tyrone estate records show the rise of a native Irish middleman, Patrick Groome O'Devin, who by 1615 was leasing the entire estate of Sir Claude Hamilton for

122 MacCuarta, 'De Renzy's Letters', 116.

123 McCavitt, *Chichester*, 157. 'Creaghting', from the Irish word for a herd, meant the keeping of mobile herds of cattle, as opposed to settled agriculture.

an annual rent of £220. In other cases members of the bardic class appear as assistants in the post-war settlement, providing translation services, genealogical information, and advice on the occupation and ownership of land. To this can be added the evidence of natives making routine use of the new legal and administrative system. Of fifty surviving chancery pleadings relating to early seventeenth-century Antrim and Down, about a quarter involved a native litigant, and two-thirds of these involved natives only. Outside Ulster, too, some found the role of collaborator preferable to that of rebel. In 1608–9 the government, as part of its continuing attempts to pacify the midland counties, transplanted a group of O'Mores from Queen's County to north Kerry. Their agent in this venture was Patrick Crosby, a crown servant from the 1580s, by his own account of English descent, but in fact, according to the earl of Ormond, one of the Mac Ui Crossanes, hereditary bards to the O'Mores. Crosby's brother John, equally adaptable, was Church of Ireland bishop of Ardfert from 1600 until 1621.[124]

A willingness to conform to the new order was not, however, the same as an ability to do so. Many Gaelic proprietors did not have the technical knowledge, or the network of contacts, required to take advantage of an expanding commercial economy. There was also the difficult transition to be made from a culture of distribution, in which status was measured in conspicuous consumption and the dispensing of hospitality to clients and retainers, to one based on profit and accumulation. To the reduction of native landownership by confiscation or the legal chicanery of the minor plantations must thus be added a significant further reduction brought about by debt-enforced sale and unredeemed mortgages. In Cavan the native share of land fell from 22 per cent at the conclusion of the plantation to 16 per cent by 1641, in Armagh from 25 per cent to 19 per cent. In Monaghan, where native proprietors had escaped the natural selection of plantation, the fall was sharper still, from 60 per cent to 40 per cent. In the barony of Iveagh, despite the political and social assimilation of the Magennises, the proportion of land in native hands fell from 85 per cent in 1610 to only 48 per cent, much of it heavily encumbered by debts, in 1641. In Sligo and Roscommon, equally, Old English gentry and merchants had by the same date acquired around 20 per cent of profitable land, once again mainly at the expense of failing native proprietors.[125]

The experience of the native Irish in the first half of the seventeenth century was thus a mixed one: military defeat and dispossession must be set against evidence of adaptation, with greater or lesser success, to a new economic and political order. The overthrow of the traditional social hierarchy had discomfited

[124] See Marc Caball, 'Pairlement Chloinne Tomáis, I: A Reassessment', *Éigse*, 27 (1993), 47–57, who suggests that, rather than upstart labourers, it was Crosby, seen as part of a 'prosperous and culturally pragmatic grouping', who was the real target aimed at in the satire.

[125] Raymond Gillespie, *The Transformation of the Irish Economy 1550–1700* (Dublin, 1991), 21–2; Harold O'Sullivan, 'The Magennis Lordship of Iveagh in the Early Modern Period, 1534 to 1691', in Lindsay Proudfoot (ed.), *Down: History and Society* (Dublin, 1997), 172.

some but benefited others—including, if *Pairlement Chloinne Tomáis* is to be taken at face value, some of the formerly despised 'churls'. The contrast in experiences is clearly seen within different branches of the same family. Tyrone's increasingly impossible position, for example, contrasts with that of several cadet branches of the O'Neills. Among the O'Briens of Thomond, similarly, the uncompromisingly anglicized fourth earl, and the two determinedly Protestant Sir Turloughs, represented a rather different form of accommodation to that of Bishop Murrough of Killaloe, eventual husband of the recusant Slaney. All four, however, stood clearly apart from the bishop's brother, yet another Sir Turlough, who in 1606 was brought before the judges of assizes at Limerick because of his association with a band of outlaws, led by Redmond Purcell and Maurice McGibbon Duff, that harassed the Clare–Tipperary border. Such sponsorship of raiding bands had once been normal practice. But Sir Turlough was clearly slower than others to see that its day had passed. It was in fact his own brother, the bishop, whose information had him and some of his sons committed as prisoners to Limerick Castle. Shortly afterwards, at Clonmel, the same judges had another of his sons hanged for a murder, committed with the same accomplice, Redmond Purcell.[126]

It is against this background of contrasting fortunes and responses that one can best understand the poems and other writings of the Gaelic learned classes of the early seventeenth century. What they reflect is a changing world, in which dispossession and decline coexisted with adaptation and opportunity, and in which traditional modes of thought and expression interacted with new intellectual influences and cultural models. Perhaps no text of the period so clearly illustrates the contradictory forces at work as what came to be known as the Annals of the Four Masters. In 1626 Michael O'Cleary, a Louvain-based Franciscan, returned to Ireland, initially to collect material for a comprehensive history of Irish saints. By 1636 , working with the aid of local collaborators, he had produced a grand synthesis of the available annalistic accounts of the Irish past, extending from earliest times to 1616. As in other cases involving the meeting of traditional learning and continental scholarship, what emerged was a fusion of old and new. Ó Cléirigh and his collaborators, unlike Keating, adhered to the annalistic style of a year-by-year chronicle. But the narrative they constructed from traditional sources was subtly reshaped. In place of the local and dynastic concerns of traditional annals what was offered was a national history, treating Gaelic Ireland as a unit with a coherent past. It was also a work steeped in the values of the Counter-Reformation, so that episodes from the 1530s onwards were interpreted in terms of a struggle between true faith and heresy that would have been recognizable to few if any of the actors involved. The final pages, likewise, contributed to the developing literature of Irish Catholic martyrdom with a graphic account of the execution of Bishop O'Devany and his companion.

[126] *CSPI 1603–6*, 471–2, 475.

If the confessional commitment of the 'Annals of the Four Masters' was clear enough, however, its politics were somewhat less so. Keating, attempting an analytical narrative, had been forced to discuss directly the legitimacy of the twelfth-century English conquest, and the rights and wrongs of the wars that had followed between colonist and native. The format of a year-by-year chronicle made such issues easier to evade. The story of the conquest begins with the arrival in 1169 of a fleet of 'Flemings', 'seventy heroes dressed in coats of mail', to assist Dermot MacMurrough in recovering the kingdom of Leinster. MacMurrough, it is true, is described as having made all Ireland 'a trembling sod' and to have died of a hideous disease by which 'he became putrid while living'. This, however, was a punishment for his plundering and burning of churches, rather than his betrayal of his nation. Thereafter the Four Masters proceed very much in the manner of their annalistic sources, offering a matter-of-fact record of raids and battles, in which 'the English' appear as one participant among many, often acting in concert with one or more Gaelic allies. Where later nationalists were to celebrate the intervention of the Scottish prince Edward Bruce as a moment of potential liberation, the Four Masters, in their entry for 1319, remained true to the spirit of their medieval sources: 'Edward Bruce, the destroyer of Ireland in general, both English and Irish, was slain by the English, through dint of battle and bravery, at Dundalk'. More striking still is the praise lavished on the ruthless Lord Grey, victor at Smerwick ('there had never come to Ireland an Englishman who, during the time he remained, was more energetic in his expeditions, more nobly triumphant, or who had been more successful in his services'), and the condemnation of the Fitzgeralds of Desmond, exterminated by God's vengeance for the crime of rebellion against their sovereign.[127]

This explicit acceptance of the legitimacy of English power is at first sight difficult to reconcile with the very different tone of the Four Masters' coverage of more recent events. A strongly worded passage describes the decision of the Ulster lords to reject the apparently favourable peace terms offered to them in 1596:

> having reflected for a long time upon the many that had been ruined by the English, since their arrival in Ireland, by specious promises, which they had not performed, and the numbers of the Irish high-born princes, gentlemen and chieftains, who came to premature deaths without any reason at all, except to rob them of their patrimonies, they feared very much that what was promised would not be fulfilled to them; so that they finally resolved upon rejecting the peace.

At this point, however, the Four Masters have simply exchanged their annalistic sources, in which English governors and provincial presidents are incorporated into a world of competing lordships, for a more recent source, a celebratory life of Hugh Roe O'Donnell, imbued with the new ideology of faith and

[127] *Annals of the Kingdom of Ireland*, ii. 1173, 1183; iii. 521; v. 1795. For Bruce see the very similar though differently worded account in *Annals of Ulster*, ii. 433.

fatherland, produced after his death by Lewis O'Cleary.[128] And their central concern remains what had always been the function of poets and historians: to celebrate and legitimize the deeds of the strong and effective leader. In the same way their record of the death in Rome of Hugh O'Neill, 'a warlike, valorous, predatory, enterprising lord, in defending his religion and his patrimony against his enemies', recalls innumerable annalistic obits across the centuries. The exact identity of O'Neill's enemies, and the precise nature of the patrimony he defended, is not so much evaded as considered unimportant. The continuity with the pragmatic politics of the past is evident in the dedication of the annals to Fergal O'Gowra, a Gaelic lord, Protestant in religion, who represented County Sligo in the parliament of 1634. The dedicatory epistle further records that they were completed 'the tenth of August, 1636, the eleventh year of the reign of our King Charles over England, France, Alba [Scotland], and over Eire'.[129]

[128] I owe this suggestion to Dr Bernadette Cunningham.
[129] *Annals of the Kingdom of Ireland*, vi. 1999, 2375; i, p. lv.

9

Epilogue: New English, New Irish?

In May 1605 Susan Montgomery, the English wife of a well-connected Scottish clergyman based in Somerset, wrote to inform a relative that the king had just appointed her husband to three Irish bishoprics: 'the names of them I cannot remember, they are so strange, except one, which is Derry: I pray God that may make us all merry'. Her response to unfamiliar placenames was more relaxed than that of the purchaser some years later of an Irish peerage, who ruled out titles derived from the towns of Granard and Lucan, on the grounds that he could find neither on a map; instead he became Baron Pope of Belturbet and earl of Down. By autumn of the following year Bishop Montgomery of Derry, Clogher, and Raphoe was installed with his wife in the town of Derry, 'in a very pretty little house, built after the English fashion'. Mrs Montgomery found it 'a better place than we thought we should, for there we find many of our country folks both of gentlemen and gentlewomen, and as brave they go in their apparel as in England'. Her main complaint was 'that the Irish doth often trouble our house, and many times they doth lend to us a louse', reminding her of her daughter's warning 'that if I went into Ireland I should be full of lice'. This was a more positive response than another member of the extended family connection, Nicholas Willoughby of Devon, who found the land good but hopelessly underdeveloped, while 'the people be so beastly that they are better like beasts than Christians'. No one, in his view, would be wise to sell land in England in order to establish himself in Ireland, although a person with ready money could do well there by buying up and exporting fish, cattle, and other produce.[1]

The assumption of cultural superiority, whether expressed in the form of condescension or positive hostility, was part of the natural armoury of settlers newly arrived in a backward dependency. Some subsequent modification was only to be expected. To see this it is only necessary to look at the earlier cohort of New English, who by the reign of James I had been settled in Ireland for a generation. Richard Boyle, earl of Cork, had shown little regard for native rights in his drive to establish himself, and remained a leading spokesman for the

[1] Susan Montgomery to John Willoughby, 20 May 1605 and *c.* September 1606 (*Trevelyan Papers*, part III, ed. W. C. Trevelyan and C. E. Trevelyan (London, 1872), iii. 78, 100); Nicholas Willoughby to John Willoughby, *c.* September 1606 (ibid. 102–3). For Baron Pope, see Charles R. Mayes, 'The Early Stuarts and the Irish Peerage', *English Historical Review*, 73 (1958), 245.

planter interest. By the early seventeenth century, however, he employed Gaelic Irish servants in his household, and had Gaelic tenants, with some of whom he seems to have established a patron–client relationship. It was presumably contact with these servants that explains why Boyle's 4-year-old son was reported in 1610 to be able to speak enough Irish to act as his father's interpreter. More striking is Cork's concern that his sons should retain the language: the tutor who accompanied two other boys to Eton reported to him on his efforts, apparently not very successful, to have them practise Irish as well as French and Latin. Cork also kept an Irish harp in his castle at Lismore.[2] In the next generation there was Sir Henry Bourghier, born in Kilmallock, County Limerick, the son of another beneficiary of Elizabethan land grants. In letters to Archbishop Ussher, written when he had been many years resident in London, Sir Henry continued to refer to Ireland as 'our own poor country' and, more remarkably, to the Catholic ecclesiastic Luke Wadding as 'our countryman'.[3]

This variety in attitudes to Ireland and Irishness needs to be emphasized, as an antidote to what is sometimes an unduly simplistic depiction of the political outlook and aims of the New English population. A newly installed elite composed disproportionately of soldiers and adventurers inevitably contained many whose prime concern was personal profit, and whose attitude to the existing inhabitants was frankly exploitative. Sir John Harrington, in 1605, alleged that some of the soldiers now installed as provost marshals, constables of strongholds, or in other positions of local power were positively anxious to provoke renewed disturbances, taking 'special care to nourish the seeds of new quarrels lest, if all were quiet, their craft would be out of request'.[4] But it would be misleading to take this characterization as typical of the New English, or even of the servitor population. Chichester and his associates did indeed assume that they were entitled to be well rewarded for their military and other services from the proceeds of a policy of plantation that would also secure control of the island for the future. But this was to take place side by side with the eventual political, cultural, and religious assimilation of a native population still in possession of a large share of landed property. In 1625 Sir William Parsons, another substantial beneficiary of the policy of plantation, offered an optimistic account of the progress made by the same policy of granting lands to 'the best Irish' with English grantees scattered among them. Free from oppression by their traditional lords, the natives 'proceed to build storehouses, make enclosures, and put their children to school. . . . Where before they purchased men now they purchase

[2] Nicholas Canny, *The Upstart Earl: A Study of the Mental World of Richard Boyle, First Earl of Cork, 1566–1643* (Cambridge 1982), 126–8.

[3] See the introduction to George O'Brien (ed.) *Advertisements for Ireland* (Dublin, 1923), p. vi. O'Brien's identification of Bourgchier as author of the work has been superseded. See above, Ch. 7 n. 104.

[4] Harrington quoted in Victor Treadwell, *Buckingham and Ireland 1616–1628: A Study in Anglo-Irish Politics* (Dublin, 1988), 33.

lands.' This policy of settlement combined with cultural assimilation was the only way forward, 'as we cannot, without too great an effusion of blood, avoid their presence here'. [5]

If leading figures in the New English establishment thought in terms of a pragmatic policy of coexistence with the indigenous population, a much smaller number showed some interest in Gaelic culture and antiquities. Of these, the most significant was Sir James Ware (1594–1666), whose father had come to Ireland as secretary to Fitzwilliam in 1588. A protégé of Ussher, Ware combined an official career as auditor general and member of the Irish privy council with a long career of pioneering scholarship. His book *De Hibernia et Antiquitatibus eius Disquisitiones* (1654) offered a cautious account of the same succession of early peoples described by Keating, along with a discussion of the Irish language, and an account of antiquities such as the medieval monastic remains at Clonmacnoise in King's County. Ware's expertise was unique—the Gaelic antiquary Roderick O'Flaherty, forty years after his death, counted him as one of only two of the New English able to read Irish—and even he seems to have relied on members of the Gaelic literary class to assist him in transcription and translation. But then it was only a small minority even of the native population who could read Irish script, or follow the archaic literary dialects used. Nor was Ware wholly alone in his interest in the Gaelic past. Two others who showed a scholarly interest in Irish manuscripts, even if they could not themselves read the contents, were the Elizabethan soldier and administrator George Carew, and the Old English but Protestant Archbishop Ussher.

An interest in Gaelic culture did not necessarily imply a benign attitude to the native population. This much is clear from the case of the other New English reader of Gaelic mentioned by O'Flaherty. Sir Matthew de Renzy, a German whose business as a textile merchant in London had failed in 1606, fled to Ireland, where he acquired an estate in King's County as well as a position in the Irish customs administration. He began learning Irish soon after his arrival, initially with the MacBruadeadha, hereditary historians and genealogists to the O'Briens. His claims to have progressed so far as to have compiled both a grammatical dictionary and a historical chronicle have been challenged, but it seems clear that he acquired a competence both in the spoken tongue and in its classical written form. None of this, however, diminished de Renzy's commitment to aggressive colonization. He used his knowledge of Irish annals and mythology to legitimize plantation, first by presenting the descendants of Milesius as an exploitative elite who had themselves subjugated the earlier inhabitants of Ireland, then by emphasizing their repeated treacherous attacks on the medieval English colony. Having thus used Gaelic traditional learning for his own purposes, he went on

[5] Parsons to Conway, n.d. [1625](*CSPI 1625–32*, 56–8). For Chichester see above, p. 290. See also the account of the attitudes of Mountnorris and other officials in Michael Perceval-Maxwell, *The Outbreak of the Irish Rebellion of 1641* (Montreal, 1994), 16–19.

to call for its extirpation. Bards and chroniclers kept alive the memory of what the natives had possessed before the English conquest. 'Therefore fit it were that those were drowned as near as it were possible, whereby they might not know in time from whence they came.' In the meantime no bonds of friendship with the native Irish, 'be it either by matching, forestering or otherwise', could allow one to be sure 'that one day they will not hope to cut our throats and put out the conqueror'. All this would suggest that de Renzy took up Irish for the same practical reasons—or, in his case, frankly exploitative ones—that led Cork to want his sons to retain their familiarity with the language. But it also seems that he remained on friendly terms with the MacBruaideadha. In 1631, three years before his death, one of their number composed a eulogy praising his learning and achievements. It gave his name in Irish as 'Mathghamhain Ó Rensi', and transferred his birthplace from Germany to Scythia, the original homeland of the Milesians. Most striking of all de Renzy was invited, presumably as a man of acknowledged status and learning, to witness a document of 1617 relating to the celebrated Contention of the Bards.[6]

Ware and de Renzy were both unusual in their engagement with Gaelic culture. But most New English settlers would have found it necessary to establish relationships with the indigenous population, as servants, labourers, tenants, or traders. The detailed depositions subsequently collected of the events of 1641 make clear that the English Protestant victims often knew their native Irish attackers. Claims for losses by merchants and others, likewise, often included debts owed by Irish creditors. There was also a degree of intermarriage. As early as 1614, in fact, the king complained of reports that undertakers in Ulster, particularly the Scots, had begun to intermarry with the Irish, and ordered Chichester to reprove offenders.[7] Sir Henry O'Neill's alliance with Martha Stafford was praised by local Gaelic poets. The sister of Audley Mervyn, heir to an undertaker's estate in County Tyrone, married Lord Maguire. In south County Down in 1621 Matthew Forde followed up his purchase of lands earlier sold off by the MacCartan family by marrying an Eleanor MacCartan. In Armagh William Brownlow, son of a Derbyshire undertaker, married Eleanor, daughter of Sir Cahir O'Doherty.

Occasionally there are glimpses of other forms of alliance or mutual accommodation. Sir Thomas Phillips in 1631 complained that the farmers who had taken over the management of the estates of the different London companies not only tolerated the presence of priests on their lands but were also guilty of 'countenancing the said priests with their usual familiarity at their tables'. He also produced two depositions to show that the sheriff of the county, Richard

[6] Brian MacCuarta, 'A Planter's Interaction with Gaelic Culture: Sir Matthew De Renzy (1577–1634)', *IESH* 20 (1993), 1–17; idem (ed.), 'Matthew De Renzy's Letters on Irish Affairs 1613–20', *Analecta Hibernica*, 34 (1987), 120, 112; idem, 'Conchubhar Mac Bruaideadha and Sir Matthew De Renzy', *Éigse*, 27 (1993), 122–6.

[7] *CSPI 1611–14*, 482–3.

Kirby, had allowed a priest to use his court to prosecute parishioners who had failed to pay their parochial fees to a supposedly illegal church.[8] In Wexford a landlord later recalled that in the summer of 1640 he had lent most of his silver plate to the local priest, so that he could entertain the Catholic bishop on his visitation, 'and had it honestly restored'.[9] Most striking of all, perhaps, Sir John Clotworthy, the austerely Protestant County Antrim landowner, appeared in London in November 1644 to testify on behalf of his former schoolfellow, Conor, Lord Maguire, and to refer to letters in which Maguire had expressed his remorse for the bloodshed that had recently taken place in Ulster.

Such accommodations were rendered easier by a reduction in the sense of imminent menace so evident in the years after 1603. Robber bands, of the kind Brereton was warned against in 1635, continued to pose a danger to travellers in many areas. But the spectre of native conspiracy and revolt that had earlier haunted the imaginations of officials and settlers appears to have faded from the late 1620s. The change was particularly evident in the case of Ulster. The conditions imposed at the time of the plantation had taken for granted the need for armed defence. Undertakers were to construct defensive bawns, round which the planners intended the English or Scottish settlement to be grouped, and were to maintain stores of weapons. Two decades, later, however, settler society was no longer militarized. A survey in 1619 indicated that there was one musket for every eight British men in the six escheated counties. By 1630, on the other hand, there was one for every thirty-three. The retreat from armed readiness appears also to have been evident in the state of the regular army. Richard Hadsor, as early as 1623, noted that soldiers were frequently married, their weapons were often borrowed, and their officers, having acquired estates and families in Ireland, were 'mollified and made effeminate with the sweet and long peace'.[10]

A greater, though still by no means complete, sense of physical security can also be detected in domestic architecture. Up to the end of the sixteenth century the Irish aristocracy and gentry had continued to live in heavily fortified dwellings, the wealthiest in castles, the remainder in the cramped, inconvenient, and functional accommodation of tower houses. In the early seventeenth century, however, the construction of tower houses came to an end, and some existing structures began to be abandoned. In their place both established occupiers and newcomers turned instead to a new hybrid, the fortified house, designed to offer its occupants a measure of continued security combined with more of the style and convenience that would have been expected in an English country mansion. The most common design was a three- or four-storey rectangular block, equipped

[8] W. P. Burke, 'The Diocese of Derry in 1631', *Archivium Hibernicum*, 5 (1916), 2, 5.

[9] Lord Anglesey, writing in the 1680s, quoted in Mary Hickson, *Ireland in the Seventeenth Century* (London, 1884), ii. 77.

[10] O'Brien, *Advertisements for Ireland*, 51. For weapons among the Ulster settlers see Rolf Loeber and Geoffrey Parker, 'The Military Revolution in Seventeenth-Century Ireland', in Jane Ohlmeyer (ed.), *Ireland from Independence to Occupation 1641–1660* (Cambridge, 1995), 73.

with the conveniences of large windows and tall chimney stacks, and laid out so as to permit internal division into different types of room. Its defensive features—corner towers providing flanking fire along the walls, gun loops permitting defenders to shoot from cover, and a surrounding bawn, with turrets and gate house, providing an outer line of defence—made clear that peace was not taken for granted. But these were defences more effective against robber bands of the sort described by Brereton than in full-scale armed conflict. A County Kerry gentleman, appealing for protection to the earl of Cork as the kingdom erupted into rebellion in late 1641, lamented his error: 'my house I built for peace, having more windows than walls'.[11]

It was against this background that a voice from an earlier age made its belated appearance in print. In 1633 Sir James Ware published *The History of Ireland*, a compendium comprising three texts: the history of Ireland compiled by the English Jesuit Edmund Campion during his period as guest of the Stanihursts in 1571, a second history by the New English clergyman Meredith Hanmer, and Edmund Spenser's *View of the State of Ireland*. Ware's dedicatory preface to the two histories, addressed to the lord deputy, Sir Thomas Wentworth, acknowledged the minor errors that could be detected in them, but recommended both for 'the good use which may be made of them by any who have leisure, desire and ability to erect and polish a lasting structure of our Irish affairs'. His separate preface to the *View* presented it too as primarily a historical text. The opening paragraph contrasted the 'happy peace' of Ware's own day with those 'former turbulent and tempestuous times'. Further on he singled out for special mention Spenser's ethnographic account of the native Irish, linking it, bizarrely, to an unpublished (and now lost) account of the Irish language by the Catholic bishop Richard Creagh.

Even in these terms, moreover, Ware found parts of Spenser's text to be a problem. His published version was in fact lightly bowdlerized. On the very first page, for example, 'that savage nation' became simply 'that nation', and a succession of similar changes quietly dropped both hostile references to specific families, notably the Butlers of Ormond, and derogatory characterizations of the native Irish in general.[12] Even with these changes, moreover, Ware found it necessary to apologize for the author's immoderate tone, which reflected 'the troubles and miseries of the time when he wrote it'.

And surely we may conceive, that if he had lived to see these times, and the good effects which the last 30 years peace have produced in this land, both for obedience to the laws, as also in traffic, husbandry, civility, and learning, he would have omitted those passages

[11] David Sweetman, *The Medieval Castles of Ireland* (Woodbridge, 1999), ch. 6; John Fitzgerald, quoted in Raymond Gillespie, 'Destabilizing Ulster 1641–2', in MacCuarta, *Ulster 1641*, 110–11.

[12] Ware's changes to Spenser's text are tabulated in Andrew Hadfield and Willy Maley (eds.), *A View of the State of Ireland* (Oxford, 1997), 162–76.

which may seem to lay either any particular aspersion upon some families, or general upon the nation. For now we may truly say, *jam cuncti gens una summus.*[13]

The final claim ('now we are all one nation') was clearly not true. Here it is necessary to make allowance, in a work dedicated to the new lord deputy, Thomas Wentworth, for an element of official propaganda, as well perhaps as for the complacency natural to those who had done well out of several decades of traumatic upheaval. But the form in which Edmund Spenser's chilling vision of the reduction of Ireland belatedly found its way into print is nevertheless a measure of the distance the Ireland of the mid-1630s had travelled since the dark days of Elizabeth's last years. It is also an indication of how little the Protestants of that Ireland were prepared for the catastrophe that was shortly to engulf them.

13 Sir James Ware, *The Historie of Ireland, Collected by Three Learned Authors* (Dublin, 1633).

APPENDIX 1

The Population of Medieval and Early Modern Ireland

ESTIMATES of population for sixteenth- and early seventeenth-century Ireland generally involve working backwards from those that can be constructed, on the basis of hearth tax returns, from the 1680s onwards. L. M. Cullen, in 1976, used a figure of 2.2 million in 1687 to suggest a population of 1 million in 1500, rising to 1.4 million by 1600, and to 2.1 million by 1641. Any lower estimates for the sixteenth and earlier seventeenth centuries, he argued, would imply an improbable rate of growth thereafter. On the same basis he inflated an estimate of 1.1 million by 1672 from the pioneering social scientist William Petty to a corrected figure of 1.7 million.[1] Critics, however, pointed out that a figure of 1.4 million in 1600 would give Ireland at that time a higher population density than rural England. Instead they argued for a figure of 1 million or slightly above.[2] Calculations of long-term trends are further complicated by the evidence of a substantial drop in population, due to war, famine, and more particularly plague, in the late 1640s and early 1650s. Padraig Lenihan has estimated a net loss of population during this period of 15–20 per cent. On this basis he suggests that the 1672 figure should be revised to 1.5 million, reflecting a plausible recovery from a low point of 1.3 million in 1652. This in turn would imply a population in 1641 of 1.5–1.6 million.[3] The case for such a downward revision of Cullen's figures is strengthened by the work of Dickson, Ó Gráda, and Daultrey, who reduced the other main benchmark, the estimate of population in 1687, from Connell's 2.2 million to just under 2 million.[4]

For the period before 1500 historians, in the absence of even the most fragile data, have worked almost entirely on the basis of extrapolation from the figures available for contemporary England. This is a hazardous procedure. Ireland is approximately three-fifths the size of England, and four times as large as Wales. But attempts to allow for what everyone agrees was a significantly lower density of population are pure guesswork. Moreover the English population figures for this period are themselves disputed. Thus an estimate that Ireland's population at its medieval peak stood at 675,000 takes as its starting point what is generally seen as an unduly low figure for England. An alternative suggestion takes Ireland as less than half as densely peopled as England, so that the conventional estimate of an English population of 4–4.5 million in 1300 suggests an Irish figure of around 1 million.[5]

There is then the problem of deciding how far this population was reduced by the Black Death and the further outbreaks of plague that followed. The suggestion that

[1] *NHI*, iii. 388–9.

[2] Nicholas Canny, 'Early Modern Ireland: An Appraisal Appraised', *IESH* 4 (1977), 64.

[3] Pádraig Lenihan, 'War and Population 1649–52', *IESH* 24 (1987), 1–21.

[4] David Dickson, Cormac Ó Gráda, and Stuart Daultrey, 'Hearth Tax, Household Size and Irish Population Change 1672–1821', *PRIA*, C, 82 (1982), 125–81.

[5] *NHI*, ii. 212–13.

Ireland in 1500 may have had significantly fewer than 500,000 inhabitants once again rests partly on a low figure for contemporary England.[6] It is also impossible to reconcile with later estimates for Ireland. Even a figure of 1 million for 1600, as Cullen has pointed out, makes the apparent rate of increase during the seventeenth century exceptionally high. Yet that in turn puts a lower limit of what can be assumed for 1500. The population of England rose by around 60 per cent during the sixteenth century, from around 2.5 million to just over 4. Ireland's population, given the lack of evidence of dramatic change in its less developed economy, can hardly have grown more rapidly. Indeed it seems likely, given the depopulation reported from Munster following the Desmond rebellion, and the famine conditions that prevailed during and immediately after Tyrone's rebellion, that growth would have been much less.[7] All this would suggest a population in 1500 closer to 750,000 than the half million often suggested. Thus:

Estimated Irish population (millions)

1300	1.0
1500	0.75
1600	1.0
1641	1.5–1.6
1652	1.3
1672	1.5
1687	1.97

That in turn would suggest a drop of 25 per cent from a peak of 1 million in 1300, a plausible figure in the light of the general European experience in the aftermath of the Black Death.

[6] Ibid. 446–7. [7] Above, pp. 179, 253–4.

Maps

Map 1. Main places mentioned in the text

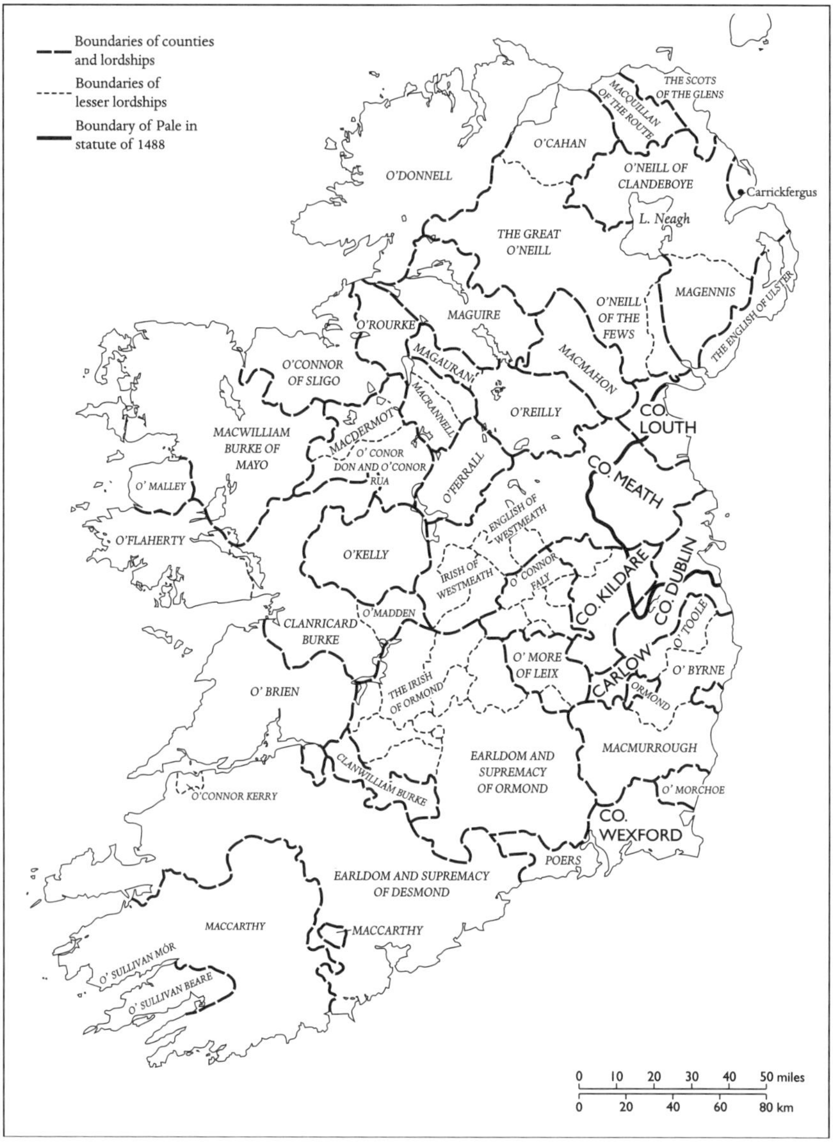

Map 2. Ireland in the Late Fifteenth Century, Showing the Boundaries of the Main Lordships (from Connolly (ed.), *Oxford Companion to Irish History*)

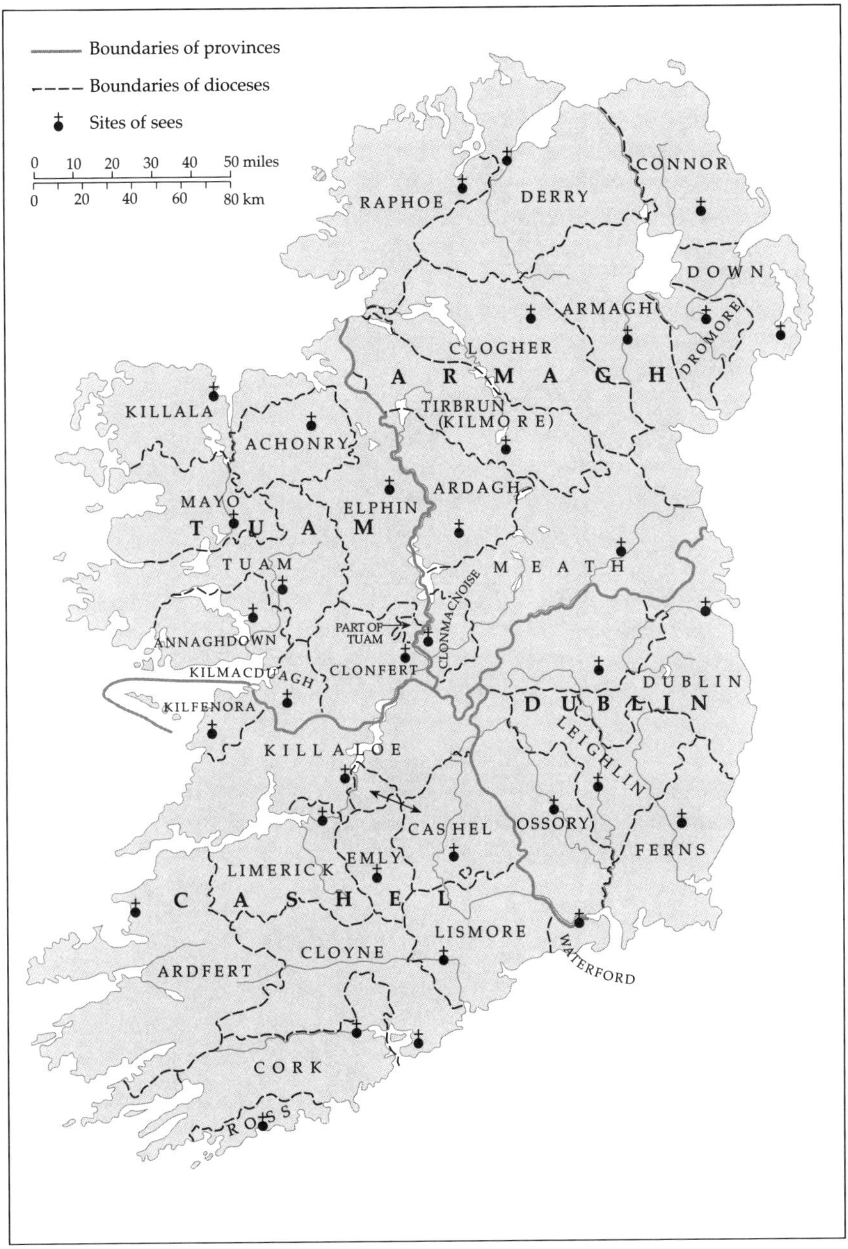

Map 3. The Dioceses of the Medieval Irish Church (from *NHI*, vol. ix)

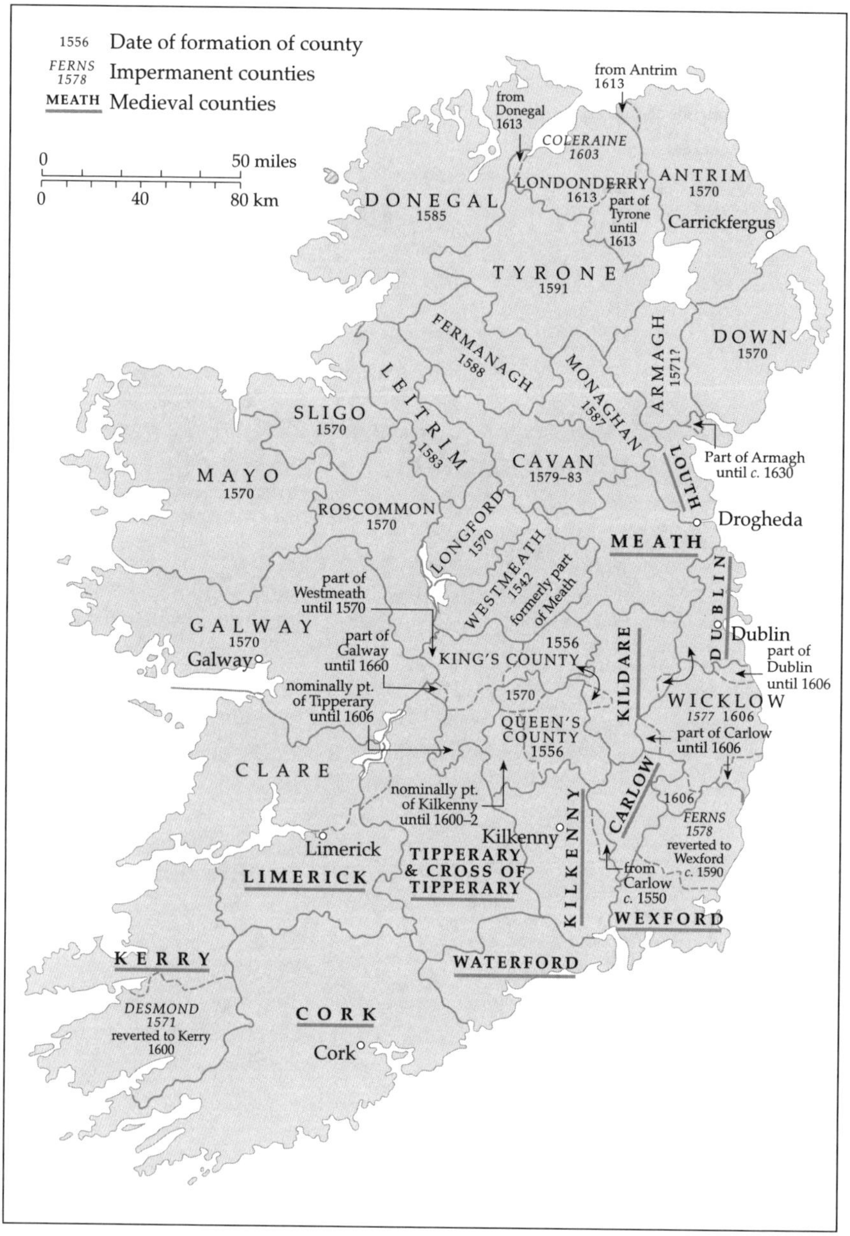

1556 Date of formation of county
FERNS 1578 Impermanent counties
MEATH Medieval counties
0 50 miles
0 40 80 km
from Donegal 1613
from Antrim 1613
COLERAINE 1603
LONDONDERRY 1613
part of Tyrone until 1613
ANTRIM 1570
Carrickfergus
DONEGAL 1585
TYRONE 1591
DOWN 1570
ARMAGH 1571?
FERMANAGH 1588
MONAGHAN 1587
LEITRIM 1583
SLIGO 1570
MAYO 1570
CAVAN 1579–83
Part of Armagh until c. 1630
LOUTH
Drogheda
ROSCOMMON 1570
LONGFORD 1570
WESTMEATH 1542 formerly part of Meath
MEATH
DUBLIN
Dublin
part of Westmeath until 1570
GALWAY 1570
Galway
part of Galway until 1660
KING'S COUNTY 1556
part of Dublin until 1606
KILDARE
WICKLOW 1577 1606
nominally pt. of Tipperary until 1606
1570
QUEEN'S COUNTY 1556
part of Carlow until 1606
CLARE
nominally pt. of Kilkenny until 1600–2
CARLOW
1606
FERNS 1578 reverted to Wexford c. 1590
Kilkenny
KILKENNY
Limerick
TIPPERARY & CROSS OF TIPPERARY
LIMERICK
from Carlow c. 1550
WEXFORD
KERRY
WATERFORD
DESMOND 1571 reverted to Kerry 1600
CORK
Cork

Map 4. The Development of the County System 1542–1613 (from *NHI*, vol. ix)

Map 5. John Goghe, Map of Ireland *c.* 1567 (reproduced from a nineteenth-century facsimile)

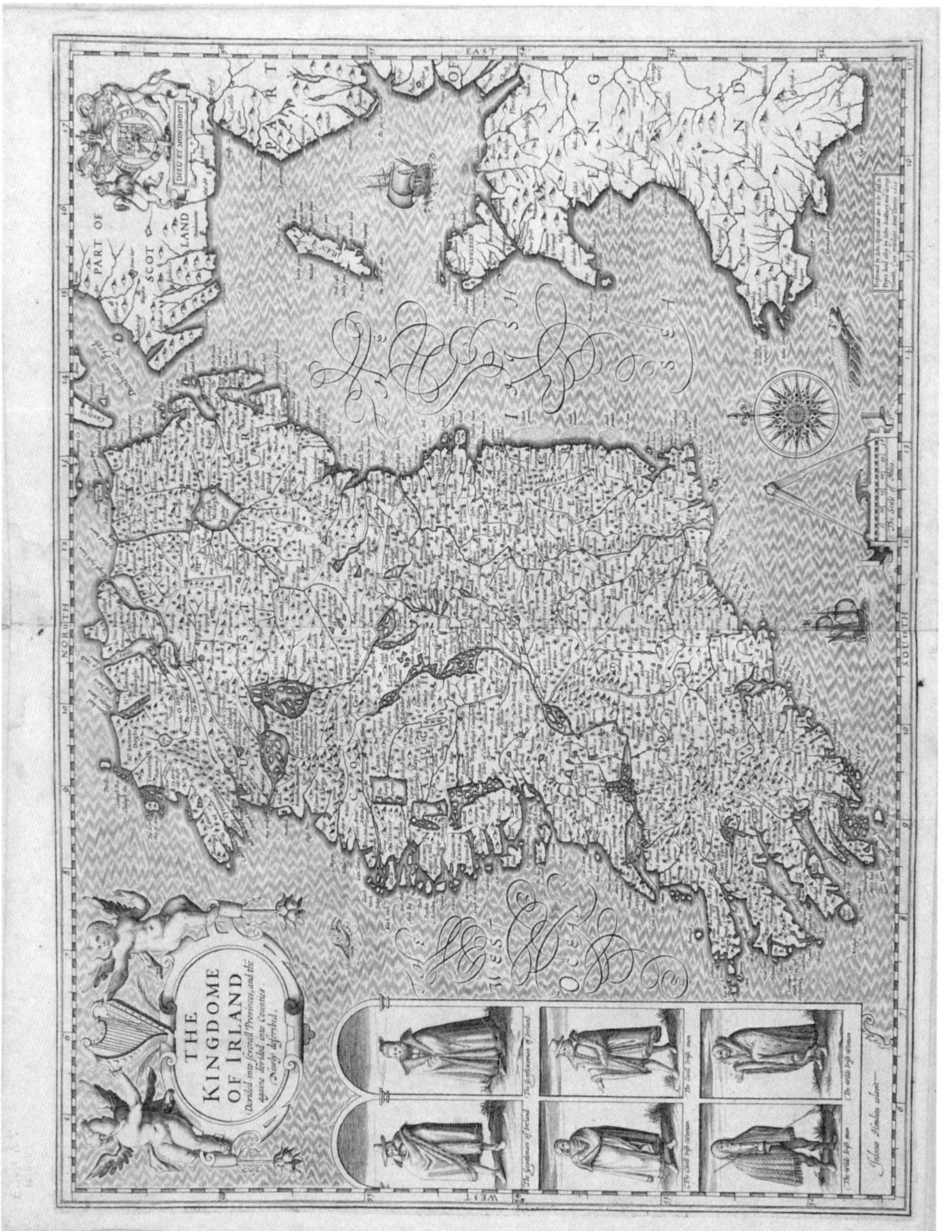

Map 6. John Speed, Map of Ireland (1611)

Index